Footprint **Cuba**

Sarah Cameron
with contributions from Claire Boobbyer
4th edition

D0977766

"City cracked open every day by the sun
and rested in silence since dusk
so that the morning finds it newly intact
with just a few papers and many kisses besides..."

Description of Havana in 'Ode to the City' by Roberto Fernández Retamar

Cuba Highlights

See colour maps at back of book

1 María La Gorda
Pristine diving with virgin reefs, caves, wrecks and an abundance of sea life.

2 Viñales
The valley is a UNESCO World Cultural Landscape for its steep-sided *mogotes*.

3 Las Terrazas
Part of a biosphere reserve, with excellent hiking and bird watching.

4 La Habana Vieja
A UNESCO World Heritage Site for its massive fortresses and elegant Spanish colonial mansions.

5 Presidio Modelo
Panopticon former prison of Fidel and Raúl Castro and other political dissidents.

6 Bay of Pigs
Site of the botched CIA-backed landing of counter-revolutionaries in 1961.

7 Matanzas
Birthplace of the rumba and other Cuban dances.

8 Santa Clara
Che Guevara's last resting place with dramatic monument and mausoleum.

9 Remedios
Colonial town famed for its pre-Christmas *parrandas*, or carnival.

USA

Florida Straits

Gulf of Mexico

HAVANA 4

3 Las Terrazas · Bauta · HAVANA 7 Matanzas

2 Viñales · MATANZAS VILLA CLARA

PINAR DEL RÍO 9 Remedios

Pinar del Río 8 Santa Clara

CIENFUEGOS

1 · 6 Cienfuegos

María La Gorda 5 Nueva Gerona 10 Trinidad

Archipiélago de los Canarreos

ISLA DE LA JUVENTUD

Caribbean Sea

N

0 km   50
0 miles   50

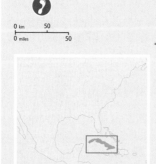

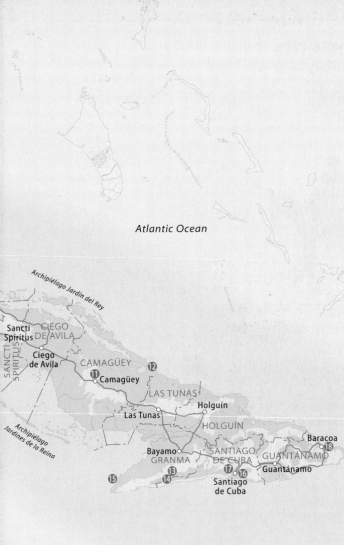

⑩ Trinidad
A UNESCO World Heritage site, frozen in time with its cobbled streets and tiled roofs.

⑪ Camagüey
Magnificent 18th-century churches and plazas characterize this colonial city.

⑫ Playa Los Cocos
A tropical idyll with coconut palms, white sand, crystal clear water and a few beach bars.

⑬ Comandancia de la Plata
Hike to Castro's secret mountain headquarters during the Revolution.

⑭ Pico Turquino
The highest mountain in Cuba and a two-day hike in the forest.

⑮ Playa Las Coloradas
Where Castro and his Revolutionaries disembarked in 1956 from the yacht, *Granma*.

⑯ Santiago de Cuba
The carnival queen and a vibrant, musical city.

⑰ El Cobre
Shrine of Cuba's patron saint, La Virgen de la Caridad is built over a copper mine.

⑱ Baracoa
The first town founded by the Spanish but accessible only by sea until the 1960s.

Contents

Paradise Found
Enjoy the idyllic beach and spectacular diving at Maria La Gorda.

National icon
The Hotel Nacional in Havana is a grand reminder of Cuba's pre-revolution days of excess.

A foot in the door

Cuba is a tropical paradise for foreign holidaymakers where residents play the lottery to get an exit visa. In city centres, from Havana to Santiago, ramshackle streets are lined with decaying colonial mansions and art deco towers, while rectangular Soviet apartment blocks dominate the suburbs. 1950s Cadillacs chug alongside horsedrawn carriages, arthritic rickshaws and sleek diplomats' saloons, swiftly overtaken by bright yellow eggshells on motorbike chassis. Out in the countryside, from the tobacco fields to the Sierra Maestra, the highways are lined with billboards extolling the virtues of the Revolution. Castro may be an elected dictator, but he eschews any personality cult, preferring instead to promote dead heroes such as Che Guevara, Camilo Cienfuegos and José Martí.

Initially a cash cow for Spanish colonial masters, Cuba became a pleasure zone for US neocolonialists in the 20th century. A heady cocktail of gambling, rum and sex lured Americans during Prohibition, when movie stars and mobsters came to sample the wares of celebrity bartenders. Rum and cigars continue to tempt today's visitors, together with other hedonistic pleasures such as sunshine, music and sensuality.

Yet life is hard for the average Cuban. The welfare state is unsurpassed but material pleasures are few and far between. Antique Russian fridges and American cars are held together with rubber bands and sticking plaster, and houses crumble into rubble-strewn alleyways. Make do and mend is the order of the day. Residents still dust off their ornaments, polish their antiques and surgically scrub their floors and, when it comes to music and dance, their rhythm, skill and innovation make Cubans world leaders.

10 Contemporary Cuba

Thirty years of isolation were swept away in the 1990s after the fall of the Soviet bloc. Castro desperately needed dollars to support his brand of Communism and the quick fix was tourism. Hotels sprang up along all the best beaches and many of Havana's ailing colonial palaces were given a makeover. Now, a decade later, nearly two million tourists come to the island every year, drawn by the prospect of sun, sea and sand and by the frisson of visiting the pariah of the USA.

The US administration predictably clamped down on Cuba in 2003 and 2004 in the run-up to the presidential elections, claiming that Cuba was fomenting the rise of left-wing governments in Latin America and denying political and human rights to its people. At the same time, Washington has, paradoxically, been preventing US citizens from their right to travel freely. Cuba is allegedly part of the 'axis of evil', but isolation and the US trade embargo have served only to fuel

Time warp town
Contemplate Cuba's colonial history in the beautiful city of Trinidad, a UNESCO World Heritage Site.

Castro's determination to stay put. Cubans see themselves as players in a David and Goliath epic and the Revolution has become part of their national identity.

The dollar is king. Cubans need dollars to buy most goods, with only a limited range available in pesos or on their rations. Some families earn dollars legally by renting out rooms to foreigners or cooking for them. Others get their dollars from relatives who fled to Miami to escape 'La Lucha' (the struggle), the gruelling life of making ends meet. Cradle-to-grave education, housing and health care hang on by a thread but other promises of the 1959 Revolution have crumbled. While the average monthly wage is US$10 and a tourist shells out US$6 for a cocktail, it's not surprising that the social fabric is unravelling. Prostitution is back and theft is on the rise. Survival depends on infiltrating the dollar economy by fair means or foul.

Drumming up enthusiasm
You're never far from a street party in Cuba; the pulsating rhythms of music and dance are everywhere.

1 *Hailing a cab. Cuba's distinctive and colourful taxis make a perfect holiday souvenir.* ▸▸ *See pages 46 and 57.*

2 *Dive Cuba's pristine off-shore waters to discover sea turtles and other marine life.* ▸▸ *See page 62.*

3 *Whether or not they're rolled on the thighs of dusky maidens, Cuban cigars are beautifully crafted and highly sought after.* ▸▸ *See page 164.*

4 *Santiago de Cuba's carnival in July is a great excuse to dress up and party.* ▸▸ *See page 349.*

5 *Take a cruise along the Malecón as the sun sets on the colonial buildings of Havana.* ▸▸ *See page 100.*

6 *The eccentric art and artefacts of Callejón de Hammel make it worth finding among the alleys of Cayo Hueso in Havana.* ▸▸ *See page 100.*

7 *When you tire of lying around in the sun, there are plenty of watersports on offer at the beach resort of Varadero.* ▸▸ *See page 194.*

8 *Fields of tobacco bask in the sun in Pinar del Río province, watched over by distinctive limestone mogotes.* ▸▸ *See page 155.*

9 *Cocotaxis may look a bit loco but they're a cheap and cheerful way to get around the capital.* ▸▸ *See page 139.*

10 *At the eastern end of the island, Santiago de Cuba has a strong Afro-Caribbean heritage and eclectic architecture.* ▸▸ *See page 326.*

11 *Korda's famous image of Ernesto 'Che' Guevara has developed from revolutionary icon to internationally recognised consumer brand.* ▸▸ *See page 404.*

12 *Taking a break from the bright sun and the even brighter costumes in Plaza de la Catedral, Havana.* ▸▸ *See page 91.*

The rhythm of life

From traditional *son* to Cuban rap via jazz and salsa, Cuba throbs to drums beating out the rhythm of the island's Afro-Cuban heritage. The sacred *cueros batá* (the three drums used in Santería rites) have been incorporated into mainstream bands, while performances of Yoruba and Congo devotional and profane song and dance are colourful spectacles, with Cubans fervidly chorusing the Santero chants and swaying to the infectious *guaguancó*. In every town there is a Casa de la Trova, where you can find old-timers crooning the traditional songs, and a club or disco where the local youth party until the small hours. Carnival festivities are exuberant and colourful; the best is in Santiago in July when rum-fuelled revellers take to the streets to dance in the conga to ear-splitting drum music.

The sun also rises

Fine, pale-golden sandy beaches stretch all along the north coast, lapped by warm, crystal clear water in shades of blue and turquoise. Many of the best bays and cays have all-inclusive hotels, often producing an unsettling form of tourist apartheid, but plenty remain as nature intended. Imagine yourself as Hemingway and go deep-sea fishing for magnificent marlin or plunge into the water to snorkel or dive reefs, walls, tunnels and wrecks. Share the sea with graceful turtles, dolphins, whale sharks, moray eels, rays and barracuda, or you can potter around in a coral garden admiring the sponges, worms, spider crabs or snails.

Cuba overflows with musical talent. Visit the Casa de la Trova in Santiago de Cuba to listen to the old soneros or join a rum-fuelled street party in Bayamo, Camagüey or Baracoa.

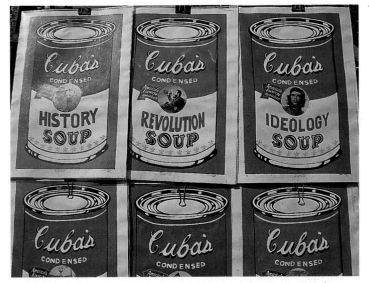

Pop goes the revolution. Art and ideology combine in a uniquely Cuban reinvention of an all-American image.

Colonial heart

The Malecón seafront road, where Cubans in love meet and old American cars lumber along, curves along the coast of Havana, bearing the scars of salt and wind erosion but still with a seductive allure. In a race against time, restoration work is putting life and colour back into this proud city and palatial mansions are being converted into boutique hotels, museums and art galleries. Away from the capital, Trinidad is a time capsule, untouched since the 19th century, but its nightlife is fully up to date and this is a great place to learn to salsa. Santiago, the carnival queen, lies in the shelter of the Sierra Maestra; a showcase for great art deco architecture and 19th-century French influences in its music and culture.

The pick of the peaks

Take off on a bike where and when you please. Cruise the cycle lane along the Malecón with the salt spray in your face and double-jointed 'camel' buses at your side. Outside Havana, quiet roads wind through flat or rolling countryside, where the majestic Royal palm towers over farmers' thatched cottages (*bohíos*), oxen are still used to work the fields and horses are the main form of transport. To test yourself and your bike, head for the mountains of the Sierra Maestra, also a hiking heaven. Trek through the forests up to Castro's base during the Revolution or up Pico Turquino, the highest mountain on the island, for amazing views amid the buzz and song of tropical wildlife.

Sunshine and showers
Cooling off in the summer heat of Santiago de Cuba.

Essentials

Planning your trip

Where to go

Cuba is the largest island in the Caribbean and nearly as big as England. Just as you could not hope to cover England in a two-week trip, do not plan to do too much in Cuba if that is all the time you have. If your time is restricted you should decide which end of the island you would prefer to see in detail. If you have got all the time in the world, then start at one end and work your way to the other. An excellent road runs all the way from Havana to Santiago down the centre of the island, passing through many of the important cities, with side roads off to other interesting places.

One-week trip
The old colonial city of **Havana** is unmissable. You need a day to see the old city with its palaces, mansions, museums and plazas and a couple of days to get round some of the major sites in the suburbs as well as take in some of the nightlife in music-mad Vedado. Use the capital as a base for day trips out to the countryside or the beaches along the coast. Places within striking distance of Havana include the lush green valley of **Viñales** and the fields of top-class tobacco in the Province of **Pinar del Río,** or the beaches to the east of the capital, **Playas del Este, Jibacoa** and the resort of **Varadero**.

Two-week trip
With two weeks you could spend more time in the western province of Pinar del Río and divers would particularly appreciate a few days at the isolated **María la Gorda** in the far west. You could stay a night at the eco-lodge at **Las Terrazas** where you can go walking in the rainforest and visit the colourful orchid gardens at **Soroa**. With two weeks, you could explore the UNESCO World Cultural Landscape of the Viñales valley with excursions to the *mogotes* (steep-sided, limestone mountains), and caves before heading up to the north coast beaches. Alternatively head east into the sugar-growing farmlands and forested mountains in the centre of the island. Allow yourself a couple of nights in **Santa Clara**, last resting place of Che Guevara; visit the Che memorial and the cays off the north coast via the charming old town of **Remedios**. **Trinidad**, the UNESCO World Heritage Site with its single-storey 18th- and 19th-century houses and cobbled streets, is a must-see on anyone's itinerary. Allow plenty of time to explore the town and surrounding areas, including the Valley of the Sugar Mills, the **Escambray mountains** and the beach at **Ancón** as well as enjoy the nightlife. The return trip to Havana could take in **Cienfuegos** for its colonial architecture and fortress, the **Bay of Pigs** and the **Zapata Peninsula** if you have your own car. The route Havana–Santa Clara–Trinidad–Cienfuegos–Havana can be done by bus.

Four-week trip
A month will give you more time to get to know both ends of the island and some places in between. The central towns are often missed because travellers concentrate on one end of the island or the other and skip the bits in between. Nevertheless, colonial **Camagüey** is well worth a day's exploration. If taking the bus or train the length of the island, make sure you break your journey in this city, preferably on a Saturday, when the streets come alive at night for an open-air fiesta: *Noche Camagüeya*. From here you can take in a day trip to the beach at **Playa Santa Lucía**. Another recommended break in the journey is at **Bayamo,** the jumping-off point for

⁙ Weather watch

Month	Jan	Feb	Mar	Apr	May	Jun	Jul	Aug	Sep	Oct	Nov	Dec
Av temp °C	22	22	23	25	26	27	28	28	27	26	24	23
Av temp °F	71	71	73	77	79	81	83	83	81	79	75	73
Av rainfall (mm)	60	45	45	55	70	160	130	140	150	170	170	55
Humidity %	75	73	71	71	74	76	75	76	78	78	75	74

hiking in the Sierra Maestra and a visit to Castro's atmospheric mountain headquarters during the Revolution. Lively **Santiago de Cuba**, Cuba's second city, is an infectious contrast to the capital, with an Afro-Caribbean culture laced with French influences, and where the climate is hotter and drier. You need up to two weeks to do justice to these eastern parts of the island: as well as experiencing Santiago de Cuba, there are excellent day excursions to **La Gran Piedra**, a tremendous viewpoint from where it is claimed that you can see Haiti and Jamaica on a clear day, and **El Cobre**, where the shrine of Cuba's patron saint is built over a working copper mine. An easterly round trip will take in **Guantánamo** (see the US Naval base through binoculars), **Baracoa** (currently one of the most popular destinations for its beaches and laid-back life-style), **Holguín** and the beaches of **Guardalavaca**, before returning to Santiago through the mountains or back to Havana. The main towns can be reached by bus or train, but places off the beaten track are difficult to get to on public transport and it is advisable to rent a car unless you like negotiating travel by truck.

> ⁙ *If you are fit and strong, you could also spend a few days exploring on a bicycle. The mountains are a challenge but there is no better way to travel.*

When to go

Climate
The **high season** is from **mid-December to mid-April**, when there are more dry days, more sunshine and less humidity. The season for **hurricanes** and **tropical storms** begins in August and can go on until the end of November. A serious hurricane does not come every year by any means, but in the last few years there have been several storms that have caused flooding and damage to houses and crops. There are also variations in climate on the island: it is hotter and drier in Santiago than in Havana, and wetter and cooler in the mountains than in the lowlands.

Northeast trade winds temper the heat, but **summer** shade **temperatures** can rise to 33°C (91.4°F) in Havana, and higher elsewhere, particularly Santiago where it can be unbearably hot in July and August. In **winter**, day temperatures drop to 20°C (68°F) and there are a few cold days, 8°-10°C (45°-50°F), with a north wind. Average **rainfall** is from 860 mm in Oriente, the east, to 1,730 mm in Havana; it falls mostly in the summer and autumn, but there can be torrential rains at any time. Walking is uncomfortable in summer but most offices, hotels, leading restaurants and cinemas are air conditioned.

Special events
Despite the heat, July is a good time to visit Santiago if you want to catch the **carnival**, although **New Year** is also lively with parades and street parties. New Year is celebrated everywhere as the anniversary of the **1959 Revolution**, so you can expect speeches as well as parties. In Havana, carnival used to be held at weekends

between July and August but in 2003 it was moved to November and it is likely to remain a movable feast. If you are staying on the Malecón you won't get much sleep. Throughout the year there are lots of excuses for music and dancing in the street, washed down with quantities of rum. Some towns even have weekly celebrations, with a special night for eating local food on the street and generally celebrating. Camagüey, for instance, has a **Noche Camagüeya** every Saturday night. In Bayamo and some other places it is called a **Noche Cubana**. ▸▸ *For further details, see also Festivals and events, page 54, and the Festivals and events section of each area's listings.*

If you are interested in attending a conference, sporting event or a cultural festival, contact the **Buró de Convenciones**, Hotel Neptuno 3rd floor, Calle 3 entre 70 y 74, Miramar, La Habana, T7-2048273, www.cubameeting.co.cu www.loseventos.cu They publish a list of events with contact names and details.

Tour operators

UK and Ireland

Cubanacán UK Ltd, T020-75377909, www.cubanacan.cu See also p24 for details of tours.
Cuba Welcome, 26 Elvaston Place, London, SW7 5NL, T020-7584 6092, enquiries@cubawelcome.com, www.cubawelcome.com Special deals, tailor-made travel, retail agents for ATOL.

Havanatour UK Ltd, 3 Wyllyotts Pl, Potters Bar, Herts, EN6 2JD, T01707-646463, sales@havanatour.co.uk, www.havanatour.co.uk
The Holiday Place, T020-74310670, www.holidayplace.co.uk
Interchange, Interchange House, 27 Stafford Rd, Croydon, Surrey, CR0 4NG, T020-86813612, F020-8760 0031, interchange@interchange.uk.com, www.interchange.uk.com

Journey Latin America, 12-13 Heathfield Terr, Chiswick, London W4 4JE, T020-8747 8315, F020-8742 1312 (London), T0161-832 1441, F0161-832 1551 (Manchester), sales@journeylatinamerica.co.uk www.journeylatinamerica.co.uk
Regent Holidays, T0117-9211711, www.regent-holidays.co.uk
South American Experience Ltd, T020-79765511, www.southamerican experience.co.uk
Steppes Latin America, The Travel House, 51 Castle Street, Cirencester, Glos, GL7 1QD, T01285-885333, F01285-885888, enquiry@steppeslatinamerica.co.uk, www.steppeslatinamerica.co.uk In-depth knowledge of Cuba, specialising in tailor-made itineraries.
Travelbag Adventures, T01420 541007, www.travelbag-adventures.com
Travelcoast Captivating Cuba, T0870-8870123, www.captivating-cuba.co.uk
Trips Worldwide, 14 Frederick Place, Clifton, Bristol, BS8 1AS, T0117-311 4402, F0117-987 2627, info@tripsworldwide.co.uk, www.tripsworldwide.co.uk

UK specialist in tailor-made holidays to Latin America and the alternative Caribbean.

Rest of Europe

STA Travel Worldwide, T01805-456422 www.statravel.de
Nouvelles Frontières, T0825-000747, www.nouvelles-frontieres.fr
Sol Meliá, T34-91-5675900, www.solmelia.es

North America

AdventureCuba.com, T310-8424148, www.adventurecuba.com
Air Transat Holidays, T1-866-3226649, www.airtransatholidays.com
Cuban Adventures Inc, T1-877-2822386, www.cubanadventures.com
Cuba Travel Services, T800-9632822, www.Cubatravelservices.com
Global Exchange, T800-4971994, www.globalexchange.org
Marazul Charters, T800-2235334, www.marazulcharters.com

Mila Tours, T1-800-3677378,
www.milatours.com
Signature Vacations, T1-866-3242883
www.signaturevacations.com
Viñales Tours, T52-52089900,
www.vinalestours.com

Australia and New Zealand

Adventure World, T02 89130755,
www.adventureworld.com.au
Travelshop, T1800-108108,
www.travelshop.com.au
Tucan Travel, T64-9-4161150,
www.tucantravel.com

Cuban tour operators

Several state-owned tour companies offer day trips or excursion packages, including accommodation, to many parts of the island, as well as tours of colonial and modern Havana. Excursions include (from Havana, 1 day, except where indicated): Viñales, including tobacco and rum factories, US$44; Guamá, US$44; Cayo Coco (by air), US$143

overnight; Soroa, US$29; Varadero, US$35 without lunch; Cayo Largo (by air), US$119 daytrip, US$170 overnight all-inclusive; Cienfuegos to Trinidad overnight US$115; Santiago de Cuba (by air) and Baracoa, US$159 including accommodation for 1 night, recommended, you see a lot and cover a lot of ground in 2 days. Tours can also be taken from any beach resort. Guides speak Spanish, English, French, Italian or German; these tours are generally recommended as well-organized and good value. On the downside, a common complaint among individual tourists is that, when they sign up for day trips and other excursions (eg Cayo Largo), they are not told that actual departure depends on a minimum number of passengers (usually 6). The situation is made worse by the fact that most tourists are on pre-arranged package tours. They are often subject to long waits on buses and at points of departure and are not informed of delays in departure times. Always ask the organizers when they will know if the trip is on or what the real departure time will be. Tourists also complain about the poor quality of the lunch provided, which is usually a set meal prepared too far in advance, so do not expect a culinary treat.

Amistur, Paseo 406 entre 17 y 19, T7-334544, amistur@amistur.cu Specialized visits to factories and schools as well as places of local historical or community interest.

Cuba Deportes, Calle 20 710 entre 7 y 9, Miramar, T7-2040945-7, F7-2041914, 247230. Arranges all-inclusive sporting holidays.

Cubamar Viajes, Av 3 esq 12, Vedado, T7-662523-4, cubamarviajes @cubamarviajes.cu Some camping resorts, student groups and diving packages.

Cubanacán, T7-2049479, www.cubanacan.cu Birdwatching and scuba diving tours or, if you prefer, hunting and fishing tours.

Gaviota Tours, 36A 3620 opposite Hotel Kohly in Havana, T7-2044781, operacion@gavitur.gav.tur.cu You can find this tour operator at all the Gaviota hotels around the country.

Havanatur, Edif Sierra Maestra, Av 1 entre 0 y 2, Miramar, T7-2042056, www.havanatur.cu Also branches in many hotels around the island and separate offices in some towns, see text for detail. Recommended for independent travellers who are looking for tailor-made but reasonably priced tours.

Horizontes, Calle 23 156 entre N y O, Vedado, Havana, T7-662004, www.horizontes.cu This operator run hotels which tend to be on the outskirts of towns and the chain provides activities for 'eco' tourists and hunters. Fly-drive tours can be arranged.

Islazul, Paseo y 19, Vedado, T7-8320402, comazul@teleda.get.tur.cu Previously for Cubans only, this operator is now moving into tourism for foreigners, offering more unusual and off-the-beaten track excursions.

Rumbos, Calle O 108 entre 1 y 3, Miramar, Havana, T7-2049626, director@viajes rumbos.co.cu Organizes excursions and runs bars and cafés.

Sol y Son, Calle 23 64, La Rampa, Vedado, T7-333271, maite.garcia@solyson.avianet.cu The travel company of **Cubana** airlines. Has offices in many hotels around the country.

Finding out more

Various colourful, glossy brochures are produced by the tourist authorities, available in tourist offices worldwide, but for hard information you are better looking on the **internet**: www.dtcuba.com has lots of details and addresses of hotels, tour companies, car hire etc. If you click on *Cocoweb* you can ask any question you like and they will reply by email. All the questions by other travellers are published every seven to 10 days, a very useful service. They also have a weekly newsletter, *Boletín Semanal DTC News*, which you can obtain for free, webmasterdtc@3milenio.com

Another excellent website is www.cubaweb.cu which has sections on news, travel, politics, business, internet and technology, health, science, art and culture, festivals and events. Many companies are linked to this website. For finding out what is going on in sport, television and radio, as well as lots of basic information and links to other companies check out www.islagrande.cu

Cuban travel agencies on the net are www.travelnet.cu in Spanish, Italian and English and the English-language www.cubalinda.com run by former CIA agent, Philip Agee, particularly helpful for travellers from the USA. You can book tickets and excursions online. They have a biweekly newsletter, *Cuba Unlimited*, keeping you updated on developments in Cuba and problems with travelling from the USA.

Get your **maps** in Cuba if you can wait, as they are generally more reliable and up to date than any of the foreign maps we have seen, although, even then, not perfect. The **Freytag and Berndt** map of Cuba has street plans of the principal towns. See also page 47.

Cuban tourist offices overseas

Argentina, Marcelo T de Alvear 928, 4th floor, Buenos Aires, T541-43267810, 541-43267995, F541-43263325, oturcuar@tournet.com.ar

Canada, 440 Blvd René Levesque, Suite 1105, Montréal, Quebec H3Z 1V7, T1-514-8758004-5, F8758006, mintur@generation.net
55 Queen St E, Suite 705, Toronto, M5C 1R6, T1-416-3620700-2, F3626799, cuba.tbtor@simpatico.ca

China, 1 Xiu Shui Nan Jie, Jian Guo Men Wai, Beijing, 100600, T/F86-10-5626704, menendez@public.bta.net.cn

France, 280 Bd Raspail, 75014 Paris, T33-1-45389010, F45389930, ot.cuba@wanadoo.fr

Germany, Ander Hauptwache 7, 60313, Frankfurt, T49-69-288322-3, F296664, gocuba@compuserve.com

Italy, Via General Fara 30, Terzo Plano, 20124 Milan, T39-02-66981463, F67380725, minturitalia@infuturo.it

Mexico, Goether 16 3rd floor, Colonia Anzures, México DF, T52-5-2555897, 2507974, F2546439, otcumex@mail.internet.com.mex

Russia, Kutuzovski Prospekt, Dom 13 kb 40, T/F7-095-2430383, cuba@com2com.ru

Spain, Paseo de la Habana54-1, Izquierda, 28036 Madrid, T34-91-4113097, F5645804, otcuba@otcuba.esp.com

Sweden, Vegagatan 6, 3rd floor, 113-29 Stockholm, augusto_h@hotmail.com

UK, 154 Shaftesbury Ave, London WC2H 8JT, T44-020-72406655, F78369265, cubatouristboard.london@virgin.net

Language

Spanish is the official language, spoken fast with some consonants dropped. In the main tourist areas you will find staff often speak several languages, but off the beaten track you will need Spanish or very efficient sign language. **English** is becoming more commonly used; it is a university entrance requirement and encouraged by the influx of Canadian and now American tourists. **German**, **Italian** and **French** are now spoken by people working in the tourist industry and tour guides are usually multilingual. Many people also speak **Russian**. ▸▸ *For a list of Spanish words and phrases, see Footnotes, pages 438-443. For details of Spanish language and other courses, see page 27.*

Specialist travel

Disabled travellers

There are few facilities for disabled people. In the resort areas new hotels have been built with a few rooms adapted for people using wheelchairs, but the older, state-run, three-star hotels usually have no facilities and neither do *casas particulares*. Cuba is not easy to get around in a wheelchair and a certain amount of determination is required. Pavements are usually built up much higher than the roads, because of rain storms and flash flooding, which makes crossing the road hazardous. Potholes and loose paving stones compound the difficulties. If you are travelling independently it is not impossible to get around and stay in private accommodation, but you will have to do plenty of research first to make sure you can have a ground-floor room and that passages and doorways are negotiable with wheels. **Víazul** is the best bus company to use if you have someone to help you, or you can hire your own vehicle. Don't be discouraged, you will not be the first disabled person to travel around Cuba and Cubans are tremendously helpful and supportive.

Gay and lesbian travellers

Cuba has in the past been notoriously homophobic and after the Revolution many homosexuals were sent to hard labour camps to be 'rehabilitated'. The Mariel exodus was characterized as being the flight of criminals and homosexuals, who could no longer stand their human rights being flouted. However, attitudes gradually changed, and although Cuba is still a macho society, there is more tolerance of gays just as there is more religious freedom. The film, *Fresa y Chocolate* (see Cuban cinema, page 418), has done much to stimulate debate and acceptance. For an excellent account of Cuban attitudes to homosexuals, before and after the Revolution and up to the present, read Ian Lumsden's *Machos, Maricones and Gays, Cuba and Homosexuality*, published by the Temple University Press, Philadelphia and Latin American Bureau, London. Gay travellers will not generally encounter any problems in Cuba, there are no laws against homosexuality and physical assaults are rare. However, in practice, there can be difficulties with accommodation if you want to stay in *casas particulares* as some owners prefer not to rent rooms to same-sex partners, particularly if one of them is Cuban.

Single travellers

Whether you are a man or a woman travelling on your own, and whatever your age and physique, you will be approached by hustlers, known as *jineteros/as* looking to make a quick buck out of you. Be careful who you allow to become attached to you, for obvious reasons, and if you choose to have a companion make sure that the terms and conditions are fully understood by both parties. Single men and women are targeted by Cubans of the opposite sex, not only for their dollars, but also as a way out of the country if they can find a marriage partner. Single women will encounter the usual macho attitudes found in all Latin American countries and can expect to receive stares, hissing and comments on their attributes. Rape is not common, but the usual precautions should be taken to avoid getting into a compromising situation, trust your intuition, as always. ▸▸ *For further details, see also sex tourism, page 39.*

Student travellers

Cuba is not well geared up to offering student discounts unless you are part of a group that has been invited for a specific project. If you are travelling around Latin America as well as Cuba get an **International Student Identity Card** (ISIC), which is distributed by student travel offices and travel agencies in 77 countries. ISIC gives you special prices on all forms of transport (air, sea, rail etc, but not in Cuba), and access to a variety of other concessions and services. The head office is in the Netherlands: **The International Student Travel Confederation**, T31-20-4212800, www.istc.org Student cards must carry a photograph if they are to be of any use for discounts in Latin America. Agencies that specialize in student travel can be found on university campuses, eg **STA Travel**, www.sta-travel.com, www.statravel.co.uk, www.statravelaus.com.au (for the USA, UK, Australia). ▸▸ *For details of Spanish language and other courses, see page 27.*

Travelling with children

Cubans love children and the experience of travelling with children in Cuba can be rewarding for both parents and offspring. The children will love the beaches and the sea of course, but inland there are lots of opportunities for entertaining them, with trips to amusement parks, caves, rivers, farms and animals everywhere. Cuba is also tremendously educational; how many children living in Europe or North America have seen sugar cane, tobacco or coffee growing? Who wouldn't enjoy taking a *bicitaxi* or a horse-drawn *coche* and watching the oxen ploughing the fields? Trinidad is recommended for families, combining sightseeing for the adults with the proximity of a beach for the kids and a relaxed atmosphere. Sightseeing can be a very hot activity for small children, but the promise of the beach in the afternoon can smooth many a path. Many of Cuba's best beach resorts are remote from places of interest for sightseeing trips, which means several hours of sitting in a bus or car to get to where the grown-ups want to go. If hiring a car or buying enough **Víazul** bus tickets, see also page 41, can be very difficult, so advance reservations are essential. For teenagers interested in music, many of the best venues in Havana offer afternoon *peñas* and discos popular with Cuban youth, see Live music and dancing venues, page 127. Apart from the sun and the need to drink plenty of water, there are no particular health problems to watch out for. Diarrhoea and vomiting are the most common problems, so take the usual precautions, but more intensively (see Health, page 71, for further advice). Breastfeeding is best and most convenient for babies, but powdered milk is generally available and so are baby foods. Papaya, bananas and avocados are all nutritious and can be cleanly prepared. The treatment of diarrhoea is the same as for adults, except that it should start earlier and be continued with more persistence. Children get dehydrated very quickly and can become drowsy and unco-operative unless cajoled to drink water or juice plus salts. Upper respiratory infections, such as colds, catarrh and middle ear infections are also common and if your child suffers from these normally, take some antibiotics against the possibility. Outer ear infections after swimming are also common and antibiotic eardrops will help.

'Wet wipes' are always useful and sometimes difficult to find, as are disposable nappies. State-run restaurants have toilets for customers' use, but not all private restaurants have them; public toilets can be found in the centre of most towns, but you cannot rely on it. There are unlikely to be any facilities for changing babies' nappies/diapers, and remember to take a good supply of toilet paper as it is not usually supplied.

Women travellers

Whether single or in pairs, all women will be hassled in the street by men offering places to stay, eat, party or their services as guides. They can be persistent and annoying, although rarely threatening or violent. You can try ignoring them, saying 'no', or politely chatting and declining their offer. It doesn't make much difference. Your size and age is no problem to potential *jineteros* and the sex tourism industry is as active for women as it is for men. Men report similar approaches from Cubanas when they are on their own. It is simply a method of relieving you of your dollars. Try not to wear clothes which are too revealing or provocative or you will be considered fair game. Going to a club on your own at night is also an open invitation to the very macho Cuban men. Do not go to remote beaches on your own, choose a well-populated beach instead where there are Cuban families or a hotel for foreigners.

Studying in Cuba

There are no private schools but **language courses** are available at the universities of Havana and Santiago. They generally start on the first Monday of the month and you study 20 sessions of 45 mins a week, Monday to Friday 0900-1320. There are different levels of study and **Cuban cultural courses** are also available. At the Faculty of Modern Languages at the University of Havana, latest prices for beginners, intermediate and advanced are one week US$100, two weeks US$200, three weeks US$240, four weeks US$300. A four-week upgrade course US$360. A Cuban culture course, held every other month is US$360 for three weeks, or you can do a joint Spanish and Cuban culture course of 320 sessions for US$960, 480 sessions US$1,392. Commercial Spanish and Intensive courses in Spanish are also available. Contact **Dr Jorge Núñez Jover** or **Carmina Sainz Padrón** ① *Oficina de Postgrado, Calle J 556, entre 25 y 27, Vedado, T7-8324245.*

Two-week courses in **Spanish language with Cuban dance** and a cultural programme are offered by **Càlédöniâ Languages Abroad** ① *The Clockhouse, Bonnington Mill, 72 New Haven Road, Edinburgh, EH6 5QG, Scotland, T0131-6217721, F0131-6217723, www.caledonialanguages.co.uk* **Julio César Muñoz Cocina** ① *José Martí 401 entre Fidel Claro y Santiago Escobar, Trinidad, T/F419-3673, www.trinidadphoto.com*, runs **photography workshops**. Cubaism ① *Unit 30, DRCA Business Centre, Charlotte Despard Avenue, Battersea Park, London, W11 5HD, toll free T0800-298 9555, toll free F0800-298 9666, T44 20-7498 7671, F44 20-7498 8333, www.cubasalsaholidays.com*, offers **dance holidays** in Cuba. It also runs **film-making holidays** (www.filmmakingholidays.com) that include pre- and post-production workshops in the UK,

Working in Cuba

Foreign workers are brought in to Cuba for specific skilled jobs, but you cannot just turn up and hope to find work. If you want to stay in Cuba for a few months on a temporary basis, it is best to contact one of the Friendship Associations listed below for volunteering opportunities. Work brigades go to Cuba for a couple of weeks or a few months, helping in farming, construction or other activities and can be a great way to get to know the country and its people at a grass roots level, while also being taken to sites of interest and being entertained with music and dance on the brigade.
▸▸ *For details of business visas, see Visas, page 29.*

Friendship associations

There are over 1,600 solidarity organizations in some 120 countries. Many organize work brigades, charity tours and donations of medical supplies and equipment to beat the US trade embargo, and produce newsletters and magazines. Their support for the government is usually uncritical. The link organization in Cuba is the **Cuban Institute for Friendship with the Peoples (ICAP)**, in Havana, T7-552395. **Australia**: Australia Cuba Friendship Association, T03-93114611. **Canada**: Canadian Cuban Friendship Association (CCFA), T416-4108254, www.ccfatoronto.ca **UK**: Cuba Solidarity Campaign, T020-72636452, www.cubaconnect.co.uk **USA**: Cuba Solidarity Network, T510-2739199, www.igc.apc.org/cubasoli/; **Pastors for Peace**, www.ifconews.org; **Center for Cuban Studies**, T212-2420559, www.cubaupdate.org7; **Global Exchange**, Cuba Project, T415-2557296, www.globalexchange.org

Before you travel

Tourist cards

Visitors from the majority of countries need only a passport, return ticket and **30-day tourist card** to enter Cuba, as long as they are going solely for tourist purposes. Tourist cards may be obtained from Cuban embassies, consulates, airlines, or approved travel agents, which is a hassle-free way of obtaining a card. Price in the UK, £15 from the consulate, or from travel agents, some other countries US$15, Can$15 or 40 Swiss francs, up to US$35 in Malaysia. To get a tourist card at a consulate you have to fill in an application form, photocopy the main pages of your passport (valid for more than six months after departure from Cuba), submit confirmation of your accommodation booking (or at least the name of any hotel) and your return or onward flight ticket. Immigration in Havana airport will only give you 30 days on your tourist card, but for US$25 you can get it extended for a further 30 days only at Immigration in Nuevo Vedado (see below) and some other towns, eg, Santiago de Cuba.

Travellers to Cuba who will be staying with friends or in any private accommodation are not normally granted a tourist card unless they have a pre-booked hotel voucher for part of their stay. If you have not obtained a voucher in advance you could be asked to pay for a minimum of three nights in a hotel upon arrival in Cuba before being admitted to the country. Officially you have to request authorization from the Immigration Office if you want to stay outside hotels, but no one ever does as far as we know. However, generally, as long as the immigration people see the name of a hotel on your tourist card they are unlikely to enquire further. If you intend to stay in private accommodation (*casas particulares*), simply fill in any hotel (eg **Hotel Plaza** in Havana).

Visas

Nationals of countries without visa-free agreement with Cuba, journalists, students and those visiting on other business must check what visa requirements pertain and, if relevant, apply for an **official/business visa**. For this you are required to submit two application forms, two passport photos, your passport (tell them whether you want the visa in your passport or on a separate piece of paper), and a letter from the Cuban organization or company which has invited you. In the UK a business visa costs £32, plus £13 for the fax that has to be sent to Cuba in connection with the application. A journalist from Trinidad and Tobago paid US$50 for a visa plus an additional US$60 for a press card in Havana. A business visa is issued for one entry into Cuba and can take at least 10 days to process. There is also a **family visa**, for those who are visiting relatives, valid for one entry into Cuba. You have to fill in an application form naming the relative who has invited you (in duplicate), submit your passport (that must be valid for six months after your departure from Cuba) and pay a fee of £45.

Visitors travelling on a visa must go in person to the Immigration Office for registration the day after arrival. The office is on the corner of Factor y Final, Nuevo Vedado. When you register you will be given an exit permit.

Travelling from the USA

The **US Government** does not normally permit its citizens to visit Cuba. US citizens should have a US licence to engage in any transactions related to travel to Cuba, but tourist or business travel is not licensable, even through a third country such as Mexico or Canada. For further information on entry to Cuba from the US and customs requirements, US travellers should contact the **Cuban Interests Section**, an office of the Cuban Government, at 2630 16th St NW, Washington DC 20009, T202-7978518. They could also contact **Marazul Charters**, 250 West 57th St, Suite 1311, New York City, 10107 New York, T212-5829570, www.marazulcharters.com or Miami, T305-2328157 (information also from **Havanatur**, Calle 2 No 17 Miramar, Havana, T7-332121/2318). US citizens on business in Cuba should contact **Foreign Assets Control**, Federal Reserve Bank of New York, 33 Liberty St, NY 10045.

Many US travellers conceal their tracks by going via Mexico, the Bahamas, or Canada, where the tourist card is stamped, but not the passport. On your return, make sure that you have destroyed all tickets and other evidence of having been in Cuba. US travellers returning through Canada are stopped at the border and threatened with massive fines. The Bush administration is taking a hard line and officers are following policy guidelines. If you are stopped by an immigration official and asked whether you have been to Cuba, do not lie, as that is an offence. If they want to take it further, expect a letter from the **Office of Foreign Assets Control** (OFAC; Department of the Treasury). This will either ask for information on your suspected unlicensed travel, in which case you should refuse to incriminate yourself, or it will be a pre-penalty notice assessing a civil fine, often US$7,500, based on the money OFAC believes you would have spent in Cuba without a licence. The latter gives you 30 days to pay the fine or request an official hearing. The **National Lawyers' Guild** has drafted specimen letters you can use to reply to OFAC in either case; for further information see www.cubalinda.com

Cuban embassies overseas

Argentina Virrey del Pino No 1810, Belgrado (1426), Capital Federal, Buenos Aires, T54-1-7829049/7829149/ 7829089/7832213, F7867713

Australia The embassy is shared with, and located in, the Philippines, but there is a consulate: 18 Manwaring Ave, Maroubra NSW, 2035, T61-2-93114611, F931155112

Austria Himmelhofgasse 40 A-C, A-1130, Vienna, T43-1-8778198, F8778130

Brazil SHIS Q1-5, conjunto 18, Casa No 1, Lago sul, Brasilia, T55-61-2484700/ 2484130, F2486778/2487559

Canada 388 Main St, Ottawa, Ontario, K11E3, T1-613-5630141/ 5630326/5630136/ 5630209

Colombia Carrera 9 No 92-54, Santa Fe de Bogotá, T57-12-2573353/2573371/ 6217054, F6114382

Denmark See Sweden

France 16 Rue de Presles 75015, Paris, T33-1-45675535, F45658092

Germany Kennedyallee 22-24, Bad Godesberg 53175, Bonn, T49-228-3090, F309244

Israel Cuba has no diplomatic relations with Israel.

Italy Via Licinia No 7, 00153, Rome, T39-06-5742347/5755984, F5745445

Malaysia 20 Lengkongan Uthant, Kuala Lumpur, T03-4516808.

Mexico Presidente Mazaryk No 554, Colonia Polanco, Delegación Miguel Hidalgo, 11560, México D.F., T52-5-2808039/2808208, F2800839

Netherlands Mauritskade 49, 2514 HG The Hague, T31-70-3606061, F3647586

Norway See Sweden

Portugal Rua Pero Da Covilha No 14, Restelo, 1400, Lisbon, T351-1-3015318, F3011895

South Africa 45 Mackenzie St, Brooklyn 0181, Pretoria, PO Box 11605, Hatfield 0028, T27-12-3462215, F3462216

Spain Paseo de La Habana No 194 entre Calle de la Macarena y Rodríguez, Pinilla, 28036, Madrid, T34-91-3592500, F3596145

Sweden Karlavagen 49, 11449 Stockholm, T46-8-6630850, F6611418

Switzerland Gesellsschaftsstrasse 8, CP 5275, 30112, Berne, T41-31-3022111/ 3029830 (Tourist Office), F3022111

UK 167 High Holborn, London WC1 6PA, T44-0207-2402488/8367886, F8362602

Venezuela Calle Roraima entre Río de Janeiro y Choroni, Chuao, Caracas, T58-2-9912911/9916661/9912566, F9935695

Customs regulations

Personal baggage and articles for personal use are allowed in **duty free**; so are one carton of cigarettes and two bottles of alcoholic drinks. Visitors importing new goods worth between US$100 and US$1,000 will be charged 100% duty, subject to a limit of two items a year. No duty is payable on goods valued at under US$100. You may take in up to 10 kg of medicine. It is prohibited to bring in fresh fruit and vegetables, which will be confiscated if found. On departure you may take out tobacco worth US$2,000 with a receipt, or only 23 cigars without a receipt, up to six bottles of rum and personal jewellery. To take out works of art you must have permission from the **Registro Nacional de Bienes Culturales de la Dirección de Patrimonio del Ministerio de Cultura**. Books that are more than 50 years old may not be taken out of the country, nor those belonging to Ediciones R. For further details on customs regulations, refer to www.aduanaislagrande.com

Vaccinations

There are no vaccinations demanded by immigration officials in Cuba, but you would do well to be protected by vaccination against typhoid, polio, tetanus and hepatitis. There is no malaria in Cuba but dengue fever has been reported and there are lots of mosquitoes in the wetlands, so take insect repellent. Travellers coming from or going through infected areas must have certificates of vaccination against cholera and yellow fever. ⏵ *For further details, see also Health, page 71.*

What to take

Bring all medicines you might need as they can be difficult to find a[...]
aid kit. You might not be offered even a painkiller if you have an accident[...]
in very short supply. Many other things are scarce or unobtainable in Cuba, [...]
everything you are likely to need other than food: razor blades; medicines and [...]
antacid tablets for indigestion; sachets of rehydration salts plus anti-diarrho[...]
preparations; heavy duty insect repellent (containing DEET for preference); strong sun
protection and after-sun preparations; sunglasses for intense sunlight; toilet paper;
tampons; condoms and other contraceptives; disposable nappies; reading and
writing materials; photographic supplies; torch and batteries.

Insurance

Before you travel make sure you take out adequate insurance. Always read the small
print. All loss must be reported to the police and/or hotel authorities within 24 hours
of discovery and a written report obtained. This is notoriously difficult to obtain in
Cuba. **Asistur** is linked to overseas insurance companies and can help with
emergency hospital treatment, robbery, direct transfer of funds to Cuba etc. Main
office Prado 208, entre Colón y Trocadero, Habana Vieja, for 24-hour service
T7-338527, T7-8671315, www.asistur.cu

Money

Currency

The monetary unit is the **peso Cubano**. The official exchange rate is US$1 = 1 peso. There
are notes for 3, 5, 10 and 20 pesos, and coins for 5, 20 and 40 centavos and 1 peso. You
must have a supply of centavo coins if you want to use the local town buses (20 or 40
centavos) or pay phones (not all work). The 20 centavo coin is called a peseta. In 1995 the
government introduced a new **peso convertible** on a par with the US dollar, with a new set
of notes and coins, used freely in the country. It is fully exchangeable with authorized
hard currencies circulating in the economy. Remember to spend or exchange any *pesos
convertibles* before you leave the country as they are worthless outside Cuba. Euros are
accepted in the major tourist resorts, such as Varadero and Cayo Largo del Sur, while US
dollars are welcomed throughout the country.

Official **casas de cambio** (**Cadeca**) rates are around 26-27 pesos to the dollar and
there is virtually no black market. Cubans are allowed to hold US$ and to have a bank
account. There will be very little opportunity for you to spend pesos Cubanos unless you
are self-catering or travelling off the beaten track and you are advised to change only the
absolute minimum, if at all. Food in the markets (*agromercados*), at street stalls and on
trains, books, popular cigarettes, but not in every shop, can be bought in pesos. You will
need pesos for the toilet, rural trains, trucks, food at roadside cafeterias during a journey
and drinks and snacks for a bus or train journey. Away from tourist hotels, in smaller
towns such as Manzanillo, you will need pesos for everything. Visitors on pre-paid
package tours are best advised not to acquire any pesos at all. Bring US$ in small
denominations for spending money, dollars are now universally preferred. You will only
be able to change a US$50 or US$100 note into smaller bills in one of the large hotels or
on production of a passport (if change is available).

Credit cards and travellers' cheques

Travellers' cheques expressed in US or Canadian dollars, sterling or euro are valid in
Cuba. Travellers' cheques issued in the US will not be accepted, so it is best to take
Visa. A British credit card issued by a US bank (eg an **Abbey National** card issued by
MBNA) is not valid. Commission ranges from 2-4%. Don't enter the place or date

hey may be refused. Visa, MasterCard, Access, Diners, ...rnet **credit cards** are acceptable in most places. No US ...o a Visa card issued in the USA will not be accepted. A ...d by a US bank (eg MBNA) is not valid. American Express, no ..., is unacceptable. Many restaurants which claim to accept credit ...cards make such a fuss that it is not worthwhile. You can obtain cash advances with a credit card at several banks, but it is best to bring plenty of cash as there will often be no other way of paying for what you need. There are no toll-free numbers for you to call if your credit card is lost or stolen. You will have to phone home to the financial institution that issued you the card in order to put a stop on its use. Make a note of this number before you leave home, together with your credit card account number and keep them separate from your card.

ATMs and exchange

ATMs are being installed in the centre of most towns but they break down frequently and may not dispense the currency you want. It is usually quicker and easier to queue at a bank to get a dollar cash advance on your credit card than to trail around looking for a working ATM. There are banks and **Cadecas** (exchange houses) for changing money legally. The latter are usually open on Saturdays when banks are shut. Non-dollar currencies can be changed into dollars. Commission charges vary widely between banks and can be different from one town to the next, or even on different days of the week. The main bank handling foreign exchange transactions is the **Banco Financiero Internacional** (BFI), which has offices in most towns of any size, but there are plenty of others, such as **Bandec**, or **Banco Popular de Ahorro**, which can usually be found around the main square.

Money transfer

If you get really stuck and need money sent urgently to Cuba, you can get money transferred from any major commercial bank abroad direct to a Cuban bank, to **Asistur** (see Insurance page 31) immediately for a 10% commission, or to **Western Union** (see Directory sections for contact information) which is used largely by Cubans abroad to send money home to relatives, but US citizens can use a Cuban name to bypass their illegal traveller status. Transactions normally take one day to process; maximum US$300 (US$25 fee), less than US$100 (US$19 fee).

Cost of living and travelling

The average state employee's monthly salary is 200 pesos (US$10) and even doctors earn only around 320 pesos a month. Housing, education and medical care is provided at no cost and some basic foodstuffs are still rationed and heavily subsidized (see Food and drink, page 50), but making ends meet is extremely hard. Most consumer goods are priced in dollars, not pesos, and families have to have access to dollars to buy nice things for their home and family. It is therefore not surprising that Cubans will do almost anything to earn dollars and many families make sure that at least one member works in the dollar economy, eg tourism. The entire peso economy is subsidized, and although there are opportunities for travellers to use pesos, it is understandable that you will be expected to pay your way in dollars. You earn hard currency, so you pay in hard currency.

It is important to remember that Cuba is competing in the Caribbean, rather than the Latin American, market and its neighbours are selling themselves as luxury destinations. Compared with islands like the Bahamas or the Virgin Islands, it is cheap, but if you have just come from a backpacking trip through Latin America and want a stop-off on an island before you go home, you will find your last few dollars don't go very far. However, by Caribbean standards, Cuba has it all. You can stay at luxury hotels (over US$100 a night for a double room), dine in elegant restaurants (up to US$50 per person) and frequent world-famous nightclubs (US$70 at **Tropicana**), or for those on a mid-range budget you can stay in pleasant colonial hotels (US$60-80 for a double room), eat reasonably well (US$15-20 for a decent dinner) and find plenty to do in the evenings in the clubs, theatres and cinemas (US$2-10). Anyone with a more restricted budget should consider staying with Cuban families in the *casa particular* system (US$15-25 per room), which is the equivalent of a bed & breakfast place in Europe. You can eat at private restaurants (US$7-15) or on the street, changing a few dollars into pesos to make resources stretch further, and head for the *Casa de la Trova* (US$1-5) for entertainment. At the bottom end of the scale you could get by on US$40 a day, including transport, but few treats. It depends what you want to do, after all, sitting on the beach is free if you don't want a sunbed. A beer can cost US$1-3 depending on where you go and a *mojito* can vary from US$1 in a local bar to US$6 in the touristy **Bodeguita del Medio**, a Hemingway haunt. Based on two people sharing, this budget would include a *casa particular* of US$20 per room, US$3 for breakfast and US$7 for dinner in the *casa particular*, US$10 for transport or an excursion and US$10 for snacks, entry fees and entertainment, assuming you manage to buy some of your food with pesos. Increasing that budget by 50% would give you flexibility to take advantage of opportunities when they arise and have the freedom to explore a bit more.

Getting there

Air

The frequency of **scheduled** flights depends on the season, with twice-weekly flights in the winter being reduced to once a week in the summer. Some of the longer haul flights, such as from Buenos Aires, are cut from once a week in winter to once a month in summer. Most international flights come in to Havana, but the international airports of Varadero, Holguín (for Guardalavaca beaches), Santiago de Cuba, Ciego de Avila, Cayo Coco, Cayo Largo, Santa Clara (for Cayo Santa María) and Camagüey (for Santa Lucía beaches) also receive flights.

Buying a ticket

A **specialist travel agency**, such as **Journey Latin America** or **South American Experience**, see above, will be able to get you better deals than anything you can find on the internet. Some airlines, such as **Air Jamaica**, will not even sell you a ticket to Havana on the internet. The state airline, **Cubana de Aviación**, flies to Europe, Canada, Central and South America and to many islands in the Caribbean. It is cheaper than competitors on the same routes but the service is worse, seats are cramped, safety is an issue, and some travel agents do not recommend it. Packages including hotels and ground arrangements can work out cheaper. Early booking is essential as agents need at least 14 days' notice to get confirmations from Havana. **High seasons** cover the Easter period, the July to August European summer and the last three weeks of December. Prices quoted below include all taxes except for Cuban departure tax, US$25.

> ✦ *Remember to reconfirm your onward or return flight 48 hours before departure, otherwise you may lose your reservation.*

Flights from the UK

Direct flights are about nine hours. **Air Jamaica** flies from London direct, while **Air France**, **Iberia** and **Martinair** operate connecting services via Paris, Madrid and Amsterdam respectively. **Air Jamaica**'s low season prices vary from £431-515, its high season prices range from £574-641. **Air France,** from London via Paris, low season quotes are £473-517. High season prices rise to £595-640. **Iberia,** via Madrid, has flights from £463-517 (low season) up to £594 in the high season. **Martinair,** via Amsterdam, offers flights in the low season from £455 up to £654 in the high season.

Flights from the rest of Europe

Direct flights are available from Amsterdam, Berlin, Dusseldorf, Frankfurt, Madrid, Milan, Munich, Paris, Rome and Shannon depending on the season and the Cuban airport. **Air Europa** offers two-month tickets from Madrid for £507-575, while Iberia fares from Madrid are £548-560 valid for three months. Other airlines offering scheduled flights include **LTU, Condor** and **Aeroflot.** All flights from Europe arrive in Havana around 2000-2130, returning overnight.

Flights from North America

Since 1962, US citizens have only been permitted to visit Cuba providing they can prove they are travelling for journalistic, cultural, sporting or scientific purposes. At the beginning of 2004, despite Congressional votes to ease restrictions, the White House tightened regulations and few permits for travel were being granted. However, despite the risk of hefty fines, US travellers are increasingly travelling via a gateway city, such as Nassau, Mexico City, Cancún, or Grand Cayman. For advice on ticketing, see www.cubalinda.com Nassau is not particularly recommended because you have to clear US customs and immigration at Nassau airport and officials may become suspicious if a flight from Cuba has just landed. Try overnighting in the Bahamas on your return as a way of covering your tracks.

Cubana offers good deals from neighbouring gateways: US$180 round trip from Cancún (US$279 **Mexicana de Aviación/Aerocaribe**), US$189 from Nassau, US$219 from Freeport, Bahamas, US$333 from Santo Domingo and US$225 from Grand Cayman. **Air Jamaica's** fares from Montego Bay or Kingston are considerably more. From Canada there are direct flights from Montréal and Toronto with high, low and shoulder seasons, the cheapest from Montréal being around Can$790 in September. There are flights to Havana from lots of Mexican cities, with connections to other Cuban airports, and also from many Central American cities with local airlines (www.grupotaca.com).

Flights from Australia and New Zealand

There are no direct flights and you have to connect in a European, Canadian or Latin American city. Get a round-the-world ticket for the best deals and tack Cuba on to a South or Central American itinerary.

Airlines and agents

Aerocaribe, www.aerocaribe.com
Aeroflot, T020-72472424 (UK),
T 7095-7535555 (Russia), www.aeroflot.ru
Air Canada, T1-888-2472262 (Canada)
www.aircanada.ca
Air Europa, T0870-2401501 (UK),
T034-971-178100 (Spain),
www.aireuropa.com
Air France, T0845-0845111 (UK),
T33-820820820 (France), www.airfrance.com
Air Jamaica, T020 8570 7999 (UK),
T1-800-5235585 in the USA and the
Caribbean, www.airjamaica.com

Condor, T01802337135 (Germany),
www.condor.de
Cubalinda, T0053-7-553980 (Cuba)
www.cubalinda.com
Cubana, T020-75377909 (UK), T537-331986,
www.cubana.cu
Cubaism, Toll-free T0800 298 9555,
www.havanaflights.com
Iberia, T0845-6012854 (UK), T34-902-400500
(Spain), www.iberia.com
LTU, T49211-9418333, www.ltu.com
Martinair, T31-206011767 (Netherlands),
www.martinair.com
Mexicana, T020-84920000 (UK),
T 800-5317921, (USA/Canada),
www.mexicana.com

Sea

Ports of entry

Before arriving in **Cuban territorial waters** (12 nautical miles from the island's platform), you should communicate with port authorities on channel HF (SSB) 2760 or VHF 68 and 16 (National Coastal Network) and 2790 or VHF 19A (Tourist Network). Not many 'yachties' visit the island because of the political difficulties between Cuba and the USA. The US administration forbids any vessel, such as a cruise ship, cargo ship or humble yacht from calling at a US port if it has stopped in Cuba. This effectively prohibits anyone sailing from the US eastern seaboard calling in at a Cuban port on their way south through the Caribbean islands, or vice versa. However, it does not seem to prevent regattas being held between Florida and Cuban marinas. It is better to rent a bareboat yacht from a Cuban marina and sail around the island, rather than include it in a Caribbean itinerary. It would be worthwhile to invest in *The Cruising Guide to Cuba*, by Simon Charles (Cruising Guide Publications, Box 1017, Dunedin, FL 34697-1017, USA, T813-7335322, F813-7348179) before embarking. ▶▶ *For further details, see also Sailing, page 69.*

Havana, Cienfuegos and Santiago receive **tourist cruise** vessels. Marinas include the Hemingway, Tarará and Veneciana (in Havana), Dársena, Chapelín, Gaviota (in Varadero) and Cayo Largo. See the noticeboards for crewing opportunities on boats to Mexico, Florida etc.

Touching down

Airport information

Cuba has several airports classified as international, but only Havana is of any size. Havana now has three terminals, the third and newest one being for international flights, with **exchange facilities** open during normal banking hours, snack bars, shops, car rental and a 24-hour tourist information bureau (**Infotur** T7-666101, limited information). The airport is safe at night, which is when the European flights come in, and taxi services are efficient. See page 82 for transport from Havana airport into the city. **Immigration** can be very slow with long queues. Coming into one of the other airports (see Getting there, Air, page 33) is a more relaxed and speedy affair with less traffic.

> ❖ *Book your flight out of Cuba in your home country, as arranging it in Cuba can be arduous. The airport departure tax is US$25 at all international airports.*

There are a couple of *casas particulares* in the Altahabana district, Boyeros, quite close to Havana airport, see page 117, but there is no airport hotel and you will need to take a taxi ride to any accommodation.

The seating everywhere at Havana airport is uncomfortable. The **restaurant** upstairs, before you go through passport control, is OK for sandwiches or full meals, welcome after a long check-in and this will be your last chance to hear a live Cuban band while eating. The food on offer in the departure lounge is awful, with a choice between a microwaved hot dog or a soggy pizza. As most European flights leave late at night this can be a problem if you have a long wait for a (delayed) **Air France** or **Iberia** flight, but you can savour your last *mojito* in this vast, uncomfortable shed. At least the toilets are free and there is unlimited toilet paper. The selection of shops is limited but there is lots of rum, coffee, biscuits, a few books, postcards and magazines on sale. The selection of cigars is poor and overpriced. Rum costs much the same as elsewhere. The *Cubita* coffee, on the other hand, is marginally cheaper than in the dollar shops in town.

⁝ Touching down

Hours of business Government offices: 0830-1230 and 1330-1730 Monday to Friday. Some offices open on Saturday morning. Banks: 0830-1200, 1330-1500 Monday to Friday. Shops: 0830-1800 Monday to Saturday, 0900-1400 Sunday. Hotel tourist (hard currency) shops generally open 1000-1800 or 1900.

Official time Eastern Standard Time, five hours behind GMT; Daylight Saving Time, four hours behind GMT. However, Cuba does not always change its clocks the same day as the USA or the Bahamas. On Sunday, 5 October 1997, Cuba moved its clocks back one hour, which appeared to take everybody by surprise in the travel industry, including Cubans, and all flight times for the following week were changed on minimal notice. Best to check in the spring and autumn so that you are not caught out with missed flights and buses etc.

Voltage 110 Volts, 3 phase 60 cycles, AC. Plugs are usually of the American type, an adaptor for European appliances can be bought at the Intur shop at the Habana Libre. In some new tourist hotel developments, however, European plugs are used, with 220 volts, although they often provide adaptors, check in advance if it is important to you. These hotels include all Cubanacán's new ones, Gaviota hotels in Varadero and Gaviota El Bosque.

Weights and measures The metric system is compulsory, but exists side by side with American and old Spanish systems.

Local customs and laws

Clothing

This is generally informal and summer calls for the very lightest clothing. Sunglasses, a high factor sun lotion and some kind of head cover are recommended for those with fair complexions. A jersey and light raincoat or umbrella are needed in the cooler months; a jersey or fleece is also needed if you plan to travel on air-conditioned internal flights, buses (particularly overnight on **Víazul** bus) or trains, which are very cold. You should be appropriately dressed to go into a church or temple. Cubans dress up to go out at night.

Gifts

If you are planning to stay with Cubans, whether with friends or in private rented accommodation, there are some items in short supply in Cuba which they may appreciate: T-shirts (preferably with something written on them), household medicines such as paracetamol, cosmetics, cotton wool, tampons, washing-up or kitchen cloths, soap, neutral shoe polish, refillable cigarette lighters, pens, pencils, notebooks and writing paper. The list of items in short supply changes according to whether foreign exchange is available to pay for imports.

Tipping

Tipping customs have changed after a period when visitors were not allowed to tip in hotels and restaurants. It is now definitely recommended. Tip a small amount (not a percentage) in the same currency as you pay for the bill (typically US$1-2 on a US$25 meal). At times taxi drivers will expect (or demand) a tip. **Turistaxis** are not tipped, but the drivers still appreciate a tip. **Víazul** porters ask for tips in some bus stations (eg

Trinidad) just for putting your luggage in the hold, but in others (eg Camagüey) they will do almost anything for you in return for a friendly chat. There is no service charge or tip for food or lodging at *casas particulares*. The attendants in toilets expect a tip in return for a sheet or two of toilet paper. Musicians in bars and restaurants depend on your tips, give generously, they are worth it. Leaving basic items in your room, like toothpaste, deodorant, paper, pens, is recommended. Tourism workers pool all their tips so that behind-the-scenes staff also benefit, and regularly donate a percentage of their tips to the national health service for the purchase of equipment for cancer treatment in children etc. However, any evidence of malpractice should be reported to the management.

Prohibitions

It is illegal to photograph military or police installations or personnel, port, rail or airport facilities. A fee is charged for photographs in some museums and national monuments. Cubans face more prohibitions than foreigners, particularly in the realm of politics and freedom of speech, but are usually happy to discuss Castro, Cuba, their past and their future with you. Cubans are not allowed to accompany you into your hotel. This can sometimes be problematic if you or your partner look Cuban.
▸▸ *For further details, see Sex tourism, page 39.*

Responsible tourism

Travel to the furthest corners of the globe is now commonplace and the mass movement of people for leisure and business is a major source of foreign exchange and economic development in many parts of the Caribbean. In many areas, such as Cuba, it is the most significant economic activity. The benefits of international travel are self-evident for both hosts and travellers: employment; increased understanding of different cultures; business and leisure opportunities. At the same time there is clearly a downside to the industry. Where visitor pressure is high and/or poorly regulated, adverse impacts to society and the natural environment may be apparent. Paradoxically, this is as true in undeveloped and pristine areas (where culture and the natural environment are less 'prepared' for even small numbers of visitors) as in major resort destinations.

The travel industry is growing rapidly and increasingly the impacts of this supposedly 'smokeless' industry are becoming apparent. These impacts can seem remote and unrelated to an individual trip or holiday (for example air travel is clearly implicated in global warming and damage to the ozone layer, resort location and construction can destroy natural habitats and restrict traditional rights and activities), but individual choice and awareness can make a difference in many instances, and collectively, travellers are having a significant effect in shaping a more responsible and sustainable industry.

In an attempt to promote awareness of and credibility for responsible tourism, organizations, such as **Green Globe** (UK), T44-020-79308333, www.greenglobe21.com and the **Centre for Environmentally Sustainable Tourism (CERT)** (UK), T44-01268-795772, www.c-e-r-t.org now offer advice on destinations and sites that have achieved certain commitments to conservation and sustainable development. Generally these are larger mainstream destinations and resorts, but they are still a useful guide and increasingly aim to provide information on smaller operations.

Of course travel can have beneficial impacts and this is something to which every traveller can contribute. Many National Parks are partially funded by receipts from visitors. Similarly, travellers can promote patronage and protection of important archaeological sites and heritage through their interest and contributions via entrance and performance fees. They can also support small-scale

⁝ How big is your footprint?

1 Spend money on locally produced (rather than imported) goods and services and use common sense when bargaining; your few dollars saved may be a month's salary to someone else.
2 Use water and electricity carefully, travellers may receive preferential supply while the needs of local communities are overlooked.
3 Learn about local etiquette and culture, consider local norms of behaviour and dress appropriately for local cultures and situations.
4 Protect wildlife and other natural resources: don't buy souvenirs or goods made from wildlife unless they are clearly sustainably produced and are not protected under CITES legislation (CITES controls trade in endangered species and Cuba is a party to CITES).
5 Always ask before taking photographs or videos of people.
6 Consider staying in local accommodation rather than hotels; the economic benefits for host communities are far greater in Cuba and there are far greater opportunities for you to learn about the local culture. In the same vein, consider eating at *paladares*, which are privately run rather than state-run restaurants.

enterprises by staying in locally run hotels and hostels (in Cuba, private homes or *casas particulares*), eating in local restaurants (in Cuba, private restaurants or *paladares*) and by purchasing local goods, supplies and arts and crafts.

Organizations, such as **Conservation International,** T1-202-4295660, www.ecotour.org **The Eco-Tourism society,** T1-802-4472121, http://ecotourism.org **Planeta,** www2.planeta.com/mader and **Tourism Concern** (UK), T44-020-77533330, www.tourismconcern.org.uk, have begun to develop and/or promote ecotourism projects and destinations, and their websites are an excellent source of information and details for sites and initiatives throughout Latin America and the Caribbean. Additionally, organizations such as **Earthwatch** (UK), T44-1865-311601, www.earthwatch.org, and **Discovery International** (UK), T44-020-72299881, www.discoveryinitiatives.com, offer opportunities to participate directly in scientific research and development projects throughout the region.

Safety

In general the Cuban people are very hospitable. The island is generally safer than many of its Caribbean and Latin neighbours, but certain precautions should be taken. See also page 26, for Single travellers and page 27 for Women travellers. Visitors should never lose sight of their luggage or leave valuables in hotel rooms (most hotels have safes). Do not leave your things on the beach when going swimming. Guard your camera closely. Pickpocketing and purse-snatching on buses is quite common in Havana and Santiago. Also beware of bag-snatching by passing cyclists. Street lighting is poor so care is needed when walking or cycling in any city at night. Some people recommend walking in the middle of the street. Dark and crowded bars can also be a haven for thieves; in one bar in Pinar del Río, nine thefts from tourists were reported in one month.

Sex tourism

Cuba had a reputation for prostitution before the Revolution and after a gap of some decades it has resurfaced. Despite government crackdowns and increased penalties, everything is available for both sexes if you know where to look. Be warned, however, that you are likely to be fleeced. The age of consent is 18 in Cuba, so if you are introduced to a young girl you are in danger of being led into a blackmail trap. Foreigners on the lookout for a sexual partner are seen as fair game. Hotels are not allowed to let Cubans enter the premises in the company of foreigners. If you or your travelling companion is dark-skinned, you may suffer from the exclusion policy in hotels as officials will assume you are Cuban until proved otherwise. Sexual encounters now often take place in *casas particulares*, private homes where there is little security and lots of risk. Regulations are being tightened, but currently vary according to province. Cubans are not allowed to stay in *casas particulares* in Trinidad, but they are in other places as long as they have their *carnets de identidad*. These are registered in the book alongside the foreigner's passport details. This protects the owner and the tourist from robbery, but if the girl/boy is found to be staying in different places with different foreigners, she/he will be 're-educated' for prostitution or put in prison. A foreign man on his own will probably not be given the key to the house in case he brings a friend back in the early hours when the family is asleep. Two men will hardly ever be permitted, two women perhaps. If you go to an illegal *casa*, you have no protection and will probably be robbed. The *casa* owners face 15-year prison sentences for running brothels if too many *chicas* stay there. If you are a man out alone at night in Havana you will find the market very active and you will be tugged at frequently, mostly by females, but around **Coppelia** ice cream parlour in Vedado the prostitutes are mostly males. Cubans who offer their services (whether sexual or otherwise) in return for dollars are known as *jineteros*, or *jineteras* ('jockeys', because they 'ride on the back' of the tourists).

In 1999 it became a serious crime to do anything to harm tourism and the penalties are extremely severe with long prison sentences. The police are usually (but not always) helpful and thorough when investigating theft. Ask for a stamped statement for insurance purposes, although this is reported to be like getting blood out of a stone from some police stations. In the event of a crime, make a note of where it happened. Visitors should remember that the government permitting Cubans to hold dollars legally has not altered the fact that some of the local population will often do anything to get hard currency, from simply asking for money or dollar-bought goods, to mugging. Foreigners will be offered almost anything on the street – from cigars to cocaine to *chicas* (girls). Buying cigars on the street is not illegal, but they are often not genuine and may be confiscated at customs if you cannot produce an official receipt of purchase.

Take extra passport photos with you and keep them separate from your passport. If you have to get more photos while you are in Cuba, there is a place in Havana next to the **International Press Centre** at Calle 21 esquina O, which produces them for US$4, with a wait of about one hour.

Getting around

The shortages of fuel and spare parts in Cuba led to difficulties in the supply of long-distance transport, a major headache for independent travellers in the past. The problems are easing now, however, and you can generally get to anywhere you want if you know how to arrange it.

Internal flights are frequent and efficient but generally only link Havana with other towns, so you can not criss-cross the island by air. Old Soviet turbo-prop aircraft built in the 1950s or 1960s are still in use. **Roads** are good and there is little traffic except in Havana, which is a bit of a nightmare if you have just arrived. Out of the city, however, roads are fairly empty and you can often travel for miles without seeing another vehicle. New **buses,** paid for in dollars, run on long-distance routes between cities commonly visited by foreigners, to supplement the existing bus network used by Cubans. You may use these buses too, but they will be less comfortable and seats for foreigners are limited. All long-distance travel by foreigners is paid for in dollars. **Tour buses** are flexible, allowing you to stay a night or two in, say, Pinar del Río, before rejoining the tour for the return to Havana. **Car hire** is available, although you may not get the car you want unless you arrange it in advance from abroad. The disadvantage of car hire is that it is expensive and petrol stations are not always conveniently located, but you will have the freedom of going where you want, when you want and you will have the roads almost to yourself. A good way of getting around and meeting the people is to hire a **private car** with driver to take you out for a day. He will want to be paid in dollars, and he runs a considerable risk because it is illegal, but if there are two or three of you it can work out cheaper and more enjoyable than taking an organized excursion on a tour bus. The **express train** between Havana and Santiago de Cuba has improved since new French rolling stock was introduced in 2001, but most rail journeys are fraught with difficulties and generally are subject to breakdowns and long delays.

Air

There are **Cubana de Aviación** services between most of the main towns. From Havana: to Camagüey (US$72 one way); Holguín (US$82); Trinidad (US$74); Baracoa (US$108); Guantánamo (US$100); Manzanillo (US$82); Moa (US$100); Nueva Gerona/Isla de Juventud (US$22); Bayamo (US$82); Ciego de Avila (US$60); Las Tunas (US$80); Santiago (US$90); Cayo Largo (US$56); Cayo Coco (US$80); Varadero (US$32); all have airports. Santa Clara and some places with airstrips are reached by **Aerotaxi** – flying buses and you often get wooden bench seating in an old Soviet aircraft. Return fare is twice the single fare. Tourists must pay air fares in US$; it is advisable to prebook flights at home as demand is very heavy, although you can get interprovincial flights from hotel tour desks if you are on a package deal. It is difficult to book flights from one city to another when you are not at the point of departure, except from Havana; the computers are not able to cope. Airports are usually a long way from the towns, so extra transport costs will be necessary. Delays are common. **Cubana** and **Aerotaxi** flights are very cold, take warm clothes and possibly some food for a long flight. Although theoretically possible to get a scheduled flight as listed above, it is often only possible for tourists to travel on excursions: day trips or packages with flights, accommodation, meals and sightseeing.

Aerogaviota is a charter airline owned by the armed forces, with national and international flights to Central America and the Caribbean, using 20-seater YAK-40 planes and eight-seater MI-8 helicopters, Avenida 47 2814 entre 28 y 34, Rpto Kohly, Havana, T7-2030668, aerogavcom@iacc3.get.cma.net

Rail

Train journeys are recommended, although long delays and breakdowns must be expected. Be at the station at least one hour before the scheduled departure time. Fares are reasonable but have to be paid for in dollars, which will usually entitle you to a waiting area, seat reservation and to board the train before the big rush starts. There is a dollar ticket office in every station. Alternatively, the tourist desks in some of the larger hotels and tour agencies, such as **Cubatur** sell train tickets to foreigners, in dollars.

Long distance trains allow only seated passengers, they are spacious and comfortable, but extremely cold unless the air conditioning is broken, so take warm clothes and a torch (needed for the toilets). All carriages are smoking areas. **Bicycles** can be carried as an express item only and often cost more than the fare for a person (see Cycling, page 46). On the *especial* a trolley passes through once with 'sandwiches' and juice, followed later by coffee (pay in pesos). Sometimes there are additional

> ✷ *Train journeys between provinces are usually booked solid days, often weeks, in advance. With time restraints, Víazul bus or an organized excursion is a better option.*

sandwiches and drinks for sale at a bar (dollars only), but it is advisable to take food with you. Availability of food can not be guaranteed on the *trece* (the most basic and slow of the three services) but sometimes cold fried meat with rice and black beans is sold in a cardboard box for 15 pesos. You have to tear off a piece of the box to use as an eating tool. This is sold soon after leaving Havana and there will be nothing else for the rest of what may be a 30-hour trip unless you can get something at station stops. Make sure you have pesos with you. Also take toilet paper.

Road

Bus (guagua)

Local The local word for a bus is *guagua*. Urban transport is varied; buses can be motorized or horse drawn (*coches*). Horses made a comeback during the crisis of the 1980s when fuel shortages limited services and are still common in provincial towns, even though buses are now back on the streets. In Havana there are huge double-jointed buses pulled by a truck, called *camellos* (camels) because of their shape, also irreverently known as 'Saturday night at the cinema' because they are full of 'sex, crime and alcohol'. In the rush hours they are filled to more than capacity, making it hard to get off if you have managed to get on. There are also regular buses in Havana and other major towns. The urban bus fare throughout Cuba is 20 centavos for *camellos* and 40 centavos for all others; it helps to have the exact fare. Urban tickets can only be bought in pesos Cubanos.

Long distance For bus transport to other provinces from Havana there are two companies offering services in dollars to foreigners, **Víazul** and **Astro**. The best service is **Víazul** (*Viajes Azul*), at Avenida 26 entre Avenida Zoológico y Ulloa, Nuevo Vedado, T7-8811413, www.viazul.cu 0900-2300, with long-distance buses and minibuses, see timetable on page 42. It is more expensive than **Astro**, but the buses are more comfortable, a/c, and films are shown on the longer journeys. You will mostly travel with other foreigners, rather than Cubans, because all tickets are sold in dollars, but it is an efficient and punctual service, which **Astro** isn't.

It is essential to book in advance during peak season and August, which can be very busy with an increased number of Cuban tourists and French travellers. Even booking up to two or three days in advance may not be sufficient to guarantee a seat, especially if you are a family with children or travelling in a group. If you are picking up a **Víazul** bus en route between Havana and Santiago, for example, it's worth bearing in mind that a minimal number of seats will be allocated.

⁞ Víazul routes, fares and daily schedules

Route	Fare	Departure times		
Havana to Santiago de Cuba	US$51	0930	1500	2000
Santa Clara	US$18	1350	1925	2340
Sancti Spíritus	US$23	1510	2045	0100
Ciego de Avila	US$27	1625	2205	0235
Camagüey	US$33	1815	2355	0420
Las Tunas	US$39	2055	0205	0650
Holguín	US$44	2200	0320	0805
Bayamo	US$44	2320	0440	0925
Santiago de Cuba	**Arrives**	0130	0650	1130
Santiago de Cuba to Havana	US$51	0900	1515	2000
Bayamo	US$7	1105	1720	2205
Holguín	US$11	1225	1840	2325
Las Tunas	US$11	1330	2000	0040
Camagüey	US$18	1610	2240	0240
Ciego de Avila	US$24	1755	0130	0435
Sancti Spíritus	US$28	1910	0200	0600
Santa Clara	US$33	2030	0320	0720
Havana	**Arrives**	1910	0705	1130
Havana to Trinidad	US$25	0100	0815	1300
Cienfuegos	US$20	0100	1220	1705
Trinidad	**Arrives**	1500	1845	
Trinidad to Havana	US$25	0745	1500	
Cienfuegos	US$6	0920	1635	
Havana	**Arrives**	1320	2035	
Havana to Viñales	US$12	0900		
Pinar del Río	US$11	1120		
Viñales	**Arrives**	1215		
Viñales to Havana	US$12	1330		
Pinar del Río	US$6	1415		
Havana	**Arrives**	1645		
Havana to Varadero	US$10	0800	0830	1600
Matanzas	US$7	1005	1030	1805
Varadero Airport	US$10	1035	1105	1825
Varadero	**Arrives**	1100	1130	1900
Varadero to Havana	US$10	0800	1600	1800
Varadero Airport	US$6	0825	1625	1825
Matanzas	US$6	0850	1645	1845
Havana	**Arrives**	1045	1845	2045

Route	Fare	Departure times	
Varadero to Trinidad	US$20	0730	
Santa Clara	US$11	1045	
Sancti Spíritus	US$16	1210	
Trinidad	**Arrives**	1325	
Trinidad to Varadero	US$20	1430	
Sancti Spíritus	US$6	1540	
Santa Clara	US$8	1705	
Varadero	**Arrives**	2025	
Trinidad to Santiago	US$33	0815	
Sancti Spíritus	US$6	0925	
Ciego de Avila	US$9	1045	
Camagüey	US$15	1330	
Las Tunas	US$12	1530	
Holguín	US$26	1645	
Bayamo	US$26	1805	
Santiago	**Arrives**	2015	
Santiago to Trinidad	US$33	1930	
Bayamo	US$7	2150	
Holguín	US$11	2310	
Las Tunas	US$11	0030	
Camagüey	US$18	0225	
Ciego de Avila	US$24	0415	
Sancti Spíritus	US$28	0545	
Trinidad	**Arrives**	0700	
Santiago to Baracoa	US$15	0730	
Guantánamo	US$10	0910	
Baracoa	**Arrives**	1220	
Baracoa to Santiago	US$15	1415	
Guantánamo	US$10	1720	
Santiago	**Arrives**	1905	
Varadero to Cienfuegos	US$16	0830	
(high season only)	**Arrives**	1300	
Cienfuegos to Varadero	US$16	1400	
	Arrives	1825	
Havana to Playas del Este	US$4	0840	1420
	Arrives	1000	1540
Playas del Este to Havana	US$4	1030	1640
	Arrives	1140	1750

Essentials Getting around

Baggage handlers in Havana, Trinidad and some other tourist towns have an irritating habit of demanding a tip even though they hardly touch your bag. Any small coin will satisfy them. **Astro** has a dollar ticket office in the Terminal de Omnibus Nacional, Boyeros y 19 de Mayo (third left via 19 de Mayo entrance), T7-8703397, daily 0700-2100. You don't have to book in advance but it might be wiser to do so as some **Astro** routes have a quota for dollar-paying passengers. Cubans often have to book tickets (in pesos) months in advance at busy times of the year and will not take kindly to dollar-paying foreigners taking up their seats. Away from the capital and off the beaten track, it is not so controversial to pay in pesos, in fact you may have no option. The **Víazul** terminal in Havana is a long way from the centre and you will have to get a taxi. In other cities **Víazul** and **Astro** use the same bus terminal. There is a weight limit for luggage of 20 kg on all long-distance bus journeys and the bus-ferry/catamaran to Isla de la Juventud. (See Sea, page 47.). In Havana and Pinar del Río some ticket sellers refuse to sell tickets until the bus arrives. Passengers in the waiting lounge are not told when it does arrive and it leaves without them. The 'helpful' ticket seller then tries to sell them a seat in a private taxi, for which he/she no doubt receives a commission.

Driving

Hiring a car is recommended, in view of difficulties of getting public transport to out of the way places and you can save a considerable amount of time, but it is the most expensive form of travel. Breakdowns are not unknown, in which case you may be stuck with your rented car many kilometres from the nearest place that will accept dollars to help you. Be careful about picking up hitchhikers, although it can be an interesting way of meeting Cubans, as well as being a useful talking road map.

Petrol stations are not self-service. Petrol for foreigners is available in **Cupet** stations, costs US$0.75 for *regular* and US$0.90 for *especial* per litre and must be

	Bayamo	Camagüey	Cienfuegos	Guantánamo	Havana	Holguín	Matanzas	Pinar del Río	Santa Clara	Santiago de Cuba
Baracoa	313	524	853	116	1051	348	989	1192	793	193
Bayamo		211	540	197	738	71	676	879	480	120
Camagüey	211		329	408	527	208	465	668	269	331
Cárdenas	628	417	171	825	146	625	56	287	148	748
Ciego de Avila	321	110	219	518	397	318	335	538	139	441
Cienfuegos	540	329		737	246	537	199	387	61	660
Guantánamo	197	408	737		935	232	873	1076	677	77
Havana	738	527	246	935		735	90	141	258	858
Holguín	71	208	537	232	735		673	876	477	155
Las Tunas	82	129	458	279	656	79	594	740	398	202
Manzanillo	60	271	600	257	798	131	736	39	540	180
Matanzas	676	465	199	873	90	673		231	196	796
Nuevitas	286	75	404	483	602	283	540	743	344	406
Palma Soriano	73	284	613	124	811	108	749	952	553	47
Pinar del Río	879	668	387	1076	141	876	231		399	999
Sancti Spíritus	395	184	145	592	343	382	281	484	85	515
Santa Clara	480	269	61	677	258	77	196	399		600
Santiago de Cuba	120	331	660	77	858	155	796	999	600	
Trinidad	468	257	72	665	318	465	271	459	122	588

Approximate distances in kilometres

paid for in US$. If possible, get the rental company to fill the car with fuel, otherwise
your first day will be spent looking for petrol. A number of hire cars use diesel, which
can be more difficult to get hold of than petrol. For example, from Santiago to Pilón
(250 km) there is only one gas station, selling petrol to Cubans only and no diesel.
Between Santiago and Baracoa diesel is only available in Guantánamo. Only the
main fuel stations sell diesel.

Autopistas were incredibly empty of traffic during the 1980s and 1990s, but as
the economy picks up traffic is increasing. Cubans have been using the hard surface
for other purposes, such as drying rice on the roadside. Oxen, horses, donkeys,
bicycles and tractors will be sharing the fast lane with you. A military band was seen
practising as though the soldiers were on a parade ground. The dogs on the side of
the road are often not dead, just asleep. Watch out for low-flying vultures preying on
any animals that really are dead. Cubans slow right down and give them a wide berth;
they can do enormous damage to your car if you do hit one. Main roads can be good
places to shop for fresh fruit and vegetables, vendors stand by the roadside (or in the
road) or sell from broken down trucks. Most ordinary roads are in reasonable
condition, but minor roads can be very badly maintained and signposting is uniformly
atrocious or non-existent. Even when there are road signs they are usually so
bleached by the sun that they are illegible until you draw level with them. Finding your
way across a large city like Havana can present problems, in spite of the courteous
assistance of police and pedestrians.

Driving at night can be extremely hazardous and is not recommended. Even in
major cities many streets are not lit. You are likely to encounter horses, cattle, pigs,
goats and sheep monopolizing the road without any semblance of lighting. In
addition, cyclists, bullock carts and other vehicles without lights are common. It is
best to travel early in the day and reach your destination before nightfall. During the
winter months, November to March, sunrise is at 0700 and sunset at 1830 (2000 in
summer months). Cubans drive on the right-hand side.

Car hire

Through state rental companies at the International Airport and most large hotels,
www.dtcuba.com/esp/transporte_tierra.asp or try the companies direct.

Cubacar: www.cubacar.cubanacan.cu **Havanautos:** www.havanautos.cu **Rex:**
www.rex.rentacar.com **Transtur:** www.transturentacar.cu **Vía Rent-a-Car:**
rentvia@teleda.gct.tur.cu Try also UK-based **Cubaism,** www.havanacarhire.com.

Minimum US$40 a day (or US$50 for air conditioning) with ❢ *During July and August,*
limited mileage of 100 km a day, and US$8-20 a day optional *it is extremely difficult to*
insurance, or US$50-88 per day unlimited mileage; cheaper *hire a car without booking*
rates over seven days. Visa, MasterCard, Eurocard, Banamex, *well in advance. It is*
JCB and Carnet accepted for the rental, or cash or travellers' *advisable to arrange car*
cheques paid in advance, guarantee of US$200-250 required; *hire from home before*
you must also present your passport and home driving licence. *you travel*.

In practice, you may find car hire rates prohibitively expensive
when small cars are 'unavailable' and a four-door sedan at US$93, unlimited
kilometres, insurance included, is your only option. Staff have been reported as
'unhelpful' in finding what you want. However, it pays to shop around, even between
offices of the same company. Cubans are not allowed to hire cars unless they have a
passport (although they may drive them), so even if you have organized a local driver
you will have to show a foreign driving licence. If you want to drive from Havana to
Santiago and return by air, try **Havanautos**. They will charge at least US$80 to return
the car to Havana, but most companies will not even consider it. **Vía Rent-a-Car**
(Gaviota) charges US$160, calculated at US$0.18 per km on a distance of 884 km
from Santiago to Havana, but this is reduced to US$0.09 if the car is hired for more
than 15 days. If you hire in Havana and want to drop off the car at the airport,

companies will charge you extra, around US$10, although this is sometimes waived if you bargain hard. Check what is required concerning fuel, you don't always have to leave the tank full, but make sure the tank is really full when you start. Fly and drive packages can be booked from abroad through **Cubacar**, part of the **Grupo Cubanacán**, who have a wide range of jeeps and cars all over the country and can even arrange a driver. Or you can do it through **Cubanacán** in the UK, who can organize rentals of Suzuki Samurai jeeps (or equivalent). Most vehicles are Japanese or Korean makes, Suzuki jeeps can be hired for six to 12 hours in beach areas, US$11-22, plus US$8 insurance, extra hours US$5. Watch out for theft of the radio and spare tyre; you will have to pay about US$350 if stolen unless you take out the costly extra insurance. **Campervans** are also available, see www.vacacionartravel.com or www.cubamarviajes.cu A suggested tour of the whole island covers 2,550 km with demarcated stops for overnight and refueling. Seven days' hire of a motorhome is US$1,015, 14 days' hire is US$1,960. **Moped rental** at resorts is around US$8-10 per hour, cheaper for longer, US$25-30 per day, US$80 per week.

Bicycles

For people who really want to explore the country in depth and independently, cycling around is excellent. A good-quality bicycle is essential if you are going to spend many hours in the saddle, although that does not mean it has to be very sophisticated. We have heard from cyclists who have toured Cuba without gears, although they did have plenty of muscle. ▶▶ *For further details, see Cycling, page 58.*

Hitchhiking

With the shortage of fuel and decline in public transport since 1991, Cubans have taken to organized hitchhiking to get about. At every major junction outside towns throughout Cuba you will find the *Amarillos*, traffic wardens who organize a queue, stop traffic to find out where the trucks or vans are going, and load them with passengers. You pay a nominal amount in pesos, for example six pesos for a four-hour ride from, say, Cienfuegos to Havana in an open truck, although some drivers will not allow foreigners on board. You can also hitchhike (*a botella*) unofficially and get rides in ancient cars without floors, trucks and other makeshift vehicles. Cubans are not allowed to carry dollar-paying foreigners in their vehicles, so if stopped it is the Cuban's problem not yours. Be prepared to tip the driver, or negotiate a fare before you get in.

Taxis

There are three types of taxi: **dollar tourist taxis**, **Cuban taxis** (*colectivos*) and **private taxis** (*particulares*). See also Transport, Havana, page 138. **Dollar tourist taxis** can be hired for driving around; you pay for the distance, not for waiting time. On short routes, fares are metered. **Cuban taxis**, or *colectivos*, also operate on fixed routes and pick you up only if you know where to stand for certain destinations. The flat rate fare is 10 pesos. Travelling on them is an adventure and a complicated cultural experience. If you are lucky enough to get into a *colectivo*, sit at the back and keep quiet. Tourists are not supposed to use this service. Cubans are not allowed to carry foreigners in their vehicles, but they do. **Private taxis**, *particulares*, are cheaper than other taxis. A *particular* who pays his tax will usually display a 'taxi' sign, which can be a hand-written piece of board, but have a private registration plate. Some have meters, in others you have to negotiate a price in either pesos or dollars, although as a foreigner you will be urged to pay in dollars. If not metered, 10 km should cost around US$5.

For long distances you can negotiate with official taxis as well as *particulares*, and the price should be around US$10 per hour. Taxis can work out cheaper than going on organized tours, if you are in a group and are prepared to bargain. As a general rule, the cost will depend on the quality of your Spanish and how well you know the area. We have received reports of a Dutch family paying US$80 to travel from Havana to Viñales by taxi, although someone else was quoted US$50 for the return journey.

Sea

There is currently only one journey you can do by public transport across the sea, and that is to the Isla de la Juventud (see page 371), although a ferry service from Havana to Varadero is proposed. To the Isla you have a ferry or catamaran, depending on which is working that day. Both leave from Surgidero de Batabanó on the coast due south of Havana, from where there are bus or train links.

Maps

Mapa Geográfico (Ediciones GEO) is one of the best maps, with a large map of Cuba, accompanied by several smaller maps of towns, regions and routes. It is one of the more accurate and up to date. The best map for drivers is the *Guía de Carreteras* (Road Guide), Directorio Turístico de Cuba (3rd edition 2000), which has proved remarkably accurate. It grades all the roads, gives distances and marks fuel stations. *Cuba, Mapa de Carreteras* (Road Map), Ediciones GEO (1999), is a good general purpose map as well as being moderately useful for drivers. Its inset map of La Habana includes details of all the major road junctions around the capital. Ediciones GEO's *Mapa Turístico* of La Habana (with Cuba, Varadero, Trinidad, Santiago, Guardalavaca, Cayo Largo and Cayo Coco on the reverse) is good in that it includes a lot of the city. For individual states and areas there are very good provincial maps going under the name of *Mapa Turístico* (Ediciones GEO), usually including the provincial capital and sometimes other places of interest, but you will probably only find them in the relevant province. **Infotur** is worth trying, see page 83.

Stanfords ① *12-14 Long Acre, London, WC2E 9LP, T020-7836 1321, F020-7836 0189, www.stanfords.co.uk*, with over 80 well-travelled staff and 40,000 titles in stock, is the world's largest map and travel bookshop. Also at 29 Corn Street, Bristol, BS1 and 39 Spring Gardens, Manchester, M2. In Cuba, one shop to try for maps of all kinds including nautical maps is the **Instituto Hidrográfico** ① *Mercaderes entre Obispo y Oficios, Habana Vieja.*

Sleeping

All hotels are state owned. The best are those with foreign investment or foreign management contracts, which are found in the resort areas. However, there are hotels to suit most budgets, even if at the lower end they are basic. Cubans stay in peso hotels, which are rarely available to foreigners. Cubans on holiday stay in campsites which occasionally accept dollary-paying foreigners. A growing segment of the market is the private sector. It is now legal to stay with a Cuban family and rent a room as long as the family is registered and pays taxes. These places are known as *casas particulares*.

Hotels

All hotels are **government owned**, solely or in joint ventures with foreign partners. The **Gran Caribe** chain owns the four- and five-star grand old hotels such as the *Nacional* and the *Riviera* in Havana. **Cubanacán** has upmarket, modern resort hotels, with an international standard of accommodation and facilities, as does **Gaviota**, owned by the military. **Horizontes** owns the two- and three-star, older hotels, often in the countryside. **Habaguanex** is in charge of the renovations of colonial mansions in La Habana Vieja and their conversion to hotels, restaurants, bars etc. **Islazul** has the cheaper end of the market, mostly for national tourism, but foreigners are welcome and many of their hotels are being upgraded. Islazul renovations of colonial mansions into boutique hotels are some of the nicest places to stay at very reasonable prices.

A three-star hotel costs US$30-50 bed and breakfast in high season, US$25-35 in low season, while a four-star hotel will charge US$80-90 and US$60-70 respectively. Most three-star hotels were built in the 1940s and 1950s and are showing their age, but some have been refurbished and are now considered four star. In remote beach resorts the hotels are usually all-inclusive. At the cheaper end of the market you can expect old bed linen, ill-fitting sheets, intermittent water and electricity, peeling paintwork, crumbling tiles and indifferent service.

Accommodation for your first day in a hotel should be booked in advance of travelling. You have to fill in an address (any hotel will do) on your **tourist card** and if you leave it blank you will be directed to the reservations desk at the airport, which is time consuming. A voucher from your travel agent to confirm arrangements is usual and hotels expect it as confirmation of your reservation. This can be done abroad through travel agencies, accredited government agencies, or through *Turismo Buró* desks in main hotels. It's a good idea to book hotel rooms generally before noon. In the peak seasons, December to February and August, it is essential to book in advance. Lack of sufficient rooms forced tourists to sleep in their cars in December 2003 in Trinidad and in the plaza in Viñales in August.

At other times it is possible to book at the hotel reception. Prices given in the text are for a double room in high season (15 December-15 March); low season prices are about 20% lower. Shop around for prices, travel agencies can get you a better deal than the hotel, which will usually offer you the rack rate. UK-based company **Cubaism** offers real-time hotel availability and online reservations for a number of hotel groups, www.cubahotelbookings.com

Casas particulares/private accommodation

Cuba is geared more to package tourism than to independent visitors, but self-employment has opened up opportunities that can prove rewarding for the visitor. Lodging with a family is possible (at US$15-30 per day or with breakfast and evening meal included, $35-40 for a single traveller or $40-45 for two people). Cubans are allowed to rent out only two rooms sleeping two people plus one child in each,

Hotel prices and facilities

LL-AL These hotels will be of an international standard, probably with a foreign partner in management. On the beach they will mostly be all-inclusive and the price will be per person with all the day and night time entertainment you could possibly need and a high quality of fixtures and fittings. In cities they are a mixture of brand new, foreign-run hotels in which you may forget you are in Cuba, and delightful renovated colonial mansions with new bathroom fittings and lots of charm. US$101-$200.

A-B These will be very good hotels with newish furnishings, a pool, tour desk and good facilities. In Havana many of them are in the old city and are 'boutique' hotels, small and intimate, colonial and newly renovated. On the beach they will be older properties, not as luxurious as the all-inclusives but they may have the best bits of beach. US$61-100.

C-D The lower end of the state hotel sector, older properties often in need of upgrading, less attactive areas of town or just off the beach, but bargains can be had and in the countryside are often delightful rural retreats. US$31-60.

E-F You wouldn't want to stay in a hotel in this range, but this is where the private sector comes in. Casas particulares cost more in Havana than in the provinces. Quality is variable; check availability of water, electricity and food, test the beds. Most are spotlessly clean and friendly. Under US$30.

subject to health and hygiene regulations and incorporation into the tax system. Hustlers on the street will offer accommodation, but it is safer to arrange rooms through our recommendations or other contacts if you can. A guide or hustler taking you to a private home will expect US$5 commission per night, which goes on your room rate. Less obvious, but still an insidious form of touting is the networking of the *casa particular* owners. Most have an address book full of owners in other towns. If you ask whether they know someone in the next town you are going to, they will happily ring up a 'friend' and book a room for you. This may be a useful service, but you will be charged US$5 extra a night for the favour, a sum which will be sent to the first owner as his commission. Some owners take this so seriously that they travel around the country in low season, inspecting the properties they recommend and getting to know the families.

You must pay in dollars. Remember that rates are likely to be negotiable if you go direct to the owners, or stay for several nights, although paying per night will keep your options open if you see better accommodation.

Making a reservation before arrival is essential during high season and is also recommended in August, when characterful accommodation is often booked weeks in advance.

Private homes vary considerably and can be extremely comfortable or very basic. Houses in the town centre can be very noisy if your room is on the street and traffic starts at 0530. Colonial houses have no soundproofing and even a door shutting can be heard all over the house at 0600. Because of shortages things often don't work, there may be water and power cuts. Take a torch, there may not be good street lighting in the area, let alone power in your house. The sheets don't always fit the bed, the pillows can be often old and lumpy, bathrooms are often shared between the two rooms but they should be exclusive to tourists' use. Towels are usually very small so take your own to complement theirs. Soap will probably be provided, but don't rely on it. Air conditioning is common but invariably noisy and will give you throat problems if you sleep with it on all the time. If there is a fan use that instead. All *casas* now have to pay a 'gastronomic' tax whether they want to provide food or not, so they usually do. Food is nearly always better at a *casa particular* than in a state restaurant or private *paladar*. The family eats at a different time and the food is prepared in stages, but it will still be fresher and made from better ingredients than in a restaurant. Remember that what Cubans can buy with ration coupons is not enough to feed a visitor and any extra food has to be bought in dollars. Theft is not a problem, as the licence would be revoked if there was a serious complaint against the owner but you should always be careful with your belongings.

It is best to check that the *casa particular* you stay in is legally registered and pays taxes. All *casas particulares* should have a sticker on their front door of two blue chevrons (changing to green in 2004) on a white background with *Arrendador Inscripto* written across, if they are legal. Those with red triangles rent in pesos to Cubans and it is illegal for them not to rent to foreigners. If you stay at an illegal residence and it is discovered, the Cuban family will have to pay a huge fine. Illegal homestays are usually reported to the police by neighbours. All clients must sign and complete address and passport details in a Registration Book within 24 hours of arrival. This book must be made available to municipal inspectors.

Camping

Official campsites are opening up all over the island; they are usually in nice surroundings and are good value. They consist of basic cabins rather than tents and are designed for Cubans on holiday rather than foreigners. Camping out on the beach or in a field is forbidden. **Cubamar Viajes**, Avenida 3 y 12, Vedado, T7-662523, www.cubamarviajes.cu cubamarviajes@cubamarviajes.cu will arrange bookings and transport to villa or cabin-style accommodation in most provinces, open from Monday to Friday 0830-1700, and on Saturday and Sunday 0830-1200. They have six campsites for tourists using camper vans, with water, power and waste disposal, at Dos Hermanos (Pinar del Río), El Abra (Habana), Planta Cantú (Sancti Spíritus), Villa Guajimico (Cienfuegos), Sierra Morena (Villa Clara) and Cayo Coco (Ciego de Avila). In each major town seek out the **Campismo** office for local campsites.

Eating

Food is not Cuba's strong point, although the supply of fresh food has improved. In Havana the peso food situation is improving but there are still shortages. It is not unusual to be told '*no hay*' (there isn't any) at restaurants where you would expect the full menu to be available (eg an Italian restaurant had no tomatoes, let alone the mozzarella and parma ham that were on the menu). The Ministry of Agriculture has set up many *organopónicos* in the city to provide the capital with fresh vegetables, grown under organic conditions and to avoid transport costs.

Outside Havana shortages are not so bad. Farmers' markets are good places to buy fruit and vegetables. The dollar shops sell mostly imported supplies such as tins of food from Spain, packets of biscuits, cookies and crackers. Tourists do not have access to local stores, or *bodegas*, as these are based on the national ration card system. Bread, rice, beans, sugar and coffee are rationed to Cuban families but they are not given enough to live on and have to purchase the balance at market prices. Milk is rationed only for children up to the age of seven. If you have dollars you can buy anything.

● *For an explanation of the sleeping and eating price codes used in hotel and restaurant*
● *listings throughout this guide, see the inside front cover.*

▪ A thirst for freedom

The first Cuban resistance fighter we know of was an Amerindian chief called Hatuey, who has now become a symbol of rebellion. He lived at the time of the Spanish invasion and when he discovered what the Spanish really wanted from his island he tried to mobilize his people. However, he was no match for the better-armed Spaniards, who chased him into the mountains, captured him and burnt him alive. The story goes that when approached by a priest and asked whether he would like to make a last request, confess and make his peace with God, he asked whether there would be Spanish people in heaven. When told that there would, he declined the offer, saying he certainly didn't want to go there.

It took nearly four centuries before Cuban freedom fighters expelled the Spanish and gained their country's independence, limited though it was, and 1998 saw the centenary of that event. Cuba's former ally, the USA, was noticeably absent from the celebrations, but Spanish investors and tourists returned in great numbers to join in the fiestas. Many thousands of other foreigners also participated, now that Cuba is firmly established on the package holiday circuit with tourist facilities of international quality. Demand for beer to quench their thirst is always strong. A Hatuey Cerveza does the trick.

Essentials Eating

Food

The national dish is *congrís* (rice mixed with black beans), roast pork and yuca (*cassava*) or fried plantain. Rice with kidney (red) beans is known as *moros y cristianos*. Pork is traditionally eaten for the New Year celebrations, so before then all the pigs that have been fattened up on people's balconies or smallholdings are on the move in the backs of trucks, cars and bicycles, to be sold privately or at the markets. Pork and chicken are the most common meats available and the cheapest.

Despite government investment in fisheries, seafood is largely found in the export and tourist markets. There is a story that the government tried to improve the diet of the Cuban people by reducing the price of fish, but all that happened was that the cats got fat. Not even price manipulation could wean Cubans off their habitual diet of pork, rice and beans. Most food is fried and can often be greasy and bland. Spices and herbs are not commonly used and Cubans limit their flavourings to onions and garlic. Salads in restaurants are mixed vegetables which are slightly pickled and not to everyone's taste. Shredded pickled cabbage and sliced cucumber are a common garnish to the main dish. Take advantage of whatever is in season as Cuba's range of tropical fruit and vegetables is magnificent. At the right time of year there will be a glut of avocados, mangoes, guavas, zapote or papaya.

> ▪ *The freshest food is found in casas particulares. As a general rule, the cleaner your surroundings and the smarter the restaurant, the less likely you are to suffer.*

Smallholders will sell their produce on the roadside or by knocking on people's doors in the street. Some *casa particular* owners freeze things in times of plenty so that you can have mango or papaya juice at any time of the year. Breakfast is usually coffee, fruit and/or fruit juice, bread, honey and eggs or a cheese and ham sandwich. Many Cubans eat their main meal at lunch time, but they expect foreigners to eat at night. Cubans are particularly hooked on ice cream, although it usually only comes in vanilla, strawberry or chocolate flavours. The ice cream parlour, **Coppelia,** can be found in every town of any size and is quite an experience, with long queues because of its popularity. There are other ice cream parlours for a change.

Drink

Rum is the national drink and all cocktails are rum based. There are several brand names and each has a variety of ages, so you have plenty of choice (see box, page 204). Do not buy cheap firewater, or cane spirit, as it is unlikely to agree with you and you may be ill for a while. The good stuff is cheap enough. Beer is good and there are regional varieties which come in bottles or cans. The locally grown coffee is good, although hotels often manage to make it undrinkable in the mornings.

The most widely available **beer** throughout the island is *Cristal*, made by **Cervecería Mayabe**, in Holguín. Found in bottles or cans at 4.9% alcohol content, it costs US$0.75 in supermarkets and US$1-2 in bars. From the same brewery is *Mayabe*, with Ordinary at 3.5% and Extra at 5%, both costing the same as Cristal and also popular with more flavour. *Hatuey*, made in Havana, is reckoned by some to be the best of Cuba's many beers, named after an Amerindian chief ruling when the Spanish arrived. It is becoming more widely available after a lengthy patent battle. *Bucanero*, from Holguín, is easily bought in the east of the island, 5.4% in bottles or cans and about US$0.60 in supermarkets. *Tínimo* (from Camagüey, good with lots more flavour than Cristal) and *Lagarto* beer are difficult to find. The former can be bought in pesos and the latter at the airport. Cuba now also produces **wines** under the *Soroa* label, grown and produced in Pinar del Río and sold for about US$3.15 in shops. It is not to be recommended except to marinate tough meat. There is also a more expensive range sold for about US$8, including Cabernet Sauvignon, Chardonnay, Tempranillo and other grapes, produced with the help of a Spanish company in a joint venture. If you want wine you are better off buying something imported.

Eating out

State restaurants/hotels

State-owned 'dollar' restaurants are recognizable by the credit card stickers on the door, where meals are about US$10-25, paid only in US dollars. Some can be quite good and there are variations in menus, so you can find Italian, Spanish or French restaurants. Be warned that the Cuban idea of Chinese food is unlike anything you might find in your home country and very sweet. You get what you pay for, and at the cheap end of the market you can expect poor quality, limited availability of ingredients and disinterested staff. Generally, although restaurants have improved in the last few years, the food in Cuba is not very exciting. Restaurants are more innovative in Havana than elsewhere and some of the *paladares* are eccentric in their tastes. Always check restaurant prices in advance and then your bill. Discrepancies occur in both the state and private sector.

Resort **hotels** tend to serve buffet meals, which can get tedious after a while, but breakfast here, and in large, urban hotels where buffets are served, is usually good and plentiful and you can stock up for the day. Breakfast in other hotels can be particularly slow. If not eating at a buffet, service, no matter what standard of restaurant or hotel, can be very slow (even if you are the only customers).

Paladares/casas particulares

Paladares are privately owned restaurants, licensed and taxed and limited to 12 chairs, as well as having employment restrictions. Some very good family-run businesses have been set up, offering a three-course meal in Havana for US$10-20 per person, less than that outside the capital. Things like olives and coffee are usually charged as extras, be sure to check what the meal includes. They are not allowed to have lobster or shrimp on the menu as these are reserved for the dollar hotels and the export market. However, if

you ask, there are often items available which are not on the menu. Remember that if 53
someone guides you to a *paladar* he will expect a commission, so you end up paying
more for your food. There are also illegal *paladares*, which will serve meals with meat
for US$1-3 per person. We do not list them. The cheapest, legal, way of getting a
decent meal is by eating in a *casa particular*. This is generally of excellent quality in
plentiful, even vast, proportions, with the advantage that they will cook whatever you
want. They usually charge US$5-7 for a meal, chicken and pork is cheaper than fish,
while some *casa* owners seem to have access to all sorts of delicacies (illegal of
course). Vegetarians can be catered for as they will cook whatever you want.
Breakfast is usually US$2-3 and far better value than in a state hotel. You can
negotiate a package of dinner, bed and breakfast which can give good value. While
quality and style of cooking naturally varies, as a general rule you will get fresher food
in a *casa particular* than you will in a restaurant or *paladar*, both of which now have
the reputation of recycling meals and reheating leftovers. If your digestive system is
delicate when travelling this is something to bear in mind.

Fast food/peso stalls

For a cheap meal you are better off trying the Cuban version of **fast food** restaurants,
such as **El Rápido**, or **Burgui**, or try one of **Rumbos'** *cafeterías*, of which there are many
all round the island. As well as chicken and chips or burgers, they offer a wide range of
sandwiches: cheese, ham, or cheese and ham, but they do come in different sizes. A
sandwich in a restaurant or bar in Havana costs about US$4, a coffee costs US$1. In a
provincial town you can pay as little as US$2 for a sandwich and beer for lunch.
Breakfast and one other meal may be sufficient if you fill in with street or 'dollar shop'
snacks. All towns and cities have **peso street stalls** for sandwiches, pizza and
snacks; change about US$10 for a two-week stay if planning to avoid restaurants. In
out-of-the-way places, you will be able to pay for food in pesos, but generally you will
be charged in dollars.

Vegetarians

For vegetarians the choice is very limited, normally only cheese sandwiches, spaghetti,
pizzas, salads, bananas and omelettes. Even beans (and *congris*) are often cooked
with meat or in meat fat. If you are staying at a *casa particular* or eating in a *paladar*,
they will usually prepare meatless meals for you with advance warning. Always ask for
beans to be cooked in vegetable oil. Some vegetarians even recommend taking your
own oil and lending it to the cook so that you can be absolutely sure that lard has not
been used. The vegetarian chain **Pekin** is also a good, cheap option with a large, varied
buffet spread, including pasta and rice dishes as well as juices, salads and fresh fruit,
where you pay in pesos. Hotels including most notably and recommended, the
Nacional also have quite extravagant all-you-can-eat buffets spreads.

Entertainment and nightlife

Of all the islands in the Caribbean, Cuba has the best and most varied nightlife with a
great music scene including Latin, jazz, folk music and rock. There are theatres for
drama and ballet, concert halls for classical music or touring bands, discos,
nightclubs, bars, cinemas showing Cuban and foreign movies, and indoor and
outdoor music venues around the country. Most of the action is concentrated in
Havana, but every town has a *Casa de la Trova* for traditional music and a *Casa de la
Cultura* for cultural events, art exhibitions and concerts, as well as a theatre and
cinema in the larger towns. Santiago is no poor relation and has its own regional
variations in music and culture.

Every visitor will experience the vibrant rhythms of Cuban music and dance, it is inescapable. Bands patrol the bars and restaurants to serenade you at every opportunity, even up to the airport departure lounge before you leave. No one wastes the chance to get up and salsa, from toddlers to grandmas, Cubans have the sexiest hip-swaying movements and are not shy about demonstrating and sharing their technique. There are even daytime events for those unable to keep going until dawn in the clubs, perfect for families. Several provincial towns, such as Bayamo, Camagüey or Baracoa have a weekly street party when stalls sell food and drink from the region, bars and restaurants spill out onto the street and there is music and dancing until late. All of this is washed down with rum of varying degrees of excellence. At many places you take the bottle of rum and they provide the ice and mixers in the price for entrance. It is easy to get a party started.

Cartelera, www.cartelera.com is a free magazine in English and Spanish where you can find out what's on in Havana. Other towns have leaflets or pin up flyers in strategic places, for example Casas de la Cultura, but your hotel or *casa particular* will be able to tell you what is happening, where and when.

Festivals and events

In contrast with other Latin American countries, there are no national religious festivals, although you will find some patron saints' days celebrated in churches (often linked to *Santería*) and Easter is an important time. Processions are usually limited to taking place within the church itself and not all round the streets of the town. **Christmas Day**, was reintroduced as a public holiday in 1997 (having been banned after the Revolution) prior to a visit from the Pope and has become a regular event with Christmas trees and tinsel, but a whole generation missed out on celebrating it and there is little awareness of what it signifies. Public holidays are political and historical events and are marked by speeches, rallies and other gatherings, often in each town's Plaza de la Revolución. **Carnival** has recently been resurrected, taking place in July in Santiago. Havana's Carnival is moved around a lot, sometimes August, sometimes October or November, you can't rely on the date. While operating with limited budgets, these events are colourful, energetic and have a raw vibrancy. Parades are accompanied by music, drumming, dancing and competitions involving children and adults and requiring lots of stamina. There are lots of cultural and sporting festivals and events held throughout the year, see below, and www.cubameeting.org

January
New Year is celebrated around the country with great fanfare, largely because it coincides with **Liberation Day,** marking the end of the Batista dictatorship, on 1 January. There is lots of music and dancing, outdoor discos and general merriment, washed down with copious quantities of rum. **Cubadanza** is a twice-yearly dance festival. **Contact Cuban Contemporary Dance**, Miguel Iglesias, T7-8796410, cnae@min.cult.cu

February
The **Havana International Book Fair** is held at La Cabaña; a commercial fair in new, purpose-built convention buildings. Look out for new book launches. Pedro Pérez Sarduy launched his novel, The *Maids of Havana*, there in 2002. Contact Iroel Sánchez, T7-8628091, presidencia@icl.cult.cu **Vuelta a Cuba de Ciclismo**, is a cycle through every province. Contact Alberto Puig de la Barca, T7-2040945, gral@cubadeportes.cu The **Cigar Festival**, introduced in the last few years, is for true aficionados of *Habanos*. Held at the Palacio de las Convenciones, you can learn about the history of cigars and there are opportrnities for visits to tobacco plantations and cigar factories. Contact Silvia Hernández, T7-2040513, shernandez@habanos.cu

March

The **International Electrical Acoustic Music Festival**, takes place every other year (2004, 2006 etc) in Havana, with workshops and performances. Contact Juan Blanco of the **Laboratorio Nacional Música Electroacústica** (LNME), T7-8303983, lnme@cubarte.cult.cu **Festival Internacional de la Trova 'Pepe Sánchez'** held at the Casa de la Trova in Santiago with concerts, roving musicians, conferences and other events, organized by the legendary Eliades Ochoa Bustamante, with the Centro Provincial de la Música 'Miguel Matamoros' and the Centro Nacional de Música Popular, www.loseventos.cu

April

International Percussion Festival 'Percuba' (3rd week of the month) at the Teatro Amadeo Roldán. Percuba (Percussion Society of Cuba) organizes a programme of theoretical and practical events and competitions to promote percussion at home and abroad. Contact Lino Arturo Neira Betancourt, T7-2038808, www.percuba.com A very popular event is the **Copa Cuba Ciclismo** for track cycle racing competitions. Contact Jackeline, T7-2040945, agenciaco@cubadeportes.cu

May

May Theatre at the Casa de las Américas with workshops and performances. Contact Vivian Martínez Tabares, T7-552706, teatro@casa.cult.cu **Havana International Guitar Festival and Competition** at the Teatro Amadeo Roldán, with performers and competitors from around the world. Contact Roberto Chorens, T7-8324521, cnmc@cubarte.cult.cu

June

International Ernest Hemingway White Marlin Fishing Tournament is one of the major events at the Marina Hemingway. Contact José Miguel Díaz Escrich, T7-2046653, yachtclub@cnih.mh.cyt.cu **Festival Internacional del Ron**, held at the Morro-Cabaña complex. For further details, contact Belkis Acosta Acosta, www.eventos.cu **International Boleros de Oro Festival** for aficionados of *boleros*, dedicated in 2004 to Brazil. Contact Dirección Promoción y Eventos UNEAC, T7-8320395, promocion@uneac.co.cu, www.uneac.com

July

Cuballet de Verano is a summer dance festival. Contact Lourdes Bermejo, T7-2650848, prodanza@cubarte.cult.cu The **Festival del Caribe** is held in the first week of July in Santiago with theatre, dancing and conferences, continuing later in the month to coincide with the Moncada celebrations on 26 July. **Carnival** in Santiago (18-27 July) is a week-long musical extravaganza taking in the city's patron saint's day, 25 July, but it traditionally stops for a day on 26 July for a day of more serious political celebrations.

August

Que Siempre Brilla el Sol baseball tournament is always a popular event. Contact Jackeline, T7-2040945, agenciaco@cubadeportes.cu **Cubadanza**, the second of the year, see January for contact details.

September

International Blue Marlin Fishing Tournament (20-25 September 2004) at Marina Hemingway. The marina fills up with mostly US fishermen eager to pit their strength against marlin and their fellow competitors, with lots of après-fishing social events. Contact José Miguel Díaz Escrich, T7-2046653, yachtclub@cnih.mh.cyt.cu

Havana Contemporary Music Festival held at UNEAC and theatres. Contact Guido López Gavilán, T7-8320194, musicos@uneac.co.cu **Festival Internacional del Son 'Matamoros Son'** at Teatro Heredia, Santiago. Music and dancing to celebrate *son* and famous *soneros*. Contact Adalberto Alvarez Zayas, www.eventos.cu **Havana International Ballet Festival** held every other year in the second half of the month at the Gran Teatro, Teatro Nacional and Teatro Mella. Run by Alicia Alonso, head of the Cuban National Ballet, T7-552948, bnc@cubarte.cult.cu **Premio Musicología Casa de las Américas**, held every other year (2005, 2007, etc) in the last week in Oct at the same time as the Coloquio Internacional de Musicología. The **Premio de Composición** is held in alternate years (2004, 2006, etc). Contact María Elena Vinuza, T7-552607, musica@casa.cult.cu **Fiesta de la Cultura Iberoamericana**, in Holguín, celebrating all things Spanish and Latin American at the Casa de Iberoamérica. Contact Alexis Triana, www.eventos.cu

November

International Tournament of Wahoo Fishing at the Marina Hemingway. Contact José Miguel Díaz Escrich, T7-2046653, yachtclub@cnih.mh.cyt.cu **Marabana** (12-15 November 2004). Havana's marathon. Contact Alberto Puig de la Barca, T7-2040945, gral@cubadeportes.cu **Festival Internacional de Teatro** held at the university in Santiago. Contact Luisa García Miranda, www.eventos.cu **International Festival of University Theatre** is held in theatres showcasing student drama. Contact Clemente González Pérez, T7-552356, luisa@reduniv.edu.cu **Bienal de la Habana** takes place every two years (2003, 2005, etc) in the Centro de Arte Contemporáneo Wifredo Lam, Centro de Arte La Casona, Parque Morro-Cabaña and Pabellón Cuba.

December

International Festival of New Latin American Cinema Shows prize-winning films (no subtitles) at cinemas around Havana. This is the foremost film festival in Latin America with the best of Cuban and Latin American films along with documentaries and independent cinema from Europe and the USA. See the stars as well as the films, as the festival attracts big-name actors and directors. Contact Alfredo Guevara, head of the Cuban Institute of Cinematographic Art and Industry (ICAIC), T7-552854, festival@icaic.inf.cu www.habanafilmfestival.com **International Jazz Plaza Festival** follows the film festival every other year at theatres and the Casa de la Cultura de Plaza. It is a great time to overload on music and cinema. It is one of the world's major jazz festivals with the best of Cuban and international jazz. There are masterclasses and workshops available and the event is organized by Grammy winner Jesús 'Chucho' Valdés. Contact Roberto Chorens, T7-8324521, cnmc@cubarte .cult.cu **Happy End of Year Regatta** at the Marina Hemingway for three days with social events that always accompany the racing fraternity. Contact José Miguel Díaz Escrich, T7-2046653, yachtclub@cnih.mh.cyt.cu

Public holidays

Liberation Day (1 January), **Labour Day** (1 May), **Revolution Day** (26 July and the day either side), **Beginning of War of Independence** (10 October) and **Christmas Day** (25 December).

Other festive days which are not public holidays are **28 January,** (birth of José Martí, 1853), **24 February** (anniversary of renewal of War of Independence, 1895), **8 March** (International Women's Day), **13 March** (anniversary of 1957 attack on presidential palace in Havana by a group of young revolutionaries), **19 April** (anniversary of defeat of mercenaries at Bay of Pigs, 1961), **30 July** (martyrs of the

Revolution day), **8 October** (death of Che Guevara, 1967), **28 October** (death of Camilo Cienfuegos, 1959), **27 November** (death by firing squad of eight medical students by Spanish colonial government, 1871), **7 December** (death of Antonio Maceo in battle in 1896). These public holidays are often marked by speeches and displays by school children.

Shopping

Where to shop

Compared with much of Latin America, Cuba is expensive for the tourist, but compared with many Caribbean islands it is not. Whereas in the 1990s most towns would have one or two dollar shops, there are now lots of supermarkets and smaller shops selling imported items in dollars. Some of these may actually have been made in Cuba in the free trade zones (see Economy, page 398), where they are allowed to sell 25% of their produce on the domestic market in hard currency. Shopping centres are springing up and the materialist culture is creeping in.

The dollar is king and there is very little you can buy in pesos apart from some food in some areas. Shoes, clothing, cosmetics, toiletries, camera film, imported food and drink are all available in dollars. Throughout the country, dollar stores are surprisingly busy, despite the small proportion of the population having direct access to dollars. All bags and receipts are checked on leaving a dollar store. It is not unusual for a *casa particular* to have two or three fridge freezers and a microwave, yet the woman will be doing the laundry in cold water in an outside sink as she has done all her life, and the family will travel on a bicycle.

> ✱ *Specialist cigar shops will provide very good advice on the various brands on offer, however if you know what you want it is much cheaper to buy the official cigars at the airport duty free shop.*

What to buy

The main souvenirs to take home with you have to be **rum, cigars** and maybe **coffee**. The street price of a bottle of rum ranges from US$2-8 depending on its age. Cigars can cost whatever you are prepared to pay, but they are still the best in the world (see box, page 164). Remember that all the best tobacco leaves go into cigar making rather than cigarettes. Make sure you buy the best to take home and don't get tricked into buying fakes, you may not get them through customs. You are only allowed to take 23 cigars out of the country without a receipt. If you are buying any souvenirs to take home, remember to keep the official receipt in case you have to show it at customs on departure.

Handicrafts are now being developed for the tourist market and there are *artesanía* markets in Havana and Varadero which hold an overwhelming amount of stock. Wooden carvings, inlaid wooden boxes for cigars, jewellery, key rings, baseball bats, model sailing ships, ceramics, Che Guevara hats and innumerable T-shirts will be offered to you. There is a considerable amount of **art work** of varying degrees of worth, but you may pick up a bargain. If you are a serious collector, skip the markets and go straight to the galleries in Havana. Taking art out of the country requires a special licence (see Havana, page 131).

> ✱ *Do not buy black coral or tortoiseshell jewellery as these are protected species and it will probably be illegal to take it in to your own country.*

⬤ *The family firm of Bacardí was the largest in Cuba for nearly 100 years. After the 1959 Revolution, when the sugar industry and distilleries were taken over by the state, the family left the island and took the Bacardí name with them. The Bacardí rum, now found worldwide, is not distilled in Cuba.*

Sport and activities

Caving

There are huge cave systems in Cuba (see Geology and landscape), some of which are developed tourist attractions. The Santo Tomás and Cueva del Indio caves in Viñales are visited by thousands of people every year, but many others are almost unknown except to professionals. Amerindian pictographs can be found in some, for example the Los Generales, Las Mercedes, Indio and Pichardo caves in the Sierra de Cubitas, Camagüey, and the Cuevas del Punta del Este on the Isla de la Juventud. The largest stalagmite in Cuba can be found in the Cueva Martín Infierno near Trinidad, 67 m high and 40 m at its base. In the Zapata peninsula there are flooded caves, which can be dived, and another, Tanques Azules, at Caletones, Gibara, near Holguín. An adventure park at the Silla de Gibara offers rock climbing, caving, potholing and cave diving. In Matanzas province there are some 350 caves, of which about 20 can be visited. The Bellamar caves receive hundreds of visitors daily, while the Saturno caverns have underwater tunnels suitable for trained cave divers: www.dtcuba.com/esp/naturaleza_ espeleologia.asp

Cycling

Cuba has an extensive network of tarmac and concrete roads, covering nearly 17,600 km. This impressive infrastructure means that the vast majority of the country is accessible to the cyclist, and there are some dramatic roads to climb and descend. There is total freedom of movement and the rewards can be immense. However, many of the roads are in a poor condition, particularly in the rural areas. After the collapse of the Soviet Union, road building and maintenance programmes were largely suspended. Road surfaces have been further damaged by recent hurricanes. A road repair programme is gradually being reintroduced, particularly in areas of tourist traffic. Despite numerous potholes, broken and rutted surfaces, most bikes can negotiate the roads. There is no need to go out and purchase a new or high specification bike for a trip to Cuba, but, with probably the best bike on the block, be prepared to receive numerous '*préstame tu bicicleta*' (lend me your bike) requests. The length of time of the loan will be unspecified. And, don't be alarmed if you are asked to provide a lift for someone at the side of the road. It is amazing how many people a bicycle can carry.

Useful words include: *Estoy ponchado* – I have a puncture (colloquial), *la cadena* – chain, *el freno* – brake, *el cuadro* – frame, *los rayos* – spokes, *la goma* – tyre, *la cámara* – inner tube, *el sillín* – seat.

The roads are gradually becoming busier with gas-guzzlers, as the economy regenerates, but in the countryside, where public transport is often scarce and unreliable, you can still find yourself the dominant form of transport. You will meet many friendly and helpful Cubans on two wheels. Cycling has become an integral part of local culture and there are an estimated 2 million bicycles in Cuba. The vast majority were imported from China, politely named *Flying Pigeon*, *Light Roadster* and *Forever Bicycle*. These heavyweight workhorses outnumber Havana's cars by almost 20:1. Cubans drive on the right-hand side. Cuban driving can be erratic and impatient, particularly in the towns and cities. Essential road signs include: *PARE* in a red upside down triangle, inside a red circle indicates a mandatory stop; *CEDA EL PASO* in a red upside down triangle, on a yellow background indicates give way. The increased availability of petrol now means that cyclists are not alone on Cuban roads. Towns and cities can be very congested with lorries, buses and cars, sometimes spewing obnoxious clouds of low-grade diesel fumes from their exhausts. Traffic is lighter in rural areas, but roads are narrower. There are numerous railway lines without barriers or warning lights that cross the roads, particularly in the sugar cane growing regions. They often look unused, but it is absolutely essential that you stop and ensure that no trains are approaching.

It is possible to reach other parts of Cuba with your bike by **train** and **plane**. When leaving Havana by train you need to arrive three hours before departure to check that there is space for the bike. Purchase the ticket for the bike at the **Departamento Expreso de Ultima Hora**, in the train station. One-way train fares for a bike from Havana to Pinar del Río US$10.60, Santa Clara US$13 and to Santiago de Cuba US$26.15. Cubans must deliver their bikes at least three days before departure, but they usually accommodate tourists on the same day as travelling, although there are no guarantees. You may have to return the following day to secure your place. It is a straightforward procedure. Show your bike, passport and *LADIS* train ticket to the official, *el aforador,* in the office. The bike will be labelled Expreso FC, you will be given a ticket for the bike, and it will be placed in the *wagón de equipaje,* usually the first carriage. Do not lose the ticket, you will not be able to retrieve the bike without it. Lock the bike securely to the carriage framework. You must follow the same procedure for the return trip. Unfortunately, bikes are not carried on the new, faster and more comfortable 01 and 02 trains running Havana to Santiago.

Before you go

Your bike must be bagged or boxed on flights to Cuba. A bike bag is easier since it can be carried with you, and used for the return flight. A suitable cardboard box can be obtained from local bike shops. Arrange to leave this at your first night's accommodation, to be picked up prior to re-boxing for the return flight. The bike is included in your luggage allowance. **Iberia**'s weight allowance is two 32 kg pieces plus 5 kg hand luggage. An average bike weighs 13-15 kg, leaving plenty of space for clothing, a small selection of tools and spare parts. Not even the seriously fashion-conscious cyclist need worry. The airline will require you to fix the handlebars parallel to the frame, let 25% of the air out of the tyres, lower the saddle and refit the pedals pointing inwards. Pipe insulation tubing can provide further protection to the frame. If you are using a bike box, limited dimensions will necessitate removing the front tyre. Arrive as early as possible at the check-in desk. Ensure the agency is aware you are travelling with a bike so that they can provide a suitable transfer vehicle to your accommodation. Pre-book internal flights and any hotels you need before you go, and ensure that all vouchers carry confirmation of the bike. A frequently experienced problem is one of unplanned arrivals at hotels. This can sometimes mean refusal at the reception desk and a lot of extra legwork to the next hotel. Private accommodation can be a better option for independent cyclists. Go for an apartment on the ground floor to avoid hikes up stairs with bike and kit. Maps of Cuba are often unreliable, where main roads soon become more hole than road and thick red lines on the map do not convert on the ground. Buy a map before you go and plan your route carefully, see Maps, page 47.

When to go

November to May is the best time to take your bike. The tropical storms have subsided and humidity is lower. Plan your route to run from east to west to avoid the strong, year-round, prevailing northeast trade winds. Temperatures are still hot and average 27° C. There can be occasional heavy downpours of rain, and clip-on mudguards and a lightweight waterproof jacket are useful. Plan to finish each ride in daylight. During the winter months, November to March, sunrise is at 0700 and sunset at 1830 (2000 in summer months). Cycling in the dark is dangerous. Outside the central districts in the main towns, roads are unlit. Drainage covers are often missing, sometimes marked by an upright tree branch, and there are large potholes, see Driving, page 44. Note that many vehicles do not have a full set of functioning headlights.

What to take

ATB (mountain) bikes fitted with semi-slick tyres with a knob pattern edge (26 cm x 1.5-2.1 mm) and hybrid bikes fitted with 700 cm x 38 mm tyres are recommended. Touring bikes can be used, but wide tyres (700 cm x 32-35 mm) and strong wheels are essential. It is best to have a wide range of gears with the emphasis on low gears, as you will encounter several hills. A minimum of 15 gears is recommended. Ensure that your bike is in good condition and that it has been recently serviced. An odometer is useful and should be calibrated in kilometres.

Carry a small range of **essential tools**, to include a pocket multi-tool, and some basic spares, including brake and gear cables and spokes, to carry out minor repairs. Suitable spare parts are not widely available in Cuba. The roads are often littered with broken glass so a puncture repair kit, pump and spare inner tube are invaluable. Alternatively, use *poncheras*, prolific private puncture repair businesses present in all towns; look out for the signs. Two water bottles are an absolute minimum. Mineral water can be purchased from dollar shops in most towns, or ask a Cuban family relaxing on their front porch – a great way to start up a conversation, and the water will be ice cold. Local food and fruit is available at roadside stalls, although scarce in remote rural areas. Take a bike lock, to ensure that your bike is securely locked at all times when left unattended; high factor sun protection lotion (minimum SPF 15); cycle helmet with visor; cycling gloves; cycling shoes or trainers with a hard sole; loose fitting cotton clothing. An early start, without stops but a long lunch, should be incorporated into your route planning. Use padded shorts and a good quality saddle, otherwise you will be forced to use a towel or similar in the critical comfort zone. Take a sweatshirt for the evenings as temperatures can drop, particularly in the Sierras. Front and rear lights are needed in case you have to cycle after dark. A map-reading case attached to the handlebars enables easy reading of route maps.

Havana and around the island

Cycling is an excellent way to see Havana. There are some cycle lanes. An absolute must is cruising the cycle lane the length of the Malecón, where the bicycle is the *de rigueur* accessory for Cuban courtship. Originally, cycle lanes were marked by ochre-coloured concrete bumps, colloquially called *mojones*, best translated as cow pats. Standard broken yellow lines are replacing these. A white bicycle in a blue circle with an arrow indicates the cycle lane and mandatory routes for bikes. Havana has numerous bicycle parking lots, *parqueo de bicicleta*, and most museums and institutions have a bicycle park. The standard charge is one peso. Always lock your bike and remove all accessories. The attendant will issue you with a numbered metal tag matching the tag attached to your bike. You must produce the tag to retrieve your bike. To wander around Vedado and Old Havana use bicycle parks at Calle 25 entre L y K and Industria esquina San José, respectively. For Miramar, use the park located at Avenida 1 esquina 46, near the *Hotel Copacabana*. They are usually open until 1800. There is also a bicycle park at the pedestrian entrance to the rear of Havana University in Calle Ronda. See page 147 for the cycling route from Havana to Matanzas.

Playas del Este

A day trip to the Playas del Este is easily negotiated. Catch the *Ciclobus*, 20 centavos, converted buses with the seats removed and special ramps at the rear of the bus for loading, designed to take cyclists through the tunnel under the harbour

Queue at Parque El Curita on Dragones, one block west of Fraternidad. Get off at the second stop, in Reparto Camilo Cienfuegos, south of the Vía Blanca. Cycle 5 km along the Vía Blanca and take the right exit to Alamar. At the roundabout in Alamar take the second exit and follow the cycle path alongside the Vía Blanca to Tarará (20 km). A large overhead sign, *Ciudad de los Pioneros*, marks the entrance, but first you must register in the office alongside the shop, by providing your name, passport number and accommodation details. You will be issued a hand-written ticket, allowing entrance to the beach and marina. There is no charge. To the left of the office is a *Pain de París* (clean, efficient service, good pizzas and coffee). Cycle down the hill to Tarará's clean, sandy beach, very popular with Cuban families at weekends. Limited facilities, cold drinks, sun beds for hire. On your return, pick up the *Ciclobus* in Reparto Camilo Cienfuegos, north of the Vía Blanca. Pass the Pan-American stadium complex and take the following exit signed Camilo Cienfuegos. At the roundabout turn left and continue the short distance to the *ciclobus* stop. It will drop you in Calle Tacón, opposite the Museo de la Música. The last bus departs at 2100.

Western Sierras

For the Western Sierras head west along Salvador Allende and Avenida Rancho Boyeros to the airport. Continue to San Antonio de los Baños. Spend the first night at **Hotel Las Yagrumas** at the entrance to the town, continue to Soroa (67 km) via Guanajay and Las Terrazas. The route includes some steep climbs after lunch, so an early start is recommended. Follow the old Carretera Central to San Diego de los Baños (58 km) and to Pinar del Río (a further 49 km). Head north, climbing up to Viñales (32 km), a good centre to tour the region. This is graded as a moderate cycle route, but includes some steep climbs. Returning to Havana, either cycle back to Pinar del Río and catch the train or cycle to San Diego de los Baños via Los Portales caves (see page 167), Che Guevara's secret military HQ during the 1962 missile crisis (61 km). From **Hotel La Ermita** turn right at the main street, at 5 km turn right, signed La Guna de Piedra. At 12.8 km take a right turning part way down the hill (very easy to miss, if you get to Mina La Constancia you've gone too far); at 43 km turn left, the sign *Los Portales* is set back from the road; at the following T-junction the route continues to the right but you can take the 2-km detour to the left to Los Portales caves. If you turn right at the T-junction, there are two demanding hill climbs through Parque La Güira, be careful on the descents as there are potholes, broken surfaces and sharp bends; follow the road through the park; at the impressive castle gates turn left to San Diego. This option is a hilly route but passes through inspiring scenery in a remote rural area, with the added possibilities of a visit to Los Portales caves and an invigorating soak in a hot thermal bath at El Balneario in San Diego (see page 161). From San Diego you can then retrace your steps back to Havana via Soroa.

Santiago de Cuba

Internal **Cubana** flights do accept bikes, at no extra charge, on the larger planes to Santiago de Cuba. Folding bikes such as Moltons may be allowed on other flights, for example to Baracoa. Arrive at least two hours before check in. Use pipe wrap to protect the frame. At Santiago the porters often try and squeeze your bike onto the conveyor belt! It doesn't fit. At least, not without considerable alteration to its design. Stand by the exit door and be prepared to knock loudly but politely on the window to advise any over-active porters. They will then open the door and pass it to you. There is a steep downhill ride into Santiago from the airport. Leave Santiago, heading west along Avenida las Américas, and cycle to El Saltón (87 km) via El Cobre. Then to Bayamo (67 km), Manzanillo (93 km), Punta Piedra (99 km), Chivirico (100 km) and return to Santiago (68 km). This is graded as a demanding route, taking in the mountainous Sierra Maestra and the outstanding coast road squeezed between the mountains and the Caribbean from Pilón to Santiago (see route description, Santiago to Manzanillo, page 339).

Trinidad

For Trinidad and the Escambray mountains take the train to Santa Clara. Cycle to Trinidad (88 km) via Manicaragua and Condado, head west along the coast road to Guajimico (44 km), Cienfuegos (43 km) and inland to Hanabanilla (51 km) via Cumanajagua. There is a steep 7-km climb to **Hotel Hanabanilla** situated on the edge of Embalse Hanabanilla. Return to Santa Clara (47 km) via La Moza and Manicaragua, turning left at the crossroads in Manicaragua. This is graded as a moderate cycle route, but includes some steep hills, particularly on the final day to Santa Clara.

Organized cycle tours

If you don't want to go it alone there are many organised **group tours**. You need to bring your own bike. In the UK, **Blazing Saddles Travels**, T020-84240483, www.blazingsaddlestravels.com organizes several one- and two-week tours to different parts of the island including visits to cultural sites, schools, hospitals and a Committee for the Defence of the Revolution (CDR) meeting. Blazing Saddles Travels also offers bespoke routes for those who want to go it alone, bike hire, ATB (mountain bikes) with 21 gears and pannier rack, US$15-20 per day including puncture repair kit for a pre-arranged hire period. The bikes will be delivered to your hotel or *casa particular*; **Havanatour UK**, T01707-646463, sales@havanatour.co.uk **Exodus**, T020-86755550, offers two weeks in the Sierra Maestra; **CTC (Cycle Touring Club)**, T0870-8730060, runs a two-week tour from Trinidad to Viñales via Che Guevara's mausoleum in Santa Clara and a beach break in Varadero; **Fietsvakantiewinkel**, Spoorlaan 19, 3445 AE Woerden, Holland, T31-3480-21844, F31-3480-23839.

You may also be able to join a group of Cuban bikers (mostly English speaking) through the **Club Nacional de Cicloturismo** (National Bike Club), Gran Caribe, Transnico Internacional, Lonja del Comercio Oficina 6d, La Habana Vieja, T7-969193, F7-669908, trans@mail.infocom.etecsa.cu They run tours of one to 28 days in all parts of the country, some with political themes.

Most tours offer a fully supported programme and have a dedicated back-up team including tour leader, mechanic and support vehicle. Even better, luggage is carried for you while you cycle. Cuba has become a popular destination for UK charities' cycle challenge events. These are large-scale events with up to 60 participants cycling over 385 km in seven days, front and rear support vehicles and support teams, including doctors and mechanics. To take part you must pay a registration fee and raise the minimum sponsorship, part of which pays for the challenge with the remainder going towards particular projects run by the charities. The **Cuba Solidarity Campaign**, T020-72636452, runs an annual sponsored bike ride in Western Cuba and delivers consignments of medical aid to a Havana Policlínico (local medical centre). See Friendship Associations, page 28, for possible contacts in other countries.

Diving and marine life

Cuba's marine environment is pristine compared with most Caribbean islands, where there has often been overharvesting and overdevelopment of the dive industry. The majority of coral reefs are alive and healthy and teeming with assorted marine life. The government has established a marine park around the Isla de la Juventud and much marine life is protected around the entire island, including turtles, the manatee

and coral. There are three main marine platforms, the **Archipiélago del Rey** (Sabana
to Camagüey), the **Archipiélago de la Reina** and the **Archipiélago de los Canarreos**.
The first one has the greatest diversity of marine species and is being explored and
classified with the aim of making it a protected zone. There are believed to be some
900 species of fish, 1,400 species of molluscs, 60 species of coral, 1,100 species of
crustaceans, 67 species of sharks and rays and four types of marine turtles around
the island, as well as the manatee.

Scuba Cuba
The main dive areas are **Isla de la Juventud, Varadero**, Faro de Luna, **María La Gorda
Santa Lucía** and close to **Santiago de Cuba**. Some 15 zones have been developed
alongside hotels around the island. Most areas offer a variety of diving, including
reefs and walls and an assortment of wrecks, from the remains of ancient Spanish
ships to many modern wrecks sunk as dive sites. Cuban diving is a new frontier in the
Caribbean and has much to offer the adventurous or trainee diver.

Cayo Levisa
Heading west from Havana, all along the northwest coast of Cuba, there is a long
chain of small islets, or cays. One that has recently been discovered by scuba divers
is Cayo Levisa, where there is a hotel. You get there by a 15-minute boat ride from
Palma Rubia, which is in turn two hours by car, 125 km from Havana. The reef runs
parallel to the cay and it drops off to over 50 m. There are about 15 dive sites
frequently dived, between 15 and 35 m deep, and boat dives are no more than half an
hour away. The underwater scenery is characterized by big sponges and enormous
black coral trees. Angel fish are very numerous, as are barracuda and schools of
jacks. The current is generally quite gentle so it is an ideal place for beginners and
experts alike. There are several bits and pieces of old galleons, most of which have
been covered by corals.

María La Gorda
In the far west of the island, María la Gorda offers some of the best diving in a warm,
sheltered bay, where visibility is good all year round. The coral formations, sponges
and gorgonians are quite spectacular and the fish are plentiful, including barracuda,
moray eels, lobsters, grunts, groupers and even whale sharks at certain times of the
year. Most dive sites, which include bits of old Spanish galleons, caves, tunnels and
drop-offs, stretch along the coast from La Bajada to Cabo Corrientes. As in most of
Cuba, you do a morning dive, return to shore for lunch and then go out again on the
boat in the afternoon. There is usually a doctor on site who specializes in hyperbaric
medicine and often accompanies divers on the boat, taking their blood pressure
before they dive. There is little else to do in this area other than dive, which, if you are
not on a package, will cost you US$30 per tank and US$7.50 a day to hire equipment.
Freshwater cave diving in blue holes is also possible, though not on offer as an
organized activity.

Isla de la Juventud
Due east of María la Gorda, now moving along the south coast of Cuba, is Cuba's most
famous and long-established dive spot, the Isla de la Juventud. From the marina on
the west coast you can reach 56 buoyed dive sites, count over 40 varieties of coral
and swim through tunnels, deep canals and valleys. It takes about one hour by boat
to reach Cabo Francés, which is where many of the best diving places are, so diving is
an all-day trip with lunch included. The west side of the island is protected from the
prevailing winds so that the water is normally calm with temperatures ranging from
24°C in winter to 28°C in summer.

There are many exciting dive sites stretching east of the Isla de la Juventud along the Archipiélago de los Canarreos, but these are really only possible on a liveaboard (some of which come from the Cayman Islands). The string of low-lying cays, with sandy beaches, mangroves, clear water and colourful reefs, has trapped many ships in the past. Divers have found the remains of over 70 ships and there is an area near Cayo Avalos, called Bajo de Zambo, that is full of them. Several would have been looking for turtle meat and today you can still find Green, Hawksbill and Ridley turtles, which are now protected in Cuba.

Cayo Largo

At the eastern end of the archipelago is the resort island of Cayo Largo, a flat, sandy island surrounded by some lovely beaches and turquoise water. You have to be keen on the water to come here, as there is nothing much else to do, and some 30 dive sites have been identified. There are two main diving areas: south of the island, along the reefs Los Ballenatos and on the nearby Cayo Rosario, there are some pretty coral patches rising from a sandy bottom in shallow water, rich in fish with easy diving, ideal for novice divers; north of the island, in the Golfo de Cazones, there is a deep drop-off with steep walls, ridges and caves where you can find large pelagics and black coral, but there is often a strong current so this is only really suitable for expert divers. The dive shop is based at Playa Sirena, T/F548300, offering a range of courses (US$350 for PADI open water), US$60 for two dives in a day, snorkelling, full day trips and night dives.

Playa Girón

Diving from Punta Perdíz (Bay of Pigs) is an easy beach entry if you are in the area, although the nearest dive shop is at Playa Girón. Nearby there is a 15- to 18-m-long Fisheries Division shipwreck, sitting in 20 m of water on a sand slope. The wreck was intentionally sunk by the government in 1995. The boat, known as a Cayo Largo boat, was built in the early 1980s from concrete and wire. Cuba is well known for building ships like this, which are expected to have a life of around 10 years and are then gutted, with everything of use being removed for a newer model. These 'throw away' boats used to be sunk in deep water, but as diving developed as a sport on the islands, the wrecks were placed in shallow waters to allow divers to explore them.

Dive sites

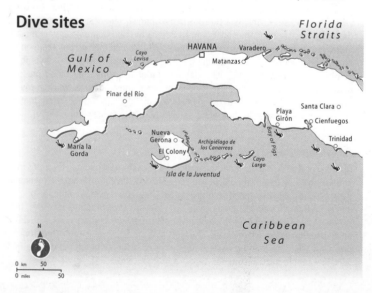

Faro de Luna

Faro de Luna, near Cienfuegos, has over 18 reef sites and a variety of modern wrecks, including seven sunk as diving sites just outside the harbour. One of the best is *Camaronero II*, a shrimp boat only five minutes from the dive shop at **Hotel Faro Luna** (Carretera Pasacaballo Km 18, Playa Rancho Luna, Cienfuegos). Most of the wrecks have been stripped of everything, but the *Camaronero II* still has her propellers which makes an interesting photo site. Built in 1974 from steel, she is 22 m long and was sunk deliberately between 1983 and 1984 in 18 m of water, totally intact. The wreck is adorned with small coral growth, small gorgonias and sponges, and seasonally large schools of red snapper, grouper, hog fish and jacks are found there. However, during the rainy season the visibility is not good because she lies near the mouth of the river. Other wrecks include: the *Camaronero I*, an 8-m wreck lying in shallow water close to shore but very broken up; the cargo ships, *Panta I* and *II*, sunk in 1988; the *Barco R Club*, a 20-m cement and steel passenger ship sunk in 1992 in 8 m; also the 20 m passenger boat *Barco Arimao* sunk in 1992 in 18 m, and the steel fishing boat *Itabo* sunk in 1994 in 12 m. There are also numerous reef sites in this area and the dive shop has identified over a dozen, of which the best include *El Bajo* in 4 m, *El Laberinto*, *La Guasa* and *Rancho Luna II* all in 12 m, and *La Corona* in 15 m (divers often see whale sharks here).

Jardines de la Reina

Jardines de la Reina is an archipelago of 3,000 sq km of islets and mangroves, 80 km south of the province of Camagüey. Unapproachable for years as they were Castro's favourite fishing spot, these islands have now been declared a natural park and you have to buy a US$70 diving licence to dive there. There are birds, iguanas, turtles and loads of fish (and mosquitoes, bring insect repellent). You get there by boat from Júcaro, it's a one-hour drive from Ciego de Avila, and then five hours by boat to the Jardines. A floating hotel, the *Tortuga*, 50 m x 15 m, has eight cabins sleeping one to four people, with air conditioning and ensuite facilities and two new compressors on board. It is moved from place to place every six months or so to reduce the impact on the reef. There is also basic accommodation on board the old and slow liveaboards: the 19-m *Explorador,* which sleeps eight in four cabins, and the 23 m *Halcón,* which sleeps up to 12 in five cabins. However, the crew is very efficient and helpful, food is

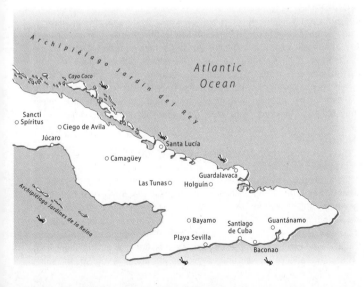

good with fresh fish and bread baked every day. The boats stay anchored for two to three days in one place or are used for a six-night trip away from the *Tortuga*. Another boat, the 25-m *MV Boca del Toro*, operates out of Trinidad but offers diving all along the archipelago. The boat is refurbished but accommodation is basic with room for 12, simple but plentiful food. There are about 40 dive sites along the southwest side of the archipelago. The reef runs parallel to the shore and usually drops down in three 'steps': the first at 10-15 m, very exposed to the surf; a second at 20 m on a sandy bottom, and a third that starts at 40-45 m and drops downward. You will find all the reef fishes here including tarpons and at one site there is shark feeding. The sea is often rough.

Santiago de Cuba

Santiago de Cuba offers a great deal of diving, with two dive shops along the coast. To the east of the city: **Sigua Dive Centre** (Carretera a Baconao Km 28), and to the west: **Sierra Mar** (Hotel Sierra Mar, Playa Sevilla, Guamá). The Sierra Maestra mountains all along this south-facing Caribbean coast offer a foretaste of what is to be found underwater, where the island platform gently shelves to a depth of 35 m and then the ocean wall drops straight down to a depth of over 1,000 m in the channel between Cuba and Haiti. Popular wreck sites near the Sigua Dive Centre include the 30-m passenger ship, *Guarico*, lying in 15 m. She lies on her port side with the mast covered in soft sponges. A ferry/tug wreck lies upside down in 35 m of water and the two vessels together span around 150 m. The metal structure is covered with large yellow and purple tube sponges. The 35-m *Spring Coral* lies in 24 m. Most of the structure is still intact with a great deal of marine growth offering many photo opportunities. An unusual site is the *Bridge*. In 1895 a large bridge broke and fell into the sea in 12 m, along with a train. Later a ship sank and was blown into the bridge underwater, adding to the mass of structures. The **Sierra Mar Dive Shop** offers a special wreck dive on the *Cristóbal Colón*, a Spanish ship lying on a slope in 9-27 m. She was badly damaged by gunfire in 1898 by the US Navy during the Battle of Santiago in the Spanish American War after a long chase. Although initially beached, attempts to refloat her were abandoned. This is an excellent shore dive with hardly any current, although in the wet season visibility is affected by run-off from the Sierra Maestra. There are four other wrecks in shallow water and they are ideal for a snorkel.

Guardalavaca

Heading northwest along the Atlantic coast back towards Havana, at Guardalavaca, there are a couple of dive shops at the resort hotels. They dive the reef and wall just offshore with mostly boat dives. There is lots of life here underwater, you can see lobsters, moray eels, huge crabs and angelfish, as well as a variety of small, colourful, tropical fish, grouper, snapper, triggerfish, eagle rays, tarpon and sometimes sharks. This area is not particularly recommended during the wet season as the sea is rough, visibility deteriorates, you have to wade and swim out to the boat with all your gear and entry and exit is tricky with high waves (the author felt rather seasick!).

Santa Lucía

Santia Lucía has two dive shops and offers one of the most interesting wrecks dived. The 66-m *Mortera* sank in 1905 on a slope of 7-27 m and is home to a host of marine life, including eight massive bull sharks, who have been hand fed by the dive masters from Sharks Friends Dive Shop since the early 1980s (very exciting to watch, no body armour worn). Other wrecks include the *Sanbinal* in 17 m and the British steel ship, *Nuestra Señora de Alta Gracia*, sunk around 1973 and completely intact, allowing divers to penetrate the entire ship, entering the engine room where all the machinery is still in place. An exciting historical site is Las Anforas, under an old fort dating from 1456. The fort was attacked several times by pirates, and artefacts from Spanish ships are scattered across the sea bed. (Four anchors were seen on one dive, with the largest being at least 2 m.) Further west along the archipelago, there is also good diving at **Cayo Coco**, where the water is beautifully clear and there is a wide variety of fish found in large quantities, including snappers, jacks, tarpon and grouper.

Varadero

Varadero is one of the most developed areas for diving. There are several sites around the offshore cays suitable for novice or advanced divers and it is an attractive ride on the boat past the beautiful islets, which are good for snorkelling and picnics. Interesting sites include the wreck of the *Neptune*, a 60-m steel cargo ship thought to be German, lying in only 10 m. This is home to a number of fish including four massive green moray eels and four very large, friendly French angelfish. The wreck is very broken up, but the boilers are still intact and there are places where the superstructure (shaft and propeller) is in good condition and interesting to explore with good photo sites. Among the many reef dive sites in the area are Clara Boyas (Sun Roof), a massive 60-sq-m coral head in 20 m of water, with tunnels large enough for three to four divers to swim through. These connect with upward passages where the sunlight can be seen streaming through. Another site, Las Brujas (the Witches), is only 6 m deep. Large coral heads protrude from the sandy bottom, with coral holes and crevices, adorned with sea fans, home for large schools of snappers. Playa Coral is a site on a 2-km barrier reef west of Varadero, beginning at Matanzas Bay, with a large variety of fish and coral. This is usually a shore dive, although if you go over the wall, where you can find black coral and gorgonians in deep water, it can be a boat dive. If you are based in Varadero on a dive package, you may be offered a trip to Playa Girón for good shore diving, and to the Saturno Caves for an inland cave dive, as part of your package.

Dive shops, tour operators and equipment

All dive shops are government-owned in Cuba, but run as joint ventures with foreign investors. There are three main companies, the largest (14 dive shops) being **Cubanacán (Marlin)**, www.cubanacan.cu The others are **Puerto Sol**, and **Gaviota**, operacion@gavitur.gav.tur.cu Most staff speak Spanish, English and often other languages such as Russian. There is nearly always a German, Italian or French speaking member of staff, depending on where most of their diving customers come from. Instructors are qualified to teach a number of courses approved by PADI, SSI, NAUI, ACUC and CMAS international agencies. Diving is usually done as part of all-inclusive packages, although dives can be booked direct with dive shops for around US$35, including all equipment. Most companies use European dive gear. In Europe for details on dive packages contact **Cubanacán UK Ltd**, T020-75377909, www.cubanacan.cu **Scuba en Cuba**, T01895-624100, www.scuba_en_cuba.com and **Regal Diving**, T0870-2201777, www.regal-diving.co.uk

Diving supplies are very limited. Good-quality, basic rental gear is available, but if you use your own you should be prepared with all spares needed for diving and photography (batteries, film, replacement parts such as a regulator mouthpiece, etc), as these are either not available or excessively expensive. In the summer months, on the south of the island, tiny jelly fish may abound and can cause stings on areas not covered by a wet suit, particularly when entering or leaving the water. A tropical hood is a good idea to protect the neck and face in jelly fish season, often referred to as *agua mala*, or 'bad water'. A well-stocked first aid kit is recommended, for although the medical profession is well trained, supplies are limited. Things you might like to take for precautionary purposes include antibiotics for possible ear or sinus infections, nasal sprays, ear drops, antihistamine cream, diarrhoea remedies and seasickness pills. Remember, however, that decongestants and antihistamine will make you sleepy and you should not dive after taking this sort of medicine.

Essentials Sport and activities

Other common problems, such as sunburn, cuts and abrasions from scraping against coral and fire coral stings, can be treated with preparatory remedies brought from home, but be particularly careful to avoid infection from any lesions and make sure you are up to date with your anti-tetanus injections. You should avoid touching any coral (which will die if you do anyway) and not go poking about in holes and overhangs, where you might get stung or bitten by something you can't see. There are now five hyperbaric chambers around the country, staffed by well-qualified medical professionals.

Dives can sometimes be delayed for a variety of reasons, including limited available fuel, Coast Guard clearance to depart port etc, so patience is needed. The authorities are very concerned about security as some dive boats have been 'borrowed' for a quick getaway to Florida.

Dolphinariums

Note that Cuba is allegedly in the habit of capturing dolphins from the wild (and selling them to other countries), a cruel practice causing considerable distress when they are separated from their pods/families and forced to perform to entertain tourists in return for dead fish and antibiotics.

Fishing

Cuba has been a fisherman's dream for many decades, not only for its deep sea fishing, popularized by Ernest Hemingway, but also for its freshwater fishing in the many lakes and reservoirs spread around the island. **Freshwater fishing** is mostly for the largemouth bass (*trucha*), which grow to a great size in the Cuban lakes. *Horizontes* is the travel company to contact for accommodation and fishing packages, which can be arranged all year round. The main places are Maspotón, in Pinar del Río, where you can fish in La Juventud reservoir or in the mouth of the Río Los Palacios or Río Carraguao; Laguna del Tesoro in the Ciénaga de Zapata, where there is a wide variety of fish; Presa Alacranes in Villa Clara province, which is the second largest reservoir in the country; Presa Zaza, in Sancti Spíritus, the largest artificial lake in Cuba, where the record catch of *trucha* is 16.5 lbs; Lago La Redonda, near Morón in Ciego de Avila province, where the clear waters hold such a concentration of fish that a group of US fishermen were able to catch 5,078 *trucha* in five days; and in the province of Camagüey on the Porvenir, Muñoz and Mañana de Santa Ana dams. Equipment can be hired, but serious fishermen will prefer to bring their own and a large quantity of insect repellent. **Deep sea fishing** can be organized at most marinas around the island, although most of the tournaments and the best facilities are at the *Marina Hemingway*, just west of Havana. The waters are home to a variety of beaked fish: marlin, swordfish, tarpon, sawfish, yellowfin tuna, dorado, wahoo, shark and a host of others are all caught here. Varadero is a good point from which to go fishing and take advantage of the Gulf Stream which flows between Key West in Florida and Cuba, but records have been broken all along the northern coast in the cays of the Archipiélago de Sabana and the Archipiélago de Camagüey. There is also good fishing off the south coast around the Isla de la Juventud and Cayo Largo. **Bonefishing** is best done off the south coast in the Archipiélago de los Jardines de la Reina, or off Cayo Largo.

For bass fishing, the fishing licence is US$20, one fishing session (three to four hours) is US$40, a double session (six to eight hours) US$70. For snook and tarpon fishing, the licence is US$20, one fishing session (three to four hours) US$90, two fishing sessions (6-8 hrs) US$170. *Horizontes* organizes an annual International Bass Fishing Tournament every February. Freshwater fishing is allowed all year round.

Golf

There are currently only two courses, in Varadero (18 holes), see page 201, and in Havana (nine holes), see page 135, but a massive construction programme of 10 professional courses is planned. Starting with one on Cayo Coco and another in San Miguel de los Baños, developed by *Rumbos* and the **UK Pro Golfers' Association**, there will be others in Havana, Trinidad, Santa Lucía, Holguín and Santiago de Cuba.

Sailing

There are **marinas** all around the country offering moorings, boat rental and a variety of services, and more are being built. Diving and fishing are on offer at many. The largest is the Marina Hemingway in Havana, with 400 slips for yachts and mega-yachts (of which 170 are equipped with water, electricity, telephone, satellite TV and security), port authorities and customs services, as well as hotels, shops, fuel, medical services, charter boats, a variety of watersports, regattas and tournaments. For technical specifications, see www.cubanacan.cu **The Hemingway Club** has links with over 200 yacht clubs worldwide, including the **Yacht Club of France**, an umbrella group for clubs in 56 French cities. Links with Spanish yacht clubs are also good and in 2001 a race was organized between Cádiz and the Marina Hemingway.

Marinas are owned by **Cubanacán Náutica** (Calle 184 123, Rpto Flores, Playa, Havana, T7-336675, comercial@marlin.cha.cyt.cu), **Puertosol** (Calle 1 3001 esquina 30, Miramar, Havana, T7-2045923, psonger@teleda.get.cma.net) and **Gaviota** (Avenida del Puerto, Edif La Marina, 3rd floor, Havana, T7-666777, gerendes @nwgaviot .gav.cma.net). **Cubanacán Náutica** runs the Marina Hemingway as well as the Santiago Marina, but also has about a dozen scuba diving centres. **Puertosol** has marinas at Tarará, Varadero, Cayo Largo del Sur, Cayo Coco, Cienfuegos, Ancón, María la Gorda and El Colony on Isla de la Juventud. **Gaviota** has a marina at Guardalavaca and at Varadero.

Shooting

Hunting and shooting birds is a popular sport in Cuba and enjoyed by a certain sort of foreigner. It takes place at most of the lodges for freshwater fishing, such as Maspotón or Morón and can also be arranged by **Horizontes** and **Gaviota** (see Cuban tour operators, page 23). All equipment and dogs are for hire and a hunting licence (US$25) must be purchased. If you want to use your own equipment you must get a permit to bring it into the country. The hunting season for most birds is from 15 September to 15 October, except for white crowned ring dove and Mexican tree duck, which is from 20 July to 30 August. One hunting session costs US$50, shotgun rental US$15. You may use your own gun, 12 gauge or 22-cal shotgun or rifle, but you have to apply for an import permit at least 15 working days before you travel. Cartridges can be bought in Cuba and cost US$10 per 25-piece box. The unfortunate victims of this sport include the mourning dove, the white winged dove, migrant ducks, snipe, guinea fowl, pheasant and quail.

Walking

The three main mountain ranges are excellent for hill walking in a wide range of tropical vegetation, where many national parks are being established and trails demarcated. The highest peaks are in the **Sierra Maestra** in the east, where there are also many historical landmarks associated with the Wars of Independence and the Revolution. A three-day walk will take you from Alto del Naranjo up the island's highest peak, Pico Turquino, and down to the Caribbean coast at Las Cuevas, giving you fantastic views of the mountains and the coastline. A guide is mandatory in the National Park. The **Sierra del Escambray**, in the centre of the island, is conveniently located just north of the best-preserved colonial city, Trinidad, and there are some lovely walks in the hills, along trails beside rivers, waterfalls and caves. The mountains of the west of the island, the Sierra del Rosario and the **Sierra de los Organos**, have some of the most unusual geological features, notably the large number of caves and the limestone *mogotes* – straight-sided, flat-topped hills rising from the midst of tobacco fields and looking almost Chinese, particularly in the early morning mist. Good large-scale maps are non-existent and you are advised to take a guide when embarking on long walks. Not only will this prevent you getting lost, but you will learn a lot more about your surroundings, as many of the guides are professional botanists or ornithologists. It is not advisable to take off for a long walk on your own in Cuba. If you are walking in National Parks a guide is compulsory.

The first months of the year are the best for walking, as they are drier, less humid and not so hot. However, temperature varies with the altitude and the higher you get in the Sierra Maestra, the cooler it will become, so take appropriate clothing. Also remember that in the rainforest there are few days when it does not rain, so expect to get wet. The months from August to November are the wettest, when the risk of hurricanes or tropical storms increases, but you can still encounter days when there is plenty of sunshine and you can get out for a good walk. It is best to start early, before it gets too hot. Always carry plenty of drinking water, some food, a hat and suntan lotion. Good footwear is essential and a walking stick is extremely useful on hilly forest trails if they are muddy and slippery after rain. The **Ramblers Association** take guided groups to Cuba, www.
Ramblersholidays.co.uk

Spectator sports

Baseball
Cuba is a baseball-mad nation and vies with the USA for poll position in the world. In 2003 Cuba came out the baseball champions in the Pan-American Games, when every television set in the island was tuned to the match. The Serie Nacional baseball season runs from November to May, culminating in the national play-offs, followed a couple of weeks later by the Liga Superior, which lasts a month. Baseball games have a fanatical following and can last up to three hours.

Basketball
Young Cuban men can be seen playing basketball in every town and village. This is the second most popular sport in the country and visitors are welcome to join in. The main stadium is the Ramón Fonst stadium near the Plaza de la Revolución in Havana and the season runs from September to November.

Boxing
Cuban boxers can always be expected to come out of the Olympic Games with a clutch of medals in all boxing weights and Cubans enthusiastically support their athletes. The best place to catch a tournament or just watch some training matches for international team events is the Sala Kid Chocolate in Havana.

There is keen interest in cycling as a sport and Cuba is a respected competitor in the Americas. Havana's professional racetrack is at the Velódromo Reinaldo Paseiro, part of the Estadio Panamericano, built in 1991 for the Pan-American Games. It is located on the southern side of the Vía Blanca, next to the swimming facilities. Cuba hosts several international competitions including Vuelta a Cuba (February), a staged road race from Baracoa to Pinar del Río. The **Federación Cubana de Ciclismo**, T7-973776, is based in Habana del Este and can be contacted for further details.

Health

Cuba has a high quality national health service and is one of the healthiest countries in Latin America and the Caribbean. Travel in Cuba poses no health risk to the average visitor provided sensible precautions are taken. It is important to go to your GP before you travel, though, to get the latest up-to-date advice and information. Medical service is no longer free for foreign visitors in Havana, Santiago de Cuba and Varadero, where there are international clinics that charge in dollars (credit cards accepted). Visitors requiring medical attention will be sent to them. Emergencies are handled on an ad hoc basis. Check with your national health service or health insurance on coverage in Cuba and take a copy of your insurance policy with you. Remember you cannot dial any toll-free numbers abroad so make sure you have a contact number. Charges are generally lower than those in Western countries. According to latest reports, visitors are still treated free of charge in other parts of the country, with the exception of tourist enclaves with on-site medical services.

Self-medication may be forced on you by lack of supplies in Cuba, see below for what to take.

The most common affliction of travellers to any country is probably diarrhoea and the same is true of Cuba. Tap water is unreliable in most areas of the country, but bottled water is widely available. There has been a water shortage for several years; when there are supply cuts, delivery to luxury hotels is in chrome tankers, the lesser hotels receive battered old water carts and the local population get supplies in converted petrol tankers. Doctors will advise you to get hepatitis A and typhoid inoculations (see below). ►► *For local health facilities see individual towns' Directory sections.*

Before you go

Ideally, you should see your GP or travel clinic at least six weeks before your departure for general advice on travel risks and vaccinations. Make sure you have travel insurance, get a dental check (especially if you are going to be away for more than a month), know your own blood group and if you suffer a long-term condition such as diabetes or epilepsy make sure someone knows or that you have a Medic Alert bracelet/necklace with this information on it.

It is risky to buy medicinal tablets abroad because the doses may differ and there may be a trade in false drugs.

Vaccinations recommended include **Polio** if none in last 10 years; **Diptheria** and **Tetanus**, again, if you haven't had one in the last 10 years (after five doses you have had enough for life); **Typhoid** if nil in last three years; **Hepatitis A** as the disease can be caught easily from food/water. **Yellow Fever** is not required unless you are coming directly from an infected country in Africa or South America. **Smallpox** vaccination is no longer required anywhere. Although **Cholera** vaccination is largely ineffective, immigration officers may ask for proof of such vaccination if coming from a country where the epidemic has occurred. Check www.cgc.gov and www.who.int for updates.

Mosquito repellents Remember that DEET (Di-ethyltoluamide) is the gold standard. Apply the repellent every four to six hours but more often if you are sweating heavily. If a non-DEET product is used check who tested it. Validated products (tested at the London School of Hygiene and Tropical Medicine) include Mosiguard, Non-DEET Jungle formula and non-DEET Autan. If you want to use citronella remember that it must be applied very frequently (ie hourly) to be effective. If you are popular target for insect bites or develop lumps quite soon after being bitten, carry an Aspivenin kit. This syringe suction device is available from many chemists and draws out some of the allergic materials and provides quick relief.

Pain killers Paracetomol or a suitable painkiller can have multiple uses for symptoms but always remember that more than eight paractemol a day can lead to liver failure.

Ciproxin (Ciprofloaxcin) A useful antibiotic for some forms of travellers diarrhoea.

Immodium A great standby for those diarrhoeas that occur at awkward times (ie before a long coach/train journey or on a trek). It helps stop the flow of diarrhoea and in my view is of more benefit than harm. (It was believed that letting the bacteria or viruses flow out had to be more beneficial. However, with Immodium they still come out, just in a more solid form.)

Pepto-Bismol Used a lot by Americans for diarrhoea. It certainly relieves symptoms but like Immodium it is not a cure for underlying disease. Be aware that it turns the stool black as well as making it more solid.

MedicAlert These simple bracelets, or an equivalent, should be carried or worn by anyone with a significant medical condition.

The climate is hot; Cuba is a tropical country and protection against the sun will be needed. To reduce the risk of sunburn and skin cancer, make sure you pack sun cream, light-coloured loose clothing and a hat. Always carry toilet paper with you, it is not always available in public toilets and even some hotels do not have it. For longer trips involving jungle treks taking a clean needle pack, clean dental pack and water filtration devices are common-sense measures.

An A-Z of health risks

Bites and stings

It is a very rare event indeed for travellers, but if you are unlucky (or careless) enough to be bitten by a venomous snake, spider, scorpion or sea creature, try to identify the creature, without putting yourself in further danger. Snake bites in particular are very frightening, but in fact rarely poisonous – even venomous snakes bite without injecting venom. Victims should be taken to a hospital or a doctor without delay. Commercial snake bite and scorpion kits are available, but are usually only useful for the specific types of snake or scorpion. Most serum has to be given intravenously so it is not much good equipping yourself with it unless you are used to making injections into veins. It is best to rely on local practice in these cases, because the particular creatures will be known about locally and appropriate treatment can be given. Certain tropical sea fish when trodden upon inject venom into bathers' feet. This can be exceptionally painful. Wear plastic shoes if such creatures are reported. The pain can be relieved by immersing the foot in extremely hot water for as long as the pain persists.

Symptoms Fright, swelling, pain and bruising around the bite and soreness of the regional lymph glands, perhaps nausea, vomiting and a fever. Symptoms of serious poisoning would be: numbness and tingling of the face, muscular spasms, convulsions, shortness of breath or a failure of the blood to clot, causing generalized bleeding.

Treatment of snake bite Reassure and comfort the victim frequently. Immobilize the limb by a bandage or a splint and get the person to lie still. Do not slash the bite area and try to suck out the poison because this sort of heroism does more harm than good. If you know how to use a tourniquet in these circumstances, you will not need this advice. If you are not experienced, do not apply a tourniquet.

Precautions Do not walk in snake territory in bare feet or sandals – wear proper shoes or boots. If you encounter a snake stay put until it slithers away and do not investigate a wounded snake.

Dengue fever

Although travellers need to take precautions against dengue fever, the risk has not increased in Cuba in recent years. Unfortunately there is no vaccine against this and the mosquitoes that carry it bite during the day. You will feel like a mule has kicked you for two to three days, you will then get better for a few days and then feel that the mule has kicked you again. It should all be over in seven to 10 days. Heed all the anti-mosquito measures that you can.

Diarrhoea and intestinal upset

Symptoms Diarrhoea can refer either to loose stools or an increased frequency; both of these can be a nuisance. It should be short lasting but persistence beyond two weeks, with blood or pain, require specialist medical attention.

Cures Ciproxin (Ciprofloaxcin) is a useful antibiotic for bacterial traveller's diarrhoea. It can be obtained by private prescription in the UK which is expensive, or in Havana at the **Camilo Cienfuegos** pharmacy, see page 142, for US$2.50 each pill. You need to take one 500 mg tablet when the diarrhoea starts and if you do not feel better in 24 hours, the diarrhoea is likely to have a non-bacterial cause and may be viral (in which case there is little you can do apart from keep yourself rehydrated and wait for it to settle on its own). The key treatment with all diarrhoeas is rehydration. Try to keep hydrated by taking the right mixture of salt and water. This is available as Oral Rehydration Salts (ORS) in ready-made sachets or can be made up by adding a teaspoon of sugar and a half teaspoon of salt to a litre of clean water. Drink at least one large cup of this drink for each loose stool. You can also use flat carbonated drinks as an alternative. Immodium and Pepto-Bismol provide symptomatic relief.

> One study showed that up to 70% of all travellers may suffer from diarrhoea or intestinal upset during their trip.

Prevention The standard advice is to be careful with water and ice for drinking. Ask yourself where the water came from. If you have any doubts then boil it or filter and treat it. There are many filter/treatment devices now available on the market. Food can also transmit disease. Be wary of salads (what were they washed in, who handled them), re-heated foods or food that has been left out in the sun having been cooked earlier in the day. There is a simple adage that says wash it, peel it, boil it or forget it. Also be wary of unpasteurized dairy products, these can transmit a range of diseases from brucellosis (fevers and constipation), to listeria (meningitis) and tuberculosis of the gut (obstruction, constipation, fevers and weight loss).

Heat

Full acclimatization to high temperatures takes about two weeks. During this period it is normal to feel a bit apathetic, especially if the relative humidity is high. Drink plenty of water (up to 15 litres a day are required when working physically hard in the tropics), use salt on your food and avoid extreme exertion. Tepid showers are more cooling than hot or cold ones. Loose cotton is still the best material when the weather is hot. Large hats do not cool you down, but do prevent sunburn. **Prickly heat** , a very common intensely itchy rash, is avoided by frequent washing and by wearing loose clothing. It is cured by allowing skin to dry off (through use of powder and spending two nights in an air-conditioned hotel!).

Remember that, especially in the highlands, there can be a large and sudden drop in temperature between sun and shade and between night and day, so dress accordingly. Warm jackets or woollens are essential after dark at high altitude.

Hepatitis

Symptoms Hepatitis means inflammation of the liver. The most obvious symptom is a yellowing of your skin or the whites of your eyes. However, prior to this all that you may notice is itching and tiredness.

Cures Early on, depending on the type of hepatitis, a vaccine or immunoglobulin may reduce the duration of the illness.

Prevention Pre-travel hepatitis A vaccine is the best bet. Hepatitis B (for which there is a vaccine) is spread through blood and unprotected sexual intercourse, both of these can be avoided. Unfortunately there is no vaccine for hepatitis C or the increasing alphabetical list of other Hepatitis viruses.

Sexual health

The range of visible and invisible diseases is awesome. Unprotected sex can spread HIV, Hepatitis B and C, Gonorrhea (green discharge), chlamydia (nothing to see but may cause painful urination and later female infertility), painful recurrent herpes, syphilis and warts, just to name a few. You can cut down the risk by using condoms, a femidom or avoiding sex altogether. HIV is not wholly confined to the well-known high-risk sections of the population, ie homosexual men, intravenous drug users and children of infected mothers. Heterosexual transmission is now the dominant mode and so the main risk to travellers is from casual sex. The same precautions should be taken as with any sexually transmitted disease. HIV can be passed by unsterilized needles which have been previously used to inject an HIV positive patient, but the risk of this is negligible. It would, however, be sensible to check that needles have been properly sterilized or disposable needles have been used. If you wish to take your own disposable needles, be prepared to explain what they are for. The risk of receiving a blood transfusion with blood infected with the HIV virus is greater than from dirty needles because of the amount of fluid exchanged. Supplies of blood for transfusion are screened for HIV in all Cuban hospitals, so again the risk is very small indeed. Catching the HIV does not always produce an illness in itself (although it may do). The only way to be sure if you feel you have been put at risk is to have a blood test for HIV antibodies on your return to a place where there are reliable facilities. The test does not become positive for some weeks.

Sun protection

Symptoms White Britons are notorious for becoming red in hot countries because they like to stay out longer than everyone else and do not use adequate sun protection. This can lead to sunburn, which is painful and followed by flaking of skin. Aloe vera gel is a good pain reliever for sunburn. Long-term sun damage leads to a loss of elasticity of skin and the development of pre-cancerous lesions. Years later a mild or a very malignant form of cancer may develop. The milder basal cell carcinoma, if detected early, can be treated by cutting it out or freezing it. The much nastier malignant melanoma may have already spread to bone and brain at the time that it is first noticed.

Prevention Sun screen. SPF stands for Sun Protection Factor. It is measured by determining how long a given person takes to 'burn' with and without the sunscreen product on. So, if it takes 10 times longer to burn with the sunscreen product applied, then that product has an SPF of 10. If it only takes twice as long then the SPF is 2. The higher the SPF the greater the protection. However, do not just use higher factors just to stay out in the sun longer. 'Flash frying' (desperate bursts of excessive exposure), as it is called, is known to increase the risks of skin cancer. Cuba is a hot, tropical country, so take a high factor sun screen, apply it regularly and stay out of the midday sun. Children need to be particularly well protected and wear a hat. The breeze at the beach is deceptive, you may not feel hot, but the sun will burn very quickly. Between May and October, the risk of sunburn is high, sun blocks are recommended when walking around the city as well as on the beach. In the cooler months, limit beach sessions to two hours. At all times of year, follow the Australians' Slip, Slap, Slop campaign: slip on a shirt, slap on a hat, slop on some sun screen.

Ticks

Ticks usually attach themselves to the lower parts of the body often after walking in areas where cattle have grazed. They take a while to attach themselves strongly, but swell up as they start to suck blood. The important thing is to remove them gently, so that they do not leave their head parts in your skin because this can cause a nasty allergic reaction some days later. Do not use petrol, vaseline, lighted cigarettes etc to remove the tick, but, with a pair of tweezers remove the beast gently by gripping it at the attached (head) end and rock it out in very much the same way that a tooth is extracted. Certain tropical flies which lay their eggs under the skin of sheep and cattle also occasionally do the same thing to humans with the unpleasant result that a maggot grows under the skin and pops up as a boil or pimple. The best way to remove these is to cover the boil with oil, vaseline or nail varnish so as to stop the maggot breathing, then to squeeze it out gently the next day.

Underwater health

If you go diving make sure that you are fit do so. The **British Sub-Aqua Club** ① *(BSAC), Telford's Quay, South Pier Road, Ellesmere Port, Cheshire CH65 4FL, UK, T01513-506200, F01513-506215, www.bsac.com*, can put you in touch with doctors who do medical examinations.

Cures Secondary infections caused by cuts, beach dog parasites (larva migrans) and sea urchins should be treated with antibiotics. Serious diving injuries may need time in a decompression chamber. ▶▶ *For further details, see Diving page 67.*

Prevention Check that the dive company know what they are doing, have appropriate certification from **BSAC** or **Professional Association of Diving Instructors** ① *(PADI), Unit 7, St Philips Central, Albert Rd, St Philips, Bristol, BS2 OTD, T0117-3007234, www.padi.com*, and that the equipment is well maintained. Protect your feet from cuts, beach dog parasites (larva migrans) and sea urchins. The latter are almost impossible to remove but can be dissolved with lime or vinegar. Keep an eye out for secondary infection.

Water

There are a number of ways of purifying water. Dirty water should first be strained through a filter bag and then boiled or treated. Bringing water to a rolling boil at sea level is sufficient to make the water safe for drinking, but at higher altitudes you have to boil the water for a few minutes longer to ensure all microbes are killed. There are sterilizing methods that can be used and there are proprietary preparations containing chlorine (eg Puritabs) or iodine (eg Pota Aqua) compounds. Chlorine compounds generally do not kill protozoa (eg Giardia). There are a number of water filters now on the market available in personal and expedition size. They work either on mechanical or chemical principles, or may do both. Make sure you take the spare parts or spare chemicals with you and do not believe everything the manufacturers say.

Further information

Websites
Foreign and Commonwealth Office (FCO) (UK), www.fco.gov.uk This is a key travel advice site, with useful information on the country, people, climate and lists the UK embassies/ consulates. The site also promotes the concept of 'Know Before You Go'. And encourages travel insurance and appropriate travel health advice. It has links to the Department of Health travel advice site, see below.

Department of Health Travel Advice (UK), www.doh.gov.uk/traveladvice This excellent site is also available as a free booklet, the T6, from Post Offices. It lists the vaccine advice requirements for each country.

Medic Alert (UK), www.medicalalert.co.uk This is the website of the foundation that produces bracelets and necklaces for those with existing medical problems. Once you have ordered your bracelet/necklace you write your key medical details on paper inside it, so that if you collapse, a medical person can identify you as someone with epilepsy or allergy to peanuts etc.

Blood Care Foundation (UK), www.bloodcare.org.uk The Blood Care Foundation is a Kent-based charity "dedicated to the provision of screened blood and resuscitation fluids in countries where these are not readily available". They will dispatch certified non-infected blood of the right type to your hospital/clinic. The blood is flown in from various centres around the world.

Public Health Laboratory Service (UK), www.phls.org.uk This site has up to date malaria advice guidelines for travel around the world. It gives specific advice about the right drugs for each location. It also has useful information for those who are pregnant, suffering from epilepsy or planning to travel with children.

World Health Organisation, www.who.int The WHO site has links to the WHO Blue Book (it was Yellow up to last year) on travel advice. This lists the diseases in different regions of the world. It describes vaccination schedules and makes clear which countries have Yellow Fever Vaccination certificate requirements and malarial risk.

Fit for Travel (UK), www.fitfortravel.scot.nhs.uk This site from Scotland provides a quick A-Z of vaccine and travel health advice requirements for each country.

British Travel Health Association (UK), wwwbtha.org This is the official website of an organization of travel health professionals.

Travel Screening Services (UK), www.travelscreening.co.uk This is the author's website. A private clinic dedicated to integrated travel health. The clinic gives vaccine, travel health advice, email and SMS text vaccine reminders and screens returned travellers for tropical diseases.

Books
The Travellers Good Health Guide by Dr Ted Lankester, ISBN 0-85969-827-0.
Expedition Medicine (The Royal Geographic Society) Editors David Warrell and Sarah Anderson ISBN 1 86197 040-4.
International Travel and Health World Health Organisation Geneva
ISBN 92 4 158026 7.
The World's Most Dangerous Places by Robert Young Pelton, Coskun Aral and Wink Dulles ISBN 1-566952-140-9.

The health section was written by **Dr Charlie Easmon** MBBS, MRCP, MPH, DTM&H, DOCCMed, who runs Travel Screening Services based at 1 Harley Street (www.travelscreening.co.uk). Additional material was supplied by Dr David Snashall.

Keeping in touch

Internet

Cubans' access to the internet is tightly controlled, so facilities are limited to dollar-paying foreigners. On January 11 2004 a new law made access to the internet even more difficult for Cubans. Only Cubans who are permitted to use the internet at home; civil servants, doctors and party representatives will be able to do so on a regular phone line paid for in pesos; others will have to pay in dollars.

Foreign tourists using the internet will invariably be asked to show their passport. The large, international hotels of four or five stars, such as the **Nacional, Habana Libre, Parque Central** and **Meliá Cohiba** in Havana and the **Meliá Santiago de Cuba** in Santiago, have business centres with computers for internet access for guests and others, but this is the most expensive way of checking emails, at anything up to US$12 for one hour. Nearly every hotel for foreigners now has internet access for its guests in some form or other and this is always worth trying even if you are not staying there. The telephone company, **Etecsa**, sells prepaid cards that give you an access code and a password code for when you log in and these cost US$15 for five hours, useful if you are in the country for a few weeks. The main telephone office in each town usually has internet access, but if not, **Etecsa** is installing mobile cabins (large blue telephone boxes) with international and national phone services and a computer for internet access. These are not yet widespread so do not rely on them. **Telecorreos** sells a different prepaid card for use in Post Offices but this is of little use to foreigners; you can send emails but you cannot surf the internet, which means that if you use Hotmail or any other system that uses the internet, you will not be able to access your inbox and you will have to set up a new account. There are very few places that could be termed internet cafés, eg in the Capitolio in Havana and in a couple of cafés in Trinidad and in Cienfuegos, where you pay in cash for the time used. Some agencies, such as Cubatur, have a few terminals using their own prepaid card.

Post

When possible, correspondence to Cuba should be addressed to post office boxes (*Apartados*), where delivery is more certain. Stamps can be bought in pesos at post offices, or at **Telecorreos** in certain hotels. Hotels will charge you in dollars, making the stamps very expensive, but they should be 45 centavos for a postcard to Europe and 75 centavos for a letter to Europe. Some postcards are now sold with postage included, look for the ones with the airmail stripe on the side. All postal services, national and international, have been described as appalling. We have had reports of postcards getting from Havana to Austria in 10 days and to Sweden in two weeks but that seems to be the exception rather than the rule, with others from Trinidad to the UK taking five weeks. Cubans will stop you in the street and ask you to take letters out of Cuba for them. Courier services are available in Havana, see page 142.

Telephone → *International code +53.*

Many public phones now take prepaid cards (*tarjetas*) which are easier to use than coins. For domestic, long-distance calls try and get hold of a peso phone card, eg 10 pesos, which works out much cheaper than the dollar cards. The furthest distance, Pinar del Río to Baracoa, costs 1 peso per minute, but if you have a dollar phone card it will cost you US$1 per minute. Most hotels have facilities for international calls and faxes which you can use even if you are not staying there. Cuba does not have a reputation for good communications; it can take time to get a line, but things are gradually improving with help from foreign telecommunications companies. The downside is that numbers and codes are frequently changing. To make a call to another province, dial o then the code and then the number. If you need the operator's help, dial o, pause, then dial o again. If you do use a phone which takes coins, they only accept 5- centavo, 20-centavo or 1-peso coins.

To phone abroad on a phone with **international dialling** facility, dial 119 followed by the country and regional codes and number. Many hard currency hotels and airports (including Havana departure lounge and Santiago) have offices where international calls can be made at high prices. Look for the **Telecorreos** or **Etecsa** signs. No 'collect' calls allowed and only cash accepted. Collect calls to some places, including London, are possible from private Cuban telephones. In a few top-class hotels you can direct dial foreign countries from your room. **Phonecards** (*tarjetas*) are in use at **Etecsa** call boxes, in different denominations from US$10-50, much cheaper for phoning abroad, for example US$2 per minute (US$1.60 1800-0600) to USA and Canada, US$2.60 per minute (US$2.20) to Central America and the Caribbean, US$3.40 (US$3) to South America, US$4 (US$3.60) to Spain, Italy, France and Germany and US$4.40 (US$4) to the rest of the world. There are two sorts of cards: '*chip*' and '*propria*', but only the latter has cheaper rates at night, otherwise they cost the same. The cost of these calls is high, connections are hard to make and you will be cut off frequently. **Faxes** can be sent from **Telecorreos** and **Etecsa** offices and major hotels. Sockets for computer users are standard US type.

Mobile phones are commonly used in Cuba. If you want to rent a cell phone you can do so from **Cubacel**, Calle 28 510 entre 5 y 7 Miramar, Havana, T7-8802222, www.cubacel.com If you plan take your own mobile phone, check www.ccom.cu for further information. To activate a mobile in Cuba call **Cubacel** on T7-8802222, or 711 on your mobile phone and they will talk you through what you must do. Your cellular phone has to be compatible with the American standard (TDMA), either dual or digital. A temporary contract costs US$2 a day to activate it and US$0.40 for calls with a one-off 'installation' charge of US$40. There is also a 'visitor's' rate of US$3 for activation, US$0.70 for outgoing calls and US$0.66 for incoming calls at peak time, better if you are there for only a short time. There is also **C-Com**, Avenida 3A 9402, entre 94 y 96, Playa, T7-2642266, www.ccom.co.cu which uses the GSM system but currently only operates in Havana, Matanzas and Varadero.

Newspapers

All newpapers are state owned. *Granma*, mornings except Sunday and Monday; *Trabajadores*, Trade Union weekly; *Tribuna* and *Juventud Rebelde*, also only weekly. *Opciones* is a weekly national and international trade paper. *Granma* has a weekly edition, *Granma International*, published in Spanish, English, French and Portuguese, and a monthly selected German edition; all have versions on the Internet, www.granma.cu Foreign magazines and newspapers are sometimes on sale at the telex centre in the **Habana Libre** hotel and in the **Riviera** hotel (also telex centre, open 0800-2000). The previous day's paper is available during the week. Weekend editions on sale Tuesday.

Television and radio

There are three state-owned national channels: *Cubavisión*, *Tele Rebelde* and *Canal Educativo*, which broadcast morning and evening. The *Sun Channel* can be seen at hotels and broadcasts a special programme for tourists 24 hours a day. Some of the upmarket hotels also have satellite TV so you can catch up with *CNN* in Spanish or English.

There are six state-owned national radio stations, although you will not be able to tune in to all of them all over the country as the strength of the signal varies. *Radio Enciclopedia*, 1260MW/94.1FM, for instrumental music. *Radio Habana Cuba*, 106.9FM, multilingual, news and information. *Radio Musical Nacional*, 590MW/99.1FM, classical music. *Radio Progreso*, 640MW/90.3FM, music and drama. *Radio Rebelde*, 670 and 710MW/96.7FM, current affairs, sport, music. *Radio Reloj*, 950MW/101.5FM, 24-hr news station. *Radio Taíno*, 1290MW/93.2-93.4FM, Cuban music with items of tourist interest.

Havana

❧ Footprint features

Introduction

Of all the capital cities in the Caribbean, Havana has the reputation for being the most splendid and sumptuous. Before the Revolution, its casinos and nightlife attracted the megastars of the day in much the same way as Beirut and Shanghai, and remarkably little has changed since then. There may be no casinos now, but Havana's bars and clubs with their thriving music scene are still a major draw for foreigners and Cubans alike. There have been no tacky modernizations, partly because of lack of finance and materials. Low-level street lighting, relatively few cars (and many of those antiques), no (real) estate agents or Wendyburgers, no neon and very little advertizing (except for political slogans), all give the city plenty of scope for nostalgia.

Havana is not a modern city in the materialist sense and is no good for people for whom shopping and eating well are the central leisure activities, although the privately run paladares offer a varied and eccentric dining experience. It is, however, probably the finest example of a Spanish colonial city in the Americas. Many of its palaces were converted into museums after the Revolution and more work has been done since La Havana Vieja (the old city) was declared a UNESCO World Heritage Site in 1982. There is also some stunning architecture from the first half of the 20th century, although most of the city is fighting a losing battle against the sea air – many of the finest buildings along the sea front are crumbling and emergency work is under way to save some of them.

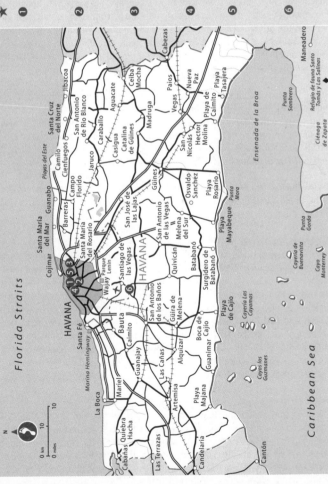

★ Don't miss...

1. **Capitolio** Grand and stately, the former houses of parliament rise above the surrounding buildings as testament to a former age of US-dominated government, page 93.

2. **Partagas cigar factory** All you ever wanted to know about how to make a cigar and a revealing insight into the labour that goes into this profitable exercise, page 94.

3. **Museo del Ron** Sugar and rum were the traditional mainstays of the Cuban economy until a recent cutback in the area under sugar cane, but rum remains king, page 96.

4. **Museo de Artes Decorativas** A treasure trove of fine art and furniture left behind by the rich who fled to Miami after the Revolution, page 103.

5. **Museo Nacional Palacio de Bellas Artes** The Cuban section is a fine illustration of the development of Cuban art from colonial times to the 21st century, page 92.

6. **Fiesta de San Lázaro** Visit El Rincón on 17 December to see pilgrims arriving on their knees at the town's gleaming white church, page 144.

Ins and outs → *Colour map 1, grid A5. Population: 2,204,300.*

Getting there

Air The José Martí international airport is 18 km from Havana and all flights from abroad use Terminal 3, the newest terminal, with the exception of flights from Cancún which arrive at Terminal 2. As many transatlantic flights arrive late at night it can be sensible to arrange the transfer from the airport to your hotel in advance with your travel agent. However, it is cheaper to get a taxi when you arrive; there are several different companies and they all charge slightly different rates – fares range from US$13-25, but US$18 is commonly asked to the old city. You will need to ask the driver who he is working for. The cheapest are **Panataxi** and **Habanataxi**. On the way back to the airport it is possible to arrange a private taxi, which may work out cheaper, if you negotiate with the driver. However, their cars are not as reliable as the state taxis and if they break down on the long drive out, you will be stuck. It is theoretically possible to get to the domestic Terminals 1 and 2 by bus (20 centavos) – or at least to within walking distance – by taking the M2 *camello* from the park two blocks west of Parque Fraternidad on Avenida Simón Bolívar, but there will be long queues, it is difficult with luggage and it will take forever. Terminal 3 is a long way from the other two (although just five minutes in a taxi) there are no connecting public buses either between the terminals or from Terminal 3 into Havana. **Víazul** operates a transfer service from some hotels for US$4; pick-up points in Vedado are Calle 1 y Paseo (**Riviera** and **Meliá Cohiba** hotels), Calzada y G (**Presidente**), Calle 21 y N (**Capri**) and Calle O y Humboldt (**Vedado**).

Bus If you are coming in by **Astro** long-distance bus, the main terminal is very near the Plaza de la Revolución in Vedado, which is central and convenient for many hotels or private accommodation. If, however, you arrive on one of the **Víazul** dollar buses for foreigners, you will be much further out and a taxi will be needed to get you to your destination. **Panataxis** wait outside the terminal and will cost around US$5 to La Habana Vieja or Centro.

Train The train station is at the southern end of the old city, within walking distance of any of the hotels there or in Centro Habana, although if you arrive at night it would be better to take a taxi to your destination. ▶ *For further details, see Transport page 136.*

Getting around

Havana is very spread out along the coast. La Habana Vieja to Miramar along the Malecón (the seafront boulevard) is more than 8 km. **Bus** Tricky for the uninitiated, involving complicated queuing procedures and a lot of pushing and shoving. **Bicitaxi** More leisurely than taking the bus is to hire a *bicitaxi* (bicycle taxi) for short journeys or longer sightseeing trips, rates negotiable but generally only a couple of dollars. **Cocotaxi** These overpriced, bright yellow motorcycle taxis are called *cocotaxis* because of their shape. **Taxi** You can opt for the traditional taxi, although those too come in lots of different styles. **Walking** Much of the city can be covered on foot, but the average visitor will be content with one district at a time and still feel well-exercised. It is also possible to hire **bikes** and **cars**. ▶ *For further details, see Transport page 136.*

Best time to visit

The driest and least humid time of the year is between December and March, when you can have completely cloudless days. From July to August is the hottest time but most public buildings have air conditioning and there is usually a breeze along the Malecón. Rain falls mainly in May and June and then from September to October, but there are wet days all year round. In recent years, the worst storms have hit between

September and November, destroying many of the decrepit houses in the city, but Havana is exceptionally well prepared for hurricanes and loss of life is rare. Carnival is a movable feast. For some years it was held along the Malecón at the end of July and the beginning of August, but in 2003 it was moved to November. There are many cultural festivals (jazz, ballet, film etc) and sporting events (baseball, cycling, boxing, fishing, sailing etc) all through the year that are worth catching. There are many festive days which are not national holidays, for example José Martí's birthday (28 January 1853), which are very important, particularly in Havana. New Year celebrations are a major event, coinciding with the anniversary of the triumph of the Revolution on 1 Jan 1959.

Tourist information

The headquarters of the **Oficina de Turismo de La Habana** is at Calle 28 303 entre 3 y 5, Miramar, T7-2040624. There is a network of kiosks run by **Infotur**, which can provide you with information and maps, www.infotur.cu At the airport, Terminal 2, T7-558733, Terminal 3, T7-666101, open 24 hrs. In Habana Vieja, Obispo entre Bernaza y Villegas, T7-333333; Obispo esq San Ignacio, T7-636884, and at the cruise ship terminal, Avenida del Puerto, daily 0830-2030. In Playa, at Avenida 5 y Calle 112, T7-247036, daily 0830-2030. At the Santa María del Mar office, Avenida Las Terrazas entre 11 y 12, Playas del Este, T7-961111/971261, guanabodir@cubacel.net daily 0800-1900, you will find maps, excursions, internet, booking for hotels, souvenirs, but with no map of the area and with limited bus information, it remains to be seen how useful they're going to be. **Infotur** is also in Guanabo at Avenida 5 entre 468 y 470, T7-966868.

If you want to book tours, do so before 1800 the day before. The state tour agencies, such as **Cubatur** and **Havanatur**, are found in hotels and other locations. Their main task is to sell tours, but they can also make hotel reservations, sell tickets for buses, trains and planes and organize pick-ups and transfers. If you are staying in a *casa particular* you will probably find your host is a mine of useful information who can fill you in on all the gossip and background detail to enrich a stay in the capital.

History

The colonial period

Havana, the capital, founded in 1519 on the present site, is situated at the mouth of a deep bay; in the colonial period, this natural harbour was the assembly point for ships of the annual silver convoy to Spain. Its strategic and commercial importance is reflected in the extensive fortifications, particularly on the east side of the entrance to the bay where there are two large fortresses, El Castillo de los Tres Reyes del Morro, built in 1589-1630 and San Carlos de la Cabaña, built in 1763-74. On the west side of the canal are the smaller, 16th-century Castillo de la Punta and the Castillo de la Real Fuerza.

The city was prey to pirate attacks as well as being a pawn in European wars. In the 18th century, the British attacked Havana and held it from 1762-63, but exchanged it for Florida. From that point, the city's importance as the gathering place for the silver convoy was superseded by trade. The local planters and merchants had briefly discovered the value of trading their crops with Britain and North America. From the second half of the 18th century to the end of the 19th century, ships came in to Havana carrying slaves, while exports of coffee, tobacco and, most importantly, sugar were the mainstay of the local economy.

19th century

From the beginning of the 19th century, the local sugar plantocracy began to move out of the city guarded by defensive walls and build neocolonial villas or country estates in what are now the municipalities of Cerro, 10 de Octubre and the high part of Marianao. One example of this architecture is Quinta del Conde Santo Venia, built in 1841, now a home for the elderly, just behind the Estadio Latino Americano. By the 1850s, the city walls had more or less collapsed and the Prado was absorbed into the old city instead of running outside the walls. A fine neoclassical example here is the Palacio de Aldama, opposite the Parque de la Fraternidad. Competition began to come from the west in the 1870s, with the rise of Vedado, which reached its high point in the 1920s, where neoclassical, romantic and art nouveau small palaces with internal courtyards vied with each other for luxury and originality. The Casa de la Amistad, on Paseo, is an example, and the Colón cemetery also reflects this bourgeois competitiveness.

20th century

By 1918, Miramar, on the western outskirts across the Río Almendares, now Playa municipality, began to take over, in another new style: that of beach resorts, exclusive seaside clubs and, of course, casinos. It was the salon of the city, American-style. In the 1950s, the development had reached as far west as the present districts of Siboney and Cubanacán (now given Amerindian names in place of their former ones of Biltmore and the Country Club) in Playa, housing some 300 wealthy families. The houses where the wealthy lived in Miramar before the Revolution are today occupied

Havana orientation

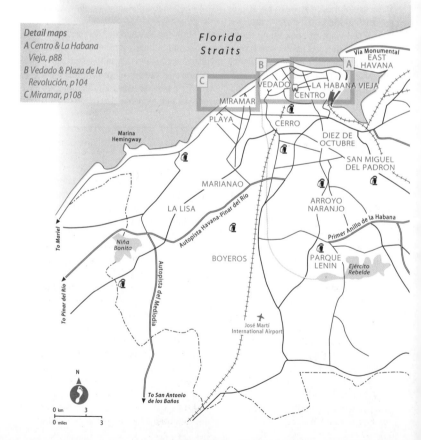

by embassies and government buildings, but there are also many abandoned villas. Major building operations took place after the two World Wars in Miramar and after the Korean war in the far western suburbs, both of which were boom periods in terms of sugar and also nickel sales for armaments. This was also the moment for the extension of Nuevo Vedado, tower buildings like the Focsa, and the Hotel Nacional. The sea was regarded as a threat during most of Havana's history and only became an asset in the 20th century. The Malecón seafront drive was built in 1901, the tunnel to Miramar (replacing a bridge) in 1950, and the tunnel leading to Playas del Este, on the other side of the bay, in 1958.

The wealthy middle class also built property for rent (80% of Havana was rented to other nationals and foreigners). Landlords lived in houses built on the *manzana* (block), architectural style. Those that were built for rent were on a smaller scale, with fewer green areas and small apartments off passageways. Working-class areas within these suburbs or municipalities were also developed, such as Pogolotti (early 1900s in Marianao), and parts of San Miguel del Padrón, in 1948. Buena Vista, in Nuevo Vedado, was also a poorer area. After the Revolution, construction was concentrated on the rest of the country, which had been largely forgotten. Havana was seen as relatively well-developed in comparison. Exceptions were service buildings, such as the Almeijeras hospital on the Malecón, and educational institutions. A whole section of the bay was also developed for the fishing industry. The municipality of Havana del Este is post-Revolution. The Camilo Cienfuegos housing estate was built in 1959-61 and Alamar in 1970. There is also the

scientific complex near Siboney in the far west of Miramar, housing a state-of-the-art genetic biology centre and a neurological hospital, among other facilities.

Contemporary Havana

Before the Revolution, Havana was the largest, the most beautiful and the most sumptuous city in the Caribbean. Today, it is rather run down and the weather has wreaked havoc on both pre- and post-Revolution buildings. Thanks to the government's policy of developing the countryside, it's not ringed with shanty towns like so many other Latin American capitals, although some reappeared in the 1990s. Nevertheless, the city is shabby and visitors are often taken by surprise by living conditions. Half the people live in housing officially regarded as sub-standard. Many buildings are shored up by wooden planks. Some of it is very old, but the ancient palaces, colonnades, churches and monasteries have undergone so much renovation that they are in considerably better shape than the newer housing.

The old city has been declared a World Heritage Site by the United Nations. Priorities include the restoration of the historic centre, under the auspices of UNESCO and the City Historian's Office, whose brief is also to rebuild communities in the widest sense of the word, with income from cultural tourism, and aid from European NGOs. Restoration will encompass the Malecón, starting from the historic centre, where housing has been badly affected by salination and sea damage, and the Bosque de la Habana, crossed by the Río Almendares, now suffering from pollution and contamination, which is a potentially rich green belt, extending over several kilometres.

Orientation

The city of Havana has 200 districts in 15 municipalities, including 14,000 *manzanas* (blocks). These municipalities are: **Playa**, **Marianao** and **La Lisa** in the west; **Boyeros** in the southwest; **Plaza de la Revolución**, **Centro Habana**, **La Habana Vieja**, **Cerro** and **Diez de Octubre** in the centre; south-central **Arroyo Naranjo**; **Regla**, **San Miguel del Padrón** going eastwards; **Cotorro** in the southeast; and in the east, **Playas del Este** and **Guanabacoa**. The centre is divided into five sections, three of which are of most interest to visitors, **La Habana Vieja** (Old Havana), **Centro Habana** (Central Havana) and **Vedado**, linked by the Malecón, a picturesque thoroughfare along the coast.

Most of the museums, palaces and churches of interest are in La Habana Vieja. Centro is largely residential and Vedado has most of the action, with clubs, bars, theatres, cinemas and hotels with murky pre-Revolution tales to tell. Beyond Vedado, west of the Río Almendares, is **Miramar**, once an upper-class suburb, where embassies and hotels for businesspeople are located. Streets have names in La Habana Vieja and Centro, but numbers or letters in Vedado and numbers in Miramar, although some of the main roads in Vedado are still referred to by names.

An **address** is given as the street (*Calle* or *Avenida*),the building number, followed by the two streets between which it is located, eg **Hotel Inglaterra**, Prado 416 entre San Rafael y San Miguel. However, sometimes this is shortened to showing merely which corner it is on, eg **Hotel Florida**, Obispo 252 esquina Cuba. A large building will not bother with the number, eg **Hotel Nacional**, Calle O esquina 21. Cubans usually abbreviate *entre* (between) to e/ while *esquina* (corner) becomes esq.

The oldest part of the city, around the **Plaza de Armas**, is quite near the docks where you can see cargo ships from all over the world being unloaded. Here are the former **Palacio de los Capitanes Generales**, **El Templete**, and **Castillo de La Real Fuerza**, the oldest of all the forts. From Plaza de Armas run two narrow and picturesque streets, Calles Obispo and O'Reilly. These two streets go west to the heart of the city to **Parque Central**, with its laurels, poincianas, almonds, palms, shrubs and gorgeous flowers. To the southwest rises the white dome of the **Capitolio** (Capitol). From the northwest corner of Parque Central, a wide, tree-shaded avenue with a central walkway, the **Paseo del Prado**, runs to the fortress of **La Punta**. The Prado technically divides the old city from Centro, having once been the edge of the city, although architecturally there is little distinction. At its north sea-side end is Havana's beguiling oceanfront highway, the **Malecón**, which snakes westward from La Punta to the residential district of Vedado.

Further west Calle San Lázaro leads directly from the monument to **General Antonio Maceo** on the Malecón to the **Universidad de La Habana** (Havana University). Further inland, past **El Príncipe** castle, is **Plaza de la Revolución**, with the impressive monument to **José Martí** at its centre and the much-photographed, huge outline of Che Guevara on one wall.

From near the fortress of **La Punta** in the old city, a tunnel built in 1958 by the French runs east under the mouth of the harbour; it emerges in the rocky ground between the **Castillo del Morro** and the fort of **La Cabaña**, some 550 m away, and a 5 km highway connects with the Havana–Matanzas road. This is an area of post-Revolution housing, designed to improve the living conditions of the average citizen. Both the **Camilo Cienfuegos** *barrio*, dating from 1961, and **Alamar**, from

1970, were built by microbrigades, with citizens helping to build their own apartments, schools and clinics. There are also vast sporting facilities, built for the Panamerican Games, which include athletics tracks, a bicycle track, swimming pool and tennis courts, as well as a hotel. The three or four decades since construction started have taken their toll, however, and the tropical climate and sea winds have eaten into the concrete and metal structures, leaving the district looking run down and depressed.

Sights

La Habana Vieja (Old Havana)

The old city is the area with the greatest concentration of sites of interest and where most work is being done to restore buildings to their former glory. New museums, art galleries, hotels, restaurants and shops are opening all the time in renovated mansions or merchants' houses. Several days can be spent strolling around the narrow streets or along the waterfront, stopping in bars and open air cafés to take in the atmosphere, although the nightlife is better in Vedado. Don't forget to look up to the balconies; Habaneros live life in the open-air and balcony life is as full and intricate as street life. ▶▶ *For Sleeping, Eating and other listings, see pages 109-143.*

Plaza de Armas

This is Havana's oldest square and it has been restored to very much what it once was. The statue in the centre is of the 'Father of the Nation', the revolutionary 19th-century landowner, Carlos Manuel de Céspedes. In the northeast corner of the square is the church of **El Templete** ① *Baratillo 1 entre O'Reilly y Narciso López*, a small neoclassical building finished in 1828 (renovated 1997). A column in front of it marks the spot where the first Mass was said in 1519 under a ceiba tree and, under its branches, the supposed bones of Columbus reposed in state before being taken to the cathedral. A sapling of the same tree, blown down by a hurricane in 1753, was planted on the same spot. This tree was cut down in 1828, the present tree planted, and the Doric temple opened. Habaneros celebrate here, every 16 November, the anniversary of the first Mass and the first town council of San Cristóbal de la Habana, the city's official name. It is also the starting point for all guided tours of La Habana Vieja. Inside El Templete there are paintings by the Frenchman, Juan Bautiste Vermay, a pupil of the Master David and the first director of the Academia Nacional de Bellas Artes, founded in 1818. His main artistic work was the creation of the paintings in El Templete. These represent the first Mass celebrated on that spot, the first *Cabildo* (local council) and the consecration of the small temple.

On the north side of the Plaza is the **Palacio del Segundo Cabo** ① *Mon-Sat 1000-1730*, the former private residence of the Captains General, now housing the **Instituto Cubano del Libro** and three bookshops, see page 131. Its patio is worth a look. On the east side is the small luxury hotel, the **Santa Isabel**, and on the south side the modern **Museo Nacional de Historia Natural** ① *Obispo 61, entre Baratillo y Oficios, Plaza de Armas, T7-8632687, museo@mnhnc.imf.cu Tue-Fri 0930-1730, Sat and Sun 0930-1630, US$3, guide US$1*, where you will find lots of stuffed animals, information (in Spanish) on Cuban bats, butterflies and endemic species. Work is being done to expand to the second floor, but this is not the most exciting museum unless you take time to read, for example, that a flock of 50,000 bats eats 200 kg a night; there are 87 species of cockroach, two thirds of

▪ *The Natural History Museum's rooftop bar, El Mirador, has excellent views over the city and the bay, and is a relaxing spot for a mojito.*

Centro & La Habana Vieja

Caleta de San Lázaro

To Havana University & Julio Antonio Mella Monument

Airline offices(Cubana, LTU)
Aerocaribbean, Aeroflot

Humboldt

25

Príncipe

Vapor

Calzada de Infanta

CAYO HUESO

Jovellar

San Lázaro

Monumento a
General Antonio
Maceo

La Inmaculada
Concepción

San Lázaro

Lagunas

Ánimas

Hamel

Ánimas

Virtudes

Concordia

Neptuno

San Miguel

San Rafael

San Martín

Márquez González

Lucena

Padre Varela (Belascoaín)

Perseverancia

Nuestra Señora
de Monserrate

La Epoca

San Francisco

Espada

Hospital

Aramburu

Soledad

Gervasio

Escobar

Lealtad

Boulevard

San Martín

Av de Italia (Galiano)

Zanja

Salud

CENTRO

Jesús Peregrino

Chávez

Nuestra Señora de
la Caridad del Cobre

Chinese

Barcelona

Pocito

Av Salvador Allende (Carlos III)

La Plaza Carlos III
Enrique Barnet (Estrella)

Sagrado Corazón
de Jesús

Parque
El Curita

Av Simón Bolívar

Maloja

Sitio

Peñalver

Escobar

Lealtad

Campanario

Manrique

San Nicolás

Rayo

Ángeles

Desagüe

Concepción de la Villa

Peñalver
Condesa

Benjumeda

Figuras

Santo Tomás

Carmen

Clavel

Rastro

Santa Marta

Corrales
Gloria

Esperanza

Atmbque

Arroyo (Av Manglar)

Av de España (Vives)

Puerta Cerrada

Diaria

To Castillo del Príncipe

To Plaza de la Revolución

A
B
C
D
E
1
2
3

N

0 metres 200
0 yards 200

Sleeping 🛏
Ana María Rodríguez
  López cp **1** *B4*
Caribbean **2** *B4*
Carlos Luis Valderrama
  Moré cp **4** *C3*
Casa Marta cp **5** *C3*
Deauville **7** *B4*
Dr Alejandro Oses cp **8** *B4*
El Parador
  Numantino cp **6** *C4*

Eugenio y Fabio cp **3** *E6*
Federico y Yamelis
  Llanes cp **17** *B4*
Jesús Deiro Rana cp **19** *C3*
Jesús y María cp **12** *D5*
Julio y Elsa cp **26** *B4*
La Casa del
  Científico **13** *C4*
Lido **14** *C4*
Lincoln **15** *C3*
Marilys Herrera

González cp **16** *B1*
Nacional de Cuba **18** *A1*
Orlando y Liset cp **20** *D5*
Residencia Santa
  Clara **22** *D4*
Rosa Artiles
  Hernández cp **23** *B4*
Sevilla **24** *C4*
Villa Colonial
  Tomy cp **21** *C2*
Xiomara cp **25** *C4*

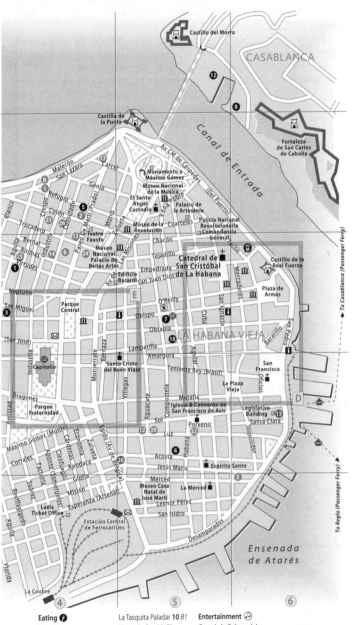

CASABLANCA

Castillo del Morro

Fortaleza de San Carlos de Cabaña

Canal de Entrada

Castilla de la Punta

Av CM de Cepedes (Del Puerto)

Malecón
San Lázaro
Cárcel
Monumento a Máximo Gómez
Museo Nacional de la Música
El Santo Angel Custodio
Palacio de la Artesanía
Museo de la Revolución
Policía Nacional Revolucionaria Comandancia General

Refugio
Colón
Genio
Blanco
Trocadero
Consulado
Paseo de Martí (Prado)
Morro
Zulueta
Chacón
Tejadillo
Empedrado
San Juan Dios de La Habana
Catedral de San Cristóbal
Castillo de la Real Fuerza

Bernal
Animas
Industria
Paseo de Martí (Prado)
Museo Palacio de Bellas Artes
Teatro Fausto
Edificio Bacardí
Plaza de Armas

Aguila
Virtudes

Neptuno
San Miguel
Parque Central
O'Reilly
Obispo
Obrapía
LA HABANA VIEJA

(San José)
Industria
Capitolio
Monserrate
Bernaza
Villegas
Santo Cristo del Buen Viaje
Lamparilla
Amargura
Aguiar
Teniente Rey (Brasil)
San Ignacio
Cuba
San Francisco
La Plaza Vieja

Dragones
Parque Fraternidad

Máximo Gómez (Monte)
Economía
Egido (Av de Bélgica)
Zulueta
Muralla
Iglesia & Convento de San Francisco de Asís
Sol
Luz
Porvenir
Compostela
Habana
Oficios
Inquisidor
Santa Clara
Legislative Building

Corrales
Cárdenas
Apodaca
Gloria
Aponte (Somerulos)
Cienfuegos
Misión
Acosta
Jesús María
Espíritu Santo

Suárez
Revillagigedo
Factoría
Ladis Ticket Office
Esperanza (Arsenal)
Merced
Museo Casa Natal de José Martí
Leonor Pérez
La Merced

Agula
Estación Central de Ferrocarriles
San Isidro
Desamparados

Florida

La Coubre

Ensenada de Atarés

To Casablanca (Passenger Ferry)
To Regla (Passenger Ferry)

which are endemic, etc. Outside in the Plaza de Armas there is a small, second-hand **book market** ⓘ *Wed-Sat 1000-1800*.

On the west side of Plaza de Armas is the former **Palacio de los Capitanes Generales,** built in 1780, a charming example of colonial architecture. The Spanish Governors and the Presidents lived here until 1917, when it became the City Hall. It is now the **Museo de la Ciudad** ⓘ *Tacón 1 entre Obispo y O'Reilly, T7-8615779, daily 0900-1930, US$3, guided visit US$4, last tour 1700, charge for photos US$2, video US$10,* the Historical Museum of the city of Havana. The museum houses a large collection of 19th-century furnishings which illustrate the wealth of the Spanish colonial community, including 'his and her' large marble, shell-shaped baths. There are portraits of patriots, flags, military memorabilia and a grandly laid-out dining room. The building was the site of the signing of the 1899 treaty between Spain and the USA. The nation's first flag is here, together with a beautiful sword encrusted with diamonds belonging to Máximo Gómez. There is a curious portrait of Calixto García featuring his unusual wound: he was shot through the neck and the bullet emerged through his forehead. Also on display is the original slave freedom charter signed by Céspedes. The courtyard contains Royal palms, the Cuban national tree. Outside is a statue of Ferdinand VII of Spain, with a singularly uncomplimentary plaque. No Spanish king or queen ever came to Cuba in colonial times. In front of the museum is a collection of church bells. The former **Supreme Court** on the north side of the Plaza is another colonial building, with a large patio. North of the plaza, the **Castillo de la Real Fuerza** is Cuba's oldest building and the second oldest fort in the New World. It was first built in 1558 after the city had been sacked by buccaneers and was rebuilt in 1582. It is a low, long building with a picturesque tower from which there is a grand view. Inside the castle is a **museum** with armour and the **Museo de la Cerámica Cubana** ⓘ *O'Reilly entre Av del Puerto y Tacón, T7-8616130, daily 0900-1830, US$1, free for under 12s, no charge for cameras,* displaying Cuban ceramic art dating from the 1940s onwards, some of which are for sale. The downstairs part is used for art exhibitions. Upstairs there is a small shop. Just off Plaza de Armas, the **Casa de la Plata** ⓘ *Obispo 113 entre Mercaderes y Oficios, T7-8639861, Tue-Sat 0900-1645, Sun 0900-1245, US$1, guide US$1, photos US$2, video US$10,* has a silverware collection of fine pieces, jewellery and old frescoes on the upper floor.

> ● *Just around the corner from the cathedral, on Empedrado 207, is La Bodeguita del Medio. More than a bar, La Bodeguita has become a museum piece to the Hemingway era and 1940s bohemia, see page 118.*

La Catedral de San Cristóbal de La Habana

ⓘ *Empedrado esq San Ignacio, T7-8617771. Open Mon-Sat 0930-1230, Sun 0830-1230. Mass Mon-Fri 2000, Sat 1700, Sun 1030.*

Heading northwest from Plaza de Armas, along Calle Oficios, brings you to one of Havana's most iconic and beautiful monuments, the Catedral de San Cristóbal de la Habana. Construction of a church on this site was begun by Jesuit missionaries at the beginning of the 18th century. After the Jesuits were expelled in 1767, the church was converted into a cathedral. On either side of the Spanish colonial baroque façade are bell towers, the left one (west) being half as wide as the right (east), which has a grand view. The church is officially dedicated to the Virgin of the Immaculate Conception, but is better known as the church of Havana's patron saint, San Cristóbal de la Habana or the Columbus cathedral. The bones of Christopher Columbus were sent to this cathedral when Santo Domingo was ceded by Spain to France in 1795; they now lie in Santo Domingo (Dominican Republic). There is much speculation over whether they were indeed the bones of Columbus. They could have been those of his brother or son, but the Dominican Republic is convinced of their authenticity.

Plaza de la Catedral and around

In the former Palacio de los Condes de Casa Bayona is the **Museo de Arte Colonial** ① *San Ignacio 61, Plaza de la Catedral, T7-8626440, daily 0900-1900, US$2, guide US$1, camera US$2, video US$10*, with exhibits of colonial furniture and other items, plus a section on stained glass. Exquisite.

The work of Cuba's most famous painter can be seen at the **Centro de Arte Contemporáneo Wifredo Lam** ① *San Ignacio 22, esquina Empedrado, just next to the cathedral, T7-8612096, Mon-Sat 0900-1630 (when art exhibitions are running), US$2.* The changing exhibition programmes feature mostly Cuban artists but also world masters. Lam directed most of his work to a non-Latin American audience.

Displays on colonial archaeology uncovered during excavation works in La Habana Vieja and the bay can be seen at the **Museo de Arqueología** ① *Tacon 12 entre O'Reilly y Empedrado, T7-8614469, Tue-Sat 0900-1430, Sun 0900-1300, permission for photos or videos must be obtained from Tacón 20, T7-8639981.* Exhibits feature Cuban and Peruvian aboriginal artefacts. The house was built in the 17th century but redesigned in 1725 by Juana Carvajal, a freed slave who inherited the building from her owner, Lorenza Carvajal. It was further expanded by the Calvo de la Puerta family, who acquired it in 1748. It was restored in 1988 and converted into a museum.

Alejo Carpentier is revered throughout Latin America as the founder of Magical Realism. The **Fundación Alejo Carpentier** ① *Empedrado 215 entre Cuba y San Ignacio, Mon-Fri 0830-1630, free*, was the setting for his novel *El Siglo de las Luces*. The foundation runs literary courses and there is a small museum of the writer's letters and books.

Castillo de la Punta and around

Built at the end of the 16th century at the northernmost part of the old city to protect the entrance to the harbour, the **Castillo del la Punta** ① *Av del Puerto y Paseo del Prado, T7-8603196, Wed-Sun 1000-1730, US$5, camera US$2*, is a squat building with 250-cm-thick walls. There are three permanent exhibition rooms covering the history of the castle, naval design and construction and marine archaeology. Opposite the fortress, across the Malecón, is the **monument to Máximo Gómez**, the independence leader.

The **Policía Nacional Revolucionario Comandancia General** is in another fortress in the block bounded by Cuba, Chacón, Cuarteles and San Ignacio. It is not open to the public but if you want to visit you can go to the offices of the **Centro Provincial de Selección PNR** ① *Tulipán y Boyeros, Mon-Fri 0830-1700*, to get permission. There are two other old forts in Havana: **Atarés**, finished in 1763, on a hill overlooking the southwest end of the harbour; and **El Príncipe**, on a hill at the far end of Avenida Independencia (Avenida Rancho Boyeros), built 1774-94, now the city gaol. The finest view in Havana is from this hill.

A small and beautifully furnished old mansion houses the **Museo Nacional de la Música** ① *Capdevila (Cárcel) 1, entre Habana y Aguiar, T7-8619846, Mon-Sat 1000-1800, Sun 0900-1200, US$2*, which displays an interesting collection of African drums and other instruments from all around the world, showing development of Cuban *son* and *danzón* and other musical styles between the 16th and 21st centuries. On the second Thursday of each month they have *peñas de tango*, US$1, and on the third Saturday of the month a show called *Con Ciertos Trovadores* at 1600, price depends on the artist. Traditional and jazz concerts are held regularly, look out for posters and notices advertising events.

The **Church of El Santo Angel Custodio** ① *Compostela 2 esq Cuarteles, T7-8610469, Tue, Thu and Fri 0900-1200, 1500-1800, Wed and Sat 1500-1800, Sun 0800-1100, 1630-1900, Mass Tue, Wed, Fri 0715, Thu, Sat 1800, Sun 0900 and 1800*, was built by the Jesuits in 1689 on the slight elevation of **Peña Pobre** hill, with the tower added in 1704. The original church was largely destroyed by a hurricane in

1846, but in 1852 it became the parish church and in 1853 José Martí was baptized here. It was rebuilt and enlarged in its present neo-Gothic style in 1868-70. It has white, laced Gothic towers and 10 tiny chapels, no more than kneeling places, the best of which is behind the high altar. There is some interesting stained glass depicting *conquistadores*. During the Christmas period some impressive figures around a manger are placed at the entrance. Other famous people baptized here include Amelia Goire (La Milagrosa), Alicia Alonso and Julián del Casal, while it is also the setting for the last chapter of the novel *Cecilia Valdés*, see Literature, page 407.

Museo de la Revolución
ⓘ *Refugio entre Monserrate y Zulueta, facing Av de las Misiones, T7-8624091/6, daily 1000-1700, US$4, guide US$2, cameras and video free. Allow several hours, explanations are mostly in Spanish.*

This huge, ornate building, topped by a dome, was once the Presidential Palace, but now contains the Museo de la Revolución. The history of Cuban political development is charted, from the slave uprisings to joint space missions with the ex-Soviet Union. The liveliest section displays the final battles against Batista's troops, with excellent photographs and some bizarre personal mementoes, such as a revolutionary's knife, fork and spoon set and a plastic shower curtain worn in the Sierra Maestra campaign. Look out for the bullet holes as you walk up the stairs. At the top of the main staircase are a stuffed mule and a stuffed horse used by Che Guevara and Camilo Cienfuegos in the same campaign. The yacht *Granma*, from which Dr Castro disembarked with his companions in 1956 to launch the Revolution, has been installed in the park facing the south entrance, surrounded by planes, tanks and other vehicles involved, as well as a Soviet-built tank used against the Bay of Pigs invasion and a fragment from a US spy plane shot down in the 1970s.

Parque Central
A very pleasant park with a monument to **José Martí** in the centre. The north side of the Parque is entirely occupied by the **NH Parque Central**, while the **Hotel Plaza** is in the northeast corner. On its west side are the **Hotel Telégrafo**, the historic **Hotel Inglaterra**, which celebrated its 125th anniversary in 2000) and the **Gran Teatro de la Habana**, a beautiful building with tours of the inside; see also Entertainment, page 126. The theatre is a neo-baroque monument dating from 1838. It is used by the National Opera and National Ballet and also houses the Teatro García Lorca. Sarah Bernhardt once performed there when the Teatro García Lorca was called the Teatro Tacón. José Martí wrote of her performance, "Sarah is flexible, delicate, svelte. When she is not shaken by the demon of tragedy, her body is full of grace and abandon, when the demon takes her over, she is full of power and nobility... Where does she come from? From poverty! Where is she going? To glory!"

Museo Nacional Palacio de Bellas Artes
ⓘ *The Arte Cubano is at Trocadero entre Zulueta y Monserrate, and the Arte Universal is at San Rafael entre Zulueta y Monserrate, for both T7-8613858/8620140, www.museonacional.cult.cu Tue-Sat 1000-1800, Sun 1000-1400, both museums cost US$5 for foreigners, but a same-day entrance to both sites is US$8, 5 pesos for Cubans, reduced rates for children and students, guide US$2, no photography permitted. Both museum sites have shops selling books, art and souvenirs.*

On the east side of Parque Central, restoration of the **Centro Asturiano** site of the Museum and National Palace of Fine Arts, has been completed after a five-year closure and extensive refurbishment estimated at US$14.5 million. Fidel Castro inaugurated this fantastic museum on 19 July 2001 and it reopened to the public on 1 August 2001.

The art collection (Arte Universal) is valued at more than US$500 million and consists of 47,628 works of art, from an ancient Egyptian sarcophagus to contemporary Cuban paintings. The impressively extended museum has two separate buildings. The exhibits are divided between the original museum in Trocadero, the 1954 Fine Arts Palace, housing the Cuban art collection (Arte Cubano) from colonial times to the 1990s including a section on the post-Revolution Art Schools, and the former Centro Asturiano, two blocks away on the east side of Parque Central on Zulueta, housing European and ancient art.

Cuban paintings in the modern building include the 20th-century painter Victor Manuel's *Gitana Tropical*, considered an important symbol of the Cuban vanguard (see Art and architecture). There are masterpieces of José Nicolás de la Escalera and Victor Patricio Landaluze from the colonial period and representations of modern-era Cuban paintings from Wilfredo Lam and René Portocarrero. Exhibited works of more recent Cuban artists include those of Roberto Fabelo and Zaida del Río and some artists who have left the country. Start on the third floor with the colonial art and work your way down to the present day. This is a truly spectacular museum and well worth a look even if you are not keen on modern art. On the ground floor there are also a small shop, café and toilets.

The colonial building designed by the Spanish architect Manuel del Busto in the early 20th century has been fabulously renovated with huge marble staircases giving access to five floors. The large collection of European paintings, from the 16th century to the present, contains works by Gainsborough, Van Dyck, Velázquez, Tintoretto, Degas et al. One painting by Canaletto, in the Italian room on the fifth floor, is in fact only half a painting; the other half of the 18th-century painting *Chelsea from the Thames* is owned by the National Trust in Britain and hangs in Blickling Hall, Norfolk. It is believed to have been commissioned in 1746-48 by the Chelsea Hospital, which is featured in the Cuban half, but the artist was unable to sell it and cut it in two just before he died in 1768. The left half was sold to the 11th Marquis of Lothian, whose family owned Blickling Hall, where it has stayed ever since. The right half was bought and sold several times until it ended up with a Cuban collector, Oscar Cinetas, who donated it to the museum before the Revolution. The museum also has Greek, Roman, Egyptian and Etruscan sculpture and artefacts, many very impressive. The unharmed Greek amphora from the fifth century BC is considered remarkable.

The museum has also included paintings from private collections left behind by rich Cuban families (including the Bacardí and Gómez Mena families) and members of the former dictator Fulgencio Batista's government who fled Cuba soon after the 1959 Revolution. The origin of these works, including Spanish artists Sorolla and Zurbarán, has been included in the catalogues. It had been rumoured that some of these collections had been sold by the Cuban government during the economic crisis of the Special Period. Additionally, there are rooms dedicated to Latin American art and 18th- and 19th-century paintings from the United States.

Capitolio
① *Paseo de Martí entre San Martín y Dragones, T7-8610261. Daily 0830-1930 but often shuts early, US$3 to go in the halls, tours available, guide US$1, camera and video charge US$2. Entry to just the Salón de los Pasos Perdidos is US$1 including photos and video. Entrance for visitors is to the left of the stairway. Internet café (see below). All bags have to be left at kiosk on the left as you go up the stairs.*

The Capitolio was built in the style of the US Capitol in Washington DC in 1929-32 by the dictator Machado in an attempt to impress his US paymasters with his loyalty. The white dome over a rotunda is 62 m high and inside there is a 17-m statue of Jupiter, representing the state. This is the tallest interior statue in Latin America and the third largest in the world. At the centre of the floor of the entrance hall is set a 24-carat diamond (or is it a fake?), which pinpoints zero for all distance measurements in Cuba. The interior has large halls and stately staircases, all most sumptuously decorated. It was initially used as the seat of parliament with the Senate and the House of Representatives meeting there, but they were dissolved after the Revolution. Now it houses the Cuban Academy of Sciences and the National Library of Science and Technology. Outside the Capitolio there are lots of old American cars waiting to offer taxi rides, as well as conventional taxis, *cocotaxis*, *bicitaxis* etc.

Partagas cigar factory

① *Industria 520 entre Dragones y Barcelona, behind the Capitolio, T7-338060. 40-min tours every 15 mins 0930-1100 and 1230-1500, US$10, English, Spanish or French-speaking guides available.*

The tour is very interesting but pricey. You are taken through the factory and shown the whole production process from storage and sorting of leaves, to packaging and labelling. Four different brand names are made here: *Partagas, Cubana, Ramón Allones* and *Bolívar*. These and other famous cigars can be bought at their shop here: open daily 0900-1700, as can rum (credit cards accepted). Cigars are also made at many tourist locations (for example Palacio de la Artesanía, the airport, some hotels). Also see box, Cigars page, 164.

Parque Fraternidad and around

The park was originally called Parque de Colón, but was renamed to mark the VI Panamerican Conference in 1892. It has been landscaped to show off the Capitolio, north of it, to the best effect. At its centre is a ceiba tree growing in soil provided by each of the American republics. Also in the park is a famous statue of the Amerindian woman who first welcomed the Spaniards: La Noble Habana, sculpted in 1837. From the southwest corner the handsome Avenida Allende runs due west to the high hill, on which stands **El Príncipe Castle** (now the city gaol). The **Quinta de los Molinos**, on this avenue, at the foot of the hill, once housed the School of Agronomy of Havana University. The main house now contains the **Máximo Gómez Museum** (Dominican-born fighter for Cuban Independence). Also here is the headquarters of the association of young writers and artists (Asociación Hermanos Saiz). The gardens are a lovely place to stroll.

Heading south along Egido, opposite the central railway station, the **Museo Casa Natal de José Martí** ① *Leonor Pérez 314 entre Picota y Egido, T7-8613778, Tue-Sat 0900-1700, Sun 0900-1300, US$1*, is the birthplace of the country's great hero (see box, page 408), with his full life story documented with photos, mementoes, furniture and papers. A tiny house which has been devoted to his memory since a plaque was first put on the wall in 1899, a museum since 1925 and restored in 1952-53.

Calle Obispo and Calle Obrapía

From the Parque Central you can walk back to the Plaza de Armas along Calle Obispo, one of the streets of La Habana Vieja which has seen most restoration, with many shops lovingly restored to their former splendour. Calle Obrapía, which runs parallel, has some magnificent colonial buildings and many of them are now museums and galleries.

Farmacia Taquechel ① *Obispo 155 entre Mercaderes y San Ignacio, T7-8629286*, displays all manner of herbs, remedies and concoctions stored in porcelain jars, glazed and gilded with herbal motifs and meticulously arranged on floor to ceiling polished mahogany shelves. The original 1896 building was the workplace of Francisco Taquechel Mirabal. In the old Ministry of Finance building the **Museo de las Finanzas** ① *Obispo y Cuba, Mon-Fri 0830-1700, Sat 0830-1230*, has a beautiful stained-class ceiling in the foyer and a huge safe, also documents, seals and coins.

Rigoberto Mena is one of Cuba's most respected contemporary artists and his studio, **Estudio Galería Rigoberto Mena** ① *San Ignacio 154 entre Obispo y Obrapía, T7-8675884*, houses a fantastic collection of abstract art. His style is deceptively simple, a meticulous composition of brilliant colours radiating from dark backgrounds.

The vintage car museum, **Museo de Automóviles** ① *Oficios 13 y Jústiz, just off Plaza de Armas, T7-8615868, daily 0900-1900, US$1, photos US$2, video US$10*, lovingly presents vehicles from the 19th and 20th centuries. There are a great many museum pieces including pre-Revolution US models, which are still on the road especially outside Havana, in among the Ladas, VWs and Nissans.

The **Museo Numismático** ① *Oficios 8 entre Obispo y Obrapía, T7-8615811, Tue-Sat 0915-1645, Sun 0915-1300*, is a coin museum which exhibits and sells coins, medals and documentation. The extensive collection of more than 1,000 pieces, including rare notes and valuable cold coins, dates from the colonial period up to the Revolution.

Casa de los Arabes ① *Oficios 16 entre Obispo and Obrapía, T7-8615868, Tue-Sat 0915-1645, Sun 0900-1230, free, donations welcome*, is a lovely building built in Mudéjar style with vines trained over the courtyard for shade. The collection includes the only mosque in Havana, jewels, Saharan robes, gold- and silver-painted weapons and rugs. Bar and restaurant, **Al Medina**, see page 119, is a relaxing place to eat.

Casa de la Obra-Pía ① *Obrapía 158 entre Mercaderes y San Ignacio, T7-8613097, Tue-Sat 0930-1630, Sun 0930-1230, no entry fee but donations welcome, photos free*, is a furniture museum, with examples from the 18th and 19th centuries, housed in a yellow building. It was built in 1665, then remodelled in 1793 by the Marqués de Cárdenas de Monte Hermoso, whose shield is over the door. The portico was made in Cádiz in 1793, but finished off in Havana. The building was restored in 1983.

Closed for repairs in 2003 the **Casa de Africa** ① *Obrapía 157 entre San Ignacio y Mercaderes, T7-8615798, africa@cultural.ohch.cu* is a small gallery of carved wooden artefacts and handmade costumes. Sculpture, furniture, paintings and ceramics from sub-Saharan Africa, including gifts given to Fidel by visiting African Presidents.

Casa de México ① *Obrapía 116 entre Mercaderes y Oficios, T7-8618166, Tue-Sat 0930-1645, Sun 0930-1245*, also called **La Casa Benito Juárez**, is more of a cultural centre than a museum, housed in a pink building draped with the Mexican flag. Exhibits include pre-Columbian artefacts and popular arts and crafts including ceramics from Jalisco.

Works donated to Cuba by the late Ecuadorean artist Oswaldo Guayasamín are displayed at the **Casa de Guayasamín** ① *Obrapía 111 entre Mercaderes y Oficios T7-8613843, Tue-Sat 0900-1645, Sun 0900-1300, donations welcome*. Exhibits are, for the most part, paintings, sculpture and silkscreens, but there are occasionally other exhibitions. Guayasamín painted a famous portrait of Fidel Castro for his 70th birthday.

On 9 April 1958 a group of revolutionaries of the Movimiento 26 de Julio attacked the business of Compañía Armera de Cuba. They were unsuccessful and four members of the group were killed. After the Revolution, the site was declared a National Monument in their honour and on 9 April 1971 a museum, the **Museo Armería 9 de Abril** ① *Mercaderes entre Obrapía y Lamparilla, T7-8618080, Mon-Fri 0900-1700, Sat 0900-1300*, was opened. At the front the original business is recreated, with some contemporary pieces, hunting and fishing accessories, including the collection of arms that Castro donated in the 1990s. At the back there is an exhibition on the events that took place there in 1958.

The **Casa de Simón Bolívar** ① *Mercaderes 158 entre Obrapía y Lamparilla, T7-8613998, Tue-Sat 0930-1700, Sun 0930-1300, free, donations welcome*, contains exhibits about the life of the South American liberator and some Venezuelan art.

Plaza San Francisco and around
The **Iglesia y Convento de San Francisco de Asís** ① *Oficios entre Amargura y Churruca, daily 0930-1830, US$2 for museum and campanario (bell tower), photos US$2, video US$10, guide US$1*, built in 1608 and reconstructed in 1730, is a massive, sombre edifice suggesting defence, rather than worship. The three-storey bell tower

was both a landmark for returning voyagers and a look out for pirates and has stunning views of the city and port. The **Basílica Menor de San Francisco de Asís** is now a concert hall (tickets for concerts are sold three days in advance) and the convent is a museum containing religious pieces. Restoration work continues. Most of the treasures were removed by the government and some are in museums. The sculpture outside the church is of the eccentric *El Caballero de París* (French Wanderer). The legendary Galician vagrant with a deluded sense of grandeur was notorious throughout the city and affectionately embraced by Habaneros. He died in 1985 in Havana's psychiatric hospital. The sculpture was the work of José Villa who was also responsible for the John Lennon monument in Vedado, see page 106.

The Corinthian white marble building on Calle Oficios, south of the Post Office was once the **legislative building** where the House of Representatives met before the Capitolio was built. The newly restored Cuban Stock Exchange building, **La Lonja**, Oficios and Plaza San Francisco de Asís, is worth a look, as is the new cruise ship terminal opposite.

The British Embassy financed the construction of the **Diana Garden** ⓘ *Baratillo, near Plaza San Francisco, daily 0700-1900*, in memory of Diana, Princess of Wales. It is dominated by a concrete tube covered in ceramics in the shape of liquorice all-sorts which don't reach to the top, symbolizing a life cut short. There is also a sculpture of the sun, representing the happiness in her life, but one triangle is missing, her heart. Around the base of the pole are rings for sadness.

Nelson Domínguez, one of Cuba's most respected and prolific of Cuba's contemporary artists, has his own studio/gallery at the **Galería Los Oficios** ⓘ *Oficios 166 entre Amargura y Teniente Rey, T7-339804, Tue-Sun 1100-1700*. Working in various mediums, he is primarily influenced by the natural environment and draws heavily on indigenous and spiritual symbolism. There are several other artists' galleries on Obispo, Oficios and Obrapía, such as **Galería de Arte Carmen Montilla Tinoco** ⓘ *Oficios 162 entre Amagura y Teniente Rey, Tue-Sat 0900-1700, Sun 0900-1300*, housed in an early 18th-century building. It was originally used as a shop below and dwelling above, then briefly as the Consulate of Paraguay at the beginning of the 20th century, but it was ruined by fire in the 1980s. The **Oficina del Historiador**, with the help of the Venezuelan artist, restored it and opened it as an art gallery in her name in 1994.

The great explorer and botanist Federico Enrique Alejandro von Humboldt, 1769-1857, lived at Oficios 254 esquina Muralla, at the beginning of 1801 when he completed his calculations of the meridian of the city. His home is now the **Museo Humboldt** ⓘ *T7-8639850, Tue-Sat 0900-1700, Sun 0900-1300, free.* Humboldt travelled extensively in Central and South America, paving the way for Darwin, who called him the greatest naturalist of his time. His scientific works were not confined merely to plants. His name has been given to the cold current that flows northwards off the coast of Chile and Peru, which he discovered and measured. He also made important contributions to world meteorology, to the study of vulcanism and the earth's crust and the connection between climate and flora. In the process he discovered that mountain sickness is caused by a lack of oxygen at high altitudes. The last years of his life were spent writing *Kosmos*, an account of his scientific findings, which was soon translated into many languages.

Museo del Ron

ⓘ *Av del Puerto 262 entre Sol y Muralla, T7-8618051, www.havanaclubfoundation .com Daily 0900-1700, US$5, under 15s free. Multilingual guides included.*

The **Fundación Destilería Havana Club** has a museum offering displays of the production of rum from the sugar cane plantation to the processing and bottling, with machinery dating from the early 20th century. The museum is well laid out but too dark and atmospheric to read the notices. There is a wonderful model railway which runs round a model sugar mill and distillery, designed and made by prize-winning Lázaro Eduardo García Driggs in 1993-94 and restored in 1999-2000. At the end of the tour you get a tasting of a six-year old **Havana Club** rum in a bar that is a mock up of the once-famous *Sloppy Joe's*. There is also a restaurant (excellent shrimp kebab) and bar (see page 125), a shop and an art gallery where present-day Cuban artists exhibit their work.

La Plaza Vieja and around

An 18th-century plaza, undergoing restoration since February 1996 as part of a joint project by UNESCO and **Habaguanex,** a state company responsible for the restoration and revival of La Habana Vieja. Many of the buildings around the plaza boast elegant balconies overlooking the large square with a fountain in the middle. The former house of the Spanish Captain General, Conde de Ricla, who retook Havana from the English and restored power to Spain in 1763, can be seen on the corner of San Ignacio and Muralla. Known as **La Casona** ① *Centro de Arte La Casona, Muralla 107 esq San Ignacio, T7-8618544, www.galeriascubanas.com Tue-Fri 0800-1730, Sat 0800-1630,* modern art exhibitions are held upstairs in the beautiful blue and white building. Note the friezes up the staircase and along the walls. There is a great view of the plaza from the balcony and trailing plants in the courtyard enhance the atmosphere. There is a museum of playing cards, **Museo de Naipes 'Marqués de Prado Ameno'** ① *Muralla 101 esq Inquisidor, T7-8601534, Tue-Sat 0900-1645,* and on the west side of the Plaza is the **Centro de las Artes Visuales** ① *San Ignacio 352 entre Teniente Rey y Muralla, T7-8629295, Tue-Sat 1000-1700,* which has a variety of art exhibitions. There are two galleries, Siglo XXI and Escuela de Plata. In one of the converted mansions, the **Fototeca de Cuba** ① *Mercaderes 307 entre Teniente Rey y Muralla, T7-8622530, Tue-Sat 1000-1700,* showcases international photography exhibitions. On the north side of the square, on Teniente Rey, is a posh and expensive restaurant, **Santo Angel,** and on the east side, on Inquisidor, the old Post Office, dating from 1909, is being renovated. In the northeast corner, Mercaderes y Teniente Rey, is the **Café Taberna.** After the English took Havana in 1762, the first coffee houses were established, and this one, the first, was called *Café de Taberna* because its owner was Juan Bautista de Taberna. It remained in operation until the 1940s and was known as a place where merchant traders congregated. It was reopened in 1999 as a restaurant with the theme of the musician, Benny Moré. Unfortunately the food is nothing special, rather greasy, and the service poor.

On the top floor of the Gómez Vila building is the **Cámara Oscura** ① *Teniente Rey esq Mercaderes, Plaza Vieja, T7-8621801, poeta@cultural.ohch.cu daily 0830-1730, US$1, free for under 12s,* where lenses and mirrors provide you with a panoramic view of the city. Donated by Cádiz, this camera obscura is the first in the Americas and one of the few in the world: two in England, two in Spain and one in Portugal.

Carlos J Finlay was an eminent Cuban doctor who discovered that the mosquito was the vector of yellow fever in the late 19th century and helped to eradicate the disease in Cuba. The **Museo Histórico de las Ciencias Carlos J Finlay** ① *Cuba 460 entre Amargura y Brasil, T7-8634824, Mon-Fri 0800-1700, Sat 0900-1500, US$1, photos US$5, video US$5,* housed in a strikingly ornate building, contains displays about science in Cuba, the history of the Royal Academy of Sciences (Academia Real de Ciencias) and exhibits on the role of the medical profession during the wars of independence.

Convento de Santa Clara

① *Cuba 610 entre Luz y Sol, Mon-Fri 0900-1500, US$2 for guided tour in either Spanish or French.*

The convent of Santa Clara was founded in 1644 by nuns from Cartagena in Colombia. It was in use as a convent until 1919, when the nuns sold the building. In a shady business deal it was later acquired by the government and, after radical alterations, it became offices for the Ministry of Public Works until the decision was made to restore the building to its former glory. Work began in 1982, with the creation of the **Centro Nacional de Conservación, Restauración y Museología** (CNCRM), and is still continuing. The convent occupies four small blocks in La Habana Vieja, bounded by Calles Habana, Sol, Cuba and Luz, and originally there were three cloisters and an orchard. You can see the cloisters, the nuns' cemetery and their cells. The first cloister has been carefully preserved; the ground floor is a grand porticoed stone gallery surrounding a large patio packed with vegetation, in it are the city's first slaughterhouse, first public fountain and public baths. The Sailor's House in the second cloister, reputedly built by a sailor for his love-lorn daughter, is now a *Residencia Académica* for student groups (and independent travellers if room). The convent is topped by an extensive tiled roof with a stone turret next to the church choir.

Casablanca

Ins and outs

To cross the bay to Casablanca, take the left-hand ferry queue for Casablanca next to the Customs House, opposite Calle Santa Clara, 10 centavos. Security is very tight here since a ferry was hijacked in 2003 for an abortive attempt to get to Miami. Everybody is searched and there are metal detectors. Access to the Castillo del Morro is from any bus going through the tunnel (20 or 40 centavos), board at San Lázaro and Av del Puerto and get off at the stop after the tunnel, cross the road and climb following the path to the left. Alternatively take a taxi, or a 20-min walk from the Fortaleza de San Carlos de la Cabaña.

Castillo del Morro

ⓘ *Casablanca, T7-8637941, daily 0830-2030. US$3 includes US$1 for the parque and US$2 for the castle. No charge for photos..*

The Castillo del Morro (El Castillo de los Tres Reyes) was built between 1589 and 1630, with a 20-m moat, but has been much altered. It stands on a bold headland, with the best view of Havana and is illuminated at night. It was one of the major fortifications built to protect the natural harbour and the assembly of Spain's silver fleets from pirate attack. The flash of its lighthouse, built in 1844, is visible 30 km out to sea. It now serves as a museum with a good exhibition of Cuban history since the arrival of Columbus.

On the harbour side, down by the water, is the **Battery of the 12 Apostles**, each gun being named after an Apostle. Every Saturday at around 1000-1100 there is a display of Afro-Cuban dancing and music. There is also a rather touristy disco, playing taped music; but it's worth a visit for the views of the harbour and the whole of Havana.

Fortaleza de San Carlos de Cabaña

ⓘ *T7-8620617, daily 0900-1800, US$3, 1800-2200, US$5 (increased charge for the cannon firing ceremony). No charge for camera or video. Access as for Castillo del Morro, see above.*

It is believed that around 1590, the military engineer, Juan Bautista Antonelli, who built La Punta and El Morro, walked up the hill called La Cabaña one day and declared that 'he who is master of this hill will be master of Havana'. His prophecy was proved correct two centuries later when the English attacked Havana, conquering La Cabaña and thereby gaining control of the port. In 1763, after the English withdrew, another

Construction lasted until 1774, when the fortress (the largest the Spanish had built until then in the Americas) was named San Carlos de la Cabaña, in honour of the king of Spain. It has a solid vertical wall of about 700 m with a deep moat connected to that of El Morro. The ditch is 12 m deep on the landward side and there is a drawbridge to the main entrance. From its position on the hill it dominates the city, the bay and the entrance to the harbour. In its heyday it had 120 cannon.

Inside are **Los Fosos de los Laureles** where political prisoners were shot during the Cuban fight for independence. On 3 January 1959, Che Guevara took possession of the fortress on his triumphant arrival in Havana after the flight of the dictator, Batista. Every night the cannon are fired in an historical ceremony recalling the closure of the city walls to protect the city from attack by pirates. This used to happen at various times and originally in the 17th century the shot was fired from a naval ship in the harbour. Now, however, it is fired from La Cabaña at 2100 on the dot by soldiers in 18th-century uniforms, with the ceremony starting at 2045. There are two museums here, one about Che Guevara and another about fortresses with pictures and models, some old weapons and a replica of a large catapult and battering ram from the 16th to 18th centuries.

Parque El Cristo
ⓘ *You can walk from the statue to the Fortaleza (10 mins) and then, from there, on to the Castillo del Morro.*

Casablanca is also the site of a statue of a very human Jesus Christ, erected in white marble overlooking Havana harbour during the Batista dictatorship as a pacifying exercise. You can get a good view of Havana's skyline from Parque El Cristo, particularly at night, but be careful not to miss the last ferry back. Go up a steep, twisting flight of stone steps, starting on the other side of the plaza in front of the landing stage. Also across the river in the charming town of Casablanca, you will find the **National Observatory** and the old railway station for the (**Hershey line**) trains to Matanzas.

Centro

The state of the buildings in Centro Habana is inclined to shock the first-time visitor, appearing to be a war zone with piles of rubble and holes like craters on the streets and pavements. Centro is not a tourist attraction, although many visitors end up staying here in one of the many *casas particulares*, conveniently placed between the architectural and historical attractions of La Habana Vieja and the nightlife of Vedado. It is separated from La Habana Vieja by the Prado, although all those buildings on the west side of the avenue are still included in the old city.

Centro is bounded on the north side by the seafront drive, the Malecón, which is in a dire state of repair because of buffeting by sea winds. Centro's main artery is Calle San Rafael, with runs west from the Parque Central. This was Havana's 19th-century retail playground, but today is spliced by ramshackle streets strewn with rubble and lined with decrepit houses. At the cross-section of Amistad and Dragones stands the gateway to **Barrio Chino**, a Cuban-Chinese hybrid. In its pre-Revolutionary heyday, this ten-block zone, pivoting around the Cuchillo de Zanja, was full of sordid porn theatres and steamy brothels. Now, a handful of restaurants strewn with lanterns, a colourful food market and a smattering of Chinese associations are all that remains of what was the largest Chinatown in Latin America.

Reopened at the end of 2003 is the **Museo Casa José Lezama Lima** ⓘ *Trocadero 162 entre Industria y Consulado, T7-8634161, mlezama@cubarte.cult.cu Tue-Sat*

⦂ Cayo Hueso

Cayo Hueso is a run down *barrio* lying in a triangle between Infanta, San Lázaro and the Malecón in Centro Habana. It was named by cigar factory workers returning from Key West and has nothing to do with bones (*huesos* in Spanish), although it was once the site of the Espada cemetery and the San Lázaro quarry. There are about 12,000 homes in the *barrio*, mostly tenements, which have been earmarked for restoration. As in La Habana Vieja, the project also involves educating the community in its own particular culture and history.

In 1924, the cigar factory workers built a social club on San Lázaro, which became the site of the José Martí People's University. San Lázaro, with the University of Havana's wide stairway at its top, was the site of fierce and determined student movement demonstrations from the late 1920s onwards. By the mid-1950s, Infanta was the Maginot line where the students faced Batista's troops. On 25 Jul 1956, Fidel Castro departed from Calle Jovellar 107 for the attack on the Moncada Garrison in Santiago de Cuba. There is a memorial plaque there now.

Cayo Hueso has lots of little alleyways, one of which, Calle Hamel, an extension of Calle Animas, between Aramburu and Espada, unites two art forms: music and visual arts. It is home to Salvador González Escalona's art studio (Hamel 1054 entre Aramburu y Hospital, T7-781661, http://salvador gonzalez.artspan.com). González is a self-taught painter and sculptor, inspired by the history of the neighbourhood and its *Santería* traditions. He has painted large bright Afro-Cuban murals on the walls of Calle Hamel, combining a mixture of abstract and surrealist design with phrases

0900-1700, Sun 0900-1300, US$2, US$3 with guide, the house where José Lezama Lima (1910-76) lived, one of the most important Cuban writers. There is a collection of his personal belongings and art by Cuban painters of the vanguard movement (La Vanguardia). ▸▸ *For Sleeping, Eating and other listings, see pages 109-143.*

Malecón

The Malecón is Havana's oceanfront esplanade, which links Habana Vieja to the west residential district of Vedado. The sea crashing along the seawall here is a spectacular sight when the wind blows from the north. On calmer days, fishermen lean over the parapet, lovers sit in the shade of the small pillars and joggers sweat along the pavement. On the other side of the six-lane highway, buildings which from a distance look stout and grand, with arcaded pavements, balconies, mouldings and large entrances, are salt-eroded, faded and sadly decrepit inside. Restoration is progressing slowly, but the sea is destroying old and new alike and creating a mammoth renovation task. Parts of the wall are also being rebuilt and there is always construction work somewhere along the Malecón.

Vedado

The largely residential district of Vedado was built in the mid 19th century, funded by the massive wealth generated by the sugar industry. According to Cuban historian Hugh Thomas, between 1917 and 1925 money flooded into the capital as Cuba supplied giving advice and warnings about danger, death and life. The project is affectionately called *Callejón de Hamel* and is recognized as the first open-air mural in Cuba dedicated to *Santería* and reflecting Afro-Cuban scenes. Salvador himself describes it as a community-based project, "from el barrio, to el barrio and with el barrio". As well as murals there are other surprises such as a typewriter pinned to the door of the gallery, painted drums and sculptures of corrugated iron and bike wheels.

Every Sunday 1200-1500 a free *Peña Cultural Alto Cubana*, known as **la Rumba de Cayo Hueso**, is held to honour the different *Orishas*. This is a very popular event, attracting large enthusiastic crowds (see Music and dance, page 127). Other community activities at Callejón de Hamel include **Té Con** on the last Friday of the month

at 2030, featuring poetry, theatre, painting and music and **Callejón de Colores** on the first Saturday of the month at 1000, a children's event in which one child is chosen to represent Callejón de Hamel. **Peña de los Abuelos**, on the second Sunday at 1000, is an event for grandparents, although all join in the fun and music. A small bar in the street sells a strong drink of rum and honey, US$2, and a stall sells herbs, representing spiritual and curative roles within *Santería*.

This is a neighbourhood of *filín* (from 'feeling'), rumba and tango. Hamel 1108 is the home of singer-songwriter Angel Díaz and the birthplace of the musical genre known as *filín*, while Calle Horno was the site of the first cultural circle dedicated to Carlos Gardel (the Argentine maestro of tango) and is another centre for cultural activities.

Havana Vedado

the United States with its entire sugar needs following the First World War. Prosperity and decadence went hand in hand as opportunistic officials grew rich on non-existent projects and gambling was allowed. The sumptous houses of Vedado (forbidden area) reflected the opulence of life under the dictatorship. However, imagination is now required with many of these beautiful residences, with crumbling but magnificent staircases, twisted wrought iron work and patched or broken stained-glass windows. Most government offices are in Vedado or around Plaza de la Revolución, which is the place to be for any demonstration, political rally or festive occasion, the scene of most of Castro's marathon speeches in the days when they lasted for hours. With the University straddling the divide between Vedado and Centro, the area is full of students, helping to make it a lively and happening part of town. The hotels here harbour many secrets and legends from the past. Some, such as the **Nacional**, were built with Mafia money and were frequented by the mob, but the **Hilton** had barely opened in 1958 before it was taken over by the victorious revolutionaries in 1959 and renamed the **Habana Libre**. Some things don't change: Vedado is still the place to come for nightlife. This is where you'll find all the hottest clubs and discos, bars and floor shows. If you are a night owl, find yourself a hotel or *casa particular* here so that you can walk home in the early hours, after enjoying salsa, jazz, *son*, boleros, cabaret, a show, theatre, cinema, ballet or a classical concert, whatever turns you on. ▸▸ *For Sleeping, Eating and other listings, see pages 109-143.*

Plaza de la Revolución

This vast open space looks more like a car park than the venue for some of the most rousing speeches and memorable gatherings including the May Day parade. Surrounded by imposing 1950s buildings housing most of the more important ministries, it is a focal point for anyone wanting to understand the charisma of Fidel and his marathon speeches. Suspended on the outside of the Ministry of the Interior is the 30-m steel sculpture of Che Guevara seen in all photos of Havana, a replica of the iconic image, originally shot in 1960, by the celebrated photographer Alberto Korda. Also overlooking the Plaza is the 17-m statue of the national hero, José Martí, carved from white marble extracted from La Isla de la Juventud. The base of the monument is where Castro stands to address the people. The long grey building behind the monument is the former Justice Ministry (1958), now the headquarters of the Central Committee of the Communist Party, where Fidel Castro has his office. The plaza was completely transformed for an open-air mass held by the Pope in January 1998 with huge religious paintings suspended over the surrounding buildings.

The **Memorial José Martí** ⓘ *Plaza de la Revolución, T7-592347, Mon-Sat 0900-1630, US$3, lookout US$2 extra*, is a beautifully restored and most impressive museum, located in the base of the memorial. Don't miss the lookout accessed by mirrored lift. This is the highest point in the city with good panoramic views of Havana. You should receive a certificate from the lift attendant on your descent. The history of the Cuban postal service is revealed at the **Museo Postal Cubano** ⓘ *Ministry of Communications, Plaza de la Revolución, T7-8815551, Mon-Fri 0900-1630, US$1, guide US$3 with prior reservation*, where you will also find a collection of stamps and the story books of José Antonio de Armona (1765).

La Rampa

Calle 23, familiarly known as La Rampa, runs through Vedado from the Malecón at its eastern end, to the Cementerio Colón and the Río Almendares in the west. The eastern end is full of activity, overlooked as it is by the grand **Hotel Nacional de Cuba**, and the infamous **Hotel Habana Libre**. There are airline offices and the International Press Centre clustered together alongside restaurants and nightclubs and the ice cream parlour, **Coppelia**, which found movie fame in *Strawberry and Chocolate*. The parlour, which occupies a whole block, is a good example of the architectural creativity of the post-Revolution years. It was built by Mario Girona in 1966, based on an idea by Celia Sánchez Manduley, a heroine of the Sierra Maestra. Just to the south is the **Universidad de La Habana** (Havana University). A monument to **Julio Antonio Mella**, founder of the Cuban Communist Party, stands across from the university's magnificent stairway.

The **Cuban pavilion** (Pabellón Cuba) ⓘ *Calle 23 entre N y M, closed Mon, music and dancing from 2100 Wed (reggae), Thu (son), Fri-Sun (disco)*, is a combination of a tropical glade and a museum of social history. It tells the nation's story through a brilliant combination of objects, photos and the architectural manipulation of space. It also hosts the annual *Cubadisco* music convention in May, a showcase for the latest Cuban music.

Near the university the **Museo Napoleónico** ⓘ *San Miguel 1159 esquina Ronda, T7-8791460, Mon-Sat 1000-1730, US$3, guide US$5*, houses 7,000 pieces from the private collection of sugar baron, Julio Lobo: paintings and other works of art, a specialized library and a collection of weaponry. Check out the tiled fencing gallery.

Avenida de los Presidentes

The Avenida de los Presidentes, or Avenida G, joins the Plaza de la Revolución in the south to the Malecón in the north, bisecting La Rampa on its way through to the sea. It is a magnificent, wide boulevard with grand houses and blocks of apartments. A very desirable place to live. Just north of the intersection with La Rampa is a statue of Salvador Allende, the murdered President of Chile. At the Malecón the avenue is blocked by a monument to Calixto García. The **Museo de la Danza** ⓘ *entrance on Línea esq G (Av de los Presidentes), T7-8312198, Tue-Sat 1100-1830, US$2, guided tour US$1*, presents an engaging collection of items from the dancer Alicia Alonso's personal collection and from the Ballet Nacional de Cuba. See box page 410.

Close to the **Hotel Nacional**, the **Monumento al Maine** is a tribute to the 265 men who were killed when the *USS Maine* warship exploded in the bay in 1898. Close by, the **Tribuna Anti-Imperialista José Martí** built during the Elián González affair shows a statue of Martí holding his son Ismaelillo and pointing towards the US Interests Section fronted by a veil of mirrored glass windows and patrolled by Cuban military personnel. The famous billboard, with a fanatical Uncle Sam towering menacingly over a young Cuban patriot, has been relocated behind the Interests Section.

Casa de las Américas ⓘ *Calle 3 52 esq G, T7-552706, Mon-Fri 0800-1700,* was founded in 1959 by Haydée Santamaría for pan-American cultural promotion and interchange. This active and welcoming centre hosts a varied programme of seminars workshops and investigative studies in addition to running its own publishing house. Exhibitions of art from all corners of Latin America are held in the Galería Latinoamericana, while contemporary Cuban art is shown in the Sala Contemporánea. On the ground floor is the **Librería Rayuela** book and music shop and a small peso bookstall. Next door is the **Galería Haydée Santamaría** ⓘ *Calle G esq 5, alongside Casa de las Américas, Mon-Fri 0800-1700, Sat 1000-1500, US$2,* which displays the work of Latin American artists. There is a good representation of mostly 20th-century styles with over 6,000 works of art including sculptures, engravings and photography. The gallery was renovated with the help of the city of Seville and reopened in 1999.

The **José Martí sports ground**,on the Malecón entre Av de los Presidentes y J, is a good example of post-Revolutionary architecture; built in 1961 opposite the Casa de las Américas, it shows a highly imaginative use of concrete, painted in primary colours.

European and Oriental art from the 16th-20th centuries is displayed at the **Museo de Artes Decorativas** ⓘ *Calle 17 502 esq E, T7-8308037, Tue-Sat 1100-1800, US$2, or if you want a guide 1100-1630, US$3,* housed in a French Renaissance-style mansion since 1964, which was originally designed by Alberto Camacho (1924-27) for José Gómez Mena's daughter, who belonged to one of Cuba's wealthiest families. Most of the building materials were imported from France. In the 1930s the mansion was occupied by Gómez' sister, María Luisa, Condesa de Revilla de Camargo, who was a fervent collector of fine art and held elegant society dinners and receptions for guests including the Duke of Windsor and Wallace Simpson. Her valuable collections were found in the basement after the family fled Cuba following the Revolution in 1959. The interior decoration was by House of Jansen and her furniture included a desk that had belonged to Marie Antoinette. There are 10 permanent exhibition halls with works from the 16th to 20th centuries including ceramics, porcelain (Sévres, Chantilly and Wedgewood), furniture (Boudin, Simoneau and Chippendale) and paintings. The Regency-inspired dining room is recommended viewing and includes a sumptuous dinner service that belonged to the dictator Batista. The attendants are very knowledgeable and informative about the exhibits, but only in Spanish.

Paseo

This is another of Vedado's grand thoroughfares, to the west of the district, running down from the Mafia-built **Hotel Riviera** on the Malecón to the Plaza de la Revolución. Many of the elegant mansions either side of the street have been converted into offices or embassies.

Casa de la Amistad ⓘ *Paseo 406 entre 17 y 19, T7-8303114, bar and cafeteria open Mon-Sat 1100-2300, Sun 1100-1800,* is a former mansion dating from 1926. A beautiful dusky, coral pink building with gardens, it is now operated by **ICAP** (Cuban Institute for Friendship among the Peoples) and housing the **Amistur** travel agency (see Tour operators), which has a reasonably priced bar and cafeteria. You can eat on the balcony overlooking the garden, serenaded by the resident quartet, the food is consistently good with large portions; there are two menus: one has lobster and shrimp, the other is a house menu. Indoors is the **Primavera** restaurant, to the right of the entrance, which

Vedado & Plaza de la Revolución

N

0 metres   200
0 yards   200

Sleeping 🛌
Adita cp **1** *A5*
Apartments 18 & 19 cp **10** *C6*
Armando Gutiérrez cp **3** *B6*
Blue Building cp **4** *A2*
Capri **5** *B6*
Colina **7** *C6*
Daysie Recio cp **8** *B4*
Eduardo cp **11** *C5*
Gisela Ibarra y Daniel Riviero cp **12** *A4*
Giuseppe y María Elena cp **31** *D5*
Habana Libre **26** *C6*
Habana Riviera **13** *A3*
Hostal Paraíso cp **30** *A3*
Jorge Coalla Potts cp **15** *B5*
Luís y Alicia cp **16** *B6*
Martha Vitorte cp **17** *B5*
Meliá Cohiba **18** *A3*
Mercedes González cp **33** *B5*
Nacional de Cuba **20** *B6*
Natalia Rodés León cp **21** *C5*
Pedro Mesa López cp **22** *C5*
Presidente **23** *A4*
Ramón y Teresa Naredo cp **25** *B4*
St John's **9** *C6*
Tamasita cp **24** *D6*
Vedado **27** *C6*
Vedado Habana **28** *B3*
Victoria **29** *B5*
Villa Babi cp **34** *C3*

Eating 🍴
Adela **7** *C4*
Amor **1** *C4*
Burgui **3** *C5*
Coppelia **4** *B5*
El Conejito **6** *B5*
El Helecho **16** *B3*

Related maps
A Centro & La Habana Vieja, p88
C Miramar , p108

Havana Vedado

Gringo Viejo **9** *B4*
La Casona de 17 **5** *B6*
La Roca **2** *B5*
La Tasquita **20** *C6*
La Torre Focsa
 & Sherezada **11** *B6, C4*
Le Chansonnier **10** *B5*
Los Amigos **12** *B6*
Nerei **13** *B5*
Pain de París **14** *B3 & D4*
Pekín **8** *C2*

Trattoria Marakas **17** *B6*
Unión Francesa **18** *B3*

Entertainment 😊
Acapulco **3** *D1*
Amadeo Roldán **16** *A4*
Cabaret Las Vegas **1** *C6*
Café El Gato Tuerto **12** *B6*
Centro de Música
 Ignacio Piñeiro **2** *B5*
Chaplin **4** *C2*

Club Atelier **8** *B3*
El Gran Palenque Bar **9** *A3*
Habana Café **13** *A3*
Hurón Azul (UNEAC) **10** *D3*
Imágenes **11** *A4*
La Rampa **5** *B6*
Las Bulerías **22** *C5*
La Zorra y El Cuervo **14** *B6*
Riviera **6** *C5*
Sala Hubert de Blanck **15** *A3*
Teatro El Sótano **17** *C5*

Teatro Mella **18** *B3*
Teatro Nacional,
 Café Cantante & El
 Delirio Habanero **19** *D4*
Teatro Trianón **20** *C6*
Tikoa **21** *B3*
Yara **7** *B5*

has elegant furniture and is expensive. There is a daily cultural event, *Atardecer Latino*, 1700-2000, free. There are Cuban music nights (Tuesday, *Noche Chan Chan*, and Saturday, *Noche Cubana*), admission US$5, where you can enjoy traditional music in a relaxed setting. It's a good place to meet Cubans, and there is no soliciting.

The recently re-landscaped and renamed **John Lennon Park** at Calle 17 entre 6 y 8, features a bronze statue of the Beatles legend sitting on a bench, sculpted by José Villa, who also sculpted the Che Guevara monument at the Palacio de los Pioneros in Tarará, in the Playas del Este area. Evocative words from Lennon's song *Imagine* have been translated into Spanish, "*dirás que soy un soñador, pero no soy el único*" (You *may say I'm a dreamer, but I'm not the only one*), and etched on the ground. It was inaugurated in December 2000, attended by Fidel Castro and Silvio Rodríguez (singer/songwriter and founder of the movement of *La Nueva Trova*). Theft of the statue's glasses has meant there is a 24-hour security guard and the replacement glasses have been permanently fixed in place. Classical guitar concerts are sometimes held here.

Cementerio Colón

ⓘ *Entrance on Zapata y 12, T7-8334196, daily 0800-1630. US$1 entrance and US$1 for good map,* Rumbos *bar opposite the cemetery gates.*

The Colón cemetery should be visited to see the wealth of funerary sculpture, including Carrara Marbles; Cubans visit the sculpture of Amelia La Milagrosa (Amelia Goire) at Calle 3 entre F y G and pray for miracles. Constructed in 1871, the 56-ha city of the dead is the second largest cemetery in the world. It was designed by the Spanish architect, Calixto de Lloira y Cardosa, who was also the first person to be buried there. The Chinese cemetery is at Avenida 26 y 31.

Miramar

Miramar is some 16 km west of the old city on the west side of the Río Almendares, and easily reached by bus. Access is via two road tunnels or bridges. Although there are many beautiful art nouveau and other houses from the early 20th century, the area is now being developed into a modern city with glossy new hotels for business people with state-of-the-art fitness and business centres. Most of the embassies are here, which always implies a certain status and level of comfort. It has the appearance of a wealthy suburb with broad avenues and neatly aligned rectangular blocks.

Avenida Primera (first) runs closest to the sea, which is rocky and not recommended for bathing (use the hotel pool instead), Avenidas Tercera (third), Quinta (fifth) and Séptima (seventh) run parallel, with the tunnels to Vedado at the end of Avenidas 5 and 7. Some of the best restaurants are in Miramar and there are good places to go at night, including the internationally famous *Tropicana* cabaret show to the south and some great places to go to listen to music and dance the night away.

To get a good idea of the layout of the city and its suburbs, visit the **Maqueta de la Ciudad** (scale model of Havana) ⓘ *Calle 28 113 entre 1 y 3. T7-2027322, Tue-Sat 0930-1715, US$3, children, pensioners and students US$1.* Opened in 1995, this is now a great attraction. The 88-sq-m model covers Havana and its suburbs as far out as Cojímar and the airport. Every building is represented. Colonial buildings are in red, post-colonial pre-Revolution buildings in yellow and post-Revolution buildings in white. Some of the model is difficult to see, especially in the middle, but there is an upper viewing gallery with two telescopes where it is a little easier to see.

Well worth a visit if you can read Spanish is the **Museo del Ministerio del Interior** ⓘ *Av 5 y 14, T7-2034432, Tue-Fri 0900-1700, Sat 0900-1600, US$2,* which details the history of the police force, canine work, drugs work and fire brigade as well as all the counter-revolutionary activity in Cuba since 1959 and plots to kill Fidel through a series of photographs and lengthy explanations (all in Spanish). Curious cases such as false money production, killer shampoo and airline terrorism through to the bombings of tourist hotels are all documented. ▸▸ *For Sleeping, Eating and other listings, see pages 109-143.*

The suburbs

Marina Hemingway

Off Avenida 5, 20 minutes by taxi (US$10-15) from Havana, is the Marina Hemingway tourist complex, in the fishing village of **Santa Fé**. Fishing and scuba diving trips can be arranged here as well as other watersports and land-based sports. The Offshore Class 1 World Championship and the Great Island speedboat Grand Prix races have become an annual event in Havana, usually held during the last week in April, attracting power boat enthusiasts from all over the world. In May and June the marina hosts the annual Ernest Hemingway International Marlin Fishing Tournament and in August and September the Blue Marlin Tournament. There are 140 slips with electricity and water and space for docking 400 recreational boats. The resort includes the hotel **El Viejo y El Mar**, restaurants, bungalows and villas for rent, shopping, watersports, facilities for yachts, sports and a tourist bureau. Building continues for more villas and apartments. The Hemingway International Nautical Club is here, a social club for foreign executives based in Cuba. Founded in 1992, it currently has 730 members from 37 countries. The notice board is a good place to find crewing opportunities. The club organizes regattas, sailing schools and excursions, as well as the Hemingway Tournament. Another club in this area is the **Club Habana** (Sol Meliá) ① *Av 5 entre 188 y 192, Playa, T245700, 243301-4*. The main house dates back to 1928 and was the Havana Biltmore Yacht and Country Club. It is very posh but has lots of facilities on land and in the water.

Cubanacán

① *Escuela Superior de Arte, Calle 120 1110 esq 9, T7-2088075 Relaciones Internacionales, T7-2089771 to arrange visits, promocion@isa.cult.cu daily 0800-1700, US$3. Visits are usually arranged by tour agencies and a specialist guide is provided. Independent visitors should phone or email at least two days in advance.*

Three architects, Ricardo Porro, Roberto Gottardi and Vittorio Garati, were involved in designing a Revolutionary national school of art, begun in 1959. The complex was to combine schools of modern dance, plastic arts, dramatic arts, music and ballet, using domestic rather than imported materials. The **Escuela Superior de Arte** is located in the grounds of the former Havana Country Club in Cubanacán, southwest of Miramar. Architects will be interested in this 'new spatial sensation', which was an ambitious project of the early 1960s. Some parts were not completed and others have been abandoned (they were not entirely practical schemes), but you can still visit the **Escuela Superior de Artes Plásticas**, a series of interlinked pavilions, courtyards and sinuous walkways designed by Porro (which most people describe as laid out in the form of a woman's body, although some see it more as the womb itself, with a cervix-like fountain in the centre).

There is also the **Escuela Superior de Artes Escénicas**, built by Gottardi, in the form of a miniature Italian hill-top town, rather claustrophobic and quite unlike Porro's sprawling, 'permeable' designs, which are full of fresh air and tropical vegetation. Porro's Dance School, although part of the same complex, is not accessible via the Country Club (now the Music School, the 1960s Music School by Garati being now in ruins). Lack of maintenance, water leaks, a faulty drainage system, structural defects, vegetation and vandalism have led to deterioration of both the finished and unfinished buildings and there is a lack of funds for drawing up a master plan as well as carrying out repairs.

Boyeros

Southwest of Havana in the district of Boyeros is **Expocuba** ⓘ *T7-447324, Wed-Fri 1400-1600, Sat and Sun 1000-1800 (times subject to change), special trains leave from the main terminal in La Habana Vieja, or take camello M6 from Calle 21, Vedado, to last stop, then bus 88 (allow up to 1 hr)*, which was completed in January 1989. A sprawling facility, past Lenin Park, near the botanical gardens, it features a score of pavilions showing Cuba's achievements in industry, science, agriculture and the arts and entertainment. It also hosts various visiting art and cultural exhibitions, sometimes including live bands. Telephone to confirm listings. Information on times (and special buses) are available from hotels in Havana.

Miramar

*Related map
B Vedado & Plaza de la Revolución, p104*

Gulf of Mexico

MIRAMAR

Maqueta de la Ciudad
Av 3
French Embassy
Museo del Ministerio del Interior
Santa Rita
Mexican Embassy
Canadian Embassy
La Maison
Av 5A
Clínica Central Ciro García

N

0 metres 300
0 yards 300

Sleeping 🛏
Guillermo Rojas Reboredo **3** *B2*

Eating 🍴
1830 **8** *B6*
Calle 10 **1** *B5*
El Aljibe **2** *B3*
El Palio **3** *A3*

El Tocororo **4** *B4*
La Cecilia **8** *B1*
La Cocina de Liliam **5** *D2*
La Esperanza **6** *A4*
La Fontana **7** *B1*

Parque Lenín

ⓘ *Northwest of Boyeros and the airport, T7-443026, Wed-Sun 0900-1700.* Parque Lenín is a huge green space on the edge of Havana, which is very popular as a weekend escape for Cuban families. There are lakes for boating, you can hire horses for riding (see page 135), there is an amusement park (very popular, with a circus show), an aquarium and an upmarket restaurant. To the south is the botanical garden and Expocuba. Hiring bikes has been recommended as a good way to visit, alternatively try getting on a *camello* (see page 136).

Jardín Botánico Nacional de Cuba

ⓘ *Km 3.5, Carretera Rocío, Calabazar, south of Havana in Arroyo Naranjo, beyond Parque Lenín. Camello M6 and omnibus 88 every 30-40 mins. Many hotel tour desks offer day trips with lunch for US$25. Taxi from Habana Vieja US$15-18 one way, good for groups. T7-549170, open daily for foreign tourists, Wed-Sun for Cubans, 0830-1600, but in practice you may not be allowed in after 1530, US$1, children US$0.50, US$3 if you take the 'train' with guide, children half price.*

The botanical garden is well maintained with excellent collections, including a Japanese area with tropical adaptations. A multilingual guide will meet you at the gate, no charge. You can take a 'train' tour along the 35 km of roads around the 60-ha site. This is an open-sided, wheeled carriage towed by a tractor, which enables you to see the whole garden in about two hours. There are few signs, so it is not as informative as it might be, and a guide is helpful, describing unusual plants in the various zones. Several inter-connected glass houses are filled with desert, tropical and sub-tropical plants, well worth walking through. There is a good **organic vegetarian restaurant** (the only one in Cuba) using solar energy for cooking. There is only one sitting for lunch, but you can eat as much as you like from a selection of hot and cold vegetarian dishes and drinks for US$12. Water and waste food is recycled and the restaurant grows most of its own food.

☻ Sleeping

Havana has a mixture of 6 and 7 digit telephone numbers many of which are likely to change in 2004. Payment for hotels used by tourists is in US$. Always tell the hotel each morning if you intend to stay on another day. Do not lose your 'guest card', which shows your name, meal plan and room number. Tourist hotels are a/c, with 'tourist' TV (US films, tourism promotion),

Entertainment ☺
Casa de la Música Egrem,
   Sala Té Quedarás **5** *C4*
Club Almendares **1** *D5*
Dos Gardenias **2** *B3*
El Río Club
   (Johnnie's Club) **3** *B6*
Salón Rosado Benny
   Moré, La Tropical **4** *E3*
Tropicana **6** *E3*

(Sidebar, right margin) **Havana** The suburbs

Hemingway's Havana or Papa Dobles on the Pilar

Marlin fishing, gambling, beautiful prostitutes: these were the things that attracted Ernest Hemingway to Cuba in 1932. At first he stayed at the Hotel Ambos Mundos in Havana, but his visits became so frequent that he decided to buy a property. In 1940 he bought Finca Vigía, a 14-acre farm outside Havana. The staff included three gardeners, a Chinese cook and a man who tended to the fighting cocks Hemingway bred.

During the Second World War, Hemingway set up his own counter-intelligence unit at the Finca, calling it 'the Crook Factory'; his plan was to root out Nazi spies in Havana. He also armed his fishing boat, the 'Pilar', with bazookas and hand grenades. With a crew made up of Cuban friends and Spanish exiles from the Civil War, the Pilar cruised the waters around Havana in search of German U-Boats. The project surprisingly had the blessing of the US Embassy, who even assigned a radio operator to the Pilar. With no U-Boats in sight for several months, the mission turned into drunken fishing trips for Hemingway, his two sons and his friends.

When Hemingway returned to Cuba after more heroic contributions to the War effort in France, he wrote the book that was to have the biggest impact on the reading public, *The Old Man and the Sea*, which won him the Pulitzer Prize in 1953. This was a period of particularly heavy drinking for Hemingway: early morning Scotches were followed by numerous *Papa Dobles* (2½ jiggers of white rum, the juice of half a grapefruit, six drops of maraschino, mixed until foaming) at the **Floridita**, absinthe in the evening, two bottles of wine with dinner, and Scotch and soda till the early hours in the casinos of Havana.

When the political situation under Batista began to grow tense in 1958, a government patrol shot one of Hemingway's dogs at the Finca. By then he was older and wearier than he had been during the Spanish Civil War, and he quietly went back to his home in Idaho, from where he heard the news of Fidel Castro's victory. Hemingway made a public show of his support for the Revolution on his return to Cuba. He met Castro during the Marlin fishing tournament, which the new president won.

Hemingway's last days at the Finca were taken up with work on *The Dangerous Summer*, a long essay about bullfighting, but his thoughts frequently turned to suicide, and he left for Florida in 1960. After the Bay of Pigs US-backed attempted invasion in 1961, the government appropriated the Finca. Hemingway committed suicide in the USA in 1961.

Bibliography: *Hemingway*, Kenneth S Lynn (Simon & Schuster, 1987).

restaurants with reasonable food, but standards are not comparable with Europe and plumbing is often faulty or affected by water shortages. Several important hotel renovation projects have been completed by **Habaguanex** in La Habana Vieja and these are now elegant places to stay, becoming known as 'boutique' hotels. Hotels in Vedado are some distance away from the colonial sites but are in a better district for nightlife. Miramar is further away still, hotels are designed for business travellers and package tourists but there are good restaurants, *paladares*, bars, clubs and Teatro Karl Marx.

La Habana Vieja *p87, map pp88, 112, 114*
Hotels
LL-LNH Parque Central (Cubanacán), Neptuno entre Prado y Zulueta, on north side of Parque Central, T7-8606627/9, F7-8606630, www.nh-hotels.com 281 rooms of international standard, excellent bathrooms, separate shower and bathtub, business centre, 2 restaurants,

2 bars, great view of Havana from pool on 9th floor, fitness centre, charming and helpful multilingual staff, efficient Dutch management, good breakfast but expensive at US$12.50.

LL-L Santa Isabel (Habaguanex), Baratillo 9 entre Obispo y Narciso López, Plaza de Armas, T7-8608201, F7-8608391. 5 star, only 27 rooms, 10 of them suites, busy with groups, height of luxury, very well-equipped bathrooms, rooms on 3rd floor have balcony overlooking plaza – great for people-watching, pool, restaurant serving Cuban and international cuisine, central patio with fountain and greenery and lobby bar. Relax with a cocktail and watch the view from *El Mirador*, the cafeteria also has a good view of the Palacio de los Capitanes Generales, El Templete and other local sights.

LL-A Conde de Villanueva, Hostal del Habano (Habaguanex), Mercaderes 202 esq Lamparilla, T7-8629293/4, F7-8629882, gerencia@cvillanueva.co.cu Named after Claudio Martínez del Pinillo, Conde de Villanueva (1789-1853), a notable personality who promoted tobacco abroad and helped to bring the railway to Cuba. Just 9 rooms and suites around peaceful courtyard, attractive red and green colour scheme, cigar theme with cigar shop, café, bar, good restaurant, highly regarded, friendly staff.

L-A Florida (Habaguanex), Obispo 252 esq Cuba, T7-8624127, F7-624117. Restored building dates from 1885, cool oasis, elegant restaurant, bar just off the street, serves great *daiquirís*, marble floors and pillars in courtyard, beautiful rooms with high ceilings, quiet a/c, TV, clean bathrooms, some balconies, some singles, good cappuccino but overpriced and poor buffet breakfast, parking.

AL-A Sevilla (Gran Caribe), Trocadero 55 y Prado, T7-8608560, F7-8608582. Recently restored but works continue, 188 rooms of 1937 vintage on edge of La Habana Vieja, most have no view, better bathrooms and equipment than at the **Plaza** but both have noisy a/c, service criticized, inviting pool (open to non-guests), shops, sauna and massage, tourism bureau, elegant restaurant and bar on top floor with great night time views over Centro and the Malecón, huge windows are flung open to let in the breeze.

AL-A Telégrafo, Prado 408 esq Neptuno, T7-8611010, F8614741. Dating from 1860,

the Telégrafo reopened in 2001. Sleek 21st-century design is fused with 19th-century architecture. 63 spacious, stylish rooms with high ceilings, elaborate bathrooms and soundproofing. Great location on Parque Central. Internet access.

AL-B Hostal del Tejadillo (Habaguanex), Tejadillo 12 esq San Ignacio, T7-8637283, F7-8638830. Great location, comfortable rooms, high ceilings, tall wooden shuttered windows, fridge, good breakfast inside or in the courtyard, lively bar with entertaining barmen and music in the afternoon/evening.

AL-B Hostal Los Frailes (Habaguanex), Teniente Rey entre Mercaderes y Oficios, T7-8629510, F7-8629718, recepcion@habaguanexhlosfrailes.co.cu In restored house of Marqués Pedro Pablo Duquesne IV, a captain in the French navy who came to Havana in 1793 and joined the Spanish marines while remaining loyal to the deposed French crown. The family continued to reside in Havana after his death there in 1834, and epitomized Franco-Cuban society. Recently converted to a small hotel with a monasterial theme; the bellboys are dressed in pseudo monks' habits. Rooms overlook the central courtyard. Pleasant, classical music (clarinets and saxophones) in the bar, 22 rooms, including 4 suites with balconies onto the street, the others don't have windows, a/c, phone, satellite TV, minibar, all meals at **La Marina** restaurant, 10 m from hotel.

AL-B Inglaterra (Gran Caribe), Prado 416 entre San Rafael y San Miguel, T7-8608595/7, F7-8608254. Built in 1875 next to the Teatro Nacional, famous former foreign guests included Sarah Bernhardt in 1887, General Antonio Maceo (one of the heroes of the Cuban Wars of Independence) in 1890, and the authors Federico García Lorca and Rubén Darío in 1910. 86 rooms, colonial style, regal atmosphere, but a bit drab and rooms don't always get cleaned every day, balconies overlook Parque Central, some single rooms have no windows but at least you won't get woken by the traffic, reasonable breakfast, lovely old mosaic tiled dining room, 1 of 4 cafés or restaurants with a variety of services and cuisines. Delightful glazed tile pictures by famous and not-so-famous artists have been set into the pavement in front.

A-B Plaza (Gran Caribe), Zulueta 267 esq Neptuno, or Ignacio Agramonte 267,

T7- 8608583/9, F7-8608869. 186 rooms, generally shabby, high ceilings, reasonable bathrooms, don't rely on toilet paper being provided, street-front rooms very noisy, ask for one in the inner courtyard, breakfast on 5th floor with fine view, poor dinner, service generally poor.

A-C Hostal Valencia (Habaguanex), Oficios 53 esq Obrapía, T7-8671037, F7-8605628, reserva@habaguanex hvalencia.co.cu Joint Spanish/Cuban venture modelled on the Spanish *paradores*. Suites and rooms – some rather past their best – are named after Valencian towns. Tastefully restored building, nicely furnished, pleasant courtyard

Plaza de Armas

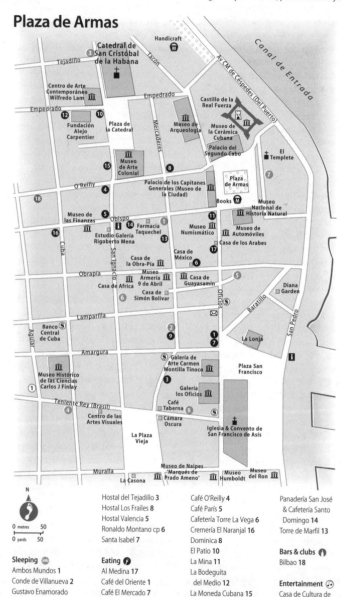

N

0 metres 50
0 yards 50

Sleeping 🛏
Ambos Mundos **1**
Conde de Villanueva **2**
Gustavo Enamorado
 Zamora cp **4**

Hostal del Tejadillo **3**
Hostal Los Frailes **8**
Hostal Valencia **5**
Ronaldo Montano cp **6**
Santa Isabel **7**

Eating 🍴
Al Medina **17**
Café del Oriente **1**
Café El Mercado **7**
Café Habana **9**

Café O'Reilly **4**
Café París **5**
Cafetería Torre La Vega **6**
Cremería El Naranjal **16**
Dominica **8**
El Patio **10**
La Mina **11**
La Bodeguita
 del Medio **12**
La Moneda Cubana **15**
Mesón de la Flota **3**

Panadería San José
 & Cafetería Santo
 Domingo **14**
Torre de Marfil **13**

Bars & clubs 🍸
Bilbao **18**

Entertainment 🎧
Casa de Cultura de
 Habana Vieja **1**

⦂ The Habana Libre – hotel as icon

The *Havana Hilton* was inaugurated on 19 March 1958, a huge tower that symbolized everything that was luxurious and decadent in the capital and attracted a high-flying and wealthy clientele. However, after the fall of the dictatorship, Fidel Castro and some of his comrades settled temporarily into the hotel. The Continental Suite, room 2324, was used as the Revolution Headquarters for the first three months of 1959 and press conferences for foreign journalists were given here. Later, the first Soviet embassy in Havana occupied two floors. In the 1960s it was used for international meetings. Castro stayed in La Castellana Suite, room 2224, for the Tricontinental conference in December 1961.

The hotel is now under the wing of *Tryp*, part of the *Sol Meliá* group (see page 115). Even if you don't want to stay there, have a walk around the lobby area. There are fascinating photos of the Revolutionaries lounging around after their success in the war, and an account of the literacy campaign in 1961.

with vines, music, good restaurant (see Eating, below). The Hostal El Comendador, next door, opened in 1999, is a discreet, well-appointed hotel on 2 floors, using the facilities of the Valencia and with the same prices. The restaurant and bar on the corner is open from 1200 and serves pizza, *tortillas*, *empanadas*, etc for lunch.

C Caribbean (Horizontes), Paseo Martí (Prado) 164 esq Colón, T7-8608210, F7-8609479. Remodelled, good security, convenient for the old town, 36 rooms, try and get one on 5th floor, fan and TV, popular with budget travellers, but avoid noisy rooms at front and lower floors at back over deafening water pump, internet access, Café del Prado at street level for pasta, pizza, snacks, daily 0700-2300.

C-D La Casa del Científico, Prado 212 esq Trocadero, T7-8638103. Beautiful colonial building, charmingly old fashioned, well preserved rather than renovated, shared or private bathroom, cheap breakfast, luxurious dining room and lounge in classic style, very pleasant atmosphere, friendly staff, reservations essential, often booked by groups, best budget option in old city, Asistur office on site.

D-E Residencia Santa Clara, Cuba 610 entre Luz y Sol, in convent buildings, T7-8613335, reaca@cencrem.cult.cu see page 97. Convent building, great value, spacious suites with colonial furnishings or small, single rooms, or dormitories. Lovely, can be noisy early morning, nice café, poor breakfast.

Casas particulares

D Jesús y María, Aguacate 518 entre Sol y Muralla, T7-8611378. Upstairs suite above the family and very private, a/c bedroom with twin beds, bathroom, living room and kitchenette with fan, fridge, also small outside sitting area, comfortable, clean.

E Eugenio y Fabio, San Ignacio 656 entre Jesús María y Merced, T7-8629877. Rooms are well equipped and spacious but dark, overlooking interior courtyard, noisy a/c. House is stuffed with antiques and bric-à-brac and meals are served in an ornate baroque dining room.

E Gustavo Enamorado Zamora – Chez Nous, Teniente Rey (Brasil) 115 entre Cuba y San Ignacio, T7-8626287, cheznous@ cemia.inf.cu 2 spacious double rooms, shared bathroom, hot water, fan, TV, balcony overlooking street, street noise, nice patio, parking, warm atmosphere, Gustavo and Kathy are kind and helpful, French spoken.

E Orlando y Liset, Aguacate 509 Apto 301 entre Sol y Muralla, T7-8675766. 2 rooms in a lovely clean apartment, great view over La Habana Vieja from the terrace, garage, elevator, help with arranging buses, taxis or accommodation in other towns.

E Ronaldo Montano, San Ignacio 205 Apto 304 entre Lamparilla y Obrapía, T7-8620109. Room with a/c, king-size bed, nice bathroom but not en suite, English spoken.

Hotels

C-D Deauville (Horizontes), Galiano y Malecón, T7-338812, F7-338148. 148 rooms, noise from Malecón but great view, balconies overlooking sea and fortress, breakfast included, pool, helpful *buró de turismo*. Restaurant **Costa Norte** offers dinner 1900-2130 for US$10 with open bar, followed by a cabaret 2200-0230, daily Tue-Sun. The pool is open to non-guests for US$5 including a cocktail, or US$2.50 for children under 12, snack bar.

D Lido (Horizontes), Consulado 216 entre Animas y Trocadero, T7-871102, F7-338814. 65 rooms, a/c, TV, not bad for the price, but looking a bit forlorn and don't expect hot water in the shower, laundry expensive, done by hand and charged per item, central, 1 block from Prado, friendly reception with internet access, restaurant downstairs, food bland and overpriced, bar and café on roof terrace much better, excellent views but slow breakfast service.

D Lincoln (Islazul), Galiano 164 esq Virtudes, T7-338209. 135 mostly refurbished and good-value rooms, convenient location, friendly, TV with CNN, hot water, a/c, clean, guests are mostly Cuban, price includes breakfast on top floor, breezy, great view but no culinary experience.

Casas particulares

E Dr Alejandro Oses, Malecón 163, 1st floor, entre Aguila y Crespo, T7-8637359. Best view in city from balcony, of entire Malecón, from El Morro to Hotel Nacional, nice place to stay although the interior rooms can be stuffy, shared bathrooms, helpful family, book ahead, always full.

E Carlos Luis Valderrama Moré, Neptuno 404 entre San Nicolás y Manrique, 2nd floor, T7-8679842. Carlos and Vivian are former teachers, he speaks English, 1940s apartment above a shop, 2 rooms, noisy front room has balcony overlooking street, good bathrooms, hot water, but very small beds.

E Casa Marta, Manrique 362 bajos, entre San Miguel y San Rafael, T7-8633078. Warm and inviting with a family atmosphere with many long-term guests. Ex-revolutionary fighter Nelsón is an excellent host. Rooms have a/c, hot water and shared bathrooms.

E El Parador Numantino, Consulado 223 entre Animas y Trocadero, T7-8627629. Argentine theme to these modern rooms only 5 mins' walk from Parque Central at the top of this price range. Private bathrooms, minibar, fans, a/c, TV, guests' reception room, breakfast US$5.

E Federico y Yamelis Llanes, Cárcel 156 entre San Lázaro y Prado, T7-8617817, llanesrenta@yahoo.es Excellent location just off the Prado and a stone's throw from the Malecón, but you have to climb 64 stairs up to the apartment on the third floor. Large, light room with tiled floor and heavy dark furniture, double bed, extra bed on request, en suite bathroom, hot water in shower, a/c, CD player, phone, desk, run by pleasant young couple, formerly lawyers, some English spoken, good breakfast with lots of fruit and juice and delicious supper.

E Giuseppe y María Elena, Valle 205 entre Mazón y Basarrate, T7-8784763, giusepperosato@hotmail.com Colonial house with patio and terrace, fan fridge, hot water, near University.

Parque Central

El Floridita 4
Gentiluomo 6
Hanoi 3
La Zargozana 5
Los Nardos 8
Pastelería Francés 9
Sevilla's Paladar 7

Sleeping
Golden Tulip
  Parque Central 1
Inglaterra 2
Plaza 3
Telégrafo 4

Eating
A Prado y Neptune 1
El Castillo de Farnés 2

Bars & clubs
Casa del Escabeche 11
Monserrate 10

Entertainment
Cine Payret 1
Gran Teatro de
  la Habana 2

E **Jesús Deiro Rana**, San Rafael 312 entre Galiano y San Nicolás, T7-8638452. An Aladdin's cave of treasures with spacious rooms, high ceilings, leafy tiled courtyard, antique clocks and furnishings, including a haughty 1870 bed to sleep in. 2 rooms with shared bathroom, all well equipped.

E **Marilys Herrera González**, Concordia 714 altos entre Soledad y Aramburu, T7-8700608, maguel20022002@yahoo.es Bathroom with warm water, fridge, a/c, TV, all modern, clean and comfortable, laundry offered, Marylis is very kind and caring, family atmosphere.

E **Ramón y Tamasita**, Valle 174 entre Infanta y Basarrate, T/F7-8794953. Large house, 2 rooms with bathroom, 1 with terrace, use of fridge, TV, a/c or fan, charming couple, English spoken.

E **Rosa Artiles Hernández**, Crespo 117 bajos entre Colón y Trocadero, T7-8627574. Excellent place, very clean and friendly, but not a family experience. The 2 rooms share a dining room, bathroom and fridge, on the top floor of the house away from the family living area, hot water, a/c, fan, radio, own key, beautiful car on ground floor, son speaks English.

E-F **Ana María Rodríguez López**, San Lázaro 160 Apto 1 entre Aguila y Crespo, T7-8637478. 1st floor apartment, 2 rooms, a/c, TV, fridge, hot water, 50 m from Malecón and short walk to old city.

E-F **Julio y Elsa**, Consulado 162 apto 2 entre Colón y Trocadero, T7-8618027, julioroq@yahoo.com 2 rooms, 1 with 2 beds, 1 with double bed, fridge, a/c, private bath, hot water and independent entrance for both. English spoken and the owners are friendly. Good and filling breakfast US$3, supper US$5-7, vegetarian food can be made.

F **Villa Colonial Tomy**, Gervasio 218 entre Virtudes y Concordia, T7-8606764, wilfredo.mtnez@infomed.sld.cu Ballet teacher Tomy is as colourful as his home, which is full of antiques and memorabilia including English tea cups, Spanish thrones, Italian Harlequin masks, Japanese screens and photos of his former pupil Carlos Acosta, now with the Royal Ballet in London. Bathroom is shared. Great rooftop terrace with murals dedicated to Oscar Wilde.

F **Xiomara**, Virtudes 216 entre Aguila y Amistad, piso 1, T7-8610656. Run by Xiomara, her husband and brother-in-law, generous and friendly and you feel part of the family. Rooms simple but cheap for Havana, excellent food. Dining room, kitchen and lounge are on the top floor, great views of Habana Vieja from terrace.

Vedado *p100, map p104*
Hotels

LL-L **Meliá Cohiba** (Cubanacán), Paseo entre 1 y 3, T7-333636, www.solmeliacuba.com International grand luxury, high rise and dominating the neighbourhood, 342 rooms, 120 suites, shops, gym, healthclub, pool, gourmet restaurant, piano bar.

LL-AL **Nacional de Cuba** (Gran Caribe), O esq 21, T7-8733564, F7-8735054. 467 rooms, some renovated, some not, good bathrooms with lots of bottles of goodies, some package tours use it at bargain rates, generally friendly and efficient service, faded grandeur, dates from 1930, superb reception hall, note the vintage Otis high-speed lifts, steam room, 2 pools, restaurants, bars, shops, business centre on lobby for emails, faxes etc, exchange bureau, gardens with old cannons on hilltop overlooking the Malecón and harbour entrance, great place to watch people and vehicles, the hotel's tourist bureau is also efficient and friendly.

L **Sol Meliá Tryp Habana Libre** (Gran Caribe), L y 23, T7-554011, www.solmeliacuba.com 606 rooms and suites in huge block, 25 floors, prices depend on the floor number, remodelled 1997, most facilities are here, eg hotel reservations, excursions, Polynesian restaurant, 24-hr coffee shop, **Cabaret Turquino** daily 2230-0300, shopping mall, includes liquor store, cigar shop, jewellery, perfume, handicrafts, shoe shop, hairdresser, **Photoservice**, **Banco Financiero Internacional**, postal service, swimming pool. See also p113.

AL **Victoria** (Gran Caribe), 19 y M, T7-333510, reserva@victoria.gca.tur.cu 4-star hotel with an elegant feel. 31 rooms, intimate and tasteful if conservative, good bathrooms, small pool, parking, good cooking. Free internet access for guests.

AL-B **Presidente** (Gran Caribe), Calzada y G (Presidentes), T7-551801, F7-333753. Oldest hotel in Havana with a distinctly Mafia vibe, refurbished, 162 rooms, 10 suites, ask for a room on the 10th floor (Colonial Floor), which has sumptuous antiques, 2 restaurants, small pool. Popular with Italian tour groups.

A **Habana Riviera** (Gran Caribe), Paseo y Malecón, T7-334051, F7-333738. 330 rooms, 1950s block, Mafia style, appearance suffers from being so close to the glitzy **Meliá Cohiba**, desolate square outside, which together with the hotel entrance is awash with prostitutes after dark, does a good breakfast, no need to eat again all day.

B **Capri** (Horizontes), 21 y N, T7-333747, F7-333750. 215 rooms, showing their age, public areas also with signs of wear and tear, a/c, pool, newly renovated luxury restaurant and cabaret, shops, barber open Mon-Sat 0900-1700, US$5, currency exchange, parking, car rental.

B **St John's** (Horizontes) O 206 entre 23 y 25, T7-333740. Convenient location steps away from Vedado nightlife, recently remodelled with sparkling new rooms and good bathrooms. Get a room on floors 9-12 for great views over either Habana Vieja or Vedado and Miramar. 24-hr internet access in lobby. Rooftop pool and nightclub daily 2230-0200.

B **Vedado** (Horizontes), O 244 entre 23 (Humboldt) y 25, T7-334072, F7-334186. Great location with good facilities, 194 basic rooms, a/c, TV, pool, gym and health centre with US$10 massages, restaurant, nightclub daily 2230-0200, admission US$10 then open bar.

D **Colina** (Horizontes), L y 27, T7-334071, F7-334104. 79 rooms, hot water, street noise, small rooms, excellent buffet breakfast, open to non-residents US$3, popular with airport **Cubatur** desk.

Casas particulares

D **Martha Vitorte**, G 301 Apto 14, 14th floor, entre 13 y 15, T7-8326475, high rise building near corner with Línea, 1 apartment on each floor, referred to as 'horizontals', beautiful modern building, very spacious, 2 rooms, en suite bathroom, a/c, security safe in each room, balcony on 2 sides for panoramic views of Havana, sea and sunsets, Martha is a retired civil servant and speaks some English and French.

E **Adita**, 9 257 entre J y I, T7-8320643. 2 spacious, comfortable double rooms with private bathrooms in a warm, family home full of antiques. The building is dilapidated but the eclectic apartment is clean and a great place to stay.

E **Apartments 18 and 19**, L 454 entre 25 y 27, close to the Habana Libre. Apto 18, T7-8324214, is run by actress María and is a light and spacious apartment. 2 comfortable double rooms with private bathrooms, a/c, and great views over Vedado. Price negotiable for long stays. Apto 19, T7-8326471, run by animated Lisette, has 1 large bedroom with the biggest bathroom in Havana. The communal rooftop terrace has great views and is a peaceful retreat.

E **Armando Gutiérrez**, 21 62 entre M y N, Apto 7, 4th (top) floor, T/F7-8321876. Large a/c rooms with 2 beds, bathroom, separate entrance, clean, hot water, Armando and his wife, Betty, and mother, Teresa, speak a little English and French and are knowledgeable on history and culture.

E **Blue Building**, 5 717 Apto 1 entre 8 y 10, www.geocities.com/bluebuilding Run by Octavio Fundora and Dr Moraima Arébalo, single or double rooms, a/c, hot water, TV, VCR, CD player, kitchen, English spoken.

E **Daysie Recio**, B 403 entre 17 y 19, T7-8305609. Spacious, light and clean. 2 airy rooms with interconnecting bathroom, one has a terrace overlooking the backyard, a/c, hot water, English spoken. Daysie is a vivacious hostess and this is a good option for families.

E **Eduardo**, 25 359 Apto B entre L y K, T7-8320956. Very nice, new, well-designed rooms, fridge, TV in room.

E **Gisela Ibarra y Daniel Riviero**, F104 altos entre 5 y Calzada, T7-8323238. Straight out of the 1950s, marble staircase, balconies, very high quality, wonderful old rooms with original furnishings, a/c, fan, fridge, TV and safety box. Gisela is an excellent hostess, running a very proper, quiet and traditional home in a residential neighbourhood. Huge, filling breakfast for US$5, laundry service offered. If she is full, her daughter Marta Díaz runs another *casa* just round the corner on Calzada 452 Apto 5, same price but rooms are smaller, darker and hotter.

E **Hostal Paraíso**, Paseo 126 Apto 4B entre 5 y 7, T7-8305160, crisjo@infomed.sld.cu Large bedroom with double bed plus wardrobe, couch, dressing table, bedside lamps, a/c, fan, phone, TV, radio, ensuite bathroom, hot water, shower, kitchenette with 4 chairs, fridge/freezer. Excellent security, own entrance and keys. Bed linen and towels changed daily, laundry on request. Very cheerful and helpful family, some English spoken.

← E **Jorge Coalla Potts**, I 456 apto 11 entre 21 y 23, T7-8329032, jorgepotts@web. correosdecuba.cu The large room with private bathroom with hot water is very comfortable. Excellent location close to the bars and restaurants of Vedado. Generous and fascinating hosts Jorge and Marisel have useful contacts throughout the island.

E **Luís Cartaya y Alicia Horta**, Línea 53 entre M y N, Apto 9, T7-8328439. Friendly couple, both doctors, Spanish speaking only, rooms cleaned daily, long stays possible, good view from 9th floor, popular so call in advance.

E **Mercedes González**, 21 360 Apto 2A, entre G y H, T7-8325846. 2 rooms, a/c, fan, good bathroom, hot water, airy rooms, 1 room has a balcony, smart, helpful and friendly, good location, near park.

E **Natalia Rodés León**, 19 376 p11B, entre G y H, T7-8328909. 2 rooms, 1 bathroom, fridge, TV, friendly lady, fought alongside Castro in the Sierra Maestra.

E **Pedro Mesa López y Tobias López Márquez**, F 609 Apto 12 entre 25 y 27, T7-8329057. Quiet area except for rooster, 3 rooms with bathrooms, fridge, a/c, only Spanish spoken by friendly couple in their 60s.

E **Teresa Naredo**, 15 605 entre C y D, Apto 1, T7-8303382, alyogan@hotmail. com Ground floor of low rise block, balcony, clean and tidy, en suite facilities, a/c, hot water, quiet embassy residential neighbourhood, often booked for extended periods.

E **Vedado Habana**, Paseo 313 Apto 43 esq 15, T7-8334174, Run by Raúl and Magaly, the former is full of tales of his dissident youth, while photos of his guerrilla wife Magaly fighting alongside Fidel in the Sierra Maestra adorn the walls. There is 1 large room with private bathroom and cheaper, smaller room with futon and shower room.

E **Villa Babi**, 27 965 entre 6 y 8, T7-8306373, www.villababi.com A must for Cuban film buffs, run by María del Carmen Díaz, second wife of the late Tomás Gutiérrez Alea, famed director of *Fresa y Chocolate* and other notable films. The walls are covered with memorabilia and the surroundings and welcoming ambience make up for the lack of plush fixtures and fittings. Popular with Italians, so call ahead for reservations.

Miramar *p106, map p108* 117

Hotels

There is a string of 4-star hotels west along the coast that are used by package tour operators; guests are often here for the first and last nights of their stay in Cuba before being whisked off round the island. They are not particularly convenient for visiting the old city, but you do get a sea view. Miramar is also popular with business people; hotels are of an international standard and the area is quiet at night.

Casas particulares

E **Guillermo Rojas Reboredo**, 40 102 esq 1, 2nd floor, Apto 5, Miramar, T7-2018727. A/c, hot water, sea view.

E **Nieves y Marlen**, 3 9401 entre 94 y 96, Apto 2, T7-2035284. Clean, spacious and modern apartment, a/c, fridge in room, hot water, balcony.

Marina Hemingway *p107*

Hotels

AL-C **El Viejo y El Mar** (Cubanacán), 248 y Av 5, Santa Fé, T7-2046336, F7-2046823. Pleasant enough hotel on seafront but out of the way and nothing to do unless you are busy at the marina, package tourists come here before going off on excursions, small pool, restaurant with buffet meals, lobby bar, clean, bath tub, tricky shower.

A **Residencial Turístico**, T7-331150-6. Rooms overlook canals, pool, snack bar, good supermarket, can be noisy with motorized watersports.

Boyeros *p108*

This quiet neighbourhood is convenient for the airport.

D-E **Magalys y Lesme**, Av Vento 9920 entre 10 y A, Altahabana, T7-441832. Large 1960s house on 2 floors with garden, garage, spacious, 2 rooms, ensuite bathroom, a/c, hot water, family atmosphere, English spoken, kitchen facilities.

D-E **Manuela y Manolito Sosa**, Parque 17010 entre A y B, T7-442437. 1960s house, 2nd floor, antiques and chandeliers, good security, garden, garage, a/c, hot water. Both houses are close to the **Hotel Altahabana**, 7 entre A y B, Reparto Altahabana, T7-578758. A small pool open to the public, US$3 for adults, US$2 children, a restaurant and snack bar.

🍴 Eating

In addition to the excellent and varied *paladares*, see Essentials, p50, for further information, and more predictable state restaurants, listed below, there are many street stalls and places where you can pick up cheap snacks, pizza etc. Note that their prices are listed in pesos even though there is a $ sign as a price indicator. These are good for filling a hole at lunchtime, but don't expect a culinary masterpiece. Make sure you eat pizza fresh from the oven, 6 pesos a piece for cheese, 10 pesos for extra cheese or meat toppings. They can be very greasy, take plenty of napkins. Very sweet juice drinks 2 pesos per glass.

For **vegetarians** there is little choice and we have received many reports that a vegetarian travelling in Cuba is bound to lose weight. Havana restaurants and *paladares* are more enlightened than those in the rest of the country. Your best bet is the restaurant in the Jardín Botánico, **El Bambú**, see p109, where lunch is served at around 1400, or try **Pekín**, see below. Many of the hotels, including the **Nacional**, see p115, serve good all-you-can-eat lunchtime buffets. Italian restaurants offer the usual meatless pizza and pasta. Some *paladares* will serve meatless meals with advance notice, but always ask for the *congris* to be cooked in vegetable oil.

There are many **fast food** outlets throughout the city: **El Rápido** (red logo) are clean with fast service and numerous locations; **Burgui**, serves hamburgers with cheese US$1.30 and fried chicken US$1.25, beer US$0.85. Branches of **DiTú** are springing up all over the city, open 24 hrs, selling pieces of chicken by weight; **El Rapidito** (red logo, not to be confused with El Rápido chain), fried chicken 25 pesos, pizzas from 8 pesos. **Pain de París**, Línea entre Paseo y A, also Plaza de la Revolución, has 24-hr service, good coffee, *café cortadito* or *café con leche* US$0.65, croissants US$0.55 and *señoritas de chocolate* (custard slices).

La Habana Vieja *p87, map pp88, 112, 114*
Restaurants
$$$ El Floridita, Obispo esq Monserrate, next to the Parque Central, T7-8671299, 1200-2400. A favourite haunt of Hemingway. It

has had a recent face-lift and is now a very elegant bar and restaurant reflected in the prices (US$6 for a *daiquirí*), but well worth a visit if only to see the sumptuous décor and 'Bogart atmosphere'. In the corner of the bar is a life-size bronze statue of Hemingway and on the bar, also in bronze, are his glasses resting on a open book. Live music.

$$$-$$ La Bodeguita del Medio, Empedrado 207 entre Cuba y San Ignacio, near the cathedral, T7-338857, restaurant 1200-2400, bar 0900-2400. Made famous by Hemingway and should be visited if only for a drink (*mojito* – rum, crushed ice, mint, sugar, lime juice and carbonated water – is a must, US$6), food poor, expensive at US$35-40 for 2, but very popular. It is here that Hemingway allegedly inscribed the now famous line *"Mi mojito en La Bodeguita, mi daiquirí en El Floridita"*. It has been claimed that one of Hemingway's drinking buddies Fernando Campoamor and the owner of *La Bodeguita* hired a calligrapher to write the line as a lucrative tourist con.

$$$-$$ A Prado y Neptuno, address of the same name, opposite Hotel Parque Central, T7-8609636, daily 1200-2400. Trendy, good views over Parque Central, excellent tiramisu and good pizza.

$$$-$$ Dominica, O' Reilly esq Mercaderes, T7-662917, daily 1200-2400. Italian, very smart, set menus US$25-30, pasta from US$6, pizza US$4.50-12 depending on size, vegetarian options, outdoor seating nice for lunch, poor service, credit cards.

$$$-$$ El Castillo de Farnés, Monserrate 361 esq Obrapía, T7-8671030, restaurant daily 1200-2400, bar open 24 hrs. Tasty Spanish food, reasonable prices, good for *garbanzos* and shrimp, also Uruguayan beef US$8 and chateaubriand US$12. Castro came here at 0445, 9 Jan 1959, with Che and Raúl.

$$$-$$ El Patio, San Ignacio 54 esq Empedrado, Plaza Catedral, T7-8671034, restaurant daily 1200-2400, snack bar open 24 hrs. Expensive, small portions, slow service, but has selection of national dishes, tables outside take up most of the square, lovely location.

$$$-$$ La Mina, on Obispo esquina Oficios, Plaza de Armas, T7-8620216, daily 1200-2400. Very much on the tourist trail, expensive, traditional Cuban food, sandwiches, pasta, lots of liqueur coffees, outdoor seating with live Cuban music.

$$$-$$ **La Paella**, Hostal Valencia, Oficios 53, T7-8671037, daily 1200-2400. Features the best paella (for two people minimum) in Havana. Good food and a traditional, charming ambience.

$$$-$$ **La Zaragozana**, Monserrate 351 entre Obispo y Obrapía, T7-8671040, open 1200-2400. Oldest restaurant in Havana, international cuisine, good seafood and wine, 3 courses about US$25, good service but generally food nothing special.

$$$-$$ **Mesón de la Flota**, Mercaderes 257 entre Amargura y Teniente Rey, T7-8629281. Restaurant-cum-tapas bar with wooden tables and impassioned flamenco *tablaos* after 2100 each evening. Reasonably priced menu with wide selection of dishes and plenty of fish and seafood, but the tapas choices are better value than the main dishes. Try the feisty *patatas bravas*.

$$ **Torre de Marfil**, Mercaderes 115 entre Obispo y Obrapía, T7-8671038, open 1200-2200. Generally good value Oriental cuisine with food surpassing anything that Chinatown has to offer in terms of authenticity, decked out with colourful lanterns and Chinese paraphernalia.

$$ **Al Medina**, Oficios 10 entre Obrapía y Obispo, T7-8671041, 1200-2300, open 1200-2300. Arab food in lovely colonial mansion, dishes priced between US$7-16, try Tangine chicken with olives, sesamo chicken and a huge vegetarian combo, appetisers US$2-3, including houmous and falafel, lovely fresh fruit juices US$1, good coffee, some seating on large cushions, trios play during opening hours, also Mosque and Arab cultural centre off beautiful courtyard.

$$ **Café del Oriente**, Oficios y Amargura, T7-860 6686, daily 1200-2400. High class food with a reasonably priced set menu and elegant surroundings.

$$ **Café El Mercado**, next to to Café del Oriente, open 24 hrs. Informal, pleasant terrace.

$$ **Gentiluomo**, Bernaza esq Obispo,T7-8671300, daily 1200-2400. Pasta, pizza, US$3.50-8, reasonable food but don't expect them to have everything on the menu, eg no fruit, no tomatoes except in season, no mozzarella, no parmesan, but the chef produces a passable pizza, friendly service, pleasant environment, a/c.

$$ **Los Nardos** (Sociedad Juventud Asturiana), Paseo del Prado 563 entre Dragones y Teniente Rey, opposite the Capitolio, T7-8632985, 1200-2400. Not obvious from the street but look out for the waiters at the entrance. Dining room upstairs lined with cabinets containing old football trophies, cups from 1936, while the heavy wooden furniture is reminiscent of a rancho. At one end are chefs in white hats busy in the kitchen while at the other you are overlooked by the stained glass windows of a pool room. Not an option for vegetarians, plenty of meat, pork, lamb or Uruguayan steak, while fish ranges from US$3.90-9 and cocktails are US$2.50. Popular with Cubans and foreigners, large, filling portions, background music is limited to golden oldies played 2-3 times during the meal.

$$-$ **Los Vitrales**, Casa del Científico, Prado 212 esq Trocadero, T7-8624511, open 0700-2200 for breakfast, lunch and dinner. Dining room has a cream and taupe baroque ceiling with a frieze of angels, marble floor and grand piano. Climb a beautiful staircase to the dining room, half way up look up for a skylight: a riot of coloured stained glass with chandeliers like buttons. American breakfast US$4. Also soups, salads and sandwiches US$2-4, fried chicken US$6-7. Tables on the balcony overlooking the Prado. More staff needed and taped music could be a few decibels lower.

$$-$ **Puerto de Sagua**, Bélgica (Egido) 603 esq Acosta, T7-8671026. Nautical theme with chrome 1950s-style bar serving great cocktails, a cheap canteen-style restaurant serving good value, well-prepared food such as pasta from US$2, big pizzas US$2-6 and prawns in tomato sauce US$4, or a more upscale, overpriced restaurant with same kitchen, serving fish, seafood, crab and frogs legs accompanied by live music.

$ **Café Habana**, Mercaderes 210 A entre Amargura y Lamparilla, T7-8610071. Café charges in pesos, dirt cheap, 8 pesos for fried egg and chips, 1 or 2 pesos for coffee.

$ **Café O' Reilly**, O'Reilly 203 entre Cuba y San Ignacio. Coffee, snacks, pizza, spaghetti, sandwiches or the usual chicken and pork. Pleasant second floor, with balcony, where there is often live music.

$ **Café París**, Obispo y San Ignacio. Serves good and reasonably priced chicken for US$3.50, beer US$1, snacks and pizza around the clock, live music, lively in evenings, pity about the hassling from harmless but irritating *jineteros*.

$ Cafetería Torre La Vega, Obrapía 114, next to the Casa de México, open 0900-2100. Cheap breakfast, bland chicken and chips US$3, better value spaghetti US$0.85, sandwiches US$0.35-1.70, *Cristal* beer US$1.

$ Hanoi, Brasil (Teniente Rey) 507 y Bernaza, T7-8671029, open daily 1200-2400. Cuban food, 3 courses for US$6, *combinados* for US$2-3, *mojito* for US$2. Plenty of food although the meat tends to be reheated and the chicken dry, but the rice and beans are good and the garlic on the potatoes will keep away vampires, live music, nice atmosphere.

$ La Dichosa, Obispo esq Compostela. Good place for breakfast or a snack, US$2-4.

$ Panadería San José y Cafetería Santo Domingo, Obispo 161 entre San Ignacio y Mercaderes, T7-8609326, open 24 hrs. Bakery and café.

$ Pastelería Francés, between the Hotels Telégrafo and Inglaterra on the Prado. Smorgasbord of pastries and cakes in a peach-coloured dining room. Popular and some of the better cakes have gone by lunchtime. The hot *pan au chocolat* and *pan con pasas* (raisins) are particularly good.

Paladares

$$$ Don Lorenzo, Acosta 260A, entre Habana y Compostela, T7-8616733, daily 1200-2400. Not a cheap option with fish and meat dishes at US$15-18 and vegetarian options for US$12, but one of the most extensive menus, with over 50 dishes offered, all types of meat and fish with a huge variety of sauces, Basque-style, French-style, cider, fruity, almond etc, an entertaining night when its full.

$$ Doña Blanquita, Prado 158 entre Colón y Refugio. Run by English-speaking lawyer, simple but good food, pork, chicken or eggs, US$7-9, upstairs, inside with fan or on balcony if dry, neon sign.

$$ La Julia, O'Reilly 506A, T7-627438, daily 1200-2400. Traditional, poplular *paladar* with meals US$10, large portions, creole food, great rice and beans. Just a few tables so reserve or arrive early.

$$ La Moneda Cubana, San Ignacio 77 entre O'Reilly y Empedrado, T7-8673852, 1200-2300. Limited choice, good fish with

salad, beans and rice with fried banana, and usually good salads prepared for vegetarians. Menus for around US$8-10. More notable for the décor of wall-to-wall currency and business cards from all over the world.

Ice cream parlours

Cremería El Naranjal, Obispo esq Cuba, Habana Vieja, T7-8632430, daily 1000-2200. Various flavours, including natural fruits.

Soda Obispo, Obispo esq Villegas, Habana Vieja, T7-8620466, daily 0900-2100. Natural and artificial flavoured ice cream, also fruit cocktails.

Casablanca *p98*
Restaurants

$$$-$$ La Divina Pastora, Fortaleza de la Cabaña, T7-8608341, daily 1200-2300. Expensive, fish restaurant, food praised.

Centro *p99, map p88*
Restaurants

$$ Los Tres Chinitos, Dragones 355 entre Manrique y San Nicolás, T7-8633388. Combination Chinese restaurant and pizzeria, the former is open daily 1200-0100, the latter 1200-2400.

Paladares

$$$ La Guarida, Concordia 418 entre Gervasio y Escobar, T7-2644940, lunch daily 1200-1600, dinner 1900-2400 with reservation. Film location for *Fresa y Chocolate*, good food, fish a speciality, seafood and vegetarian paellas delicious, slow service, always busy, popular with US tourists, 'street guides' may not take you here because the owners do not pay commission to them.

$$$ La Tasquita, Jovellar (27 de Noviembre) entre Espada y San Francisco, T7-8734916, daily 1200-2400. Wonderful food and great atmosphere. Good for vegetarians with delicious sweet potato and Cuban fried eggs, served on mountains of rice and beans, plus good salads, run by Santiagüera Aralicia. Potent *mojitos*. No smoking.

$$ Bellomar, Virtudes 169A entre Industria y Amistad, T7-8610023, daily 1200-2300. Good fish and chicken dishes, generous salads, rice and beans, served in a fun, kitsch setting with friendly and obliging hosts.

Barrio Chino p99

At Zanja y Rayo, 1 block west of Galiano, there are several restaurants in a small street. Tables inside or outside, menus on view, you will be pestered for your custom. Do not expect authentic Chinese cuisine or you will be disappointed. Chop suey or chow mein is about the most Oriental you can get, 'sweet and sour' not recommended as it is very sweet and fruity. Spring rolls bear no relation to anything you might find in China. Meals around US$5-10. Food can be very good if there is water, if there is cooking gas and if there is any food – problems that affect all the restaurants around here. Lots of flies during the daytime. All prices in pesos or dollar equivalent, therefore very cheap.

Restaurants

$$-$ Tien Tan (Templo del Cielo), Cuchillo 17, entre Zanja y San Nicolás, T7-8615478, taoqi@enet.cu daily 1100-2400. Always full, chef from Shanghai, pesos or dollars accepted, cheapest dish US$0.60, most expensive around US$18.

$ El Flamboyán, Cuchillo de Zanja entre Zanja y San Nicolás, T7-8621490, Mon-Thu 1100-2400, Fri-Sun 1100-0300. Soup, main course, fried rice, dessert, drink and coffee for under US$10.

$ Sociedad Chang Weng Chung Tong, San Nicolás 517 entre Zanja y Dragones, T7-8621490, bar, café and restaurant, Mon-Wed 1200-2400, Thu-Sun 1200-0300. Part of the **Sociedad China de Cuba**, Chinese and *criollo* food.

$ Tong Po Laug, Cuchillo 10, www.geocities.com/tongpolaug daily 1200-2400. Cheap, pesos accepted. The most expensive dish is US$8 or peso equivalent, or you can have chop suey, fried rice, vegetables and salad for US$2, Cuban beer US$1, imported beer US$1.50.

Vedado p100, map p104
Restaurants

$$$ La Torre, 17 y M, at top of Edif Fosca, T7-8327306, daily 1200-2400, French chef, best French food in Havana, about US$40 per person but worth it, great views over Havana, a/c.

$$$ Polinesio, in the Habana Libre Hotel, with access from the street, daily 1200-2400. Smart, dark and cool, a mix of Chinese and Indonesian dishes, US$12-20, and the **Bar Turquino** on the 25th floor (spectacular views of Havana which makes the food acceptable, service bad). Cabaret 2230-0430. Bar daily 1030-0430.

$$$ Unión Francesa, 17 esq 6. Attractive colonial building, rooftop restaurant has good views, relaxed, nice atmosphere, photos of Fidel and Chirac, excellent wide menu, under US$25 per person including a beer. Live music.

$$$-$$ La Roca, 21 102 esq M, T7-334501, 1200-0200. Restored 1950s building with stained-glass windows dating from when it was a guest house. Sleek but stark dining room, international menu for a range of budgets, *croquetas de pollo* US$1.50, onion soup US$1.50, spaghetti carbonara US$2.50, plus more expensive dishes. Piano music while you eat. From 2230 there is a comedy show, US$3 including a cocktail, but this might change.

$$ El Conejito, M esq 17, T7-8324671, daily 1200-2400. Specializes in rabbit in several different styles and sauces, average US$6, with alternatives of chicken, pork or fish if you prefer, 24-hr bar attached which offers karaoke Thu-Sun 2000-0200.

$$-$ Casa de la Amistad, Paseo entre 17 y 19 (see p103), 1100-2300. Serves chicken, snacks and pizza. Inside the main building is **Restaurant Primavera**, daily 1200-2400, is more elegant and expensive with antique furniture and good table service.

$$-$ La Casona de 17, 17 60 entre M y N, T7-334529, daily 1200-2400. Elegant peach mansion with colonial terrace, once home to Castro's grandparents. House dish is *arroz con pollo a la chorrera*, US$3.50. Also good is *paella Casona*, at US$7.50, or there is always a half roast chicken (bit greasy) with bacon, rice'n'beans, chips and salad. Adjoining Argentine *parillada* serves up mixed grills. Nice for a relaxing lunch.

$ Cafetería La Rampa, Hotel Habana Libre, with access from the street as well as the hotel, open 24 hrs. Breakfast, sandwiches, pizza (US$3.50 plus toppings US$1-2) and pasta (US$2.20-6), burgers (US$4.50-6.50) and main meals.

$ Centro de Prensa Internacional, 23 2502 esq O. Basement bar open until 1900, good hamburgers for US$1, CNN news (Spanish) on TV, good place to wait your turn for email access upstairs.

$ Dinos Pizza, 23 y L in the same building as Cine Yara, open 24 hrs. Small and family-sized pizzas for US$1.40-5. Also beer, soft drinks, juices and ice cream.

$ Pekín, 23 1221 esq 12, close to Cementerio Colón, T7-8334020, daily 1200-2200. A great choice for vegetarians, this peso restaurant serves over 50 vegetable dishes on a buffet-style spread. Aubergines stuffed with soya, vegetable paella, lasagne, salads, stir fries, juices and soups etc. You can fill a couple of trays for less than 40 pesos. Unfortunately there are usually huge queues and slow service, the food is cold, tepid at best and the selection usually shrinks by closing time. The best branch is on Calzada entre D y E, in the loveliest area of Vedado, with pleasant outdoor seating, great views of Teatro Amadeo Roldán, and smaller queues.

$ Trattoria Marakas, O entre 23 y 25, part of St John's Hotel, with separate entrance on the street, T7-333740, daily 1200-2345. Good Italian, even has mozzarella and olive oil, pizzas US$3.95-6.50, pasta US$4.25-5.50, peppermint green decor, canteen-style, uncomfortable plastic furniture.

Paladares

$$$ Adela, Calle F 503 entre 21 y 23, T7-8323776. Call ahead for opening hours. Adela is an artist and this *paladar*, though legal, is primarily an art gallery. Clients come to buy art and stay to eat. Appetisers include cinnamon-baked bananas, fried malanga, corn and chorizo stew and others, although the choice of main course is limited. Prices around US$20-25 per person.

$$$ Hurón Azul, Humboldt 153 esq P, T7-8791691, daily Tue-Sun 1200-2400. Traditional Cuban food with unusual sauces and Mediterranean influences, try the chicken in mustard sauce or fish stuffed with tuna, olives, peppers and tomato, a/c.

$$ Amor, 23 759 entre B y C, daily 1200-2400, T7-8338150. Reopened end-2003 after extended closure. Welcoming atmosphere, large eating area with elegant furniture, great food, good portions, fried chicken, peanut sauce, rice and beans, salad and beer for US$10. Try and go on the first Sun in the month for the musical gathering on the rooftop. Local artists perform, great fun, entrance by donation to the local hospital.

$$ Gringo Viejo, 21 454 entre E y F, T7-8311946, daily 1200-2300. Nice atmosphere with wall-to-wall cinema memorabilia, good portions, main course of fish, chicken and pork with fruity or spicy sauces accompanied by rice, beans and salad average US$8.50, maximum US$10.

$$ Le Chansonnier, J 257 entre 15 y Línea, T7-8321576, daily 1900-2400. Very personal service from Hector and his mother in a pink colonial mansion and all the silver service trimmings. Some sauces are a little rich and greasy, but redeemed by the bountiful fruit and vegetable salad. All main courses, served with fries and rice are US$10.

$$ Los Amigos, M entre 19 y 21, opposite Victoria, T7-8300880, daily 1200-2400. Good, US$12 including drinks but check your bill. Convenient location for après-dining entertainment, popular with locals and ex-pats, dining among Christmas decorations, religious artefacts and wind chimes.

$$ Nerei, 19 110 esq L, T7-8327860, daily 1300-2400. Good food, main courses include lamb with pepper, chicken and beer, turkey with wine and grilled squid average US$11 with salad and rice, tables outside on the veranda, English spoken.

$ El Helecho, 6 203 entre Línea y 11, T7-8313552, daily Wed-Mon 1200-2230. One of the few *paladares* still charging in *moneda nacional*, straightforward Cuban food served in dining room at the front of the house, main dishes with *congrí* and salad range from 117-208 pesos.

Ice cream parlours

Coppelia, 23 y L, Vedado, Tue-Sun 1100-2230. A visit to the most famous ice cream parlour in Cuba is recommended, see also p102. With a capacity for 707 seated ice cream lovers, there are several separate outdoor areas to eat in, each with their own entrance and queue in the surrounding streets, or inside in La Torre. Extremely popular with Cuban families. If you pay in pesos, you will almost certainly have to queue for an hour or so, particularly at weekends, not unpleasant as the design is integral with the characteristic *copey* trees, which provide plenty of shade. A dedicated attendant (brown uniform) controls the queue and directs you into the seating area as tables become free. Alternatively, pay in dollars to avoid the queue, in the upstairs section or the

⣿ Mojito

Every barman makes a slightly different *Mojito*, some are sweeter than others, but all are refreshing, and light enough to drink at any time of day. Since the 1920s, the place to drink a *Mojito* is the **Bodeguita del Medio** in Havana, surrounded by graffiti through the ages; imagine yourself rubbing shoulders with the likes of Ernest Hemingway, the most famous boozer of them all. To make a *Mojito* yourself, put half a tablespoon of sugar, the juice of half a lime and some lightly crushed mint leaves in a tall glass. Stir and mix well, then add some soda water, ice cubes, 1½ oz light dry rum and top up with soda water. Serve with a garnish of mint leaves and, of course, a straw.

Fuente de Soda kiosks outside (said to be open 24 hrs but often closed after midnight). Bring your own plastic spoons for the tubs as they invariably run out. US$2 for small portion, many different flavours, depending on availability (chocolate is still the top flavour), and styles (all come with a glass of water): *ensalada* (mixture of flavours), *jimaguas* (twins), *tres gracias*. After devouring your first choice you can stay and order a second portion without queuing. Alternatively, sample the **Coppelia** ice cream in the tourist hotels and restaurants and some dollar food stores. Another ice cream shop is **Bim Bom**, 23 y Calzada de Infanta, Vedado, while several street stalls specialize in ice cream (*helado*), 21 esquina K, near to **Coppelia** but no queues, 3 pesos per cone.

Miramar *p106, map p108*
Restaurants
$$$**El Tocororo** (national bird of Cuba), 18 302 esq Av 3, T7-2042209, Mon-Sat 1200-2400, bar 1400-0200. Excellent food at US$40-60 a head, old colonial mansion with nice terrace, great house band, no menu, ostrich steak, prices fluctuate widely but one of the best restaurants in town.
$$$**La Cecilia**, 5 entre 110 y 112, T7-2041562, daily 1200-2400. Good international food, mostly in an open-air setting. Thu-Sun features live bolero and salsa bands 2200-0300 with dancing outside, US$20 cover charge.
$$$-$$**1830**, 7 1252 entre 20 y 22, T7-553091, daily 1200-2400. High-class dining with cabaret shows from 2200 and local bands in a wonderful setting at the mouth of the Río Almendares. French and Cuban cuisine, from US$12.50 for fish with

lime and capers, to US$16.25 for tenderloin with blue cheese sauce and lobster at US$36.
$$$-$$**La Ferminia**, 5 18207 entre 182 y 184, T7-336555, daily 1200-2400. A beautiful neoclassical residence with an elegant atmosphere. Training school for chefs with varied cuisine, good for vegetarians or carnivores, vegetable pies, pasta and buffet, or *churrasquería* with skewers of Uruguayan beef, chips and rice for US$12.95.
$$**El Aljibe**, 7 entre 24 y 26, T7-2041583, daily 1200-2400. Originally opened in 1947 as *Rancho Luna*, drawing 50's movie stars like Eva Gardner and Errol Flynn with its secret recipe for roast chicken. Following the Revolution the restaurant closed in 1961, but reopened again as El Aljibe by state-run **Cubanacán** in 1993 and the original owner Sergio García Maciás began to bring his famed *pollo al Aljibe* to a new generation of movie stars, including Jack Nicholson, Steven Spielberg and Danny Glover. Open, breezy, framework design and friendly atmosphere. Generous portions of delicious black beans, rice, fried potatoes and salad, with more if you want, US$12 per person.

Paladares
$$**Calle 10**, 10 314 entre 3 y 5, near Teatro Karl Marx, T7-2096702, daily 1200-2400. Mansion setting, outdoor seating with open-air grill and tiki bar. Specials include *ropa vieja* (shredded beef), plenty of pork dishes and a good salad Niçoise. Attentive service, upbeat atmosphere, English spoken, main course plus beer US$10.50.
$$**El Palio**, Av 1 entre 24 y 26. Open air, Italian, fresh fish with choice of creative sauces, although portions can be rather small and atmosphere lacking.

$$ La Cocina de Liliam, 48 1311, entre 13 y 15, T7-2096514, Sun-Fri 1200-1500, 1900-2200, closed 2 weeks in Aug, 2 weeks in Dec. Very good, imaginative Cuban food with tables outside in a lovely garden. Great appetizers and fresh fish and crab dishes. Popular with locals, reservations recommended, main course plus beer US$12, excellent service.

$$ La Esperanza, 16 105 entre 1 y 3, T7-2024361, 1900-2330, closed Sun. Small sign, very popular with Cubans and foreigners, traditional food, meal and drinks around US$15 per person, reservations advisable, run by Hubert and Manolo in their inviting living room surrounded by their paintings and antiques.

$$ La Fontana, 3-A 305 esq 46, T7-2028337, daily 1200-2400. Good Cuban food, extremely popular with Cubans, tourists and diplomats, ask for the *menu de la casa* for non-inflated prices, under US$15, arrive early or make a reservation, essential at night.

$$ Mi Jardín, 66 517 esq Av 5B, T7-2034627. Good Mexican and Italian food, under US$15.

The suburbs *p107*
Restaurants

$$$-$$ El Rancho Palco (Cubanacán), Av 19 y 140, Playa, T7-2089346, daily 1200-2300. Set in lovely jungle garden near the Palacio de las Convenciones, very popular with ex-pats for its Argentine steaks, good barbecued chicken, meats, typical *criollo* cuisine and international food, expensive, good live music provided by a quartet.

$$-$ Palenque, beside Expocuba pavillions 17 y 190, Siboney. Cheap, good food, speciality suckling pig US$6, open air, popular with locals and ex-pats. At Marianao beach there are also some cheaper bars and restaurants.

$$$-$$ Los XII Apóstoles, in the Morro-Cabaña complex, T7-8638295, daily 1230-2300. Fish and good *criollo* food, good views of the Malecón. Outdoor daily 2100-0200, US$5 per couple including one drink.

Boyeros *p108*
Restaurants

$ La Casa del Dragón, Cortina de la Presa y 100, off the main road to the right soon after entrance from Arroyo Naranjo, look for the sign, T7-443026 ext 176, Tue-Sun 1200-2000. Chinese, only 4 tables, bamboo furniture, good food, reasonable prices, spring roll, sweet and sour pork, rice and salad US$6, beer US$0.85, nice walks nearby.

Fast food outlets

$ El Rodeo, roundabout opposite Ciudad Deportiva, Rancho Boyeros y Vía Blanca, open 24 hrs. Large, loud, popular snack bar, good place to head after a sports match.

Parque Lenín *p109*
Restaurants

$$$ Las Ruinas, 100 esq Cortina de la Presa in Parque Lenín, T7-443336, daily 1200-2400. One of the best restaurants in Havana, the ruined plantation house has been incorporated into a modern structure. There's a great resident pianist, but watch out for mosquitoes at dusk. Tours of Parque Lenín often include a meal at Las Ruinas, otherwise you'll have to take a taxi, US$15, but try to persuade the driver to come back and fetch you, as it is difficult to get back into town.

🍸 Bars

Ordinary bars not on the tourist circuit will charge you in dollars, if they let foreigners in at all. If it is a local bar and the Cubans are all paying in pesos, you will have to pay in US dollars. Even so, the prices in most places are not high by Caribbean standards. You will find musicians in most bars. Have a ready supply of small change. Many play only 3 or 4 songs, then come round with the collecting bowl trying to sell their CDs, and move on, to be replaced by another band who do the same thing, adding quite a premium to your evening beer or cocktail.

La Habana Vieja *p87, map pp88, 112, 114*
Bar Dos Hermanos, Av del Puerto esq Sol, opposite the ferry terminals, T7-8613514, daily 0800-2400. Good, down to earth bar, bohemian atmosphere, popular with Cubans, just off the tourist circuit so lower prices, local *son* band usually blast off after 2300, ask the barman who's playing.

Bar El Louvre, Hotel Inglaterra, Prado 416, Parque Central, T7-8608595. A pleasant place for an outdoor evening drink, where you can watch the sun going down catching the newly clean cream of the Museo de Bellas Artes through the Royal palms. Roving live musicians who don't stay long and expect a generous tip, making your excellent US$2 daiquirí rather pricey. Very slow service.

Bar Monserrate, Monserrate y Obrapía, daily 1100-2400. Beer US$1.50, *mojito* US$2.50, plenty of flavour but not very generous shots of rum, hot dogs US$2.50, filling meal featuring unidentifiable meat in breadcrumbs US$6.50, interesting to sit and watch comings and goings, high level of prostitutes/*jineteras*, although bar staff seem to have unwritten agreement whereby girls are allowed in with a foreigner, or if they buy a drink, but if girl to punters ratio gets too high, some of the girls have to leave, hustling is not excessive though.

Bilbao, O'Reilly entre Cuba y Aguiar. A shrine to Atlético Bilbao. An earthy bar off the main drag. You pay in pesos but at tourist dollar equivalent. Go for the experience.

Café de París, Obispo 202 esq San Ignacio, daily 0800-2400. Predominantly tourist clientele but good location for people watching as long as you can fend off the *jineteros*. Cocktails from US$3 and barmen often bring you another even if you haven't ordered one. Live music 1200-1500, 2000-2400 except Thu.

Café O'Reilly, O'Reilly 203 entre Cuba y San Ignacio, daily 1000-2400. Tour groups are often taken here for a *mojito*, pleasant leafy, upstairs with balcony.

Casa del Escabeche, Obispo esq Villegas, T7-8632660, daily 0800-2400. Tiny bar but popular and welcoming, as well as very cheap, house quartet from 1200, cocktails US$1-1.50, *Cristal* beer US$0.90, *Bucanero* US$0.80, imported beer US$1.15.

El Castillo de Farnés, Monserrate 361 esq Obrapía, T7-8671030, see Eating above.

Restaurant at the back 1200-2400, lively bar open 24 hrs, serves snacks and breakfast.

El Floridita, see Eating above. A favourite with tour groups for a mid-morning daiquirí.

La Bodeguita del Medio, see Eating above. The bar not to miss in the old town for Hemingway fans.

Lluvia de Oro, Obispo esq Habana, open 24 hrs in winter, 1000-2400 in summer when there is no music. Good place to drink rum and listen to loud rock music or salsa, food is also served.

Mirador de la Bahía, Obispo 61 entre Oficios y Baratillo, T7-8613652, daily 1200-2400. A sun-trap by day on the roof terrace of the Natural History Museum, great views of La Habana Vieja, and the ceremonial cannon firing from across the water at 2100. Good cocktails, but overpriced snacks and meals.

Museo del Ron, Av del Puerto 262 entre Sol y Muralla, T7-8618051. As well as the Rum Museum, daily 0900-1730, there is also a shop selling Havana Club souvenirs, an art gallery 0900-1730, a courtyard restaurant and 2 bars, 1 with nightly music, 0900-2400. Serves good *Cuba Libre* and sometimes showcases quality live bands.

Centro *p99, map p88*

Palermo, San Miguel y Amistad, T7-8619745, daily 1200-2400. Bar-cafetería serving chicken, sandwiches, steak and pork. Local beer 10 pesos, Cristal or Bucanero US$0.90, imported beer US$1.15-1.50. Taped music and TV with video.

Vedado *p100, map p104*

Casa de la Amistad, Paseo 406 (see above), bar with a beautiful garden extension, tasty cheap light meals optional, very peaceful surroundings.

Casa de las Infusiones, 23 y G, Vedado, open 24 hrs. Very cosy, lots of plants, an ideal place to read or talk.

⊙ Entertainment

Cabaret

La Habana Vieja *p87, map pp88, 112, 114*
Cabaret Nacional, San Rafael y Prado, entrance to the side of Gran Teatro,

T7-8630736. A cheap version of the Tropicana, see below, daily cabaret shows 2100-0200, US$5 entry but expensive drinks. Lots of prostitutes. Also traditional music *peñas* Wed, Fri, Sat 1500-1930, US$3, and rock *peña* on Sun.

Centro *p99, map p88*

La Terraza, Hotel Lincoln, Virtudes 164 esq Galiano, Centro Habana, T7-8628061, daily 2100-2400, Fri and Sat until 0200, US$1. Rooftop club with great views, low prices means it is a popular venue for Cubans, live show at weekends.

Vedado *p100, map p104*

Cabaret Las Vegas, Calzada de Infanta 104, T7-8707939, daily 2200-0500. Minor salsa bands, entrance US$5, hot and raw.

Copa Room, at the Habana Riviera, Paseo y Malecón, T7-334051 for reservation. Recently refurbished and has gone back to its pre-Revolution name (formerly *Palacio de la Salsa*). Traditional music including the boleros of Benny Moré. Glitzy Cuban cabaret *A lo Riviera*, skimpy outfits and sequins, Mon, Wed and Thu 2030-2430, show followed by taped music Fri, Sat, Sun, 2030-0300, show followed by salsa band, US$25 including cocktail, meal from US$50 per person.

Parisien, at Hotel Nacional, T7-333564/7, daily 2100-0230. Excellent show for US$35, lasts longer than **Tropicana** and of equivalent standard, make a reservation.

Salón Rojo, Hotel Caprí, 21 entre N y O, T7-333747. US$20 including drinks. Newly renovated luxury restaurant and cabaret, **Tropicana**-style show with disco afterwards for dancing until 0300. The *Caprí* was Meyer Lansky and Lucky Luciano's turf in the days of the Mafia wheeling and dealing in the 1950s. Scenes from the *Godfather II* were filmed here.

Turquino, at Hotel Habana Libre, 25th floor, T7-334011, daily 2230-0300, US$15, cabarets start at 2300 and 0100. Great setting with amazing views. The roof opens and you can dance under the stars. Expensive drinks at US$6. Unaccompanied males are likely to be fleeced as soon as they walk through the door.

The suburbs *p107*

Tropicana, 72 4504 entre 43 y 45, Marianao, T7-2670110, daily 2030 until everyone stops dancing some time after midnight. Reservations 1200-1600. Internationally famous and open air (entry refunded if it rains). Prices vary and there are good deals around. Best to take a tour, which will include transport, as a taxi from La Habana

Vieja costs US$12. **Rumbos** offers 3 prices: US$65, US$75 and US$85, depending on location of seat and whether you drink 3-, 5- or 7-year old *Havana Club*. Transport, a snack or dinner can be added. If you fancy a cheap drink or snack go to **Rodneys**, daily 1200-0100, a pseudo 1950s bar and restaurant designed by Cuban painter, Nelson Domínguez, just beyond the entrance to the show.

Cinemas

Comprehensive weekly listings of all films from Thu-Wed posted in cinema windows. Most have a/c. **Annual Film Festival** in Dec (overlaps with Jazz Festival, above) in all cinemas. International films, no translations into English. Information in **Hotel Nacional**.

La Habana Vieja *p87, map pp88, 112, 114*

Payret, Prado 513, esquina San José, T7-8633163. Films continuously from 1230.

Vedado *p100, map p104*

Acapulco, 26 entre 35 y 37, Nuevo Vedado, T7-8339573, from 1630.

Chaplin, 23 1155 entre 10 y 12, T7-8311101. Arty films at 1700 and 2000, shop good for film memorabilia.

La Rampa, 23 111 esq O, T7-8786146. 2 films from 1630, dodgy toilets.

Riviera, 23 507 entre Av de los Presidentes y H, Vedado, T7-8309564.

Yara, L 363, opposite Habana Libre hotel, T7-8329430. From 1230, late weekend showings, 2 video lounges show recent US releases, but sound quality is sometimes poor in Salon B. Often sold out at weekends.

Dance

Gran Teatro de la Habana, Prado y San José, Parque Central, T7-8613078, dir.gth@cubarte.cult.cu US$10. Opened in 1838, this wonderful baroque building, which seats 1,500 with 2 galleries, has seen countless famous performers on its stage. The **Cuban National Ballet** and **Opera** companies perform here in the Sala García Lorca. The **Conjunto Folklórico Nacional** and **Danza Contemporánea** dance companies sometimes perform here. It also hosts the **International Ballet Festival**.

Dancing lessons

Casa del Tango, Neptuno 309 entre Galiano y Aguila, T7-8630097. Tango dance classes at 1600. The **Escuela Danzamor** also operates out of here. Ask for **Adelaída and Wilki**, Lázaro and Moraima, Aguiar 361 apto 5, 4th floor, entre Obispo y Obrapía, T7-8638835. There are several people who give salsa and other dancing lessons.

Jazz

See also Live music venues below which often feature jazz sessions.

Vedado *p100*
All jazz venues are in Vedado. During the annual Jazz Festival in Dec you can hear international as well as Cuban stars, free or US$5-10 per show, based at **Hotel Riviera** but in the 2 weeks before there are also events at the **Nacional** and the **Habana Libre**. Information from the **Instituto de la Música**, 15 452 entre E y F, T7-323503-6, ask for schedule from Rita Rosa. Fri nights at **Meliá Cohiba** from 2100. **Hotel Riviera** sometimes features jazz sessions in the bar off the lobby, entrance after Copa Room, recommended, but phone first to check listing.
Jazz Café, Galerías del Paseo esq 1, T7-553302, 1200-0200. US$10 *consumo mínimo*. Sleek and savvy venue with class acts, a laid-back welcoming ambience and a highly appreciative audience. Star-studded line-up includes legendary pianist Chucho Valdés. Excellent for jazz lovers.
La Zorra y el Cuervo, 23 y O, T7-662402, daily 2130-0200, US$10 (US$5 *consumo mínimo*). The fox and the crow is one of the best nights in Havana for jazz enthusiasts. The small cellar space on La Rampa is entered through a fine reproduction red British telephone box. High-calibre jazz musicians playing to an appreciative crowd. Get there before 2300 if you want a table with an unobscured view of the stage. Cuban bands often feature visiting US musicians.

Live music and dance venues

See also Jazz above. Havana clubs are late night/early morning affairs with most Cubans arriving around midnight and staying late. Expect queues at the weekends. Cubans dress up for club nights and most clubs have a smart dress code, strictly enforced by the door staff. This includes no shorts or sleeveless T-shirts for men. No one under 18 is admitted. The emphasis is on dancing, be it salsa and Latin dance styles, R and B, hip hop or rock. Many places are frequented by *jineteros/as* and lone travellers have reported feeling uncomfortable with the unwelcome attention. Several venues now feature earlier shows, aimed at young Cubans, with entrance in pesos.

Radio Taíno FM 93.3, English- and Spanish-language tourist station, gives regular details of a wide range of venues and Cuban bands playing, particularly in the programme *El Exitazo Musical del Caribe*, daily 1500-1800 presented by Alexis Nargona. Also **Radio Ciudad de la Habana**, 94.9 FM, 820 AM, in Spanish. Up-to-the-minute salsa programmes, *Disco Fiesta 98*, Mon-Sat 1100-1300, provides accurate information about musical events in Havana, *Rapsodia Latina*, Mon-Fri 1630-1730. The newspaper, **Opciones**, also has a listing of what's on and **Cartelera**, available free of charge every Thu, is found at most hotel reception desks.

La Habana Vieja *p87, map pp88, 112, 114*
Casa de Cultura de Habana Vieja, Aguiar entre Amargura y Teniente Rey, T7-8634860. Vibrant and welcoming cultural centre with varied programme. Rumba by *Tambor Llévame Contigo* on the 2nd and 4th Sat of the month 1800-2000, free, *Sonora Habana* every Wed 2000-2300, 40 pesos, *Descarga en Casa* 1st and 3rd Sun 1700-2000 free, *Con Té Teatro* last Sun 1900-2100, free, *Peña Chapotín y sus Estrellas* (*son*), every Fri 2100-2400, 40 pesos.

Centro *p99, map p88*
Callejón de Hamel, Hamel entre Aramburu y Hospital, Centro Habana. A fast, kicking *rumba* show with invited guests and community artists every Sun 1200-1600, a responsive audience and electric jam sessions make this a hot venue, recommended (see Music in Havana, p129). Take lots of sun screen and water. Rum and honey for sale US$2.
Casa de la Cultura del Centro Habana, Av Salvador Allende 720 entre Soledad y Castillejo, T7-8784727, borysmundo@yahoo.com for

details or call ahead. Hours vary according to schedule of events. Extensive programme from blasting rock on the 1st Sun of the month from 1500 to sedate *peñas campesinas* on Sat from 2100, and on the 4th Sun of the month from 1500 frenetic rap and hip hop threaten to bring the house down.

Casa de la Música Galiano, Galiano 255 esq Neptuno, T7-8624165, cmh-eco@egrem.cult.cu Music shop, restaurant and dance floor with popular bands. Daily matinée 1600-2000, US$5, beer US$1, *mojito* US$1.50, evening performances 2200-0300, US$10-25, beer US$2.50, *mojito* US$3.50.

Casa de la Trova, San Lázaro, entre Belascoaín y Gervasio, T7-8793373, Thu-Sun 1900-2200. Where locals go to hear traditional Cuban music, US$5, thoroughly recommended.

Casa del Tango Edmundo Daubar, Neptuno 309 entre Aguila y Italia, T7-8630097. Musical venue/museum with fascinating collection of tango memorabilia dating back to the 1940s, from record sleeves to all manner of Carlos Gardel idolatry.

La Madriguera, Quinta de los Molinos entre Av Infanta y Salvador, entrance on Jesús Peregrino (Final), after crossing over Infanta. T7-8798175. This is the **Casa del Joven Creador de Ciudad Habana** and the headquarters of the **Asociación Hermanos Saíz in Centro**, with arts, crafts and musical workshops for all ages and talents. Hip hop, rap, rumba and more traditional Cuban rhythms are all here; fascinating glimpse into Cuban youth culture. Mon-Sat 1800-2400, although best Thu-Sat. The 1st Sat of the month from 2000 there is a '*Narración Oral Escénica, Poesía, Trova*', free. On the 2nd Fri '*Obsesión por el hip-hop*' (*Peña de Rap*), from 2000, 5 pesos. On the 3rd Fri from 2000, '*Peña de Rock*', 5 pesos. On the last Fri, '*El Viernazo*' (*Peña de Trova*) from 2000, 5 pesos. On the 1st Fri and 3rd Sat a '*Peña de Literatura*' from 2000, free. Cocktails for sale during *peñas* but no beer. There is also a gallery with various art exhibitions, daily 0800-1700, and also open when there are *peñas*, and special events and fiestas throughout the year.

Palermo, San Miguel y Amistad, Sun-Fro 2100-0300, Sat 2100-0400, US$2. Cabaret show from 2400 every night with weekend showcase feature of *Odelquis Revé y su Changüí*, followed by salsa disco.

Vedado *p100, map p104*

Café Cantante, Teatro Nacional, Plaza de la Revolución, Paseo y 39, T7-8796011, daily 2200-0330, US$5, US$10 or US$15 depending on who is performing, matinées Tue-Sun 1600-2000, US$5. Highly regarded venue, top bands play here, popular with local musicians and others in the business. Start your night in *El Delirio*, see below, then head down to the basement for the last hour of *Café Cantante* (the doorman may let you in with no charge at this late hour). Matinées are particularly popular with Cuban youth.

Café El Gato Tuerto (the one-eyed cat), O entre 17 y 19, T7-552696/662224. *Consumo mínimo* US$5, *Son*, *trova* and boleros performed 2400-0300. Bohemian people and post-modern decor, funky bordering on pretentious, local legends often perform here, *filín* and boleros, intimate stage with audience participation encouraged.

Casa de la Amistad, Paseo 406 entre 17 y 19, T7-8303114 (see above). US$3 admission plus US$2 *consumo mínimo*, US$5 for *Noche Chan Chan* or *Noche Cubana*. One of the best settings for listening to great traditional music with a welcoming atmosphere. A traditional *son* group, *La Peña del Chan Chan*, plays every Tue at 2100. Sat feature more up-tempo salsa and bolero groups. Dancing on the veranda afterwards or in the gardens, Tue until 2400 and Sat to 0200. Thu is *trova* night from 1800 and Sat is *Noche Cubana* with *son* and *guaracha*. A good tourist to Cuban mix and soliciting is rare. Very limited toilet facilities.

Centro de Música Ignacio Piñeiro, 17 y K, Vedado. The last Fri of every month, showcases new local salsa bands, young and very energetic crowd.

Cine Riviera, 23 entre G y H, Vedado, T7-8309564, 1900-2300. 3rd Fri of each month the cinema is given over to a live music event with an ecological theme, Cuban reggae and jazz bands, young, friendly and relaxed, mostly Cuban crowd. 5 pesos.

Club Atelier, 17 esq 6, corner of Parque John Lennon, every night 2200-0400. Small L-shaped dance floor, pool table, beer US$1.50, various house styles from salsa to rap, US$5.

El Delirio Habanero, Teatro Nacional, Plaza de la Revolución, Paseo y 39, T7-8735713. Piano bar upstairs on the 5th floor (lift sometimes not working) where you can hear quality music, *nueva trova*, bolero, etc, US$10

▪ Music in Havana

Havana is buzzing with musical activity. Rumba, conga, son, danzón, charanga, salsa – you'll hear it all, as Cuba's greatest musicians converge on the capital. This is the place to be if you want to hear Cuba's established artists – *Los Van Van, Sierra Maestra, NG La Banda, La Charanga Habanera, Isaac Delgado, Buena Vista stars* – all regularly liven up the theatres, hotels and parks. You might even get to wave a flag at Silvio, Sara or Pablito if the UJC are holding a rally in the Plaza de la Revolución.

Havana offers more than star quality, however. Fancy a conga? The revived carnival parade is in November. Many of the *comparsa congas* parade regularly throughout the year down Paseo Martí and through La Habana Vieja, and a newly established Christmas Day parade gives you another chance to go wild with the *farolas* and *tambores*. A rumba? The unmissable *Sábados de La Rumba* are held Saturdays 1500-1700, by the **Grupo**

Folclórico Nacional at Calle 4 entre 5 y 7 in Vedado, you can *Guaguancó* with some of the best drummers and dancers in the land. There is also an outdoor rumba venue at **Callejón de Hamel**, where the action takes place around 1200-1500 on Sundays.

You might want to practise your *son* – there are plenty of willing partners at the **Casa 10 de Octubre** (Calzada de Luyanó entre Reforma y Guasabacoa, Santos Suárez, south of Cerro), where the *septetos* turn back the clock to the Havana of the 1920s. More up to date sounds can be heard at the annual Jazz Plaza festival in December, where Cuba's finest join forces with international stars for a world class event. You can peruse Cuba's musical history at the **Museo Nacional de la Música** (see page 91). For a real history lesson, don't miss the ancient *Orquesta Típica* playing old *Danzones* with gusto in the Plaza de la Catedral. None of the band looks a day over 80.

consumo mínimo, daily 2200-0600, matinées on Sun 1600-2000. Resident band *Los Tres Habaneros* Thu and Sat for salsa. Rumba *peña* Sun 1600-2000. Great views of floodlit José Martí monument and Plaza de la Revolución. Take the big red sofa seats under the windows. Busy at weekends with a mostly Cuban crowd, phone to reserve the best tables. Delicious cocktails, good-value snacks, attentive service. Recommended, energetic clubbers leave here and head for the sweaty *Café Cantante* (see above) in the basement for the last hour. Downstairs in the theatre there are live concerts such as a *Nueva Trova* show.
El Gran Palenque Bar, 4 entre Calzada y 5, T7-339075. On Sat at 1500-1700 the courtyard of this open-air café/bar is taken over by the acclaimed Conjunto Folclórico Nacional de Cuba for an upbeat rumba show: *Patio de la Rumba*. US$5.

El Pico Blanco, Hotel St John, O 206 entre 23 y 25, T7-333740, daily 2200-0300. Spectacular rooftop setting but predictable variety show of comedy followed by salsa disco. US$10 for open bar. At the weekend there is a show in the Restaurant La Plaza called *Café Concierto* 2230-0200, US$5 (US$3 *consumo mínimo*), with karaoke, comedy and recorded music.
Habana Café, in the Meliá Cohiba, Paseo entre 1 y 3, T7-333636. Very touristy and largely frequented by Meliá guests. A 1950s American pastiche, which has replaced the bombed-out disco. Old cars, small Cubana plane hanging from the ceiling, memorabilia on the walls, Benny Moré music and large screen showing brilliant film of old Cuban musicians and artistes. Food expensive and meals not recommended, overpriced cocktails US$6. US$10 minimum entry fee for show at 2100, Thu-Sat live bands, US$15, 1 Sun a month US$15 to see Pablo Milanés.

Hurón Azul, 17 351 entre Av de los Presidentes y H, T7-8324571. The headquarters of UNEAC (artists' and writers' union) in a majestic, colonial mansion. An inviting intelligentsia hang-out, the lovely, welcoming bar hosts regular upbeat afternoon *peñas*. Wed alternate between *Trova sin Traba* and *Peña del Ambia* 1700-2000. Sat bolero 2100-0100.

Imágenes, Calzada 602 esq C, T7-333606, daily 2130-0300 with musical comedy show at 2400 Tue-Sun. US$5 includes 1 drink. Cocktails US$2-2.50. Intimate, classy piano bar, great for low-key evening. Local pianist Mario Romeu, also karaoke, salsa disco and *nuevo imagen*, a showcase for new talent.

Las Bulerías, L entre 23 y 25, T7-8323283, daily 1200-0200. Tapas bar serving glow-in-the-dark chorizo, spongy tortilla and gnarled ham. From 2300-0200 karaoke during the week, salsa disco at weekends.

Sherezada, Edificio Focsa, M y 19, next to Teatro Guiñol, T7-323042, open 24 hrs. Disco and show, US$2.50.

Tikoa, 23 entre N y O, T7-8309973, 2100-0200. Live music and karaoke, US$2, Mon-Thu live singer, Fri, Sat *Salsa Mi Son*, weekend matinées 1600-1900 US$1. Popular with travellers and locals, this small and sweaty basement club swings with a strong Afro-Cuban vibe.

Miramar *p106, map p108*
Casa de la Música Egrem, Sala Té Quedarás, 20 3308 esq 35, T7-2040447. CD shop daily 1030-2400. One of the top venues to listen to the cream of Havana's musical talent. Tue-Sun live music with important bands 2200-0330, US$15, normally *Adalberto y Su Son* play Wed, *NG La Banda* play Fri when in Cuba. Other bands cost US$10. Upstairs at the *Diablo Tun Tun* traditional music is played by small groups daily 2300-0600, US$10. Matinées Mon 1600-2100, Tue-Sun 1600-2000, US$5. Food service from the *parrilla* daily 1200-2400.

Club Almendares, Márgenes del Río Almendares, 49 y Av 28, Kohly, Miramar, T7-2044990. The Salón Chévere (*Disco Temba*), daily 2200-0300, US$10 with open bar, all types of music. At the swimming pool Fri, Sat, Sun 2300-0300, there is a live show called a *Noche Cubana*, US$5, mosquitoes can be troublesome as you are in the Bosque de la Habana.

El Río Club, A entre 3 y 5, T7-2093389. Locals still refer to it as *Johnnie's Club*, its previous name before the Revolution. Salsa disco, hot and sweaty dance floor, current favourite with Havana's dance crowd.

La Macumba, 222 esq 37, La Coronela in La Giraldilla tourist complex, T7-330568. Variable programme, Sun-Wed recorded music, fashion shows, karaoke and dancing 2200-0400 US$10, Thu-Sat 2200-0400 US$15, live bands play only Thu. Top Havana nightspot, open-air disco with two large dance floors for Latin and R&B, popular with Cubans and foreigners.

Salón Boleros en Dos Gardenias, 7 esq 26, Miramar, T7-2042353, daily 2200-0300, US$5. Upmarket *bolero* venue, 4-5 live shows every night, elegant, well-dressed crowd with popular Chinese restaurant and bar.

Salón Rosado Benny Moré, La Tropical, 41 y 46, T7-2061281. Raunchy, popular dance venue with some of the best salsa in town but under renovation at end 2003.

Theatres

All productions are performed in Spanish. Tourists pay in dollars, 1 peso = US$1.

Vedado *p100, map p104*
Amadeo Roldán, Calzada y D, T7-8321168. The fabulously renovated concert hall, Sala Caturla, is where you can hear the **Orquesta Sinfónica Nacional** as well as visiting international symphony orchestras, including several from the USA. **Opus** bar is open daily 1500-0300.

Sala Hubert de Blanck, Calzada 654 entre A y B, T7-8335962. Specializes in classical and contemporary music concerts but has also staged major works by García Lorca and Cuban playwright Abelardo Estorino, and contemporary dance companies, **Danzabierta** and **Danza Contemporánea**.

Teatro El Sótano, K 514 entre 25 y 27, T7-8320630. Shows contemporary drama, somewhere to find fringe theatre and home of the **Rita Montaner Company**.

Teatro Guiñol, M entre 17 y 19, T7-8326262. A children's theatre that specializes in marionette shows.

Teatro Mella, Línea 657 entre A y B, T7-8335651. 8-10 pesos, depending on seat. Specializes in modern dance but stages lots of other drama performances as well. **Galería**

Tina Modotti bar, daily 1800-2200, also a garden where you can eat, daily 1000-2200. **Teatro Nacional de Cuba**, Paseo y 39, T7-8735713. There's always lots going on here: concerts in the theatre downstairs, a piano bar, **El Delirio Habanero** and in the basement is the **Café Cantante**, see above. **Teatro Trianón**, Línea entre Paseo y A, Vedado, T7-8309648. Part cinema, part theatre. Small and in good condition.

The seats have quirky pull-out extensions for you to rest your thighs on.

Miramar *p106, map p108*
Teatro Karl Marx, Av 1 1010 entre 8 y 10, T7-2030801, T7-2091991. Renovated in 2000 and now famous for hosting the first rock concert by a Western band, Manic Street Preachers, who played here in 2001 in the presence of Fidel Castro.

⊛ Festivals and events

The year in Havana is crammed with festivals of one sort or another. The most popular cultural events are the cinema and jazz festivals in **Dec**, but there are also several **ballet** and **contemporary dance** festivals as well as **folk** and **classical** music events. There are **book fairs**, many **sporting events** and even a **cigar festival**, while at the Marina Hemingway there always seem to be **regattas** and **fishing tournaments** in progress. For further details, see Festivals and events, p54.

⦿ Shopping

Art
Feria de Artesanías, between Tacón and Av del Puerto by Castillo de la Real Fuerza (see below). A platform for many talented young artists to show off their skills, you may pick up a bargain, or you may be asked to pay Miami-type prices. You need documentation to take works of art out of the country or you may have them confiscated at the airport; galleries will provide the necessary paperwork and even vendors in the market can give you the necessary stamp.
Galería del Grabado, at the back of the Taller Experimental de Gráfica de la Habana, Callejón del Chorro 62, Plaza de la Catedral, open all day, closed Sun, T7-620979, F7-338121. Original lithographs and other works of art can be purchased or commissioned directly from the artists. You can watch the prints and engravings being made and specialist courses are available for those who want to learn the skill for themselves, for 1 month, US$250, or 3 months, US$500.
Galería Forma, Obispo 255 entre Aguiar y Cuba, T7-8620123, daily 1000-2000. Formerly the bookshop, *Exlibris Swan* from 1927-60, now an art gallery belonging to the **Fondo Cubano de Bienes Culturales**, selling paintings, artesanías, ceramics, jewellery and sculpture.
La Exposición, San Rafael 12, Manzana de Gómez, in front of Parque Central. Reproductions of works of art.
La Victoria, Obispo 366 entre Compostela y Habana, T7-8627914, daily 1000-1900. An art gallery with a large choice of paintings at good prices, and books, owned by artist Natividad Scull Marchena.
Taller Serigrafía, Cuba 513. Another big workshop, making screen prints; again, you can watch them being made and buy things.

Bookshops
There are second-hand bookstalls outside on the Plaza de Armas where you may be able to pick up a treasure if you know what you are looking for.
Casa Editorial Abril, at end of El Prado, opposite the Capitolio. English, French, German books, but selection poor, lots of scientific and cultural books on Cuba, in Spanish.
El Navegante, Mercaderes 115 entre Obrapía y Obispo, T7-8613625, Mon-Fri 0830-1700, Sat 0830-1200. Maps and charts, both national and regional, also prepaid phone cards.
Fernando Ortíz, L 460 esq 27, T7-8329653. Quite a wide selection, mostly in Spanish, and some beautiful postcards.
Instituto Cubano del Libro, Palacio del Segundo Cabo, O'Reilly 4 y Tacón. The

Cuban all stars

Celebrities have always had a fascination for Cuba and there has always been a steady stream of rich and famous visitors to the 'Pearl of the Antilles'. In 1898 the young Winston Churchill narrowly missed being hit by a bullet on his 21st birthday when he visited to see what the Spanish-American War was all about. He returned, older and wiser, to paint and to smoke cigars, creating the ever-popular image of the wartime British leader puffing on a great fat *Habano*.

The US Prohibition Act of 1919 gave tourism in Cuba an unexpected boost, when drinking customers and whole bars moved to the island. The Irish-owned Donovan's Bar was relocated, lock, stock and barrel to a building opposite the Capitolio in Havana, and Cuban bartenders became world famous for their cocktails. Constante Ribalaigua, at the **Floridita**, was already an established expert before Hemingway discovered his *Daiquirís* (he allegedly regularly drank 11 double, sugarless daiquirís before 1100), but the author gave him the crowning touch by writing about his cocktails in the novel *Islands in the Stream*. He also invited his friend Marlene Dietrich to sample them and she became a regular visitor to Havana. Another actress visitor, Mary Pickford, had a cocktail created for her in the **Hotel Sevilla Biltmore**.

George Gershwin was so taken with the music and rhythms of Cuba that he composed the *Cuban Overture*, first performed in 1932. Frank Sinatra was a regular visitor and even had a modernist house in the former Country Club district. Many others came down in their yachts to sail around the cays and drink in the bars. Photos of Errol Flynn, Gary Cooper, Spencer Tracy, Ava Gardner, Carmen Miranda and other glamorous figures still grace the walls of the **Bodeguita del Medio** bar.

There were also, of course, the less salubrious visitors – gangsters like Al Capone, Lucky Luciano, Meyer Lansky and George Raft – who were attracted by the money to be made in the casinos and by bootlegging alcohol. George Raft had a penthouse apartment (now a restaurant) on top of the **Capri** casino hotel. The **Hotel Nacional** and the **Riviera** were also linked to mafia money. The bar of the *Nacional* has a rogues' gallery of photos of its famous guests.

Today, celebrities continue to flock to this last bastion of Communism in the western world. Famous names have recently included Sir Paul McCartney, Francis Ford Coppola, Naomi Campbell, Kate Moss, Leonardo di Caprio (whose entourage was so large he took over whole hotels), while the annual Latin American Film Festival attracts a clutch of actors and directors, notably Robert de Niro, Arnold Schwarzenegger, Ken Loach, Jack Nicholson, Helen Mirren and Kevin Costner. In 2001, the Welsh band, the *Manic Street Preachers*, performed to crowds of adoring fans in the **Karl Marx Theatre**, with Fidel Castro in the audience.

institute has 3 bookshops: **Librería Grijalba Mondadori**, which has an excellent selection of novels, dictionaries, art books, children's books from around the world, all in Spanish; **Librería Bella Habana**, T7-8628091-3, which has Cuban and international publications, and **Librería UNESCO Cultura**, which stocks UNESCO publications, books on Cuba, a few thrillers in English and postcards.

La Moderna Poesía, Obispo 527 esq Bernaza, T7-8616953, libreria@lamoderna poseia.ohch.cu daily 1000-2000. Biggest in Cuba, modern design, literature, sciences, art materials, CDs, posters, cards, café.

Food

For food shopping, there is the **Focsa Supermarket** on 17 entre M y N (at the base of the big tower block) or the **Amistad**, on San Lázaro, just below Infanta. The **Isla de Cuba** supermarket on Máximo Gómez entre Factoría y Suárez has the best selection of food in La Habana Vieja, with prices stamped on the goods to prevent overcharging. Opposite the Plaza Hotel is the **Peerless** and inside the small shopping centre is **El Cristal**, both of which also mark the prices on the goods. One which doesn't is **El Juvenil**, or **Los Fornos**, on Neptuno, just round the corner from the Hotel Inglaterra, where overcharging is common. If you eat at the restaurant here ask to see a price list as they overcharge too. Both are housed in a repainted shell of an old building.

There are tourist mini-stores in most hotels, but they do not sell fresh food. **International Press Centre** (open to the public) on La Rampa sells items like chocolate for dollars in a shop to the right of the entrance. Bread is available at the **French bakery** on 42 y 19 and in the **Focsa** supermarket, see above.

Food markets

Farmers are allowed to sell their produce (root and green vegetables, fruit, grains and meat) in free-priced city *agromercados*. You should pay for food in pesos. There are markets in Vedado at 19 y B and a smaller one at 21 esq J; in Nuevo Vedado, Tulipán opposite Hidalgo; in the Cerro district at the Monte and Belascoaín crossroads; and in Centro, the **Chinese market** at the junction of Zanja and Av Italia where you can eat at street food stalls (avoid Mon, not a good day). **Cadeca** exchange bureaux at the first and last listed. The last Sun of every month there is a large and very busy food market held in Paseo, between Calzada de Zapata and the Teatro Nacional. Good value and lots of produce, black beans 4 pesos/lb, oranges 10 centavos each, 1 hand of green bananas 2 pesos. Loaded lorries arrive in the early hours and some people start to queue at midnight to get the best cuts of meat. Similar markets held on the same day in other Havana neighbourhoods. New state market Plaza del Cerro, Vía Blanca y Boyeros opposite Ciudad Deportiva entrance, Tue-Fri 0800-1800, Sat 0700-1700 and Sun 0700-1200. **Cadeca**

exchange bureau, car and bike park. **Jardín Wagner**, Mercaderes 113 entre Obispo y Obrapía, Habana Vieja, T7-669017, Mon-Sat 0900-1700, Sun 0900-1300. Flowers for sale, including artificial flowers and pot plants.

Handicrafts

Asociación Cubana Artesanos y Artistas (ACAA), Obispo 411 entre Compostela y Aguacate, T7-8666345, Mon-Sat 1000-1800. Handicrafts, clothing, humidors, glassware and musical instruments.

Casa del Abanico, Obrapía 107 entre Oficios y Mercaderes, La Habana Vieja, T7-8634452, Mon-Fri 0900-1700, Sat 0900-1200. Beautifully decorated fans for sale from luxury silk to everyday cotton. Lots of historical details. You can have one customized to your own design, just as the criollo ladies used to.

Palacio de la Artesanía, Palacio Pedroso (built 1780) at Cuba 64 entre Peña Pobre y Cuarteles (opposite Parque Anfiteatro). A mansion converted into boutiques on 3 floors with musicians in the courtyard. A large selection of Cuban handicrafts is available. It also has things not available elsewhere, such as American footwear (trainers), as well as clothing, jewelry, perfume, souvenirs, music, cigars, restaurant, bar and ice cream. Visa and Mastercard accepted, passport required.

Handicraft markets

Many open-air markets, handicraft and tourist souvenir markets and *ferias de artesanías*, have sprung up.

Feria del Malecón, Malecón, entre D y E, Vedado. Including shoes, jewellery, lamps and the ubiquitous booksellers. Che Guevara and religious *Santería* items lead the sales charts. Illegal cigar sellers operate here.

Feria del Tacón, Av Tacón entre Chacón y Empedrado, La Habana Vieja, Plaza de la Catedral end, daily, Wed-Mon 0800-1900. Havana's largest craft market, a multitude of products and if they don't have what you want someone will know someone who does. Tourist souvenirs, clothing, paintings, the list is endless. Also sold here are carvings, crochet, ceramics, boxes, jewellery, T-shirts, baseball bats and black coral (illegal to bring in to many countries, so avoid).

Feria del 23, 23 entre M y N, Vedado, Mon-Sat 0900-1800. Not a great selection, carvings and beads predominate.

Music, cigars and souvenirs

Artex, L esq 23, T7-8320632, Mon-Sat 1000-2100, Sun 1000-1900. Excellent music section and tasteful T-shirts and postcards, **Caracol chain**, in tourist hotels (eg Habana Libre) and elsewhere. Tourists' requisites and other luxury items such as chocolates, biscuits, wine, clothes, require payment in US$ (or credit cards: Mastercard, Visa).

Casa de la Música Galiano, Galiano 255 esq Neptuno, Centro, T7-8609640, cmh-eco @egrem.cult.cu daily from 1000 until events finish. Shop specializes in music, extensive list of titles, past and contemporary.

Casa del Habano , 7 y 26, Miramar, T7-2042353. Mon-Sat 1030-1830. Full range of cigars, one of many branches of state cigar shops. See Cuban cigars, p164.

Casa del Tabaco, y Ron Obispo esq Monserrate, La Habana Vieja, daily 1000-1900. Wide range of rums of all ages and tobacco.

EGREM, Casa de la Música, see Live music and dancing venues above. A good selection of CDs and music.

El Siglo de las Luces, Neptuno esq Aguila, T7-8635321, near Capitolio. Good place to buy *son*, *trova* and jazz (rock) records.

La Maison Calle 16, 701 esq 7 in Miramar. Luxurious mansion with dollar shops selling cigars, alcohol, handicrafts, jewellery and perfume. There is live music in the evening 2030-2450, in a lovely open-air patio, and fashion shows displaying imported clothes sold in their own boutique, US$10. However, as with all shops depending on imports, the quantity and quality of stock is variable and can be disappointing. The Piano Bar is open daily 2200-0300, karaoke and comedy show as well as live music, US$5. The swimming pool has a bar and café daily 1000-1800, US$3.

Longina Música, Obispo 360 entre Habana y Compostela, La Habana Vieja, T7-8628371, Mon-Sat 1000-1900, Sun 1000-1300. You can buy drums and other instruments here as well as CDs and Hi-fis.

Perfumería Mercaderes, 156 entre Obrapía y Lamparilla, T7-8613525, daily 1000-1800. Manufacture and sale of perfumes and colognes from natural essential oils.

Photography

Kodak film can be bought in a number of tourist locations at reasonable prices.
Photoservice, 23 esq P, Vedado, daily 0800-2200. Films developed and also camera repairs (0800-1700), T7-335031.
Post Office, Plaza de la Revolución, Mon-Sat 0830-2030. Sells camera film, floppy discs, stationery.
Publifoto, Edif Focsa, M entre 17 y 19. Films developed.

Shopping centres/department stores

Shopping centres tend to get very busy at weekends. Taxis and *bicitaxis* wait outside. Bags must be left outside shops in designated storage areas called *guardabolsas*; you should receive a numbered badge to identify your bag. Items purchased will be checked against receipt by security when you leave each shop. The large department stores are along Galiano (Av Italia) near San Rafael and Neptuno.

Galerías de Paseo, 1 entre Paseo y A, Vedado, opposite Meliá Cohiba, T7-553475, Mon-Sat 1000-1800, Sun 0900-1300. 3 levels, car showroom (for foreigners), supermarket, sports and clothes shop, café, photographic service (Fotovideo), Mon-Sat 1000-2100, Sun 0900-1300. Jazz café on 3rd floor (see Live music venues, above).

Harris Brothers, Av de Bélgica 305, entre O'Reilly y Progreso, La Habana Vieja, T7-8611615, daily 0900-2100. 4 floors, supermarket, fashion stores, children's clothes, snack bars and café.

La Epoca, Av de Italia (Galiano) y Neptuno, Centro Habana, T7-8625065, Mon-Sat 0900-1900, Sun 0930-1330. 5 floors, including clothes shops and supermarket.

La Plaza Carlos Tercera, Av Salvador Allende (Carlos III), entre Arbol Seco y Retiro, Centro Habana, Mon-Sat 1000-1900 and Sun 1000-1500, 3 levels, Western Union money transfer service, Mon-Fri 1000-1700 and Sat 1000-1200. ATM gives pesos convertibles for credit card transactions. Wide range of shops including clothing, cigars, photography, sports, supermarket and household appliances. 'Everything for a Dollar' shop. Bank, Mon-Fri 0800-1500, last working day of the month 0800-1200. Selection of cafés and snack bars.

▲▲ Activities and tours

Sport

Baseball

Estadio Latinoamericano, Pedro Pérez 302, Cerro, T7-8706576. South of the centre, in Cerro district, this is the best place to see baseball (the major league level). Opened in the 1950s, it has a capacity for 55,000 spectators and is home to the 2 Havana teams, **Industriales** (Los Azules) and **Metropolitanos**. The *Serie Nacional* baseball season runs Nov-May, culminating in the national play-offs, followed a couple of weeks later by the *Liga Superior*, which lasts a month. Baseball games have a fanatical following and can last up to 3 hrs. Follow the evening's game by visiting the Parque Central in La Habana Vieja the next day, the traditional venue for groups of passionate fans to congregate and discuss match details using frantic hand gestures to illustrate their opinions. Games at 2000 Tue-Sat, 1400 Sun, US$3 for the best seats and US$1 for the regular stand.

Basketball

Ramón Fonst stadium, Av Independencia y Bruzón, Plaza de la Revolución, T7-8814196. Local team is **Capitalinos**. No fixed match dates.

Boxing

Sala Kid Chocolate, Paseo de Martí y Brasil, La Habana Vieja, T7-611547. Sports centre hosts regular matches during boxing season. Also here are judo, weightlifting, chess and handball and for international events it hosts tennis, boxing and badminton, when tickets are US$1. A monthly programme of events is put on the notice board.

Cycling

See also Essentials, p58, and Cycling from Havana to Matanzas, p147. Cycling is a good way to see Havana, especially the suburbs, you can reach the Playas del Este beaches and surrounding countryside quickly and easily; some roads in the Embassy area are closed to cyclists. The tunnel underneath the harbour mouth has a bus designed specifically to carry bicycles and their riders, from Parque El Curita, Aguila y Dragones, to Reparto Camilo Cienfuegos after the tunnel. Take care at night as there are few street lights and bikes are not fitted with lamps. **Poncheros**, small private businesses that crudely fix punctures, are everywhere.

Golf

Club de Golf, Carretera de Vento, Km 8, Capdevila, Boyeros, towards the airport, T7-338919, cgolf@continental.cubalse.cu US$30 for 18 holes, US$20 for 9, US$10 for a ½ hr lesson . Non-members are welcome. There is also a miniature bowling alley, billiards (3 tables), tennis (bring your own rackets), squash and grubby pool, US$5 (US$8 in summer) including a drink, a bar and a poor restaurant/snack bar, **La Estancia**.

Gyms

Some of the hotels have facilities that can be used by anyone. At the **Hotel Nacional** there is a small range of machines and free weights, sauna and massage available. Lockers provided, US$5 including towel and shower (free to guests). The Hotel **Meliá Cohiba** has better facilities and range of machines, US$10 including sauna, massage from US$15. There is also a gym in the Barrio Chino, run by the **Sociedad Chang Weng Chung Tong**, San Nicolás 517 altos entre Zanja y Dragones, T7-8621490, Mon-Sat for aerobics, Taibo, apparatus, US$25 for monthly membership. Restaurant attached, see Eating, above.

Horseriding

You can go riding at **El Rodeo** near Las Ruinas in Parque Lenín, T7-443026, for US$5 per hr, including a guide. It is mostly for Cubans and you may be able to pay in pesos. No reservations, just turn up. Horses well cared for.

Running

Havana's marathon, Marabana, is held in Nov annually, US$10, including a marathon jersey. Another race is **Terry Fox** on 2 Feb each year to raise money for cancer treatments.

Sports centres

Ciudad Deportiva, at the roundabout on Avenida Boyeros y Vía Blanca, T7-545001. Camello M3 and M2 and bus P2 pass outside. The "Sports City" is a large circular sports stadium seating 18,000 spectators, enclosed by a dome with a roof diameter of 88 m. The architects were Nicolás Arroyo and Gabriela Menéndez; the complex was inaugurated on 26 Feb 1958. At the time it was considered one of the world's best indoor sports facilities. Entrance 2 pesos for seats and 1 peso for concrete benches in upper tiers. Buy tickets in advance at venue. International matches are usually a sellout. Volleyball (very popular), basketball, martial arts, table tennis. Great atmosphere, crowded, limited food and drink facilities. Large neon sign outside '*listos para vencer*' (ready to win).

Watersports

Club Habana (Sol Meliá), Av 5 entre 188 y 192, Reparto Flores, Playa, T7-2045700, F7-2045705. A club for permanent residents with annual membership of US$1,500. Tennis, squash, pool, diving (with certification), windsurfing, training golf course, child care, shops, meetings facilities, sauna and massage, bar and restaurant, expensive. All motorized watersports were withdrawn in 2003 following a security clampdown.

Club Náutico Internacional 'Hemingway', at Residencial Turístico 'Marina Hemingway', Av 5 y 248 Playa, T7-2041150-6, F7-2045280. **Cubanacán Náutica**, formerly Marlin 'Marina Hemingway', same address, VHF 16 and 72, direccion@prto.mh.cyt.cu Office open Mon-Fri 0800-1700, but activities 24 hrs. Boat trips, sport fishing, US$450 half day, catamarans, sailing lessons in dinghies, diving and snorkelling. The dive centre, **Centro de Buceo La Aguja**, takes up to 8 divers on the boat.

Tour operators

Guides

Many Cubans in Havana tout their services in their desperate quest for dollars, they are a considerable nuisance and nearly all tourists complain of being hassled. If you feel you trust someone as a guide, make sure you state exactly what you want, eg private car, *paladar*, accommodation, and fix a price in advance to avoid shocks when it is too late. *Casas particulares* can often be a good source of information on reputable guides. You may find, however, that the police will assume your guide is a prostitute and prohibit him or her from accompanying you into a hotel.

State owned travel agencies

There are lots of state-owned travel agencies, which co-operate fully with each other and have bureaux in all the major hotels (see Essentials, page 23).

As well as local trips to factories, schools, hospitals etc, tours can be arranged all over Cuba by bus or air, with participants picked up from any hotel in Havana at no extra charge. Examples include a tour of the city's colonial sites (US$15, 4 hrs); a trip to the **Tropicana** cabaret (US$65, 75 or 85, depending on quality of seat and the age of the rum you drink); Cayo Largo for the day by air with boat trip, snorkelling, optional diving, lunch (US$137, 12 hrs); Cayo Coco for the day with flight, all-inclusive package and changing room (US$143); Cayo Levisa day trip by bus and boat with snorkelling and lunch (US$65); Guamá and the Península de Zapata with a stop en route at the Finca Fiesta Campesina, tour of crocodile farm, lunch (US$65, 9 hrs); Viñales and Pinar del Río, visiting mogotes, caves and tobacco factory, lunch (US$44, 9 hrs); a day on the beach at Varadero (US$50 with lunch, 10 hrs, and you get a changing room with shower and towel); Trinidad and Cienfuegos overnight, visiting the colonial city and the Valle de los Ingenios (US$115 per person based on two sharing a room); ecological tour of Las Terrazas with walking and river bathing, lunch (US$44, 10 hrs). In practice, prices vary between agencies and you can negotiate a reduction without meals.

⊙ Transport

Local

Bicycle hire

See also Essentials, p58. **Blazing Saddles Travels**, in the UK, T020-84240483, www.blazingsaddlestravels.com rents out mountain bikes at US$15-20 per day, provides puncture repair kits and spare inner tubes. Bikes can be delivered to your hotel. Cycling tours can also be arranged. Bikes can be hired in La Habana Vieja from **Fénix SA** (*Bicicletas Cruzando Fronteras*), San Juan de Dios y Aguacate, T7-8608531, bicicletas cuba@enet.cu Prices depend on length of hire and type of bike (4-21 gears), US$2 per hr, US$12 1 day, US$20 for 2 days, spare parts and accessories provided, daily 0900-1700. **Cubalinda** hires touring bikes (Peugeot or Norco) for US$11 a day, less for longer, from Edif Someillan, O 2 entre Línea y 17, Piso 27, Vedado, T7-553980, reservations @cubalinda.com Bikes and scooters (*motos*) can be hired at **Rumbos**, Av 3 entre 28 y 30, Miramar, T7-2045491, daily 0800-2000, call for assistance if you break down. *Motos* US$24 a day for 1-2 days, US$21 for 3-10 days and US$18 for over 11 days.

Buses/camellos

Town buses have been in crisis since 1993 but the service is now slowly recovering; buses are more frequent but still very crowded. Always start moving to the exit before your stop and be prepared to shout to the driver to stop if the bus starts to move off before you've got out: '*chofe, dame un chancecito*'. There is a regular service on the *camellos*, long articulated buses on a truck bed, 20 centavos, the cheapest way of getting around. Entrance is at the middle double doors, there is a conductor here to collect the fare.

The M2 starts at Parque El Curita, esq Reina y Avenida Italia (Galiano). Previously they had all started at nearby Parque de la Fraternidad, but since its redevelopment as part of La Habana Vieja restoration programme it was decided to change some of the *camellos*' starting points. The M4 and M7 start from Fraternidad near to Calle Máximo Gómez (Monte). They are hot and sweaty and uncomfortably crowded at all times. Habaneros insist they carry more people than a Boeing 747 and refer to them as *La Película del sábado* (Saturday Night Movie), since like the content advice prior to the film starting, they contain bad language, violence and sex scenes. Maybe a slight exaggeration, but be aware of pickpockets.

They cover the main suburbs: M1 (pink) Calle G, Vedado, via Carlos III and El Floridita to Alamar; M2 (blue) Parque El Curita, via Plaza de la Revolución, Boyeros and airport terminals 1 and 2 to Santiago de las Vegas; M4 (green) Parque Fraternidad, via Marianao,

La Lisa to San Agustín; M3 (yellow) Ciudad Deportiva, via Lawton, Guanabacoa to Zone 8 in Alamar; M6 (brown) Calle 21, Vedado, via Malecón and La Víbora to Reparto Eléctrico (near Lenin Park). Ask for the right queue. The queue may look disorganized but it is actually highly functional. Discover who is last (*el último*, you have to shout loudly) for the bus you want (*por el camello*); when identified, ask him/her who they are behind (*detrás de quién*), as people mark their places and then wander off until the bus comes. When the bus comes everyone reforms in an orderly queue. That's the theory. However, things may deteriorate at night, particularly if there has been a long wait, when the elbow becomes the preferred mode of queuing.

Other than the *camellos*, buses (blue) cost 40 centavos. The 222 and 264 buses run from Egido near the train terminal to Miramar and Playa, via Vedado, respectively. *Taxibuses* (green) at 1 peso, run from the train terminal to airport terminals 1 and 2 along Rancho Boyeros. They are fairly infrequent, but are restricted to a fixed number of passengers, making a more comfortable journey. Consequently, when they are seen arriving many in the *camello* queue will make a frantic dash for them. P1 and P2 both originate in San Miguel del Padrón. P1 travels through Luyanó, Infanta, Vedado and along Línea. P2 travels through Lawton, La Víbora, Ciudad Deportiva, **Víazul** bus terminal, Vedado 26 y 41 to Miramar. Both routes cost 40 centavos and pass every 20 minutes.

Driving

Hiring a car is not recommended for getting around Havana, roads are badly signed and there have been many accidents with tourists driving rental cars, see Essentials, p44. Most of the hotels have car hire agencies in the reception area. Many streets around tourist locations have unofficial 'supervisors' who monitor car parking spaces and expect a US$0.50 payment on your return. If you want the real experience, **Gran Car**, T7-335647, rent classic cars (including Oldsmobiles, Mercury '54, Buicks and Chevvy '55) with driver, maximum 4 passengers, US$15 per hr or US$18 per hr for cars without roofs (go for the Oldsmobile '52). A trip to the beach at Playas del Este is US$15, a tour of the city US$15-18.

Havana Transport

Petrol stations Most widespread petrol chain is **Cupet-Cimex** (green logo) at Av Independencia y 271, Boyeros (near Terminal 2), Av Independencia esq Calzada de Cerro, Plaza (near Plaza de la Revolución), Paseo y Malecón (near Hotel Riviera), L y 17 and Línea y Malecón all in Vedado, 112 y 5, Miramar and Vento y Santa Catalina, Cerro. All open 24 hrs. Attached shops sell drinks, snacks and food. Second chain is **Oro Negro**, at 86 y 13, Miramar, and 7, entre 2 y 4, Miramar. Also open 24 hrs.

Ferries

There are ferries from La Habana Vieja to **Casablanca** and **Regla**, 10 centavos, which depart from Muelle de Luz, San Pedro opposite Bar Dos Hermanos. If you are facing the water, the Casablanca ferry docks on the left side of the pier and goes out in a left curve towards that headland, and the Regla ferry docks on the right side and goes out in a right curve. There are lots of security checks with X-ray machines and body searches following the 2003 hijacking of a ferry.

Taxis

Taxis are plentiful and there are numerous companies. It is a safe and easy way to travel around Havana, but relatively expensive. The cheapest taxis are the very smallest. Ask for the '*oferta especial*' or '*servicio económico*' and you will be charged only US$0.45 per km, T7-335539-42. For longer trips some companies charge by the hour and some by the kilometre, eg for an excursion including Cojímar, Santa María del Mar and Regla, Panataxi, see below, quoted US$25 while Habanataxi , see below, quoted US$35. Note that on Av 5 in Miramar, no one is allowed to pick up or set down in case Castro comes along, so don't try and hail a taxi here. **Panataxi**, T7-555555. This call-out service is one of the cheapest although Panataxis also wait outside most hotels and at the airport, or ask your hotel to call one. They are identified by their yellow colour and have a new fleet of a/c Citröen cars, so they are the most comfortable service as well as being the most reliable and still the cheapest dollar service, at under US$15 from the airport to Vedado. At the airport you will be asked if you want a taxi as soon as you leave baggage collection and you will have to insist on a Panataxi (if you want this service), since the person organizing

the taxi queue will want to put you in a more expensive taxi. Even for short journeys, Panataxi is the cheapest, cheaper even than a *cocotaxi*, see below. Panataxi also have minibuses, or big taxis, useful if you are a group with lots of luggage, T7-332020. Other call out services include:
Fénix, T7-639720 /639580.
Havanataxi T7-539086/539090.
Panautos, Línea y Malecón, Vedado, T7-553255, Av 26 y Zoológico, Nuevo Vedado, T7-666226, Av 3 y 42, Miramar, T7-227684, Terminal 2 at the airport, T7-330306, Terminal 3, T7-330307, 24-hr reservations T7-553286, panatrans@dpt.transnet.cu
Taxi OK, T7-2040000. Relatively expensive.
Transgaviota, T7-2672727 (also minibuses),

Cuban peso taxis

Licensed Cuban peso taxis are mostly reserved for hospital runs, funerals etc, but after completing their quotas they can now freelance. They are navy and yellow and usually have some kind of taxi sign. In the older taxis there are no meters and there is normally a fixed charge between points in or near the city. The fare should be fixed before setting out on a journey. Several private car owners operate as taxi drivers, some legitimately, others without a licence, always for dollars. Registered private taxis have yellow licence plates, indicating private ownership, and a red sticker 'Pasaje' on the near side of the windscreen. Beware of private moonlighters without the licence sticker on the windscreen; they could charge you over the odds, generally are not paying any taxes and you have no come-back in the case of mishaps.

Taxi *colectivos* ply their trade up and down main thoroughfares, usually stopping at bus stops to pick up passengers. They are large old American gas guzzlers in variable condition, usually poor, and you will be squeezed in with the other passengers. Tell the driver where to drop you. Routes include Parque Fraternidad going out of town to Santiago de las Vegas along Rancho Boyeros and the central parking area outside the Capitolio to Alamar. Standing on the corner opposite **Hotel Telégrafo**, Parque Central, peso cabs will drop you in Vedado, on Calle 23. Indicate to the driver where you want to get out. Fixed 10 pesos fare.

Bicitaxi/cocotaxi

In La Habana Vieja and Vedado, bicycle or tricycle taxis are cheap and readily available, a pleasant way to travel. A short journey will cost US$1, La Habana Vieja to Vedado US$3, or pay around US$5 per hr, bargaining is acceptable.

There is also the *coctaxi/cocomóvil*. If you can handle being driven around in a bright yellow vehicle shaped like a coconut shell on a 125cc motor bike, then these are quick and readily available. They take 2 passengers, no safety belts, plenty of pollution in your face. The fare is fixed in dollars, but agree the fare before the journey. A typical fare from the Hotel Nacional to La Habana Vieja is US$3. Less conspicuous are the **Rentar una fantasía** vehicles, using the same 125cc engine but the vehicle is designed as a pre-1920s motor car.

Long distance

Bus

Some ticket sellers refuse to sell tickets until the bus arrives. Passengers in the waiting lounge are not told when it does arrive and it leaves without them. The 'helpful' ticket seller then tries to sell them a seat in a private taxi, for which he/she no doubt receives a commission.

Buses leave from the Terminal de Omnibus Interprovinciales, Av Rancho Boyeros (Independencia) 101 entre 19 de Mayo y Bruzón, by the Plaza de la Revolución, T7-8709401/8703397. There are 2 ticket offices, the one painted blue is for foreigners and you pay in dollars. You can buy tickets for both **Víazul** and **Astro** buses here. **Víazul** buses often call in here after leaving their own terminal but you can't rely on seats being available. At the entrance, turn right and go to the end of the corridor. Long-distance buses have become a very popular and reliable way of travelling around Cuba and the 24-hr office is often busy with tourists. Monitors indicate departure times. Good facilities here: shop, cafés, including **Pain de París**, open 24 hrs, good coffee. **Bandec** bank Mon-Fri 0830-1500.

The dollar tourist service, **Víazul**, leaves from Av 26 entre Av Zoológico y Ulloa, Nuevo Vedado, T7-8811413/8811108/ 8815652, F7-666092, viazul@transnet.cu with a/c buses or minibuses to most cities, with lots of intermediate stops. Viazul's terminal is smaller, but there is a **Caracol** dollar shop where you can buy food and drinks, a poor snack bar upstairs, toilets, and outside there is an **Etecsa** cabin for local and long distance calls. See Essentials, p41, for advance booking addresses, and individual destinations for times and fares. **Astro** buses are US$5-10 cheaper than **Víazul**, but journey times are longer, buses are older, break down frequently and do not all have a/c.

Trains

Trains leave from the Estación Central on Egido (Av de Bélgica) y Arsenal, Havana, to the larger cities. The Estación Central has what is claimed to be the oldest engine in Latin America, *La Junta*, built in Baltimore in 1842. Get your tickets in advance as destinations vary, the departure time is very approximate. Tickets are easily purchased from **LADIS** (Ferrocuba) office on Arsenal y Aponte, daily 0800-2000, T7-8624971, pay in US$, passport needed, spacious, food and drink on board. There are 3 services to **Santiago de Cuba**. An *especial* train (number 1) leaves every other day for Santiago at 1805, arrives 0625, US$62 first *special*, US$50 *special*, returning at 1705, arriving 0600. If the train arrives more than 1 hr late, barring certain conditions, the cost of the ticket will be refunded. The trains have a/c, folding tables, clean toilets and are comfortable with good lighting. The *regular* train (number 11) also leaves every other day at 1515, about 14-15 hrs on a good day, returning 2025, US$30. On Sun and Wed a *coche motor* (number 31) leaves at 1735, arriving 0610, US$42. The trains stop at every town along the way and have to give way for a goods train, so there are always delays.

There are also daily trains to **Pinar del Río** (number 21), 2235 arrives 0420, US$6.50 and **Matanzas**, several from 0940, US$3. A long distance bus or dollar taxi may well do the same journey in a fraction of the time, eg **Havana–Pinar del Río**, 2 hrs or less by taxi, 7-8 hrs by train. It is not unusual for the trains to break down, in fact Cubans refer to this as 'normal service'. It will be mended and carry on, but be prepared to spend a serious amount of time travelling. The '*Hershey*' electric train with services to **Matanzas** no longer starts from the Casablanca station but from La Coubre, around the corner from the main station, T7-8621006.

❶ Directory

Airlines

Most are at the seaward end of Calle 23 (La Rampa), Vedado. In 1 block on 23 entre P y Infanta, you can find **Cubana, LTU, Aerocaribbean** and **Aeroflot**. Another group can be found on the ground floor of the Hotel Habana Libre further up the same street: **Grupo Taca (Aviateca, Lacsa, Nica, Taca), Air Europa, Aeropostal**. Cubana, www.cubana.cu For international sales, 23 64, esq Infanta, T7-334446/334950, Mon-Fri 0830-1600, Sat 0830-1200, for national sales, Infanta esq Humboldt, T7-8709430. **Aerocaribbean**, T7-8797524, or at the airport, T7-451024. **Aeroflot**, T7-333200, T7-335432. **Aeropostal**, Hotel Tryp Habana Libre lobby, T7-554000, Mon-Fri 0900-1200, Sat 0900-1300. **Air Europa**, Hotel Habana Libre, T7-2046904, Mon-Fri 0800-1630, Sat 0900-1300, also office in Miramar next to Iberia. **Air France**, 23 esq P, T7-662642, arruiz@airfrance.fr Mon-Fri 0830-1630, Sat 0830-1230; at the airport, T7-669708. **Air Jamaica**, Hotel Meliá Cohiba, T7-662447, Mon-Fri 0830-1630, and at airport, Terminal 3, T7-330212. **Iberia**, Av 5 y 76, Centro de Negocios Miramar, Edif Santiago de Cuba, Planta Baja, T7-2043444, Mon-Fri 0900-1600. **LTU**, 23 64 esq Infanta, T7-333524-5, Mon-Fri 0830-1200, 1300-1600, at the airport T7-335359. **Martinair Holland**, 23 esq E, T7-8333729, Mon-Fri 0800-1600. **Mexicana de Aviación**, 23 64 esq P, T7-333532, geventashav@mexicana.com.mx Mon-Fri 0830-1630, Sat 0830-1200. **TACA**, T7-333114, reservas@enet.cu at the airport T7-666042, www.taca.com

Banks

For dollar services, credit card withdrawals, TCs and exchange, open Mon-Fri 0800-1500, last day of the month until 1200, **Banco Financiero Internacional**. In Vedado: Línea 1 esquina O, T7-333423, F7-662190, in Habana Libre complex, T7-554429, F7-554795; in La Habana Vieja: Teniente Rey esq Oficios, T7-8609369, F7-8609374; in Centro: Centro Comercial Carlos III, T7-8736496; in Miramar: 18 111 entre 1 y 3, T7-2042058, F7-2042454, Av 5 esq 92, T7-2675500, Edif Sierra Maestra, Av 1 y O, T7-2039764; charges 3%

commission for foreign exchange deals and gives credit card cash advances in US dollars. **Banco Internacional de Comercio**, 20 de Mayo y Ayestarán, Plaza de la Revolución, T7-555485, Mon-Fri 0830-1400. Branches at Empedrado y Aguiar, La Habana Vieja, T7-666408, Av 3 y 78, Playa, T7-2043607, both open Mon-Fri 0830-1500. **Banco Metropolitano**, Av 5 y 112, Playa, T7-2049188, Línea 63 esq M, Vedado, T7-553116-8, Monserrate (Av de Bélgica) esq San José, T7-8633953, Mon-Sat 0830-1500, cheapest (2%) for changing TCs, most hotels and airport cambios charge 4% for changing TCs. **Netherlands Caribbean Bank**, Av 5 6407 esq 66, Miramar, T7-2040419-21, Mon-Fri 0800-1700. (See also under Currency, p31.)

Cadecas (exchange houses): Obispo 358 entre Compostela y Habana, T7-8618501, daily 0800-2200; Neptuno 161 entre Consulado e Industria, T7-8636853, Mon-Sat 0800-1800, Sun 0800-1300; in Hotel Sevilla daily, 0900-1900; in Hotel Nacional, 0800-1200 and 1230-1930, credit card cash advances. **Buró de Turismo** in Tryp Habana Libre also gives credit card cash advances.

ATMs A Visa ATM outside the business centre of the NH Parque Central issues convertible pesos and is a safe place to get money out. There is also an ATM in the Plaza Carlos III shopping centre, Av Carlos III, but again, it only issues *pesos convertibles*. It is far easier to queue at a *cadeca* or bank to get dollars with a credit card than to hunt down an ATM, which will probably not be working when you get there.

Embassies and consulates

All in Miramar, unless stated otherwise: **Argentina**, 36 511 entre 5 y 7, T7-2042972, F7-2042140. **Austria**, 4 101, esq Av 1, T7-2042825, F7-2041235, Mon-Fri 0900-1200. **Belgium**, 8 309 entre 3 y 5, T7-2042410, F7-2041318. **Brazil**, Lamparilla 2, La Habana Vieja, T7-669051. **Canada**, 30 518 esq 7, T7-2042516, F7-2042044, Mon-Thu 0830-1700, Fri 0830-1400 (Consular section). **France**, 14 312 entre 3 y 5, T7-2013131, F7-2013107, Mon-Thu 0830-1230. **Germany**, B 652 esq 13, Vedado, T7-332569, F7-331586. **Greece**, Av 5 7802, esquina 78, T7-2042995, F7-2041784. **Italy,** Av 5 esq 4, T7-2045615, F7-2045661, Mon-Fri 0900-1230 (Consular section). **Japan,** Av 3 esq 80, Centro de Negocios, 5th floor, T7-2043508, F7-2048902, Mon-Fri 0900-1700. **Mexico,** 12 No 518 entre 5 y 7, T7-2042498, F7-2042294, daily 0900-1200, Mon-Fri. **Netherlands,** 8 307 entre 3 y 5, T7-2042511, F7-2042059, Mon-Fri 0830-1130. **Peru,** 30 109 entre 1 y 3, T7-2042477, F7-2042636. **Portugal,** 7 2207 esq 24, T7-2042871, F7-2042593, Mon-Fri 0900-1230. **South Africa,** 5 4201 esq 42, T7-2049671, F7-2041101, Mon-Fri 0900-1200. **Spain,** Cárcel 51 esq Zulueta, La Habana Vieja, T7-338025, F7-338015, Mon-Fri 0900-1300. **Sweden,** 34 510 entre 5 y 7, T7-2042831, F7-2041194, ambassaden.havanna@foreign.ministry.se Mon-Fri 0930-1130. **Switzerland,** Av 5 2005 entre 20 y 22, T7-2042611, F7-2041148, Mon-Fri 0900-1200, swissem@enet.cu **UK,** 34 702 y 704 entre 7 y 17, T7-2041771, F7-2048104, embrit@ceniai.inf.cu (Consular Section), Mon-Fri 0800-1200. **US Interests Section of the Swiss Embassy,** Calzada entre L y M, Vedado, T7-333551/7-334401, Mon-Fri 0830-1700. **Venezuela,** 5 1601, T7-2042612, F7-2042773.

Hospitals and clinics

Clínica Central Cira García, 20 4101 esquina 41, Miramar, T7-2042811/14, F7-2041633, www.cira.sld.cu Payment in dollars, emergency health care, also the place to go for emergency dental treatment. There are other branches at the Hotel Comodoro, Sevilla, Habana Libre, Marina Hemingway, Terminal 3 at the airport and at Clínica Playas del Este, Villa Tarará, and Villa Panamericana to the east. **Hotel La Pradera Pharmacy and Treatment Centre,** 230 entre 15A y 17, Reparto Siboney, T7-337473-4, water therapy, yoga, sauna, physiotherapy, Mon-Sat 0800-1700. **Servimed Biotop,** Av 412206 esq 22, T7-2042377, F7-2042378. Body and facial aesthetics, stress management, revitalizers, innovative techniques for psychological and physical evaluations, alternative non-invasory techniques.

Opticians Optica Miramar, 11 14614 esq 146A, Siboney, Playa, T7-2086257, also branches at 7 y 24, Miramar, T7-2042269. **Optica Miramar Arrinda,** Neptuno 411 entre Manrique y San Nicolás, Centro, T7-8632161, arrinda@opticam.cha.cyt.cu Mon-Fri 1000-1800, Sat 1000-1300; **Optica El Almendares,** Obispo 364 entre Habana y Compostela, La Habana Vieja, T7-8608262, Mon-Sat 1000-1800; and other locations, www.opticas-miramar.com Ophthalmology consultants, contact lenses, photochromic brown and grey lenses, lightweight glasses, plastic and metal frames. Lenses from US$35, bifocals US$44, varifocals US$75.

Internet

Access is available at a limited number of places. Most hotels now have 1 or 2 terminals in the lobby, which are not reserved for guests but they will be more expensive than **Etecsa.** Prepaid Etecsa cards (see Keeping in touch, p77) can be used in the **International Press Center** on La Rampa, Vedado, where there are also long queues.

The best place in La Habana Vieja is Etecsa's **Telepunto,** Obispo entre Compostela y Habana, T7-8660089, daily 0830-2030, which has a communications centre with phones and fax service as well as 8 new terminals for internet access, US$3 for 30 mins and US$0.10 each subsequent min. At the **Lonja del Comercio,** Plaza San Francisco de Asís, T7-8662824, Mon-Fri 0830-1700, 4 terminals. There is a cybercafé in the **Capitolio.** Go in the main entrance and it is diagonally opposite to your right. There are 6 old terminals, US$3 for 30 mins, open 0830-1800 (although 2000 is advertized but the Capitolio is shut by then). You may have to wait up to 45 mins for 1 to be free.

Hotels The cheapest place is the **Hotel Telégrafo** on the Parque Central, US$2.50 for 30 mins. There are only 2 terminals and often queues, but the bar alongside serves great *daiquirís* to ease the wait. **Plaza,** US$4 for 30 mins, **Lido,** US$6 for 1 hr (unused time can be saved for another day), **Caribbean,** 2 terminals US$6 for 1 hr. The large hotels of 4 or 5 stars, such as the **Habana Libre,**

For an explanation of the sleeping and eating price codes used in this guide, see inside the front cover. Other relevant information is provided in Essentials, pages 48-53.

Nacional, Parque Central, Meliá Cohiba, all have business centres with computers for internet access, as well as telephone, fax and telex facilities, but they charge a lot more, eg US$5 for 30 mins at the **Nacional** and US$7 for 30 mins, US$20 for 2 hrs at the **Parque Central** (business centre on 1st floor, ext 1911, 1833, daily 0800-2000).

Language schools
See Essentials, p 25, for information.

Laundry
It is best to take your own washing powder and softener (buy in local shop). Leave a bag and you can collect your washed and dried clothes later for a small dollar tip. Always telephone first to ensure the water supply is working.

Aster, 34 entre Av 3 y 5, Miramar, T7-241622, Mon-Fri 0800-1700, Sat 0800-0200. US$2 per machine with 6 kg load, US$1 for drying. Ironing and delivery service available. Another in Vedado at J y 19, T7-302909. **Alaska**, Villegas 256 entre Lamparilla y Obrapía, La Habana Vieja, T7-8630463, Mon-Sat 0600-1700. **Amistad**, Amistad 357, T7-8636893, Mon-Sat 0600-1800. Girbau machines (relatively modern Spanish) cost 1.5 pesos per machine with up to 7 kg load.

Pharmacies
The pharmacy at the **Clínica Central Cira García** (see above, open 24 hrs) sells prescription and patent drugs and medical supplies that are often unavailable in other pharmacies, as does the **Farmacia Internacional** (Cubanacán Turismo y Salud), Av 41, esq 20, Miramar (T7-2042051, daily 0900-2100). **Camilo Cienfuegos Pharmacy**, L y 13, Vedado, T7-333599, daily 0800-2000.

Places of worship
Afrocuban Asociación Cultural Yoruba de Cuba, Prado 615 entre Monte y Dragones, La Habana Vieja, T7-8635953, daily 0900-1700.
Baptist William Carey, J 555, Vedado, T7-8322250, lirio@enet.cu Sun 1000 Sunday School, 1100 Worship. **Islam** Casa de los Arabes, Oficios 16 entre Obispo y Obrapía, La Habana Vieja, T7-8615868. Not authorized for services, more an exhibition within the museum, Tue-Sat 0915-1645, Sun 0900-1300.
Jehova's Witnesses Casa Betel, Av 15 4608 entre 46 y 48, Playa, T7-2035577,

Mon-Fri 0800-1100 and 1300-1600, Sat 0800-1100. **Jewish** Bet Shalom Temple, synagogue and community centre, I entre 13 y 15, Vedado, T7-328953, F7-333778, beth_shalom@enet.cu office and library, Mon-Fri 1000-1600, services Fri 1900-2000, Sat 1000-1200. **Methodist** K 502 entre 25 y 27, Vedado, T7-8320770, services Wed, Sat 2000, Tue, Thu, Sat 0900, Sun 0900, 1230, 1700 (English). **Presbyterian** Salud 222 entre Campanario y Lealtad, Centro Habana, T7-8621219, www.prccuba.org presbit@enet.cu Service Sun 1030. Rev Héctor Méndez is the Secretary General of the Cuba YMCA. **Roman Catholic** Catedral de la Habana, Empedrado 156, La Habana Vieja, T7-8624979, Mass Mon-Sat 0800, 1630, Sun 0800, 0930, 1630, **Sagrado Corazón**, Reina e Belascoín y Gervasio, Centro Habana; **Iglesia del Carmen**, Infanta entre Neptuno y Concordia, Centro Habana, T7-8785168, Mass Mon-Sat 0800, 1830, Sun 0830, 1130, 1830, and many others. **Seventh Day Adventist** Gertrudis 109, Lawton, T7-986566, Calle 168 31504 entre 315 y 317, Rpto Lutgardita, Rancho Boyeros, T7-6833729.

Post offices/courier services
Post Offices sell stamps in pesos, but hotels will charge in dollars, making them very expensive.

Línea y Paseo, T7-8305138, open 24 hrs, also internet access, US$4.50 for 3 hrs, but only for sending messages, you can't check your inbox, incredibly busy, long queues. Oficios 104 entre Amargura y Lamparilla, opposite the Lonja, open 24 hrs, T7-8625795, and postal facilities in the **Hotel Nacional**. Also on Ejido esq Arsenal, next to central railway station, T7-8622174, 24 hrs, and in the same building as Gran Teatro de La Habana.

Couriers Cubanacán Express, Av 3 8890 entre 88A y 90, Miramar, T7-2047848, cubex@courier.cha.cyt.cu national and international courier service. **DHL** in Miramar on Av 1 102 esq 26, T7-2041578, F7-2040999, and at Calzada 818 entre 2 y 4, Vedado, T7-8322112.

For **stamp collectors** the Círculo Filatélico, which belongs to the Federación Filatélica de Cuba (FCC, Mon-Fri 0800-1500), is on San José 1172 entre Infanta y Basarrate, T7-8705144, FFC@correos.enet.cu Wed 1300-1500, Sat 1200-1600, Sun 0900-1200. There is a shop on Obispo 518, Tue-Sat 1230-1700, with an excellent selection (Cuban stamps are very colourful and high quality). A philatelic shop has opened in Vedado on 27 esq L, just around the corner from the Fernando Ortíz bookshop.

Telephones

There are phone boxes all over the city, taking coins or phone cards; it is written on the side whether they are for local, national or international calls. **Cubacel Telefonía Celular** is at 28 510 entre 5 y 7, Miramar, T7-8802222, F7-8800000. **Empresa Telecomunicaciones de Cuba** (Etecsa) is on 18 3303 entre 33 y 31, Miramar, T7-2041828. **Ministerio de la Informática y las Comunicaciones**, Av Rancho Boyeros entre 19 de Mayo y Aranguren, Plaza de la Revolución, T7-668000.

Useful information

Ambulance T7-405093-4. **Fire** T7-8675555. **Insurance claims** Asistur is linked to overseas insurance companies, can help with emergency hospital treatment, repatriations, robbery, direct transfer of funds to Cuba, financial and legal problems, travel insurance claims etc. For (24-hr) emergencies go to Paseo Martí 208 entre Trocadero y Colón, La Habana Vieja, T7-338527/8671315, F7-338087, asistur @asistur.cu see Essentials, page 74. **Police** T7-8677777. Main police station is at Dragones entre Lealtad y Escobar, Centro, T7-8632441. **Weather reports** Observatorio Nacional, T7-8670721-6.

Around Havana

Several places of interest on the outskirts of Havana and in the Province of Havana can easily be reached as a day trip from the capital, with the option of staying a night or two if you wish. Readers of Ernest Hemingway novels will be fascinated to see his former home, now a museum dedicated to his memory, just as he left it, or Cojímar, the setting for his novel The Old Man and the Sea. *Alternatively you can base yourself on the beach and come in to Havana for sightseeing. The best beaches are east of Havana, at Playas del Este, an easy cycle ride or taxi from the city, or further afield at Jibacoa where you can explore the countryside as well as the sea.* ▶▶ *For Sleeping, Eating and other listings, see pages 151-154.*

West of Havana

Playa Baracoa and El Salado

Heading out of the city west along the north coast, on the *autopista* La Habana– Mariel, you come to Playa Baracoa, which is a nice place to go for some relaxation on the beach. El Salado, 25 km west of Havana, is another beach, although some parts are rocky, but there is good snorkelling as a result. The water is slightly polluted and locals bring their pigs here for a bath, but the pigs enjoy it at least. Further along the coast there is a completely abandoned holiday village with empty swimming pool and then the remains of a military coastal defence system, also deserted. There is a hotel here, described by one reader as a bungalow park, **Villa Cocomar**, see Sleeping below. Parties of day- trippers come to use the swimming pool and there are lots of watersports on offer in season, including rowing boat hire and scuba diving. The **Centro de Buceo Blue Reef** is based here, taking up to eight divers to 30 dive sites ranging from 5-35 m.

Mariel

Don't expect a beach at Mariel, further west from El Salado along the coast and scene of the mass exodus in 1980 known as the Mariel boatlift. This is a major industrial town, with the largest cement plant on the island, a shipyard, a thermal electricity plant and a duty-free industrial zone. If you continue along the coastal road, you enter the province of Pinar del Río on the way to Viñales.

San Antonio de los Baños

The capital of Havana Province is **Bauta**, near the beginning of the Carretera Central, the old route to Pinar del Río. South of Bauta is San Antonio de los Baños, a pleasant country town of some 30,000 people, set in an agricultural area where citrus and tobacco are grown. The Río Ariguanabo flows through the town, going underground by a large ceiba tree near the railway station. The town is large enough to have two museums: the **Museo del Humor** ① *Calle 60 y Av 45, Tue-Sat 1100-1800, Sun 0900-1300, US$2*, which has an unusual collection of cartoons, drawings and other humorous items, worth visiting if you are in the area, and the **Museo** Municipal ① *Calle 66 entre 41 y 43, Tue-Fri 1000-1800, Sat 1300-1700, Sun 0900-1300*, which has exhibitions of local historical interest. The **Galería Provincial Eduardo Abela** ① *Calle 58 3708 entre 37 y 39, closed Mon, US$1*, is also an art gallery displaying the work of local artists.

Outside the town, in the middle of a grapefruit plantation off the Nuera Vereda road, is the **Cuban film school**, approached down an avenue of magnificent palm trees. It is not, unfortunately, open to the public unless you obtain prior authorization to visit with 24 hours' notice. The reason most people come here, though, is because of the hotel **Las Yagrumas**, see Sleeping and Activities and tours below.

El Rincón

Northeast of San Antonio de los Baños, on the way back to Havana, is **El Rincón**, another country town that comes alive once a year for a fiesta. The day of San Lázaro, 17 December, is marked by the arrival of pilgrims on their knees, making their way to a very smart, brilliantly white church. Festivities start on 16 December and last until early 18 December, with many pilgrims asking Lazarus to cure them of illnesses. Behind the church is a leper hospital, with a good reputation for curing people. The Lazarus worshipped here is a mixture of the Lazarus of Bethany, who Jesus summoned to get up and walk, and Lazarus the beggar with leprosy. Additionally, African slaves merged the image with one of their Orishas, producing Babalú Ayé.

East of Havana

Cojímar

The former seaside village, now a concrete jungle, featured in Hemingway's *The Old Man and the Sea*, is an easy excursion (15 minutes by taxi) from central Havana. He celebrated his Nobel prize here in 1954 and there is a bust of him opposite a small fort. The coastline (no beach) is covered in sharp rocks and is dirty because of effluent from tankers. **La Terraza**, founded in 1926, is a restaurant with a pleasant view, see page 153.

Regla

Regla is to the east of La Habana Vieja, across the harbour. You can take a ferry from near the Customs House, opposite Calle Santa Clara in La Habana Vieja (or the Ruta 6 bus from Zulueta entre Genios y Refugio inland), to Regla, which has a largely black population and a long, rich and still active cultural history of the Yoruba and *Santería* (see Afro-Cuban religion, page 425). The main street, Martí, runs north from the landing stage up to the church on your left. Next to the church, the **Museo Municipal de Regla** ① *Martí 158 entre Facciolo y La Piedra, T7-976989, phone to check it is open, Tue-Fri 0900-1800, Sat 0900-1900, Sun 0900-1300, US$2*, has an extension room with information and objects of Yoruba culture, but it is not always open. Three blocks further on is the **Casa de la Cultura** ① *Martí 212, T7-979905*, which has very occasional cultural activities.

Guanabacoa

ⓘ *5 km to the east of Havana and reached by a road turning off the Central Highway. Take a 40-centavo bus Ruta 195 (1 hr) from Calle 23 esq J, Vedado, Ruta 5 (1 hr) from 19 de Mayo, Ruta 3 from Parque de la Fraternidad, or launch from Muelle Luz (at the end of Calle Santa Clara, La Habana Vieja) to Regla, then by bus direct to Guanabacoa.*

Guanabacoa is a small colonial town. Sights include the old parish church which has a splendid altar; the monastery of San Francisco; the Carral theatre; the Jewish cemetery; and some attractive mansions. The **Museo Histórico de Guanabacoa** ⓘ *Martí 108 entre Versalles y San Antonio, T7-979117, US$2, US$3 with guide, US$5 photos, US$25 video (30 mins)* is a former estate mansion, with slave quarters at the back of the building. The Sala Yoruba is a section devoted to African religions. The *Festival de Raíces Africanas Wemilere* is held here in the last week of November, each year dedicated to a different African country. The **Cementerio de Judíos** (Jewish Cemetery) was founded in 1906-10 and is set back behind an impressive gated entrance on the left on the road to Santa Fé. There is a monument to the victims of the Holocaust and bars of soap are buried as a symbolic gesture. Saúl Yelín (1935-77), one of the founding members of Cuban cinema is buried under a large flamboyant tree and you can also see the graves of the *Mártires del Partido Communista*, victims of the Machado dictatorship.

Museo Ernest Hemingway

ⓘ *San Francisco de Paula, San Miguel del Padrón, 12½ km from the centre of Havana, T7-910809, Wed-Mon 0900-1630, closed Tue and rainy days. US$2 without guide, US$3 with guide, camera US$5, video US$25. Hemingway tours are offered by hotel tour desks for US$35. No toilets. Bus P1 from Línea and P2 from Calle 26 y 41, Vedado. The signpost is opposite the Post Office, leading up a short driveway.*

Hemingway fans may wish to visit **Finca La Vigía**, where he lived from 1939 to 1961, now the Ernest Hemingway Museum. Visitors are not allowed inside the plain whitewashed house, which has been lovingly preserved with all Hemingway's furniture, books and hunting collections, just as he left it. But you can walk all around the outside and look in through the windows and open doors. There is a small annex building with one room used for temporary exhibitions and from the upper floors there are fine views over Havana. The garden is beautiful and tropical, with many shady palms. Next to the swimming pool (empty) are the gravestones of Hemingway's pets, shaded by a shrub.

Playas del Este

This is the all-encompassing name for a truly tropical string of beaches within easy reach of Havana, which arguably surpasses Varadero's brand of beach heaven. The only blot on the picture postcard landscape is the ugly concrete mass of hotels, which erupt sporadically along the coastline. Travelling east, the first stretch is the pleasant little horseshoe beach of **Bacuranao**, 15 km from Havana and popular with locals. At the far end of the beach is a villa complex with restaurant and bar. Then comes **Tarará**, famous for its hospital where Chernobyl victims have been treated, and which also has a marina and vast hotel complex, and **El Mégano**.

Santa María del Mar is the most tourist-oriented stretch of beach. A swathe of golden sand shelves gently to vivid crystal blue waters, lined with palm trees, and dotted with tiki bars, sun loungers and an array of watersports facilities; the hip spot to chill out, flirt and play. For more undistracted sun worship, continue further eastwards to the pretty, dune-backed **Boca Ciega**, a pleasant, non-touristy beach 27 km from Havana. At the weekend cars roll in, line up and deposit their cargo of sun worshippers at the sea's edge transforming the beach into a seething mass of baking flesh. For a more authentic seaside ambience, head to the pleasant, if rather more rough-hewn, beach of **Guanabo**. Most facilities here are geared towards Cubans. The small town of Guanabo is very laid-back, there is no hassle and it also enjoys a lush, green park between Avenida 474 y 476 and a children's playground. Generally, it is cheaper than Santa María del Mar and it's where a cluster of *casas particulares* are located. The quietest spot is **Brisas del Mar**, at the east end.

Tourism bureaux offer day excursions (minimum six people) for about US$15 per person to Playas del Este, but for two or more people it's worth hiring a private car for the day for US$20-25 or just taking a taxi. Cheap packages and all-inclusive holidays can be booked here from Canada and Europe, which can be good if you want to combine a beach holiday with excursions to Havana. However, most people report getting fed up after a few days of sitting on the beach here and the food is monotonous, so if you are the sort of person who likes to get out and about, avoid the all-inclusive deals. ▸▸ *For details of watersports, see Activities and tours, page 153.*

Vía Blanca

The main road along the coast towards Matanzas and Varadero is called the **Vía Blanca**. There are some scenic parts, but you also drive through quite a lot of industry, such as the rum and cardboard factories at **Santa Cruz del Norte**, a thermal electricity station and many smelly oil wells. The **Hershey Railway** runs inland from Havana, more or less parallel to the Vía Blanca, and is an interesting way to get to Matanzas. This electric line was built by the Hershey chocolate family in 1917 to service their sugar mill, at what became the Central Camilo Cienfuegos after the Revolution, now dismantled with the decline of the sugar industry. From Santa Cruz del Norte, you can drive inland via the former Central Camilo Cienfuegos to **Jaruco**, and 6 km to the west, the **Parque Escaleras de Jaruco**. The *escaleras*, or stairs, are geological formations in the limestone and there are caves, forests and other rocks to see, set in a very picturesque landscape. There is a hotel in the park, but it is for Cubans only. The restaurant at the entrance is only open at weekends for lunch, but there is a nice coastal view from the terrace.

Jibacoa

Continuing east from Santa Cruz del Norte, some 60 km east of Havana is Jibacoa beach, which is good for snorkelling as the reefs are close to the beach and it is also a nice area for walking. It is pretty, with hills coming down to the sea, and is a pleasant place to go for a weekend away from Havana. You can be served freshly caught

Playas del Este

Sleeping
Aparthotel Horizontes Atlántico **1**
Aparthotel Las Terrazas **2**

Casa Alex cp **11**
Club Arenal **5**
Club Atlántico **3**
Gran Vía **4**

Hugo Puig Roque cp **10**
Miramar & Los Jazmines **9**
Norma Martin cp **12**
Tropicoco Horizontes **6**

0 metres 500
0 yards 500

lobster for lunch on the beach, by a man who spreads a white tablecloth on a table laid especially for you. Someone else will arrange horses for a ride up into the hills afterwards to work off the lobster. They are poor old nags, but it is a great trip. Some 14 km east of Jibacoa is the **Puerto Escondido marina**, at Vía Blanca Km 80, which has boat trips, fishing, snorkelling, scuba diving and a cafetería.

Cycling from Havana to Matanzas → *4 days, 127 km.*

On this moderate graded cycle ride, with some steep hills, you will cycle through the lush agricultural interior region of Havana and Matanzas provinces, characterized by sugar cane fields, Royal palms dotting the landscape, busy market towns and sleepy villages. You have the option of returning along the same route or on the train from Matanzas. Mountain bikes are strongly recommended, since there are sections of badly broken road surfaces with numerous potholes. The route crosses several railway lines without barriers, check both directions for trains as these lines carry frequent services. Several girder bridges are marked in the route description, care must be taken when crossing and, if the ground is wet, dismount and walk across. The grid surface is very slippery when wet. Each day ends at a hotel, although in Matanzas there is ample opportunity to stay at a *casa particular*.

Day 1 Habana Vieja to Rancho Mi Hacienda
→ *A short 20-km ride on undulating terrain.*
Catch the ferry, *La Lanchita*, from Muelle de la Luz, Calle San Pedro opposite Calle Santa Clara, Old Havana. A 15-minute crossing, every 45 minutes, 10 centavos. Pass through Regla and Guanabacoa, very busy suburbs with poor road surfaces and crowded streets, to the agricultural interior region of Havana Province. **Rancho Mi Hacienda** (Gran Caribe), Carretera de Jústiz Km 4, Minas, T335485. Accommodation in original mansion or cabins along bank of Río Itabo, swimming pool, boating and horseriding.

o km Disembark from the ferry. Distance markers operate from this point. Cycle past the blue **Central Termoeléctrica Antonio Maceo** plant on the right. Immediately after, take the compulsory right turn. Follow the road round to the left. The park is on the left. Go straight across the crossroads into **Calle Maceo**. Continue to the top of the hill.

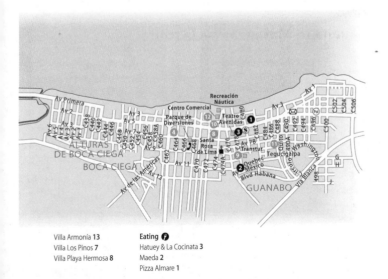

Villa Armonía **13**
Villa Los Pinos **7**
Villa Playa Hermosa **8**

Eating 🍴
Hatuey & La Cocinata **3**
Maeda **2**
Pizza Almare **1**

1.3 km Turn left at the T-junction. The **Cementerio de Regla** is in front of you. A formidable ochre-coloured entrance. Stay on this road. The surface is potholed in parts.

2.3 km Go straight across at the major crossroads with traffic lights. Enter **Municipio Guanabacoa**. Sign on the left. Continue straight on and up the hill through Guanabacoa.

3.4 km Keep to the right where the road divides. Pass a park on the right, with a statue of Antonio Maceo, and a walled school , Escuela Pías (written on the gates), on the left . The road surface deteriorates here, with numerous potholes. Continue straight on.

6.2 km Pass **Policlínico Docente Andrés Ortíz** on the left. Soon afterwards pass a Hebrew cemetery with imposing walls and gated entrance, set back from the road on the left. Pass under a road bridge (Vía Monumental).

8.3 km Enter **Santa Fé**. Pass Hogar de Ancianos (residential unit for the elderly) on the left. Stay on this road and pass through **Bacuranao**. There is a *guarapo* stall on the right at 11.3 km selling sugar cane juice. An energy boosting drink and well worth a stop. Soon afterwards cross a small girder bridge and leave town. Distinctive Royal palms dot the landscape.

12.8 km Go up a short hill and pass through **La Gallega**. Stay on this road and pass **Motel Villa Romance** on the right.

15.8 km Enter **Las Minas**. Pass a brightly painted blue and white *Ponchera* (small private puncture repair business) on the right. Keep to the left at the junction (Arango is to the right here). Leave town, go downhill and pass **La Granja Rosita** on the right.

18.1 km Leave Municipio Guanabacoa and keep straight on at the unmarked junction. **Rancho Mi Hacienda** is on the right at 19.5 km.

Day 2 Rancho Mi Hacienda to Playa Jibacoa
→ *60 km, undulating to hilly terrain.*

The route runs alongside the **Escaleras de Jaruco** and climbs to the Atlantic coast, passing through a rich agricultural landscape and several small, busy towns and villages. There is a steep climb to **Jaruco**. The latter part of the ride includes a 7-km stretch along the busy Vía Blanca dual carriageway. Stay at **Campismo El Abra** (see page 153).

0 km Leave the hotel and turn left.

1.4 km At the unmarked junction turn left. The junction is easy to miss. There is a faded, blue-painted building on the left-hand corner, with two telephones on the wall. There are numerous potholes here. Stay on this road. Pass **Agrupación Maquinaria** on the right. There are good views of the **Escaleras de Jaruco** in the distance.

Havana to Matanzas cycle route

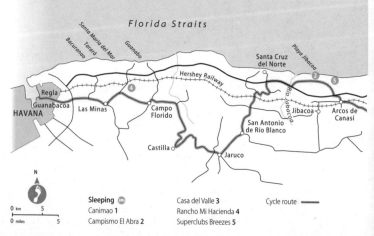

Sleeping 🛏
Canimao **1**
Campismo El Abra **2**

Casa del Valle **3**
Rancho Mi Hacienda **4**
Superclubs Breezes **5**

Cycle route ━━━

6.8 km Descend a short hill and enter **Campo Florido**. Pass a park on the right with a statue of a Revolutionary with a gun. At the crossroads with the main street, turn left, signed 'Jaruco and Guanabo'. There are usually street vendors selling fruit and vegetables on the right here. Pass **Banco Popular de Ahorro** on the left (green logo) and immediately after turn right, signed 'Jaruco'. There is a green and white pizzeria on the corner. Bear to the left, cross a bridge and leave town. Stay on this road.

13.1 km Leave Municipio Ciudad de La Habana. Immediately after turn right at unmarked junction. There is a blue painted house, number 604, on the left. (Tumba Cuatro is straight on here.) Pass through several small towns, including **San Miguel de Casanovias**. Cross a railway bridge. The road starts to climb.

20.5 km Enter **Castilla**. There are good views of the hills in the distance. The rural landscape is marked by banana plantations, palm trees and small *bohíos*.

24.6 km Pass through columns of palms lining the road as it starts to climb. Stay on this road. Cross a white-washed railway bridge. Go down the hill.

29.1 km Enter **Pachuco**. Cross a bridge over a small river, follow the road round to the right. Pass a faded pink 'Acueducto' building on the left. Continue past a row of small houses on the right and climb up the steep hill to **Jaruco**. Almost at the top of the hill, at the small crossroads turn left into Calle 28. There is a rust-coloured house, number 2801, on the right here. Continue to the top of the street and turn right. This is the suggested lunch stop, in the park opposite the church (San Juan Bautista, 1778). In the park there is a small monument to Motherhood. On the other side of the park there is a good, private pizzeria which serves generous sizes for 4 pesos. Continue along this street to the crossroads. There is a police station on the left corner, painted blue. Turn right. At the following crossroads turn left (to the right is a pedestrian boulevard). Follow this street through town. Pass **Radio Jaruco** building on the left. Cross a railway line. At the offset crossroads turn left, signed San Antonio de Río Blanco, pass under overhead road sign. Stay on this road, passing through fields of sugar cane.

37.4 km Enter **San Antonio de Río Blanco**. Pass a park and church on the left. Stay on the main street. Leave town and continue through fields of sugar cane. Pass Las Mercedes Station. Cross a railway line at Tremoleda Station. Enter **Loma del Travieso**. Climb up the hill through the town. Pass primary school Máximo Gorki on the right. Go down the hill and leave town. There is a large factory with a tall chimney in the distance. Go straight across at the crossroads towards the factory. Pass sign 'Bienvenido a Santa Cruz'. Enter **El Comino**. Stay on this road.

43.7 km Cross a railway line at Chucho Jaguey Station. Pass the Central Camilo Cienfuegos sugar mill on the left. At the T-junction turn right. Take care, there are sharp, steep curves on the downhill section. At the top of the hill bear to the left. (There is a solitary bus stop on the right and a block of flats on a hill in the distance to the right.) The Atlantic Ocean is in front of you in the distance, as is Cuba's largest rum factory (**Ronera Santa Cruz**). Go down the hill. Continue straight on at the junction and pass a large sign 'Bienvenido a la Perla del Norte' on the right.

47.4 km Keep to the right at the junction, signed 'Jibacoa'. Pass a large paper mill factory on the right. Immediately after turn right, signed 'Matanzas'. Keep to the right and join the

Vía Blanca. Take care, this is a busy dual carriageway. Stay in the right hand lane, near to the kerb. The Atlantic is to the left. Cross Río Jibacoa.

55.5 km Immediately before the overhead bridge marked 'Matanzas/Varadero' take the right exit off the Vía Blanca. Give way and turn right at the next junction. Then turn right, signed 'El Abra'. Follow the road round and go under the Vía Blanca. Stay on this road through a shaded, tree-lined section. Follow the signs to **El Abra**. The road winds through numerous beach huts and camping grounds close to the sea. The entrance is on the left at 59.6 km. Follow the driveway down to the *carpeta* (reception).

Day 3 Playa Jibacoa to Mena → *32 km, undulating, with some short climbs.*
The road surface has very badly deteriorated from Arcos de Canasí through the picturesque Yumurí valley, and there are numerous potholes. A definite boneshaker. Stay at **Hotel Casa del Valle** (see page 190).

0 km Leave *El Abra* and turn left. Pass La Laguna and **Villa Trópica** hotels on the left.

1.3 km After **Villa Trópica** bear to the right. Stay on this road as it winds inland.

5.6 km At the main highway, the Vía Blanca, turn left. Remember you are cycling on the right-hand side and must cross to the far side of the highway. Take care, this road carries fast-moving traffic. Stay on this road for about 0.5 km. Immediately before an unfinished, overhead bridge turn right to **Arcos de Canasí**. Continue to the top of the short hill. There is a tall factory chimney in front of you.

6.5 km Turn left at the junction. Pass the factory on the right. Go down the hill. Pass Puerto Libre. Keep straight on at the following junction (Jibacoa is to the right here). Enter **Arcos de Canasí**. Go down the hill and pass under the railway bridge. Follow the road round to the left. At the T-junction, with the **El Manubrio** shop in front of you, turn left. Pass **Cine Canasí** and **Banco Popular de Ahorro** on the right. Cross a bridge and leave town. Stay on this road passing several turnings-off to farmsteads and agricultural co-operatives. This is the **Yumurí Valley**, a lush, green tranquil landscape with numerous Royal palms and dramatic mogotes (limestone hills) of the Sierra de Camarones in the distance to the right. Guava trees line the road. A small thirst-quenching fruit. Wash the skin and eat the whole fruit. Pass through **San Antonio** village.

21.5 km Enter **Corral Nuevo**. Pass the local baseball ground on the left. Rows of small houses with rocking chairs on the verandas line the main street. Pass a church next to a small park, with benches and a statue of José Martí on the right. This is the suggested lunch stop. Continue on the main street. At the end of the street, bear to the right. **La Bodega La Esquina** is in front of you. Pass Templo Bautista on the right. Bear to the left and leave town. Stay on this road. Pass **Campomento Bautista** on the left. This is a rural retreat for baptist families. Pass through the small village of **San Miguel**.

29.5 km At the junction turn left, signed 'Chirino'. (Matanzas is straight on here.) Be careful, this turning is easy to miss. Cross over a girder bridge and cross the Hershey railway line at Mena Station. Stay on this road to the mid-range **Hotel Casa del Valle** (T52-253584/F52-253300) on the left at 31.5 km. The gated entrance is lined by Royal palms and the Cuban flag flies outside.

Day 4 Mena to Matanzas → *17 km.*
The ride starts with a demanding hill climb, followed by a steep descent through the narrow busy streets of Matanzas. Staying at **Hotel Canimao, you will have plenty of time to explore the nearby Río Canímar (see page 189).**

0 km Leave the hotel and turn right. Cross the railway line and girder bridge.

1.8 km At the T-junction turn left to Matanzas. Go through the village, passing Escuela Minerva Duarte on the right, and climb up the steep hill. Great view behind you at the summit.

4.7 km Pass a garage on the right and turn left at the T-junction. After 0.5 km bear right at the fork. Pass **Parque René Fraga** on the left, a good view of the city and harbour from here. This is a steep descent along a one-way street, Calle 83. Pass

Radio 26 on the right. At the bottom of the hill pass **Parque de la Libertad** on the left. A good place to stop and watch Matanceros coming and going.

7.2 km At the end of the street turn right into **Plaza de la Vigía**. Pass **Teatro Sauto**, the oldest theatre in Cuba, on the left. At the traffic lights, go straight across. Pass the small neoclassical fire station on the left. Go over **Puente Calixto García**, a girder bridge, crossing Río San Juan. Follow the cycle lane to the end of the street. At the T-junction, with traffic lights, turn left. Pass the bus station on the right and cross a railway line. Stay on this road. Pass **Los Pinos** garage on the left.

14 km At the T-junction turn right, a wooden building, La Paz Chita, is on the right. Pass a **Servi-Cupet** garage (green logo) on the left, a good stop for cold drinks. Keep to the left at the fork and pass a small bandstand on the right. Cross **Río Buey Vaca** and climb up the hill, passing **Matanzas University** on the right.

16.7 km Turn right alongside restaurant El Marino, a blue building on the right, into the **Hotel Canimao** entrance. Continue up to the hotel. If you cross Río Canímar you have missed the turning.

The south coast

The southern coast is mostly swamp and wetlands, but there is access by sea to the Isla de la Juventud. There is no coastal road, as along the north coast, which means that although there are several nice beaches within striking distance of Havana, they are difficult to get to and beach hopping is tricky. The easiest to get to from Havana is probably **Playa Majana**, in the west of the province, access to which is off the Carretera Central, the old road to Pinar del Río. From here, northwards to the **Bahía de Mariel**, is the island's narrowest point. The main town on the south coast is **Batabanó**, 51 km from Havana. There has been a settlement here since the 16th century, but most travellers are only passing through on their way to **Surgidero de Batabanó**, to catch the ferry or catamaran to Isla de la Juventud. The latter is a ramshackle fishing town of wooden houses. There are several small restaurants selling fried fish, which makes a change from fried chicken, but they are poor quality and not worth making a detour for. There is only peso accommodation which may not accept foreigners. The beach, 2 km east of the port, is dirty and muddy with the outflow from several rivers and there are mangroves.

● Sleeping

Cojímar *p144*
Casas particulares
D **Raquel**, Martí 460 entre 32 y 33, T7-652975, www.cubamania.com (Villa Estrella). Independent, 2 rooms, a/c, 2 bathrooms, fridge, central heating, kitchen, swimming pool.
E **Yohana Ferra Veloso**, 30 96 entre E y F, T7-933907. 2 rooms, 2 bathrooms, a/c, hot water, kitchen and living room for guests use only, interior garden.

Playas del Este *p145, map p146*
Hotels
LL-A **Villa Los Pinos** (Gran Caribe), Av de las Terrazas 21 entre 4 y 5, Santa María del Mar, T7-971361-7, informatica@pinos.gca.cma.net

Standard rooms plus 26, 1-, 2- and 3-roomed houses, most with pools or near the beach, grill restaurant, café and pizzeria, popular with Italians, Spanish and French in that order, lots of repeat guests, comfortable, private, good for entertaining friends, very flexible, friendly management, multilingual staff. But the place could do with a lick of paint and an upgrade.
AL **Club Atlántico** (Gran Caribe), Av Las Terrazas entre 11 y 12, Santa María del Mar, T7-971085-7, www.club-atlantico.com 92 rooms, only booked through Italian tour companies. It's all-inclusive with all mod cons and it's right on the beach.
AL **Hotel Club Arenal** (Horizontes), Laguna Itabo entre Santa María del Mar y Boca Ciega,

T7-971272, F7-971287. All-inclusive, 166 a/c rooms, good accommodation in 4, 2-storey, buildings around a large pool with terrace bar and barbecue, beach reached by footbridge over Itabo lagoon, non-motorized watersports and bicycles included, restaurant, disco, shop.

AL-D **Villa Armonía Tarará**, 9 esq 14, Tarará, T7-971616-18, www.cubanacan.cu 75 houses with 268 rooms (2-5 rooms per house), situated in a massive, closed-off complex which has security like a prison. Most staff are totally unfriendly. Houses have TV, fully equipped kitchens, porch and parking, marina, restaurant, snack bar, grill, disco, watersports, gym, shop, and free shuttle to Havana.

A-D **Aparthotel Las Terrazas**, Av de las Terrazas entre 10 y Rotonda, Santa María del Mar, T7-971344. 84, 1-3 bedroomed apartments, a/c, each with extremely well-equipped cooking facilities (if only there was such variety of food in Cuba to merit), in a rather unattractive block opposite the beach, 2-tier swimming pool, restaurant, bar, tourist bureau, car rental, great location but rather run down. Not the best of what's on offer around here but service with a smile which can't be said for everyone in these parts.

B **Aparthotel Horizontes Atlántico**, Av Las Terrazas entre 1 y 12, Santa María del Mar, T7-971494, horiatla@hatlant.hor.tur.cu This has 61 apartments, 93 rooms, a restaurant, bar and pool. It was undergoing renovations at the time of going to press

B **Hotel Horizontes Tropicoco**, Av Sur y Las Terrazas, Santa María del Mar, T7-971371, reception@htropicoco.nor.tur.cu The architecture here is ugly (it's in the same hideous style as the hotel at Playa Ancón and Hotel Pasacaballos in Cienfuegos. It has a pool, restaurant, and three bars and is an all-inclusive. It is conveniently placed opposite the beach where most tourists are deposited on day trips from Havana so if you need drinks or the toilet, best stop here.

E **Gran Vía** (Islazul), 5 Av y 462, T7-962271, between Boca Ciega and Guanabo. Friendly service, better food than at the Horizontes hotels, no hot water and no single rooms, US$3 for TV, US$5 key charge.

E **Villa Playa Hermosa** (Islazul), Av 5 entre 470 y 472, Guanabo, T7-962774. 33 rooms or chalets with a/c, fridge and TV, but no hot water and the pool is only half full. Still, the hotel is good value, and is often used by party faithful and honeymooners. There is a bank on the premises.

E-F **Miramar**, 478 esq 7B, Guanabo, T7-962507/8. A small, pleasant hotel where the 3rd floor rooms are the best in terms of quality and the view; some rooms can be joined up for family reasons. 8 rooms out of 24 have hot water. All have TV, fridge, clock and safety box. The pool is clean and there is 24 hr electricity. Restaurant daily 0730-2300, bar daily 1000-2200 and 24-hr reception.

Casas particulares

E **Casa Alex** 486 7B07 entre 7B y 9, Guanabo, T7-966057/960060, cell T2635240. Alex and his mother Prieta have rooms with a/c, *cocina*, TV, music. People who stay there can use the pedalos for free at **Recreación Náutica**. Telephone service and *parqueo*.

E **Norma Martín**, 472 1A06 entre 3 y Playa, Guanabo, T7-966734. 2 rooms in small house with a/c and hot water. This place is a stone's throw, literally, from the beach.

E-F **Hugo Puig Roque**, Av 5 47203 entre 472 y 474, Guanabo, T7-963426. 1 apartment with private bathroom, a/c, and kitchen, good location, friendly. Prices negotiable, depending on season and length of stay.

Jibacoa *p146*

Hotels

B **SuperClubs Breezes Jibacoa**, Playa Arrojo Bermejo, Vía Blanca Km 60, T692-85122, www.superclubscuba.net Price per person per night depending on season and view, all-inclusive, no children under 16, 250 rooms and suites in 2-storey buildings, attractive setting with hilly backdrop and curved, sandy bay, well equipped, comfortable, good bathrooms, nice beds, buffet, Cuban or Italian restaurants, good food, vegetarian options, tennis, basketball, bicycles, hiking, snorkelling, diving, catamaran, sunfish, kayaks, gym, windsurfing, no motorized watersports to protect reef, excursions available, indoor games room, pool, piano bar, nightclub, beach bar, wheelchair accessible, 2 rooms for disabled guests, evening entertainment disappointing, but around the headland is a Cuban camping resort where they know how to party during the summer holidays.

D **Villa La Loma** (Islazul), Playa Jibacoa, Km 57, T692-83612. 39 rooms in a/c *cabañas*, private bathroom, TV, restaurant, bars, sports, currency exchange, parking.

E-F **Campismo El Abra**, further along rough track, T692-85120. Essential to book through **Cubamar** in Havana, people who arrive without a reservation are turned away. 87, 2-3-bed cabins with fan or a/c, small rooms, very basic, hot, small shower, organized activities incl bicycles, small horses, badminton, *pelota*, bar, restaurant, Post Office and *Cambio*, enormous but murky pool, small, rocky beach, best to walk east or west, extensive grounds, lots of greenery and mosquitoes. This resort does accept foreigners, but about 70% of guests are Cuban. However, there are several other places for Cubans, such as **Laguna Camping**, which do not, and which may be open only in the Cuban summer holiday season.

Playa Baracoa and El Salado *p143*
Hotels
C-D **Villa Cocomar** (Cubanacán), Carretera Panamericana Km 23.5, Caimito, T680-258890, F680-258889. 41 rooms in bungalows, fridge, hot water, a/c, TV, clean towels daily, in pretty setting, lots of coconut palms, pool, reasonably priced restaurant, US$4 for steak and bananas, tours offered, nightclub on Fri and Sat.

San Antonio de los Baños *p144*
Hotels
D **Las Yagrumas** (Islazul), Calle 40 y 210, T7-335238, root@yagrum.hab.cyt.cu Popular with Canadians, Mexicans and Ecuadorians, on the banks of the Río Ariguanabo 5 km outside the town, 22 km from Havana and 19 km from the airport, in a lovely setting. It is a low key resort of 120 rooms in a 2-storey building, the rooms overlooking the river are quieter than those looking over the pool. You can take boat trips or go fishing on the river and there is tennis and an indoor games room, see Activities and tours below.

🍴 Eating

Cojímar *p144*
La Terraza, Real 161 esq Candelaria, T7-939232, daily 1200-2300. Over-priced seafood meals at US$20 for terrible fish, paella is the house speciality. Photographs of Hemingway cover the walls.

Playas del Este *p145, map p146*
Many reasonably priced *paladares* in Guanabo and elsewhere. There are cafés, bakeries, restaurants and *heladerías* on Av 5 entre 478 y 480 in Guanabo, including, **La Hatuey**, a chilled, dark, wooden bar, and **La Cocinita**, which has a pool table, on Av 5 esq 480. There's also a great little bakery just past the *Cadeca*.

Restaurants
$$ **Maeda**, Quebec 115 entre 476 y 478, Guanabo, T7-962615, daily 1200-2400. This is a beautiful setting with outside seating under flower-filled terracing. There is also seating in an air-conditioned room. International and Cuban food is served as well as a *parillada* along with wines and a selection of puddings. Starters range from US$2-9 and from US$4-9 for a *plato fuerte*. Run by the welcoming Miguel. Reservations advised for the evenings as it's a popular spot for visiting Habaneros.
$ **Café River Ristorante**, behind Villa Playa Hermosa entre 472 y 474, daily 1200-0200. Dishes under US$3, beer US$0.85, cosy, funky.
$ **Los Jazmines**, close to Hotel Miramar, Guanabo, daily 1000-2200. Serves *comida china* in an airy dining room or outdoor terrace but it mostly offers non-Chinese cuisine including cheap sandwiches and ice cream. There is a **Caracol tienda** next door.
$ **Pizza Almare**, Av 5 y 482, Guanabo. A huge variety of pizzas ranging from US$1.50-4.

🎭 Entertainment

Playas del Este *p145, map p146*
There are several cabarets on Av 5 in Guanabo: **Guanimar** entre 466 y 468, **Rincón Azul** on 486 and **Tokio** entre 470 y 472.

▲▲ Activities and tours

Playas del Este *p145, map p146*
At Playas del Este, the hotels provide some non-motorized watersports.
Marina Tarará, run by Marinas Puertosol, Vía Blanca Km 19, Tarará, Playas del Este, T7-971462, F7-971313, VHF77. Moorings for 50 boats, VHF communications and provisioning, yacht charters, deep sea fishing (US$250-450 per day depending on type of boat) and scuba diving, all of which can be arranged through the hotel tour desks.

Mi Cayito Recreation Centre, Av de las
Terrazas, Laguna Itabo, Santa María, near
Boca Ciega, T7-971339, daily 1000-1800.
Equipment for hire includes a pedal boat
(US$1 per person per hr) with four seats,
water skiing in the lake, US$10 for 15 mins
and kayak hire. Showers and changing
rooms available. The **Restaurant El Pelícano**
is on site but set back from the lake.
Recreación Náutica, beach at the end of Av
474, Playas del Este, daily 1000-1800. Run by a
bunch of friendly guys. Pedalos, US$7.50 per
hr, catamaran US$15 per hr with sailor, 2½ hr
trip with snorkelling, US$15 per person. Sun
lounger US$2 per day, umbrella US$2 per day.
Bar service and food served on the beach.

San Antonio de los Baños *p144*
At **Hotel Las Yagrumas**, see Sleeping above,
you can get a day pass to use the facilities. Use
of the pool for day visitors is US$3 Mon-Fri, or
US$5 at weekends. 2 people can get a day pass
for US$15 to use the facilities and have lunch of
a half chicken, vegetables and 8 beers. The
tennis courts at the hotel are reasonable;
rackets and balls are supposed to be available
but don't rely on it, there is a gym and massage
is offered, although not really worth the US$5
charge. Bicycles (US$2 per hour), rowing boats
(US$1 per person) and motor boats (US$3 per
person) are in variable states of repair.

O Shopping

Playas de Este *p145, map p146*
There is a **farmers' market** in Guanabo
selling fresh fruit and vegetables 6 days a
week and a supermarket for bread and
tinned goods. The **Centro Comercial de
Guanabo** shopping centre, behind
Recreación Náutica has a supermarket.

⊜ Transport

Bus
For the **Playas del Este**, the 400 bus (40
centavos) from Egido near the Estación
Central de Trenes can get you to **Bacuranao**,
Santa María and **Guanabo**. The 405 and
the 464 also leave from **Guanabacoa**. For
Jibacoa, Víazul bus Havana–Varadero will
drop you off at the beach, US$7, but ask for
the Playa, not the hotels, or you could get
stranded a long way from anywhere.

Cycling
Cycling is a good way to get to the **Playas
del Este**. Use the *ciclobus* from Parque El
Curita, Aguila y Dragones, Centro, via the
tunnel under Havana Bay, or the 20-centavo
ferry to **Regla** from near the Aduanas
building, and cycle through Regla and
Guanabacoa. Be careful of the very poor
road surfaces and frequent roadworks.

Taxi
The standard private taxi price from Havana
to the **Playas del Este** is US$15 (fix the price
before you set off); opposite Hotel Miramar
in Guanabo is **Transtur** taxi service, 476 esq
7B, open 24 hours, T7-966666, T7-963939. A
Panataxi from **Baracoa** to the airport costs
US$20 and to Miramar, **Havana**, US$15.

❻ Directory

Banks
Banco Popular de Ahorro, Guanabo, Playas del
Este, open Mon, Thu, Fri 0830-1530. Wed
0830-1900. Visa and MC accepted. **Cadeca**,
Av 5 entre 476 y 478, Guanabo, Playas del Este,
daily 0800-1300, 1400-1800. Visa and MC
accepted. Credit card advances from *cadecas*
incur a standard 1.5% handling charge.

Hospitals and clinics
All hotels have a doctor on permanent duty,
US$25 per consultation. The **Clínica
Internacional** is at Av de las Terrazas 36, Santa
María del Mar, Playas del Este, T7-6872689.
Clínica Internacional Santa Maria del Mar, Av
de las Terrazas, Santa María del Mar,
T7-971032, open 24 hrs all year. Includes all
types of medical service from consultation to
ambulance service to dentistry. A consultation
between 0800-1600 is US$25, between 1601
and 0759, US$30. It also sells nappies, sanitary
towels and medicines. **Clínica Central Cira
García**, Clínica Playas del Este, Villa Tarará,
www.cira.sld.cu Payment in dollars,
emergency healthcare, also the place to
go for emergency dental treatment.
For branches in Havana, see p141.

Post office
At Playas del Este, the Post Office is on Av Las
Terrazas entre 10 y 11, Santa María del Mar,
Playas del Este. Here you will also find a
Telecorreos and **Transtur** car hire.

Pinar del Río

❖ Footprint features

Introduction

The west of Cuba is blessed with an exotic landscape of limestone mogotes, caves and mountains, forested nature reserves and tobacco plantations. This is where you will find the world's best dark tobacco, which is hand-processed into the finest cigars. There is world-class scuba diving, and there are good beaches and wetlands for migrant water fowl. The Sierra del Rosario contains the Biosphere Reserve at Las Terrazas, a must for anyone with an interest in ecology and tropical forests, as well as the orchidarium at Soroa and the opportunity to pamper yourself at the San Diego spa.

The capital of the province and the major city west of Havana, Pinar del Río, can be a good base for excursions as transport starts from here, while María La Gorda is a diver's dream, low key, laid back and friendly. The small town of Viñales attracts thousands of visitors, both independent and package tourists. Its position beside the mogotes provides spectacular views and good walking opportunities. Its beauty has been internationally recognized and the Viñales Valley has been declared a UNESCO world cultural landscape.

★ **Don't miss...**

❶ **Las Terrazas** Hike through the old coffee plantations in the Biosphere Reserve and see if you can spot a tocororo, page 160.

❷ **Soroa** The orchid farm is a glorious riot of colour with over 700 different orchids, page 160.

❸ **María La Gorda** Scuba diving off the Península de Guanahacabibes is pristine and fascinating at any time of year, page 168.

❹ **Valle de Viñales** Sit and enjoy the view of mogotes and the valley from the pool terrace at Hotel Los Jazmines, pages 174 and 178.

❺ **Caridad's garden** A shady botanical garden first planted 70 years ago in Viñales with a huge variety of fruits and flowers, trees and shrubs, page 174.

Ins and outs

Getting there

Pinar del Río is the main transport hub of the area. **Air** It has a domestic airport, the only one in the west, but flights are few and far between. **Rail** There is a railway line between Havana and Pinar del Río, with a slow and unreliable service, usually at night. The line continues on to Guane for local services. **Road** There are plenty of **Víazul** and **Astro buses** to the city, continuing on to Viñales. Local services to smaller towns fan out from Pinar del Río. A dual-carriage highway has been completed almost as far as Pinar del Río. It takes two hours to get to Pinar del Río on the *autopista*, see Havana to Pinar del Río below. Some slip roads are unsurfaced, just mud and stones. **Car hire** is available in Pinar del Río and Viñales for independent excursions. There are also plenty of tours to caves, cigar factories, tobacco farms and other local attractions.

Tourist information

Tour agencies such as **Cubatur, Rumbos, Cubanacán** and **Havanatur** operate as tourist information offices, although their main purpose is to sell tours. They can help with hotel reservations, tickets and transfers.

Best time to visit

The weather is wettest from September to November, but you can get rain in the hills at any time of year, usually in the afternoon. Pinar del Río holds its carnival in July and Viñales has one in September.

Land and environment

The western end of the island is dominated by one of the island's three main mountain ranges, the **Cordillera de Guaniguanico**, which is divided into the **Sierra del Rosario** in the east (rising to the **Pan de Guajaibón**, its highest point at 699 m) and the **Sierra de los Organos** in the west, which form a curious Chinese-looking landscape with steep-sided limestone hills and flat, fertile valleys. A fault line creates a sharp boundary between these mountains and a wide expanse of rolling farmland in the southern part of the province, centred on the pleasant but unspectacular provincial capital of Pinar del Río. The province contains three major nature reserves:

Las Terrazas

Sleeping 🛏
Moka 1

Paths & trails 🥾
Cañada del Infierno Trail 1
San Juan River Trail 2

Buenavista Coffee
Plantation Trail 4
La Serafina Path 6

a 260 sq km Biosphere Reserve in the Sierra del Rosario, a 132-sq-km National
Monument in the Sierra de los Organos around Viñales, and a 1,175-sq-km Biosphere
Reserve in the Guanahacabibes peninsula at the western tip.

Pinar del Río grows about 70% of Cuba's tobacco crop and almost every agricultural
area is dotted with *vegas*, curious tent-shaped windowless structures made of palm
thatch, which are used for drying tobacco leaves, a process that takes at least 45 days
(easy to enter and take photographs). The fields are ploughed, mostly with oxen, in
September and October. The crop is transplanted into the fields in November, with the
leaves picked over the following months. The cigar factory in Pinar del Río has regular
tours and in the harvest season it is possible in most villages to visit an *escogida de
tabaco*, where the best leaves are selected for further processing. The flat lands of San
Juan y Martínez are where the very best tobacco is grown. See page 164.

Sierra del Rosario → *Colour map1, grid B4.*

*Heading west from Havana the land is initially low-lying and unimpressive. Soon,
however, green mountains come into view, stirring anticipation of exploration and
discovery. The Sierra has a 260 sq km of Biosphere Reserve, giving recognition to its
ecological diversity and richness. Birdwatching is rich and rewarding around Las
Terrazas, the main centre for nature tourism. Lovers of flora will appreciate the
orchidarium at Soroa, while anyone who has hiked up and down the hills can relax
their exhausted muscles at the San Diego spa baths.* ▶ *For Sleeping, Eating and other
listings, see pages 161-163.*

Ins and outs

Getting there The easiest way of getting to Soroa is to book yourself on an organized
tour from Havana. A day trip (10 hours) to Las Terrazas, with walking, river bathing and
a ghastly lunch is around $44 at any tour agency. Other trips include overnight stays
at the hotels and some take in Soroa as well. Alternatively, hire a **car** and take your
time, but rooms at **Hotel Moka** need to be booked in advance. Public transport is
negligible. Long-distance **buses** go along the *autopista* but not to Las Terrazas or
other sites of interest. **Taxis** are expensive and can only be arranged in Havana, Pinar
del Río or Viñales.

Best time to visit The driest time is from January to April, when it is easiest to hike in
the mountains. The orchids at Soroa are good then too. The wet season begins
around May, while storms can be expected between September and November.

Havana to Pinar del Río

The *autopista* journey from Havana to Pinar del Río is a rather surreal experience, with
modern motorway junctions but virtually no traffic using them except horse-drawn
buses running to nearby villages. Watch out for dogs sleeping peacefully in the fast
lane or bicycles heading towards you in the wrong lane. Vultures can be seen circling
overhead. The *autopista* passes through flat or gently rolling countryside, with large
stretches of sugar cane, tobacco fields and some rice fields, with scattered Royal
palms and distant views of the Cordillera de Guaniguanico, separated sharply from
the southern plains by a geological fault. There are also large uncultivated areas used
as rough pasture, with hump-backed zebu and other cattle, as well as white cattle
egrets which help rid them of parasites. You can see traditional houses built of palm
planks, thatched with palm leaves, and plenty of *vegas*.

An alternative route is to leave the *autopista* at **Candelaria** or **Santa Cruz de los Pinos** for the Carretera Central, quite a good road, which adds only 20 minutes to the journey. It passes through more intensively farmed countryside, with citrus and other fruit trees. Villages straggle along the road, with colonnaded single-storey traditional houses and newer post-Revolution concrete block structures.

Las Terrazas

On the *autopista*, 51 km west of Havana, the Sierra del Rosario appears on the right and a roadside billboard announces the turning to Las Terrazas/Moka, 4 km north of the *autopista*. However, after that there is little signposting through a confusing series of side roads; you will have to ask the way. There is a barrier at the entrance to the **Biosphere Reserve** ① *admission US$7*, which covers 260 sq km of the eastern Sierra del Rosario. Admission to the reserve includes a horrible lunch, unless you have a reservation at the hotel. Las Terrazas was built in 1971 as a forestry and soil conservation station, with nearby slopes terraced to prevent erosion. It is a pleasant settlement of white-painted houses and a long apartment block overlooking the lake of San Juan, which now houses an ecological research centre. In Las Terrazas there is a *paladar* (US$7), as well as craft workshops, a gym, a cinema and a museum which sometimes holds *canturías* or folk music sessions. Nearby there are waterfalls where you can picnic. There is a lovely car park and they may be building cabins.

Following the death in a car accident of the popular singer, Polo Montañez in 2002, his house was opened as a museum, run by his brother. In nearby San Cristóbal, a clay statue of the singer has been put on display. Once a woodcutter, he rose to fame as a singer/songwriter with many hits in the three years before his death, touring Latin America and Europe.

Hiking around Las Terrazas

The hills behind the hotel rise to the **Loma del Salón** (564 m). There are several easy hiking trails: to the partly restored 19th-century **Buenavista** coffee plantation (restaurant has *pollo brujo*, US$10 for hotel guests, US$12-15 for others); 3 km along the San Juan River to the old **La Victoria** coffee plantation and sulphur springs; 4 km along **La Serafina** path to the ruins of the 19th-century **Santa Serafina** coffee plantation, excellent for seeing birds like the Cuban trogon, the solitaire, woodpeckers and the Cuban tody; 8 km along the Cañada del Infierno valley to the **San Pedro** and **Santa Catalina** coffee plantations. There are also more demanding whole-day hikes: a day hiking with a professional ecologist as guide is US$33-41 for one person, falling to US$14-18 per person with six people. Other activities include riding (US$6 per hour), mountain bikes (US$1 per hour), rowing on the lake (US$2 per hour) and fishing.

Soroa

If travelling by car, you can make a detour to Soroa, a spa and resort in the Sierra del Rosario, 81 km southwest of the capital, either by continuing 18 km west then southeast from Moka through the Sierra del Rosario, or directly from the *autopista*, driving northwest from Candelaria. As you drive into the area from the south, a sign on the right indicates the **Mirador de Venus** and **Baños Romanos**. Past the baths is the **Bar Edén** (open till 1800), where you can park before walking up to the *mirador* ① *25 minutes, free on foot, US$3 on a horse*. From the top you get fine views of the southern plains, the forest-covered Sierra and Soroa itself. There are lots of birds, butterflies, dragonflies and lizards around the path; many flowers in season and birdwatching is very popular here.

Further north is a **Jardín Botánico Orchidarium** ① *guided tours daily 0830-1140,*
1340-1555, US$3, birdwatching, hiking and riding US$3 per hr, with over 700 species
of which 250 are native to Cuba, as well as ferns and begonias (check if the orchids
are in bloom before visiting). Alberto, at the desk, speaks good English and some
French and there is also a restaurant, **Castillo de las Nubes** (1200-1900, US$5-6).
There is an excursion to **El Brujito**, a village once owned by French landlords, where
the third and fourth generations of slaves live. Across the road from the Orchidarium
is a **waterfall** ① *250 m along a paved path, US$2,* worth a visit if you are in the area. A
day trip from Havana costs US$29, or you can stay overnight for US$43 per person.

San Diego de los Baños

Nearer Pinar del Río, another detour north off the Carretera Central at Entronque de
San Diego, also in fine scenery, is to the spa of San Diego de los Baños and the
Parque Nacional La Güira. In the wet season a nearby irrigation lake, the **Embalse La
Juventud**, often floods and then this diversion becomes compulsory. San Diego de los
Baños is a pretty little village, with colonnaded houses and a tree-lined square, right
on the southern edge of the Sierra del Rosario. Its mineral waters have made it one of
the most popular health farms in Cuba, but not everyone who comes here is sick.

Parque Nacional La Güira
A few kilometres west of San Diego, an impressive neo-Gothic gateway leads to the
Parque Nacional La Güira. Inside, there are extensive neglected 19th-century gardens,
pools and statues, with the ruins of a Gothic mansion. There is a small bar near the
entrance. Behind, the road winds up through the hills to an army recreation centre;
behind this there is an enormous, cheap (US$3 main course) and rather run down
restaurant. The holiday *cabañas* further up this road are closed and the ones at the
entrance are for Cubans only. The **Cueva de las Portales** just north of here was Che
Guevara's HQ during the Cuban missile crisis and there is a small exhibition of
military and personal relics.

Maspotón

To reach Maspotón, near **Alonso Rojas** in the mangrove wetlands close to the south
coast, leave the *autopista* at Los Palacios and drive south for 25 km. This is an
interesting wildlife area close to the bird migration route from North to South America,
but is run by **Horizontes** as a 134-sq-km hunting resort, where migratory ducks,
long-tail and white-wing doves, quail, guinea fowl and pheasant can all be shot, and
there is also freshwater fishing. **Horizontes** also organizes hunting at Alonso Rojas.

◉ Sleeping

Las Terrazas *p160, map p158*
Hotels
AL-B **Hotel Moka** (Gran Caribe),
T/F82-78600, reservas@commoka .get.tur.cu
Run in co-operation with the Cuban
Academy of Sciences as an ecotourism
centre, breakfast US$5, other meals US$15,
breakfast and dinner packages available,
transfer from Havana US$32, a/c, satellite TV.
Above the village is this 26-room hotel

complex, beautifully designed and laid out in
Spanish colonial style with tiled roofs. Staff
are friendly and knowledgeable, gardens
behind the hillside site have a tennis court
and a pleasant pool where you can have
food and drinks. Vegetarian restaurant just
below the hotel. This is an unusual
opportunity to stay in a nature reserve with
tropical evergreen forests, 850 plant species,
82 bird species, an endemic water lizard, the

world's second smallest frog and world-class experts on tap. Even the hotel receptionist has an ecology PhD.

Casas particulares

F**Villa Juanita**, Las Pastora 601, Cayajabos, Artemisa, 3 km from las Terrazas. 2 rooms, small kitchenette, meals available, good food, very welcoming *casa particular*, no English, but expressive, slow Spanish spoken.

Soroa *p160*
Hotels

C-D**Horizontes Villa Soroa**, T8-852122, www.horizontes.cu 49 cabins and 10 self-catering houses, a/c, phone, radio, some have VCR and private pool, restaurant **El Centro** (quite good), lunch US$8, dinner US$10, disco, bar, Olympic-sized swimming pool, bike rental, riding nearby and handicrafts and dollar shop. A peaceful place. The hotel runs 1-day, gently paced hikes around the main sights of the area with picnic for US$10, to caves for US$12.

Casas particulares

E**Casa Azul**, 300 m outside Soroa next to a primary school. 1 big room with private bath, hot water, balcony overlooking a huge garden, fruit trees, coffee bushes and mountains, free parking, meals available, daughter speaks some English.

San Diego de los Baños *p161*
Hotels

Hotel Libertad, just west of the plaza, is for Cubans only.

Pinar del Río

0 metres   200
0 yards   200

C-D **Hotel Mirador**, on Calle 23 Final, T82-78338, tsalud@sermed.cha.cyt.cu 3 star, spa with warm sulphur baths, massage, pool (US$1), car rental, rooms have a/c, phone, satellite TV, disco US$1.

Casas particulares

F **Caridad Gutiérrez y Julio Gil**, Calle 29 4009 entre 40 y 42, opposite the *balneario*. 2 rooms, 1 with a/c, 1 with fan, 1 has fridge, hot water, meals and drinks available, garage US$1, porch overlooks garden, near river where locals swim, nice people.

F **Carmen Suárez González**, Calle 34 2310 entre 23 y 33. 1 room, 3 fans, no a/c, fridge, garage US$1, colonial architecture with tiled roof, huge garden, building a new room, meals available.

Maspotón *p161*

Hotels

D **Club de Caza Maspotón**, Granja Arrocera La Cubana, Los Palacios, T7-660581, www.horizontes.cu 16 a/c rooms, with restaurant, bar, shop and swimming pool, hunting equipment for rent.

❼ Eating

Havana to Pinar del Río *p159*

There are *paladares* in some villages, including a rooftop one in Candelaria: **Fusilazo**, US$5-10, 3 blocks south of the Carretera Central and 500 m east of the junction with the road for Soroa.

San Diego de los Baños *p161*

Paladar Sorpresa opposite *Libertad*, west of the plaza.

▲▲ Activities and tours

Soroa *p160*

Tour operators

Rumbos, Soroa, T8-771402, open Mon-Fri 0800-1130 and 1400-1700, Sat 0800-1200. Run by English-speaking Yania. **Aerotaxi** and **Víazul** bookings, phone cards and tours.

Pinar del Río → *Colour map 1, grid B3.*

The capital of Pinar del Río province gives a good taste of provincial Cuba. It is a lively city and there is always something going on but it is not particularly attractive. The centre consists of single-storey neoclassical houses with columns, some with other interesting architectural detail. Under the porches, there is a thriving trade in one-person businesses, from selling snacks to repairing cigarette lighters. Horse-drawn vehicles vie for space alongside bicycles and battered old cars on the roads, while the pavements are full of people jostling and weaving in and out of the pillars and other obstacles. ▸▸ *For Sleeping, Eating and other listings, see pages 168-173.*

Ins and outs

Getting there There is an **airstrip** but services are not well-developed, apart from an aerotaxi you can catch from Isla de la Juventud. There is a **train** from Havana, which is cheap but has the disadvantage of being very slow with lots of stops and is very dark, so there is a risk of theft. You have to hang on to your bags all the time and take particular care of your pockets in the tunnels. The **bus** station is reasonably central and all buses use the same terminal. There is a choice of **Víazul** air-conditioned dollar buses or **Astro** buses from Havana on a route that continues to Viñales. On arrival in Pinar del Río you must expect to be hassled by crowds at the bus or train stations, who are touting for your business (see Sleeping page 168). One particularly large, bald man who looks like a Gladiator is known as 'Morro'. Even if you come in by car they will be waiting for you at the road junctions. Young men on bicycles are a particular hazard and very persistent. One was killed recently by a tourist's car when he tried unsuccessfully to force the driver to stop, but that has not deterred the others. Always say you have a reservation. ▸▸ *For further details, see also Transport, page 172.*

Cuban cigars

During Columbus' second journey to the New World, he landed at Gibara in Cuba. Forays inland brought reports that the local inhabitants were smoking roughly rolled dried leaves for ceremonial or religious purposes, which they called *cohibas*. The Spaniards soon acquired the taste for tobacco and in the 17th century introduced it to the European market with great success. The first tobacco plantations in Cuba were established by the Río Almendares (Havana), in the centre of the island and around Bayamo. Tobacco planting spread in the 18th century, becoming particularly successful in the west and by the 19th century tobacco planters and merchants were extremely prosperous. By the time Cuba achieved its independence there were 120 cigar factories around the island.

Nowadays tobacco is cultivated in the west of Cuba in the province of Pinar del Río, in the centre in the provinces of Villa Clara and Sancti Spíritus and in the east in the provinces of Granma and Santiago de Cuba, although the tobacco regions are known as Vuelta Abajo, Semi Vuelta, Partidos, Remedios and Oriente. Only Partidos and Vuelta Abajo can grow tobacco of a high enough quality for the Grandes Marcas of cigars (*Habanos*), and only Vuelta Abajo produces all the leaves necessary for a cigar. Lower quality tobacco is made into cigarettes. Tobacco is extremely labour intensive and in Cuba it is grown, harvested and processed entirely by hand. Seedlings are transplanted from the nursery in October-December when they are 18-20 cm, taking great care not to damage the delicate roots. After a week they are weeded and after two weeks they are earthed up to maintain humidity and increase the plants' assimilation of nutrients. This is done with the help of oxen rather than a tractor, to avoid compacting the soil. When the plant reaches 1.4-1.6 m, side shoots are removed and the plant is encouraged to grow tall with only 6-9 pairs of leaves. Harvesting takes place in January-March, during which time the leaves are collected by hand, two or three at a time, every five days, starting at the bottom. They are then taken to a huge, thatched barn, where they are sewn together in pairs and hung on a pole to dry. The leaves turn yellow, then reddish gold and are considered dry after about 50 days. They are then piled in bundles or stacks for about 30 days, during which time the first fermentation takes place at a temperature not exceeding 35°C, before being classified according to colour, size and quality for wrappers or fillers. At this stage the leaves are stripped off the main vein, dampened, flattened and packed in bigger stacks for up to 60 days of fermentation at a temperature not exceeding 42°C. Finally they are stored and aged for months, or maybe years, before being taken to be rolled by the expert hands of factory workers.

Five types of leaves are used in the manufacture of a cigar. In the middle (*tripa*) are a mixture of three types, *ligero, seco* and *volado*. These are wrapped in the *capote*, which is then enveloped in the *capa*, which is the part you see and determines the appearance of the cigar. There are two types of tobacco plant: the *corojo*, and the *criollo*. The former produces only the *capa*, but it comes in several colours. It is grown beneath vast cotton shrouds to protect it from the sun's radiation and keep it soft and silky. The latter provides the other four leaves needed to make up the cigar, which determine the flavour. It is grown in full sunlight to get intense flavours. Each of the five leaves is processed and aged differently before reaching the factory floor for mixing according to secret recipes and rolling.

Hundreds of workers sit at tables in the factory, equipped only with a special knife called a *chaveta*, a guillotine and a pot of gum. A skilled artisan (*torcedor*) makes an average of 120 cigars a day as he or she sits and listens to readings from the press or novels, a tradition which has been carried on since 1865 and has never been replaced by the radio or taped music. Although many of the people rolling cigars are women, it is unfortunately a myth that Cuban cigars are rolled on the thighs of dusky maidens. The women sorting the leaves do, however, place them across their laps on each leg and this may have been where the erotic image originated.

Quality control is rigid. Any cigars which do not meet the standards of size, shape, thickness and appearance are rejected. Those which do make it are stored at a temperature of 16°-18°C at a humidity of 65-70% for several weeks until they lose the moisture acquired during rolling. A specialist then classifies them according to colour (of which there are 65 tones) and they are chosen for boxes, with the colours ranging from dark to light, left to right. They have to remain exactly as they are placed in the cedar wood box and the person who then labels each cigar has to keep them in the same order, even facing the same way.

Finally the boxes are stamped and sealed with the government's guarantee, which looks rather like a currency note and carries the words: 'Cuban Government's warranty for cigars exported from Havana' in English, French and German as well as Spanish.

Always buy your cigars from a state shop, not on the street, where they are bound to be fakes, no matter how good a deal they appear. Check the quality of each cigar. They should be tightly rolled, not soft; they should have no lumps or other protuberances; if you turn them upside down nothing should come out; the colour should be uniform and the aroma should be strong. The box should be sealed with the four-language warranty, which should not be a photocopy, and on the bottom you should find the stamp: Habanos s.a. HECHO EN CUBA *Totalmente a mano*. You may take only 23 cigars out of the country without a receipt, but if you buy them in a state shop and get a valid receipt you can buy cigars up to a value of US$2,000 (unless you are returning to the USA, of course, where the embargo forbids you to import Cuban cigars of any worth).

Cigars are like fine wines or whiskies and there are many different types from which to choose. Castro used to smoke *Cohiba* cigars, which were created in 1966 exclusively for the diplomatic market. In 1982 the *Cohiba Lanceros*, *Coronas Especiales* and *Panatelas* were created for public sale, followed in 1989 by the *Espléndidos*, *Robustos* and *Exquisitos*, which together make up the Classic Line (*La Línea Clásica*). In 1992, to mark the 500th anniversary of the landing of Columbus, they brought out the 1492 Line (*La Línea 1492*), with its five centuries: *Siglo I, II, III, IV, V*. The *Espléndidos* now sell for up to US$383 a box.

As well as the *Cohiba* brand, there are *Montecristo*, *Romeo y Julieta*, *Bolívar*, *Punch*, *Hoyo de Monterrey*, *H Upmann*, *Partagas*, *Quintero*, *La Flor de Cano*, *El Rey del Mundo* and *Rafael González*, all of which have their company histories and logos, mostly dating from the 19th century.

Getting around The town is one of several that have changed street names but continue to use the old ones as well as the new official names. It can be confusing when names on the map conflict with what people really call the streets, for example 20 de Mayo is now Primero de Mayo, Vélez Caviedes is also Ormani Arenado, while Virtudes is also Ceferino Fernández. Pinar del Río is not large and it is easy to **walk** around the centre and to most of the places of interest, such as the rum and tobacco factories. For a short excursion out of the town, it is easy enough to get a **bus** to Viñales, stopping at places on the way, but public transport is very limited to towns in other directions. **Car hire** is the most convenient way of getting about, but you can also commission a local driver/guide and use his/her car for a day trip, or hire a taxi.

Best time to visit Carnival is in July but it is not on the scale of Santiago's or Havana's. At any time of year you can find something going on in and around the city. Expect rain in between September and November, although heavy showers can happen at any time, usually in the afternoon.

Sights

The main shopping street and centre of activities is José Martí, which runs west-east through the town. At the west end is the **Centro de Artes Visuales** ⓘ *Martí, opposite Parque Independencia, T82-752758, Mon-Fri 1000-1700, Sat 0800-1200, 1 peso or US$1*. Walk along José Martí to the east to a renovated building opposite the Wedding Palace: the **Palacio de Computación** ⓘ *Martí esq González Coro, Mon-Sat 0800-2100, theatre, cafeteria and classrooms for teaching computer skills,* which was inaugurated by Fidel Castro in January 2001. It is very photogenic if taken from Parque de la Independencia. The **Casa de la Cultura Tito Junco** ⓘ *Martí esq Rafael Morales, Mon-Sat 0800-1800,* is in a huge, recently renovated colonial house and includes an art gallery, a hall for parties and seven classrooms for teaching dancing, painting, singing etc. There are evening activities according to scheduled programmes. The old **Globo** hotel, right in the centre near the corner of José Martí and Isabel Rubio, is closed pending renovation, but it has a beautiful tiled staircase worth a peep. The **Museo Provincial de Historia** ⓘ *Martí 58 entre Isabel Rubio y Colón, T82-754300, Mon-Sat 0800-1700, US$0.25,* details the history of the town and displays objects from the wars of independence. On the same side of the street is the **Teatro José Jacinto Milanés** ⓘ *Martí esq Colón*. Built in 1883, this is one of the most beautiful theatres in the country. Further along Martí is the **Museo de Ciencias Naturales Tranquilino Sandalio de Noda** ⓘ *José Martí 202 esq Av Comandante Pinares, T82-758037, Mon-Sat 0800-1700, US$1,* with geological and natural history, not large, not much explanation, not much on typical Cuban animals. The great thing, however, is the eclectic building, formerly the Palacio Guasch, which is the most ornate in the region, with Gothic towers, spires and all sorts of twiddly bits.

There is a **cigar factory**, Fábrica de Tabaco Francisco Donatién ⓘ *Maceo 157, T82-7 23424, Mon-Sat 0800-1700, US$5 for a short visit,* one of the town's main tourist attractions, but it was closed for remodelling in 2003. It reputedly makes the best cigars in Cuba and even when the factory is shut you can still buy the very finest cigars in the town. Avoid the youngsters selling cigars outside. Workers in the factory will also try and sell you cigars. Buy from the shop opposite, **Casa del Habano**, and you'll get the genuine article, even if it is pricey. Remember there is a limit on the number of cigars you can take out of the country without a receipt so any illegally bought cigars should be smoked in Cuba. Also worth a visit, if you're interested, is the **rum factory**, Fábrica de Guayabita ⓘ *Isabel Rubio 189 entre Ceferino Fernández y Frank País, Mon-Sat 0800-1700, US$2, tour and stop at the tasting room,* which makes a special rum flavoured with miniature wild guavas,

Armed guards around the cigar factory are to protect tourists from hassling.

are cheaper than those in the shops. Between the two is the pretty cream-coloured
cathedral of **San Rosendo** ⓘ *Maceo 2 Este esq Gerardo Medina.*

Around Pinar del Río

South to the coast

The nearest beach, 25 km to the south of Pinar del Río, is **Las Canas,** near **La Coloma**.
From La Coloma you can take a boat trip to the **Cayos de San Felipe** ▸▸ *For further details,
see Activities and tours, page 170.* The Cays are unspoilt and fabulous.

The Carretera Central continues west from Pinar del Río through pleasant farming
country with villages strung along the road, sugar and tobacco fields, citrus trees and
pasture. There are distant views of the mountains to the north and clearly marked side
roads lead south to the fishing town of **Boca de Galafre** and the beach for Cubans at
Bailén, where there are small A-frame cabins, popular with Cubans during the summer
▸▸ *See Sleeping, page 169.* The beach is spoilt by the run-off from the Río Cuyaguateje, which
makes the water muddy and there is no reef to snorkel on. It is cleared at the beginning of
April but then left to get dirty, muddy and smelly. The beach is slightly better further east.

There is a bus from Pinar del Río in the morning, returning in the afternoon, but it
often fails to appear. Several kilometres down the road to Playa Bailén and 1 km before
you get to the beach, there is a **crocodile farm** ⓘ *daily 0900-1700, US$3, photographs
US$10, video cameras US$50,* where you can get uncomfortably close to the babies and
can hold them. However, unless you are lucky, or come at feeding time, you are a 500 m
telephoto lens away from the 4-5 m beasts. Note that small cars are likely to get bogged
down in the sandy drive of the farm.

West to Península de Guanahacabibes

Back on the Carretera Central, **Isabel Rubio** has a gas station with a dollar shop selling
drinks, toiletries and canned foods. From Isabel Rubio, a very pretty way to return to
Pinar del Río (about one hour) is through Guane, Los Portales and Sumidero. **Guane,** a
large, attractive village with old houses and a little baroque church, is also the railway
terminus. The road runs through limestone hills, crossing the pretty **Río Cuyaguateje**
several times and passing through the **Valle de San Carlos,** a spectacular narrow
valley with cliffs and steep wooded hills rising on either side. Farmers grow fruit,
vegetables and tobacco, with ox-drawn ploughs furrowing the bright red soil and
tent-shaped tobacco drying sheds, *vegas,* everywhere.

After Isabel Rubio the countryside becomes completely flat. The villages are less
lively and the agricultural landscapes less varied, with plantations of Caribbean pine
in some stretches. On the north side of the road, 7 km west of Isabel Rubio, is the
turning for **Laguna Grande,** a lake where you can fish or swim. A few miles further on at
Punta Colorada is a small beach.

The main road continues through **Sandino** and **La Fé** to **Manuel Lazo**. After this
village, potholes are more common. The last 15 km or so to the coast are through
semi-deciduous dry coastal woodland. On reaching the coast at **La Bajada,** a very
desolate little village, an immigration post will ask to see your documents. Private
taxis are not allowed to take you any further, you will have to wait and hitch a lift with
official tourist transport, which may mean a long wait.

The **Península de Guanahacabibes,** which forms the western tip of Cuba, is a
Natural Biosphere Reserve. The reserve covers 1,175 sq km but has not yet been
developed for ecotourism. The peninsula is formed of very recent limestone, with an
irregular rocky surface and patchy soil cover. There are interesting fossil coastlines,
caves and blue holes; but with dense woodland on the south coast and mangrove on
the north, the peninsula is uninviting for the casual hiker. However, for keen

naturalists there are 12 amphibian species, 29 reptiles including iguana species, 10 mammals (including *jutia carabalí* and *jutia conga*) and 147 bird species, including nine of the 22 which are endemic to Cuba. There is a scientific station at La Bajada. Permits are required for entering the reserve. The Science Academy, T84-3277, offers a Safari Tour with an English-speaking guide, Osmani Borrego, for US$6 per person. You can climb to the Radar for US$1 for a good view of the forest and the sea.

To the west of La Bajada, a track for four-wheel-drive vehicles continues to **Cabo de San Antonio**, where there are a few houses and a lighthouse built in 1849 and named after the then Spanish governor, Roncalli. The coastline has several pretty white-sand beaches and clear waters, but is otherwise lonely and desolate. A large hotel is planned.

The main road continues 12 km south, hugging the coast, to **María La Gorda**, in the middle of nowhere, reputedly the best diving centre in Cuba and an idyllic spot for relaxing or doing nothing but **diving**. There are several wrecks off the western peninsula and freshwater cave diving in the blue holes is also possible, though not on offer as an organized activity. The dive boat tours usually go a short distance to dive sites, mostly reef or wall dives, where there are lots of fish of all sizes, rays, turtles, barracuda and maybe whale sharks. The sea is very clear, very warm and calm, even when it is too rough to dive anywhere else in Cuba. There is good snorkelling with small coral heads close to the white sand beach, or you can go out on the dive boat, but from September to December there are sometimes jelly fish. They inflict only a mild sting, but they make swimming uncomfortable. ▸▸ *For further details, see Activities and tours, page 171.*

● Sleeping

Pinar del Río *p163, map p162*
Hotels
C **Hotel Pinar del Río**, José Martí final, towards the *autopista*, but within walking distance of the city centre, T82-750707. Staff friendly and helpful, swimming pool, nightclub, car hire, in need of updating, beds too soft, sheets too short, hot water in the evenings only, poor lighting, no bedside light, poor TV reception, poor breakfast.

Casas particulares
There is a mafia of young men on bicycles who will meet you on arrival, whether by car, bus or train, and pester to take you to a *casa particular*, *paladar*, or whatever. Sometimes they say they are from **Formatur**, the tourism school. Sometimes they tell you there is a salsa festival in town to get you to stay here rather than go on to Viñales. They are after a commission, set by them at US$5 per person per night and have been known to be violent with Cuban landlords who refuse to pay. Avoid them if you can and make your own way using the map. If you accept any help with directions they will ask the Cuban family for money. If you are given the card of a *casa particular* in Havana, by a bus ticket seller or a taxi driver, be aware that they too are receiving a commission. Taxi drivers are in the same game; if your driver says

he can't find the address, refuse to pay unless he goes to the right house. He will try and take you somewhere else to get his commission. Drivers have even been known to state that the owner of a *casa* is in prison rather than take you there.

F **Bertha Báez**, Pedro Téllez 53 entre Ormani Arenado e Isidro de Armas, T82-754247. 2 rooms, the 2nd floor is reserved for guests, hot and cold shower, a/c, fans, garage US$1.

F **Eloína Arteaga**, Isabel Rubio 18, Apto 4, opposite the Baptist Church. 1 room and meals available. Only women live here, Eloína and her 2 daughters and 3 grand daughters.

F **Hospedaje Torres**, Adela Azcuy 7 entre Gerardo Medina y Isabel Rubio, no phone. Run by nice lady, room with fan or a/c, clean and safe, excellent breakfast and dinner.

F **Ivan Lorenzo**, Gerardo Medina 241 entre Frank País y 2. 1 room, a/c, hot water 24 hrs, meals available.

F **José Antonio Mesa**, Gerardo Medina 67 entre Adela Azcuy y Isidro de Armas, T82-753173. Colonial building, spacious, breakfast available, nice family but involved in paying commissions so unpopular with other renters.

F **Noelia Pérez Blanco**, Gerardo Medina 175 entre Ceferino Fernández y Frank País, T82-753660. Run by elderly lady, most of the house is used by tourists, although there is only 1 bedroom, 2 beds, fan or a/c, TV, hot water, garage US$2, roof with table and chairs, a little English spoken.

F Salvador Reyes, Alameda 24 entre Volcán y Avellaneda, opposite phone company, T82-773145. 1 room, a/c, fan, hot shower, nice terrace, some English and German spoken, nice family, a little far from the centre.

F Traveller's Rest, Primero de Mayo 29 entre Isidro de Armas y Antonio Rubio, Apto 16, sign outside, T82-751792, http://geocities.com/travellers_rest_pinar 2 rooms with 2 beds, hot shower, a/c or fan, fridge, good meals available, book exchange, garage US$1 a day. Run by Juan Carlos Otaño, also known as 'The Teacher', he speaks French, English, some Swedish, Italian and German, very friendly and helpful. Only he and his mother live in the apartment. Excursions and trips locally and around the island.

F Villa Lolo, Martí 57 entre Isabel Rubio y Colón. 1 room, private, a/c, fan, hot and cold shower, little English spoken, dog, watch out for hustlers seeking commission.

F Zunilda Rodríguez Hernández, Acueducto 16 entre Méndez Capote y Primera, Rpto Celso Maragota, T82-754639. 2 a/c rooms, private bath, hot water, breakfast and dinner, garage, her husband Julio fought with Che and Fidel.

South to the coast *p167*
Hotels
E Villa Playa Bailén, Bailén, on the beach, T82-33401. A sprawling resort stretching 2 km along the sand, with small A-frame cabins on the beach and concrete houses with self-catering facilities behind. It is very popular with Cubans in the summer months and even at other times of the year foreigners are likely to be told it is full. Cubans are allowed here Apr-Sep for a very basic beach holiday. Foreigners may come all year round. The small, A-frame cabins are little more than camping. Further east, away from the river, the cabins are larger, better and have water. The beach is nicer here too, but it is all rather rundown.

West to Península de Guanahacabibes *p167*
Hotels
C-D María La Gorda, T/F84-78131. Jul-Aug are most expensive, Nov-Easter high season, 3 meals US$31 per person, nowhere else to eat, package of accommodation, meals and 2 dives

daily is US$100 per person. Lovely location, rooms open onto the beach, hammocks between palm trees, excellent value, nicely decorated, simple but comfortable, a/c, hot water, minibar, TV. 20 new *cabañas* have been built in the forest, but these attract mosquitoes. Good service, friendly staff, buffet meals, bar, not much entertainment, shop, *Telecorreos*.

E Villa Internacional Aguas Claras, Carretera de Viñales Km 7, T82-778426. Two-star, 50 basic rooms in small chalets in beautiful landscaped garden around unchlorinated pool, mosquitoes, restaurant has usual pork and chicken of poor quality.

E Villa Turística Laguna Grande (Islazul), Granja Simón Bolívar, Municipio Sandino, T84-2430. 12 gloomy, thatched, A-frame cabins, with a/c, bar and restaurant. A quiet, pleasant and rural location, but not much going on. Rather neglected but clean.

Camping
There is a booking office where you can make campsite reservations on Isabel Rubio entre Martí y Adely Azcuy, T82-755316, open Mon-Fri 0800-1200 and 1300-1700, Sat 0800-1200.

⊙ Eating

Pinar del Río *p163, map p162*
Restaurants
The best peso pizzas are on Gerardo Medina opposite Doña Neli bakery; Mon-Sat 0900-1700, 6-10 pesos.

$$ Pinar Café, Gerardo Medina, opposite Coppelia, open daily 1800-0200. Expensive restaurant, US$5 for soft drink, beers, bottle of rum and potato chips, also a show at 2130, Afro-Cuban show Tue. Beware of theft.

$ Coppelia, Gerardo Medina, open daily 0800-2330. Ice cream can be bought in pesos, very cheap.

$ Doña Neli, Gerardo Medina 24. Dollar bakery, open daily 0700-1900 for bread, 0830-2300 for pastries and cakes.

$ Doña Yuya, José Martí 68, entre Isabel Rubio y Colón, open 1130-1430 and 1830-2130. Pay in pesos, beautiful architecture, but terrible food.

$ La Taberna, Coro 103 opposite La Paquita amusement park for children, open daily from 1800. Pesos only, very cheap, dinner around 50-60 pesos, beer 8-10 pesos, bar and patio.

$ **Mar Init**, José Martí, opposite Parque de la Independencia, T82-754952, open Tue-Sun 1930-2130. Pay in pesos, fish is the speciality of the house.

$ **Rumayor**, 2 km on Viñales road, open 1200-2200, closed Thu. State-run restaurant which specializes in *pollo ahumado* (smoked chicken), overpriced at US$6.50, grim toilets, cabaret at night, see below.

$ **Terrazina**, Antonio Rubio y Primero de Mayo, open 1130-1500 and 1800-2200. Pay in pesos, pizza, spaghetti, beer, all-you-can-eat for less than US$1.

$ **Vueltabajo**, Martí y Rafael Morales, daily 0930-2000. Food available, also bar selling rum, beer, soft drinks.

Paladar

$ **El Mesón**, Martí, opposite the Museo de Ciencias Naturales, T82-752867, Mon-Sat 1100-2400. A *paladar* run by Rafael, a former teacher, nice place, the only place outside a *casa particular* where you can get a decent meal, lunch or dinner US$6-7.

◉ Entertainment

Pinar del Río *p163, map p162*
Cinema
Cine Praga, Gerardo Medina, next to Coppelia, Mon-Sun 1400-2400. 2 pesos.
Cine Zayden, Martí 111. 1 peso.

Music
The town is very lively on Sat nights and, to a lesser extent, on Fri. There is live music everywhere, salsa, *son*, Mexican music, international stuff. During the day in **Parque Roberto Amarán** you can hear traditional music (mambo, rumba, cha-cha-cha, *danzón*) Wed and Sat 1400-1520, Sun 0900. There is often boxing at 1000 in the same *parque*.
Bar La Esquinita, on Isabel Rubio, daily 2000-0200. Live music, usually guitarist.
Callejón de Corina, Primero de Mayo. A *Proyecto Socio-Cultural*, held at weekends (Sat or Sun) 1500-1730, show of folkloric music (rumba, Guaguancó) and children perform with dance and a fashion show.
Casa de la Cultura, Rafael Morales esq Martí. Band play every Sun evening with a dance contest for the elderly, fantastic, free, photos allowed.

Casa de la Música, on Gerardo Medina next to Coppelia. Live music daily except Mon, 1 peso, no drinks, but you will also find it all along José Martí, with competitions and displays.
Disco Rita, on González Coro. An open-air venue popular with teenagers, where they play loud, US-style disco music, entry 2 pesos, the only drink on sale is neat rum at 25 pesos a bottle.
Hotel Pinar del Río, see Sleeping above, Thu-Sun 2000-0400. Classy disco, US$1, very popular, full every night, young crowd, nice atmosphere. Next door is the **Cafét D'Prisa**, open 24 hrs, rowdy, frequent fights, avoid.
La Picauala, at the back of the Teatro Milanés, Sat, Sun 2100 for the best bands and a fashion show, 10 pesos.
Rumayor on Viñales road, see Eating above. A *Tropicana*-style show, Fri, Sat and Sun US$5, very good, lots of security. Starts 2300 (get there before 2200 to get a table) and lasts about 1½ hrs, followed by disco until 0300 or so. Held in small amphitheatre with proper sound and lighting system. No photography or videos allowed. The complex is in a pleasant garden with lots of trees. Don't bother with mid-week *Noche Cubana*, held on a different stage, the show is no good and the place is full of *jineteros*.

Nightclubs
Artex, Martí 36, opposite Photo service, open daily 0900-0200.
The Wedding Palace, Martí 125, bar open Tue-Fri 0800-2400, Sat and Sun 1000-0200. Beer, rum, snacks, TV, a/c, a lovely place.

Theatre
Teatro José Jacinto Milanés, Martí esq Colón. There are 3 theatre groups, 1 children's and 2 adults, which give occasional performances.

▲ Activities and tours

Boat trips
Ecotur-Alcona SA, Km 2.5 Carretera Luis Lazo, T82-793844. From Coloma there are boat trips to the Cayos de San Felipe. Prices range from US$38, if there are 10 of you, to US$166 per person if there are only 2, for a day trip that includes a visit to a lobster ground, a coral reef for snorkelling, Cayo Sijú, bird-watching, lunch

and a spell on the beach. You can also go diving or fishing. Also available is a liveaboard boat on which you can spend 7 days and 6 nights, including 10 dives and all meals, for US$570. In winter you can watch turtles and at any time you can see crocodiles and iguanas watching you while you have lunch.

Diving
Dive shop at María La Gorda, T84-771306, T/F84-78131, see p168. Doctor specializing in hyperbaric medicine. Good boat with shade, pleasant Spanish-speaking staff. The dive boat leaves 0930 and 1530 for the offshore reef (US$30 per dive, plus US$7.50 a day to rent equipment for those not on a package).
Cubamar and **Puertosol**, see Essentials pxxx, organize a package including accommodation, food, diving (US$100 per person a day, minimum two people) and transfers from Havana (US$70 each way, 4-5 hours).

Kids' activities
There is a children's amusement park, 'Paquito' on Coro, opposite **Restaurant La Taberna**, open 1600-2200 during the week and 0800-2200 at weekends.

Sailing
For visitors arriving by yacht, María La Gorda is a port of entry. There are 4 moorings, max draft 2 m, VHF channels 16, 19, 68 and 72.

Tour operators
Cubanacán, Martí. Tours, reservations, tickets, internet 0830-2100.
Cubatur, Martí 51, esq Ormani Arenado, T82-778405, daily 0800-1700.
Ecotur-Alcona, see Boat trips above, also offers horse riding (US$3 per hour or US$10 per day), hiking (US$8 with a guide), jeep safaris, caving and hunting (US$130 per day).
Rumbos, Martí, next to La Casona, Mon-Fri 0800-1700, Sat 0800-1200, T82-771802, F82-771401, arumcupr@ip.etecsa.cu Excursions to beaches, tobacco plantations, etc, also maps and phone cards for sale, car rental.

☺ Festivals and events

Pinar del Río *p163, map p162*
1st week of Jul Carnival lasts for for 5 days, Wed-Sun.

◘ Shopping

Pinar del Río *p163, map p162*.
Bookshop
Vietnam, Martí 5, Mon-Fri 0800-1700, Sat 0800-1200.

Cigars and rum
Do not buy cigars on the street from a young man calling himself 'Teacher', he is an imposter called Osmany dealing in fakes.
Casa del Habano, opposite the cigar factory, for all brands of cigar from the Vueltabajo region. Smart, upmarket, bar at the back, open same hours as the factory.
Casa del Ron, Maceo esq Antonio Tarafa, 50 m from cigar factory, for all your rum needs.

Hair and beauty
Barber, Martí 60, open Mon-Sat 0800-1800. Another on Primero de Mayo, opposite Traveller's Rest, 2 pesos for a shave, 5 pesos for a hair cut, popular.
Beauty Parlour, Martí 41A, opposite Artex, Mon-Sat 0900-1800. Pay in pesos, body massage US$2 per hour with Erik, who only works until midday.

Handicrafts
There is a craft shop on Martí esq Gerardo Medina, daily 0800-1700.

Markets
There is a fruit market opposite the railway station on Av Rafael Ferro, Mon-Sat 0800-1600, Sun 0800-1300, pay in pesos. A new a/c market is opposite the Banco Financiero Internacional, next to Coppelia on the corner of Gerardo Medina and Isidro de Armas, daily 0900-1700.

Photography
Photo service, on Isabel Rubio 2 entre Martí y Máximo Gómez, open Mon-Sat 0800-1800,

---

● *For an explanation of the sleeping and eating price codes used in this guide, see inside the* ● *front cover. Other relevant information is provided in Essentials, pages 48-53.*

Sun 0800-1200, also Martí 35, T82-78346, daily 0800-2200.

⊖ Transport

Air

Alvaro Barba airport is on the road to La Coloma, 8 km from town, T82-755542, bookings 0800-1200. To **Isla de la Juventud**, Tue and Thu 1240, US$22 1 way, rather like a flying bus, DC3 taking 20 Cubans and 10 foreigners. Reservations at **Rumbos**, Martí, next to La Casona, Mon-Fri 0800-1700, Sat 0800-1200, T82-771802, F82-771401, arumcupr@ip.etecsa.cu or call Cristino at the airport.

Bus

In Pinar del Río some ticket sellers refuse to sell tickets until the bus arrives. Passengers in the waiting lounge are not told when it does arrive and it leaves without them. The 'helpful' ticket seller then tries to sell them a seat in a private taxi, for which he/she no doubt receives a commission.

The bus station is on Colón, north of José Martí, near Gómez. Downstairs for tickets for provincial buses and trucks, upstairs for buses to **Havana** and tickets in US dollars. 24-hr café opposite the bus station. Víazul, T82-752571/755255, runs a daily bus service from Havana to **Viñales** which leaves at 0900. It stops on request at **Las Terrazas** (US$6) and **San Diego de los Baños** (US$8), and gets to **Pinar del Río** (US$11) at around 1120 with no stops. The return bus leaves Viñales at 1330, stopping in Pinar del Río around 1400 and getting to Havana at 1645. You may have to wait until the bus comes in so they know how many seats are free.

Astro also runs daily from Havana at 1700 to Pinar del Río, cheaper at US$7, but the bus regularly breaks down and is slower. May be necessary to book in advance in peak travel periods. The *Víazul* fare between Pinar del Río and Viñales is US$6, but if you get a local peso bus your name has to be on the list. To **La Palma**, 1730, 2 pesos, **Bahía Honda**, 1820, 4 pesos, **Puerto Esperanza**, 1930, 2.60 pesos, **Sandino**, 1800, 2 pesos, **Guane**, 2 pesos, **Mantua** 3 pesos.

Víazul runs a minibus from Pinar del Río to **María la Gorda**, timed to leave after the bus from Havana has arrived in Pinar del Río, returning 1500, max 8 passengers, US$80 for whole bus. Unreliable in low season. Alternatively visitors come on package tours with US$70 transfers from Havana or rented car. Local buses run unreliably to María La Gorda from the equally remote villages of Las Martinas and Sandino.

Car hire

Havanautos and **Transautos** both have offices in Hotel Pinar del Río. Distances from Pinar del Río are 157 km to Havana, 159 km to María La Gorda, 103 km to Las Terrazas, 88 km to Soroa, 25 km to Viñales. From Havana to Pinar del Río takes around 2 hrs 50 mins by the highway, 4 hrs 10 mins on the main road.

Taxi

Long distance travel by taxi is possible but you will need very good Spanish to negotiate effectively. Pinar del Río to Viñales in a state taxi is US$10, although locals can hire a taxi for the same distance for about US$5. **Panataxi**, T82-758458, driver Israel Machado is good and has a comfortable car. US$50 one way to María la Gorda. Private taxis charge around US$30 from Pinar del Río to La Bajada, where they have to leave you at the checkpoint, but they have effectively been sidelined by the introduction of the Víazul service.

Train

The railway station in Pinar del Río is on Av Comandante Pinares, T82-752106. From **Havana** at 2140, arriving at 0310. Take a torch, hang on to your luggage, don't sleep, noisy, train stops about 29 times, very slow. The line continues to **Guane**, 3 pesos or US$3. Trains to Havana leave at 0900 on alternate days, and cost US$7.

⊕ Directory

Pinar del Río *p163, map p162*
Banks
Banco Financiero Internacional (BFI), Gerardo Medina, opposite Coppelia, T82-778183, F82-778213, open Mon-Fri 0800-1500. **Cadeca**, Gerardo Medina, next to Coppelia, open 0830-1800. Also on Martí 50 next to Artex bar. **Banco Popular de Ahorro**, Martí 113, opposite the chess academy, Mon-Fri 0800-1700. Money on credit cards.

Chess academy
Martí 110, Mon-Sat 0800-2000.

Hospitals and clinics
Policlínico Turcios Lima, opposite cathedral, Gerardo Medina 112, open Mon-Sat 0800-1700. **Dentist**, Martí 162, T82-773348, open 0800-1700.

Internet
Etecsa, on Av Alameda. US$15 for 5 hrs with *tarjeta*. **Cubanacán**, Martí, internet access 0830-2100, 2 terminals, prepaid cards US$6 for 3 hrs.

Language schools
Andrés Bello, Maceo 20, Mon-Thu 1730-2030. French, German, English, Italian and Spanish classes.

Pharmacies
Camacho, Martí 62. Open daily 0800-2300. Piloto, under El Globo Hotel, open daily 0800-2400 with emergency service.

Post office
Martí esq Isabel Rubio, Mon-Sat 0800-1700.

Telephone/fax
Etecsa, Av Alameda IIA, Parque de la Independencia, T82-754585-7. A 24-hr phone centre is at Gerardo Medina esq Juan Gualberto Gómez, domestic and calls abroad, phone cards for sale. **Telecorreos**, Hotel Pinar del Río. Fax service US$10.20 a page. At the **Post office**, see above, a fax service abroad is available, US$8 per page.

Viñales → *Colour map 1, grid B3.*

North of Pinar del Río, the road leads across pine-covered hills and valleys for 25 km to Viñales, a delightful, small town in a dramatic valley in the Sierra de los Organos. Viñales itself is a pleasant town, with an avenue of pine trees and wooden colonnades along the main street, with its red-tiled roofs. Visitors come here to relax, hike in the hills and maybe visit a beach on the north coast. The valley has a distinctive landscape, with steep-sided limestone mogotes rising dramatically from fertile flat-floored valleys, where farmers cultivate the red soil for tobacco, fruits and vegetables. As in so much of rural Cuba, horses, pigs, oxen, zebu cattle and chickens are everywhere, including on the main road. ▶▶ *For Sleeping, Eating and other listings, see pages 176-180.*

Ins and outs

Getting there There is no **airport**, but the one at Pinar del Río is not far away. The nearest train station is at Pinar del Río. **Víazul** has a daily **bus** service from Havana via Pinar del Río and there are local buses between villages.

Getting around The town is little more than a village and it is easy to **walk** around. Many visitors hire a **car** or **scooter** to get around the nearby attractions, although there are also **horses** for hire and **peso buses**. Illegal **private taxis** will take you anywhere, although you may have to get out of the car and walk some sections to avoid police checks.

Best time to visit The mountains attract a fair amount of rain and you can expect wet afternoons, particularly from September to November. Carnival is in September.

Sights

The main street is Salvador Cisneros and a walk along the avenue of pine trees will reveal nearly all the attractions Viñales has to offer. Streets running parallel or across it are residential and contain many *casas particulares*. **Víazul** drops you off half way along the street, opposite the main square with a little-used church. There is also a little municipal museum on Salvador Cisneros and a **Casa de la Cultura** on the square with an art gallery. An informative curator here speaks English. There are

Rocks, caves, valleys and mogotes

The rocks around Viñales are pure limestones formed in the Jurassic period around 160 million years ago. Unlike most other rocks, limestone can be dissolved by rainwater. Rivers and streams often flow underground through extensive cave systems; most of the 10,000 recorded caves in Cuba are in the western province and one cave system in the Valle Santo Tomás consists of a total of 25 km of underground passages. Where a valley is formed in tropical limestone, often by downwards faulting of the rock, it may be filled with fertile red soil. Rotting vegetation increases the acidity of the groundwater on the valley floor. This 'aggressive' water eats into the valley sides, undercutting the rocks and producing steep cliff-like features. The valley floor is broken by isolated steep-sided hills, known to both English- and Spanish-speaking geologists by their Cuban name: mogotes. Other valleys (narrow gorges) are produced when the roof of a large cave collapses. Similar tropical limestone landscapes can be seen in parts of Puerto Rico and Jamaica.

Rapid drainage of rainwater into the rock produces dry growing conditions for plants. The limestone hills have a distinctive vegetation type, with palms (including the curious cork palm), deciduous trees, succulents, lianas and epiphytes. More than 20 species are endemic, found only in the Viñales area. The isolation of the mogotes has also produced distinctive animal species, with some types of snail found only on a single mogote.

several bars and restaurants along Salvador Cisneros, but hardly of the quality to warrant the thousands of visitors who come here every year. Indeed, in August 2003, there were so many tourists that the town couldn't cope and several had to sleep in the plaza.

On the edge of Viñales is **Caridad's Garden** ① *turn left at the gas station at the end of Salvador Cisneros, no entry fee, but a tip of US$1 is appreciated*. The garden contains a beautiful collection of flowers from Cuba and around the world and fruit trees. Chickens scratch about in the shady undergrowth with their chicks. Currently run by two elderly sisters, the garden was first planted by their parents in the 1930s. A guide will show you around, pointing out all the different species and you will be invited to try all the different fruits. They are generous with their produce but appreciate contributions to the upkeep of the garden.

Around Viñales

Hiking around Viñales

An area of 132 sq km around Viñales has been declared a National Monument. A visitors' centre is under construction on the main road heading out to Pinar del Río, near **Hotel Los Jazmines,** which should open in 2004. Hiking in the valleys is perfectly safe, however if venturing into the mountains themselves, it would be sensible to take a local guide, at around US$5 a day, but they don't all speak good English. You can find one at the museum opposite **Artex.** Martín Luís López is recommended; a former ecology and geography university lecturer, he speaks English, French and some German and knows Viñales like the back of his hand. You may find him at Caridad's garden.

Mural de la Prehistoria

Two kilometres west of Viñales is the Mural de la Prehistoria, painted by **Lovigildo González**, a disciple of the Mexican Diego Rivera, between 1959 and 1976, generally disliked as a monstrous piece of graffiti. If you are fit and active you can climb up the rocks to the top for a great view. No guide needed. One hundred metres before the mural is **Restaurant Jurásico**, from where you can see the paintings and there is a swimming pool nearby.

> ⁞ *It's worth seeking out Cirilo in the Valle del Ancón, the area's oldest man. He can show you antique farm tools and talk about times gone by and old farming customs.*

Los Acuáticos

Four kilometres from Viñales is the community, **Los Acuáticos**, where the villagers worship water. It was founded in 1943 by Antoñica Izquierdo, a *santera*, who recognized the importance of hygiene and clean water for health. The few families in the hamlet on the mountainside are self-contained and they bathe three times a day. Despite excellent rural healthcare in Cuba, the community refuses medical assistance for anyone who has an accident or is sick. Women on their own should take care as local boys reportedly lurk in the bushes with no clothes on.

Caves

Six kilometres north of Viñales is the **Cueva del Indio**, a cave which you enter on foot, then take a boat ⓘ *US$3, avoid 1130-1430 when tour parties arrive, not enough boats, long delays*, with a guide who gives you a description, very beautiful. There is a restaurant nearby where tour parties are given a lunch of suckling pig (*lechón*). The **Rumbos** tour includes lunch but not the cave, and no drinks; even water is an 'extra'. Beyond the restaurant is a small farm, well kept, with little red pigs running around, oxen and horses. There are day trips to a disco in the **Cueva de San Miguel**, west of Cueva del Indio (much better to go on your own and have the cave to yourself), short hiking trips to a *mogote*, visits to various caves and **El Palenque de los Cimarrones**, a restaurant and craft shop with a display of Cuban folklore. These are advertized as daily events, but don't rely on it. ▸▸ *See Entertainment, page 179.*

The **Valle de Santo Tomás** (with 25-km cave system) contains the **Gran Caverna Santo Tomás** 17 km southwest from Viñales in a community called El Moncada. A guide will show you the cave; prices depend on which walk you choose. Near El Moncada is the 3-km ecological path, **Maravillas de Viñales**.

North of Viñales to the coast

It is a lovely drive southwest through the valley and then north up to the coast through El Moncada (see above), Pons and the former copper mining centre of **Minas de Matahambre** up to **Cayo Jutías** on the north coast near Santa Lucía, 50 km. The road is well signed on the way there, but not at all on the way back. The coastal road around the western end of Cuba through **Mantua** to Guane is long and rather tedious, too far inland to see the sea. It is mostly good but you can't relax, it is full of potholes and other surprises.

Cayo Jutías

Cayo Jutías, a 6.7-km cay, is attached to Cuba by a long causeway through mangroves. Only foreigners and Cubans with passports are allowed in, US$5 per person, which includes one drink. **Rumbos** has a restaurant/bar on the beach (open daily 1300-1800, bar 1000-1800) and there are thatched shade umbrellas and a toilet. The beach is a narrow strip of curving white sand with mangroves at either end. The sea is calm, warm and multi-coloured but there is weed and not much snorkelling unless you can swim quite far out to the reef, which is marked by buoys. There is some good brain coral and anemones and, although there is a good variety, the fish are quite small. There is a lot of sand and sea grass on the way out to the reef, which can get stirred up with poor visibility, but this changes once you are over the reef, which is shallow with excellent visibility, especially when the sun is shining. A kiosk rents snorkelling equipment for US$2.50 per hour or US$5 per day (individual bits can be rented separately) on production of identity documents. Sunbeds cost US$1 per day. **Mégano**, an islet just offshore, is reached by boat, 12 minutes. An excursion there with lunch costs US$20.

Cayo Levisa

Puerto Esperanza, 24 km from Viñales, is a fishing town and not worth going to for beaches. There are *casas particulares* and plenty of food on offer, eg lobster and fish.

Further east is Cayo Levisa, part of the **Archipiélago de los Colorados**, with a long, sandy beach and reef running parallel to the shore, with good snorkelling and scuba diving (lots of fish). There are about 15 dive sites between 15m and 35 m deep and no more than 30 minutes away by boat. In season you can windsurf or go on sailing and snorkelling trips to other cays and beaches, but from September when the sea gets rougher there is less available. Check beforehand: if you pay in advance for diving but the boat does not go out, it is time consuming to get a refund. To get to Cayo Levisa go to Palma Rubia, from where it is 15 minutes by boat to the island. The last ferry across is at 1130, returning 1700 (US$15 includes drink), but you get there too late for the snorkelling tour (US$12, 45 mins). The jetty is on the south side and you follow a boardwalk through the mangroves to get to the hotel on the north side. Take insect repellent. Day trips or longer stays are organized by **Horizontes**; you can even visit by helicopter. Hired cars can be left at **Horizontes'** terminal building at Palma Rubia. Dives are US$25 for one tank, US$45 for two.

⊜ Sleeping

Viñales *p173, map p177*
Casas particulares
There are a huge number of registered *casas particulares* and people meet you off the buses. A torch is necessary if you stay off the main street, and even on it, because of power cuts.
F **Caridad Naveda**, opposite Caridad's garden, Salvador Cisnero 8, no phone. Private room, a/c, fan, garage US$1, meals.
F **Casa Maura**, Salvador Cisneros 131, opposite Don Tomás. Big breakfast included, dinner US$5, hot water, bikes US$3 per day.
F **Doña Inesita**, Salvador Cisneros 40, T8-793297. Energetic and friendly Inés Núñez Rodríguez and her husband, both in their 80s, offer an upstairs apartment with own entrance, 2 bedrooms each sleep 3, sitting room, aged bathroom, cold water, balcony, terrace, a/c, but cheaper without, substantial breakfast US$5, vast dinner US$8, fruit, eggs and meat from their own garden, even coffee is home-grown and roasted.
F **Estévan Orama Ovalle**, Orlando Nodarse 13, T8-793305. Very knowledgeable and

friendly hosts, big room, clean and safe, excellent breakfast and dinner, good *mojitos*.
F **Garden House**, Salvador Cisnero 44, T8-793297. 1 room, terrace overlooking big garden, garage US$1, meals available.
F **Marcelino y Yamile Arteaga González**, Salvador Cisneros 6, near the Cupet station, on the road to the cemetery, no phone. Welcoming and kind, great breakfast US$3 and tasty dinner US$6.
F **Silvia Guzmán Collado** (Berito), Camilo Cienfuegos 60A, T8-793245. 1 room, sleeps up to 6, fans, private, hot shower, garden, English spoken, meals available, try 'Berito's chicken', drinks (beer, *mojito*).
F **Villa Azul**, Km 25 Carretera Pinar del Río, T8-793288 (neighbour). Large room for up to 5 people, private bath, parking, fruit and coffee from own garden overlooked by terrace, caring couple offer security and comfort.
F **Villa Blanca**, Salvador Cisneros, Edif Colonial 2 Apto 12, T8-793319. Friendly couple, 2 bedrooms, fans, shared bathroom, balcony, breakfast and dinner.

F **Villa Chicha**, Camilo Cienfuegos 22. Charming, typical single-storey house with rocking chairs outside, private bathroom, entertaining family.

F **Villa El Pollo**, Salvador Cisneros, by Bandec. Run by nephew of Garden House owner and often used as overspill. Suite at back of house with independent entrance, very large room, dining room and bathroom. No hanging space for clothes but lots of room to spread out. A/c, no fan, rocking chairs outside front door, good food, fish excellent, chickens in back yard.

F **Villa Ernesto**, Salvador Cisneros 20, T8-793162. One room with two beds, fan, hot shower, breakfast US$3, lunch/dinner US$7, *mojitos* US$1. Nice elderly couple, Don Ernesto makes the best *mojito* in Viñales, having worked for over 30 years as barman at Los Jazmines.

F **Villa Mirtha**, Rafael Trejo 129. Run by Martha Fernández Hernández, double room with 2 double beds, bathroom, hot water, good breakfast included, dinner US$6 for fish, beans, rice and salad, son David speaks French but no English.

F **Villa Neyda**, Camilo Cienfuegos 41. Comfortable rooms, wonderful hospitality, good food with choice of meat or fish, Neyda's sister, at Camilo Cienfuegos 42, also rents rooms, same quality.

F **Villa Yolanda Tamargo**, Salvador Cisneros 186, T8-793208. 1 large room, hot and cold shower, fan, colonial architecture, parking US$1, terrace overlooking garden with fruits and orchids, nice place, meals.

F **Yolanda y Pedro Somonte Pino**, Interior 7A (behind the *Secundaria*), no phone. Nice family, quiet, relaxing, little garden, 1 room with 2 beds, fan, bathroom, hot water, simple but clean, good breakfast with lots of fruit from the garden, dinner available.

Around Viñales *p174, map p178*

C **Horizontes La Ermita**, Carretera de la Ermita Km 2, 3 km from town with magnificent view, T8-893204. 62 rooms, a/c, phone, radio, shop, tennis court, wheelchair

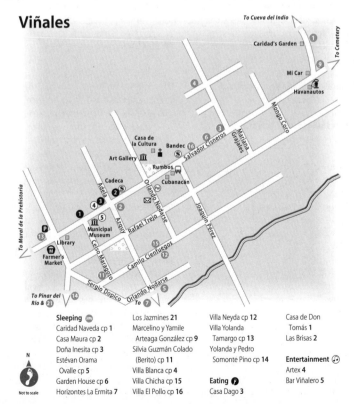

Viñales

access, pool (not always usable), food better than at **Los Jazmines**, breakfast included, lunch US$10, dinner US$12, nicer public areas than at **Los Jazmines**.

C **Los Jazmines** (Horizontes), Carretera de Viñales Km 23.5, 3 km before the town, in a superb location with travel brochure view of the valley, T8-936205/210, F8-936215, but booking is best done through Horizontes in Havana, T7-334042, F7-333722. 62 nice rooms and 16 *cabañas*, nightclub, breakfast buffet US$5 if not already included, lunch US$10, dinner US$12, unexciting restaurant, bar with snacks available, shops, swimming pool (US$5 including towels for day-visitors and US$5 in vouchers for bar drinks), riding, easy transport.

D **Horizontes Rancho San Vicente**, Valle de San Vicente, near Cueva del Indio, T8-893200. 20 a/c *cabañas*, bar, restaurant, breakfast included, lunch US$8, dinner US$10, nightclub, shop, tourist information desk, nice pool, open to day-visitors, good for lunch after visit to caves, spa with warm sulphurous waters, mud baths with steroids, hormones, antibiotics and vitamins, other facilities on offer include physiotherapy, massage, acupuncture, digitopuncture, medical checkups, a full-body massage is US$20, with mud pack on the face US$5, mineral baths US$3 with use of pool.

Around Viñales

Lomas de
San Vicente

Valle de Ancón

Valle del
Ruiseñor

Cueva de
San Miguel

Valle de la Guasasa

To Los Acuáticos

To Valle de Santo
Tomás & El Moncada

Mural de la
Prehistoria

Mogote
del Valle

Mogote Dos
Hermanas

Mogote
la Feita

Cueva del
Indio

Cueva del
Cable

Mogote la
Esmeralda

Mogote
Coco Solo

Valle de Viñales

Viñales

Loma
del Puerto

N

To Pinar del Río

Sleeping
Horizontes La Ermita **1**   Rancho
Los Jazmines **2**   San Vicente **3**

0 km   1
0 miles   1

North of Viñales to the coast *p175*
Book your hotel before you arrive as everywhere is often full.

AL-A **Cayo Levisa**, T7-335030 in Havana. Packages include transport from Havana, some or all meals and often watersports, book in Havana through any tour agency that deals with **Horizontes** or **Cubamar**. 20 cabins on beach, thatched, with verandahs, a/c, TV, comfortable but not luxurious, spacious, restaurant, bar, live music.

F **Casa Alexis**, Zona L 33, Sandino, T04-3282. 2 rooms with a/c, breakfast US$3, lunch/dinner US$5-7. On the road to María La Gorda, the house has a sign.

F **La Almendra**, La Sabana, Santa Lucía. 1 room, fan, no a/c, parking US$1, breakfast US$3, lunch/dinner US$7.

Camping
F Basic cabins, no tents, dirty linen, water intermittent, at Aguas Claras and Dos Hermanas (2 km from Viñales next to Mural de la Prehistoria, swimming pool), US$15 lodging, US$3 breakfast, US$7 dinner, disco, bar, horse riding, guides.

● Eating

Viñales *p173, map p177*
$$-$ Casa de Don Tomás, Salvador Cisneros. The oldest house in Viñales (1879), state owned, features in **Horizontes** brochure. Food very average, eggs the only option for vegetarians, cocktails are good and it's pleasant to sit and listen to live music with a Ron Collins or Mary Pickford. Most cocktails are US$1.50, but the house special, *Trapiche*, is US$2 (rum, pineapple juice, honey, sugar cane syrup). A bottle of rum is not much more than in a shop and a shot of rum starts at US$0.20. Begging dogs can be a nuisance although they are regularly chased away by staff and security guard.

$ **Casa Dago**, Salvador Cisneros. Popular restaurant/bar with good jazz salsa band, run by extraordinary character with impressive 1927 Ford Chevrolet, food indifferent, but once the music gets going and the rum starts flowing you could be dancing all night.

$ **Las Brisas**, formerly Valle Bar, T8-93183, on the main street. Small, friendly, recommended, *pollo frito* US$4, spaghetti

US$2.50, steak, or just have a beer, US$1, and listen to the live music in the evening, talk to Osmany Paez Arteaga who plays percussion in the band, helpful advice on local attitudes and information.

Around Viñales *p174, map p178*
$ **Jurásico**, Mural de la Prehistoria. Bar open daily 0800-1630 for lunch US$7-8, beer US$0.85, soft drink US$0.50, water US$0.60.

North of Viñales to the coast *p175*
$ **Paladar Jesús Carus Gallardo**, Frank País 87, Puerto Esperanza. Tasty food, inexpensive, help with accommodation if needed.

⊙ Entertainment

Viñales *p173, map p177*
Live music
Artex, Salvador Cisneros, soon moving to the plaza, bar 24 hrs, shop 1000-2200, live music.
Bar Viñalero, Salvador Cisneros, next to the museum. Live music in evenings, inside and outside seating. Varied music, from traditional to rock, then move on to **Artex**.
Los Jazmines, see Sleeping above. Disco 2000-0300, US$5.
Palenque de los Cimarrones, 4 km north of Viñales at km 32 Carretera a Puerto Esperanza. **Rumbos**-run, show Mon-Sat 2230-2400, followed by recorded music, US$5 for foreigners.

✺ Festivals and events

Viñales *p173, map p177*
Jul Parades including beauty pageant.
Sep Carnival is in the middle of the month lasting for 4 days, Thu-Sun.

○ Shopping

Viñales *p173, map p177*
El Mogote, open daily 0900-1900. A *Caracol* dollar shop on main street. There is also a **bakery** close to the farmers' market.

▲ Activities and tours

Riding
Yosbel Reyes Crespo, Camilo Cienfuegos s/n. US$5 per hour. Yosbel does a 5-hr tour taking in the Cueva del Indio, which is probably more than enough on a horse. Well worthwhile and a good way to see the countryside.

Tour operators
Cubanacán, on Salvador Cisneros 63C, next to the bus terminal, 0800-1700. Motocross rental, US$30 per day, phone cards, lodgings, car rental.
Havanatur, the other side of Cubanacán. Tours, reservations and ticket sales.
Rumbos, next door to Cubanacán. Same tours, reservations, tickets etc.

⊙ Transport

Bus
Bus terminal at Salvador Cisneros 63A.
Viazul daily from **Havana** via Pinar del Río at 0900, US$12, arrives 1215, returns 1330, arrives in Havana at 1645 depending on the number of stops. **Astro** from **Havana** 0900 via Pinar del Río, returns 1430, arrives in Havana 1820, US$8, cheaper but less comfortable and unreliable. Local buses from **Pinar del Río** to **Puerto Esperanza**, **La Palma** and **Bahía Honda** all pass through Viñales. Tour buses from Havana will drop you off if you want to stay more than a day and collect you about 1600 on the day you want to return.

Cycling/scooters
On the plaza **Cubanacán**, daily 0900-1900. Rents bicycles for US$1 per hr, US$12 a day, scooters for US$9-12 per hr, US$20-24 a day.

Car hire
Mi Car and **Havanautos** are both at the end of Salvador Cisneros by the gas station. The former is hardly ever open, despite official opening hours of Mon-Fri 0800-1700, Sat 0900-1300, but if you can find someone there they are reputed to have the cheapest

---

● *For an explanation of the sleeping and eating price codes used in this guide, see inside the* ● *front cover. Other relevant information is provided in Essentials, pages 48-53.*

car hire in town. You can negotiate a deal for 2 weeks for a little as US$27 per day, plus insurance and fuel. Havanautos, T8-796305, Mon-Fri 0830-1800, has **Suzuki Vitaras** for US$64 a day including insurance of US$15, or a/c cars for US$56 a day, cheaper for longer.

Taxi

There are several taxi companies, but Beta, who works for **Cubataxi**, is the only driver who speaks any English. Look out for him in his green Peugeot, he is of Jamaican origin. An official taxi to **Cayo Jutías** is US$60-70, as they charge by distance and for waiting time, with a surcharge later in the afternoon. A private car costs US$35-40, but there are drawbacks. You have to avoid patrols, which may mean getting out of the car while the driver goes round the block, or even walking 5-10 mins through the countryside, cutting off corners where there are police stations.

❶ Directory

Viñales *p173, map p177*
Banks

Banco Popular de Ahorro, Salvador Cisneros 54A, does not do credit cards, open Mon-Fri 0800-1200 and 1330-1630. **Bandec**, Salvador Cisneros 58, for credit card transactions. **Cadeca**, Salvador Cisneros 92, open Mon-Sat 0800-1800. Only gives pesos convertibles,

Matanzas

• Footprint features

Introduction

Matanzas province, to the east of Havana, is mainly associated with the mega-resort of Varadero. This tourist enclave incorporates some 14,000 hotel rooms squeezed onto a finger of land stretching out into the Caribbean. All budgets are catered for but you won't find a double room under US$50-60 in high season. The white sand, the handsome palm trees and the inviting sea, along with watersports, some good hotel food in a few places and some winning deals at all-inclusives make this a popular holiday spot. However, for all that it represents of Cuba it might as well be another country. Close to Varadero and in contrast to it are the low-key towns of Matanzas and Cárdenas where there is no engineered tourism. Both have had their heyday: Matanzas as the birthplace of rumba and danzón and Cárdenas as an industrial superstar. The outstanding Cuevas de Bellamar and the luscious Valle de Yumurí, studded with thousands of Royal palm trees, are also worth visiting.

The second largest province in the country also has a southern coast with one of Cuba's most notable geographic features, the Ciénaga de Zapata, a huge marsh covering the entire coast and the peninsula of the same name. It is a nature reserve, protecting many endemic species of flora and fauna, as well as numerous migrating birds. The diving in the deep-blue sea off Playa Girón and Playa Larga is exceptional. Also here, in the Bay of Pigs, the disastrous American-backed invasion is remembered in two museums.

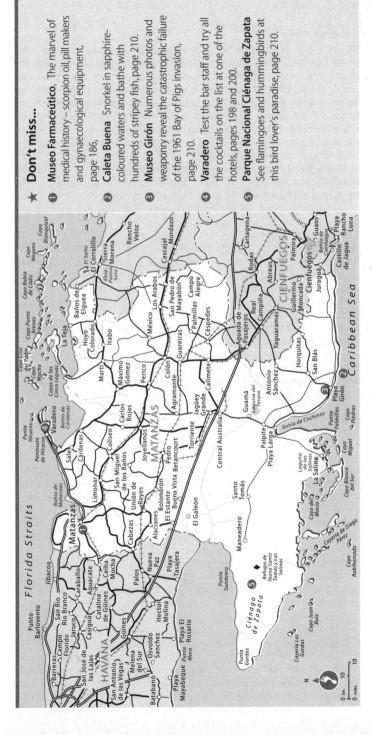

★ **Don't miss...**

1. **Museo Farmacéutico**, The marvel of medical history – scorpion oil, pill makers and gynaecological equipment, page 186.

2. **Caleta Buena** Snorkel in sapphire-coloured waters and bathe with hundreds of stripey fish, page 210.

3. **Museo Girón** Numerous photos and weaponry reveal the catastrophic failure of the 1961 Bay of Pigs invasion, page 210.

4. **Varadero** Test the bar staff and try all the cocktails on the list at one of the hotels, pages 198 and 200.

5. **Parque Nacional Ciénaga de Zapata** See flamingoes and hummingbirds at this bird lover's paradise, page 210.

Ins and outs

Getting there

Air There is an international airport at Varadero, which receives scheduled and charter flights from Europe and Canada. **Rail** Connections by rail are reasonable with Matanzas on the main line between Havana and Santiago and on local lines to other towns, however service is poor. A feature of rail transport is the Hershey electric line between Havana and Matanzas, which used to service the Hershey chocolate factory before the Revolution, but it breaks down frequently and timings are very approximate. **Road** There is a good road out from Havana along the north coast to Matanzas and Varadero with an excellent bus service provided by **Víazul**. Local buses run to other towns such as Cárdenas but public transport is limited to the Zapata peninsula. **Viazul** stops at Entronque de Jagüey with taxis as an option for onward transport. There are plenty of tour buses to take you there on an excursion, but car hire is recommended if you want flexibility. ▸▸ *For further details, see also Matanzas below, Varadero page 192, Cárdenas page 205 and Zapata peninsula and the Bay of Pigs, page 208.*

Tourist information

State tour agencies can be found in Matanzas and in all the hotels in Varadero and the Bay of Pigs. They operate as tourist information offices although their main purpose is to sell tours. They can help with hotel reservations, tickets and transfers. Infotur has a branch in Matanzas and is planning an office in Varadero.

Best time to visit

The winter season between December and April has the best weather but the highest prices. The wettest time of year is between September and November, but if there is a cold front off the eastern seaboard of the USA in the winter you can expect rough seas and a smaller expanse of sand as a result. The Bay of Pigs is more protected from the weather but has been hit in the past by hurricanes coming up from the Caribbean between September and November.

Matanzas → *Colour map 2, grid A1. Population: 115,000.*

Matanzas is a sleepy city with old colonial buildings, a remarkable pharmacy museum and a legendary musical history. It sits on the Bahía de Matanzas and is freshened by the sea breeze. On the opposite side of the bay is the busy, ugly industrial zone (there are oil storage facilities, chemical and fertilizer plants, sugar, textile and paper mills and thermal power stations). Both the rivers Yumurí and San Juan flow through the city and you can walk along the riverside at dusk and watch the fishermen or take in the tranquillity and murmur of fellow observers.

Most of the old buildings are between the two rivers, with another colonial district, Versalles, to the north of the Río Yumurí. This area was colonized in the 19th century by French refugees from Haiti after the revolution there. The newer district, Pueblo Nuevo, also has many colonial houses. ▸▸ *For Sleeping, Eating and other listings, see pages 190-192.*

Ins and outs

Getting there The town lies 104 km east of Havana along the Vía Blanca, which links the capital with Varadero beach, 34 km further east. If you are travelling by **car** the drive is unattractive along the coast and can be smelly because of the many small oil wells producing low-grade crude en route, but once you get into the hills there are good views of the countryside. There is a particularly spectacular lookout with a view

Music in Matanzas

Matanzas is a quiet town in all senses but one. If you listen carefully you can hear its unique heartbeat: one, two, one two three.

With its docks and warehouses, Matanzas provided the ideal birthplace for the rumba and it is still the world capital of this exhilarating music and dance form. Families here are virtually born into the rumba: the latest incarnation of the *Muñequitos de Matanzas* has a young boy keeping the beat on the bamboo *guagua*. The *Muñequitos* are the fathers and mothers of contemporary rumba, having set the standards for *rumberos* on their tours across the globe. Of course, the *rumba Matancera* bears not the slightest resemblance to its ballroom namesake.

The rumba at the *Casa de la Trova*, which used to be on Calle 85, was famous for its intricate drumming, vocal improvisations and dancing, which is by turns graceful, audacious, devotional and downright dirty.

Rumba is a communal art form – the *Columbia* style was created by workers on the Columbia railway line; however, great names of the past are recalled in *Columbias* such as '*Malanga Murió*'. On your way to a rumba, don't forget to stop at a bar and put a record by Matanzas' own Arsenio Rodríguez on the 1950s jukebox. Without Arsenio, there would have been no *conjunto son* and thus no Latin salsa. If you've got time, go and pay homage at the site of the dance hall where on a hot January night in 1879 Miguel Faílde created the *danzón Cubana*, still the only authentic, unselfconscious marriage of orchestral sounds with African rhythms. It is now the *Sala de Conciertos José White de Matanzas*, Calle 79 entre 288 y 290. *Danzón* is currently enjoying a revival: across Cuba, music is being reissued and orchestras formed and there is a European *danzón* orchestra based in Holland. The world has much to thank Matanzas for.

of the Yumurí valley, called the *Mirador de Bacunayagua*, overlooking a viaduct spanning a gorge, the highest bridge in Cuba. Most buses make this a rest stop. Long-distance **buses** between Havana and Varadero all pass through Matanzas and you can request a stop here. You can also get here by **train**, either *regular* or *especial* service en route from Havana to Santiago. However, the 2½ to four-hour journey via the Hershey Railway, the only electric train in Cuba, which runs from Havana to Matanzas, is memorable and scenic if you are not in a hurry. ▸ *For further details, see also Transport, page 191.*

Getting around Most of the places of interest are within walking distance, but if you get tired you can board a **horse-drawn coche**, or hail a **bicitaxi**. **Excursions** with transport can be arranged with a travel agency, see Activities and tours, page 191, or you can hire a **local driver** to take you around for a day trip out of town.

Tourist information Infotur, Parque de la Libertad, Milanés esq Sta Teresa y Matanzas, T45-253551, infotur@tuisla.cu daily 0800-2300. Also offers tours, see Activities and tours. Matanzas has its own website: www.atenas.inf.cu

History

The town dates from 1693, when immigrants from the Canary Islands founded a settlement they called San Carlos y Severino de Matanzas, between the rivers San Juan and Yumurí. Before that, the area was known mainly for an attack on the Spanish fleet in 1628 in the Bahía de Matanzas, by the Dutch Admiral Piet Heyn. Spain and Holland were at war at the time and the fleet was considered war booty, with the 4 million ducats of gold and silver captured being used to finance further battles. The name Matanzas is thought to come from the mass slaughter of wild pigs to provision the fleets, but it could also refer to the killing of the Amerindians who lived here and called the bay Guanima. Around the time of the founding of the city, a fortress, the Castillo de San Severino, was built on the northern shore of the bay to keep out pirates and any other invaders.

The town became prosperous with the advent of sugar mills in the 1820s, followed by the railway in 1843. Most of the buildings date from this time and by the 1860s it was the second largest town in Cuba after Havana, with all the trappings of an important city, such as a theatre, newspaper and library. It even became known as the 'Athens of Cuba' because of all the musicians and writers living there.

Sights

City centre

Parque de la Libertad is the main square, with a statue of José Martí in the middle and dominated by the former **Palacio del Gobierno** on its eastern side. The **Sala de Conciertos José White** (see below) is on the northern side and next to it is the abandoned **Hotel Velasco**. Just beside the hotel is the **Teatro Velasco**, now a cinema.

On the south side of the plaza is the beautifully preserved **Museo Farmacéutico** ① *Milanés 4951 entre Santa Teresa y Ayuntamiento, T45-223197, Mon-Fri 1000-1800, Sun 0800-1200, US$3, camera charge, US$1 per picture,* containing the original equipment, porcelain jars, recipes and furnishings of the Botica La Francesa, opened in 1882 by the Triolet and Figueroa family. Both men founded a pharmacy in Sagua la Grande before visiting Matanzas together and establishing the new pharmacy; Triolet later married into the Figueroa family. The pharmacy shelves are all made of cedarwood and divided by Corinthian columns – all made from one tree trunk. All the shelves are filled with 19th-century French porcelain jars, which are full of medicinal plants and imported European products and North American goods. The museum exhibits lists with all the formulas in it, displays pill makers, the original telephone, baby bottles, gynaecological equipment and scorpion oil. It was a working pharmacy until 1964, when it was nationalized and then converted into this fascinating museum, believed to be unique in Latin America. Curator Patria Dopico is very helpful.

❦ *Although you'll find numbers written on the streets, locals still refer to names or a mixture of the two. North-south old town streets have even numbers, east-west streets have odd numbers. Where possible we have listed names and numbers on our map.*

East of the plaza is the former home of local poet, José Jacinto Milanés (1814-63), on the street that bears his name; it is now the **Archivo Histórico**. There is a statue of the poet outside the elegant **Catedral de San Carlos Borromeo**, further down on Milanés (83), first built in 1693, but rebuilt in 1878 after a fire in a neoclassical style with frescoed ceilings and walls.

Further east is the **Plaza de la Vigía**, dominated by the **Teatro Sauto** ① *daily 0830-1600, US$2.* There are 14 performances a month and ticket prices vary. A magnificent neoclassical building, built by Daniel Dallaglio, an Italian, who won the commission by competition; Dallaglio also built the church of San Pedro Apóstol, see page 188. The theatre dates from 1862-63 and seats 650 people in cream, wrought-iron seats in three-tiered balconies for performances that have included in the past Enrico Caruso and Anna Pavlova, who toured Cuba in 1917. French actress Sarah Bernhardt, musician José White, singer Rita Montaner and Alicia Alonso, director of the Cuban national ballet, have all appeared here. It was restored after the Revolution. In the entrance there are Carrera marble statues of Greek goddesses (and a painting of Piet Heyn, the Dutch admiral) and, in the hall, the muses are painted on the ceiling. Most unusually, the floor can be raised to convert the auditorium into a ballroom. Opposite the theatre is the restored, pale orange **Palacio de Justicia**, built in 1826 and rebuilt in 1911.

The **Museo Palacio de Junco** ① *Milanés entre Magdalena y Ayllón, T45-23195, Tue-Fri 1000-1800, Sat 1300-1900, Sun 0900-1200, US$1*, a pale, royal-blue building overlooking the theatre, houses the provincial museum, built by a wealthy plantation owner and dating from 1840. The historical exhibits include an archaeological display

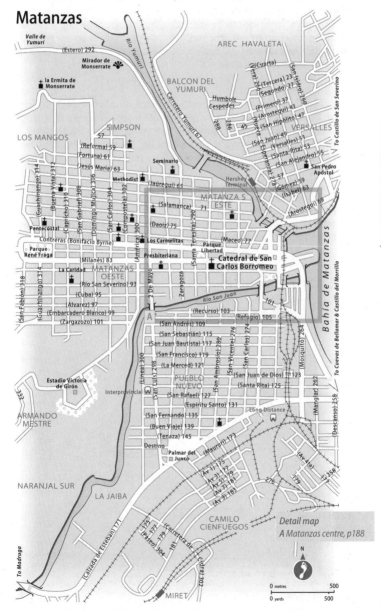

Matanzas

Detail map
A Matanzas centre, p188

0 metres 500
0 yards 500

and the development of sugar and slavery in the province. It's not that interesting apart from the exhibit of the remains of a slave who was thrown into a pit with his chains still attached and stocks to hold the feet of slaves. There are guns and pistols from the capture of silver boats of Dutchman Piet Heyn on 8 September 1628. Upstairs is the doziest curator in Christendom.

There are several bridges in the town, but the one you are most likely to notice is the steel **Puente Calixto García**, built in 1899 at the edge of Plaza de la Vigía and next to the neoclassical fire station, **Parque de los Bomberos**. Just below the bridge is a **mosaic memorial to Che Guevara**. Opposite the fire station is **Ediciones Vigía** ① *daily 0900-1600*, where you can see books being produced, ranging from fairy tales to those commemorating important events. These are all handmade and in first editions of only 200 copies, so they are collectors' items, particularly if you get one signed. The **Galería de Arte Provincial** ① *also on the plaza, daily 0900-1700*, has rotating displays of contemporary Cuban art.

North of the city centre

North of the Río Yumurí in Reparto Versalles near the Hershey terminal is the **Iglesia de San Pedro Apóstol** ① *Calle 57 y 270, open Mon-Sat mornings and 1530-1930*. Cross the park in front of the terminal and walk up the street in the far corner. The church will soon be towering above you on the left. There is a rather lovely stained glass of Saint Peter. The interior is mustard yellow and there is an imposing altar piece with four Ionic columns.

Beyond Reparto Versalles, towards the northeast on Avenida del Muelle is **Castillo de San Severino** ① *Mon-Sat 0900-1700, Sun 0900-1300, US$2, US$1 for pictures, US$5 for a video camera.* This muscular, colonial castle was a solid lookout post on the Bay of Matanzas built to prevent pirate attack. The original coat of arms is still above the main entrance. Originally water lapped at the castle entrance but a road was built in front of it in 1910. The moat, however, was never filled with water.

Matanzas centre

N

0 metres 100
0 yards 100

Sleeping	Luis Alberto Valdés **5**	Café Velasco **4**	**Entertainment**
Casa Manolo **4**	Luis Felipe Pilotz **6**	El Louvre **2**	Sala de Conciertos
Enriqueta y Exposito **2**		El Rápido **5**	José White **2**
Hostal Alma **3**	**Eating**	La Ruina **1**	Teatro Sauto **3**
Louvre **1**	Café Atenas **3**		

San Severino was also used as a prison until the 1980s. A man was incarcerated here for six years for being a Jehova's witness. It is said the prison was divided by a wall: on one side were political prisoners and on the other homosexuals. The castle was built in 1693 and is in the process of restoration and, with UNESCO support, is being turned into a **museum of slavery**. This will include displays of ceramics and pipes and other materials found at the castle as well as exhibits on Afro-Cuban religion.

La Ermita de Montserrate, a good hike north up Domingo Mujica (306), northwest of the Parque de la Libertad, was built in 1872 in honour of the Virgin of Monserrat. It is now storm-ruined and the roof has caved in. But, from the hilltop it is perched on, you can see the city and the bay rolled out before you and on the other side the verdant **Valle de Yumurí** although the perfection of the view is slightly marred by the pylons marching towards the horizon. This is an excellent place to walk and there is an accommodation option.

Around Matanzas

Castillo del Morrillo and Caves

The road out to Varadero goes past the university and the Escuela Militar. One kilometre past the university you come to the **Río Canímar**, which flows into the Bahía de Matanzas. Trips along the river can be arranged from Varadero. Just before the bridge over the river, take the road running alongside the river towards the bay to the **Castillo del Morrillo** ① *Tue-Sun 1000-1700, US$1 entrance, US$1 for guide*, built in 1720 to protect the area. The castle is now a museum in memory of Antonio Guiteras Holmes, who was shot with the Venezuelan revolutionary, Carlos Aponte Hernández, by Batista's troops near the bridge. Bronze busts of the two men can be seen underneath a mahogany tree. Guiteras Holmes was a student leader who started a revolutionary group called *Joven Cuba* (Young Cuba) in 1934. He served briefly in the government that replaced Machado, but fell foul of the rising Batista. It was when he and Aponte came to Matanzas in 1935 to try and find a boat to take them into exile in Mexico that they were caught and executed. The castle also has a *sala* of aboriginal archaeology and a large rowing boat.

‡ *Between Matanzas and Varadero you will see fields of henequén, typical of the region; even the local baseball team are nicknamed Los Henequeneros.*

Southeast of town at Finca La Alcancía are the **Cuevas de Bellamar** ① *daily 0900-2030, T45-253538, US$5, US$8 includes the extra 100 m stretch, parking US$1, US$5 for cameras with flash and video cameras*. Trips leave daily at 0930, 1030, 1130, 1315, 1415, 1515, 1615. The caves close at 1700. This cave system, discovered in 1862 by somebody working the land, stretches for 23 km, and is stuffed full of stalactites, stalagmites (one 12 m tall) and underground streams. Tour parties come from Varadero so you may get herded along with a bus load but, in any case, you are not allowed in unaccompanied along the 750-m trip through the caves; you can go a further 100 m with torches. There is a small museum with items found in the caves and explanations in English and Spanish. There is a tourist train (on wheels), which has no timetable, but leaves from the Parque de la Libertad. The complex has a restaurant, shop and children's playground, and a swimming pool is planned.

‡ *Neptune's Cave, between Matanzas and Varadero, has an underground lagoon, stalagmites and stalactites, evidence of Amerindian occupation, and was used as a secret hospital during the war of independence.*

There are also caves at **Las Cuevas de Santa Catalina**, near Carbonera, 20 km east of Matanzas, where there are believed to be 8 km of tunnels. Amerindian paintings have been found here, close to the entrance, and the caves were used as a burial site. Another cave, **Refugio de Saturno**, is a large cave often visited by scuba divers (see Diving, page 67), although anyone can enjoy a swim here. It is 1 km south of the Vía Blanca, 8 km east of the Río Canímar.

● Sleeping

Matanzas *p186, maps p187 and p188*
Hotels
D-E **Hotel Louvre**, on south side of Parque de la Libertad, T45-244074. A beautiful 19th-century building which has seen better days. Variety of rooms and prices, opt for the a/c room with bathroom and balcony overlooking the square, beautiful mahogany furniture, rather than the small, dark, cupboard room in the bowels of the hotel, water (0700-1900), lush garden in patio. There is a large and mostly empty, dark wood café (0630-2200).

Casas particulares
E-F **Enriqueta y Exposito**, Contreras 29016 entre Sta Teresa (290) y Zaragoza (292), T/F45-245151. Enriqueta has 2 pleasant rooms although 1 is up a precarious staircase. Both rooms have a/c and fan and there's use of a fridge. This place is often full and so it might be wise to ring in advance.
F **Casa Manolo**, Manzano (77), (also known as Maceo) 28805 entre Ayuntamiento (288) y Sta Teresa (290), T45-247893, 1 block from the centre. This is a basement house (enter a large entrance hall and then take the steps down to the right), with 1 clean room with a wall fan above the bed. The bathroom is shared with the owner who provides amusing company.
F **Hostal Alma**, Milanés 29008 Altos entre Sta Teresa (290) y Zaragoza (292), T45-247810, alberto@tuisla.cu Huge and grand 19th-century house with beautiful *vitrales*, terrace and fabulous roof view, with 2 rooms on the second floor with private bathroom, a/c, fridge, hot and cold water, minibar. 1 room can hold a couple and child. Breakfast US$3, supper US$6 including pudding. Dinner is also offered to non-guests, but ring beforehand to book. The friendly family and their attractive house make this a highly recommended option.
F **Luis Alberto Valdés**, Contreras (79) 28205 (2nd floor) entre Jovellanos y Ayuntamiento (288), T45-243397, luis.alberto@tuisla.cu Luis has 2 rooms, 1 able to house a couple and a child. Shared bathroom with hot water in clean, first floor flat. Fans available but there may be a/c by the time you read this. Breakfast offered (US$2-3) dinner (U$5-6).
F **Luis Felipe Pilotz**, Cuba esq Manzanera.

An 1882 house with beautiful taupe and blue tiles. There's use of a fridge, washing machine, and 2 shared bathrooms. Large patio. The 2 rooms have fan. There is also use of a parking spot 30 m away. Breakfast US$3, dinner US$6-8. Welcoming family.

Around Matanzas *p189*
Hotels
E **Canimao**, Km 4.5 Carretera Matanzas a Varadero, T45-261014, F45-262237. A modern, but nice-looking hotel on the outskirts of Matanzas opposite the **Tropicana** cabaret. It has 120 rooms on a hill above the Río Canímar, with good restaurant, nightclub, pool, excursions offered on the river or to caves. Nearby is a natural canyon, the Cueva de Los Cristales, which had evidence of aboriginal infanticide.
C-D **Casa del Valle** (Horizontes), Carretera de Chirino, Km 2.5, Valle de Yumurí. T/F45-253300, www.horizontes.cu A gorgeous setting amid the lush Valle de Yumurí in the 1940s house and grounds of the former police chief of the area. The heat is unrelenting, but there is an attractive pool to wallow in and some of the *senderos* around the hotel are shaded. There are 40 rooms, 6 bungalows and 8 apartments, all with the usual facilities. There's also a bowling alley, gym, billiards and tennis plus a centre for massage (US$10), acupuncture (US$10), lassotherapy, diet therapies and mud treatments. Horseriding (US$5 per hr) and guided walks offered.

Casas particulares
There are several rooms to rent along the coast road to Varadero, right on the sea front, in Reparto Playa, once you get past all the bridges. They are quite a long way from the town centre with a good view of the tankers.

● Eating

Matanzas *p186, maps p187 and p188*
You are better off eating in your *casa particular* in Matanzas.
$$ **La Ruina**, just past Puente Calixto García on Calle 101, open 24 hrs. Very attractive **Rumbos** restaurant converted from sugar warehouse, dinner US$2.50-10, delicious

pastries, great ice cream, pesos and dollars accepted, live music at weekends.

$$ Restaurante El Louvre, Parque de la Libertad. This restaurant has absolute zero atmosphere and the eating experience is like that of a 1940s train station café, but the service is speedy and the portions are enormous, which means you definitely won't go hungry.

$ Café Atenas, Calle 83 y 272, (Plaza de la Vigía), daily 1000-2200. A modern, highly air-conditioned all-plastic café opposite Teatro Sauto, snack food, but also pizzas, spaghetti, grilled fish, chicken and ice cream.

$ Cafe Velasco, next to Sala de Conciertos, in the former lobby of Hotel Velasco. It sells mostly snacks and sandwiches and again, is like eating in an even larger train station waiting room.

$ El Rápido, behind the cathedral. Serves up the usual pizza, snacks and cola combinations. Service is very quick.

⊕ Entertainment

Matanzas *p186, maps p187 and p188*
The **Centro de Promoción y Publicidad Cultural**, Independencia (85) entre Ayuntamiento (288) y Sta Teresa (290) has a *cartelera* in the window displaying all entertainment fixtures.

Live music and dance
The Plaza de la Vigía is the place to go in the evenings; locals congregate here to chat, play dominoes or draughts, or make music. The **Sala de Conciertos José White de Matanzas**, on Contreras (79) on the plaza, was formerly the *Lyceum Club* and is famous for being the place where the *danzón* was danced for the first time in 1879 (there is a plaque outside); music is performed here and all events are free. The **Teatro Sauto**, see also Sights, page 186, usually has live performances at the weekends.

Around Matanzas *p189*
Cabaret
Tropicana Matanzas, Autopista Varadero Km 4.5, T/F45-265555, reservas@tropimat .co.cu daily 2030-0230, show 2200-2330, Wed-Sun $35 which includes a cocktail, ¼ of a bottle of rum and 1 soft drink. The Matanzas version of the famous cabaret in a spectacular outdoor setting opposite the Hotel Canimao.

⊛ Festivals and events

Matanzas *p186, maps p187 and p188*
20-26 Aug From the Tue-Sun is the Carnival de Matanzas.

⊙ Shopping

Matanzas *p186, maps p187 and p188*
Next door to the Galería de Arte Provincial, on Plaza de la Vigía, is a large building housing **Vigía Crafts**, Mon-Fri 0900-1800, for crafts, ceramics, clothing. **Librería Viet Nam** on Calle 85 y 288 for books, behind El Rápido. **Photo Service** on Ayuntamiento (288) esq Independencia (85). **Supermercado La República** Ayuntamiento (288) entre 83 (Milanés) y 85 (Independencia), daily 0830-2030. A fairly well-stocked, but small, dollar supermarket.

▲ Activities and tours

Tour operators
Infotur, see also Ins and outs, Tourist information, p184. Tours to the Refugio de Saturno, daily 0900-1500, US$5, and Cuevas de Bellamar daily 0900-1800, US$4. Prices include transport. Tours to the Valle de Yumurí in Aug only including horse riding and swimming, 1000-1900 daily. Infotur also sells maps and can arrange car hire.
Campismo Popular, Buro de Reservaciones, Independencia (85) entre Zaragoza y Sta Teresa (290), T45-243951, T45-244628, daily 0800-1700.

⊖ Transport

Bus
The long-distance bus station, T45-291473, open 24 hrs, is at Calle 131 y 272, Calzada Esteban esq Terry (Coppelia is opposite the terminal). There are taxis and *coches* at the bus station. However, if you arrive later in the day you might just be left with a *taxi particular*, in which case, if you have an address when you arrive at the house insist that you did so by your own means otherwise the taxi driver will get a US$5 commission for every day you stay in a *casa*.

Víazul, T45-916445, passes through on its **Havana-Varadero** route, 3 daily, see timetable, p42. The interprovincial terminal is at 298 y 127, both in Pueblo Nuevo. For foreigners, the only peso bus leaving from here that's worth noting is the one to Jagüey: 0500, 0700, 1100, 1300, 1700. Returning 1315, 1420, 1525, 1630.

Astro 0530 and 1335 to **Havana**, US$4 (from Havana 0910 arrives around midday, US$4); 1040 to **Santiago**, US$30.50; 0900 to **Camaguey**, US$18.50; 1100 to **Cárdenas**, US$5.

Taxi
Taxis wait alongside the cathedral.

Train
There are 2 stations: the Hershey terminal and main terminal. There are 5 trains daily on the electric Hershey Railway to and from Casablanca in **Havana**. It uses a station north of the Río Yumurí in Versalles at 282 y 67. There are no facilities here and the ticket office has erratic opening hours. Trains from **Hershey** leave at 0433 (getting in to Casablanca at 0720), 0830 (1102), 1243 (1532), 1633 (1918), 2034 (2318), returning from Casablanca at 0606, 0947, 1411, 1805, 2204. Tickets are in pesos, but you may never get charged.

The newer, main station south of the town at Calle 181, Miret, (open 24 hrs, T45-292409), receives *regular* and *especial* trains from Havana en route to Santiago. Horse-drawn *coche* to market area, 1 peso or

US$1. The **Santiago**-bound train stops at **Santa Clara**, **Ciego de Avila**, **Camaguey** and **Las Tunas**. The train to **Bayamo** and **Manzanillo** stops at **Jovellanos** and **Colón** as does the **Holguin** train. To **Havana** U$3, **Santa Clara** US$7, **Santiago** US$27.

---

❶ Directory

Matanzas *p186, maps p187 and p188*
Banks
Banco Nacional, at 83 (Milanés) y 282, diagonally opposite the cathedral. **Bandec**, esq 282 y 85, Mon-Fri 0800-1500. Visa and MC. **Banco Popular**, Medio (Independencia) (85) opposite the church, Mon-Fri 0800-1530.

Medical facilities
Facilities for foreigners are available in Varadero, but there is a **pharmacy** here, open 24 hrs, at 85 y 2 de Mayo.

Post office
At 85 entre 290 y 288, daily, 24 hrs.

Telephone/internet
Telepunto, Milanés y 282, daily 0830-2130. Telephone service and internet, US$0.10 per min. Internet also at **Infotur**, on the plaza, see Tourist information above p184. US$5.75 per 3 hrs.

Varadero ➜ *Colour map 2, grid A1.*

Cuba's chief beach resort, Varadero, is built on the Península de Hicacos, a 20-km-long thin peninsula, along the length of which run two roads lined with dozens of large hotels, some smaller ones, and several chalets and villas, many of which date from before 1959. Sadly, some of the hotel architecture is hideous.

Varadero is still undergoing large-scale development and joint ventures with foreign investors are being encouraged, with the aim of expanding capacity to 26,000 rooms by 2010. Despite the building in progress it is not over-exploited and is a good place for a family beach holiday. The beaches are quite empty, if a bit exposed, and you can walk for miles along the sand, totally isolated from the rest of Cuba, if not other tourists. ➜➜ *For Sleeping, Eating and other listings, see pages 195-203.*

Ins and outs
Getting there Varadero's international **airport** is 23 km from the beginning of the hotel strip. If you are booked into one of the new hotels at the end of the peninsula, you will have a journey of some 40 km. The **Víazul** bus pulls in here on its way to the central bus terminal. If you are travelling **by car** from Havana there is a good dual

carriageway, the Vía Blanca, which runs to Varadero, 144 km from the capital. The toll at the entrance to the resort is US$2 for cars and motorbikes. The easiest way to get to and from Havana is on a **tour** or **transfer bus,** booked through a hotel tour desk, which will pick you up and drop you off at your hotel. There are several daily **buses** from Havana with **Víazul** or **Astro,** and also from Trinidad via Sancti Spíritus and Santa Clara with **Víazul** (see timetable, page 44). A taxi from Havana to Varadero airport costs US$60. ▸▸ *For further details, see also Transport page 203.*

Getting around Distances are large. Avenida 1, which runs southwest–northeast the length of the peninsula, has a tourist **bus** service, see Transport page 203. It takes about an hour to cover the length, taking into account dropping off times. Calle numbers begin with lowest numbers at the southwest end and work upwards to the northeast. Most hotels rent **bicycles**, often without gears and very unsophisticated, or **mopeds**, which will allow you to get further, faster. **Taxis** wait outside hotels, or you can phone for one. There are also **horse-drawn carriages** for a leisurely tour.

Tourist information Infotur is planning on setting up an office in Varadero. In the meantime your hotel tourist desk should be able to answer all your questions. If not, all tour operators can help. A lot of places now accept Euro in Varadero. All hotels, restaurants and excursions must be paid for in US dollars or in some cases Euro.

History
Salt was the first economic catalyst in the area, followed by cattle, timber and sugar. A plan was drawn up in 1887 for the foundation of a city, but development of the peninsula did not really begin until 1923, when it was discovered as a potential holiday resort for the seriously rich. There are some old wooden houses left, with rocking chairs on the verandahs and balconies, but the village area was not built until the 1950s. The Dupont family bought land in the 1920s, sold it for profit, then bought more, constructed roads and built a large house, now the **Mansión Xanadú**.

Sights
The relatively recent development of Varadero means there is little of historical or architectural interest; visitors spend their time on the beach, engaging in watersports or taking organized excursions, rather than sightseeing. The southern end of the resort is more low key, with hustlers on the beaches by day and *jineteros* in the bars at night, but they are no worse than anywhere else in Cuba. The village area does feel like a real place, not just a hotel city, and, in contrast to some other tourist enclaves (such as the northern cays), Cubans do actually live here. A couple of hotels are reserved for Cubans, foreigners are not admitted, and you are as likely to meet Cubans as foreigners on the beach up to around Calle 60. The far northeastern end is where international hotels are; you can pay to use their facilities even if you are not staying there. Apart from their own hotel shops, they are very remote from the shopping area and independent restaurants. As a result, most of the hotels at the far end are all-inclusives.

The **Museo de Varadero** ① *C 57 y Av 1, daily 1000-1900, US$1*, is worth a visit if you want something to do away from the beach. The house itself is interesting as an example of one of the first beach houses. Originally known as *Casa Villa Abreu*, it was built in 1921 by architect Leopoldo Abreu as a summer house in blue and white with a lovely timber verandah and wooden balconies all round, designed to catch the breeze. Restored in 1980-81 as a museum, it has the usual collection of unlabelled furniture and glass from the early 20th century, stuffed animals in a natural history room (a revolutionary guard dog, Ima, appears to be suffering from mange), and an Amerindian skeleton (male, aged 20-30, with signs of syphilis and anaemia). However, the most interesting exhibit is a two-headed baby shark washed up on these shores. There are several old photos of the first hotels in Varadero, including Dos Mares (1940), Internacional (1950) and Pullman (1950), as well as items of local sporting history, a shirt of Javier Sotomayor and a rowing boat from the Club Náutico de Varadero. The **Parque Josone**, Avenida 1 y 57, is a large park with pool, bowling, other activities and a café.

At the far end of the peninsula the land has been designated the **Parque Natural de Varadero** (Parque Natural Punta Hicacos) ⓘ *Centro de Visitantes for the reserve is at the road entrance to Hotel Paradisus Varadero, 0900-1630, T45-613594.* The reserve includes 700 m of beach with different plant species including scrub and cactus, with a lagoon where salt was once made, several kilometres of sandy beach and two caves. Half way between Marina Chapelín and Marina Gaviota are the caves, **Cueva de Ambrosio** i *30 mins walk from the main road, daily 0900-1630, US$3,* where dozens of Amerindian drawings were discovered in 1961. **Cueva de Musulmanes** contains aboriginal fossils (same hours and price). There is also a beach trail for the same price as the two caves. If you do all three walks a discount on the entrance fee is possible. On the entrance road to Beaches Varadero is a Dolphinarium, see Activities and tours, page 201.

Beaches, watersports and the cays

Varadero's sandy beach stretches the length of the peninsula, broken only occasionally by rocky outcrops which can be traversed by walking through a hotel's grounds. Some parts are wider than others and as a general rule the older hotels have the best bits of beach. For instance, the **Internacional,** which was the *Hilton* before the Revolution, has a large swathe of curving beach, whereas the brand-new, upmarket **Meliá Las Américas** and its sister hotels, **Meliá Varadero** and **Sol Palmeras,** have a disappointingly shallow strip of sand and some rocks. However, the sand is all beautifully looked after and cleaned daily. The water is clean and nice for swimming but snorkelling is not worth the effort. For good **snorkelling** take one of the many boat trips out to the cays. There are three **marinas,** all full service with **sailing tours,** restaurants, **deep sea fishing** and **diving**. All services can be booked through the tour desks in hotels. You can indulge in almost any form of watersport, including **windsurfing, parasailing, waterskiing, jet skiing, non-motorized pedalos** and **water bikes**. If you are not staying in any of the Varadero hotels you may organize activities yourselves, but it will be a bit more difficult.

❧ *Beach vendors will try to sell you T-shirts, crochet work and wooden trinkets. Don't buy the black coral, it is protected internationally and you may not be allowed to take it in to your country.*

There are many **sailing tours** to the offshore cays, which usually includes lunch, an open bar and time for swimming and snorkelling. Submarine tours in glass-bottomed boats are also a popular option.

Varadero

Detail map
A Varadero centre, p196

0 km   1
0 miles   1

The **cays around the Hicacos Peninsula** were once the haunt of French pirates and it is supposed that the name 'Varadero' comes from the fact that ships ran aground here, becoming *varados* (stranded). **Cayo Mono** lies five nautical miles north northeast of Punta de Morlas. During the nesting season in mid-year it becomes a seagull sanctuary for the 'Gaviota Negra' (*Anous stolidus*) and the 'Gaviota Monja' (*Sterna fuscata* and *Annaethetus*), during which time you can only pass by and watch them through binoculars. **Cayo Piedra del Norte** is two miles southeast of Cayo Mono. On the cay is one of the 18 lighthouses which *Marinas Puertosol* intends renovating, with facilities for passing yachts. Other cays visited by tour boats include Cayo Blanco, Cayo Romero and Cayo Diana. ▸▸ *For further details, see Activities and tours, page 62.*

⬤ Sleeping

Casas particulares are not legal in Varadero but they do exist. Between Cárdenas and Varadero there are oil wells. The air smells of sulphur, which drifts as far as Varadero if the wind is in the wrong direction when gas is released from the wells, often in the middle of the night. It is particularly obvious if you stay at the southwestern end of the peninsula.

The building of new hotels and renovation of older ones is continuing all along the Varadero peninsula, with some encroaching on the edge of the nature reserve. Overdevelopment is a real issue. Unless you want an all-inclusive beach holiday in an international hotel, it is best to stay in the mid-town area, where restaurants, bars and shops are within walking distance, hotels are smaller and more intimate and the beach is just as good. Someone booking from abroad as a package will get a better deal than those who try and book from Havana where you'll get a rack rate. Prices quoted here are rack rates. There are weekend deals, mid-week deals, daily rates etc.

All-inclusive hotels include a pool (many beautifully designed), children's pool, tennis courts, gardens (often exceptionally well landscaped), restaurants, watersports, karaoke and other day and nighttime entertainment. Some offer all drinks included, others do not. Watersports include sailing, windsurfing, snorkelling, kayaking, catamaran use. Some hotels include motorized watersports in the price, others do not and some do not offer them at all for environmental reasons. Some incl gym use. Facilities not incl: laundry, massage, baby sitting, internet, telephone, post office service, doctor and hairdresser, car hire, moped hire and baby sitting. Tipping is not permitted in any *SuperClubs* hotel which seems dreadfully unfair on Cuban staff.

LL Meliá Varadero Beach & Incentive Resort, Av Las Américas, T45-667013, www.solmeliacuba.com This is by far the most expensive all-inclusive hotel on the strip with 490 rooms, 5 stars, on rocky promontory, tennis, watersports, nightclub, spa. It did win a **Green Planet** award in 2001, probably as motorized watersports are not permitted.

Matanzas Varadero: listings

LL Sol Club Coral, Carretera Las Américas entre H y K, T45-667009, jefe.reservas.sco@solmeliacuba.com The former *Sol Club Las Sirenas* and *Sol Club Coral* have combined. Both buildings are on the beach with the usual emphasis on sports (diving lessons are included in the price here, but motorized sports are not) and evening entertainment, restaurants, large curving pool, children welcome, very comfortable. The all-inclusive has 8 restaurants and 8 bars. There are 705 rooms and 3 pools. The *Habana Café* next to the enlarged complex is no longer open to the public, only to hotel guests which is a shame.

LL Sol Club Palmeras, Av Las Américas, T45-667009, F45-667008. This comes in as the second most expensive hotel in Varadero with 375 rooms, 32 suites, 200 comfortable bungalows, well-landscaped, quiet, shady, attractive, cool lobby bar. Discounts for guests at the golf course.

LL-L Meliá Las Américas Suites & Golf Resort, Carretera de Las Morlas, T45-667600, www.solmeliacuba.com An all-inclusive with 250 rooms, suites, 125 luxury bungalows, comfortable, glitzy public areas, 5 restaurants, breakfast recommended, nice pool but cold, good beach, golf, tennis, watersports, gym, disco, **Plaza América** shopping centre alongside. Children from 3-12 get free food and lodging whereas at other **Meliá** hotels it costs 50% of the adult price. Discount on the golf available. Very professional staff.

L Arenas Blancas (Gran Caribe), 64 entre Av 1 y Autopista, T45-614450, F45-611832. Huge and ugly, all-inclusive with 358 standard rooms, facilities for disabled people. In addition to the standard facilities it offers archery, mini golf and a kids' playground.

L Iberostar Bella Costa, Carretera Las Américas, Km 4.5, T45-667210, www.iberostar.com A good, all-inclusive with 386 rooms at the end of one section of a sandy beach with rocky shore, landscaped gardens, attractive, well run, good service. Pool with swim-up bar, watersports (motorized sports are not included in the price), tennis, lovely fish restaurant on small cliff overlooking sea, see pxxx.

L-AL Club Amigo Varadero (Cubanacán), Carretera Las Morlas, 1 km west of Punta Francés almost at the end of the peninsula, T45-668243, F45-668230, 331 bungalows, 24-hr drinks and snacks, non-motorized watersports, day and night entertainment, well-run, 4-star all-inclusive.

L-AL Tryp Peninsula Varadero Hotel Resort, Parque Natural Punta Hicacos, T45-668800, jefven@tpeninsula.solmelia.cu This is the most attractive all-inclusive hotel on the entire peninsula. Nothing else comes close. It is built in wooden, plantation-style villas painted in pastel and white shades. The lobby bar is attractive with wicker chairs. There are 591 rooms and 5 suites which are in bungalows, some with sea view. Watersports included.

Varadero centre

AL SuperClubs Puntarena (Gran Caribe), Av Kawama y Final, T45-667120, reservations manager@superclubspuntarena.cu A very isolated all-inclusive ugly-looking hotel with watersports included. Rooms with ocean view cost more. Lots of activities available.

AL-A Brisas del Caribe (Cubanacán), Carretera Las Morlas Km 12, T45-668030, F45-668005, ventas@bricar.var.cyt.cu 440 comfortable a/c rooms with satellite TV, phone, terrace or balcony and sea or garden view; 4 suites have Jacuzzis, 2 restaurants, grill on the beach, 6 bars, lots of sporting facilities, pool, gym, games room, entertainment.

AL-A Club Med Varadero, Autopista Sur Km 11, T45-668288, www.clubmed.com/ Villages-Clubmed/village_VARC.html For ages 12 and up, 487 rooms including 18 suites, a/c, phone, TV, safety box, 3 restaurants and 3 bars, of which 1 is reserved for cigar smokers, lots of sports including catamarans, windsurfing, kayaks, aerobics, gymnasium, volleyball, basketball, 8 tennis courts, circus school, pool, dancing lessons, pétanque and indoor games, other things can be arranged outside the *Club* such as horseriding, deep sea fishing and scuba diving and the usual excursions offered by all the hotel tour desks.

AL-A Cuatro Palmas Accor Coralia, Av 1 entre 60 y 61, T45-667040, F45-667583. 343 a/c rooms, also in bungalows and villas hacienda style, on the beach, opposite Centro Comercial Caiman and good for

shops and restaurants, very pleasant, pool has built-in sunbeds just under the water, with pleasant hacienda-style sitting room and bar overlooking the pool area. Lots of services. This is definitely one of the more attractive places to stay.

AL-A Hotel Varadero Internacional (Gran Caribe), Carretera Las Américas, T45-667038, reserva@gcinter.gca.tur.cu Formerly the *Hilton*, renovated in 1999-2000 when many of its period features were obliterated and instead of the garish pink it is now painted in tasteful but characterless shades of cream. Watersports are not included if you take the all-inclusive option. There is a famous cabaret, Cuban art gallery, and the best bit of beach on the whole peninsula. The **Cabaret Continental** (El Ritmo de Tambor) stars Tue-Sat at 2200. US$25. On Sun there is a smaller one.

A Beaches Varadero (Cubanacán), Carretera Las Morlas Km 14.5, T45-668470, F45-668335, www.beachesvaradero.com All-inclusive hotel with 350 rooms, buffet and 3 other restaurants, 4 bars, no under 16s, diving, fitness centre, sauna, tennis, car rental, watersports (all included), lots of services and entertainment. A new hotel is being built next to this one.

A SuperClubs Breezes, Carretera de las Americas Km 3, T45-667030, F45-667005 (In the UK, T020 83394150), www.superclubs cuba.net 166 rooms for singles and couples, no children under 16, a/c, phone, satellite TV, lots of activities and sports (all included),

Matanzas Varadero: listings

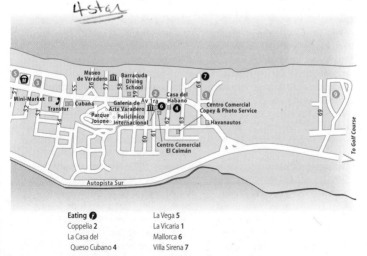

4 star

Cuban cocktails

Most bars have their own specialities, but there is a range which is fairly common to all. However, even the standard cocktails will taste different when made by different barmen, so don't expect a *Mojito* in Havana to be the same as a *Mojito* in Varadero. Cocktails come in all colours and flavours, short or long, and some are even striped or multicoloured. All should be presented as a work of art by the barman, who has probably spent years at his training.

A **Cubanito** is a Cuban version of a Bloody Mary, with ice, lime juice, salt, Worcester sauce, chilli sauce, light dry rum and tomato juice. Note that tomato juice is not always available everywhere.

An **Ernest Hemingway Special** is light dry rum, grapefruit juice, maraschino liqueur, lime and shaved ice, blended and served like a *Daiquirí*.

An **Havana Special** is pineapple juice, light dry rum, maraschino liqueur and ice, shaken and strained.

A **Mulata** is lime juice, extra aged rum, *crème de cacao* and shaved ice, blended together and served in a champagne glass.

The old favourite, **Piña Colada**, can be found anywhere: coconut liqueur, pineapple juice, light dry rum and shaved ice, all blended and served with a straw in a glass, a pineapple or a coconut, depending on which tropical paradise you are in.

Another old recipe best served in a coconut is a **Saoco**, which is just rum, coconut milk and ice.

One to finish the day off, and maybe even yourself, is a **Zombie**, a mixture of ice, lime juice, grenadine, pineapple juice, light dry rum, old gold rum and extra aged rum, garnished with fruit.

---

plenty of equipment, free sunbeds for guests, 5 bars, 3 restaurants, disco, theme parties, indoor games room, gym, sauna, Jacuzzis, Olympic-size pool, tennis, diving and other watersports, such as sailing and waterskiing, popular, crowded even in low season. Discount golf rates available.

A-C Kawama (Gran Caribe), Carretera de Kawama y 1, T45-614416, reserva@kawama .gca.tur.cu On the beach, 202 double rooms and 30 triples, a/c, balcony or terrace, minibar, bathroom, TV, phone, safe in room, snack bar, buffet and à la carte restaurant, disco, entertainment, watersports included, kids' club, pool, tennis, gym, sauna, massage, hairdresser, medical services, PO, cambio, email services, moped and car rental, taxis, tourism bureau.

B Los Delfines (Horizontes), Av 1 entre 38 y 39, T45-667720, F45-667496. Built across Av Playa so traffic has to go around, 3 floors, green windows and balconies, cream walls, package business, marketed exclusively by **Press Tours** of Italy. The interior is pretty revolting with 80s style architecture and primary green splashed everywhere. Pink columns adorn the foyer and a dolphin sculpture completes the masterpiece. There are 103 rooms with all mod cons. The staff are exceptionally helpful and friendly here but some of the European clientele leave a lot to be desired.

B Villa Punta Blanca (Gran Caribe), Reparto Kawama, T45-668050, F45-667004. 4 star, 320 rooms, made up of a number of former private residences with some new complexes. The green house on the right on the way down to **SuperClubs Puntarena** belonged to President Grau. This was closed for repairs and an upgrade at the time of going to press.

B Villa Sotavento, 13 entre Av 1 y Av Playa, T45-667132 F45-667229, facturas@acua .hor.tur.cu 110 mini apartments with the same facilities as **Varazul** and TV, kitchen shared, next to beach, clean, with bath, breakfast, US$5, buffet, very good. Guests can use all the facilities at **Acuazul**.

B-D Villa La Mar (Islazul), Av 3 entre 28 y 29, T45-613910, T/F45-612508, vlamar@teleda.get.tur.cu Friendly staff, rooms available from B&B up to all-inclusive. 264 rooms with a/c, TV, hot water, smart and clean, pool, kids' pool, bar, excursions, buffet breakfast included but nothing special, cheap hotel for package deals booked from abroad. Convenient for the **Víazul** bus and the banks. One of the best value places in the lowest price range on the peninsula.

C Acuazul, Av 1 entre 13 y 14, T45-667132, F45-667229, facturas@acua.hor.tur.cu 78 rooms in a blue and white concrete block, with pool. Older-style hotel, but quiet and one of the more reasonably priced. The kitsch aquaerobics entertainment is unmissable.

C Dos Mares, Calle 53 y Av 1, T45-612702, www.horizontes.cu One of the oldest hotels, dating from 1940, small, friendly and full of character, across the road from the beach, breakfast included, rooms adequate, some with good-sized bathrooms, others small, a/c, TV (CNN), safe, bar. Closed for an upgrade at the time of going to press.

C Pullman, Av 1 entre 49 y 50, T45-612702, www.horizontes.cu One of the oldest hotels in Varadero notable for its turret and style of a castle. Small, not directly on the beach, low key, breakfast included, a/c, TV. Closed for repairs and an upgrade at the time of going to press.

C Varazul, Av 1 entre 14 y 15, T45-667132, F45-667229, facturas@acua.hor.tur.cu 69 mini apartments which include kitchen, dining room and bathroom in a quiet part of town. Facilities at **Acuazul** can be used.

C Villa La Caleta (Gaviota), 20 y Av 1, T45-667080-1. 46 a/c rooms with baths, phone, TV, minibar, restaurant, room service, pizzeria, grill, bar, pool, scooter and bike hire, parking, convenient for nightlife.

D La Casona, 51 y Playa, T45-612389, F45-667219. This is a charity project, the **Social and Educational Services Centre** (CESERSE), run by Nacyra Gómez Cruz (who speaks English). The Centre works with Grandparents' Clubs to bring senior citizens and children with special needs or terminal illnesses from around Cuba to the house for a holiday. Church groups are also involved and Pastors for Peace donated a bus. The centre offers dinner, bed and breakfast from Nov-Mar, mainly to groups of people, as part of fundraising for these visits. It will organize excursions too.

Eating

Food is nothing special here but, outside the hotels, dishes are improving in quality, although if you find much beyond the usual staples you will have hit the jackpot. There are just 1 or 2 exceptions to the mediocre eating experience that is Varadero.

Hotel restaurants

$$$ **El Mirador**, at Iberostar Bella Costa, T45-667210, daily 1200-2300. On a cliff overlooking the sea. Lovely fish restaurant, with lobster and shrimp as the tempting options.

$$$ **Las Américas**, Av Las Américas, T45-667600, daily 1200-2215. International food, beautiful setting, food good 1 night, inedible the next.

$$$ **Oshin**, in grounds of Sol Club Palmeras, T45-667009, daily 1200-1500 and 1800-2300. Chinese, popular, reservations essential.

Along Camino del Mar

$$ **Mi Casita** (book in advance), Camino del Mar entre 11 y 12, T45-613787, daily 1800-2300. Meat and seafood.

$ **La Cabañita**, Camino del Mar esq 9, T45-616764, daily 1900-0100. This is right on the beach under a thatched roof with a lovely bit of sand opposite which appears to be family-orientated. Good combos are available: US$5 for chicken or fish, rice, fries and a drink.

East on Av Primera and Playa

$$$ **Mansión Xanadú**, Carretera Las Américas, Km 8.5, T45-668482, www.varaderogolfclub.com The mansion was established between 1928 and 1930. It has more than 100 wines. Restaurant 1900-2230 serving up such mouth-watering delights as octopus with sliced paprika on mango, and shrimps in sherry. **Bar Mirador Casa Blanca** daily 1000-2345. There are also 2 rooms with sea view: **AL** but **LL** over Christmas. For guests the green fee is free and unlimited.

$$$-$$ **Casa de Al**, in among Villa Punta Blanca, see Sleeping above. A stone building with blue painted wooden attributes, which used to belong to Al Capone. It's a quiet spot for a sunset drink (with outdoor tables on the terrace) or a meal of Mafia Soup, Godfather Salad, Fillet Mignon "Lucky

Luciano" and cold blood ice cream. The service is a little on the slow side but not annoyingly so. Worth a visit.

$$$-$$ La Casa del Queso Cubano, Av Playa y 64, daily 1200-2300. A highly air-conditioned restaurant with smart tables serving a variety of fondues including lobster fondue and chocolate fondue as well as breaded pork, chicken and grilled fish. Vegetables sometimes lacking although advertized on the menu.

$$$-$$ La Vega, Av Playa entre 31 y 32, T45-611430, daily 1200-2300. A charming, wooden restaurant with baskets hanging from the staircase and with outdoor seating on wooden decking. Serving a large range of *mariscos* including squid, paella and crêpes for pudding. Cheaper dishes are available. There is a gorgeous giant leaf sculpture outside.

$$ Castelnuovo, Av 1 y 11, T45-667794, daily 1200-2345. Italian restaurant with a smart-ish indoor dining area and a rundown, but pleasant, outdoor area. The pizzas are massive and the service is very efficient.

$$ El Criollo, esq 18 y Av 1, T45-614794, daily 1200-2330. A thatched-roof bar with ambient Cuban music and more efficient service than the nearby "Bellamar". Offerings include, *filete de res mechado con* bacon, *camarones* and roast pork.

$$ Lai-Lai, Av 1 y 18, T45-667793, daily 1200-0300. Bar/restaurant serving up spring rolls, Chinese soup and other oriental cuisine as well as the usual Cuban fare.

$$ Ranchon Playa "Bellamar", Av 1 entre 16 y 17. Pleasant, thatched-roofed roadside restaurant delivering up large portions of food, including breaded fish fillet, pizza, red snapper, lobster and vegetable salad. Don't eat anything for hours beforehand and bring earplugs if you can't bear blaring western 70s hits.

$ Coppelia, Av 1 entre 44 y 46, in the town centre, T45-612866, daily 1000-2245. Ice cream US$0.90.

$ Deportivo Kiki's Club, Av 1 y 8, T45-614115, daily 1200-2345. Sports theme. Serves Italian food in a restaurant that's partially open air.

$ La Vicaria, next to Los Delfines hotel. A part-thatched covered restaurant, which, apart from doing a whole heap of chicken like everywhere else on the strip, actually serves salads, which are hard to come by.

$ Mallorca, Av Playa y 62, T45-667746. Seafood, spaghetti, pizza, snack bar. US$2-5.

🍷 Bars

Every hotel has several bars to choose from and it can be fun to work your way through the barman's list of cocktails during your holiday. Even here, however, you may be told '*no hay*', with tomato juice and other mixers often unavailable. Stick to the traditionally Cuban and you won't be disappointed. Outside the hotels, the **Bar Mirador Casa Blanca**, on the top floor of the **Mansión Xanadú** at the Golf Club is worth a visit for the view and relaxed atmosphere, if not the prices. See Eating above.

🎭 Entertainment

La Casa de la Cultura Los Corales, Av 1 entre 34 y 35. A *cartelera* in the window advertizes local events.

Cinema
Cine Varadero, Av Playa entre 42 y 43. Shows Cuban and foreign films.

Discos
Most large hotels have one including:
La Patana, Canal de Paso Malo, T45-667791, daily 2100-0300. Floating disco at entrance to the laguna.

Nightclubs and cabaret
Cabaret Continental, at Hotel Internacional. See Sleeping, above.
Cabaret Cueva del Pirata, Autopista Sur Km 11, T45-61389, Mon-Sat 2200-0300. Show in a cave.
Mambo Club, Carretera Las Morlas Km 14, next to Club Amigo Varadero, daily 0900-1600. US$10. The *Orquesta Tarafa* plays here, they were famous in the 1950s.
Palacio de la Rumba, Av Las Américas, Km 4, T45-668210, daily 2200-0300, Mon-Thu US$10 entrance, Fri-Sun US$15, Sun 1600-2100 US$5, includes bar, live salsa bands at weekends. Popular with Cubans and foreigners.

🎉 Festivals and events

Jan Carnival involves lots of tourist participation, encouraged by the hotel entertainment teams.

Some years an **arts festival** is held in Varadero, lasting a week, which attracts some of the best artists in South America. Entrance US$2-10 per day.

O Shopping

Arts and handicrafts
Handicraft markets offer all manner of souvenirs, from elaborately decorated wooden *humedores* to keep your cigars temperature-controlled, to T-shirts and keyrings, which are easier to pack. The main market area is in the Parque de las Mil Taquillas. **Casa de la Artesanía Latinoamericana**, Av 1 y 64, T45-667691.
Galería de Arte Sol y Mar, 34 y Av 1, T45-63153.
Galería de Arte y Taller de Cerámica Artística, Av 1 entre 59 y 60, daily 0900-1900.

Cigars
Arte Nuevo, Av 63 entre 1 y 2, T45-61256. For cigars, rum and coffee.
Casa del Habano, Av 1 esq 39 and 63 entre 1 y 3 in the Centro Comercial Copey. Also in the restaurant **La Vega**, daily 0900-2100. Also **Bar Tienda Maqueta** and Casa del Habano next to La Casa del Queso Cubano, daily 0900-2300.

Food and general provisions
On the corner of Av 1 y 43 is a **bakery**. There's a small, but decent, **mini-market** on Av 1 entre 53 y 54 selling food, drink, shampoo and sunscreen etc, while for those on the southwestern end of the peninsula, there's a **grocery store** on C13, daily 0900-1800, close to the Canadian consulate.

Music
Max Music, Centro Comercial Copey, Av 3 entre 61 y 63, for CDs and other music.

Opticians
Opticas Miramar, Av 1 entre 42 y 43.

Photography
Photo Express is at Av 1 entre 41 y 42, T45-667015, open 24 hrs.
Photo Service has 2 outlets: Av Playa y 44, open 24 hrs, and Centro Comercial Copey, 63 y Av 3, T45-667753, daily 0900-2100.

Shopping centres
Centro Comercial Copey, Av 3 entre 61 y 63; **El Caimán**, Av 1 entre 61 y 62; **Plaza América**, by the Sol Meliá hotels.

▲ Activities and tours

Diving
Centro Internacional de Buceo y Escuela Barracuda, (Cubanacán), C 59 y 1 Av, T45-613481, F45-667072, ventas@aqwo.var.cyt.cu daily 0800-1730. There are some 30 dive sites off Varadero. Bay of Pigs excursion offered too (US$45) as well as night diving, cave diving, wreck diving (including a l00-m-long Russian wreck) and lessons. 1 dive US$35, 2 dives US$60, then from 3 dives at US$85 up to 8 dives at US$190. ACUC open water diver US$365, dive master US$800. English, Italian, French, German, Russian and Hungarian spoken. Most trips are 0830-1430 but a trip to Playa Girón lasts all day.
Recompression chambers in Varadero, Cárdenas and 2 in Havana, 24 hrs. **Marina Gaviota**, and **Marina Dársena**, see Marinas above, also offer diving as does **Marina Chapelín**, which is partnered with Barracuda.

Dolphinarium
Delfinario, autopista sur, at entrance to Hotel Beaches Varadero, daily 0900-1700. Shows 1100, 1430, 1630. Show is US$10, swimming with the dolphins US$65, camera US$5, video camera US$10, see pxxx.

Golf
There is a Canadian-designed golf course on Av Las Américas Km 8.5, upgraded in 1996-98 to 18 holes, par 72. The original 9 holes were set out by the Duponts around their mansion, built in 1928-30, which is now the **Mansión Xanadú**, and the new ones extend along the **Sol Meliá** resorts.
Varadero Golf Club, T45-667788, T45-668180, www.varaderogolfclub.com daily 0700-1900. With 2 putting greens, a chipping green and a driving range and Pro-shop and equipment rental at Caddie House. Green fee 18 holes, $60. Beginner's lesson US$12 per 30 mins. The course is open from 0700 until dusk. Special offers are available at certain times of the year with

shared powered golf carts (which are compulsory) thrown in. Reservations with 24 hrs notice are advised especially Sep-Dec.

Hotel sports facilities

The large hotels all offer **tennis** courts, some have **squash** courts and **volleyball** is played on the beach, usually organized by the hotel entertainment staff. **Table tennis**, **billiards** and other indoor games are available if the weather deteriorates or you have had enough sun.

Marinas and water-based activities

Marina Chapelín, Carretera Las Morlas, Km 12.5, T45-667550/093, direccion@marlinv .var.cyt.cu VHF 16 and 72, daily 0800-1900. **Moorings** for 20 boats, maximum draft 30 m, boat rental and laundry. There's an on-site restaurant and staff are friendly. Ring at least 1 day beforehand to book your activity. This is by far the busiest marina, see Diving pxxx. **Snorkelling** is offered Mon-Sat 0930-1430 at a coral beach and in Saturno Cave; a **seafari** to Cayo Blanco includes a dolphin show, transfer, equipment, open bar, lunch and an Afro-Cuban show, US$75 per person, daily 0900-1630; **fishing**, daily 0900-1430, US$300 (1-4 people) including open bar and equipment; **yacht trips**, daily 0900-1430, US$30 including open bar and snorkelling (minimum of 8 people required). *Noche Pirata*, a trip out in a galleon with entertainment on board, dinner and drinks included, US$39, daily 1700-2100. For **sportfishing** consult www.aquaworld varadero.com Prices vary but includes transfer, all drinks, all fishing gear, licences and crew. Offshore: *Peto* (wahoo) Oct-Feb, *Dorado* Apr-Sep; Sierra (sailfish) Apr-May; *Atún, bonito* Apr-Sep. Reef: Barracuda all year; *Aguají* (grouper) all year; *Pargo* (snapper) May-Jul best, Aug-Apr good. Bay: *sábalo* (tarpon); *jinawa* (yellow jack) Feb-Apr best, rest of year good.
Marina Dársena, Carretera de Vía Blanca Km 31, T45-668063, VHF 16, 19, 68, 72. Moorings for 70 boats, maximum draft 5 m, boat rental, showers, laundry, restaurants, bar, **fishing**, shops, day charters, **diving**, liveaboard for 20 people. The Mundo Mágico submarine that sets off from here goes down to a depth of 35 m with 46 passengers for 55 minutes.

Marina Gaviota, Peninsula de Hicacos Km 21, T45-66755/756, dir.marina@delvar .gav.tur.cu VHF 16. Moorings for 10 boats, 3 m draft, showers, laundry, restaurant, bar. **Sea safaris** in catamarans with a visit to Cayo Cangrejo, yacht rental, fishing, swimming with dolphins and diving.

Sky diving and parachuting

Aeroclub Varadero, Km 0.5, Vía Blanca, opposite Marina Dársena, T45-667256 /667260. Parachuting/skydiving can be done here. Courses or tandem jumps are on offer, see the price list on the wall at the airstrip. It is approximately US$135 for a lesson and a jump/fall/fly.

Tour operators

Every hotel has a tour agency on-site offering local and national excursions, boat trips, multilingual guides, transfers, booking and confirmation of air tickets, air charters, car rentals, reception and representation service.
Cubatur, Av 1 y C33, T45-667401/217, varadero@cubatur.cu daily 0830-1230, 1330-2030.
Gaviota, T45-667684; Rumbos, C13 1301, esq Av 1, T45-612384, F45-611858, direccion@rumboscuba.co.cu
Islazul, C1 3504 entre 35 y 36, T45-612517, F45-667023.
National tours Trips to Havana, Cárdenas (see p205), Valle de Yumurí, Pinar, Cayo Largo, Bay of Pigs, Guama-Cienfuegos -Trinidad, Pinar by plane, Tropicana, Santa Clara.
Local excursions The following excursions can all be booked at all hotel tourism bureaux and through tour operators:
Challenge Tour, T45-668000, altius@atenas.inf.cu Based out of Marina Chapelín, see above. This is a multi-adventure day out – a jeep tour with boat ride, horseriding and lunch all included. US$74 per person.
Jolly Roger Catamaran Cruises, Km 125, T45-667757, www.jollyrogervaradero.com A seafari to Cayo Blanco including snorkelling and a dolphin show and open bar. Sunset cruises available. It is not a pseudo pirate ship as in other parts of the Caribbean, but a comfortable catamaran. US$70.
Jungle Tour, Carretera Las Morlas, Km 12, T45-668440, www.jungletour-cuba.com next to Marina Chapelín, opposite Brisas del Caribe.

Parque Turístico Río Canímar, Km 106 Vía Blanca, T45-261516. Boat ride, lunch, horseriding, fishing, hammocks and a visit to Cueva Saturno and Playa el Coral. **Varasub**, sales office: Av Playa entre 36 y 37, T45-667027. The Varasub is a Japanese semi-submersible carrying 48 passengers. A reef tour is followed by a trip to Cuevas Bellamar and Matanzas, US$37. 6 departures a day from **Hotel SuperClubs Puntarena**, 1½ hrs.

⊖ Transport

Air
The Juan Gualberto Gómez **airport** (VRA), T45-613016, receives international scheduled and charter flights. There are domestic flights from **Havana** and **Santiago**.

Bus
The interprovincial bus station is at Autopista Sur y 36, T45-663254, T45-662626, daily 0700-1800.

Víazul, T45-614886, has 3 daily buses **Havana-Varadero** via **Matanzas** and **Varadero airport**, 0800, 0830, 1600, 3 hrs, US$10, returning 0800, 1600, 1800. **Varadero-Trinidad** 0730, 6 hrs, US$20, with stops in **Cárdenas** US$6, **Coliseo** US$6, **Jovellanos** US$6, **Jagüey** US$6, **Santa Clara** US$11 and **Sancti Spíritus** US$16, returns from **Trinidad** 1430.

Astro bus twice a day (0805 and 1600) from **Havana** bus terminal to **Varadero**, which stops off at **Varadero airport**, US$8, reserve 1-2 days in advance. To **Havana** 0820,1050; to **Santa Clara** 1415, 1815; to **Cienfuegos** 0845, 1315. To **Cárdenas** 0730, returning 1100. The buses to **Santa Clara** and **Cienfuegos** also pass through **Cárdenas**.

Tourist bus Varadero Beach Tour. There are several bus stops along the peninsula (all clearly marked). The bus passes every hour (a red open-top double decker); the timetable is posted clearly at every bus stop. US$2 for a day ticket where you can get on and off.

Car/moped hire
Hire a car rather than jeep to avoid having your spare wheel stolen, insurance covers 4 wheels, not the spare (see Essentials, page 45). **Cubacar** (Cubanacán) at many of the hotels, main office: T45-667341. **Transtur**, Av 1 y 55, or through many of the hotels. **Nacional** (Gaviota)

at 13 entre Av 2 y 4, T/F45-667663. **Transautos**, Av 2 y 64, T45-667336, or Av 1 entre 21 y 22. **Petrol stations** Servi Cupet, 54 y Autopista, 17 y Autopista, Vía Blanca Km 31.

Moped/bicycle hire
Hiring a moped is a good way to see the peninsula but you will have no insurance and no helmet. Many of the hotels do moped rental and bicycle hire, US$1 per hr. **Moped Rent Rumbos**, Av 1, entre 37 y 38, US$6 per hr, US$24 per 24 hrs. Also hires bicycles up to US$6 for 3 hrs. **Havanautos**, Av 1 y 64, Moped hire up to US$20 per day.

Taxi
Horse-drawn vehicles act as taxis, usually just for a tour around town. Taxis charge US$0.50 per km. Beware of being fleeced on arrival at the bus station. A 2-min taxi ride can cost US$3 and up for the innocent newly-arrived. The best place to hail a taxi is at any hotel as they usually wait there for fares. **Transgaviota**, T45-619761/2; **Turistaxi**, T45-613763; **Taxi OK**, T45-667341. A reliable taxi driver who is open to negotiations for excursions is **Pedro Rodríguez Carmenate**, C Libertad 954, Santa Marta, T45-619560, T45-619811 (home).

⊕ Directory

Banks
Banco Popular de Ahorro, esq Av 1 y 36, has an ATM for Visa only, but accepts MC inside, Mon-Fri 0830-1530. Banco Financiero Internacional, Av 1 y 32, Mon-Fri 0900-1500, last working day of month 0900-1200. Cash advance service with Visa and MC available. Bandec, Av 1 y 36, has an ATM but it accepts Visa only.

Internet/telephone
For cellular phones, **Cubacel** is at 25 y Av 1, Edif La Cancha, T45-667222/198, F45-667222. **DHL**, next to Casa del Habano, Av 1 y 39, daily 0800-2000. It also has a cyber café, daily 0800-2000, with phone service. **Etecsa**, Av 30 y 1, daily 0800-0700, closed for lunch Sat and Sun, US$3 per 30 mins for internet.

Medical facilities
Policlínico Internacional, Av 1 y 61, T45-668611, T45-667710-1, F45-667226,

Cuban rum

Sugar was first introduced to Cuba by Christopher Columbus, who brought sugar cane roots from the Canary Islands on his second transAtlantic voyage. The first rudimentary mills produced sugar cane juice, but as they became more sophisticated the juice was turned into alcohol. A clear wine was made, which, when distilled, several times became a basic rum. In the 19th century a new manufacturing process was developed, which considerably improved the quality of Cuban rum, and the industry rapidly expanded with the construction of hundreds of sugar mills all over the country. The cities of Havana, Santiago de Cuba, Cienfuegos and Cárdenas all produced rum of export quality under the labels of *Havana Club* (founded in 1878), *Bacardí, Campeón, Obispo, San Carlos, Jiquí, Matusalem, Bocoy* and *Albuerne*.

The family firm of *Bacardí* was the largest in Cuba for nearly 100 years, building substantial wealth on the back of rum. After the 1959 Revolution, when the sugar industry and the distilleries were taken over by the state, the family left the island and took the Bacardí name with them. The Bacardí rum, now found worldwide, is not distilled in Cuba. Many labels can be found in Cuba, including the venerable *Havana Club, Caribbean Club, Caney, Legendario, Matusalem, Varadero, Bucanero* and *Siboney*.

Rums of all different ages can be found. Generally, the younger, light rums are used in cocktails and aged, dark rums drunk on the rocks or treated as you might a single malt whisky. Light, dry rum in Cuba is aged (*ron añejo*) for three years, has little body and is between 40° and 60° proof. Old gold, dry rum is aged for five years, is amber in colour and can be drunk straight or added to cocktails for an extra kick. Extra aged rum is aged for seven years and is usually drunk neat in a brandy glass.

Cocktails first became popular after the development of ice making in the USA in 1870 and were introduced to Cuba soon afterwards. The first Cuban cocktails were the *Cuba Libre* and the *Daiquirí*, the former developed when US intervention forces brought in bottled cola drinks during the war of independence against Spain at the end of the 19th century, and the latter invented by an engineer in the *Daiquirí* mines in eastern Cuba.

Cocktails boomed in the 1920s with an influx of bartenders and global visitors, many of whom were escaping prohibition in the USA. Recipes were named after visiting film stars and other dignitaries and developed at *La Bodeguita del Medio* or *El Floridita*, bars still flourishing today. The *Hemingway Special* was created for the writer by the famous bartender, Constante, at *El Floridita*. Others include a Greta Garbo, Lilian Gish and a Mary Pickford.

clinica@clinica.var.cyt.cu International clinic, doctor on duty 24 hrs, a medical consultation in your hotel will cost US$50. The clinic has an excellent international **pharmacy** attached. Any diver needing treatment for the bends will be taken to the **recompression chamber** at the Centro Médico Sub Acuática at the Hospital Julio M Arístegui, just outside Cárdenas. For further details, see also p201.

Post office
Av 1 entre 36 y 37, open at 0800. Most hotels have post offices where you can buy stamps for use and for collectors. Internet, phone and fax services are usually available but rates vary.

Useful addresses
Immigration and Police: 39 y Av 1. Immigration, Mon-Fri 0900-1200, 1350-1630 for visa extensions. **Canadian consulate**, 13 y Av 1, close to a mini grocery store.

Cárdenas → *Colour map 2, grid A1. Population: 75,000.*

Cárdenas is 18 km southeast of Varadero on the Bahía de Cárdenas. The town's architecture is attractive, in the traditional 19th-century Spanish colonial style of houses with tall windows, intricate lattices, high ceilings inside, ceramic tiled floors and interior gardens. However, its glory days are over and it's a good place to come to see a working Cuban town. It is trapped in a time warp, empty of tourists, friendly and a good place to meet Cubans. There is none of the aggressive hustling found in hotel districts or more tourist-oriented cities and no police harassment of Cubans associating with foreigners. However, the flip side of this relaxed attitude is that romantic liaisons, which once took place in Varadero, are being squeezed out to Cárdenas. ▶ *For Sleeping, Eating and other listings, see pages 207-207.*

Ins and outs

Getting there Most long-distance transport is via Varadero where you will find the nearest **airport**. The **railway** is for local services only and there is not much in the way of long-distance **bus** transport, although there are **Astro** services from Havana, Matanzas and Varadero, and **Víazul** stops here on its way between Varadero and Trinidad.

Getting around Cárdenas is a slow city, with traffic moving at the pace of the horse. Transport is limited to **coches**, **bicycles** and pedestrians. The city is set out in very regular grid form, with Calles running parallel to the sea in consecutive numbers and Avenidas crossing them. The main street is Avenida Céspedes and Avenidas are numbered from here, with those running northwest starting from Avenida 1 oeste in odd numbers, and those running southeast starting from Avenida 2 este in even numbers. However, as in many places, people refer to old names rather than the numbers. Use the TV tower as a landmark. The tower is on Avenida Céspedes y Calle 11, called Coronel Verdugo. The three main museums are around Plaza Echeverría, just two blocks from Avenida Céspedes.

Best time to visit Like Varadero, hurricane season can be wet and stormy although there are plenty of fine, bright days. Between December and April is the driest time.

History

Cárdenas was founded in 1828. It was once one of the most important cities in Cuba with its wealth built on sugar. It had the first alcohol refinery, the first electricity plant and the first gynaecological hospital in Cuba; and its Plaza de Mercado is unique in Latin America. Its main claim to fame is that the Cuban flag was first raised here in 1850 by the revolutionary General Narciso López, a Venezuelan who tried unsuccessfully to invade Cuba by landing at Cárdenas with an army of 600 men (only six of whom were Cuban), who had sailed from New Orleans. Cárdenas was also thrust onto the world stage in 1999-2000 after the Miami boat boy Elián González was finally returned to his home town after a geopolitical wrangle involving the USA, Cuba, the families and the law. His story is commemorated in a new museum, see below.

Sights

Cárdenas is a city with a sense of humour: it commemorates the mundane with bizarre memorials. On Calle 13 there is a *coche* statue, equipped with a white, stone horse. Behind the **Fuerte Roja** (a bar in a tower) is a bicycle that stands high on a thin metal plinth as if it was balancing on the gymnastics beam. Outside the hospital a large, fibreglass nose provides a bus shelter: its giant nostrils the gaping way in to the waiting area. (Apparently, the *nariz* is in homage to the majority black population of

Cárdenas); and at the entrance to the city (approaching from the Varadero end) a giant crab welcomes visitors. However, the sculptor's lack of marine knowledge has left a biological mutant on the roadside: the Cárdenas crustacean has a large right pincer (normal *cangrejos* sport the large claw on the left).

Where Avenida Céspedes ends at the sea, there is the **Monumento a la Bandera** with a huge flagpole commemorating the flag-raising event on 19 May. There is also a plaque at the **Hotel Dominica,** which Narciso López occupied with his men and is now a National Monument. Unfortunately, the General's attempts to free Cuba from colonial rule were unsuccessful, as he failed to get local support. One of the town's other claims to fame is that it contains the oldest **statue of Christopher Columbus** in the Western Hemisphere, now in front of the cathedral in Parque Colón on Avenida Céspedes, five blocks from the flagpole. It was the work of a Spanish sculptor, Piquier, in 1862. **Plaza Malacoff** is worth a visit to see the decaying, iron market building, put up in the 19th century on Avenida 3 oeste and Calle 12. It was built in the shape of a cross and the two-storey building is surmounted by a 15-m dome made in the USA. The market is a great public gathering place for gossip and beer-drinking. On Calle 2, overlooking the water, is the **Fábrica de Ron Arrechabala,** which makes both the *Varadero* and *Bucanero* label rums. The site has been a rum factory since 1878, when the *Havana Club* company was founded here.

One of Cárdenas' most celebrated residents is the boy, Elián González, who hit the headlines in 1999 when he was shipwrecked off the Miami coast (see History, page 397). His father, who works locally in the tourism industry, was finally able to take him home from the US after seven months of legal wrangling, and Elián has resumed near-normal life in school. In July 2001, Fidel Castro opened the **Museo a la Batalla de Ideas** ① *C 12 y Plaza Echeverría, Tue-Sat 0900-1700, Sun 0900-1300, US$2, kids free, camera US$5, video US$25, guide US$2, mirador US$1*. This small museum, housed in the 1873 fire station, is a veritable shrine to Elián. Everything Elián and his family said or did is featured here. Two displays include the T-shirt worn by the fisherman, Sam Ciancio, who hauled Elián out of the sea. There are also letters from the likes of Guatemalan Nobel Prize-winning author Rigoberta Menchú and the Uruguayan exiled writer Mario Benedetti saying that Elián must be reunited with his father. There is a *maqueta* (model) of the Tribuna Antiimperialista José Martí, a demonstration ground built in front of the US Interests section in Havana during the whole saga. The large bronze statue of José Martí in the museum foyer was the original statue on the parade ground during the demonstrations against his staying in Florida. The one in Havana is a replacement statue. There is also a large display about the Miami Five.

The **Museo Municipal Oscar María de Rojas** ① *Plaza Echeverría entre Av 4 y 6 este, Tue-Sat 0800-1600, Sun 0800-1200, US$2*, exhibits art, geology specimens and local and natural history. A local, 20th-century hero is remembered in his birthplace, now a museum. **Museo Casa Natal José Echeverría** ① *Av 4 este y Plaza Echeverría, Mon-Sat 1000-1800, Sun 0800-1200, US$1, guide US$2, US$1 per photo*, dates from 1703, but Echeverría was born here in 1932. He was a student leader killed by Batista's troops in 1957. Exhibits are scarce but those on show relate to 19th-century independence struggles downstairs and the 20th-century Revolution upstairs. Of note are a giant doll used to hide clandestine objects and a photo of the man himself, blood-drenched in the street after being mown down. The park outside is named after Echeverría and there is a monument to him in the park. The **Salón Massaguner art gallery** ① *Av Céspedes 560, one block south of the TV tower*, has high-quality works from Matanzas province artists. There is the *art naif* of Olga Vallejo and political works of Francisco Rivero, among others, including sculptures.

Around Cárdenas

About 10 km from town is the **Central Azucarero José Smith Comás**, where an 1888 steam engine is still used to haul sugar to the main railway lines. Take the road to Santa Clara, turn right at the fork by an old paper mill. Some 24 km south of Cárdenas

is **Jovellanos,** a large town with a pleasant colonial centre, Parque Central and church.
It is a junction of the roads from Varadero to the Zapata peninsula and from Matanzas
to Santa Clara. It is of no particular interest to travellers except that as a result of
slavery and enforced migrations, the Arara people of Benin came here via Haiti and
brought the sort of music with them that is normally only heard around Santiago de
Cuba. There is a bus from Cárdenas, 2 pesos.

The main road from Matanzas runs east from here to **Colón,** on the main railway line
from Havana. This is another 19th-century town with abundant neoclassical architecture
and faded grandeur. For adventurous independent travellers exploring rural Matanzas,
you will be well off the tourist trail; you can stay in peso hotels here and spend pesos in
restaurants and on transport. Carnival is 15-17 October. The **Astro** bus from here to Santa
Clara leaves at 1100 daily, but is usually booked two weeks in advance. You can pay for
train tickets here in pesos, only 7 pesos to Guayos, the Sancti Spíritus station.

Sleeping

Cárdenas *p205*
F**Dominica**, Av Céspedes y C Real, T45-521501.
25 rooms in an old sugar warehouse, converted
to hotel in neoclassical style in 1919 and now a
National Monument, big rooms and suites,
some with balconies, but the rooms are pretty
filthy and the reception is grotty. Unfortunately,
the beautiful cosmetic makeover of the exterior
which has a lovely duck egg blue façade, has
not been extended to the interior.

Eating

Cárdenas *p205*
There are a couple of *cafeterías* where you
can get a sandwich and a beer and peso
snack stands along Av Céspedes, but
otherwise Cárdenas is not a great culinary
experience. The public market has plenty of
fresh fruit and vegetables.
$**Café Spiriu**, Plaza Echeverría, 2 blocks east of
Av Céspedes, daily 0800-2200. Popular,
attractive with lovely *vitrales* above its doors,
criollo food, great ice cream, reasonable prices,
main course less than US$4, best place in town.
$**El Rápido**, diagonally opposite the cathedral
and another branch opposite Plaza Malacoff.
Good for a quick fix.
$**Las Palmas**, Av Céspedes y 16. In large,
walled, colonial building with imposing
dining room, mostly a drinking place,
sometimes drunken brawls late at night.

Bars

Cárdenas *p205*
There's a beer bar opposite El Rápido, see
Eating above, which seems popular at

weekends. **La Fuerte Roja**, a small turret,
that's more of a dusty pink than red, is a
popular and quirky spot for a beer with
wooden, roadside tables standing firm in the
middle of a small and quiet traffic island in
front of the memorial to a bicycle.

Transport

Bicycles/coches
Local There is not much in the way of local
transport; bicycles, or *coches*, are the only
carriers, 1 peso. Cárdenas is an easy bike ride
from **Varadero** and there are bike park areas
where a guard will watch your bike for 1 peso.

Bus
The bus station is on Av Céspedes y 22, with
services to **Matanzas**, **Colón**, **Jagüey Grande**,
Havana and **Santa Clara**. To get to **Varadero**
catch a bus from the corner of Av 13 oeste y
Calle 13, they should leave every hour, but as
the principal demand is from hotel workers
they are more likely to run according to shifts.

Víazul stops in Cárdenas on its **Trinidad-
Varadero** route, US$6 from **Varadero**, US$10
from **Santa Clara**, US$18 from **Trinidad**.
Alternatively, **Astro** from **Havana** 0845, US$6,
or **colectivo taxi**, US$15. Astro returns to
Havana 1340 via **Varadero** and **Matanzas**.
There are no facilities to charge in dollars and
if you show your ticket stub from your arrival
they will charge you only 6 pesos for your
return. Get there early, or buy a reserved ticket.

Taxi
Taxi from **Varadero** US$25 round trip with
waiting time.

Zapata Peninsula and Bay of Pigs

This is one of the most famous places in the world: for every Cuban it signifies a great victory; for the Americans, a failure of monumental proportions. Historian of Cuba, Hugh Thomas, said the disaster of the CIA-backed invasion in April 1961 was so politically dismal for JFK that he went out and ordered the US space agency to land a man on the moon before the decade was out. In his history epic 'Cuba' he wrote, "perhaps a victory for the US in Cuba might have deprived mankind of that achievement in 1969". Unfortunately, there is little to see at the Bay of Pigs (Bahía de Cochinos) relating to the air and sea attack except crosses on the roadside marking the fallen and a museum about the invasion. However, this is extremely interesting and is full to overflowing with photos for those who don't read Spanish and there is a feeling of achievement and importance in making it to such an historical site that is a little off the beaten track.

Nowadays, there is more to the region than just its history. The whole of the south coast of the Matanzas province is taken up with the Zapata peninsula, an area of swamps, mangroves, beaches and much bird and animal life. Much of it is a national park – Parque Nacional Ciénaga de Zapata, the largest ecosystem on the island containing the Laguna del Tesoro, a 9.1-sq-km lagoon over 10 m deep. It is an important winter home for flocks of migrating birds. There are 16 species of reptiles, including crocodiles. Mammals include the jutía and the manatee, while there are more than 1,000 species of invertebrate, of which more than 100 are spiders.

Near Playa Girón is a stunning natural pool area, Caleta Buena, brimming with sapphire-coloured water and teeming with tropical fish. Between Playa Larga and Playa Girón the sea is an exceptional colour, like lapis lazuli flecked with aquamarine. The diving in these beautifully coloured waters is highly rated. ▶▶ *For Sleeping, Eating and other listings, see pages 211-212.*

Ins and outs

Getting there and around Entronque de Jagüey on the main highway marks the 'entrance' to the peninsula. There is also a backroad from Cienfuegos. Public transport is limited. **Viazul** is planning a Habana-Entronque-Girón-Cienfuegos route. A few local **buses** run to Playa Girón and Playa Larga **Tour buses** and **taxis** are the usual method of transport but the most convenient way of getting around is to hire a **car** so that you can get to out-of-the-way places and stay as long as you like. **Hiking** is good in the National Park, but you will need to carry water as it is very hot in the swamps.

Zapata Peninsula

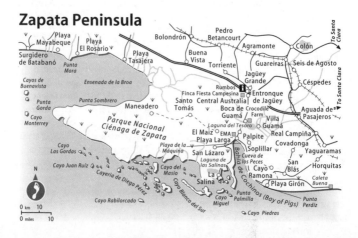

Café at Entronque de Jagüey, on the national highway, T459-3224, daily 0800-2200, and provides local information and sells a map of the zone. It can arrange taxis down to Playa Larga, US$15-20, and to Playa Girón, $25-30. For national park information, see EMA, below. The dry season is from December to April. Winter is also the time when migratory birds visit the peninsula so birdwatching is especially rewarding.

South to the Bahía de Cochinos (Bay of Pigs)

Due south of Jovellanos you head towards the Zapata peninsula and the countryside becomes flat and uninteresting. This area was particularly badly hit by Hurricane Michelle in November 2001, with lots of houses and the sugar mill damaged or destroyed. The storm ripped through the Zapata peninsula and its tourist attractions. **Jagüey Grande** is just north of the central highway from Havana to Santa Clara.

Finca Fiesta Campesina① *just south of the Entronque de Jagüey, daily 0900-1800*, is a large country farm. The large, shady garden contains caged animals as well as a bar, shops and toilets. You can watch a man push sugar cane through a mangle so that you can try a glass of *guarapo* (sugar cane juice) mixed with lime (and rum if you want it) for US$1. Animals include a snake called a *Majá de Santa María*, the *jutía*, a large-eared rat, and a prehistoric fish called a *manjuarí*, which has a long bill with lots of teeth and eyes set far back, making it look a bit like a platypus crossed with a crocodile. There is a *cabaña* complex in the grounds providing accommodation.

Central Australia, is a sugar mill that looks like an ailing dinosaur, built in 1872, and decommissioned in 2002. It had its moment of fame when Castro used the administration office (built 1915) as his centre of operations to repel the Bay of Pigs invasion (Operation Pluto). The office is now the **Museo Memorial Comandancia de las FAR**① *Tue-Sat 0900-1700, Sun 0900-1200, $US1 plus $US1 with guide*. It is a singularly unimpressive museum considering its historical importance. There are photos of destroyed planes and victory pictures and one showing the name of Fidel written on a wall in the blood of one of the Cuban victims. There are also some pictures of José Ramon Fernandez, Director of Operations, who is now a member of the Comité Central. The phone used by Fidel is still in situ and there is an anti-missile machine in the lobby. Outside the museum is the wreck of a plane shot down by Castro's troops. The guide will tell you that the dead American pilot was kept frozen in an institute in Havana as the US did not want to claim him and thereby admit responsibility for the invasion. The serviceman was not reclaimed until his daughter came to collect him in 1989.

Boca de Guamá

① *Daily 0900-1800. Entrance to the crocodile farm US$5, US$2.50 for children, shows 0900-1630 including crocodile meat tasting. The boat trip (1000 and 1200, 45 mins, return after 1 hr, 20 mins) from Boca de Guamá to Villa Guamá is US$10, US$5 for children under 12. Speed boats run if there are enough visitors. Life jackets on board.*

At Boca de Guamá is a tourist centre of shops, a ceramic factory, a restaurant and a crocodile farm (*Criadero de Cocodrilos*) where they breed the native Rhombifer (*cocodrilo*; see also page 431) and which is also home to turtles (*jicotea*), *jutía* and what they call a living fossil, the *manjuarí* fish. From here it is possible to take a boat to **Villa Guamá**, a hotel (see Sleeping below), and **Aldea Taína**, an Amerindian complex in the **Laguna del Tesoro**. On one of the islets a series of life-size statues of Amerindians going through their daily routines has been carved by the late Cuban sculptor Rita Longa, which you can see by following a boardwalk. In the middle is a replica of a *caney*, a large house belonging to the *cacique* (chief), where actors do a lot of wailing, blow a conch, daub your face black and expect you to give them a generous tip. This is not obligatory. Birdwatchers are advised to spend a few nights, or go on a tour one day and return with the next tour the following day. You will see most at dawn before the tour buses arrive.

The road south down the peninsula meets the coast at Playa Larga, at the head of the Bahía de Cochinos, commonly known as the **Bay of Pigs**. The US-backed invasion force landed here on 17 April 1961 but was successfully repelled. There is a small monument but most of the commemorative paraphernalia is at Playa Girón (see below). See History, page 390, for more information. The beach is open and better than that at Playa Girón. Some *casas particulares* have beach access.

Playa Larga is also a good place to come to explore the **Parque Nacional Ciénaga de Zapata**, also known as Parque Natural Montemar, a bird lover's paradise. There are 21 endemic species of birds inside the park. The smallest of these is the hummingbird. The best time to see flamingoes and migratory birds is from December to March. Other sightings include magnificent frigates, sandhill crane, Cuban parakeet, nighthawks, owls and pied billed grebe. Sport fishing is also offered. The park Headquarters, the EMA office, is just before you reach Playa Larga on the main road.

The **Laguna de las Salinas**, 25 km southwest, is the temporary home of huge numbers of migratory birds from December to April. The rest of the year it is empty. At the end of the road, at the forest technical station at La Salina, you can get a boat to one of the outlying islands, **Cayo Venado**, where there are iguanas and *jutías*. West of Playa Larga, a track leads to **Santo Tomás** where, in addition to waterfowl, you can see the Zapata wren, the Zapata rail and the Zapata sparrow.

East around the bay, **Cueva de los Peces**ⓘ *daily 0900-1600, US$1, restaurant and bar*, is a *cenote* that is full of fish and is good for diving and snorkelling, particularly early in the day. Two kilometres southeast of Playa Larga is **Playa de la Máquina**, a sandy beach frequented by locals where you can see lots of old trucks, caravans and other 'machines'. Between Cueva de los Peces and Playa Girón is **Punta de Perdiz** ⓘ *0900-1630*, where there is a restaurant, snorkelling, a dive centre and boat trips.

Playa Girón → *Colour map 2, grid B2.*

The resort at Playa Girón is isolated and small with little entertainment or nightlife. It is named after a 17th-century French pirate, Gilbert Girón, who frequented the area and presumably also appreciated its isolation. A stay of a few nights would be plenty to explore the area, visit the Bay of Pigs museum and take advantage of the scuba diving and snorkelling. The beach is walled in and therefore protected, but the sea is rocky. The **diving** and **snorkelling** is excellent and you can walk to the reef from the shore. The dive operation at the resort offers courses and packages of dives which can be tied in with accommodation, see Sleeping below. Further along the shore, however, there is another long sandy beach, and 8 km southeast is **Caleta Buena**, a pretty cove with lots of coral and fish. There is a small tourist centre, perched on some craggy rocks and the water is excellent for snorkelling. The pale blue, natural swimming pools are teeming with shoals of multi-coloured fish. There are also **caves** in the area for divers to explore. If you have your own transport, find a beach along the road between Playa Girón and Caleta Buena, there will be no people and good snorkelling 100 m offshore.▸▸ *For further details of watersports, see Hotels Playa Girón and Playa Larga, page 67.*

At the site of national pilgrimage where, in 1961 at the **Bay of Pigs**, the disastrous US-backed invasion of Cuba was attempted (see History, page 390), is the **Museo Girón**ⓘ *T459-4122, daily 0900-1700, US$2, plus US$I for guide, under 12s free, video show US$1, use of camera US$1, video camera US$1, also sells postcards, books and posters*. It shows how the invasion was repelled within 72 hours, with 200 CIA-trained Cuban exiles killed, 1,197 captured and 11 planes shot down. Monuments to those who died are scattered along the coast. Outside the museum is a British Sea Fury fighter aircraft, used by Castro's air force against the invaders. The tank outside is a replica of the original in Havana that destroyed *USS Houston*. The remains of an American B-26 are also in the gardens. It came down on the *pista* on 17 April 1961. There are also tanks and boats belonging to the mercenaries (Brigade 2506).

● Sleeping

Entronque de Jagüey *p209*
Hotels
E **Bohío de Don Pedro**, T459-3224. Next to the **Finca Fiesta Campesina** is a complex of 6 a/c *cabañas* with plans for expansion. They can be booked with **Rumbos**.

Casas particulares
E **Casa de Zuleida**, C 15A 7211 entre 72 y 74 (behind the hospital), Jagüey Grande, T459-3208. 2 big rooms, a/c, hot water, garage, informative and helpful family.

Guamá *p209*
Hotels
D **Horizontes Villa Guamá**, Laguna del Tesoro, T459-5515. 59 a/c rooms in thatched *cabañas* on stilts on islands in the style of a Taíno village, with bath, phone, TV, restaurant, bar, cafeteria, nightclub, shop, information desk, excursions, fishing in the lake. Take plenty of insect repellent. **Rumbos** will book rooms here.

Playa Girón *p210*
Hotels
B-C **Hotel Playa Girón**, (Horizontes), T459-4110, reservas@pgirón.esimtz.co.cu 292 rooms in large bungalows with shared bathrooms, a/c. It's an all-inclusive with buffet meals, bar, pool, diving, **Cubatur** office, horse hire, shop, car rental. There's a disco opposite. If there are few people staying at the hotel you can use the pool for US$8, lunch included. For non-guests, dinner is US$11, breakfast US$5. It has its own diving centre: US$25 each dive, package US$100, 4 dives and you get 1 free. Caleta Buena is US$6 if you are a hotel guest.

Casas particulares
When you enter the village from its northern aspect (which is now the only way in), on your left are 2 apartment blocks. The 1st block is edificio 2, while the one behind, at an angle, is edificio 1. Opposite are a line of houses, some of which are *casas particulares*.
F **Hostal Luís**, Carretera a Cienfuegos esq Carretera a Playa Larga, a house with blue and green gates with lion-topped columns closest to the hotel, T459-4121, www.cuba.tc/cuplaya giron.html Owned by Luís A García Padrón, 1 bedroom, a/c, hot water, parking, very clean and super-friendly.

F **José García Mesa (Tito) y Yaquelín Ulloa Pérez**, opposite edificio 2, T459-4252, (neighbour Hortensia's phone). Room with bathroom, hot and cold water 24 hrs, parking, secure, very nice people in a house with purple, plastic furniture to boot!
F **Miguel A Padrón y Odalys Figueredo**, behind edificio 1, T459-4100. Brand-new house, exceptionally clean, fan, helpful.

Playa Larga *p210*
Hotels
C **Hotel Playa Larga**, (Horizontes), at Playa Larga, T459-7294, www.horizontes.cu Sometimes fully booked with tour groups, 50 a/c spacious rooms in 1- or 2-bedroomed bungalows with bath, TV, restaurant, bar, nightclub, shop, pool, tour desk birdwatching and watersports. Most people prefer to travel on to stay at Playa Girón. Used to be fairly basic but it is currently undergoing a major revamp.

Casas particulares
All the *casas particulares* are in Barrio Caletón which is just west of the public park in Playa Larga. When you arrive in Playa Larga take an immediate right in front of the public park and swing round the edge until you arrive at the small residential area. Ask directions as you go.
E **Josefa Pita Cobas** (known as Fefa), Barrio Caletón, T459-7133, yosvanyps@correo deaba.com Small, but pleasant house with sea view but the water laps at the back wall and so there is no access to the beach. A/c and hot and cold water in shared bathroom. Rooms with 2 beds. Single person discount offered. Fefa's son teaches diving.
E-F **Ernesto Delgado Chirino**, T459-7278. Run by the cousin of Roberto Mesa Pujol, see below. Waterfront property, 1 room to rent.
E-F **Fidel Silvestre Fuentes**, Barrio Caletón, T459-7233, yosvanyps@correodeaba.com Very friendly and welcoming family with 1 a/c room with hot and cold water in a shared bathroom and access right onto the beach from a pleasant patio. *Comida criolla* for supper.
F **Roberto Mesa Pujol**, Caletón, Playa Larga, T459-7307. 1 room, a/c, private bathroom, hot water, garage, marvellous location with garden opening onto white-sand beach, palm trees, volleyball net, billiards table, not as especially friendly as they used to be.

● Eating

Boca de Guamá *p209*
The restaurant by the crocodile farm caters for tour parties and you get a bland and uninteresting set lunch with either fish, pork or chicken. However, if you ask, you can try a small portion of crocodile, US$5, which is chopped and fried. It tastes like fishy chicken with the texture of tough pork.

Playa Larga *p210*
On the road to Playa Larga is **Rumbos'** **La Casa del Mar**, bar and grill, 1000-1800. See also, **Hotel Playa Girón**, above.

● Shopping

South to the Bay of Pigs *p206*
Opposite the Museo Girón is a block of shops including **Tienda Playa Girón**, daily 0830-1630 (food, drinks and souvenirs) and **Artex** (souvenirs). Other shops sell dive equipment. At the end of Principal is a 24-hr **Rumbos** bar and **Tienda Imagen** for souvenirs, daily 0800-1600.

▲ Activities and tours

Diving
See **Hotel Playa Girón**, Sleeping above, for details.
EMA, Playa Larga, T459-7249, emavg@enet.cu, daily 0800-1630 Trips to the Río Hatiguanico, Las Salinas, Los Arrollones, Los Sábalos, Bermejas and Santo Tomás. Each trip costs US$10 and includes food, drink and *lancha*. The guides are all bird specialists and some speak English. Visitors need their own transport and tips are not included. **Rumbos** also sells some of these tours run by its own staff for US$15. EMA can also arrange visits to a fish, turtle and bird reproduction centre, US$2. Sport fishing is also offered but you need to ring the office for information and prices.
Tourist centre, Caleta Buena, T459-5589, daily 1000-1800. Entrance to the cove US$12 adults, US$6 children, including lunch (1230-l500) and all drinks (1000-1700). There are sun loungers and *casitas*. Snorkelling US$3/day, diving US$25 per dive, massage US$15. There's also a volleyball net. Highly recommended day or half-day trip. You need your own car or a taxi to get here.

Tour operators
Both hotels **Playa Girón** and **Playa Larga** have tour desks, see Sleeping above. See also **Rumbos**, Tourist Information, p209.

● Transport

Bus
In high season, **Víazul** runs a daily bus **Varadero-Guamá-Girón-Cienfuegos**, US$16, 4½ hrs, departing Varadero 0830, returning from Cienfuegos 1400.
The Fri/Sat/Sun **Astro** bus from **Playa Girón** passes through **Playa Larga** on its way to Havana. To **Playa Larga** from edificio 2, 0630, 30-40 mins, 1.45 pesos.

Car hire
Between **Playa Girón** and **Playa Larga** in a car is 25-30 mins; from **Guamá** to **Playa Larga** is 10 mins; from **Entronque de Jagüey** to **Guamá** is 15 mins.
Petrol station Petrol Cupet-Cimex, diagonally opposite Museo Girón, open 24 hrs.

Taxi
For **Playa Larga**, organize a taxi with **Rumbos** at Entronque de Jagüey. **Playa Girón** and the **Bay of Pigs** can also be reached by truck or taxi from **Cienfuegos** (1½ hrs).
There are several **Transtur** offices; in Hotel Playa Larga, T459-7294; opposite Hotel Playa Girón, T459-4126/44, daily 0900-1700; inside Hotel Playa Girón, T459-4110. **Juan Carlos González González**, at the above numbers, nemuri@esimtz.co.cu will do a 1-day tour of the area for US$37. **Havanautos**, opposite Hotel Playa Girón, daily 0800-1200 and 1300-2000. All taxi and rent-a-car staff are sleepy here though.
A private taxi will charge about US$70 to **Havana**. Better to get a lift with a tour bus returning to **Havana** or **Varadero**, US$25-30. Alternatively, the hotel runs day trips to Havana, but ring to check days and times beforehand, a 1-way ride will cost about US$25.

● Directory

There is a **post office** near the Museo de Girón and a **laundry** opposite.

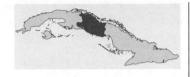

Centre West

Footprint features

Introduction

From the early Spanish settlements and sugar plantations built on slavery to magnificent 19th-century merchants' mansions and opulent theatres, this region is generously endowed with architectural delights. The memories of heroes of the wars of independence and other struggles for liberation including the Revolution, are preserved in monuments and street names. The three provinces of Cienfuegos, Villa Clara and Sancti Spíritus in the centre west share the lush, forested Montañas de Guamuhaya, their boundaries meeting close to the highest point, Pico San Juan, in the legendary Sierra del Escambray. The mountains are a habitat for many birds, butterflies, frogs and other creatures of the forest and offer great hiking, river bathing and birdwatching.

The coastal city of Cienfuegos has some architectural highlights, particularly the theatre and the Palacio de Ferrer, both late 19th-century masterpieces. The diving is good, with some pleasant dive lodges. The 1958 battle for the city of Santa Clara was crucial to the outcome of the Revolution and this lively university city is now a shrine to the Argentine guerrillero and icon, Che Guevara.

The northern part of Villa Clara is mostly flat and the coastline is protected by an archipelago of cays with some spectacular white coral sandy beaches. Heading south, the provincial capital of Sancti Spíritus was one of the seven towns founded by Diego Velázquez in 1514, but the star attraction is the colonial town of Trinidad, awarded UNESCO World Heritage Site status to protect its cobbled streets, single storey, pastel-coloured houses with red tiled roofs, its churches and its planters' mansions. It also has the advantage of being close to a beach, with access to the mountains, and has some outstanding live music performances.

★ Don't miss...

❶ **Castillo de Jagua** Climb the spiral staircase up the tower and take in the views across the city, the entrance to the bay and up to the mountains beyond, page 219.

❷ **Che Guevara monument** Visit the Mausoleum in Santa Clara to see where Cuba pays homage to the revolutionary whose guerrilla tactics did so much to hasten the end of the Batista dictatorship, page 230.

❸ **Christmas Eve in Remedios** Experience the exuberant celebrations and *parrandas* at the end of carnival week, pages 243 and 247.

❹ **Playa Ensenachos** Drive along the 48-km causeway from cay to cay off the north coast and spend a few hours on this untouched beach, page 245.

❺ **Trinidad** Stay in a *casa particular* in one of the old colonial homes and soak up the atmosphere of this beautiful World Heritage Site, page 254.

❻ **Topes de Collantes** Take a walking stick and hike in the steaming mountains, cooling off in the waterfalls and pools of the rivers in the rainforest, page 259.

Ins and outs

Getting there

There is an international airport outside Santa Clara which receives mostly charter **flights** from Canada in season, otherwise you fly to Havana or Varadero and transfer from there overland. Santa Clara is on the main east-west highway from Havana to Santiago and communications by land are excellent, with frequent **buses** in both directions. Direct buses run daily to Cienfuegos from Havana, continuing to Trinidad, or you can get to Trinidad from Varadero via Santa Clara and Sancti Spíritus. There is also a daily service Trinidad-Santiago de Cuba, with several stops along the way. Santa Clara and Cienfuegos can be reached by **train** from Havana, but Trinidad is not on the main line and only local services operate from here. ⏵ *See also Getting there, pages 216, 227, 242, 248 and 254.*

Tourist information

Tour agencies such as **Cubatur**, **Rumbos**, **Cubanacán** and **Havanatur** can be found in all the main towns and operate as tourist information offices although their main purpose is to sell tours. They can help with hotel reservations, tickets and transfers.

Best time to visit

If you enjoy watersports and festivals related to the sea, then March is a good time to go to Cienfuegos. May is busy in Santa Clara, where there are film, music and dance festivals, but the best time is around 28 December, when the populace celebrate the end of the Revolution and the Plaza de la Revolución is alive with revellers enjoying a concert. The week leading up to Chrismas Eve is the time to be in Remedios, when the *parrandas* are in full swing, and September is ceremonial in Trinidad, with followers of Catholicism and *Santería* joining parades through the streets in honour of the Virgen del Cobre, patron saint of Cuba, whose day is 8 September.

Cienfuegos → *Colour map 2, grid B3. Population: 386,100.*

Cienfuegos, on the south coast, is an attractive, breezy seaport, sometimes described as the pearl of the south, with a Caribbean feel to the place. Once known as Fernandina de Jagua, it has its fair share of legends about pirates and corsairs. A couple of dive lodges to the south, a brand-new marina club and a dolphinarium add to its nautical emphasis, although the beaches in this area are pleasant but not worth going out of your way for. Most of the city's festivals are based on seafaring activities and there are many regattas and races for yachts, power boats, kayaks and rowing boats. French immigrants at the beginning of the 19th century influenced the development and architecture of the city, which is a fascinating blend of styles including a heavy presence of art deco buildings in its residential streets. Highlights are the Tomás Terry theatre and the Ferrer palace both remarkable buildings from the 1890s, the heyday of Cienfuegos' prosperity. ⏵ *For Sleeping, Eating and other listings, see pages 221-225.*

Ins and outs

Getting there **Trains** run on alternate days from Havana and Santa Clara. The railway station is on Calle 49 esquina Avenida 58, not far from the old centre. Cienfuegos is 80 km from Trinidad and 70 km from Santa Clara. There are regular daily **buses** from both these cities as well as from Havana, and every other day from Santiago de Cuba and Camagüey. The bus station is on Calle 49, esquina Avenida 56, close to the railway station. ⏵ *For further details, see also Transport, page 225.*

Getting around Much of the city can be seen **on foot**, or you can use a horse-drawn **coche** for longer distances. For excursions out of the city, **car hire** is the most convenient, or hire a state or private **taxi** to take you around, or take a **tour**.

Tourist information Tour operators such as **Cubatur, Cubanacán** and **Rumbos** are the best places to seek official information but if you are staying in a *casa particular*, you will find your hosts very knowledgeable about what is going on in the area. All the tour operators offer trips and hotel and nightclub reservations. As well as trips to Trinidad and Havana etc, more local trips include El Nicho, a city tour, dolphinarium, tobacco factory, boat trips and the botanical gardens.

Sights

City centre
The main street, running north-south, is Calle 37, called the **Prado** with a central promenade down the middle of the road where people stroll or sit. It is called the **Malecón**, further south, between Avenida 40 and Avenida 22, where the Prado runs beside the water. The palm trees and the view across the Bahía de Cienfuegos make this a lovely walk. The bay can be seen from quite a few places in the centre of the city, but there is no beach and the land by the water is usually dirty. Part of Avenida 54, from Calle 29 to the Prado, is closed to traffic. Known as the Boulevard, it has small trees, cafés and restaurants as well as many shops.

Centre West Cienfuegos

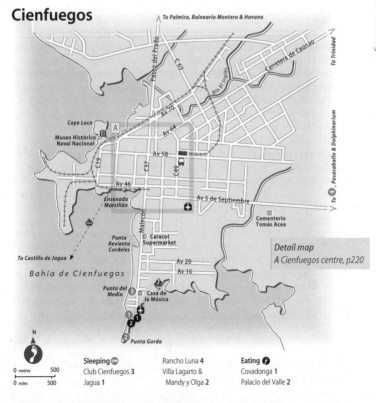

Cienfuegos

To Palmira, Balneario Montero & Havana

To Trinidad

Paseo del Prado

Río El Inglés

Carretera de Caunao

Av 70

Cayo Loco

Av 64

Museo Histórico
Naval Nacional

Av 58

To 4, Pasacaballo & Dolphinarium

C 19

C 37

C 49

Av 46

Ensenada
Marsillán

Av 5 de Septiembre

Cementerio
Tomás Acea

Malecón

Punta
Revienta
Cordeles

Caracol
Supermarket

To Castillo de Jagua

Bahía de Cienfuegos

Av 20

Av 16

*Detail map
A Cienfuegos centre, p220*

Punta del
Medio

Casa de
la Música

Punta Gorda

N

| 0 metres | 500 |
| 0 miles | 500 |

Sleeping
Club Cienfuegos **3**
Jagua **1**

Rancho Luna **4**
Villa Lagarto &
Mandy y Olga **2**

Eating
Covadonga **1**
Palacio del Valle **2**

The central square is **Parque José Martí**, which is a pleasant plaza with benches, a rotunda bandstand and a statue of the ever-present José Martí. The arch on the west side of the square symbolizes the entrance to the city and is supposed to be similar to the Arc de Triomphe in Paris, having been built by the French founders of Cienfuegos. There is a cluster of colonial buildings around the Parque José Martí. On the east side on Calle 29 is **La Catedral Purísima Concepción** built in 1868, which has a somewhat neo-Gothic interior with silvered columns. On the north side, on Avenida 56, is the majestic building of the old **Colegio San Lorenzo**, now a secondary school, **5 de Septiembre**, not open to the public but a site of former resistance. A civilian and naval uprising in Cienfuegos was quashed by Batista on this day in 1957 and there are several memorials and references to the event across the city. If you do get permission to enter, there is a memorial to the martyrs who died and their pictures are in a glass cabinet.

Next door is Cienfuegos' *pièce de résistance*, the **Teatro Tomás Terry** ① *T432-513361, daily 0900-1800, US$1 including a guided tour, see also Entertainment page 224*, built in 1889 after the death of the Venezuelan Tomás Terry, with the proceeds of a donation by his family. It was inaugurated in 1890 in front of an audience of 1,200. The lobby has an Italian marble statue of Terry and is decorated with fine paintings and ornate gold work. The interior is largely original with wooden seats. Note the ceiling with exquisite paintings of muses and also two portraits of Cuban writers. Over the stage is a large grinning mask representing comedy. The two sets of theatre boxes nearest the stage were traditionally used by mourners who were not supposed to be at the theatre, but did not wish to miss the performance. They had a separate door so that they could enter and leave the theatre and watch the performance unseen by the rest of the audience.

The most notable building on the west side is the Palacio de Ferrer, now the **Casa de Cultura Benjamín Duarte** ① *T432-516584, Mon-Sat 0830-1900, Sun 0830-1400, US$0.50 (including the tower), guided tours in Spanish, English and French*. It is a beautiful building dating from 1894, with a magnificent tower on the corner designed to keep an eye on the port and shipping (great views of the park and the sea if you climb the tower). The opera singer, Caruso, stayed at the Palacio de Ferrer when he came to Cienfuegos to sing at the theatre in 1920. It is a little neglected now, but worth seeing for the marble floor, staircases and walls, carved in Italy and assembled at the palace. Also note the Italian ceramic wall tiles in gold, white and blue, which change colour in the sunlight, and the plasterwork on the walls and ceiling. Several rooms are used for music, dance, theatre and art, especially geared for children.

The grand grey and white building on the south side of the square is the **Antiguo Ayuntamiento**, the former town hall where Fidel Castro spoke to the people on 6 January 1959. At the **Museo Provincial** (formerly the casino) ① *Av 54, on the south side of Parque Martí, T432-519722, Tue-Sat 1000-1800, Sun 0900-1200, US$2, camera and video cameras US$1*, exhibits include an aboriginal skeleton, a necklace made from vertebrae, small zoomorphic statues and stones, art nouveau doorways, a *maqueta* of the 5 September 1957 uprising and plenty of explanations about the event, but one of the most interesting things in the museum is a gigantic pair of red, fibreglass, high-heeled shoes – the vast heels hanging over the toilet walls. On the north side of the park, the **Centro de Arte** ① *Av 56 entre 25 y 27, Mon-Fri 0900-1800, Sat 0800-1000, Sun 0900-1200*, is a large colonial house with changing exhibits of modern works.

Ten minutes' walk south along Prado is the **Museo de la Clandestinidad Hermanas Giral Andreu** ① *Av 42 entre 37 y 39, Tue-Fri 1000-1800, Sun 0900-1200, free*, which has a few exhibits about the 1959 Revolution, including an unusual propaganda instrument – a man's shaver sporting the words "Batista es el hombre" and some grainy black and white pictures of the 5 September 1957 uprising. Revolutionaries Lourdes and Cristina Giral were born here. The sisters were murdered in Havana in 1958 during the Batista regime.

Some ten minutes walk west along Avenida 62 is the **Museo Histórico Naval Nacional** (Naval Museum)① *Cayo Loco, Tue-Fri 0900-1700, Sat-Sun 0900-1300, US$1*, a much more interesting museum than it looks. There are rooms dedicated to the 1957 uprising and then a number of interesting documents, such as Cuba's declaration of war against Germany, Tokyo and Rome; the *bandera* that was on the Maine and on the Granma; items and documents relating to the Granma, the Playa Girón invasion and coins found on sunken Spanish ships.

About 3 km east of the centre is the **Cementerio Tomás Acea** ① *Mon-Sat 0900-1700, US$1 guide included*, noted for its grand replica of the Parthenon at the entrance. There is a striking monument to the fallen of 5 September 1957 inside.

Around Cienfuegos

Palmira

The Parque Central of **Palmira**, about 8 km north of Cienfuegos, is rather unusual. The church looks like it is decorated with *Terry's Chocolate Orange* segments and the southern side features an ornate Grand Masonic Lodge. The fascinating lodge interior features statues of Minerva, Venus and Hercules and the severed John the Baptist's head as well as unusual swords. There are human skulls on display, although questions about their origins are sidestepped. Ask at the lodge social club next door if you would like to be shown around. Palmira is famous for its *Santería* processions and the time to be in town is 3-4 December. On 3 December animal sacrifices are made; on the following day processions can be seen in the streets. At the **Museo Municipal de Palmira** ① *southeast corner of the park, T43-544533, Tue-Sat 1000-1800, Sun 0900-1300, US$1*, the very friendly staff will explain all the exhibits in the three sections dedicated to *Santería* especially the three principal sects in the area: Cristo (dating from 1913), San Roque (1915) and Santa Barbara (1917). The museum also arranges folkloric shows. Ring for information or ask at one of the tour operators in Cienfuegos.

Balneario Jesús Montane Oropesa Ciego Montero

① *North of Palmira, open all year except the last 2 weeks of Dec, T86 (ask for a llamada por distancia), US$13 in taxi from Cienfuegos. There is a train from Cienfuegos (0700) on alternate days, 1 hr, to Baños station, which is a few minutes' walk from the balneario, return train 1700, bus at 1420 from Cienfuegos, returning 0600, daily.*

These thermal baths are close to the famous water factory from where millions of bottles of mineral water are transported around the country. The sulphurous waters with temperatures of 37-38° are good for rheumatism, arthiritis, psoriasis and traumas. Treatments last from 10 days to six months and range from hydromassage, body massage (US$25), fangotherapy (US$10), immersion in thermal pools (US$4-6) to acupuncture. There are three rooms for tourists who eat separately from the Cubans. US$27.50 per person per night, including all food. There are no facilities nearby except, bizarrely and incongrously, a small dollar store selling alcohol (which is not permitted at the *balneario*) and fast food the other side of the railway track.

Playa Rancho Luna and Castillo de Jagua

① *Castillo open Mon-Sat 0900-1700, Sun 0900-1300, US$1, guides are available. There is a ferry from Cienfuegos to the castle from Av 46 entre 23 y 25. 0800, 1300, 1730, 45 mins, returning 0630, 1000, 1500, US$0.50, car US$3. Regular crossings, 5 mins, US$0.50 from close to Hotel Pasacaballo to the village around the castle. There is also a guagua (bus) from Pasacaballo to Cienfuegos every 1½ hrs, 1 peso.*

220 If you are in need of some sea and sand, the Playa Rancho Luna is about 14 km from Cienfuegos, on a road lined with mango trees, near the **Hotel Rancho Luna**, Sleeping, page 222. The beach is quite nice but nothing special and there is a rundown restaurant. However, the diving, organized at the hotel, is very good.

If you continue along the road for about 3 km past the beach you get to the **Hotel Pasacaballo**. There is a jetty here and another further along a rough track to the left, from where you can get a little ferry which plies across the mouth of the Bahía de Cienfuegos to the village on the western side, site of the **Castillo de Jagua**. The castle was built at the entrance to the bay in 1733-45 by Joseph Tantete of France. There is only one entrance via a still-working drawbridge across a dry moat. There are views of the narrow entrance to the bay and the Escambray mountains beyond. The vista is impressive minus the eyesore of the **Hotel Pasacaballo** and the eerie structures and housing projects of Ciudad Nuclear, which were built for a nuclear power station whose construction was abandoned halfway through the project. The courtyard of the castle has a prison and a chapel. Inside the castle is the **Museo Nuestra Señora de los Angeles de Jagua** with five exhibition rooms full of legends and historical explanations. There is a bar and small restaurant (*camarones* US$8).

Cienfuegos centre

Sleeping
Andrés Haro Cuellas cp **1**
Casa de la Amistad cp **2**
Hector Ferrer Gatell cp **3**
Isabel Martínez
   Cordero cp **8**
Jerónimo García
   Escoriza cp **5**
Margarita Jiménez
   Marín cp **4**
María Núñez
   Suárez cp **6**
Unión & 1869 **9**

Eating
Coppelia **7**
Doñaneli Panadería **1**
El Rápido **5**
El Criollito **2**
Helados Alondria **3**
La Verja **4**

Bars
El Palatino **6**

El Polinesio &
   Restaurant **8**
La Fernandina **9**

Entertainment
Casa de la UNEAC & Bar **1**
Cine Luisa **2**
Cine Prado **3**
Club El Benny **4**
Teatro Tomás Terry **5**

Close to the **Hotel Faro Luna,** see Sleeping page 223, is a **Dolphinarium** ① *Km 17 Cienfuegos-Pasacaballo, T43-548120, Fri-Wed 0930-1700 (subject to change), shows at 1000, 1400 (dolphins), 1600 (sea lions), US$5 and US$3.* The dolphins are kept in seawater pens. You can swim with the dolphins – US$35, under 12s US$23 (including entrance and show). There is a bar and showers on site. See Essentials for further information about dolphinariums in Cuba.

Jardín Botánico de Cienfuegos

① *Pepito Tey, daily 0800-1700, US$2.50, children US$1, bar for drinks. Look out for 2 rows of palm trees leading to the garden from the entrance at the road. Bus from Cienfuegos stops outside, 20 centavos, or take an organized tour.*

Some 23 km east of Cienfuegos, on the road to Trinidad between the villages of San Antón and Guaos, is the Cienfuegos botanical garden, a national monument founded in 1901 by Edwin F Atkins, the owner of a sugar plantation called Soledad, nowadays called Pepito Tey. Atkins turned over 4.5 ha of his sugar estates to study sugar cane, later introducing other trees and shrubs that could be used as raw materials for industry. In 1919 Harvard University became involved in the studies and the site became known as the Harvard Botanical Station for Tropical Research and Sugar Cane Investigation. After the Revolution, the State took charge of the gardens in 1961, renaming them and employing scientific personnel to preserve and develop the many tropical species now found there. Different sections of the gardens are devoted to areas such as medicinal plants, orchids, fruit trees, bamboos and one of the world's most complete collections of palm trees. It is a fine garden and a nice place to wander around. See if you can get a guide (Spanish speaking, tip welcomed) as it will be much more interesting.

Eastern Cienfuegos

In the east of the province at **Martín Infierno**, off the road between Cienfuegos and Trinidad there is a 67-m-high stalagmite, said to be the tallest in the Americas. You will need a four-wheel-drive vehicle for this trip and so it's recommended to take a tour. **Rumbos** in Cienfuegos, 46 km away, advertizes an excursion to **El Nicho,** a series of cascading waterfalls up to 35 m high surrounded by forest in the Escambray mountains (see also page 233). Situated on the western spur of the lake in Cienfuegos province, there are pools, caves and paths and, of course, a lunch stop. A beautiful spot in the forested hills on the edge of the Parque Natural Topes de Collantes. There is almost no public transport to the lake despite assurances of the occasional bus from Manicaragua, so car hire or private transport is essential.

◉ **Sleeping**

Cienfuegos *p217, maps p217 and p220*
Hotels
AL **La Unión** (Cubanacán), 31 esq Av 54, T432-551020, comercial@union.cfg.cyt.cu Built in 1869 and recently restored, this very attractive hotel in colonial style is painted an attractive duck-egg blue with white, wrought-iron balcony railings. 49 rooms and some suites are equipped with pleasant, dark wood furniture and all mod cons. The hotel is decorated in pretty tiles and the swimming pool is beautifully sunken into the patio, there being no difference in the ground and water level. There's also a sauna, Jacuzzi, gym, laundry, pharmacy, internet centre, tourism bureau, car hire, shop, 3 bars and the 1869 restaurant, see Eating below. There is a discount on stays of 4 nights or more. Non-guests can use the pool for US$5.
A **Jagua** (Gran Caribe), Punta Gorda, 37 y 0, T432-551003, reserves@jagua.co.cu 147 a/c rooms (most with twin beds), 2 suites, with view over bay. **Restaurant Escambray** and 24-hr café next to a very nice pool. The **Palacio del Valle** restaurant is also next door to the hotel. There is a shop, internet access and

nightly cabaret, (except Wed, 2200, US$5pp includes one cocktail), which is extremely colourful, good and worth the entry fee.

Casas particulares

E-F Jerónimo García Escoriza, 35 5806 entre 58 y 60, T432-516549. 1 room with a/c and wardrobe and private bathroom with a very large bath and sink. This is quite an interior with neoclassical columns resting on marble plinths balancing on a lovely, tiled floor. Jerónimo's son-in-law speaks English. Kind and helpful household and the food has been described as the best in Cuba. Opposite this house is a lovely pink, but fading, art deco building.

E-F Margarita Jiménez Marín, Av 60 3503 entre 35 y 37, T432-555185, isidroherrera@ correosonline.co.cu A royal-blue colonial home with 2 rooms and a small patio. 1 room has natural light, the other does not. Food is offered by the kind and friendly family who set the rule that you will only get your own key to the house if you are a couple.

F Andrés Haro Cuéllar, Av 62 3922 entre 39 y 41, T432-527078. 1 room in a colonial apartment above a busy street, however, the room does not face onto the street. The room has a massive bathroom, large wardrobe, fan and small, attached dining area. For the pet-friendly, as Andrés has a very sweet dog.

F Casa de la Amistad – Armando y Leonor Martínez, 56 2927 entre 29 y 31, T432-516143, amistad@correosonline.co.cu Delightful and knowledgeable elderly couple who are English speaking. Armando fought at the Bay of Pigs and is an economist, and will provide frank and informative conversation. Large, 2nd floor of a colonial house with 2 rooms that have their own private bathroom. Very popular, essential to book ahead. They have extensive knowledge of the area, and can find other *casas* if they are full. Good food is served.

F Hector Ferrer Gatell y Ilia Espinosa Coll, Av 54 4314 entre 43 y 45, T432-517006, hectorj@jagua.cfg.sld.cu This exceptionally friendly and helpful family has 1 room with wardrobe and a/c and a pink bathroom. Laundry service and domestic calls are free. Delicious meals and good value. The owners are very helpful with organizing taxi trips,

getting information about the city and Cuban way of life, interesting discussions.

F Isabel Martínez Cordero y Pepe, Av 52 4318 entre 43 y 45, T432-518276. 2 a/c rooms, but with little natural light, in a pleasant house with private bathroom and fridge. There is a car park nearby. The house is known for its good vegetarian food.

F Mandy y Olga, 35 apto 4D entre Litoral y 0, Punta Gorda, T432-519966. Next to **Villa Lagarto** and part of the same family. There are 2 rooms with an adjoining shared bathroom. Each room has a fridge, closet, TV and a/c. There is an independent entrance to the accommodation but you will probably want to hire both rooms as there's only 1 entrance to the 2 rooms and bathroom. Coffee and juice are free.

F María Núñez Suárez, Av 58 3705 Altos entre 37 y 39, T432-517867. 2 rooms sharing an adjoining private bathroom (the red, plastic loo seat makes a welcome, comfortable change), a/c and ceiling fan, plus fridge. Breakfast and dinner served on the apartment's balcony. Ask María's husband, Oscar ("El Pure"), and friends to tell you stories about when they were young, fighting with Che in the Sierra Maestra, at the Bay of Pigs or working in Ethiopia.

F Villa Lagarto, 35 apt 4B entre Av 0 y Litoral, Punta Gorda, T432-519966, (mob) T558085, villalagarto@yahoo.es Tony and Maylin have 2 upstairs rooms with open balcony. 1 has 2 beds, fridge and a/c, the other has a double bed and fridge. There is a pretty patio with fabulous views over the water and towards the mountains. There is a small, salt-water swimming pool with a lizard sculpture which spouts water from its mouth. The pool is also home to 2 beautiful turtles. Welcome cocktail on arrival.

Around Cienfuegos *p219*
Hotels

B Rancho Luna (Horizontes), Km 18, T43-548012, rancholuna@ranluna.co.cu 222 small rooms, 2 restaurants, massage, Jacuzzi and gym facilities. The pool is very large but in an older style. Mini-golf, horseriding, car hire, watersports, internet and diving centre, see Diving p225. The lobby music is extremely and unnecessarily loud. Bring earplugs if you want any peace. Popular with Canadians in winter.

B-C **Carrusel Faro Luna** (Cubanacán), Carretera de Pasacaballo Km 18, Playa Faro Luna, T43-548030, aloja@fluna.cfg .cyt.cu The Faro Luna is a much smaller and much more attractive hotel than the **Rancho Luna**. Its pool is also a lot more attractive and its 46 rooms are larger and nicer. Only some rooms have fridge. The beach is 100 m away at **Rancho Luna**.

C **Hotel Pasacaballo** (Islazul), Carretera a Rancho Luna, Km 22, T43-548013-18. This is a truly ugly hotel, where you live among the vegetation as the building is very open plan. There are 188 rooms with all the usual facilities but the nearest beach, Playa Rancho Luna, is some distance away. Apparently it may be undergoing a much needed facelift.

C **Villa Guajimico**, Carretera a Trinidad Km 42, Cumanayagua, T43-451205, F43-451326, best to book through **Cubamar**, in Havana, www.cubamarviajes.cu Overlooks mouth of Río La Jutía, great location, surrounded by cliffs, caves, coral reefs and small beaches accessible only by boat. 3 star, 54 cabins, some triples, white with red tiled roofs, a/c, bathroom, pool, restaurant serving average food, bar, parking, hobicats, good for excursions, but more than anything it is a great dive resort, see Diving p225, 3 meals US$31, sailing US$10.

🍴 Eating

Cienfuegos *p217, maps p217 and p220*
Restaurants
$$$ **Palacio del Valle**, next to Hotel Jagua, Tue-Sun 1000-2200. The place to go for its style, if not for the food. The building dates from 1894, with a mixture of architectural styles but with Arab influences predominating. It has incredibly ornate ceilings and other decorations. The building was bought by Alejandro Suero Balbín and given to his daughter as a wedding present upon her marriage to Sr Valle. Speciality seafood, including *paella Cienfuega* and lobster, with cheaper options such as fried shrimps and omelettes.
$$ **1869**, Hotel La Unión, T432-551020, daily 0700-2145. The service is good and the decor handsome but some of the food is second rate. Oyster in creole sauce and squid in tomato sauce are better options than the chicken dishes.

$$ **La Verja**, Boulevard (Av 54) entre 33 y 35, T432-516311, daily 1100-1500 and 1800-2400. Offers fried fish, breaded shrimp, goulash and salads (a rarity) plus all the usual culprits in a lovely dining room with dark wood carved features, with scarlet tablecloths and curtains. There's a bar as well as patio dining. A bronze chandelier hangs from the ceiling and the floor is studded with blue, diamond-shaped tiles. Also does *bocaditos*. Good service.
$$-$ **Covadonga**, opposite *Hotel Jagua*, T432-516949, daily 1230-1530 and 1800-2200. Large restaurant in a pleasant seaside setting. Lobster US$8, fish US$5.55.
$$-$ **El Polinesio**, 29 5410 entre 54 y 56, T432-515723, daily 1200-2300. Chicken, fish and *empanadas* served in a very dark restaurant completely decked out with stuffed sharks, fish and netting on a nautical/Polynesian theme. Quite bizarre.
$ **Coppelia**, Prado y 53, Tue-Sun 1000-2300. The national ice cream parlour.
$ **Doñaneli Panadería**, Parque Villuenda, daily 0900-2215. Sells hot biscuits and fancy cakes.
$ **El Rápido**, Boulevard entre 35 y 37, Mon-Sat 0900-2100, Sun 0900-2200. Fast food chain.
$ **Helados Alondria**, between Teatro Terry and Colegio San Lorenzo, daily 0800-0100. More of an Artex shop than an ice cream parlour. There are still ice creams but the variety has deteriorated. There is a pleasant covered patio to sit in.

Paladares
$ **Alex y Juana**, Av El Mar 401, in the village near Castillo de Jagua, T43-96456. Seafood for US$7.
$ **El Criollito**, 33 5603 entre 56 y 58, T432-515540, 1200-2400. Meals include salad, chips, rice and coffee, tasty fish, chicken and *bistek* in this front-room *paladar*.

🍸 Bars

Cienfuegos *p217, maps p217 and p220*
Bar Jardines de la UNEAC, on the west side of Parque José Martí, Calle 25, daily 1200-1800, 2000-2200. Set in a tranquil garden/patio which is completely covered in bougainvillea. Live music nights are posted on the gates.

El Palatino, on the south side of Parque José Martí entre 25 y 27. An old man makes cigars here – if you give him 2 cigarettes, he'll roll a cigar for you. Live music at night, jazz Mon evening, but during the day you can see Pepe the saxophonist together with Ezequiel.
El Polinesio, 29 entre Av 56 y 54, Tue-Sun 1000-1600, 1830-2200. Next to the restaurant of the same name. A dark dive.
La Fernandina, Prado y 52. A small, popular, but cosy bar.
Palacio de Valle, see Eating above. On the roof is a bar, daily 1000-1700. Good views and another restaurant in the garden, US$1 to enter *terraza* and get a cocktail.

⊕ Entertainment

Cienfuegos *p217, maps p217 and p220*
Live music
Casa de la Música, 37 entre 4 y 6.
T432-552320. Entrance price varies according to band/show but is posted outside on the ticket booth. This is a large venue on the sea front with afternoon and evening entertainment posted outside the entrance. There is a rather lovely seafront stage with great views across to the Escambray mountains. Also a music shop with helpful staff, Mon-Sat 0830-1700, Sun 0830-1200.
Casa de la UNEAC, on the west side of Parque José Martí, Calle 25. Rather like a *Casa de la Trova*, with live local music. Videos are also shown. Events are held next door at the **Casa de la Cultura Benjamín Duarte**.
Club El Benny, Av 54 2904 entre 29 y 31, Mon-Fri 2100-0100, Sat 2100-0200, US$3 per person, couples US$8, *consumo mínimo*. Nightclub with live entertainment. Nightly offerings of comedy, karaoke and *bolero*.
Cultural Municipal, Av 56 entre 25 y 27. *Boleros, peñas* and *danzón*.
Parque Villuenda, between 62 y 64. Live music by *Guajiros* in this park on Sun at 1000.

Theatre
Teatro Tomás Terry, 56 entre 27 y 29 2701, T432-513361. *Cartelera* ts posted outside.

⊕ Festivals and events

Cienfuegos *p217, maps p217 and p220*
First week of Mar Feria Internacional del Mar (FIMAR) is a commercial exhibition which coincides with the **Fiesta de los Amigos del Mar**, a sporting event including sailing, rowing, water skiing, motor boats, kayaks, swimming, as well as cycling, beach volleyball, karting etc. Later in the month there is a national motorboat competition for the **Copa 26 de Julio**.
Apr International **rowing** competition.
End of May A **sailing** tournament.
Mid-Jul The bay of Cienfuegos roars to the sound of speed boats when the **Grand Prix, Formula T-1**, is held, with competitors from the USA, Mexico, Venezuela, Costa Rica and Cuba, among others.
Oct **Carnival** with stalls and plenty of boozing along the partially shut off Malecón.
Dec **Christmas** is celebrated with a huge street party; rum is drunk from all manner of containers and there is dancing to a band on the **Hotel Jagua** promenade.

⊙ Shopping

Cienfuegos *p217, maps p217 and p220*
Art
Galería Maroya, Fondo Cubano de Bienes Culturales, Av 54 2506, south side of park, Mon-Sat 0900-1830, Sun 0900-1300. Original art works, papier maché goods, wooden items, jewellery, clothes, etc, antiques, showcase for local artists, courtyard at the back with art on the walls.

Dollar shops
There are quite a number of dollar shops on the pedestrian section of Boulevard:
El Embajador, Av 54 esq 33. Sells all top tobacco, rum and coffee.
El Fundador, Boulevard (Av 54) esq 29, Mon-Sat 0900-1900, Sun 0900-1300. Sells T-shirts, rum, water, music and postcards.
Glamour (Tienda Panamericana) on 35 entre Av 56 y 54. Sells some food and clothes.

Food
Caracol, Prado, daily 0900-1900. A well-stocked supermarket.
El Paraíso supermarket, Av 58 esq 33, Mon-Sat 0830-1730, Sun 0830-1200.

Photography
Photo Service on Boulevard (Av 54) entre 31 y 33, open 0800-2200, and a larger branch at Punta Gorda on 37 opposite Hotel Jagua.

▲ Activities and tours

Diving

There are 2 dive operations in the area: at **Hotel Rancho Luna** and **Villa Guajimico**. **Villa Guajimico**, see p223, www.cuba marviajes.cu or www.DivePackage.html Offers various dive packages with accommodation. **Whale Shark Scuba Center** Run by Cubanacán Náutica SA at Hotels Carrusel Faro Luna, see p223 and Rancho Luna, see p222, but based at Hotel Rancho Luna, T43-548087. English, French, German and Italian spoken. 5 dives, US$116, 10 dives US$220, night dive US$40. Every 10 dives get 1 free. Open water diver certification US$299, advanced US$250. There are 40 sites including 8 sunken ships. Open daily, price includes all equipment and transport etc. Instructor is Omar Alvarez Morales (mpsolcfg@enet.cu).

Sailing

Club Cienfuegos, 37 entre 8 y 12 Av, Punta Gorda, T432-512891, contacto@club.cfg .cyt.cu daily 1000- 0100, until 0200 Sat. A pure white Parisian-style mansion built in 1920 is now this club/marina. There is a restaurant under a pleasant, stretched canopy. Facilities include a shop selling sporting and fishing equipment, car and moped hire, billiard table, bumper boats (US$0.50 for 3 mins), go-karts (US$1 for 4 mins) and minigolf. Planned for the future are boat trips around the bay, a beach club, tennis courts and a charter base.

Tour operators

Cubanacán, Av 54 2903, T432-551680, cuba.viajes@cfg.cyt.cu daily 0830-1730. **Cubatur**, 37 y 0, T432-451242. **Havanatur**, Boulevard (Av 56) 2906, T432-511150, dolores_vaquero@cimex.com.cu Mon-Fri 0830-1200, 1330-1630, Sat 0830-1200. **Rumbos Cuba**, 37 entre 12 y 14, T432-451121, F432-451175, also office at Hotel Jagua, T432-451226. Trips to waterfalls (see El Nicho, p221, Lake Hanabanilla, p233), and other local and extended tours. **Transtur**, T432-551172/551600.

⊖ Transport

Bus

Terminal at Calle 49 esq Av 56, T432-515720/516050. Tickets may be purchased 1 hr or so in advance from the small office with a brown door, next to the *Salón Reservaciones*.

Víazul, office inside the main bus station, T432-518114/515720, daily 0800-1700, passes through Cienfuegos on its **Havana-Trinidad** route. New service to **Pinar del Río**, 0945, 5½ hours, US$35. To **Matanzas** and **Varadero**, 1015, 4½ hrs, US$20, only a minibus and reservations are required at least 1 day beforehand. In high season, **Víazul** runs a daily service **Varadero-Guamá -Girón-Cienfuegos**, US$16, leaving Varadero 0830, 4½ hrs, returning from Cienfuegos 1400.

Astro to **Havana**, daily, 0600, 1000, 1230, 1500, 2350, 5 hrs, US$14, bus with a/c US$17. From Havana, 0630, 1220, 1630, 1945, 2130. To **Santiago de Cuba**, every other day, 1600, US$25.50, or US$31 for bus with a/c. To **Camagüey**, every other day, 0800, 5 hrs, US$13 *regular*, US$16 *especial*. To **Trinidad**, 0630, 1130, 2 hrs, US$5. To **Santa Clara**, 0500, 0910, 1¼ hrs, US$2.50. **Astro** has a daily 1430 service to **Matanzas**, US$9.50 *regular*, US$12, *especial*, via **Cárdenas** and **Varadero**, but check if it is running. Sun is a good day with people returning to work in Varadero. The bus station personnel will tell you that there is an **Astro** bus to **Playa Girón** at 0320 and 1520, but it only goes to **Yaguaramas**, 4 hrs, 2.35 pesos, which is quite a long way from Playa Girón. It would be unwise to take this hoping for onward transport. **Astro** to **Palmira**, 0705, 1 hr 15 mins. (*Colectivos* to **Palmira** from 37 y 60, 5 pesos, 20 mins.) To **Baños**, 1620.

There is a daily *camión* to **Playa Girón** from Av 56 esq 51, 1 block from bus station, at 1230, unreliable and the driver may refuse to take tourists, see also taxi below.

Car/moped hire

Havanautos, C 37 y Av 20, T432-451154, 451211. As well as car hire, you can also hire mopeds at US$22/day. **RentaCar**, Hotel Jagua car park, C 37 y 2, Punta Gorda, T432-451645. **Petrol stations** Servi Cupet Cimex petrol station is at C 37 entre 16 y 18, and also on the way to Rancho Luna. The **Bahía** filling station, at Autoimport, is at C 37 esq Av 40.

Coches

Coches charge a couple of pesos.

Taxi

Cuba Taxi, T432-519145. The cheapest operator and recommended. To **Rancho Luna**, US$8, to **Pasacaballo** US$11. A private but illegal **taxi** for **Playa Girón** can be bargained down to US$25.

Train

Terminal at C 49 esq Av 58, T432-3403 /5495. All services generally slow and uncomfortable. To **Havana**, direct or via **Santa Clara**, on alternate days, 1030, 9 hrs, US$9.50, or 1430, arrive Santa Clara 1700, US$2.10, Havana 2300, US$9.50.

❶ Directory

Cienfuegos *p217, maps p217 and p220*
Banks

Banco Financiero Internacional, Av 54 esq 29, Mon-Fri 0800-1500, 3% commission on TCs. Cash advances on credit cards. **Bandec**, Av 56 esq 31, Mon-Fri 0800-1500. Visa and MC accepted. **BPA**, Boulevard y 33, Mon-Fri 0800-1600, Visa and MC accepted. **Cadeca**, Av 56 entre 33 y 35, Mon-Sat 0830-1800, Sun 0800-1230.

Hospitals and clinics

International Clinic, C 37 202, opposite Hotel Jagua, T432-551622, F432-551623. Offers 24-hr emergency care, consultations, laboratory services, X-rays, pharmacy and other services. There is usually someone who speaks a language other than Spanish. If the front door is shut, knock. Visa and MasterCard accepted.

Internet

Cibercafe Enmi-Cuba, 0800-2400. US$3/hr. Fast service. Also at Etecsa, see below. **Post office**, C 35 esq 56, 0800-1800. **Telecorreos**, Av 56 entre 35 y 37, 0800-2045.

Pharmacies

There is a pharmacy on Prado esq Av 60, open 24 hrs every day.

Telephone

Etecsa/Telepunto, C 31 entre 54 y 56. Phone, fax and internet, US$6 per hr, daily 0830-2130.

Useful address

Immigration Av 48 esq 29. Open for visa extensions, Mon-Fri 0800-1200, 1300-1500.

Santa Clara

Detail map
A Santa Clara centre, p232

Central University of Las Villas

Río Cubanicay

Circunvalación

R Chivas

Carretera de Maleza

Av de la Libertad

Loma el Capiro Monument

To Parque de Recreación Arco Iris

Parque Leoncio Vidal

RPTO CENTRO

A

Carretera Central

RPTO VIGIA

International Law Office

Carretera Central

Dollar Store

Long Distance Bus Station

Oquendo

Che Guevara Mausoleum

Plaza de la Revolución Ernesto Guevara

Prolongación de Marta Abreu

Rafael Trista

Municipal Bus Station

Carretera Central

Cuba

Colón

La Pastora

Río Belico

Comandante

Prolongación de Colón

González Coro

Raúl

Roberto Fleites

Sancho

Circunvalación

To Manicaragua & Embalse Hanabanilla

N

To ❷

0 metres 500
0 yards 500

Sleeping 🛏	Eating 🍴	Entertainment 🎵
Los Caneyes **2**	El Mandarín **2**	El Bosque **1**
Villa La Granjita **1**	La Concha **3**	

Santa Clara → *Colour map 2, grid B4. Population. 215,000. Altitude: 112 m.*

Santa Clara is best known for being the site of the last and definitive battle of the Revolution, when Che Guevara and his men captured an armoured troop train and subsequently the city. Che's body is interred here and his mausoleum is a major visitor attraction. Long underestimated by tourists on their way to somewhere else, Santa Clara is a pleasant university city lying in the heart of Cuba, with a sense of urgency and purpose. It is a cultured city and, as well as the monumental mausoleum, there are several art galleries and museums to stroll around and parks to sit and take in the atmosphere. Santa Clara's nightlife is humming, with any number of clubs and music venues where you can take in traditional or more contemporary Cuban styles, or there is the beautiful old theatre where you can find dance or drama performances of an international standard. South of the city, the land rises gently to the Alturas de Santa Clara, a range of hills reaching 464 m at its highest point, and then the magnificent Sierra de Escambray. There are lakes and reservoirs in the hills, where you can hike, birdwatch or fish in a peaceful and picturesque landscape.➤➤ *For Sleeping, Eating and other listings, see pages 234-241.*

Ins and outs

Getting there There are no domestic **flights** to Santa Clara but international charters come from Canada with **Air Transat, Sky Service** and **Air Canada,** while flights from Europe are expected soon. On the cays, an airstrip receives short-hop flights and air taxis (**Gaviota**). Santa Clara is on the main cross-island railway line. Daily **train** services join the city with Havana and Santiago de Cuba and with most of central Cuba's towns. The railway station is quite near the middle of the town. If you are travelling by **car**, the arterial *autopista* running from Havana to Santiago de Cuba links the city with these two major urban centres and other provincial capitals. Lesser roads go north to the cayos and south to Trinidad. Daily **bus** services make Santa Clara easy to get to on any route through the island. The long-distance bus station is about 2 km from the centre (a taxi to the centre is US$2).➤➤ *For further details, see also Transport, page 240.*

Getting around It is easy enough to **walk** round the town centre but the main attraction, the Che Guevara mausoleum in Plaza de la Revolución, is some way out. Walking takes about 30 minutes. You can get a horse-drawn **coche** or hire a **bicitaxi** to take you around. **Car hire** is available at the hotels if you want to make excursions further afield, or there are guided tours for the cays from some of the travel agencies in town. Limited services are available from the municipal bus station to Remedios and other local towns. If you are staying in a *casa particular* ask if anyone in the family offers their services as a driver and/or guide, which will be cheaper than an official taxi but you will not be allowed to go out to the cays.

Tourist information There is no tourist office as such, but several state tour agencies in town can give you information on trips and excursions, as well as make hotel reservations and reconfirm flight tickets. If you are staying in a *casa particular* you will probably find your hosts to be a mine of information worth tapping into. They will usually make phone calls for you to arrange transfers or accommodation at your next destination. The hotels all have a *buró de turismo*, which sells organized tours and little else.

History

The village of Santa Clara was founded on 15 July 1689, when 17 families from San Juan de los Remedios migrated from the coast to the interior. Land was parcelled out and a powerful landholding oligarchy was formed. The settlement grew and the economy prospered on the fortunes of stockbreeding, tobacco, sugar, other crops and the exploitation of the Malezas copper mines, while taking advantage of the favourable location on the main trading route through the island. In 1827 when the island was divided into three departments, Santa Clara was one of the sections of the central department. In 1867 the town became a city and in 1873 the railroad arrived, linking it with Havana. In 1895 when the island was further divided, this time into six provinces, Santa Clara became the capital of Las Villas, which included within its boundaries what is now Villa Clara, Cienfuegos, Sancti Spíritus and the Península de Zapata. The 1975 administrative reorganization sharply reduced the provincial territory, renaming it as Villa Clara, with Santa Clara as its capital and dividing it into 13 municipalities. Aside from Santa Clara, where most of the heavy industry is concentrated, other important urban centres are Caibarién, Camajuaní and Remedios to the northeast, Placetas to the east and Sagua La Grande to the north.

Santa Clara was the site of the last battle of the Revolution in December 1958 before Castro entered Havana. Batista was on the point of sending an armoured train with military supplies, including guns, ammunition and soldiers, to Santiago de Cuba to counter-attack the revolutionaries. However, when the train arrived in Santa Clara on 24 December it could go no further because the rebels had destroyed several bridges. Che Guevara had his command post in the university and his troops were hiding in the outskirts of Santa Clara. The train was parked near the Loma El Capiro and soldiers on board climbed up the hill to see Che's troops advancing. They opened fire but were defeated and the rebels took the Loma. Che moved his command post to the building which is now the seat of the PCC Provincial and from there made plans to derail the train, which took place at dawn on 29 December. At around 1500 the same day, the train retreated but was ambushed by 23 men. Fighting for the train was over within an hour, but the battle for the city lasted until 1 January 1959 when news spread that Batista had fled the country. It is said that the capture of the train was the decisive factor in the triumph of the Revolution and it is now a major tourist attraction (see under Sights below).

Sights

City centre

Parque Leoncio Vidal is the central plaza of the city, a pleasant park with trees, a central bandstand, and a bronze statue of **Marta Abreu de Estévez**, one of the benefactors of Santa Clara. It is busy day and night and local people love to listen to the band playing or just stroll around in the evening with their friends and families. There are plenty of benches where you can sit and take in the atmosphere but be prepared to be joined by interested Cubans. The roads around the edge are for pedestrians only and until 1894 there was racial segregation, with a fence dividing the inner and outer footpaths: white people walked in the centre of the park, while blacks were only allowed around the edge. In 1996 the plaza was declared part of the National Heritage. In one of the fountains on the north side of the Parque is a sculpture by José Delarra dating from 1989 (replacing a statue placed here in 1925 which was damaged in 1959), called **El Niño de la Bota Infortunada**. It is of a boy of about six or seven years old, representing those who, during the war of secession in the United States, used their boots to carry water to the sick and injured, much of it often spilt or lost through holes in the shoe. There are plans to renovate some of the buildings around the square and turn one or two into hotels.

On the north side of the Parque, on the corner of Calle Máximo Gómez, is **Teatro La Caridad** ① *Parque Vidal, T42-208548, Tue-Sun 0900-1700, US$1, tickets for performances around US$4-10.* It was built in 1884-85 with money raised by Marta Abreu de Estévez containing frescoes by artist Camilo Salaya (Philippines). In its heyday it attracted artists such as Enrico Caruso, Libertad Lamarque, Lola Flores, Alicia Alonso, El Ballet Nacional de Cuba, Chucho Valdés etc. It is a Monumento

Nacional and has been restored several times but contains more original features than any other theatre in Cuba, such as furniture, mirrors, paintings and busts in the lobby. You can also see the original stage machinery, with over 4.5 km of ropes, levers, pulleys and counterweights, possibly the only machinery of this period still in use anywhere in the world.

Round the corner from the theatre is the largest art gallery outside Havana, the **Galería Provincial de las Artes Plásticas** ① *Máximo Gómez 3 entre Marta Abreu y Barreros, T42-207715, Tue-Sat 1000-1800, Sun 0900-1300, free.* Originally built in the 19th century as a family house, it became the headquarters of the Colonia Española at the beginning of the 20th century. After the 1960s it was used for other purposes and has recently been rebuilt with all its former glory. There are three rooms for temporary exhibitions of paintings, drawings, crafts, sculpture and other works by national and international artists.

On the same side of the Parque as the theatre is the **Museo de Artes Decorativas**, ① *Martha Abreu entre Lorda y Luis Estévez, T42-205368, Mon-Thu 0900-1800, Fri 1300-2200, Sat 1300-1800, Sun 1800-2200, check times as they can vary, US$2.* The house was built at the end of the 18th century and belonged to a *criollo* family. Furniture, paintings, porcelain and glassware are exhibited in rooms around a central courtyard, each furnished in the style of the 18th, 19th or 20th centuries. The courtyard is also used for small concerts, fashion shows etc. Half a block away, just off the Parque is the **Centro Provincial de Patrimonio** ① *Céspedes 10 y Plácido, T42-205051, Mon-Fri 0830-1630, free.* Dating from the beginning of the 19th century when it was a domestic building on two floors, the first floor is now an art and photographic gallery. There is evening entertainment the first and third Saturday of the month at 2100. A little further on and round the corner is the **Casa de la ACAA** (Asociación Cubana de Artesanos y Artistas) ① *Maceo 7 entre Bulevar y Céspedes. 0900-1700.* Here you can find locally made handicrafts and works of art for exhibition and sale in a recently restored colonial house (1840). Two blocks from the Parque is the Catholic Church, **Nuestra Señora del Buen Viaje** ① *Pedro Estévez (Unión) esq Buen Viaje, T42-206332, daily 0900-1200, Mass Tue-Fri 0730, 1700, Sat 1500, 1700, Sun 0730.* Some of its architectural elements date from the 18th century, although the building was deeply modified later, especially during the 20th century and it is a mixture of styles. Next to the church, the former monastery built by the priests is now the Bishopric of Santa Clara. Another Roman Catholic church to the south of the Parque is **la Santísima Madre del Buen Pastor**, or 'La Divina Pastora', built in the 19th century and part of the Capuchin Order.

Also on the Parque is the **Biblioteca Provincial José Martí**, housed in the neoclassical **Palacio Provincial** ① *T42-206222, Mon-Fri 0800-2100 general rooms, 0800-1600 special rooms, Sat 0800-1600 all rooms, Sun 0800-1200.* It was the seat of provincial government (Las Villas) and one-time headquarters of Batista's police force. It was attacked by the Revolutionaries on 29 December 1958, surrendering the next day. It was also the place from where General Máximo Gómez addressed the people on 13 February 1899. Its stock of books is limited but the architecture rewards a visit. On the west side of the Parque is the **Hotel Santa Clara Libre**, an ugly green tower block whose bullet-marked, art deco façade is a reminder of Che's battle for the city. Just behind Teatro La Caridad runs Santa Clara's main commercial thoroughfare, best known as the Boulevard, which heads east as Calle Independencia to the Tren Blindado. Art exhibitions and cultural events are held during the day and evenings at the **Casa de la Cultura** ① *T42-203041, Mon-Fri 0900-1700, Sat 0900-1300, or until 2300 for concerts, 1 peso.* The building is architecturally interesting and worth a look. See Entertainment below, for details of events.

If you walk two blocks away from the Parque along Marta Abreu and then turn right along Zayas, heading up to the Boulevard, you enter what has traditionally been the Chinese part of town. The architecture ranges from traditional colonial to art deco and you won't find Chinese temples here, but around 20% of the residents are of

Chinese origin and until recently the Chinese Consulate was here (now a school, 13 de Marzo). The **Casa de la Ciudad Atípica** ① *Boulevard esq Zayas, T42-205593, Mon 0800-1200, Tue-Fri 0800-1200, 1300-1700, Sat 1300-1700, 2000-2300 or later, Sun 1600-1830, US$1,* is mostly an art gallery showcasing local artists. Built in the 19th century, it has beautiful stained glass windows and colonial architecture. It was initially a family house belonging to a man called Rivalta, from Barcelona; it became the Casa de la Ciudad in 1990. There are 12 exhibition rooms (permanent and temporary) containing art, furniture, photography (provincial social and political themes), local heraldry and local folkloric legends. Other artists of national and international stature are hung here, including several paintings by Ruperto Jay Matamoros (1912), Amelia Pelaez (1896-1968) and Wifredo Lam (1902-1982). There is also a room about tobacco and cigar making with a map of the growing areas. Concerts and *peñas* are held in the central patio. ▸▸ *See Entertainment, page 240.*

Some 425 people, of which three quarters are women, work at the **Fábrica de Tabacos** ① *Maceo entre Julio Jover y Berenguer, T42-202211, Mon-Fri 0700-1200, 1300-1600, workers go home at 1600, US$2. There is a shop opposite (see Shopping),* the largest cigar factory outside Havana occupying most of one block. Tours are available during working hours. Note the cigar labels used as paper chain decorations.

The cathedral, **Iglesia Parroquial Mayor de las Santas Hermanas de Santa Clara de Asís** ① *Calle Marta Abreu, entre Alemán y Lubián, T42-202078, daily 0900-1200, Mass Tue 2015, Thu 1730, Sat 1515, Sun 0800, 1000, 1700,* dates only from the 20th century. It is a relatively modern construction, having been consecrated in 1953 after a decade of works, and has some interesting stained-glass windows donated in the memory of loved ones. It became the cathedral of the new Diocese of Santa Clara in 1995. The main attraction is the 3-m-high white marble statue of the Virgin Mary at the main door, officially known as La Inmaculada Concepción, but also called La Virgen de la Charca (Virgin of the pond). The statue was commissioned by a local association of Roman Catholic women and blessed on Mother's Day, 12 May 1957. It stood originally at the entrance to the city but in the 1960s it was discarded in a ditch. It remained there until 1986 when it was disturbed by road building machinery and attracted huge interest with hundreds of people helping to clean up the Virgin. However, it was not until 1995 that the rather damaged and soiled Virgin was put inside the cathedral.

There are other churches scattered around the city, such as **Nuestra Señora del Carmen** ① *Parque El Carmen, T42-205217, Mass Mon and Tue, Thu and Fri 1730, Wed 2030, Sat 1600, Sun 0730, 2100.* This small church with a beautiful altar was built in the 18th century on the same hill where the founders of Santa Clara celebrated the first Mass, in 1689. It was once used as a prison for women in 1868-78. Part of the Silesian Order, there are connections with Don Juan Bosco and Italian saints, whose portraits adorn the walls. Father José Vandor, a Silesian priest and deeply holy man, was a mediator in the historic Battle for Santa Clara in December 1958. He was much loved by his parishioners and the process for his canonization has recently been opened. In the pleasant square, Parque El Carmen, outside, there is a 1951 marble monument to the 12 families who founded the city. It is a semi-circular spiral construction supported by 12 pillars and in the middle is a tamarind tree. Also in the square is a monument to Roberto Rodríguez 'El Vaquerito', a troop commander who was killed here in one of the battles for Santa Clara in December 1958.

Plaza de la Revolución

A monument to Che has been built on one side of the **Plaza de la Revolución Ernesto Guevara** , about a 20-minute walk from the city centre, and this is the focal point of the national obsession with the Argentine *guerrillero*. A huge bronze statue of Che carrying a machine gun stands on top of a large concrete plinth, a bas-relief scene depicting Che in battle and an inscription of a letter from Che to Fidel when he left Cuba. It is on Prolongación Marta Abreu after the Carretera Central forks to the south;

Ernesto 'Che' Guevara: rise and fall of the 'New Man'

Every visitor to Cuba learns to recognize the face of Che Guevara, the Cuban Revolution's unofficial emblem. Born in Rosario, Argentina, Ernesto Guevara was a medical student when he began travelling around Latin America by motorcycle, bus, truck and even as a stowaway on ships. In 1954, Guevara was in Guatemala when the CIA toppled that country's elected government. His hopes for peaceful change in the hemisphere were dashed and Guevara found his natural enemy: imperialism. Months later in Mexico he met his natural ally, the exiled Cuban lawyer, Fidel Castro. Guevara joined Castro's invasion force as a doctor, but once in Cuba quickly showed himself a brilliant field commander as well and rose during three years of warfare to lead the guerrilla army's second column. Repeatedly wounded, Che led from the front lines and was lionized by his Cuban soldiers, many of whom would follow him for the rest of their lives. On 27 December 1958, Che's badly outnumbered guerrillas ambushed a troop train at Santa Clara, Cuba, the decisive victory that sealed the fate of the Batista regime. It was the apogee of Guevara's career. Within days he had entered Havana and the realm of revolutionary politics, a field of battle far more dangerous than the mountains of the Sierra Maestra.

Following the triumph of the Revolution on 1 January 1959, Cubans rallied to Guevara. Nicknamed 'Che' after an Argentine figure of speech, Guevara routinely spoke at Castro's side and was seen as the Revolution's second leader. His position was won through public support; a charismatic orator, Guevara appealed to the idealism of the young, calling for the birth of a 'New Man', or a revolutionary society based on moral, rather than material incentives. His eloquence on behalf of the poor and dispossessed made him a global spokesman for the Third World.

Once in power, Guevara endorsed show trials and summary executions of opponents and later, as head of the Central Bank and the Ministry of Industry, his Socialist economic reforms produced chaos even by his own account. Frustrated by Fidel Castro's increasing reliance on the Soviet Union, Guevara quit Cuba in 1965, first to join a doomed rebellion in the Congo, then, in late 1966, to launch his own guerrilla column in Bolivia.

On 8 October 1967, in an operation co-ordinated by the CIA, Guevara was captured and executed by Bolivian troops. His remains were repatriated to Cuba 30 years later, to be interred in a bronze mausoleum at the site of his great victory in Santa Clara.

Guevara remains an enigmatic figure, seen as both an inspiring idealist and an inflexible ideologue. Despite his position as the Revolution's greatest hero, 'El Che' has also become a symbol of dissent for those Cubans who recall his energy and optimism at a time when the Cuban Revolution seems to lack both. See also page 404.

entrance on Calle Rafael Tristá, which runs parallel. The Plaza de la Revolución has enough spotlights to light a football stadium, major speeches and commemorative events take place here, such as on May Day or 8 October, the day of Che's death. On 28 December there is an annual concert with Cuban and Latin American singers.

The monument complex, inaugurated on 28 December 1988, was designed by **José Delarra** (1938-2003), who went on to construct 14 further sculptures symbolizing the feats of the guerrilla and his invading forces in Villa Clara province. Under the monument is a **Mausoleum**. The remains of Che and his comrades who fell in Bolivia have been interred at this site, with architecture designed to be in keeping with the harsh surroundings in which they fought. Fourteen Royal palms to the left represent the date, 14 June, while the additional 14 Royal palms to the right, making a total of 28, represent the year of Che's birth: 1928. The mausoleum is open to the public, numbers limited to 20, and the chamber is a place of contemplation and calm. There are now 38 tombs but only 30 are occupied; see History, page 382. Beside the mausoleum is the **Museo Histórico de la Revolución** ① *T42-205985, Tue-Sat 0800-2100, Sun 0800-1700, free, bags should be left at the entrance.* The museum has good displays in Spanish and sometimes a video about Che's life and role in the Revolution, with many photos, uniforms and personal effects, including his famous leather jacket, the clothes he wore when he was murdered in Bolivia, as well as displays of the battle in Santa Clara. Recommended. To get to the museum from the city centre, you can take a *bicitaxi* US$1 per person, but make sure you agree on a price in advance, as the drivers are notorious for moving the goalposts.

Santa Clara centre

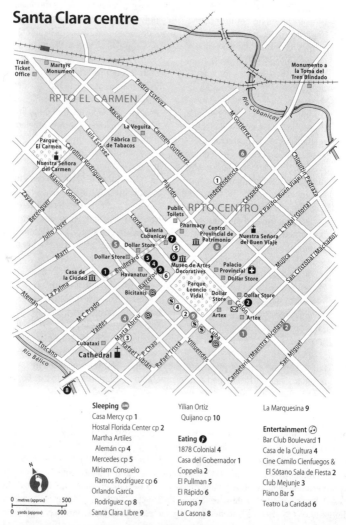

0 metres (approx) 500
0 yards (approx) 500

Sleeping
Casa Mercy cp **1**
Hostal Florida Center cp **2**
Martha Artiles
Alemán cp **4**
Mercedes cp **5**
Miriam Consuelo
Ramos Rodríguez cp **6**
Orlando García
Rodríguez cp **8**
Santa Clara Libre **9**

Yilian Ortiz
Quijano cp **10**

Eating
1878 Colonial **4**
Casa del Gobernador **1**
Coppelia **2**
El Pullman **5**
El Rápido **6**
Europa **7**
La Casona **8**

La Marquesina **9**

Entertainment
Bar Club Boulevard **1**
Casa de la Cultura **4**
Cine Camilo Cienfuegos &
El Sótano Sala de Fiesta **2**
Club Mejunje **3**
Piano Bar **5**
Teatro La Caridad **6**

Monumento a la Toma del Tren Blindado

ⓘ *Independencia, heading east towards Camajuaní, between Río Cubanicay and the railway line, T42-202758, Tue-Sat 0800-1830, Sun 0800-1200, US$1.*

Three of the five carriages of Batista's troop train and a bulldozer used to derail the train are preserved here. Is Cuba the only place in the world where a bulldozer sits on a plinth? The train, carrying 408 heavily armed troops and weapons, was attacked and taken on 29 December 1958 by 23 guerrillas under the command of Che Guevara in a heroic battle lasting only one hour. The carriages are arranged in a small park among clusters of angular pillars and an inscription on an obelisk describes the event. There is a museum inside the wagons showing weapons and other things carried on the train as well as photos of the aftermath.

El Che de los Niños

On the outskirts of Santa Clara as you head towards the cays (opposite the PCC offices, which were Che's HQ in 1958), there is another statue of Che, a bronze cast by Casto Solano of Spain. It is known as El Che de los Niños and shows Che striding along holding a small child in one arm, a cigar in the other hand and lots of tiny details reflecting events in his life. On his shoulder is an Amerindian man on a goat, signifying him telling his story to the child. On one of his boots is the bike he travelled on through South America with his friend Alberto Granados. Don Quijote is on one of his pockets, while on his belt is his troop.

> ‡ *There is also a monument on top of El Capiro, the hill which Che and his troops captured during the battle with the troops on the train. You can get an excellent view of the city from here, just as Che did in 1958.*

Around Santa Clara

Parque de Recreación Arco Iris

About 4 km from the centre, on the Carretera Central heading east towards Placetas, is this huge recreational park ⓘ *T42-293374, open Tue-Sun*, in a rural undulating setting, popular with families of all ages. There are two children's playgrounds, camping, mini golf, Expocentro Convention Centre, swimming pool, motocross and lots of other activities, as well as four restaurants including a pizzeria. The Casa de la Música Longina is also here, so you can extend your entertainment into the night.

Embalse Hanabanilla

The **Sierra del Escambray**, part of the Montañas de Guamuhaya, occupies most of the land between Santa Clara and Trinidad and can be visited from either city. Although not the highest mountain range in Cuba, it is one of the most beautiful, being coated in forest and home to a variety of plant and animal species. The peaks are intersected by streams, waterfalls and fertile valleys, where thatched *bohíos* are home to farming families eking out a living from growing bananas, coffee and livestock. There are several lakes and dams in the province of Villa Clara and the province boasts the largest river to drain into the Atlantic, Río Sagua la Grande, at 144 km long. Embalse Alacranes, 45 km north of Santa Clara, is the second largest reservoir in the country, while man-made Embalse Hanabanilla, the third largest, is very attractive and used for recreational purposes as well as water supply, with hunting and fishing both popular. Thirty kilometres south of Santa Clara, the road to Trinidad passes through **Manicaragua**, a large town of some 80,000 inhabitants set in rolling hills covered with tobacco fields, and then rises into the mountains. **Hanabanilla reservoir** has the largest hydroelectricity station in the country, but looks like a natural lake. It is in a very attractive landscape with lovely views. It has been a resort area for a long time because of its popularity with the shooting/fishing fraternity. The lake is stocked with largemouth bass and other fish and there are plenty of wild duck, quail, pheasant and other game birds. This does, of course, also make it interesting for twitchers. You can take a boat trip on the lake (boat rentals US$20 per hour) to the **Restaurante Río Negro** (7 km from the **Hotel Hanabanilla** and accessible only by boat) and the Trucha Falls, and go hiking or horse riding in the mountains. The resort area can get crowded with Cubans at the weekends, but you don't need to walk far to get peace and quiet. Embalse Hanabanilla can be visited as a day trip from Santa Clara, Cienfuegos, Trinidad or Sancti Spíritus, but an overnight stay would be more rewarding and it is a convenient place to stay between the towns.

● Sleeping

If you want to be in the city centre then you are recommended to stay in a *casa particular*, of which there are several excellent ones to choose from with knowledgeable and helpful host families. Beware of *jineteros* outside who may tell you the house is full and offer to take you somewhere else, or concoct some other story. Ring the bell and get the facts from someone inside. For a more rustic feel, there are state hotels on the outskirts of the city and in the hills, but these are usually booked for people on package tours.

Santa Clara centre *p228, map p232*
Hotels

D-E **Santa Clara Libre** (Islazul), Parque Vidal 6, T42-207548, F42-205171, hscl@ip.etecsa.cu Central, 1956 dilapidated metal-concrete building on Parque Vidal with bullet holes on the façade, preserved from the December 1958 battle when some of the police were using the building to defend the city from the revolutionaries. 145 spartan rooms, but comfortable, with a/c and fans, phones, some rooms have TV, water shortages, lifts also erratic and ancient, straight out of Batman's Gotham, noisy, car rental, shops (**Tienda Caracol** 3rd floor), dollar pharmacy (2nd floor, ext 220, 0900-1700), tour agency (3rd floor), observation deck with bar on top of the building from where you get a great view of the city, cinema. Sala de Fiestas in the basement and **El Topet** disco on the roof, see Entertainment page 237.

Casas particulares

Private homes in Santa Clara are nicer places to stay than the state hotels on offer.
E-F **Casa Mercy**, San Cristóbal (Machado) 4 entre Cuba y Colón, T42-216941, omeliomoreno@yahoo.com Run by Omelio (engineer) and Mercedes (social worker)

Moreno and family, who speak several languages. 2 good rooms, upstairs overlooking the street, private and separate from the rest of the house, stocked fridge in each, 1 bathroom, towel and soap provided, double bed, a/c, fan, kitchen facilities, laundry, iron, hearty food served on the roof terrace or in ante-room. Friendly family with dog, very central. Parking.
E-F **Hostal Florida Center**, Candelaria (Maestra Nicolasa) 56 entre Colón y Maceo, T42-208161. Delightful colonial house with 2 rooms opening on to verdant garden in patio where there are parrots, a dog and cats. Rooms have double bed with extra single bed, basin in room, private bathrooms, a/c, TV, fridge and minibar, antique furniture. Hospitable host Angel Martínez is an excellent cook and speaks some English, French and a little Italian.
E-F **José Ramón de Zayas Lara y Lisnay Amador Prieto**, Máximo Gómez 208 altos entre Yanes y Berenguer, T42-207239. Short walk from Parque Vidal and train station. José Ramón is a young architect who designed this tasteful room; he and his wife are helpful and informative. 1 room, hot shower, a/c, TV, VCR, lookout terrace, quiet.
E-F **María y Jorge García Rodríguez**, Cuba 209, Apdo 1, entre Serafín García (Nazareno) y E P Morales (Síndico), T42-202329, garcrodz@yahoo.com 2 a/c rooms, clean, comfortable, owners very helpful and informative.
E-F **Martha Artiles Alemán**, Marta Abreu 56 altos, entre Villuendas y Zayas, T42-205008, martaartiles@yahoo.es Central but quiet, sizeable colonial house with balcony views towards Parque Vidal, the cathedral and the Che mausoleum, *bicitaxi* outside and car parking. Large rooms, a/c, fan, bathrooms with hot and cold water, laundry, clean, parking, own key to house. Martha is a

retired anaesthetist who knows Santa Clara from A-Z and is extremely helpful.

E-F Mercedes, Máximo Gómez 51 altos, entre Independencia y Martí. Central, rooms with own bathroom and terrace, high standard, friendly family, Mercedes practices *Santería*.

E-F Noely González González, Bonifacio Martínez 18, entre Serafín García (Nazareno) y EP Morales (Síndico), T42-216193. Large room with 2 big beds, fan, a/c, hot water, private bathroom, parking.

E-F Olga Rivera Gómez, Evangelista Yanes 20 entre Máximo Gómez y Callejón del Carmen, T42-214973. Lovely art deco house in front of Nuestra Señora del Carmen church. A lush green vineyard in the inner patio is home to a dozen parrots and canaries singing in their cages. 2 rooms, hot shower, a/c, fridge, TV, parking, terrace, helpful owner.

E-F Orlando García Rodríguez, Buen Viaje 7 entre Parque y Maceo, T42-206761. 2 rooms, a/c, fan, shared fridge, shared bathroom, lovely house, eating area on the roof, guitar/singer, excursions arranged.

E-F Santiago Martínez y Lidia Viera, Bonifacio Martínez 58A altos entre Síndico y Caridad, T42-204474. 2 nice rooms, hot shower, a/c, fridge, friendly family.

F Eduardo Alvarez Chaviano (Casa Suiza), Colón 170 entre Nazareno y San Miguel, 3 blocks from Parque Vidal, T42-206190. 1 cosy room with private bathroom, hot shower, a/c, fridge, kitchenette, parking. Eduardo is a geography teacher, a good cook, an expert on Santa Clara and has travelled to Switzerland.

F Ernesto y Mireya, Cuba 227 altos entre Pastora y Síndico, opposite Iglesia La Pastora, T42-273501. 2 double rooms with shared bathroom, Ernesto is funny and helpful, will arrange collection from bus station if you pay for taxi.

F Hostal IDO, Céspedes 24 entre Maceo y Parque Vidal, T42-202489. Run by the very helpful and hospitable Babi and brother, relatives of Martha Artiles. Very central, independent rooms, a/c, private bathrooms with all-day hot water and car parking.

F Maykel Pérez y Aidé Yanes, A 119 entre 3 y 4, Reparto Vigía, T42-271104. Walking distance from city centre and the Sandino food market. Maykel speaks a little English and is young and easy going, Aidé is his mother and his sister is living in Italy.

Independent upstairs rooms with hot shower, a/c, fridge, parking.

F Miriam Consuelo Ramos Rodríguez, Independencia 265 Este Apto 1 entre Pedro Estévez y San Isidro, T42-202064. Ernesto's cousin, English spoken, huge room with 2 double beds and bathroom, Miriam Consuelo is a 1-person tourist office, she knows everything, large family and comedy dog.

Around Santa Clara *p233, map p226*

Hotels

C Villa La Granjita (Cubanacán), outside town at Km 2.5 on Maleza road, T42-218191, aloja@granjita.vcl.cyt.cu   75 rooms in thatched *cabañas* among fruit and palm trees, emphasis on nature and tranquillity, TV, a/c, phone, internet access, pool, bar, shop, buffet restaurant, horses, nighttime entertainment around the pool. *Sala de fiestas* (US$6, free bar 2200-0130). 24-hr medical services, massage (45 mins US$10, 20 mins US$5).

D Los Caneyes (Horizontes), Av de los Eucaliptos y Circunvalación, T42-218140. Thatched public areas with 90 cabins designed to look like Indian huts in a park-like setting, a/c, hot showers, TV, facilities for disabled people, pool, disco 1800-0200, enthusiastic evening entertainment by the pool, good buffet, supper US$12, breakfast US$4, excellent value, car rental, internet access, medical services, shop, tourism bureau, hairdresser, game shooting and fishing can be arranged, popular hotel for tour parties and hunters. Day passes are available whereby you can use the pool and eat and drink until 1800, but note that although they are sold as all-inclusive deals (US$10 Fri-Sun, US$5 Mon-Thu), they are in fact credit slips and anything you eat or drink over that amount will be charged at the end of your visit.

D-E Hanabanilla, Salto de Hanabanilla, Manicaragua, on the northwest edge of the lake, T42-202399, carpeta@hanabanilla.vcl .cyt.cu   Rates vary with the season, 125 rooms in Soviet-style block, a/c, phone, radio, pool, bar and grill, restaurant with Cuban and international food. Mirador Bar on the top floor, excellent view, disco, tours offered, fishing tackle available.

🍴 Eating

The best food can be found in *casas particulares*, although some of the *paladares* are also worth trying. Most *casas* offer food, with breakfast at around US$3, dinner US$7-8, depending on what meat you choose, recommended, better than restaurants. In the city centre you can find snack bars such as **Rápido** and **Di-tú** serving sandwiches, biscuits, ice cream and little else. Begging can be persistent if you eat outside at a street café.

Santa Clara centre *p228, map p232*
Restaurants

$$ **1878 Colonial**, Máximo Gómez 8, near the Boulevard, T42-202428, daily 1000-1100 for snacks, 1200-1445 lunch, 1900-2245 dinner. Reopened after renovation in 2003. Offers a variety of *criollo* dishes, mainly pork in different styles, bar in the patio, long trousers required for men at night. Pesos or dollars accepted.

$ **Casa del Gobernador**, Boulevard. In old colonial building, not very hygienic, open daily for lunch 1200-1500, *merienda* (tea/snacks) in the patio 0900-2300, dinner 1900-2245. Nightclub Tue-Sun 2100-0100.

$ **Coppelia**, Colón esq Mujica just off Parque Vidal, T42-206426, Tue-Sun, 1000-2330, ice cream, seriously cheap. The 2nd floor belongs to the **Viaten** chain, Tue-Sun 1000-1630 and 1800-2345, ice cream, sweets, pastries and drinks.

$ **Doña Neli**, Maceo y San Miguel, T42-218189. Dollar coffee shop serving fast food meals. At weekends a small stage is erected inside with live music and nightly fun shows. The bar/restaurant is open 0900-2100, the bakery 0700-1900.

$ **El Marino**, Paseo de la Paz y Carretera Central, T42-205594, daily 0700-2245, with lunch at 1200-1500, and dinner 1900-2245. Seafood, paella a speciality, snacks available outside formal meal times, cheap, dollars or pesos accepted.

$ **El Pullman**, Independencia. Peso snack bar, 4 pesos for a pizza or 9 for an *especial*, drinks, cocktails and rum in dollars.

$ **El Rápido**, Lorda 8 near Parque Vidal, T42-207659, daily 0830-0500. Fast food, sandwiches, biscuits, ice cream, pasta, beer and little else, only US dollars.

$ **Europa**, on the corner of Boulevard and Luis Estévez, T42-218016, daily 0700-0200. A good place to sit and watch shoppers and drink a cool beer, dollars only, cheap café.

$ **La Carreta**, Carretera Central, T42-271662, daily 1200-1445 and 1900-2245, servi-bar. *Criollo* food in cosy environment, cheap, pay in pesos or dollars.

$ **La Marquesina**, next to theatre, T42-218016. Cheap 24-hr café serving coffee, tea, rum and not much else, pesos or dollars accepted, pleasant place for a drink, popular with young people at night.

$ **Park View**, Hotel Santa Clara Libre, Parque Vidal, daily 0800-0200. Bar, *cafetería*, serving coffee, soft drinks and beers, sandwiches, hamburgers, hot dogs and pasta, nice view overlooking the park, a/c, TV.

$ **Salón Juvenil** (Cubanacán/Palmares), Marta Abreu 10 entre Máximo Gómez y Villuendas, T42-208534. Mon-Fri 0900-2300 and Sat-Sun 0930-2400. *Cafetería*, drinks, cocktails, cybercafé (internet use US$1.25 for 15 mins).

Paladares

$ **Bodeguita del Centro**, Villuendas 264 entre San Miguel y Nazareno, T42-204356, daily 1200-2300. Run by Soledad and José, this singular, bohemian restaurant with graffiti-covered walls recalls Havana's **Bodeguita del Medio** and is worth trying. Good *criollo* food is served for as little as US$3, pesos and dollars accepted.

$ **El Alba**, Rolando Pardo (Buen Viaje) 26 entre Maceo y Parque, daily 1200-1500 and 1900-2030. Standing counter only catering mainly for Cubans and charging in pesos, although dollars are accepted. Takeaway food also available. Meals are mostly pork dishes with *congrí* and green salad, cheap and practical, US$1-3.

$ **El Castillito**, San Miguel 9 entre Villuendas y Cuba, Wed-Mon from 1200 as long as there are customers. Pesos or dollars accepted. Meals such as pork, *congrí* and salads are served at a standing counter, US$1-3.

$ **La Casona**, Carretera Central 6 entre Padre Chao y Marta Abreu, just by Río Bélico, T42-205027, daily 1200-2400. Nice old house with beautiful tiled floor but no tables or chairs, tasty food served at standing counter to avoid *paladar* regulations, like a takeaway service, friendly hosts.

Restaurants

\$\$ Cubanicay, 15-min walk east of the centre, on the top floor of a 12-storey building on Av El Sandino beside the baseball stadium in Reparto El Sandino, T42-207888, daily 1200-1500 and 1900-2400. Panoramic views, nice decor. Cheap, dollars or pesos accepted, only of average standard.

\$\$ El Mandarín, Carretera Central beyond bus stations, T42-291010, daily 1900-2245. Chinese, pay in pesos or dollars.

\$\$ La Concha, Carretera Central esq Danielito, 1 km to the east of the centre, T42-218124, F42-204260, Mon-Fri 0900-2400, Sat and Sun 1100-0200. Good international and *criollo* cuisine, Italian speciality, dollars only, extensive range of bar drinks, pleasant place.

⊕ Entertainment

Santa Clara centre *p228, map p232*
Cartelera is a pamphlet with what's on in Santa Clara, Remedios, Caibarién.

Cinema

Cine Camilo Cienfuegos, on the ground floor of the Hotel Santa Clara Libre on Parque Vidal, T42-203005. Check billboard outside for show times and what's on. This is Santa Clara's only cinema and entering is like stepping back in time. Seriously cheap, 2 pesos.

Live music

Bar Club Boulevard (Carishow), Independencia 225 entre Maceo y Unión, T42-216236, daily 1300-1900 and 2100-0200, Carishow US\$1.50, Fri-Sun US\$2. Nightclub, very trendy, small, phenomenal dancing and lethal supplies of rum although drinks more expensive than other places, also used for social occasions, birthdays etc, show with different acts, singers, comedians etc.

Casa de la Ciudad, Boulevard esq Zayas. Typical Cuban music in the inner courtyard of a lovely colonial house. Be sure to pin down what's going on and when. Usually, *Peña de Música Tradicional Cubana* on the 2nd Fri of the month at 2100, *Peña del Bolero* on Sun at 1600, *Noche del Danzón* 2nd Sat of the month at 2100, *Tardes de Tradiciones* 3rd Thu at 1600, *Ateneo Cultural* last Thu 1530, *Concierto en Casa* some Sats with professional groups. Seriously cheap, pay in pesos.

Casa de la Cultura, Parque Vidal, T42-203041. A variety of cultural activities with local and provincial artists: *Noche del Danzón* first Wed in the month 2100, *Noche de Trova Tradicional* third Wed 2100, *Noche de la Cultura* first Thu 2100, *Peña de Freida Anido* third Thu 2100, children's karaoke night every Fri 2100, *Tarde de Recuerdos* 2nd Sat 1400, *Quinteto Criollo* with dancing every Sat 2100, *Peña Campesina* 2nd Sun 1400, *Peña de Abel* (trova) 3rd Sun 1500, *Tarde de Tradiciones* 4th Sun 1500, *Festival de Casino* with dancing 3rd Sun 2130.

Club Mejunje (mishmash), 2½ blocks west from Parque Vidal, Marta Abréu 107 entre Alemán y Juan Bruno Zayas, T42-282572, open weekdays at variable hours, Sat 2100-0200, Sun 1600-2100, US\$1 for foreigners, 5 pesos for Cubans. The best place to go to sample what Santa Clara has to offer in the way of nightlife. Cultural centre in a backyard full of trees, ruins, artefacts and graffiti-covered walls. Composers, singers, musicians and friends sing, play and drink together, friendly, welcoming, enjoyable. Rock night Tue, *Trovuntivitis* Thu with very good *trovadores*, both young and traditional, Fri is *Viernes de la Buena Suerte*, traditional Cuban music and occasionally the internationally famous *Los Fakires*, Sat is the night for gays with a show, and Sun there is dancing 1600-2100. Larger events are staged in the courtyard, wide variety ranging from concerts to theatre, from shows for kids to (transvestite) shows for gays (popular at weekends).

El Bosque, Centro Cultural, Av El Sandino y Carretera Central, Vigía, 1 km from Parque Vidal, T42-204444, Wed-Sun 2100-0100, Sat 2100-0200. Tree-ringed, outdoor venue for live and taped music and nightlife, cabaret, fun shows, US\$5, including bottle of rum and 4 colas and table for the show. After midnight it eventually becomes a disco. Heady atmosphere and good dancing. 24-hr patio bar charges in dollars.

El Sótano Sala de Fiesta, Hotel Santa Clara Libre, Tue-Sun 2100-0200, *consumo mínimo* US\$3 per couple. 1hr show and taped music afterwards.

El Topet, Bar La Terraza, Hotel Santa Clara Libre, T42-207548 ext 1000, from 2100 onwards. Rooftop, open-air bar and disco with a bird's eye view of Santa Clara where rain is the only drawback. Easy to meet local people here.

Longina (Casa de la Música), Arco Iris leisure complex 2.5 km from the centre towards the east along the Carretera Central to Placetas. Authentic Cuban music for dancing, Fri-Sun live music, Tue-Thu taped music from 2100, drinks available.

Piano Bar, Luis Estévez 13 entre Independencia y Parque, T42-215215, closed Thu, restaurant daily 1000-2145, *comida criolla*, the piano bar opens 1200-1900 for drinks, cocktails and snacks and 2100-0100, live music with the pianist Freyda Anido and band, invited singers, national and international music, couples only.

Theatre

Teatro 2, Independencia entre Maceo y P Estévez, T42-204038. Base for Teatro Estudio Teatral and Teatro 2, both from Santa Clara. Experimental or alternative theatre, occasionally visiting companies from abroad. 2 theatre halls seat 120 and 60 people, varied programme, see billboard at the theatre.

Teatro Guiñol, Tristá entre Alemán y Carr Central, T42-207860. Children's theatre and entertainment, Sat 1700, Sun 1000 and 1700.

Teatro la Caridad, Calle Máximo Gómez, Parque Vidal, T42-208548. Look in *Cartelera* or the billboard outside for what's on, you might catch a performance by a top ballet company and the annual National Dance Festival is held here. Bring a fan, it is hot inside. Tickets US$4-10, performances at 2100.

⊛ Festivals and events

There are 2 annual **film** festivals: **Festival del Cine Cubanacán** in **Nov** and **Festival del Cine Profilm** in **May**, dates variable, with premières, critics, discussions.

Jan A *trova* festival is held, called the **Festival Longina Canta a Corona**, with subsidiary events in Caibarién.

Mar Santa Clara is the base for the **Festival 'A Tempo' con Caturla**, a young person's concert also held in Remedios.

First week of May At the **Festival Nacional de la Danza** (National Dance Festival) there is traditional music and dancing in theatres and all around Parque Vidal, and every 4 years international groups participate.

12 Aug There is a popular jazz festival called

La Verbena de la Calle Gloria, celebrated since the beginning of the 20th century in honour of Santa Clara de Asís, patron saint of the city.

End of Oct, beginning of Nov The week-long **Festival de Rock Ciudad Metal** held on Calle Tristá and Carretera Central.

Dec Every 2 years (Dec 2004) the **Festival de Creación Musical 'Gustavo Rodríguez'** In Memoriam is held, in which composers and songwriters release their new works. On 28 Dec there are lots of commemorative activities in the Plaza de la Revolución, celebrating the last successful battle of the Revolution in 1958 with concerts and music festivals attracting Cuban and Latin American singers and musicians.

⊙ Shopping

Santa Clara centre *p228, map p232*
The road behind the theatre, which runs between Maceo and Juan Bruno Zayas, is known locally as *Boulevard*. It is pedestrianized and locals shop here in dollars for clothes, electrical, domestic and household goods, some food and other items. Shops are open daily 0900-1700 unless otherwise stated.

Bookshops

Pepe Medina, Colón y Parque Vidal, T42-205965. 1 of the best in town.

Viet Nam Heroico, Independencia 106, T42-203233. Reasonable selection with dollar shop next door selling postcards.

Cigars

La Veguita (Cubanacán), Maceo 176 entre Berenguer y Martí, T42-208952, economia@univer.vcl.cyt.cu Opposite the tobacco factory, sells cigars, rum and coffee, English spoken, very informative, large stock.

Clothing

La Isla, Colón 6 entre Machado y Parque, Mon-Sat 0900-1700, Sun 0900-1200. Boutique selling clothes, shoes and perfume, all brands.

Tienda Candilejas, Independencia (Boulevard) y Máximo Gómez, T42-208883, Mon-Sat 0900-1700, Sun 0900-1200. Clothes and sports wear, shoes, perfume, jewellery, international brand names and designer labels.

Markets

Agromercado El Sandino, Av Sandino, Tue-Sat 0800-1800, Sun 0800-1200, and **Mercado de la Calle San Miguel**, Tue-Sun 0800-1800, both sell fruit, vegetables and pork, in pesos. El Sandino has the best variety.

Photography

Fotografía Trimagen, Colón 8 entre E Machado y Parque, T42-206991, Mon-Sat 0830-1830. Cameras, film and accessories.
Photo Club Cubanacán, Marta Abreu 10 entre Máximo Gómez y Villuendas, beside *Salón Juvenil*, T42-208534, open Mon-Fri 0800-1800, Sat 0800-1200. Cameras and accessories, film developing and printing, photocopying, scooter rental.

Souvenirs

Next to the theatre on the corner of Parque Vidal and Lorda is a small shop selling T-shirts, books about Che, cassettes and CDs, nicknacks and maps.
Artex, south side of Parque Vidal. A dollar store selling a few handicrafts, cassettes, CDs, toiletries, drinks, a few books in English principally on Fidel and Che, T-shirts and nicknacks. There is another Artex, nearby on Colón 16 entre Machado y Parque, Mon-Sat 0900-1700, Sun 0900-1200. Sells artesanías, Che souvenirs, percussion (drums, bongos), wind (saxophones, trumpets) and string (acoustic and electric guitars) instruments.
Galería Cubanicay, Luis Estévez 9, daily 0800-1830. Wide choice of handicrafts, art as well as furniture and shoes made locally.

▲ Activities and tours

Baseball

Played from Nov until around Apr at the **Augusto César Sandino** stadium, Av Sandino y 6, T42-203838. Tickets 2 pesos. Take drink and snacks. The local team is Villa Clara. Nearby is the **Natilla Jiménez** mini-stadium built for children's baseball, great matches, unforgettable.

Fishing and shooting

Expeditions are organized to Embalse Alacranes and Embalse Hanabanilla, contact **Flora y Fauna**, Carr Central Km 306, Banda Placetas, T42-206285, Mon-Fri 0800-1630, equipment rental, guide.

Health clubs

Centro de Estética Personal, Biobel, Luís Estévez 57 entre Martí y Jover, T42-204752, Mon-Fri 0900-1800, Sat 0900-1300, café open until 2200, gym, sauna, body massage, also shaving for men and waxing for women.

Hiking

In the Escambray mountains.

Kayaking

Cayo Fragoso in the north.

Swimming

You can swim at the **Hotel Los Caneyes** for US$5 (Mon-Thu) or US$10 (Fri-Sun), which entitles you to US$4 or US$8 worth of food and drinks in summer. In winter the rate is US$5 every day. Bring your own towel.

Tour operators

Cubatur, Marta Abreu 10 entre Máximo Gómez y Villuendas, T/F42-208980, cubaturvc@ip.enet.cu daily 0900-2000. Also at **Hotel Los Caneyes**, T42-208982, and Cayo Santa María. Excursions to every possible tourist site in west and central Cuba as well as **Víazul** tickets, flight confirmations etc. Helpful and informative personnel. Internet access, prepaid card US$6 for 6 hrs, also phone cards.
Havanatur, Máximo Gómez, 13 entre Independencia y Barreras, T42-204001, Mon-Fri 0830-1700, Sat 0830-1230. Air tickets, car hire, tours etc. Excursions to Cayo las Brujas US$27 (transfer, lunch and beach time), Cienfuegos US$23 (city tour, lunch and beach, US$16 without lunch), Trinidad US$29 (city tour, lunch and beach), to Hanabanilla and Elguea on demand.
Islazul, Lorda 6 entre Parque Vidal y Boulevard, just off Parque Vidal by the theatre, T42-217338, Mon-Fri 0800-1130, 1300-1545. Dealing mainly with Cubans, mostly hotel and restaurant reservations, but in season they organize excursions to Hanabanilla for US$3. Prices and times vary, always check first.
Imagen y Destino, Hotel Santa Clara, T/F42-208979, staclara@imagenydestino .com Mon-Fri 0900-1700. Full service of air and bus ticket reservation and purchase, accommodation, transfers and excursions in the area as far as Trinidad and Cienfuegos.

Air

Abel Santa María international airport is on Carretera de Malezas, Km 11, north of the city, T42-209138. Charter flights come in from Canada, at the moment there are no domestic flights. **Airlines** No airline office in Santa Clara, but ticket purchase and reconfirmation can be done through tour operators.

Bus

Local There are some buses, 20 centavos. Horse-drawn *coches*, or taxi-buses, go all over town and down Marta Abreu to the bus stations, 1-2 pesos. They stream up and down the main streets, taking 8 passengers and there are always queues.

Long distance The provincial bus station for destinations within Villa Clara is on Marta Abreu esq Pichardo, T42-206284/203470, 1 km from centre, white building. The interprovincial bus station for long distances is on Carretera Central (Av Cincuentenario) 483 entre Independencia y Oquendo, Virginia, T42-292114, 1 km further out, building remodelled and renovated in 2003 with a/c, dollar snack bar.

For Víazul services, see table, page 42, to **Havana** US$18, **Santiago** US$33, **Varadero** US$11, **Camagüey** US$15, **Trinidad** US$8, and to most of the provincial capitals.

Astro to **Havana** daily at 2350 (arrives 0430), US$12; to **Santiago** via **Camagüey** alternate days 1900, 12 hrs, US$22.50 (US$10.50); to **Cienfuegos** daily at 0710 (arrives 0900), US$2.50, 1120 (1230), US$2.50; to **Trinidad**, 1320, 3½ hrs, US$6; to **Varadero**, daily 0900 (arrives 1300), US$8; to **Matanzas**, 1210, 4 hrs, US$8; to **Sancti Spíritus**, 0825 and 1700, 2 hrs, US$3.50. To **Remedios**, 1435, 1 peso; to **Caibarién**, 1020, 1520, 1.50 pesos, or change at Remedios. Frequent delays, get numbered ticket then stay near departure gates until bus is ready and then join the scrum.

Car hire

Both economical and de luxe cars available, prices are seasonal, around US$45-65 a day for a small car. Mopeds US$15-20 a day. **Havanautos**, Av Eucaliptos y Carretera Central, T42-205895. **Micar**, Servicentro Oro Negro, Carretera Central y Calle San Miguel, T/F42-204570, US$35-75 including insurance. **Transtur**, Hotel Santa Clara, Parque Vidal, T42-218177, also at Maceo y Carretera Central and in the towns of Remedios, Caibarién and Sagua la Grande. **Veracuba**, Tristá y Amparo, T42-202020 /202040, cars, taxi, transfers.

Petrol stations **Servicentro Oro Negro**, Carretera Central y San Miguel, T42-204570, open 24 hrs daily, shop, fuel, repairs, payment in dollars. Also **Servicentro El Capiro**, Av Liberación, Santa Catalina, T42-204184, and **Servicentro Las Villas**, Carretera Central y Maceo, T42-208879, offering the same services.

Taxi

The best taxi company is **Cubataxi**, T42-202691/206903, good drivers, reasonable prices, about US$60 for a whole day's tour to the **cays** and **Remedios**.

Bicitaxi costs US$1 to most places in town, fix a price beforehand or they will overcharge you. We have received numerous complaints about charming drivers who rip you off. Apparently it is illegal for them to take foreigners, so you might like to take down his ID registration number (on the back) if there are any problems.

Train

The Martha Abreu railway station is north of Parque Vidal on Estévez at Parque Mártires, and is much more central than either of the bus stations. It is a very impressive station with a shady square outside, the usual bust of Martí and a monument to martyrs that looks like a stone totem pole which someone has taken a bite out of where it has eroded at the top. The ticket office (and a Post Office) is across the square, T42-202895-6. Reservations T42-200854. There are daily trains to **Havana** and to **Santiago**; the *especial* stops here every other day, arriving at 2155 and heading east at 2205 (to **Camagüey** US$19 1st class, US$15 2nd class, to **Santiago** US$41 1st, US$33 second, 9 hrs), and then the next day coming back at 0155 and heading west at 0205 (to **Havana** US$21 1st class, US$17 2nd class, 4 hrs). There are trains to **Bayamo** (9½ hrs), **Camagüey** (3¼ hrs), **Sancti Spíritus**

⦿ Directory

Banks
Banco Financiero Internacional, Cuba 6 entre Tristá y E Machado, just down from Parque Vidal, T42-207450, F42-218115, open Mon-Fri 0800-1500, but closes at 1200 on the last working day of the month, also Visa and MasterCard. **Bandec**, Vidal esq Cuba, Visa, MasterCard, Cabal, Red, Tran$card, Mon-Fri 0800-1500. The **Cadeca** office for changing currency and TCs (4% commission) is at Parque Vidal, Rafael Tristá esq Cuba, T42-205690, Mon-Sat 0830-1800, Sun 0830-1200. **Western Union** branches at La Riviera, opposite the bus station, Carretera Central, Bda Esperanza, T42-218166, and at Tienda Praga, Independencia y Máximo Gómez, T42-209134, open Mon-Fri 1000-1200, 1300-1700, Sat 1000-1200.

Hospitals and clinics
The best hospital for foreigners is the **Arnaldo Milián Castro Hospital**, referred to as Hospital Nuevo, at Circunvalación and Av 26 de Julio in the Reparto Escambray area to the southeast of the town, T42-272016 /271234. **Ambulance**: T42-202259.

Internet
There are several places on Martha Abreu for internet access, prices vary. No printing service is offered anywhere. At **Cubatur** (see Tour operators) it costs US$6 for 3 hrs; at the **Palmares** snack bar next door US$5 for 1 hr, 0900-1800, at **CITMA** (CIGET) half a block away on Martha Abreu 55 entre Villuendas y J B Zayas it is US$0.10 for 1 min. **Salón Juvenil** (Cubanacán/Palmares), Marta Abreu 10 entre Máximo Gómez y Villuendas, T42-200974, Mon-Fri 0900-2300, Sat and Sun 0930-2400. Cafeteria, drinks, cocktails, cybercafé (US$1.25 for 15 mins). See also Etecsa, below.

Pharmacy
Farmacia Campa, Independencia y Luís Estévez, T42-201643, 24 hrs, 0800-2200

sales of medicine to the public, after 2200 only official prescriptions. There is a pharmacy at Luis Estévez 8 on the corner with Boulevard, T42-281643, daily 0900-1900. Another pharmacy is in **Hotel Santa Clara Libre**, 2nd floor, T42-207548 ext 220, selling medicines, cosmetics and other health products.

Places of worship
For Catholic Churches see Santa Clara, p228 above. Baptist Church **La Trinidad**, R Tristá esq JB Zayas, T42-203861, a neoclassical church built at the end of the 19th century and recently restored, Sunday school and worship 0800-1200, worship 2030. **Seventh Day Adventist Church**, JB Zayas 8 entre Marta Abreu y Santa Bárbara, services Wed, Fri, Sun 2000, Sat 0900. **Los Pinos Nuevos**, Paseo de la Paz 61, T42-214095. Methodist Church, Villuendas 152, T42-204352.

Post office
Colón 10 entre Parque y E Machado, T42-202203, just off Parque Vidal, opposite Coppelia ice cream parlour, Mon-Sat 0800-2200, email service with prepaid cards, US$4.50 for 3 hrs. **DHL**, at Telecorreos, Cuba 7 entre Tristá y E Machado, T42-214069, for courier service, Mon-Fri 0800-1600, international express documents up to 0.05 kg US$25-30, parcels up to 0.5 kg US$39-49.

Telephone
Etecsa has a *cabina* on Cuba esq Machado (San Cristóbal), T/F42-217898, daily 0900-2100. For domestic, foreign calls, fax (42-204050), internet access US$0.10 per min.

Useful addresses
Immigration There is an immigration office for visa extensions on Sexta 9, entre Carretera Central y Av Sandino, T42-212523. English spoken, but patience required, Mon-Fri 0900-1630, Sat 0800-1200.
Police The Police Station is on Colón entre Serafín García (Nazareno) y Morales (Síndico), near Parque Vidal, T116. **Services** There is a public toilet at the corner of Luis Estévez y Boulevard in Parque de las Arcadas, small charge for admission.

Remedios and the north coast

The province of Villa Clara has plenty of lesser known attractions to offer including the delightful colonial town of Remedios, famous for its Christmas-time festival but a pleasant place to visit at any time of year. Off the main tourist drag, it is a fine example of an unspoilt provincial town, where foreigners are welcomed but not hassled. Its museums, churches and galleries are well cared for and worth visiting. Caibarién, an old fishing town on the coast, has fewer charms but work is being done to restore its old buildings to their former glory. The northern coast is low lying and there are mangroves and swamps, but it is fringed with coral cays with sandy beaches and crystal clear water in the Archipiélago de Sabana. Some of the cays are being developed as a major new beach resort, while the most northwesterly point of the province is an established health spa.▸▸ For Sleeping, Eating and other listings, see pages 246-248.

Ins and outs

Getting there There are domestic **flights** to the Abel Santamaría international airport north of Santa Clara from Havana and Varadero and international charters from Canada with **Air Transat, Sky Service** and **Air Canada** in high season. It is 116 km from the airport to Cayo Santa María, the furthest resort. On the cays, an airstrip receives short-hop flights and air taxis. **Train** services are slow (2 hrs) and designed for local people to get to work in Santa Clara, rather than for tourist excursions. If you are travelling by **car**, a good road leads northeast from Santa Clara through Camajuaní to Remedios and Caibarién, from where a stone causeway has been built to link several cays. The causeway is a toll road. There are a few **buses** from Santa Clara to the towns, but none to the cays.

Getting around Hiring a car or a taxi is the best way of touring the region as public transport is intermittent and unreliable. In any case, there is no other way of visiting the cays except on an organized tour.

Best time to visit The driest time of year is from December to April, so if you are thinking of sitting on the beach this is the ideal time. There are fascinating and enjoyable festivities in the week running up to Christmas Eve in both Remedios and Caibarién.

San Juan de Remedios → *Colour map 2, grid B4.*

The colonial town of San Juan de Remedios is 43 km northeast of Santa Clara. Remedios was the eighth *villa* founded by the Spaniards, around 1513-15, by Vasco Porcallo de Figueroa and for 160 years it was the main settlement in the area. It was never given the status of one of the original *villas* because Porcallo de Figueroa refused to allow the construction of a city hall. Its location was changed a couple of times, however, in 1544 and 1578, and when pirate attacks and other commercial incentives encouraged some of the inhabitants to move inland to Santa Clara, it began to decline. Not long after the founding of Santa Clara, a fire in 1692 hastened this trend. The present town was built following the fire and there are many beautiful colonial buildings, particularly around the pleasant Plaza Martí, which has some Royal palms and a gazebo in the centre.

Sights

This is the only town in Cuba where there are two churches on the plaza. **Iglesia Buen Viaje** is in a poor state and leaking, so it is unused and awaiting funds for renovation. The **Iglesia San Juan Bautista de Remedios** was built in 1692 on the remains of a 1570 church, making it one of the oldest churches in Cuba. It was renovated in 1944-53 by

an American millionaire who traced his family roots to Santa Clara. He discovered that
one of his ancestors had been a founding member of the town and therefore must
have come from Remedios, where he found birth records in the church. He spent
US$1 million renovating the roof and walls and altar, taking off a false ceiling and
whitewash on the beams to reveal gloriously painted and carved beams. The altar is
cedar and was covered in gold leaf, but it shone so much you couldn't see the detail,
so some of it is now painted over to give more definition and contrast. Buried in the
church are Juan de Loyola (parish priest 1685-1775) and 17 of his relations. If the doors
are shut, go round to the back of the church where you will probably find the church
warden, Esteban Granda Fernández (born 1922), who sits and waits for visitors. He
knows all there is to know about the church and the town and is a fascinating guide.
He likes to recount (in Spanish) that he has spent all his life with this church and if he
didn't love women so much he would have been a priest. Donations requested for the
upkeep and further renovation of the church.

Also on the square is the **Museo de Música Alejandro García Caturla** ① *Mon-Sat
0900-1200, 1300-1700, Sun 0900-1300, 50 centavos*. García Caturla was born in
1906 and in the 1920s he studied both music and civil law at the university of Havana.
He formed the jazz band *Caribe* with a group of students but he was strongly
influenced by the Grupo Minorista which contributed to bringing the African influence
into Cuban mainstream music. He met the writer, Alejo Carpentier, and under his
protection he went to Paris where he continued his cultural education by going to the
Ballet Russes and the *Folies Bergères*. On his return to Cuba he created the *Orquesta
de Conciertos de Caibarién*, which gave its first concert in 1932. His music then took a
back seat and he concentrated on law, rising through the ranks of the local judiciary,
but he was murdered in 1940, aged 34, shot by an unknown assassin allegedly for
upsetting the local social order by working with the poor. The museum has copies of
newspaper articles about his death, including one by Nicolás Guillén, the poet.

There is also an interesting **Museo de Parrandas** (festival museum) ① *walk past
the Hotel Mascotte down Máximo Gómez away from the plaza, the museum is one
block on the right, Tue-Sat 0900-1200 and 1300-1700, Sun 0900-1300, US$1,* which
should not be missed. Two sections of the town compete against each other in games
and festivities in the week leading up to 24 December, with the winning district being
the one to make most noise, although no one really wins. The event originated with
the local priest telling children to wake everyone in the town for midnight mass by
making as much noise as possible and it soon became a tradition. The mayor
complained to Spain about the 'music from hell' and asked for it to be banned, but
the *parrandas* continued and developed into what they are today. The two districts,
named Carmen and San Salvador, prepare long in advance, building towers in secret,
which have a different theme each year and are transported and erected at the
corners of the plaza. There is music, based on the *polka*, which varies slightly
between Carmen and San Salvador, fireworks and floats. However, in contrast to
carnival elsewhere, the people on the floats do not dance, in fact they do not even
move, they are there simply as a tableau. An informative guide will explain all about
the *parrandas* in English or Spanish, starting with a model and map of the city
showing how the festival boundaries have changed over the years from eight groups
to two, Carmen and San Salvador. There are replicas of several towers constructed
during the 20th century, photos, costumes, musical instruments and mascots.

Museo del Vapor

① *Reforma* village, 400 m on the left of the road from Remedios to Caibarién,
T42-363586, Mon-Sat 0800-1700, US$2.

Many redundant sugar mills in the country are now being converted into museums
and this is one of them, in the old Central Marcelo Salado. The museum is dedicated

to the history of the sugar industry in Cuba with an exhibition area made up of all the different installations of a sugar mill, its tools, machinery and boiling rooms. There are several working steam engines, a video room and a tour of the nearby **Rum Museum** (US$2). If a group of visitors can be got together, they will pick you up in Remedios or Caibarién and put you on an open-sided railway carriage to take you by steam train one hour through the countryside to the museum so that you can see the surrounding area. The train stops at the **Finca Curujey** restaurant, see below.

Caibarién and around → *Colour map 2, grid B5.*

The town's full name is Cayo Barién, but it is always referred to as Caibarién. It is a fishing town and the main port for the province. There is a dirty beach on the edge of town, although beach tourism for foreigners is now being directed offshore to the cays. Founded in 1832, Caibarién, a small town, with distinctive 19th-century architecture, has become rundown and scruffy in parts. Many buildings have fine wooden porches with a French influence, and some are quite grand, although there is an atmosphere of the Wild West, emphasized by the number of horses in town. Bicycles and horse-drawn buses are everywhere. The pavements, unusual in Cuba, are made of large stone slabs set in concrete. Caibarién is as yet untouched by tourism and the visitor can wander around unmolested by hustlers. The Malecón is lined with numerous warehouses used for storing sugar cane in the 19th century, most of which are now in ruins. Recent investment in the seaside boulevard has led to the construction of a new Malecón to the fishing zone in the east with a new road, coconut palms and several bars and cafés where you can sit and admire the view. At the centre of the town there is a large square, with an 1850 church and the impressive neoclassical Lyceo (1926), where the **Museo Polivalente María Escobar Laredo** ① *Parque Central, 2nd floor, Tue-Sat 1000-1800, Sun 0900-1300, free*, has recently opened. There are permanent and temporary exhibitions as well as the furniture belonging to María Escobar Laredo, who was one of the benefactors for the city. The gazebo in the centre of the plaza was built in 1915, the largest in Cuba and famous for its excellent acoustics. There are concerts by local bands on Thursday and Sunday nights. Also on the plaza is a shop, now a Panamerican store, which was, during the first decade of the 20th century, a bespoke tailor's called **London City**.

There is a legend that says recently transported slaves who escaped from their masters in Santa Clara fled northwards towards the coast, believing that they were still in Africa but had merely been shipped along the coast of their continent. Upon reaching Caibarién, they despaired to find that they could not go any further, and reluctantly settled there. Much of the local culture is influenced by slavery and African traditions. Like Remedios, Caibarién also has its *parrandas*. Christmas Eve is a non-religious celebration, inaugurated in 1892 with the banging of a drum by a 110-year-old former slave called Juan de Jimagua. The public then followed him plus many other conga players around the town, a tradition still maintained today. The members of each *barrio* build an artistic creation on the plaza, based on local legends and folklore; they are ostensibly judged, but this is usually just a friendly, heated discussion of which is the best creation.

The cays

The nearest cay to Caibarién is **Cayo Conuco**, accessible by ordinary road (not the new causeway) just offshore. This is a biosphere reserve with lots of flora and fauna, and a campsite. Take insect repellent. There are the ruins of a former cholera hospital, built by the slaves in the 19th century to quarantine victims of the disease.

Extensive development is under way on the coast, with several new hotels being built or renovated. Entirely funded by Cuban money, this project is said to be of particular interest to Fidel Castro. He used to fish here when he was younger and for many years he kept it undeveloped. A 48-km stone causeway, from Caibarién to the three cays off the north coast, was completed in 1996 having taken seven years to build. There are plans to extend it to Cayo Guillermo. If driving from Santa Clara, when you reach Caibarién turn right at the statue of a huge crab at the entrance to the town and then right at the next junction, avoiding the town centre. Carry on to a bridge, go under it and turn right in order to go over the bridge and effectively turn left. There are signs. There is a toll booth (*peaje*) at the start of the causeway, US$2 cars, US$4 RVs, for admission. Passports are checked. Beware of unscrupulous officials charging you twice; the toll fee applies to a return journey. The road takes you through mangroves and open water and it is an impressive drive. If you want a few days of peace and quiet on unspoilt beaches then the cays are perfect, but they are remote and you need to be aware that there are no facilities outside the current two hotels, one small and the other huge and all-inclusive.

Driving along the new causeway, the first (undeveloped) cay is **Cayo Herradura**, so named because it is in the shape of a horseshoe, part of a group of islands known as Cayos de la Herradura. At bridge 36 is the airport at **Cayo Las Brujas**, the first of the cays to be developed for tourism. The airstrip is used for day trips from other parts of the country. There is a small hotel, **Villa Las Brujas**, on the cay, pleasant restaurant and bar, open to non-guests, and with a wooden observation deck up on the rocks overlooking the beach and the sea. You can visit the hotel for the day (providing you buy lunch; hamburgers US$4), and have use of their facilities, including the hotel beach; this a recommended way to experience the cays. Watch out for biting insects at dawn and dusk. **Scuba diving** trips can be arranged for around US$30 and there are other trips which leave from the jetty, eg to San Pascual, a moored American cargo ship built in 1920 which only sailed once and has been here since 1933. It was once used as a molasses warehouse and there are still barrels of molasses (*miel*) in it, being used as ballast. There are murals by the famous Cuban artist Leopoldo Romañach. Both he and Ernest Hemingway stayed here. After bridge 42 look out for a sign, 1 km to beach. The track is in poor condition and after rain parts of it flood, but it is worth the effort. Look out for iguanas. The beach, **Playa Ensenachos**, is deliberately being left wild and there are no hotels or facilities, just several stretches of perfect soft sand between rocks, sea grapes and mangroves.

The last and largest cay, **Cayo Santa María**, is under major development. One new, luxury hotel has been built and another is soon to be inaugurated (Gaviota). The beach here is long, sandy, wild and unspoilt, but it does get rough at certain times of the year. The sea is calmest from June to August, it can be rough after then if there is a cold front off the eastern seaboard of the USA, and then in January and February the waves can be huge. Go to Playa Ensenachos if it's too rough for you, the beach there faces a different direction and is quieter. The new hotel, **Cayo Santa María**, has 760 m of beach, but you can walk much further.

Camajuaní

The road from Santa Clara to the cays and the coast leads first to Camajuaní, a typical 19th-century town stretching along the main street of Independencia. All the houses in Camajuaní have columns and verandas and an extremely grand railway station evokes a prosperous past. There is a **Rumbos** bar on the main street if you need to stop for refreshment.

Baños de Elguea

In the extreme west of the province, 136 km from Santa Clara, is Baños de Elguea ⓘ *Circuito Norte, Corralillo, Villa Clara, T42-686298, F42-208072, elguea @esivic.cu for further details, see also Sleeping, below.* The Elguea *balneario* is a hotel and health resort with sulphur springs which are used to treat arthritis, rheumatism, skin diseases and tourists in need of pampering. The waters healing properties were discovered accidentally when a slave of the Elguea family was freed. He had a skin disorder and it was feared he might contaminate the rest of the slaves. He was later found to be cured after he had frequently bathed in the springs. A small hotel was then built to exploit the waters' beneficial properties, now replaced by the hotel and spa. Thermal waters are different temperatures (average 45°C) and there are medicinal muds for a variety of complaints including stress and obesity. Qualified medical assistance is available, along with masseurs for general pampering. If you stay more than five days it's US$35 a night including all food and treatments. The health centre is open 0730-1600. Prices range from US$5 for a full body mud wrap to US$8 for a sauna to US$12 for a full body massage. The mud bath (US$10) is recommended as is immersion in a thermal bath with high-powered Jacuzzi (US$10) – absolute heaven. The hotel organizes excursions into the nearby Bay of Cádiz, US$45 per person (if there are two people), which includes lunch. To say that the hotel is remote is understated. The transport situation is a nightmare and if you don't have your own transport, which is very wise, make sure you arrange it in and out with security. There can be a few mosquitoes at night but not enough to affect your stay.

There are beaches at **El Salto** and **Ganuza**, nearby, where there are no hotels but you can find accommodation at local resorts and at local *campismo* resorts, if there is space for non-Cubans. The hotel at Baños de Elguea offers excursions here for US$3 per person. Hiring a car in Santa Clara is a good idea and you will need a good road map.

● Sleeping

San Juan de Remedios p242
Hotels
C-D **Mascotte**, Máximo Gómez 112, T42-395144. 10 lovely rooms in restored mansion, those in front overlook the square, those at the back look over old tiled roofs, new bathrooms, basin in room, a/c, cable TV, radio, bar, restaurant, charming patio used for entertainment, car rental.

Casas particulares
E **Jorge Rivero Méndez**, Brigadier González 29 entre Independencia y José A Peña, in front of the old Post Office, T42-395331. Room with twin beds, bathroom, a/c, hot water, parking, beautifully restored house.
F **Alberto Pelato Alfonso**, Av Heriberto Duquesne 9 entre Céspedes y Morales Lemos, T42-395102. At entrance to town, opposite the police station. 1 room, a/c, ceiling fan, private bathroom.
F **Gladys Aponte Rojas**, Brigadier González 32 altos entre Independencia y Pi Morgal, T42-395398. Central, close to main square. 2 rooms, 1 double, 1 triple, 1 bathroom, no a/c.
F **Hospedaje San Carlos**, José A Peña 75C entre Maceo y La Pastora, T42-395624. A modern house run by Annia González with 2 comfortable double bedrooms upstairs, shared bathroom, hot water, a/c, fan, fridge with mini bar, central, some English spoken, clean, laundry service, breakfast and dinner offered. Car parking.
F **La Casona Cueto**, Alejandro del Río 72 entre Enrique Mararé y Máximo Gómez, T42-395350. Colonial house from the 18th century with its original façade, floors and roof, beautiful interior windows and curved wooden staircase leading to a room upstairs, as well as medallions symbolizing the Soles y Rayos de Bolívar conspiracy. Renny Cueto has 2 large rooms with double bed, shared bathroom, hot water, windows onto the street, fan, interior patio with fountain, 2 dogs, doves and turtles. Breakfast and dinner offered, safe car parking.

Caibarién p244
Hotels
Accommodation is hard to find when Cubans are on holiday in the summer.
F **Brisas del Mar**, Reparto Marazal, T42-364212. Very rundown on small beach away from centre but with lovely sea views, mostly Cuban guests (who pay in pesos), intermittent water, no toilet seats, restaurant, bar.

Casas particulares
There are many families offering rooms in their houses; touts will find you when you get off the bus or stop you as you drive into town.

F **Casa Jorge**, Av 7 1815 entre 18 y 20, T42-364277. A modern house run by Jorge F Amador, upstairs, 2 rooms with shared bathroom, hot water, a/c, fan, seafood and typical Cuban food.

F **Casa Virginia**, Ciudad Pesquera 73, T42-363303. Run by Osmani and Virginia, he is a fisherman and can lend you snorkelling gear, she is very kind and chatty. Private downstairs area for guests, 2 rooms with private bathroom, hot water, fridge, a/c, fan, TV, terrace with hammock and plants, independent entrance. Very good food, seafood a speciality.

F **Casa Yayo**, Av 35 10-16B entre 10 y 12, T42-364253. 50 m from the sea with sea view, terrace on the 3rd floor, 2 rooms with private bathroom, hot water, fridge, a/c, fan, parking, breakfast and dinner offered. Run by Eladio Herrada Bernabeo, the house is in an area where fishermen live.

F **Julio Gómez González**, Bloque 21 Apto 13, Reparto Van Troi, T42-363113. Nice apartment and helpful owners.

The cays *p244*
Hotels
LL-AL **Sol Cayo Santa María** (Gaviota), T42-351500, www.solcayosantamaria. solmelia.com All-inclusive, 300 rooms, of which 11 superior with hydro-massage, 2 suites, 3 for wheelchair users, connecting rooms for families in 2-room bungalows, TV, fridge, phone, lots of bathroom goodies, hair dryer, safe, balcony with great view of sea for about half the rooms, others have partial view or look south over mangroves. 3 pools, gym, sauna, tennis, kids' club, piano bar, disco, several restaurants, diving, sailing, windsurfing, waterbikes, all non-motorized watersports included, fishing and massage at extra cost.

B **Villa Las Brujas** (Gaviota), Cayo Las Brujas, T42-204199, F42-207599. A small complex of 24 good-quality red-roofed *cabañas* (19 have sea view) connected by wooden boardwalk above rocks and between mature bushes, all with colour TV, a/c, sea views, balconies and verandas on stilts, quiet and peaceful, access to a good sweep of curving beach, soft, pale sand, a few umbrellas and hire of watersports. Restaurant with open air or a/c seating and view down to the beach. Car hire and tours arranged, **Cubatur** on site.

D-E **Baños de Elguea**, Circuito Norte, Corralillo, Villa Clara, T42- 686298, elguea@esivic.cu

● Eating

San Juan de Remedios *p242*
Restaurants
$$-$ **Curujey** (Cubanacán-Minaz), 1 km from the steam museum. Tour parties are taken here. Rural location, farm surroundings, large grove of trees, turkeys, chickens and you can watch them milking the cows.

$$-$ **El Louvre** (Rumbos), overlooking the square, T42-395639, daily 0700-0200. Said to be the oldest restaurant in Cuba, colonial building with wooden bar and counter, tables inside and out, snacks and drinks, nice place to stop for lunch and watch the school children on their break. Snacks from around US$5, steak and main meals US$8-10.

$ **Di Tú** (Palmares), Máximo Gómez 098C, Mon-Fri 1000-2400, Sat and Sun 1000-0200. Light meals and drinks.

Caibarién *p244*
Food can be bought in the **Panamerican** store on the plaza; there is a bakery nearby.

$ **Pizzería al Mare**, Calle 8 entre 5 y 7, daily 0900-1500, 1520-2120. Eat inside or out for people watching. The food is not good, but you can pay in pesos. Street food and drinks sold outside on the corner at lunchtime.

$ **Rumbos**, Av 9 entre 18 y 20, T42-363305, on your left just as you come into town, turning left at the crab statue, open 24 hrs. The usual Rumbos fare with snacks and main meals.

$ **Saramar**, Calle 14 1502 entre 15 y 17, open 1100-2300. Good prices and excellent cooking at this *paladar*, can be paid in pesos or dollars, in which case prices start at US$5.

● Festivals and events

San Juan de Remedios *p242*
Dec Apart from its architecture, Remedios' other claim to fame is its carnivals, (*parrandas*), held on 16-24 Dec; the best night being 24 Dec, when celebrations go on until dawn.

Caibarién *p244*
Last weekend in Aug Carnival.
Oct Caibarién has a new annual fiesta, dating from 1999, celebrating the founding

of the town on 26 Oct.

Dec Like Remedios, Caibarién also has *parrandas* at the same time.

▲▲ Activities and tours

Havanatur, Av 9 entre 8 y 10, on plaza next to the Liceo, Caibarién, T42-351171, Mon-Fri 0830-1200 and 1330-1630, Sat 0830-1200. **Rumbos**, Av 9 entre 18 y 20, Caibarién, T42-363305. Located in 24-hr Cafetería La Parrillada, but open office hours.

⊙ Transport

Air
Cayo Las Brujas airport has flights to **Havana**, **Santiago** and **Varadero**. International flights use the airport north of Santa Clara.

Bus
The San Juan de Remedios bus station is at the entrance to the town on the right coming from Santa Clara, T42-395185. Taxis and *bicitaxis* wait outside. The Caibarién bus terminal, Calle 1 entre 6 y 8, has regular buses to **Santa Clara** at 0430, 0820, 1400, 1 hr. To **Remedios** at 0605 and 1630. *Carros particulares* (private cars) can be found for trips to other destinations. Fares are all in pesos, get a numbered ticket when you arrive at the terminal, seats are sold only when the bus arrives. If going to **Santa Clara**, many private cars will take you from outside the terminal for about US$2-3 per person. There is no public transport out to the cays, soyou have to arrange car hire or pick up an official taxi.

Car hire
Transgaviota, 24 esq 29, Caibarién, T42-35153.

Train
There is a (*ferroviario*) slow train from **Caibarién** via **Remedios** to **Santa Clara**, departing at 0421, arriving 0650, returning 1735, so no use for a day trip from Santa Clara. US$1.90 from Caibarién, US$1.65 from Remedios.

❶ Directory

Banks One on Av 11 entre 4 y 6, Caibarién, with an ATM machine. Another at Av 9 entre 6 y 8, Caibarién. **Western Union**, T42-364440, Mon-Fri 1000-1200 and 1300-1700, Sat 1000-1200. **Post office** Calle 10 entre 11 y 13, Caibarién, T42-363208, daily 0800-1200 and 1400-1800. Card phones on the main plaza. **Useful addresses** Immigration: Av 7 entre 6 y 8, Caibarién, open 0800-1200, 1300-1500.

Sancti Spíritus → *Colour map 2, grid B4. Population: 80,000.*

Sancti Spíritus, the provincial capital, is one of Cuba's seven original Spanish towns and has a wealth of buildings from the colonial period, although many of them have been altered and there has been lots of new building. Tourism is now being developed around the town. Hotels have been renovated and remodelled, Rumbos *has developed a large tourist restaurant on the river and* Havanatur *and* Havanautos *have opened an office on the Plaza. So far foreign tourists get little unwanted attention. The local people are friendly and helpful when approached, but are generally indifferent to foreigners.*

» *For Sleeping, Eating and other listings, see pages 252-253.*

Ins and outs
Getting there There are no scheduled **flights** to the airport north of town. Main line **trains** from Havana to Santiago stop here. The train station is 15 km away at Guayos, but you will be met by **taxis**, both state-owned and private. The former cost US$10 into town, the latter can be negotiated. About 80 km northeast of Trinidad and 90 km southeast of Santa Clara, the town can be reached by road from Cienfuegos, Santa Clara or Trinidad. Long-distance **buses** come to Sancti Spíritus from both ends of the island, but the bus station is 2 km from the centre, so if you are not up to walking with your luggage you will have to get a taxi. » *For further details, see Transport, page 253.*

Getting around The old city can be toured **on foot** without much difficulty. For excursions by **car** ask at a *casa particular* for a private driver, or find one outside the bus station and negotiate a price. Trinidad can be visited as a day trip by bus or car, but it is better to stay in Trinidad and visit Sancti Spíritus as a day trip.

Tourist information There is no tourist office in Sancti Spíritus, but the office of **Havanatur** on the square can provide information.

History

The town was founded by Diego Velázquez in 1514. Originally situated on the Río Tuinicúe, it was moved to its present location on the Río Yayabo in 1522 and was sacked by pirates in 1665. The town grew as sugar and livestock became important and its geographical position made it an excellent agricultural market town. In the San Luis valley, or Valle de los Ingenios (Valley of the Sugar Mills), between Trinidad and Sancti Spíritus, are many ruined sugar mills, plantation houses and slave quarters, including Manaca Iznaga (see page 260). There are many sites commemorating those who fought in the 19th-century wars of independence, the local hero being Major General Serafín Sánchez Valdivia. At the end of the Cuban Revolution in 1958, rebel forces were led into the city under the command of Armando Acosta Cordero and Sancti Spíritus was liberated on 23 December. Fidel Castro arrived on 6 January 1959 and spoke from the balcony of the library. With the administrative changes in 1976, Sancti Spíritus became the capital of the new province of Sancti Spíritus.

Sights

City centre

Parque Serafín Sánchez is the centre of activity in the city where all major roads converge. Around the square are the cinema, library, banks, Havanatur/ Havanautos and the beautiful baby blue *Hostal del Rijo*, renovated to its colonial splendour. Just to the east of the square is the **Museo Provincial de Sancti Spíritus** ① *Céspedes 11 Sur entre Ernesto V Muñoz y Av de los Mártires, T41-27435, Tue-Sun 0900-1700, US$1.* Here you have the usual exhibits on local history and culture in a building that dates from 1740. There are collections of Amerindian artefacts, items from the colonization and African slavery, the wars of independence and the Revolution plus coins and decorative arts.

Just north of the square **El Lyceo/Sociedad Cultural de Negros** was the first school for blacks, opened in 1859. It is behind **Hostal del Rijo** and is now a society for veterans of the Revolution.

The **Galería de Arte Universal Oscar Fernández Morera** is in the house of the local artist Oscar Fernández Morera on Céspedes 126 Sur, whose works are on permanent display. There are exhibits of originals as well as reproductions.

On Plaza Honorato, south of Parque Serafín Sánchez, the **Iglesia Parroquial Mayor del Espíritu Santo** ① *Jesús Menéndez 1 entre Honorato y Agramonte, Tue-Sat 0900-1100, 1400-1700,* dates from 1522 when it was a wooden construction. The present Romanesque and baroque building made of stone, replaced the earlier one, but it is acknowledged as the second oldest church in Cuba because it still stands on its original foundations. It was finished in 1680, having taken 60 years to build. The church has been declared a National Monument. Fray Bartolomé de las Casas gave a famous sermon here, marking the start of his campaign to help the indigenous people. He was a Dominican missionary and polemist, who devoted his life to the cause of Amerindian liberty. He spent many years on Hispaniola (now the Dominican Republic and Haití), where he wrote the *Brief Relation of the Destruction of the Indies*, a horrifying catalogue of atrocities that took place at the time. He was appointed Protector of the Indians in 1516 and spent the next 10 years trying to prove that free Amerindians could be converted to Christianity without use of force or enslavement. However, the experiment came too late for the Amerindians of the Greater Antilles, as the Spanish could not do without slave labour and the Amerindians would not work without coercion.

The **Museo de Arte Colonial** ⓘ *Calle Plácido 74 Sur entre Guairo y Pancho Jiménez, T41-25455, Tue-Sat 0830-1700, Sun 0800-1200, US$2, guided tour US$3, photos US$1*, is housed in the former palace of the Iznaga family, who made their fortune out of sugar and were hugely influential with links to the military and bureaucracy of the province. Built in 1750, the house has 100 doors. It contains collections of porcelain from France, England, Germany and Spain, oil paintings and decorative fans, and in the music room there is one of the oldest pianos in Cuba.

East of the church, a cultural institute is being established in the newly renovated 1926 building, **Colonia Española**, on Independencia Sur esquina Agramonte. It is a fine building in the eclectic style with neoclassical ceilings and CE on the windows, once a cultural centre for the high society.

Sancti Spíritus

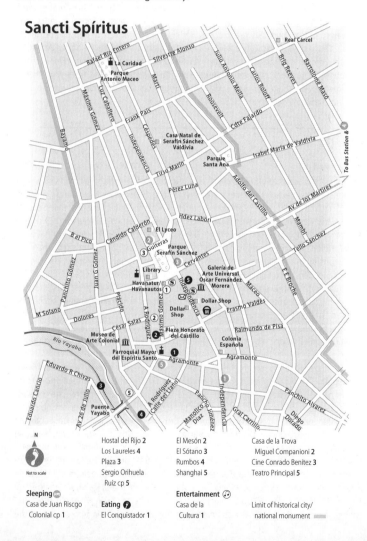

Sleeping 🛏		
Casa de Juan Riscgo Colonial cp **1**	**Eating** 🍴	El Conquistador **1**
Hostal del Rijo **2**	El Mesón **2**	Casa de la Trova Miguel Companioni **2**
Los Laureles **4**	El Sótano **3**	Cine Conrado Benítez **3**
Plaza **3**	Rumbos **4**	Teatro Principal **5**
Sergio Orihuela Ruíz cp **5**	Shanghai **5**	
	Entertainment 🎭	
	Casa de la Cultura **1**	Limit of historical city/ national monument ▬

The **Puente Yayabo** is considered a particular feature of Sancti Spíritus and is the only one of its type left on the island. The bridge was inaugurated on 12 June 1825 with five arches made of lime, sand and bricks. It is now also a National Monument and is the only one of its type left in the country. The river itself has given its name to the *guayaba*, or guava, which grows along its banks, and also to the *guayabera*, a loose man's shirt without a tail, worn outside the trousers and without a tie.

The former **Teatro Principal** next to the bridge was built in 1839 and was the scene of all the major cultural, social and political events of the city. **Calle Llano** is a twisty street, with cobblestones right to the edge of the Yayabo River.

North of the centre

Walk up Céspedes and you will pass the **Casa Natal de Serafín Sánchez Valdivia** ① *Céspedes 112 Norte, entre Sobral y San Cristóbal, T41-27791*. Sánchez Valdivia was born here on 2 July 1846, going on to fight in three wars in the 19th century. He collaborated with José Martí and reached the rank of Major General before being killed in battle in 1896. **Parque Antonio Maceo**, on which stands the **Iglesia de la Caridad**, was the place where the Communist Party of Sancti Spíritus was founded on 7 December 1930. If you head east along Frank País out of the historic centre, you will come to the old prison, **Real Cárcel** (Royal Prison) ① *Bartolomé Masó entre Anglona y Mirto*. The building has been preserved as a site of historical interest. It was built in the mid-19th century and used initially to incarcerate runaway slaves and then to imprison hundreds of Cubans who fought for independence.

Around Sancti Spíritus

Many of the excursions included in the Trinidad section, page 254, can also be done from here, particularly the Valley of the Sugar Mills, which lies between the two towns. ▶▶ *See Activities and tours, page 267, for excursions around Trinidad.* The flatlands of the northern coast of the province rise to the Sierra de Meneses, and the flatlands of the southern coast rise in the west to the Montañas de Guamuhaya. Much of the province's economy depends on sugar cane and cattle, but there is some tobacco grown on the hills and rice in the low lying south. A lot of the southeast of the province is flat, with mangroves and wetlands along the coast, and this area contains the largest man-made reservoir in the country, **Embalse Zaza**, through which flows the Río Zaza, 144.7 km long. Embalse Zaza is a popular excursion for hiking, birdwatching, shooting and fishing, or just to go to the hotel (see page 252) and laze around the pool. The hotel can get busy at weekends. In September there is an annual international fishing tournament here.

For those with their own transport (or hired private car), you can tour the north coast, where there is a beach at **La Victoria**, a spa at **San José del Lago** and a cave system at **Cueva Grande de Judas**. **Mayajigua** is the main town in this area, founded in 1820, and reasonable for a break in the driving.

The road to Playa Victoria is virtually the only road to the north coast where there are mangroves and caves of the **Parque Nacional Caguanes**, a UNESCO Biosphere Reserve, see under National Parks, in Background. None of the park is over 25 m above sea level and it is notable for its caves, pictographs and underground treasures rather than its scenic beauty. **Lago Martí** in the park has fresh water sponges.

North of Mayajigua is **Punta de Judas** on a road which stops just short of the coast. Here there is the Cueva Grande de Judas, which is at the eastern side of the Parque Nacional Caguanes, where there are several caves: Cueva Grande, Cueva del Pirata, Cueva Humboldt and Cueva de los Chivos. There are archaeological sites in the caves and pictographs.

● Sleeping

City centre *p249, map p250*

Hotels

D-E Hostal del Rijo (Cubanacán), Honorato del Castillo 12 esq Máximo Gómez, T41-28588, damaris@hostalrijo.co.cu Built in 1818-27 the building has been converted from the ruins of the old family home of a doctor, Rudesindo García Rijo, facing onto the Parque. It is a typical example of colonial architecture with stained-glass windows, arches downstairs for shade and balconies with wrought iron fretwork upstairs, all painted in a variety of beautiful blues. An inner courtyard has a fountain, plants and dining tables outside, overlooked by the landing giving access to the 16 spacious (some bigger than others) and well-furnished rooms with wooden shutters at the windows, high ceilings, a/c, bathroom, safety box, minibar, radio, room service, TV, facilities for wheelchairs, restaurant, *cafetería*, snack bar, currency exchange, post office, internet/fax, laundry.

D-E Plaza (Islazul), Independencia 1, Plaza Serafín Sánchez, T41-27102, F41-22562. 29 rooms, CP, in an old colonial building, first built in 1854 but destroyed by fire in 1973 and subsequently restored and opened to the public in 1994. High-ceilinged rooms, refurbished in colonial style, some with balconies overlooking plaza, triples available, a/c, TV, bar, restaurant, car hire, internet access.

Casas particulares

Ask around in the Parque and in restaurants for other accommodation (mostly**E-F**).

E-F La Pantera, Independencia 50 entre Fajardo y Laborí, T41-25435. Beautiful colonial house built in 1806, lovely marble pillars and high ceilings. Rooms with private bathrooms, communicating doors if you want them, good food, friendly family. Pity about the posters on the walls of girls in provocative poses.

F Casa de Juan Riscgo, Independencia 56 entre Agramonte y Onorato. 2 rooms, good bathroom, fan, meals, convenient location.

F Ricardo Rodríguez, Independencia Norte 28. Local taxi driver, friendly, good price.

F Sergio Orihuela Ruíz, room in apartment, Agramonte 61, Apto 5 Altos entre Jesús Menéndez y Llano, CP 60 100, T41-23828. Opposite Iglesia Parroquial Mayor del Espíritu Santo, English spoken, meets most trains.

Around Sancti Spíritus *p251*

B-C Carrusel Rancho Hatuey (Cubanacán), 4 km north of town, 2 km from the airport, just off Carretera Central at Km 383, T41- 28315, F41-28350. Modern hotel with 78 double and 3 triple rooms in main building or in modern *cabaña*, pool, various meal plans, restaurant, bar, quiet, hunting for ducks and doves.

D-E Zaza (Islazul), T41-28512, hzaza@esiss .colombus.cu 10 km outside the town on the Zaza artificial lake, at Finca San José. 105 a/c (old and noisy) rather cramped rooms with balconies overlooking pool, phone, restaurant, bar, nightclub, games room, shop, car rental, medical services, tourism bureau, rather rundown but pleasant and good value, shooting and fishing can be arranged.

E Los Laureles (Islazul), T41-27016, F41-23913, Carretera Central Km 348, 5 km north of town. Set in nice gardens with mature trees, 48 rooms, in semi-detached a/c chalets with solar power, large pool with bar, loud music, almost exclusively Cuban guests, foreigners are stared at, extravagant Tropicana-style show and cabaret Sat nights, overpriced, restaurant staff unwelcoming, occasional buses into town, taxis difficult to organize, private taxi US$10, reasonably convenient for Guayos train station.

● Eating

City centre *p249, map p250*

Restaurants

$ El Conquistador, Agramonte 52 Ote, open until 2200, closed Mon. Delightful building, friendly staff, mainly Cuban dishes.

$ El Mesón, Máximo Gómez 34, on Plaza Honorato del Castillo, T41-28546, daily 1100-2300 if there are customers. In a building that was the first post office. *Criollo* food, probably the best restaurant in town, crowded at lunchtime, popular with tourists. Good seafood, or try *garbanzo* soup or *ropa vieja*.

$ Quinta Santa Elena, Padre Quintero entre Llano y Manolico Díaz, T41-29167, daily 0900-2400. Popular with tourists at lunchtime. Near the river and bridge in colonial house with patio garden, traditional Cuban food and music, show on Sat evening.

$ Saratoga, on the plaza. **Rumbos** café serving drinks and snacks, and a restaurant overlooking the river.

$ **Shanghai**, Independencia, just off the plaza. Chinese, mostly Cuban clientele. You may be able to pay in pesos.

Paladares

There are several *paladares* just across Puente Yayabo, then turn left or right. Try: $ **El Sótano**, Eduardo R Chivas 18C entre 26 de Julio y Jesús Menéndez, T41-25654, daily 1100-2400. Good peso *paladar*. One of the tables is on a balcony overlooking river (mosquitoes), ask in advance for vegetarian food, large portions, good food, nice family.

Street stalls also sell snacks including pizza, which are good value.

🎭 Entertainment

City centre *p249, map p250*
Cinemas

There are 3 cinemas on Parque Sánchez, 60 centavos for a film, 2 pesos for a video.

Live music

Most nightlife happens around the Parque. **Bar La Hermina**, over Puente Yayabo. A boat on the river and tables on the grass.
Bar La Quinta Helena, on the left just before Puente Yayabo. Large, pleasant terrace, garden, patio, live music and concerts.
Casa de la Cultura. For all things cultural. Holds ad hoc art exhibitions, poetry readings and live music. There is usually rock music on Sat night and irregular performances of more traditional *boleros* on other nights.
Casa de la Música, Padre Quintero 32, T41-24963. Open-air seating and a stage, terrace overlooking Río Yayabo, US$1, shows Fri and Sat nights.
Casa de la Trova Miguel Companioni, Máximo Gómez Sur 26. Live music.

🛍 Shopping

City centre *p249, map p250*
There are **dollar stores** on Independencia Sur and a peso **market** on Erasmo Valdés, good for meat, fruit and vegetables.
Fondo de Bienes Culturales, Independencia Sur 55. Art and handicrafts.
Librería Julio Antonio Mella, Independencia Sur 29. A reasonable bookshop; there is a second-hand bookshop nearby at Independencia Sur 25.

❓ Activities and tours

City centre *p249, map p250*
On the square, at Cervantes 1, are **Havanatur**, T41-28308, for flights and tours, **Havanautos**, T41-28403, for car hire, and **Islazul**, T41-26390, for hotels and tours.

🚍 Transport

Bus

Local Horse drawn buses for short journeys around town. **Long distance** The bus station is 2 km east of town on the Carretera Central. Walk out of town along Cervantes, follow signs to Ciego de Avila along Carretera Central, about 5 blocks past the zoo, the bus station is on your right. **Astro** buses to **Trinidad**, several daily, 70 km, 2 hrs, trucks are often used, crowded and uncomfortable; **Ciego de Avila** 2 daily, 75 km, 2 hrs; **Santa Clara** several daily, 86 km, 2 hrs; also long-distance **Víazul** or **Astro** buses on the **Havana** to **Santiago** or **Trinidad** to **Santiago** routes daily, but you may not get a seat.

Taxi

Local *Bicitaxis* will get you around town if you don't want a taxi. **Long distance** A private taxi (*particular*) will take you to **Trinidad** for US$25 or less, and to **Santa Clara** for around US$30, depending on the quality of your Spanish. Find a driver outside the bus station.

Train

Station at Guayos, 15 km north. Taxi into town US$10. Touts offer transport and accommodation. Daily trains to **Camagüey** 0900, 1510, 1930, 2-3 hrs, US$6.50. The *especial* to **Havana** at 2145, 9 hrs, US$14 and to **Santiago** at 2213, 8 hrs, US$22.

ℹ Directory

Banks Banco de Crédito, on the plaza, Mon-Fri 0800-1500. Cash advance on credit cards. **Cadeca**, Independencia 31, just off plaza, for TCs and currency exchange, Mon-Sat 0830-1800, Sun 0830-1230, commission on TCs is 3% weekdays and 4% at weekends. **Pharmacy** Independencia Sur at the southwestern corner of Parque Maceo. **Post office** Independencia Sur 8, south of Parque Serafín Sánchez.

Trinidad → *Colour map 2, grid B4. Population: 60,000.*

Trinidad, 133 km south of Santa Clara, is a perfect relic of the early days of the Spanish colony: beautifully preserved streets and buildings and hardly a trace of the 20th century anywhere. It was founded in 1514 by Diego Velázquez as a base for expeditions into the 'New World' and Hernan Cortés set out from here for Mexico in 1518. The five main squares and four churches date from the 18th and 19th centuries and the whole city, with its fine palaces, cobbled streets and tiled roofs, is a national monument. Architecturally, Trinidad is perhaps Cuba's most important town: its preserved and colourful colonial buildings are suspended in a time warp and since 1988 it has been a UNESCO World Heritage Site. Many of the families who live in the old houses rent out rooms and this is one of the best places to lodge privately. There is good hiking among picturesque waterfalls and abundant wildlife in the forests up in the mountains overlooking Trinidad. Playa Ancón, nearby, is a reasonable beach to relax on and a good base for boat trips and watersports.

▶▶ For Sleeping, Eating and other listings, see pages 262-268.

Ins and outs

Getting there There is a small airport which only receives charter **flights**. A taxi into the colonial centre will cost you a few dollars. Trinidad is not connected to the national **rail** network and there are only local and tourist services. The most convenient independent way of getting to Trinidad is by **Víazul bus** (see timetable, page 44), with services from Havana via Cienfuegos, or from Varadero via Santa Clara and Sancti Spíritus. There is also **Astro,** less comfortable buses from these towns and some trucks for those who like to rough it. Do not believe the taxi drivers who say there are no buses from Sancti Spíritus – there are, but they are irregular. Most visitors to Trinidad arrive on tour buses from Havana and Varadero and do a day trip, although it is possible to extend your stay and rejoin the bus a day or two later. The drive from Sancti Spíritus through the Valley of the Sugar Mills is very attractive.▶▶ *For further details see also Transport, page 267.*

Getting around The old city should be toured **on foot**. The cobbled streets make wheeled transport rather uncomfortable. All the main sites are within easy walking distance of each other. For local excursions many people hire a driver and **car**, although some prefer to **cycle** to the beach (fine on the way there, harder work on the way back), and organized tours are recommended for **hiking** in the mountains to avoid getting lost and to make sure you go to all the right places.

    Maps of Trinidad can be unbelievably difficult to follow because of the use of old and new street names. Locals of course switch from one to the other. The old ones have been painted over in white on the streets and are still legible. The new names are in black letters on white, often on the opposite side of the street.

Tourist information There is no tourist office, but information is freely available from the state tour operators: **Cubatur, Rumbos** and others (see Tour operators, below). However, they are concerned to sell their own tours, so for impartial advice and for how to get off the beaten track it is worth asking your hosts, if you are staying in a *casa particular*. They will know of private, usually illegal, taxi drivers and guides who can show you something a bit different from the organized tours.

Best time to visit September is good for religious processions around the 8th of the month, Cuba's patron saint's day, but at any time of year you can find music, dance and other festivities. Expect heavy rain between September and November, when the cobbled streets become torrents of rushing water, but in the mountains it can rain any day, turning paths into muddy, slippery slopes.

A thriving economy soon grew up around the settlement, originally based on livestock, exporting leather, meat and horses. This prize inevitably attracted the attention of adventurers and there was a particularly severe period of attacks between 1660 and 1688. Mansfield from Port Royal in Jamaica and Legrand from Tortuga, off Hispaniola, looted and set fire to the town, destroying the original archives of the church and the city hall. Unlike other populations who moved inland to escape pirate attacks, the inhabitants of Trinidad decided to stay and defend their wealth with their own fleet, inflicting several defeats on British and Dutch corsairs in the 17th and 18th centuries. After the British took Havana in 1797 they tried and failed to invade Trinidad and Sancti Spíritus, an event which is portrayed in the coats of arms of both cities.

After a time, sugar was introduced, most successfully, and by 1797 there were 56 sugar mills and 11,697 slaves imported to work in the sugar cane fields. Trade, the arts and sciences all expanded on the back of the sugar prosperity: Alexander von Humboldt visited and studied the fauna and flora around Trinidad; the first printing press was opened and the first newspaper began to circulate; schools of languages, music and dance were opened; a wide variety of artisans set up businesses, including gold and silversmithing; and in 1827 the Teatro Cándamo opened its doors. The well-off patricians built huge mansions for themselves (now museums) and sent their children to European universities. However, the Industrial Revolution and the increase in sugar beet grown in Europe sounded the death knell for an economy based on slave labour and in the second half of the 19th century Trinidad went into decline. Construction ceased and the city remained frozen in time with its cobbled streets and red-tiled roofs.

Sights

Plaza Mayor

The Plaza Mayor is the centre of the town, an elegantly adorned square with white wrought iron railings and ornate lamp posts in the middle shaded by a few towering Royal palms. Cobbled streets run round the outside and the occasional horse or ox and cart provide ideal photo opportunities in this picturesque spot. Some of the very few two-storey buildings can be found here, denoting the importance of the plaza and all are painted in pretty pastel colours with red-tiled roofs. On the east side of the plaza is the cathedral, **Iglesia Parroquial de la Santísima Trinidad** ① *Casa Parroquial at Fco J Zerquera 456, opposite the church, T419-3668, F419-6387, daily 1030-1300 for sightseeing and photos; Mass daily at 2000, Sun at 0900.* The church was built between 1817 and 1892. The later altars are made of precious woods, such as cedar, acacia, mahogany and grenadine and were built in 1912-22 by a French priest, Amadeo Frieory, a Swiss Brother Lucas and two Cuban carpenters. It is the largest church in Cuba and is renowned for its acoustics. On the left of the altar is a crucifix of the brown-skinned Christ of Veracruz, who is the patron of Trinidad. If you want to make a charitable donation of any sort, the church is the place to do it.

Next to the church is the **Museo Romántico** ① *Hernández 52, T419-4363, Tue-Sun 0900-1700, US$2, no cameras allowed.* The museum has an excellent collection of porcelain, glass, paintings and ornate furniture, which belonged to several families from the area. The ground floor was built in 1740 by Santiago de Silva and in 1808 the second floor was added by Don José Mariano Borrel y Padrón. The Conde de Brunet family lived there from 1830-60, during what is known as the Romantic period. The Conde de Brunet, a local dignitary, whose full name was Nicolás de la Cruz Brunet Muñoz, made his fortune from sugar and cattle. At his death he owned 700 slaves and two sugar mills as well as lots of land and cattle. The exhibits are displayed in the colonial mansion, with beautiful views from the upper-floor balconies. Locals come here for their wedding photos.

Other museums worth visiting around Plaza Mayor include the **Museo de Arqueología Guamuhaya** ① *Simón Bolívar 457, esq Villena, Plaza Mayor, T419-3420, Sat-Thu 0900-1700, US$1,* which presents a general view of developments from pre-Columbian to post-conquest times. **Museo de Arquitectura Colonial** ① *Desengaño (Ripalda) 83, T419-3208, Fri-Wed 0900-1700, US$1,* exhibits specifically on the architecture of Trinidad, particularly aspects of the 18th and 19th centuries. It also offers tours of the city with a guide and video showings. The **Museo**

Trinidad

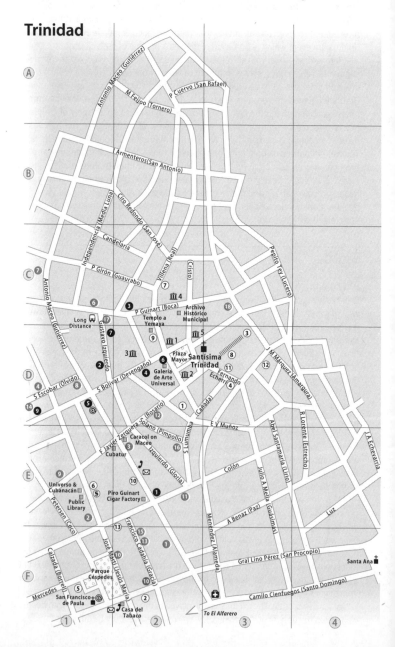

Nacional de Lucha Contra Bandidos ① *Hernández esq Piro Guinart, T419-4121, Tue-Sun 0900-1700, US$1,* housed in the old San Francisco de Asís convent, features exhibits on the 1960s counter-revolutionary campaign in the Escambray mountains. There is a small shop selling T-shirts of Che, postcards etc. **Museo Municipal de Historia** ① *Calle Simón Bolívar 423, T419-4460, Sat-Thu 0900-1700, US$2,* is an attractive building, but with rather dull displays in eight rooms

‡ These museums are very popular with tour parties and can get very crowded, particularly on Wed.

N

0 metres 100
0 yards 100

Sleeping 😴
Balbina Cadahía Benavente cp **1** *F2*
Carlos Gil Lemes cp **2** *E1*
Casa Arandia cp **3** *E2*
Casa Muñoz cp **4** *D1*
Dra Mariela Susana de Fernández y Sergio Fernández cp **14** *D1*
Hospedaje Yolanda cp **6** *C1*
Hostal Sandra y Victor cp **7** *C1*
Hugo P Bastida Saenz de Buruaga cp **8** *D1*
José y Fátima cp **9** *E1*
La Ronda **10** *F2*
Lazara Borrell Farías cp **11** *E2*
Mabel Ortíz Durán cp **12** *D2*
María Esther Pérez cp **13** *F2*
Martha Puig Jiménez cp **15** *F2*
Mercedes Padrón Jiménez cp **16** *E2*
Pedro Aliz Peña cp **17** *C1*
Rafael Soler Valdés, Casa de Huéspedes El Rústico cp **18** *C3*

Eating 🍴
Colonial **1** *E2*
Don Antonio **2** *D1*
El Jigüe **3** *C2*
El Mesón del Regidor **4** *D2*
Las Begonias **5** *D1*
Plaza Mayor **6** *D2*
Ruinas de Leonci **7** *D1*
Santa Ana **8** *F5*
Sol y Son **9** *D1*

Bars 🍸
Daiquirí **10** *F2*

Entertainment 🎭
Bar Las Ruinas de Segarte **12** *D3*
Casa de la Cultura **1** *D2*
Casa Fischer **2** *F2*
Casa de la Música **3** *D3*
Casa de la Trova **4** *D3*
Cine Romello Cornello **5** *F1*
Coppelia **6** *E1*
La Bodeguita de Trinidad **13** *F2*
La Chanchánchara **7** *C2*
La Escalinata **8** *D3*
La Parranda **9** *D2*
Las Ruinas de Brunet **10** *E2*
Palenque de los Congos Reales **11** *D3*

Museums 🏛
Museo de Arqueología Guamuhaya **1** *D2*
Museo de Arquitectura Colonial **2** *D2*
Museo Municipal de Historia **3** *D2*
Museo Nacional de Lucha Contra Bandidos **4** *C2*
Museo Romántico **5** *D2*

To Los Cuevas
(Buen Retiro)
Plaza Santa Ana
8
5

of scientific, historical and cultural exhibits, walk up the tower for a good view of Trinidad instead.

Also close to Plaza Mayor is the **Casa de la Cultura** ① *Francisco Javier Zerquera 406 entre Muñoz y Lumumba, T419-4308, daily 0700-2300,* which has an art gallery and a *sala* for teaching drama, painting, music and dance, open for special events. The **Casa de la Música** next to the church has two entrances. Its main entrance is at the top of the steps next to the church. Its other entrance, leading to a large "greenhouse" venue is on JM Márquez. There is a music shop selling CDs, cassettes and also instruments, with a small display of the history of music in Trinidad. These two places join back to back. Located in an open-air shell of a house is the **Casa de la Trova** ① *entrance on Fernando Echerrí, Mon-Sat from 2200 until late for music performed by live bands, Sun from 1400 until late for singing groups, followed by música mecánica.*
➤➤ *See also Entertainment, page 266, for live music venues.* The **Galería** ① *Plaza Mayor, free,* exhibits local art. Upstairs, a shop sells paintings, clothes and handicrafts.

The **Templo a Yamaya** ① *Villena 59 entre P Guinart y S Bolívar,* is an Afro-Cuban shrine. It is open to the public and you can watch *Santería* celebrations take place. Initiations are held here for anyone who wants to become a *Santero*. In September 2003 the first procession was permitted through the streets of Trinidad, coinciding with the celebrations on 8 September for the Día de la Caridad de Cobre, patron saint of Cuba. After lighting candles in the temple, the Virgin was paraded around the block to the accompaniment of trumpet and drums, similar to many Catholic processions. However, it was followed by ceremonies back at the Templo involving *Santería* drumming when dancers became possessed by spirits.

Centre West Trinidad

Parque Céspedes to the southwest of the centre has shaded archways of vines and trailing plants. To the west is the fine building of the local government, Poder Popular Municipal, and to the south is the **Iglesia de San Francisco de Paula**. There is also a cinema and telephone offices. The **Plaza Santa Ana** is at the extreme southeast of the colonial zone. On the north side is the ruined church, the **Ermita de Santa Ana**, and on the east, a yellow colonial building houses the **Restaurante Santa Ana**, see page 265.

You can also visit the **Piro Guinart Cigar Factory** ① *Maceo esq Colón, opposite Restaurante Colonial, Mon-Sat 0700-1200, 1300-1600*. It is not very big and the tour is free; note that only a few people work on Sat. Tips are gratefully received; it is acceptable to take photos. Note that the **Fábrica de Tabacos** makes tobacco for cigarettes while the **Casa de Tabaco** makes cigars.

South of Parque Céspedes is **El Alfarero** ① *Calle Andrés Berro, go east on Maceo until 1 block after the hospital you get to a blue house on a corner, turn left, El Alfarero is the low yellow building 2 blocks on the right, Mon-Sat 0730-1200 and 1300-1600*, which is a ceramics factory, making earthenware pots. There is no organized tour but it is open for you to wander around, watch the pots being thrown and glazed, and buy anything if you want. The factory used to belong to the Santander family, but was taken over by the government. The standard of pottery declined and only utilitarian pieces are now produced. The elderly Sr Santander still lives opposite the factory, but now devotes his time to breeding birds. He has 400 or so birds in his house and yard: finches, budgerigars, parakeets etc, which are exported around the world by the government. The Santander family have now been allowed to set up their own factory again on the other side of the road and are successfully making pots and souvenirs at **La Casa del Alfarero (Casa Chichi)** ① *Andrés Berro 51, T419-3146*. The house is very smart and prosperous with urns on the wall. Go down side entrance to the left of the house to the workshop at the back. Cuba is known for its old 1950s American cars, but this family owns a 1914 Ford model T car, which has been used in several movies.

Around Trinidad

South of Trinidad to Playa Ancón

About 8 km west of Trinidad is the small, pleasant fishing village of **La Boca**. The beach here is not cleaned daily as it is on Playa Ancón in front of the hotels, but Cubans come here on holiday and there is a cheerful if rough and ready atmosphere about the place. Many people prefer it to Playa Ancón as it is lively with the facilities of *casas particulares* and places to eat. There are some buses to La Boca or you can get a taxi, or rent a bicycle from local people for about US$3 a day. You can also hire a private car or taxi for about US$5 one way or a cocotaxi for US$2 to take you from Trinidad to La Boca.

Casilda is a rather scruffy fishing village 5 km south of Trinidad across a tidal flat where there are lots of birds. It is a run down port used mainly for exporting sugar. Its sights include the ruined Catholic church, **Ermita de Santa Elena**. There is private accommodation available, but it is still about 11 km to the beach. If you are cycling this route you may be pleased to know that there is a breezy bar at the point where the road La Boca-Ancón meets the road Casilda-Ancón, where you can get a coke for US$1.

The best beach resort near Trinidad is **Playa Ancón**, not a town as such, just three resort hotels of varying quality. The beach is white sand with clean turquoise water, but sandflies appear after 1600. Inland there are swamps and lakes, so be prepared for mosquitoes at certain times of the year. The best part of the beach is right in front of the **Hotel Ancón**, where there are straw sunshades and beach loungers. The rest of the beach has little shade. People are sometimes disappointed when they come here and expect something more spectacular, but it is very pleasant for a day trip out of Trinidad. A return taxi fare is about US$12-16, try **Cubataxi** at the bus station, but

⁞ Salto Javira by horse

Off the beaten track is the Salto Javira, reached on horseback across the Valle de los Ingenios from Trinidad, up into the Escambray mountains. A very pretty and pleasant trip through farmyards, bean fields and sugar cane, before you climb a rocky path through forest to the waterfall. The river cascades down a smooth rock face into a deep green pool, surrounded by cliffs and caves inhabited by bats, which fly in and out of the darkness. It is great for a cool swim and very photogenic. The only drawback is the quality of the poor horses, which would be rescue cases in the countries from where the tourists come. I rode an ex-racehorse, which had once won its owner sizeable amounts of money at *fiestas*, but now has one back leg twice the size it should be, with an untreated wound, and is reduced to carrying tourists around. All had sores from their rough saddles and bridles and festering wounds in other places. However, their feet were shod and in reasonable condition and I was told that they are treated once a year against parasites. As long as the horse can still stand up and do its job, Cubans appear to care little for its welfare. It is up to tourists to complain and campaign for better treatment of the horses. Changes have been made in other areas of tourism when foreigners have made their feelings known.

Horses cost US$15 on an organized tour, or US$10 if arranged unofficially through your *casa particular*. Ask to see the horses before you hire. Similarly, the park entrance is US$6.50 with a tour but US$5 when privately arranged.

bargain hard and don't pay any money until the driver returns to collect you. There is good **diving** less than 300 m offshore (see Diving and fishing, page 266). The drop-off is at about 25 m and there is plenty to see.

Cayo Blanco de Casilda

Offshore and southeast of Playa Ancón is Cayo Blanco de Casilda, where there is a beautiful beach with lovely white sand, 1½ hours by boat. A small cay to the east, **Cayo Macho**, is excellent for watching seabirds and pelicans, while to the west of Cayo Blanco there is some lovely coral 18-40 m deep where you can find a wide variety of fish, turtles, lobster and crab. In places the coral has been damaged by storms but in other patches it is plentiful with brain coral, sea fans and lots of fish and starfish. A day trip on a catamaran with snorkelling is organized by hotels and tour companies for US$32 with lobster lunch, US$25 without if you want to take your own picnic (children half price). Huge iguanas and hermit crabs clean up all the leftovers round the back of the kitchen. Sometimes the iguanas come round to the tables and effectively beg for fruit. Take plenty of water. There is a bar on the island but not on the boat. You get a lovely view of the Sierra Escambray from the sea and it is a worthwhile excursion. ▶▶ *For diving, sailing and deep sea fishing, see page 266.*

⁞ *This natural park is run by the military, and it is very secure, with controlled entry.*

Parque Natural Topes de Collantes

Inland from Trinidad are the beautiful, wooded Escambray mountains, whose highest point is **Pico San Juan**, also known as La Cuca, at 1,140 m. Rivers have cut deep valleys, some of which, such as the Caburní and the Guanayara, have attractive waterfalls and pools where you can swim. The **Parque Natural Topes de Collantes** ① *entrance to the National Park US$6.50*, is a 110-sq-km area of the mountains which contains many endemic species of fauna and flora. There are several paths in the area and walking is very rewarding with lovely views and lush forest. There is no public transport, but day trips are organized to Topes de Collantes by **Cubatur, Cubanacán** or **Rumbos,** which are recommended.

A **Jeep Safari** for six hours costs US$25 per person, minimum four passengers, lunch not included, take water and snacks if you think you'll get hungry. There is a fair amount of hiking, which is hard work when the return journey is uphill. The **Rumbos** five-hour trip includes a stop at a farm house for fruit, mashed plantain with garlic and lime, *guarapo* (sugar cane liquor) and coffee for an extra US$1. A **Truck Safari,** minimum eight passengers, including lunch, costs US$37. All take in swimming in a waterfall. You can see lots of wildlife, butterflies, hummingbirds and the *tocororo*, the national bird of Cuba. These are great days out in luscious surroundings. Recommended. Hiring a private car with driver to Topes de Collantes and the **Salto de Caburní** will cost you about US$20-35 with up to four people. Private tours do not go to the same places as jeep tours, whatever anybody tells you. Bargain hard for a good price but do not go if it has been raining recently, it gets very muddy and it is dangerous to walk in the hills. A walking stick is recommended, as is a guide. Make sure the driver takes you to the right place. The path which begins at the village of Topes is not the right place. The official start of the path to the waterfall is at the **Hotel Escambray,** but private cars cannot take you to it, so you have to walk from the village to the hotel and ask for directions there. Guides can be picked up in the village, or take an official tour at the hotel, which is much better value as you go to all the right places. You may find horses for hire half way up the hill if the climb is too much for you. ▸▸ *For further details, see Activities and tours, page 266.*

To get to the **Salto Vegas Grandes,** another waterfall, turn right immediately after the barrier when entering the village from Trinidad. You go into a cul-de-sac with several high-rise apartments. Continue along the track at the end of the last block for about 1½ km. Eventually the track descends steeply along a narrow path (very tricky, good footwear required – do not attempt after rain). Another 2 km walk leads west from the hotels to **La Batata,** a cave with an underground river making pools in which you can swim. The temperature of the water never exceeds 20°C. Just northwest of here, but best reached on another path, is the restaurant at **Hacienda Codina,** T42-540117, (serving *comida criolla*) often combined with a trip to the Cueva del Altar, the orchid gardens and a mirador

Some 12 km north of Topes near Guanayara, there is another waterfall, the **Salto El Rocío,** with swimming in the Poza del Venado by the Río Caballero. There is a restaurant nearby, the **Casa de la Gallega,** where you can have a chicken lunch Galician style.

Alberto Delgado monument

About 4 km from Trinidad, on the Cienfuégos road on the way to the turning for the Topes de Collantes National Park, there is a small monument to Alberto Delgado. Turn south on the road by the stone wall with his name on it and there is a small monument and cave by the Río Guaurabo. Alberto Delgado was a revolutionary who infiltrated the group of US-backed counter revolutionaries known as G2, working from the Escambray mountains. As a result of his activities, a group of 90 counter-revolutionaries was caught in the early 1960s. However, intelligence sources in Cuba and Miami identified him as a spy and a message to that effect was sent from *Radio Swan* (on Swan Island near Miami) to G2 in the mountains. Delgado was captured and executed by the counter-revolutionaries by being hung from a tree in the vicinity of the monument. On the other side of the river from the monument is the house of the Finca Maisinicú, where Alberto Delgado lived.

Torre de Manaca Iznaga and Valle de los Ingenios

The Torre de Manaca Iznaga ① *15 km from Trinidad on road to Sancti Spíritus, daily 0900-1600 or 1700, US$2,* in the village of the same name has now been given UNESCO World Heritage status alongside Trinidad city, because of its historical importance The legend goes that there were two rival brothers, one who wanted to build a tower and the other who wanted to dig a hole as deep as the tower was high. In fact there is only a tower, which was built between 1835 and 1845. It is 43½ m high, has seven floors and 136 steps to the top. It was built as a lookout to watch the slaves working in the valley at the sugar mills. There were two bells in the tower, one was rung when it was time for the slaves to stop work and take a meal in a communal eating house, the other was rung if an escape was discovered, alerting the slave catchers, or *rancheros*. One of the bells, dating from 1846, can be seen on the path leading to the tower. There is a great view of the surrounding countryside, including the Valle de los Ingenios (Valley of the Sugar Mills) and the Escambray mountains as well as the rooftops of the village below. Look out for the large sugar cauldrons lying around the village. The **Manaca Iznaga** restaurant is in the old plantation house, a yellow colonial building (daily 0900-1700, meals US$7-8) and there is a small shop. Tour operators offer day trips, see page 267, or you can hire a private car to take you for about US$10. See Transport, page 267, for train details.

On the same road, 5 km from Trinidad, is a mirador, from where you get a fine view of the Valley of Sugar Mills and the Escambray mountains, with the sea on the opposite side. There is a nice bar at the mirador, and if a tour group turns up there is often a demonstration of a sugar press.

Around Trinidad

0 km 1
0 miles 1

Sleeping
Ancón **1**
Brisas Trinidad del Mar **2**

Costa Sur **3**
Las Cuevas **5**
Villa de Recreo Ma Dolores **4**

ing

254, map p256

as (Horizontes), Finca
T419-6133, F419-6161,
reservas@cuevas.co.cu On a hill 10 mins'
walk from town (good road), with caves in
the grounds and a caving museum, nice
view of the sea. Recently remodelled, 109
comfortable rooms and mini-suites in
chalets and apartments with a/c, phone,
radio, hot water, very clean, 2 swimming
pools, bar with excellent *daiquirís* and great
view, show in the hotel 2120, disco in cave
below. Reception 2200-0200, entrance
US$10 (most rooms are far enough away not
to be disturbed by noise), internet access,
games room, tennis, 24-hr medical service,
dollar shop, post office, exchange facilities,
restaurant with poor buffet meals, breakfast
US$5, evening meal US$11.

C **Villa de Recreo Ma Dolores** (formerly
Finca María Dolores) Carretera Circuito Sur,
T419-6481, F419-6410, 1½ km from Trinidad
on the road to Cienfuegos. Garden setting
near Río Guarabo, 12 brick *cabañas* and 26
bungalows with kitchen, recently renovated,
a/c, shower, clean, restaurant, shop, pool bar,
quiet spot but noisy in the evening as it is an
all-dancing, all-singing tour group
destination, horseriding, volleyball,
basketball, fishing, river excursions.

E **La Ronda** (Islazul), José Martí 238 entre
Colón y Lino Pérez, T419-4011. Small rooms
around a leafy patio, few outside windows,
TV, clean, restaurant and lively roof bar with
friendly staff. Usually full with Cuban
business travellers and almost impossible to
get a room, so don't turn up on spec.

Casas particulares

E **Casa Muñoz**, José Martí 401 entre Fidel
Claro y Santiago Escobar, T/F419-3673,
trinidadjulio@yahoo.com Very friendly,
English speaking, run by Julio César Muñoz
Cocina and Rosa Orbea Cerrillo with their 2
children and 2 splendid dogs. Great house,
one of the grandest in Trinidad, built in 1800
with lofty ceilings and cool, intricately tiled
floors, 2 rooms with 2 double beds, new
bathrooms, a/c and fans, roof terrace,
parking, very popular so book in advance.
Base for photographers and film makers;

Julio is a photographer and can
arrange workshops and study
groups, www.trinidadphoto.com

E **Hostal La Rioja**, Frank País 389 entre
Simón Bolívar y Fco J Zerquera,
T419-4177/3879, tereleria@yahoo.com.mx
Run by friendly and helpful Teresa Leris
Echerri, 2 rooms with double and single beds,
the one upstairs has access to a small kitchen,
bathrooms, noisy a/c, fan, hot water, patio
garden at rear, table outside in the shade for
meals, dachshund, garage, some French and
English spoken, several good reports.

E **Hostal Sandra y Victor**, Maceo (Gutiérrez)
613 entre Piro Guinart (Boca) y Pablo Pichs
(Guaurabo), T419-6444,
hostalsandra@yahoo.com Family lives
downstairs, 2 guest rooms upstairs, gives
privacy and security, well cared for property,
good bathrooms, a/c, fan, fridge, balcony to
the front off the dining room, spacious and
comfortable with friendly hosts who provide
delicious and hearty meals.

E **María Esther Pérez**, Francisco Cadahía 224
(Gracia) entre Colón y Lino Pérez, T419-3528.
Nice extension with 2 rooms attached to old
colonial house, antique beds in both, 1
communal bathroom, a/c or fan, fabulous
fish meals, run by herbalist, using plants from
her own garden, parking 5 doors away.

E **Teresa Cerrillo**, Frank País 372 entre Mario
Guerra y Francisco J Zerquera, T419-3673
(Casa Muñoz), teresacerrillo@yahoo.es Pink
house with patio at the rear full of plants and
greenery, 2 double beds in large room,
ensuite bathroom, a/c, ceiling fan, fridge.

F **Balbina Cadahía Benavente**, Maceo 355
entre Lino Pérez y Colón, CP 62600,
T419-2585. Extremely nice family, old
colonial house, hot water shower, will
arrange trips, friendly, good reports.

F **Carlos Gil Lemes**, José Martí 263 entre
Colón y Fco J Zerquera, T419-3142, next to
library. Beautiful late-19th century house
with sumptuous tile decoration, English
spoken, 2 rooms with shared bath, hot
water, fans, garden courtyard, neighbour has
a garage for rent, US$1 per night.

F **Casa Arandia**, Maceo 438 entre Colón y
Rosario Trinidad, T419-3240. Very nice
restored house, guest room has own
courtyard and garage.

F **Casa de Hospedaje El Fausto**, Simón Bolívar 220 entre Clemente Pereira y Frank País, T419-3466. Exceptionally clean and newly modernized colonial house, nice rooms with 1 or 2 beds, fan and bathroom, fridge. Several terraces around the house to sit and relax. Friendly family, only Spanish spoken, he is a sculptor, lots of fun with music, salsa and fiesta atmosphere.

F **Gisela Borrell Bastida**, Frank País (Carmen) 486 entre Fidel Claro y Santiago Escobar, opposite Gaviota, about 200 m from bus station, T419-4301. Bedroom with double and single bed on ground floor, bathroom with hot shower, use of own dining room, sitting room, own entrance, lots of space.

F **Hospedaje Yolanda**, Piro Guinart 227 entre Izquierdo y Maceo, opposite the bus station. Very nice rooms in enormous colonial house including 1 up a spiral staircase with 2 double beds, terrace and views of sea and mountains, hot water shower, a/c.

F **Hostal La Candelaria**, Antonio Guiteras (Mercedes) 129 entre P Zerquera y A Cárdenas, T419-4239. Run by Elvira and Eddy, both teachers but no English spoken, friendly and generous, humble accommodation, but spotlessly clean, 2 rooms, hot water, a/c, fans, nice garden, great food, cheap.

F **Hugo P Bastida Saenz de Buruaga**, Maceo 539 entre Santiago Escobar (Olvido) y Piro Guinart (Boca), name above the door, T419-3186. Typical dark colonial home with high ceilings run by elderly gentleman, 1 lovely room, bathroom attached, 24-hr hot shower, a/c, very friendly dog, Sr Bastida speaks English and his wife is an excellent cook, good-value meals.

F **José y Fátima**, Francisco J Zerquera 159 (Rosario) entre Frank País y Francisco Petersen, T419-3898. Upstairs rooms, 1 with double bed, the other with double and single beds, a/c, fan, nice new private bathrooms, hot water, door and windows open onto balcony for lots of fresh air, table on the patio for meals (lots of dishes, whatever you want) and roof terrace with laundry facilities and washing machine and a great view over the rooftops

F **Lazara Borrell Farías**, Colón 312 entre Maceo y Jesús Menéndez, T419-2454. 2 rooms each with bathroom, huge house in historic centre, friendly, good English.

F **Mabel Ortíz Durán**, Francisco J Zerquera 360 entre Ernesto V Muñoz y Gustavo Izquierdo, T419-2220. Own key to room and house, huge room with 2 double beds, hot water, fans, huge portions of food with lots of fruit and vegetables, will cook whatever you want, beautiful colonial building 2 mins from main square, feels almost like a museum, generous and hospitable family.

F **Dra Mariela Susana de Fernández y Sergio Fernández**, Santiago Escober 158 (Olvido) entre José Martí y Frank País, T419-3410, www.cubanaweb.com 1 comfortable room with a balcony and view of the centre. A/c and private bathroom. The spiral staircase up to the room takes some skill, especially after a few cocktails. Food available. Spanish only, friendly and helpful.

F **Martha Puig Jiménez**, Francisco Cadahía 236, entre Colón y Lino Pérez, T419-2361. Speaks fluent English, free coffee, house and courtyard spotlessly clean, fans, shared bathroom, hot water, friendly, informative, car parking arranged.

F **Mercedes Padrón Jiménez**, Manuel Solano 7 (Pimpollo), T419-3068. 2 rooms, 1 with own bathroom, more privacy than some, owner is former teacher and speaks the kind of Spanish that even people who don't speak Spanish can understand, phone ahead, popular.

F **Pedro Aliz Peña**, Gustavo Izquierdo 127 (Gloria) entre Piro Guinart y Simón Bolívar, T419-3776/3025, just by bus station where Víazul buses stop. Old house with high ceilings, patio, quiet, 2 spacious rooms, fans, simple but clean, new bathrooms, hot water, Pedro and Teresa are sociable and helpful, only Spanish spoken.

F **Rafael Soler Valdés**, Casa de Huéspedes **El Rústico**, Juan M Martínez 54A entre Piro Guinart y Simón Bolívar, 1 block from Plaza Mayor, T419-3024. 5 rooms, a/c, bathroom shared, very clean. Rooms on top floor private, roof terrace, view over town, only problem is having to ring doorbell if you come home late.

South of Trinidad to Playa Ancón
p258, map p261
Hotels
AL Brisas Trinidad del Mar (Cubanacán), Playa Ancón, T419-6500-7, reservas @brisastdad.co.cu 4-star all-inclusive hotel

opened in 2001, 241 rooms and junior suites in 2/3-storey multicoloured blocks in a circle around free-form pool, 2 rooms for wheelchair users, a/c, TV, phone, radio, internet access, medical centre, massage, beauty parlour, shops, laundry, fax and email, car and bike rental, tourism desk, buffet and à la carte restaurants, Jacuzzi, tennis, gym, sauna, games room, watersports, entertainment including karaoke, on good beach, reef-protected sea, nice sand with sea grapes behind.

B Ancón (Gran Caribe), Playa Ancón, T419-6120, F419-6121 (reservations). Concrete block of 279 rooms, showing its age, price room only, although they encourage you to go all-inclusive, including 3 meals, 24-hr drinks (although the snack bars are often unstocked and drinks watered down) and extras such as snorkels, bicycles. The hotel has an hexagonal pool, disco and many facilities, including scuba diving and watersports, best beach here, lots of families stay, but lots of complaints. Offices of Cubanacán, Rumbos and Transtur for excursions and car hire.

B-C Costa Sur (Horizontes), Playa Ancón, T419-6174-8, www.horizontes.cu Standard (71) or superior rooms (39) in a block or chalets (20) in front of them, built above rocks with beach to north of hotel where there is a natural swimming pool and bar on the sand. Hotel is rundown and shabby, a/c, bath, phone, balconies with mostly broken chairs, breakfast included, dinner buffet US$10, not bad, also Italian seafood restaurant, bar, beer US$1.50, *mojito* US$2.50, nightclub show at 2130, pool, billiards, shop, internet access, car rental and taxis.

Casas particulares

A couple of hostels are on the main street.
E Hostal Vista al Mar, Calle Real 47, La Boca, T419-3716. Owned by Manuel (Manolo) Menéndez, 2 rooms, a/c, parking, overlooking the sea.
E Ruddy Marrero, Av del Sol, La Boca, T419-5131 (call Anita), or just turn up. Ruddy lived in the USA and speaks excellent English, if he is full he can recommend alternatives, bicycles for hire, friendly and reliable.
E Villa Sonia, Av del Mar 11 entre D y E, La Boca, T419-2401. 2 rooms with private bathrooms, parking, overlooking the sea, porch with hammocks, meals available.

F Elsa Hernández Monteagudo, Av del Mar, Casa 5, La Boca, T419-3236. 5 double rooms, 2 bathrooms (ants on floor, harmless), huge, tasty meals, bike rental US$2 per day, rocking chairs on terrace for sunset watching, great hospitality.

PN Topes de Collantes *p259*
Hotels

There is a huge hospital in the mountains at Topes de Collantes, the 4-star **Kurhotel Escambray** (Gaviota), T42-540219/97, F42-540288. It offers special therapeutic treatments for patients from all over the world, but has the usual hotel services, too.
E Villa Escambray. Villas for tourists behind the Dirección General by the path to Salto de Caburní.
E Los Helechos (Gaviota), T42-540330, F42-540117, southwest of Topes de Collantes village. 48 a/c rooms, restaurant, bar, *cafetería*, thermal pool, gym, massage, sauna, steam baths, bowling alley, shop, tourism bureau, car hire.

● Eating

The price of beer in some restaurants drops from US$2 to US$0.60 after 1700 when the tourist tours leave, but all the state-run places shut then too. Family-run restaurants, *paladares*, are not as popular as before because most people eat in *casas particulares* where the food is excellent and cooked to order. Breakfast is usually US$2-3 and dinner US$5-10.

Trinidad *p254, map p256*
Restaurants

$ Colonial, Maceo 402, esquina Colón, daily 0900-2200. US$7-8, nice place, popular.
$ El Jigüe, Real 69 esq Guinart, T419-6476, daily 0900-2230. Live music, good food and atmosphere, most dishes US$7-8, chicken special US$8.
$ El Mesón del Regidor (Rumbos), Simón Bolívar 426 entre Ernesto V Muñoz y Villena, opposite Toro, T419-6572, daily 0900-2200. US$7-8. Also in the complex is a bar, internet terminal and 4 rooms to rent.
$ Las Begonias, Maceo esq Simón Bolívar, daily 0900-2200. The only café in town with the added attraction of 6 computer terminals for internet access. Fast food dishes around US$5-8. Ice cream parlour opposite.

$ **Plaza Mayor**, Villena 15, just off Plaza Mayor, T419-6470, plazamayor@enet.cu daily 1200-2130. Elegant setting with pink tablecloths, live music, lobster US$19, steak and seafood, buffet US$8, pleasant courtyard at the rear and a couple of internet terminals although they don't both always work.

$ **Restaurante Don Antonio**, Izquierdo 118 entre Piro Guinart y Simón Bolívar, T419-6548, daily 1130-1700. A nice old colonial house with ornate columns and tiled floor, meals US$6-8.

$ **Ruinas de Leonci**, Gustavo Izquierdo entre Simón Bolívar y Piro Guinart, T419-6498, daily 0900-2300. Bar and restaurant with cosy small garden, pleasant wooden tables and chairs inside.

$ **Santa Ana**, Plaza Santa Ana, daily 0900-2200. House special pork US$4.65, other dishes US$5-6.

$ **Sol y Son**, Simón Bolívar 283 entre Frank País y José Martí, daily 1200-1500 and 1900-2300. Run by English-speaking ex-architect Lázaro in 19th-century house, nice decor, courtyard, mixed reports, some say it is the best food in Cuba, others that it is overpriced with average food, vegetarian special, excellent pork, tasty stuffed fish, around US$10 with drinks.

Peso restaurants

There is a sit-down pizza restaurant where tourists can pay in pesos on Martí at Parque Céspedes. Lots of pizza stalls on Lino Pérez entre Martí y Maceo, but the best on Francisco Cadahía y Lino Pérez.

South of Trinidad to Playa
Ancón *p258, map p261*
There are several bars all along the beach in La Boca. In Playa Ancón there is very little choice apart from the hotels listed above.

$ **Grill del Caribe**, Playa Ancón, along the beach northwest of the Hotel Ancón. Makes a change from hotel food but is poor value, a salad (plate of tomatoes) is US$1.

$ **Ranchón Playa La Boca** (Islazul), La Boca, T419-6618, daily 0700-2100. Serves seafood, bar open 24 hrs.

🍸 Bars

Trinidad *p254, map p256*
Bar Daiquirí, Lino Pérez entre Cadahía y José Martí, daily 0800-2400. Fast food, beer US$1, *mojito* US$2, zombie US$4.

Círculo Social de Obreros, Martí. Serves rum in pesos, tourists welcome, an authentic drinking experience.

🎭 Entertainment

Trinidad *p254, map p256*
Cinema
Cine Romello Cornello, Parque Céspedes. Show at 2000, 40 centavos. For up-to-date times and programme see the billboards just inside the doors. Some American action films are shown here.

Music and dance
Lots of people offer 'unofficial' salsa lessons for about US$4 an hour; Trinidad is a good place to learn and you'll soon be dancing with Cubans in local bars.

Bar Las Ruinas de Segarte, Alameda entre Márquez y Galdós, open 1000-2400. Set in a ruined courtyard, also does fried chicken for US$1.50 or other fast food, traditional music, live bands play in the day, Afro-Cuban dance, amazingly energetic and incredible to watch, variety show at 2100.

Casa de la Música, up the steps past the church in Plaza Mayor, daily 1000-0200. Full of tourists and Cubans, salsa, live performers, show at 2200, restaurant with expensive snacks 1000-2200, internet, shop selling CDs, cassettes, music magazines.

Casa Fisher (Artex), Lino Pérez 306 entre Cadahía y José Martí. In a nice old colonial house built in 1870, outdoor bar 0900-0100, US$1 for show at 2130 with dancing, live music and karaoke.

Coppelia, Martí, opposite the public library. Still open after everything else is closed, music, popular with Cubans, open for breakfast at 0700, restaurant food 1000-2100, disco at 2200, special show Fri-Sun at 2300, US$1 for show and disco, karaoke.

Casa de la Trova, daily 0900-0100. Entry free during the day, US$1 at night. One block from the church is the excellent live Cuban traditional music and *trova* with a warm, vibrant atmosphere. There are mostly Cubans here, of all age groups, and it's a great place to watch, and join in with, the locals having a good time. All drinks paid for in dollars, quite expensive.

La Bodeguita de Trinidad, Colón entre Martí y Maceo, daily 0900-2400. Not as legendary as its Havana namesake, but a nice little music bar, open courtyard and with quaint sheltered booths for couples, *trova* group every night 2100-2400, entry free, beer US$1, food available.

La Canchánchara, Villena 78, daily 0900-2100. Another venue for live music, fast food, serves a drink of the same name created out of rum, honey and lime in small earthenware pots. More touristy than **Casa de La Trova** (cigar and souvenir shop), but good traditional music with different groups playing during opening hours.

La Escalinata, on the terrace leading up the steps next to the church, before you get to the Casa de la Música, daily 1000-2000. Live bands all the time but not when it rains.

La Parranda, Villena 59, in the patio of the Templo de Yemaya just off Plaza Mayor, open 0900-2400. An outdoor bar/music venue, very ad hoc farmyard atmosphere, but excellent live music every night, good place to learn salsa, watched from semi-circle of seats, cocktails US$2, dancing.

Las Cuevas (see Sleeping, p262). Good disco, dance merengue and salsa with Cubans between the stalactites in a cave below reception, from 2200, entrance US$10.

Las Ruinas de Brunet, Maceo entre Colón y Francisco Javier Zerquera, daily 0900-2400. Nightly Afro-Cuban show at 2100 for tourists in ruined colonial courtyard, very tacky and unauthentic, also *trova* from 1600, percussion classes 0900-1100, dance classes 1300-1600. Bicycle and scooter rental.

Palenque de los Congos Reales, Fernando H Echerri entre La Escalinata y Casa de la Trova, bar daily 0900-0100. During the day there are sometimes groups playing and at 2200 there is an Afro-Cuban show.

⊙ Shopping

Trinidad *p254, map p256*
Art
Galería de Arte Universal, Villena 43, opposite the Plaza Mayor, T419-4432, Fri-Wed 0800-1700. Contemporary Cuban art for sale, **Tienda de Arte Amelia Pelaez**, Simón Bolívar esq Valdés Muñoz, T419-3590.

Food
There is a store on Zerquera esq Izquierdo, daily 0930-2130, which sells some food and drink with a good selection, and another on Maceo esq Lino Pérez which sells food, clothes and toiletries. Fruit and vegetables are bought from vendors in the street or at doorways. Look out for what is on offer or in season and pay in pesos.

Handicrafts
All along S Lumumba and EV Muñoz are handicraft stalls, especially crochet and needlework, with some books and stamps and sometimes a band playing.
It is called Candonga, or Mercado Popular de Artesanía.

Photography
Photoservice, José Martí entre Colón y Lino Pérez, daily 0800-2000. Film about US$5-7 per roll, also sometimes has bread. Most dollar shops sell film.
Photoclub, José Martí 254, T419-4539. Development and printing 35 mm film in 1 hr.

Souvenirs
Bazar Trinidad, Maceo 451, esq Zerquera, on the opposite corner from Caracol. Postcards, curios, pictures, T-shirts, typical Cuban handicrafts.
Caracol on Maceo, esq Zerquera. Souvenirs, T-shirts, postcards, etc.
Tienda La Cochera, on Simón Bolívar, round the corner from the Museo Romántico. Another dollar store with a small selection of souvenirs, drinks, postcards, toiletries, T-shirts.
Tienda Panamericana, Lino Pérez entre Cadahía y José Martí. A dollar store selling some food, clothes and toiletries.
Universo, Martí entre Rosario y Colón. Sells shoes, clothes, department store, also **Cubanacán** tour company on site.

▲ Activities and tours

Diving
Puertosol, by Hotel Ancón, Cayo Blanco de Casilda. Offers diving and underwater photography: US$30 for 1 dive, US$50 for 2, US$130 for 5 dives, a night dive is US$40, CMAS certification course US$300, equipment rental US$15.

Fishing
The sales office at the marina, T419-6205, see below, organizes fishing (fly, deep sea,

trawling and liveaboards), sea safaris to Cayo Blanco, snorkelling, sunset sails with dinner, etc. A boat for a party of 4 to go deep sea fishing all day costs around US$250, while fishing from a launch is US$50 per day.

Marina
Marina Cayo Blanco, Península Ancón, Cayo Blanco de Casilda, VHF 16, 19, 68, 72. Six moorings, 1.8 m draft, showers, laundry, rental.

Sailing
Sunsail Cuba, at the marina, Cayo Blanco de Casilda, T419-6290, sunsailcuba@syc.co.cu Base daily 0800-1230 and 1300-1800 for sailing and yacht hire.

Tour operators
Excursions are all much the same price, for example: US$15 for a city tour including the Valley of the Sugar Mills *mirador*, the tobacco and ceramics factories, museums and *La Canchanchara*; US$65 for a trip to the Zapata peninsula, minimum 8 people; US$25 for a sea safari from Playa Ancón marina (not including transfers) to Cayo Blanco with snorkelling, US$32 with seafood lunch; US$45 to Guanayara including lunch and jeep (0900-1600, 2 km walk); US$28 to Caburní (0900-1400, 3-km walk down, 3-km struggle up); US$20 by horse to El Cubano including entrance to National Park, drink and transport (0900-1400). Bicycles and horses are for hire, which you can book through **Cubanacán** etc, but you may find your *casa* owner knows the man they subcontract to and can arrange it cheaper. Try and use the legal operators as you will be better covered in case of emergency and the horses and bikes will be better quality.
Brisas Trinidad del Mar, T419-6695. Arranges tours and excursions and is a useful information resource for travellers. Staff speak French, English, German and Italian.
Cubanacán, in the Universo store on Martí entre Rosario y Colón, T419-6142, Mon-Sat 0800-1900, Sun 0800-1400. Tours to waterfalls with horses or jeeps, catamaran and other offshore excursions.
Cubatur, Maceo esq Zerquera, T/F419-6314, 0900-1200 and 1300-1800. Much the same tours and prices as **Rumbos** and hotel reservations. In the office there is also a bank, T419-6310, and the office of **Transtur Rent a Car**, T419-6110.

entre Maceo y Cadahía. In the same building you will also find **Veracuba**, T419-6317, **Cubacar** and **Taxi OK**.
Paradiso, Lino Pérez 306 y Martí (Casa Fischer), T419-6486, paradiso@artextdad.co.cu Tour operator specializing in promoting cultural tourism. The building has a lovely courtyard with white wrought iron tables and chairs for events and an Artex shop at the entrance.
Rumbos Cuba, Simón Bolívar 430 esq Maceo, T419-6495, daily 0900-1800, also in Hotel Ancón, T419-6640.

⊖ Transport

Air
No regular flights, only charters.

Bicycle/scooter hire
Cycling on cobbled streets is difficult to say the least. Scooters and bicycles can be hired from **Ruinas de Brunet**, see Entertainment, p266. Bicycles can also be hired through tour companies or *casas particulares*.

Bus
Long distance   Terminal entrance on Gustavo Izquierdo, near the corner with Piro Guinart, office daily 0600-1700, T419-4448. Transport (other than with **Víazul**) to the east of Cuba is difficult from Trinidad as it is not on the Carretera Central. Best to go to Sancti Spíritus through beautiful hilly scenery (see below) and take the bus or train from there.

Víazul from **Havana** 0815, 1300, via **Cienfuegos**, arriving 1400, 1800, US$25, returning 0700, 1515; from **Varadero** (US$20) via **Santa Clara** (US$8) and **Sancti Spíritus** (US$6) at 0730, arriving 1405, returning 1440. Víazul also runs **Trinidad-Santiago** 0815, 12 hrs, US$33, via **Sancti Spíritus, Ciego de Avila, Florida, Camagüey, Sibanicú, Guáimaro, Las Tunas, Holguín, Bayamo** and **Palma Soriano**, returning from **Santiago** at 1900 overnight.

Astro daily services to **Havana, Sancti Spíritus, Cienfuegos, Santa Clara**, cheaper, slower, less comfortable.

Havanautos, at ServiCupet on the way out of Trinidad towards Casilda, T/F419-6301. Rent a Car Vía (Gaviota), at the airport, T419-6388. Transtur, Maceo esq Zerquera, T419-5314, cars and buses. Transautos, T419-5336.

Petrol stations Cupet gas station on Frank País esq Zerquera.

Taxi

Cubataxi, T419-2214, at the bus station. Also cocotaxis and bicycle rental. Taxi OK, T419-6302. Transtur, T419-5314. Cubataxi to **Playa Ancón**, up to 5 people, from the bus terminal US$10 1 way, 15 mins. To **Topes de Collantes**, up to 4 people, US$25 return with 3-hr wait there.

Train

The station is south of the town, walk south straight down Lino Pérez until you get to the railway line, then turn left. The old building once used for the trains has been renovated as the School of Art; the office is now about 100 m to the right, T419-3348. Local services only. Tourists can take a trip on a 1907 steam train to **Manaca Iznaga** daily in high season at 0930, US$10. Best to buy ticket at an agency (Rumbos, Cubatur etc).

⊙ Directory

Trinidad *p254, map p256*
Banks
Bandec, José Martí 264 entre Zerquera y Colón, T419-2405, Mon-Fri 0800-1700, Sat 0800-1600. Changes TCs for dollars and cash advances on credit cards. Cadeca, Martí 164, T419-6262, half a block from Parque Céspedes, open Mon-Sat 0830-1800, Sun 0830-1200.

There are **cambios** in Hotel Las Cuevas, Hotel Ancón and Hotel Costa Sur, where you can change TCs for dollars. Western Union cabin in ServiCupet beside Havanautos for receiving money from abroad, takes 24 hrs. Used mostly by Cubans getting money from the USA, maximum US$300 (US$25 commission).

Hospitals and clinics

The Clínica Internacional is on Lino Pérez 103 esq Anastasio Cárdenas, T419-6492, F419-6240. Modern, with out-patient consultations, laboratory tests, X-rays, pharmacy, dentistry, massage and 24-hr emergency care. It is better to go there rather than to the general hospital as they have more medical supplies. A consultation fee is US$25, a call-out fee US$50.

Internet

Las Begonias, Maceo entre FJ Zerquera y Simón Bolívar, 6 terminals, US$1 for 10 mins, US$5 per hr, Mon-Fri 0900-1300 and 1500-2100, Sat and Sun 0900-1300. Etecsa, on Parque Céspedes. Email facilities using the prepaid card system, recently remodelled, 6 terminals, fax, phones and cards. Restaurante Plaza Mayor, see Eating above, has 2 terminals at the back of the restaurant which don't always both work, US$0.10 per minute.

Library

The **Public Library** is on José Martí 265 entre Zerquera y Colón, Mon-Fri 0800-2200, Sat 0800-1700. **Archivo Histórico Municipal de Trinidad** , Piro Guinart 320 entre Hernández y Villena, T419-6321, open 0800-1700. The literary archives of Trinidad, with historical documents on Trinidad going back to 1724.

Places of worship

Templo a Yemaya, Villena 59 entre Piro Guinart y Simón Bolívar. A place of *Santería* worship which anyone can visit, open 24 hrs, where you will see dolls on the altars and Afro-Cuban symbols on the walls. See above for details of services at the Iglesia Parroquial.

Post office

Antonio Maceo 418 entre Zerquera y Colón, also for international **telephones** and **fax**, Mon-Sat 0900-1800, Sun 0900-1700. Another small Post Office and Etecsa **telephone/fax/internet** office on Gral Lino Pérez, Parque Céspedes, beside Iglesia San Francisco, daily 0700-2300.

Useful addresses

Immigration T419-6650. Rumbos on Simón Bolívar 430 can renew visas and tourist cards within a day or less, daily 0800-2000. **Police** The main police station is 1 km from the centre of town on Calle 1 in Reparto Armando Mestre. There is a sub-station at the corner of Colón and José Martí. For any problem ring T419-3901.

Centre East

Footprint features

Introduction

The three provinces of Ciego de Avila, Camagüey and Las Tunas make up a large area of mostly flat, agricultural land with few natural features of outstanding beauty, although the landscape is pleasing with livestock grazing in the meadows. The city of Ciego de Avila has little to recommend it and it is not a tourist attraction. North of the city, however, is one of the island's main beach resorts: Cayo Coco. Its extensive beaches of pale sand are now a magnet for the all-inclusive tourist market. Many other cays in the Jardines del Rey archipelago are being developed for tourism, either with hotels or as destinations for scuba diving or deep sea fishing.

The only city of note in the region is Camagüey, which is an ideal place to stay a few days if travelling from one end of the island to the other. The old colonial heart of the city has been restored to its former splendour while the shopping area is full of magnificent 19th-century buildings which have stood the test of time better than in seaside cities such as Havana or Santiago. North of the city is the long-established beach resort of Playa Santa Lucía, with hotels now starting to show their age. However, this beach and the nearby cays are irresistible for lovers of sun, sea and sand, while the diving is superb, especially if you like sharks. Las Tunas is another city where people mostly just keep going, preferring instead to visit the north-coast beaches, which are so far relatively undeveloped with few facilities.

★ Don't miss...

1 Flamingoes Some 30,000 birds wade happily in the shallow waters surrounding the north coast cays and can be seen year round on Playa Los Flamencos, page 274.

2 Churches Camagüey has a number of beautiful old churches in various states of renovation, each with a story to tell, pages 281-284.

3 Camagüey Saturday night is the night for a Noche Camagüeya, a weekly street fiesta, page 290.

4 Playa Los Cocos Spend a relaxing day on the beach and lunch on freshly caught lobster, page 285.

5 Cayo Sabinal This unspoilt, undeveloped cay has changed little since Hemingway sang its praises, page 286.

Ins and outs

Getting there

Air There are international airports north of Ciego de Avila, on Cayo Coco and north of Camagüey, and a domestic airport near Las Tunas. Charter flights from Canada and Europe bring visitors to the cays. **Rail** The three provincial capitals are linked by rail and road, being on the main routes from Havana to Santiago de Cuba. Trains are unreliable and pass through at unsociable hours in the middle of the night. **Road** **Víazul** has a good daily bus service either from Havana or Trinidad to Santiago, stopping at all major towns along the way. ›› *For further details, see also Ins and outs for Ciego de Avila below, Camagüey page 279 and Las Tunas page 293.*

Tourist information

State tour agencies can be found in all the main towns and at hotels in the beach resorts and these operate as tourist information offices although their main purpose is to sell tours. They can help with hotel reservations, tickets and transfers.

Best time to visit

These three provinces have not been badly hit by a hurricane or tropical storm for some time, but you will still find plenty of wet weather if you come here between June and November, with most of the rain falling in the three months at the end of that period. Snow birds come in the winter months to the north-coast beaches but there can be rough seas bringing weed and debris from November to February if there is a cold front further north. Generally the driest time of year is between December and April.

Centre East Ins and outs

Ciego de Avila

To Airport

To Morón

Plaza de la Revolución Abel Santamaría

Embalse la Turbina

Plaza Camilo Cienfuegos

Museo Provincial

Honorato del Castillo

Marcial Gómez

A Delgado

O Hernández

A Ramírez

Cuarta

Serafín Sánchez

Máximo Gómez

Joaquín Agüero

Galería de Arte Provincial

Parque Martí

Echevarría

Agramonte

Antonio Maceo

Simón Reyes

Teatro Principal

San Eugenio de la Palma

Ayuntamiento

Libertad

Independencia

José Martí

N López

Candelario Agüero

JA Mella

To Camagüey

Chicho Valdés/Carretera Central

Zoo

N

0 metres 200
0 yards 200

Sleeping 😴
Ciego de Avila **1**
Santiago-Habana **2**
Sevilla **3**

Eating 🍴
Cafetería 12 Plantas & Solaris **1**
Don Pepe **3**
El Colonial **2**

Entertainment 🎭
Casa de la Trova **1**

Ciego de Avila → *Colour map 2, grid B6. Population: 85,000.*

Ciego de Avila was founded in 1840 on the site of a hacienda granted to Alonso de Avila, one of Velázquez' commanders, and consequently is short of fine historical architecture and monuments although there are plenty of columns, portals and tiles to decorate the 19th-century buildings. It is an agricultural market town with a large thermal electricity plant. The main road from Havana to Camagüey passes straight through the middle of town; most people just keep going. The Province of Ciego de Avila is most often visited for the beach resorts off its northern coast. The islands of Cayo Coco and Cayo Guillermo have excellent deep sea fishing, diving and snorkelling. Many new luxury hotels are opening for package tourism but they are very remote and isolated from the rest of Cuba. Scuba divers also rate highly the cays off the south coast that make up the western half of the Jardines de la Reina archipelago. Dive packages must be organized in advance but the unspoilt underwater environment makes the effort well worthwhile. Elsewhere in the province, game shooting is organized and freshwater fishing must be about the best on the island. However, lovers of colonial architecture may be disappointed as there is little of historical interest. Not many visitors bother to stop long in the provincial capital, most of them head for the water. ▸▸ *For Sleeping, Eating and other listings, see pages 276-278.*

Ins and outs

Getting there Two **flights** a week come in from Havana to the airport 24 km north of Ciego de Avila, but notably these connect with flights coming from 15 Mexican cities. The new international airport on Cayo Coco is more convenient if that is your destination, saving a long bus ride out to the cays. So far it is receiving scheduled international flights from Frankfurt, Milan and Canada, as well as domestic flights from Havana and Varadero, and charter flights according to season and demand. The railway station is central and **trains** on the Havana to Santiago route stop here, but usually in the middle of the night. **Víazul buses** are more convenient, running from Havana to Santiago and Trinidad to Santiago, several daily. However, if you break your journey here, make sure you have a reservation well in advance for the onward bus, as the long-distance buses are usually full when they go through town. c

Getting around Much of the city can be seen **on foot**, or you can use a **coche** for longer distances. For excursions out of the city, **car hire** is the most convenient, or you can hire a state or private **taxi** to take you around, or take a tour.

Tourist information The hotels have *burós de turismo* which can give information, although their main purpose is to sell tours. These can be convenient if you do not have a car.

Sights

The main square is the **Parque Martí**, with a statue of José Martí dating from 1925 in the centre. On the south side are the church, **Iglesia de San Eugenio de la Palma**, patron saint of the city, and the former town hall, **Ayuntamiento**, built in 1911, and now the provincial government headquarters. The **Teatro Principal** ① *Joaquín Agüero y Honorato del Castillo, T33-222086*, built in 1927, is considered one of the best in the island for its acoustics. For an insight into local artists, visit the **Galería de Arte Provincial** ① *Calle Independencia entre Honorato del Castillo y Maceo, T33-223900*. The **Museo Provincial** ① *José Antonio Echevarría 25, T33-228128, Tue-Sat 0800-1200, 1300-1700, Sun 0800-1200, US$2*, is in an old school building the other side of the railway, with exhibitions of local history including the region's part in the 1959 Revolution.

Around Ciego de Avila

Ciego de Avila is sandwiched between the provinces of Sancti Spíritus and Camagüey. It is the flattest province with none of its land rising above 50 m. The northern coastline is low lying and swampy with mangroves. Offshore, but connected to the mainland by a long causeway, is Cayo Coco and other cays where tourism is being developed and several large hotels built. The central part of the province is used for cattle ranching. Sugar is grown widely and there are citrus and pineapple plantations. To the south, there are more mangroves along the coast and more cays with a wealth of marine life (see Diving and marine life, Essentials page 65).

The two main cities of Ciego de Avila and Morón lie in the centre of the province. In the late 19th century the Spanish built a road, sentry towers and other fortifications north-south from Morón to Júcaro via Ciego de Avila to try and contain independence fighters. The ruins of some of these fortifications can still be seen in places. They were unsuccessful in keeping out the rebels: in 1876 General Manuel Suárez took Morón, in 1895 General Antonio Maceo crossed the line north of Ciego de Avila, as did Camilo Cienfuegos in 1958.

Morón → *Colour map 2, grid B6. Population: 50,000.*

Morón was founded in 1750 and is about 40 km northeast of Ciego de Avila. It is promoted as the Ciudad del Gallo (Cockerel City) with a monument to the bird. There is a **Museo de Arqueología e Historia**, Calle Martí, showcasing the archaeology and history of the city, and there is a Casa de la Trova on Calle Libertad entre Martí y Narciso López.

Apart from visitors passing through here on their way to Cayo Coco, the main visitors to this area are here for the **shooting** and **fishing**. Northeast of Morón, **Horizontes** organizes shooting for game birds and waterfowl at **Aguachales de Falla** and other lakes close by. The hunting season runs from 15 November to 15 March and a licence costs US$25. On top of that you pay for the hire of a 12-bore shotgun, about US$8 per day, ammunition US$12 and transport rental US$0.80 per km.

North of Morón to the west of the road is the **Laguna de la Leche** (Milk Lake), Cuba's largest natural lake at 68.2 sq km. It is so called because of its cloudy white appearance, caused by lime deposits under the water. Its salinity makes it very popular with several thousand flamingoes. It is the location for the **Aquatic Carnival** of Morón and now one of the sites for the **World Championship Formula T-1** speed boats.

About 11 km from Morón, beside the road and before the Isla de Turiguanó, is **Laguna La Redonda**. It covers an area of 26 sq km, with four main canals and a channel network, with an average depth of 1 m. Red mangroves grow in abundance and you may see the *tocororo*, the national bird. The lake is full of fish, principally the largemouth bass. A record was set in the 1980s when a group of Americans caught 5,078 fish in five days. There is a **Puertosol** marina at the lake, where you can arrange fishing trips and hire rods, boats and guides, and a restaurant/bar where non-fishing visitors can sit and watch the water. Fishing is available all year, there is no closed season.

About 40 km west of Morón, where the land becomes more hilly and picturesque, is **Florencia**. This is a place where organized excursion parties come from the cays to sample Cuban country life. Horse riding is available in the hills, you can swim in the mineral waters of a river pool, have a lunch of suckling pig on the banks of the river and watch a rodeo. Independent travellers may not get the rodeo, but if a visit is timed not to coincide with a tour party, they could benefit from all the other activities in peaceful surroundings.

Cayo Coco → *Colour map 2, grid B6.*

Cayo Coco has become a focal point in the government's 'ecotourism' interests, although the hotels are large, luxury resorts built and operated with foreign investment. It is very isolated and nearly all foreigners are here on a package of a week or so and do not go far. There are plans to build an average of 1,000 hotel rooms a year, all four or five star, until Cayo Coco has 16,000 and the other cays have a further 6,000. There will be other development for tourism on Media Luna, Antón Chico and Paredón Grande. Cayo Coco is a large island, 374 sq km, of mostly mangrove and bush, which shelter many migratory birds as well as permanent residents. The first hotels on Cayo Coco are 62 km from Morón. The island is connected to the mainland just north of Morón by a 27 km causeway cross the Bahía de Perros. This used to be the main way for visitors to arrive on the cay, using the international airport north of Ciego de Avila, but now Cayo Coco has its own international airport. Contact tour operators, see Activities and tours, to arrange excursions if you do not have your own transport.

The Atlantic side of the island has excellent beaches, particularly **Playa Los Flamencos** (15 minutes' drive from hotels), with some 5 km of white sand and shallow, crystalline water. Year round you will see flamingoes, after whom the beach is named. Flamingoes nearly died out here in the 1970s but, with some encouragement, have increased to some 30,000 birds in the cays. Beach bars, barbecues and horses for hire. The beaches are quite difficult to get to and some of the hotels restrict access to guests only.

Anyone looking for solitude can explore **Playa Prohibida**, appropriately named as the government has banned construction here in the interests of ecology. A nature trail starts from near here leading into the centre of Cayo Coco, ending at a dune, the highest point in the area at 212 m. There is a cave, **Cueva Jabalí**, 6 km from **Tryp Cayo Coco hotel**, where shows and discos are held. The cave is divided into interconnecting rooms. A golf course is being built. **El Bagá nature park** ① T33-301064, is a recently protected 70-ha area designed to preserve the wildlife as well as make it accessible to visitors. It is named after a local tree, the roots of which are used for floats in fishing nets. Among its facilities are an Indian village, a lookout, farms to raise *jutías*, bats, crocodiles, butterflies and flamingos, a dock, a museum on piracy and cafeterias.

Cayo Guillermo

Cayo Guillermo, a 13-sq-km cay with 5 km of beach, is connected to Cayo Coco by a causeway and there are plans underway to build a 35-km causeway to link it with Cayo Santa María to the west. Cayo Guillermo is protected by a long coral reef which is good for diving with plentiful fish and crustaceans, while on land there are lots of birds. Sand dunes, covered in palms and other vegetation, are believed to be among the highest in the Caribbean. The environment is protected by the **Santa María National Park**. The author Ernest Hemingway came here to fish, which is why there are frequent references to him. Fishing is still superb around here and if you tire of deep sea fishing you can make an excursion to one of the freshwater lakes mentioned above.

Jardines de la Reina

The Jardines de la Reina archipelago is uninhabited and generally visited only by liveaboard dive boats. The cays run along the south coasts of the provinces of Ciego de Avila, Camagüey and Las Tunas. Access is usually from **Júcaro** on the coast. Dive boats leave here. A new 20-km causeway is being built out over the sea to Cayo Providencia, opening up the south of the province to tourism. Other cays are expected to be developed as the road is extended to Cayo Caoba in the gulf of Ana María. Fishing and diving will be promoted among these virgin cays with empty beaches. Of all the cays there is only one with any infrastructure for visitors, and that is still limited. **Cayo Caguama** is just off the south coast of the province of Camagüey. It is earmarked for development but has not got much more than an airstrip so far. There is a beach where turtles nest and iguanas run around under the trees. Diving and snorkelling are available and there are several restaurants. Package tours cost US$105 and include the flight by air taxi, food, diving and snorkelling, as a day trip from Santa Lucía on the north coast; contact **Rumbos** or **Fantástico** tour agencies in the resort hotels. ▸▸ *For further details, see Diving and marine life, Essentials page 62.*

● Sleeping

Ciego de Avila *p273, map p272*
Hotels
C-D Hotel Ciego de Avila (Islazul), Carretera de Ceballos, about 2 km outside Ciego de Avila, T33-228013. 143 standard, functional rooms in a modern, 5-storey block, large pool, taxis, **Havanautos** car hire, good food.
D-E Santiago-Habana (Islazul), Honorato del Castillo entre Joaquín Agüero y Chicho Valdés, T33-225703, F33-227262. 76 rooms on the main road through town, rundown but convenient.
D-E Sevilla, Independencia 57 entre Honorato del Castillo y Maceo, T33-225603. Central, renovated, a/c, TV, video, radio, room service, restaurant, café, bar, car and motorbike hire, disco.

Morón *p274*
Hotels
B-C Carrusel Morón (Cubanacán), off Av de Tarafa, T335-2230, hhmm@hmoron .cav.cyt.cu 3-star, concrete block type of hotel, 144 rooms and suites with balcony, 3 restaurants, 2 coffee shops, bars, disco, large pool, games room, good a/c and food, tourism bureau, medical service, car hire, currency exchange, shop, shooting arranged with guide and dog.
D La Casona de Morón (Horizontes), Cristóbal de Colón 41, T335-2236, F335-2128. Also known as the *Club de Caza y Pesca*, 2 star, 7 a/c rooms, yellow colonial building, TV, minibar, restaurant, grill, bar, nightclub, pool, *cambio*, used by hunters.

Casas particulares
F Alcides Pérez Torres, Calle 11 edif 9 Apto 23, T335-54552.
F Juan Clemente Pérez, Castillo 189 entre Serafín Sánchez y San José, T335-53823. Nice family, helpful and friendly, 2 rooms, a/c, private bathroom, simple but clean, hot water available, Spanish only.
F Onaida Ruiz, Calle 5 46 esq 8, T335-3409.

Cayo Coco and Cayo Guillermo *p274*
All the hotels on Cayo Coco and Cayo Guillermo are all-inclusive. Some of them are huge; they are all new and in good condition. All offer several restaurants, entertainment and watersports. The rate will vary depending on how long you are staying and the time of year. Although most people who stay here are booked on packages from abroad, independent travellers can book their own stays at short notice once they are in the country. In high season there is limited availability for rooms of less than a week's rental, but out of season rooms are filled on a daily basis. There are lots of 2-3 day packages or weekend breaks offered from Havana. Details of **Sol**, **Meliá** and **Tryp** hotels on www.solmelia.es or www.solmeliacuba.com The full list is on www.dtcuba.com At the end of 2001 there were 3,200 hotel rooms in the Jardines del Rey archipelago.

Camping
The Reservations office for **Campismo Popular** is at Honorato Castillo entre Independencia y Libertad, Edificio 12 Plantas, T33-222708. All 5 sites in the province are reserved for national tourism, but exceptions can be made. 3 are inland with river bathing, at Boquerón, near Florencia, T33-69318, Los Naranjos, near Ciro Redondo, T33-36700, and El Charcazo, near Primero de Enero, T33-82568. On the north coast at Máximo Gómez, near Punta Alegre, T33-66112, and on Cayo Coco, Km 14, T33-301105.

● Eating

Ciego de Avila *p273, map p272*
Restaurants
$ **Cafetería 12 Plantas**, Parque Martí, same building as **Solaris**, below, open for breakfast, lunch and dinner. State-run, low quality.
$ **Don Pepe**, Independencia 103 entre Simón Reyes y Maceo, T33-223713. Cuban food, open for lunch and dinner until there are no customers.

$ **El Colonial**, Independencia 110, entre Simón Reyes y Maceo, T33-233595, open for lunch and dinner. Nice courtyard but Spanish food nothing to write home about.
$ **La Romagnola**, Carretera Central entre M Gómez y Honorato del Castillo, T33-225989, open for lunch and dinner. Italian.
$ **Solaris**, Honorato del Castillo entre Independencia y Libertad on the west side of Parque Martí, top floor of 12-storey building, T33-222156. 24-hr **Rumbos** bar serving fried chicken and cold beer as well as 'international' food.

Morón *p274*

$ **Doña Neli**, Serafín Sánchez 86 esq Martí, T335-4216. 24-hr snack bar and bakery.
$ **La Fuente**, Martí 169 entre Libertad y Agramonte, T335-5758. Creole and international food.
$ **San Fernando**, Rotonda de Morón, Km 34, at entrance to the city, T335-5440. Restaurant open 24 hrs, international food, with 2 rooms to rent, a/c, private bathroom. Outside town is La Cueva de la Laguna de la Leche, which has a *parrillada*.

● Entertainment

Ciego de Avila *p273, map p272*
Music and dance
Batanga, Hotel Ciego de Avila, T33-228013. Hotel disco, open until 0200 or later.
Casa de la Trova, Libertad 130 y Simón Reyes, Ciego de Avila. Traditional and folklore live music.
La Cima, Hotel Santiago-Habana, T33-225703.
La Macarena, Hotel Sevilla, T33-225603. Bar and disco.
Moscú, Carretera Central 78 y Maceo, T33-225386. Bar and disco.
Paraíso Las Palmeras, José Martí 382 entre Sergio Antuña y Dimas, T33-225328. Disco with taped music.

Morón *p274*
Disco en La Casona, Hotel La Casona. Outdoors, lots of people, popular.
Discoteca, Hotel Carrousel Morón, T335-3901. From 2200 but best after 2400.

Cayo Coco *p274*
All the hotels offer nighttime activities, night clubs, discos, piano bars etc.

▲ Activities and tours

Diving
Avalón (Marinas Puertosol), near Cayo Caballones off the south coast at Júcaro, Jardines de la Reina, T33-98104. CMAS resort courses and open-water courses, snorkelling, equipment rental, 2 liveaboard boats, shark diving, night diving. This is the only dive centre in the area, where there is also a small floating hotel, *Hotel Flotante Tortuga*, for divers and fishermen.
Blue Diving, Hotel Meliá Cayo Coco, T33-308179.
Coco (Cubanacán Náutica), Tryp Cayo Coco, T33-301323 ext 741. Equipment rental for diving and snorkelling. Resort courses and open water certification with CMAS, ACUC, SSI. Capacity for 32 divers a day on the boats.
Jardines del Rey (Cubanacán Náutica), Rotonda Villa Océano, Cayo Guillermo, T33-301738. ACUC, CMAS and SSI courses at all levels of training. Snorkelling and equipment rental.
Meliá Cayo Guillermo (Cubanacán Náutica), at Meliá Cayo Guillermo, T33-301627.
Scuba Cuba, Sol Club Cayo Guillermo, T33-301760. Diving and snorkelling gear for rent, resort courses and open water certification as well as windsurfing, water skiing, catamarans, glass-bottom boats and trips to other cays.

Fishing and shooting
Horizontes, Morón, www.horizontes.cu Organizes shooting for game birds and waterfowl at Aguachales de Falla and other lakes close by. The hunting season runs 15 Nov-15 Mar and a licence costs US$25. On top of that you pay for the hire of a 12-bore shotgun, about US$8 per day, ammunition US$12 and transport rental US$0.80 per km. *Puertosol*, Laguna la Redonda, Morón. Marina where you can arrange fishing trips and hire rods, boats and guides, and a restaurant/bar where non-fishing visitors can sit and watch the water. Fishing is available all year, there is no closed season.

Marinas
Marina Cayo Coco, Casasa, VHF 16 and 72, commissary, minor repairs, fuel, water, boat rental, fishing, dive centre.

Marina Cayo Coco-Guillermo (Cubanacán Náutica), Faro Paredón Grande, Cayo Guillermo, T33-301637, VHF 16, 19. 6 berths, 30 m draft, fuel, water, electricity, commissary, restaurant, bar, boat rental, fishing, diving, snorkelling, excursions. **Marina Júcaro** (Puertosol). Moorings for 6 boats, maximum 5 m draft, catering and VHF/HF communications systems (VHF 16, 19, 68, 72, HF 2182, 2790, 7821). Bonefishing is available.

⊖ Transport

Air

There is an airport at Ceballos, 24 km north of Ciego de Avila, Aeropuerto Máximo Gómez (AVI), T33-266626/32525, which receives weekly scheduled flights from European cities, as well as twice weekly flights from **Havana** with **Cubana**. Charter flights also use this airport from time to time to get holiday-makers out to the resort hotels on **Cayo Coco** but it is being replaced by a new international airport on **Cayo Coco** which opened in 2002. Cayo Coco airport receives flights from **Havana** and **Varadero** as well as international flights with aircraft carrying no more than 150 passengers.

Airlines Cubana, Carretera Central 83 y Honorato Castillo, T33-266627/225316. **Aerotaxi** at Cayo Coco airport, T33-301245.

Bus

The Ciego de Avila bus station is on the Carretera Central just east of the zoo. **Víazul**, T33-225109, stops here on its **Havana-Santiago** route. Víazul, to **Havana, Trinidad, Cienfuegos**. Also a Víazul minibus going out to the **cays**. Check with Víazul about the timetable and price. Only tour buses and the Víazul minibus go to **Cayo Coco**, there are no public buses and a checkpoint at the beginning of the causeway effectively prevents Cubans without permission from visiting the cay.

Astro, to **Santa Clara**, **Havana** and **Camagüey**.

There are other, cheaper buses to all the places on the main road from **Havana-Santiago** and a lot of others besides, such as **Manzanillo, Holguín** and **Niquero**. However, by the time the long-distance buses get here they are nearly always full. **Morón** bus terminal at Martí entre Poi y Céspedes.

Car hire

Agencia de Transporte para Turistas, Av Tarafa, Morón, for car rental and taxis. **Cubacar**, head office for the area at Cayo Coco, T33-308197. **Havanautos** is at the Aeropuerto Máximo Gómez, T33-223312. **Micar**, Libertad esq Agramonte, Morón, T33-266157, and on Cayo Coco, T33-266216. **Transautos**, is at Hotel Ciego de Avila, T33-228013, and at Sol Club Cayo Guillermo, T33-301760 ext 266.

Petrol stations Most tourists move around on tour buses, but if you have a car, there are **Cupet-Cimex** gas stations at Carretera de Morón, Circunvalación Km 2.5, Ciego de Avila, Crucero Campo Hatuey, Majagua, and Carretera de Morón, Vía Cayo Coco. Oro Negro station is at Carretera Central e Independencia Km 444, Ciego de Avila.

Taxi

Cubataxi, Reparto Ortiz, T33-266666. **Taxi OK**, central office on Cayo Coco, T33-308197. **Turistaxi**, in Ciego de Avila, T33-222997, and on Cayo Coco, T33-301712.

Train

3 trains daily to **Ciego de Avila** to and from **Havana**. Most trains go through at night to **Holguín, Matanzas** and **Santiago**. **Morón** is on the **Santa Clara-Nuevitas** railway line. Every other day to **Santiago** and **Havana**, 2 daily to **Camagüey**.

ⓘ Directory

Ciego de Avila *p273, map p272*

Banks Banco Financiero Internacional, Honorato Castillo 14, T33-266310. **Bandec**, Independencia 73 y Maceo, T33-23002.
Hospitals and clinics Clínica Internacional de Cayo Coco, Hotel Tryp Club Cayo Coco, T33-301205. Facilities for tourists. **Post office** At the corner of Chicho Valdés y Marcial Gómez.
Telephone Note that phone numbers are changing, some have 6 digits, some still have 5. Salón de Llamadas Nacionales e Internacionales, on Parque Martí, Ciego de Avila, in the 12-storey building.

Camagüey

Camagüey is the largest of Cuba's 14 provinces and is an excellent place to break your journey if you are crossing the island from one end to the other. The unexceptional yet attractive countryside is flat and fertile, with cattle roaming the grasslands which are dotted with Royal palms. The colonial capital city of Camagüey is recommended for a stay of a few days, as there is much of historical importance and lots of sites of revolutionary interest from the 19th and 20th centuries. Significant restoration works are taking place in the city on churches, plazas and mansions. Culturally, Camagüey has lots to offer, with street parties on Saturday nights, an excellent ballet company and lots of music and art. Camagüey has been politically and historically important since the beginning of the 16th century. Many generations of revolutionaries have been associated with Camagüey and several key figures are commemorated, the most notable being Ignacio Agramonte, who was killed in action in 1873. However, most tourists head instead for the north coast to Santa Lucía beach resort for sun, sea and sand. This is another of Cuba's remote hotel developments and it can be difficult to organize worthwhile excursions unless you have a car. Trips to cays off the south coast are now being offered by plane or liveaboard boat, which are very popular with divers, snorkellers and turtle watchers.▶▶ For Sleeping, Eating and other listings, see pages 287-291.

Ins and outs

Getting there All major routes pass through Camagüey province and as the city is squarely in the middle, it is well located as far as communications are concerned. The international **airport** is 9 km north of the city and you may be lucky enough to find a bus that will bring you into Parque Finlay, otherwise you will have to catch a taxi, state or private, US$5. Most tourists arriving at the airport are taken by bus straight to their resorts on the north coast, not into Camagüey. There are **flights** from Havana and international scheduled and charter flights, although these vary with the season. The **railway** station is just north of the centre, within walking distance of several hotels and *casas particulares*, and on the main line from Havana to Santiago. The **bus** station is further out, the other side of the river from the centre, with several daily buses from Havana and Santiago, as well as good connections with neighbouring towns. Taxi from here to the town centre, approximately US$5.▶▶ *For further details, see also Transport, page 291.*

Getting around The active will be able to **walk** to most sites of interest in the city, otherwise you can pick up a **bicitaxi** for around US$1. Many provincial towns can be reached by **bus** or **truck**, but check your return journey before setting off. **Car hire** is available, or you can arrange for a Cuban to drive you in his car.

Tourist information All the main hotels have tourist agencies who can provide information, although their main aim is to sell tours. In Camagüey, the **Havanatur** agent at the Gran Hotel is a mine of knowledge about the province (see below, tour operators). The **Cubatur** office in Camagüey is of very little use except that there are computers for internet access, even their tours are sold only from Playa Santa Lucía and you cannot sign up for one from the city unless you are part of a large party.

History

The capital of the province was originally called Puerto Príncipe, until 9 June 1903. The village of Santa María de Puerto del Príncipe was first founded in 1515 at Punta del Guincho in the Bahía de Nuevitas, but the site was unsatisfactory for development because of a lack of water and poor soil fertility. In 1516 the first settlers moved to

⁞ Tinajón – vessel of love and bondage

The logo of Camagüey is the *tinajón* and the city is known as the city of the *tinajones*. This story goes back to the time when the first settlers had serious problems with their water supply. However, it rained a lot in the region and the Spanish potters found a solution by storing water in pots similar to those brought from Spain containing wine and oil. From that time on the *tinajón* became a feature of every Camagüeyan house or patio. Legend has it that if a girl offers a visitor water from a *tinajón*, he should not refuse it, but before accepting, he should know that if he drinks he will fall in love with the girl and never leave the city.

Caonao (an Amerindian word for gold or place where gold can be found), an aborigine chiefdom near the Río Caonao. However, in 1527 enslaved Amerindians rose up against the Spanish colonizers and burned down the town. The settlers then moved again, further inland, between the Río Tínima and the Río Hatibonico, where the village was finally established.

Moving inland was no protection against pirate attacks. During the 17th century, as the settlement became prosperous on the back of raising livestock, and later sugar, it was the target of the Welshman Henry Morgan in 1668 and of French pirates led by François Granmont in 1679. However, despite the looting, the town continued to grow throughout the 18th century, although its architects took the precaution of designing the layout to foil pirate attacks. No two streets run parallel, and this creates a maze effect, which is most unlike other colonial towns built on the grid system. On 12 November 1817, Fernando VII, the king of Spain, declared Puerto Príncipe a city with a coat of arms.

Several revolutionary events of the 19th century are remembered in Camagüey. In 1812 eight black slaves fighting for independence under the command of José Antonio Aponte, were executed. In 1826, revolutionary Agüero Velazco was hanged in what is now Parque Agramonte. Joaquín de Agüero y Agüero and his followers took arms against the colonial power in 1851, but their movement failed and they were executed by firing squad. In 1868, when Carlos Manuel de Céspedes initiated the struggle for independence, many Camagueyans supported him, including Ignacio Agramonte, Salvador Cisneros Betancourt, Maximiliano Ramos, Javier de la Vega and others who are remembered in street names, monuments and museums.

Land and environment

Camagüey is the largest province in the country covering more than 14,000 sq km. It is mostly low lying. Its highest point, at 330 m, is in the Sierra de Cubitas to the north of Camagüey city. The Atlantic north coast is broken by a series of large coral cays, which make up the Archipiélago de Camagüey. There is great potential for tourism here, with long sandy beaches, crystal clear water and fantastic diving on the reef, but so far there has been little development except at Playa Santa Lucía in the east. Behind the protective cays, the land is marshy, until it rises gently to the Sierra de Cubitas where there are caves and rocky spurs. Nuevitas is the main port on the north coast and there is considerable heavy industry in the area. The southern, Caribbean coast of the province is mostly swampy. There is a fishing port at Santa Cruz del Sur, but otherwise little habitation in the wetlands. Offshore, the sea is dotted with tiny uninhabited cays, which are part of the Archipiélago Jardines de la Reina. Previously one of Fidel Castro's favourite fishing spots, the cays are now visited mostly by scuba divers on liveaboard boats.

Beef and dairy farming occupies much of the land and many of the province's traditions revolve around cowboys and their activities, such as rodeos. There are also many poultry farms in the central part around Camagüey and Minas. Sugar cane is grown in the north and south of the province, with sugar mills near Florida, Carlos Manuel de Céspedes, Brasil, Senado, Vertientes, Batalla de las Guásimas, Cándido González, Haití and Hatuey. There are also rice fields in the west around El Trece and El Alazán. Some citrus is grown and processed in the north near Solas.

Sights

City centre

Colonial buildings of the 17th to 19th centuries are interspersed with more modern constructions of the 20th century and walking around the city will reveal many architectural gems being used for everyday purposes. There are plazas, museums and churches being restored to attract tourism, but this is not a tourist city.

Santa Iglesia Catedral is on the south side of Parque Ignacio Agramonte. Construction was started after the town fire of 1616 with the intention that it should be the largest parish church in Puerto Príncipe, with two chapels and a cemetery. In the 19th century the chapels were demolished and a different shape was given to the building in 1875. In 1937 the sculptor Juan Albaijez carved a statue of Christ which was placed inside the church. After being closed for some time for renovations it reopened in 2001 with a newly painted exterior and very smart interior. The Parque has also had a facelift, with lots of marble and a cleaned up statue of Ignacio Agramonte on horseback. The Casa de la Trova is on the west side of the square, together with the library. One block away on Agüeros esq Cisneros is the **Casa Natal de Nicolás Guillén Batista**. The building may have been the poet's birthplace, but he only lived here until he was two. The building is now used as an art and cultural studies school although staff are very happy to show you round and there are a few pictures and some of his poems on the walls. See also page 407.

A couple of blocks south of the Parque is **San Juan de Dios**, another national monument, built in 1728 as a church with a hospital attached, the first hospital in the village for men. It also contained a home for the aged. Apparently this is the only church in Latin America that has the Holy Trinity as its central image. The **Plaza San Juan de Dios** was created at the beginning of the 19th century when two houses were bought to make the plaza. At around this time the San Juan de Dios church tower was moved to the front. On 12 May 1873 the body of Ignacio Agramonte was deposited in the hospital for identification before being taken to the cemetery. In 1902 the hospital was closed and later converted to a military infirmary. It was used to house the homeless after the hurricane in 1932 and was inaugurated as a modern hospital in 1952. Cobblestones were laid in the plaza in 1956. The hospital building changed hands several times before the **Centro Provincial de Patrimonio Cultural** occupied it. There are plans to turn it into a luxury hotel. The plaza is closed to traffic. There is a small handicraft market, **Tienda Caracol**, and a couple of restaurants.

Casa Jesús Suárez Gayol, now the **Museo Estudiantil Camagüeyano** ① *República 69, T32-297744, closed lunchtime,* was the home of one of the Cuban guerrillas who lost his life in Bolivia in 1967 alongside Che Guevara. The museum has exhibits about Camagüeyans, particularly students, who were active revolutionaries in the struggle for independence.

East of the cathedral along Luaces is the **Parque Martí**, also known as the **Plaza de la Juventud**. The **Sagrado Corazón de Jesús**, on Luaces, overlooking the Parque Martí, is a beautiful neo-Gothic church built in 1920. It used to have wonderful stained-glass windows depicting scenes from the gospel, but most were destroyed by stone throwing after the Revolution. Restoration work also started here in January 2001, with a new roof

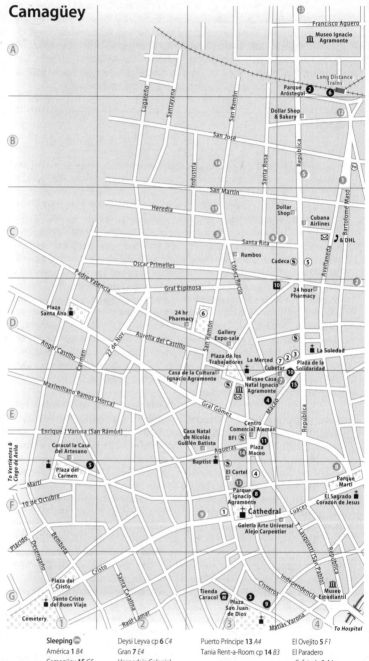

N

Not to scale

Sleeping	Deysi Leyva cp **6** C4	Puerto Príncipe **13** A4	El Ovejito **5** F1
América **1** B4	Gran **7** E4	Tania Rent-a-Room cp **14** B3	El Paradero
Camagüey **15** G5	Hospedaje Colonial		Cafetería **6** A4
Caridad García	Los Vitrales cp **8** F4	**Eating**	La Volanta **8** F3
Valua cp **2** D4	Isla de Cuba **10** D4	Cafetería Ditú **2** A4	Parador de los
Casa Blanca cp **3** C3	Jorge Rovirosa cp **9** F3	Campana de Toledo **3** G3	Tres Reyes **9** G3
Casa Manolo cp **4** C3	Jorge Sáez Solano cp **11** C3	Coppelia **4** E3	Pizzería la Piazza **10** E4
Colón **5** B4	Plaza **12** B4	Doñaneli **15** E4	Rancho Luna **11** E3

Bars & clubs 🎶
Bar el Cambio **13** *F3*
Bar Las Ruinas **14** *E3*

Entertainment 😊
Casa de Trova **1** *F3*
Cine Encanto **2** *D4*
Cine Casablanca **7** *D4*

Colonial Galería **3** *D4*
Disco Café **4** *F3*
Disco Labarra **5** *C4*
Teatro Principal **6** *D3*

among other works. Good progress is being made on the church and a building on the west side of the square is also shored up with timber supports prior to its renovation.

North of Parque Ignacio Agramonte, if you walk up Independencia, you come to Plaza Maceo, a busy junction of several roads with shops, banks and places to eat. One block north of here is the **Plaza de los Trabajadores**. **Nuestra Señora de la Merced**, a National Monument on Avenida Agramonte on the eastern edge of the Plaza de los Trabajadores, was built in 1747 as a church and convent at what was then the edge of town but is now in the centre. Over the years it has been transformed into a baroque church and a diocesan house where specific activities are held by the church. In the courtyard there are abandoned cannon used by the Spanish military in the 19th century. In 1906 a fire burned the altar, which was reconstructed in Spain in a neo-Gothic style. As the city expanded, the cemetery had to be closed, but the catacombs can still be seen. The entrance is either side of the altar; you will be followed by a warden down the steps into the mini-museum. The original wooden cross on the bell tower was moved into the catacombs in 1999. You can also see bones, skulls and several 18th-century artefacts from the church. The ceiling of the church shows early 20th-century paintings in a swirling pre-Raphaelite style, although it badly needs to be restored. On the walls are four 17th-century and eight 18th-century paintings, but the most important treasure in the church is the Santo Sepulcro, a silver coffin, constructed in 1762 with the donation of 23,000 silver coins. Before the Revolution, it was carried in procession along the streets of Camagüey; now it is kept inside the church. The church has been under restoration for many years and is still not completed. It has an external clock, which was the first public clock in Camagüey, and a library. There is always someone around to show visitors the church and provide information.

Also on the square is the **Museo Casa Natal Ignacio Agramonte**① *Av Ignacio Agramonte 49, opposite the church on Plaza de los Trabajadores, T32-297116, Tue-Sat 1000-1800, US$2.* The museum is for serious students of revolutionary history. Ignacio Agramonte y Loynaz, one of the national heroes of the struggle against the Spanish, was born here on 23 December 1841. Agramonte, a lawyer and cattle rancher, led the rebellion in this area and in July 1869 forces under his command bombarded Camagüey. However, he died on 11 May 1873 after being wounded in action. When he took up arms against the colonial power in 1868 shortly after finishing his studies at university in Spain and Havana all his goods were confiscated by the state. The ground floor and courtyard of this lovely house were turned into a market while the second storey was occupied by the Spanish council. Later the ground floor became a bar and a post office. In the second half of the 20th century the house was restored and now the top floor is a museum exhibiting objects relating to the life of this revolutionary, while other rooms are used for lectures, art exhibitions and offices.

East along Ignacio Agramonte is the tiny Plaza de la Solidaridad, formerly Plaza del Gallo, little more than a junction of five roads. **Nuestra Señora de la Soledad** is on República esquina Ignacio Agramonte on the edge of the Plaza. It is the oldest church in town. In 1697 the Presbyterian Velasco started the construction of a hermitage which was concluded in 1701 and transformed into a parish by the bishop Diego Evelino de Compostela. In 1733 the current church was started, although construction was not finished until 1776. The outside is of brick, while inside there are attractive painted friezes on the arches, a carved wooden roof and a painted cupola (which needs renovation).

West of the centre

Iglesia Nuestra Señora de Santa Ana, along General Gómez, was started in 1697 with a single nave. Over the years it was gradually enlarged with a tower added in the middle of the 19th century.

Nuestra Señora del Carmen, on the west side of Plaza del Carmen, was started in 1732 by Eusebia de Varona y de la Torre, who wanted to build a three-nave temple for the Jesuits. However, they did not like its location, which at that time was on the outskirts of the town, so they demolished it. One hundred years later, her heirs with the help of Padre Valencia, built the women's hospital of Nuestra Señora del Carmen, which was finished in 1825. A church was built alongside the hospital, originally with only one tower, but a second was added in 1846, making it the only two-towered church in Camagüey. Part of the church collapsed in 1966 but restoration started in January 2001. The façade has been replastered and work continues inside. The hospital alongside is now the **Sede del Historiador de la Ciudad**. The whole of the **Plaza del Carmen** has been renovated, a task which included housing as well as smart new restaurants and tourist shops. An amusing feature are the clay statues of very lifelike people going about their ordinary tasks: women gossiping over coffee, a man pushing a cart, another man reading a newspaper and a couple with their arms around each other. It's pleasant to sit on a bench with them and watch the world go by.

At the west end of Calle Cristo is **Santo Cristo del Buen Viaje**, built as a small hermitage in 1794 by Emeterio de Arrieta with one nave. In the 19th-century two naves and a tower were constructed. It is rather dilapidated and the walls are deteriorating, but the large cemetery behind it is kept very smart with grand tombs. The square in front of the church, **Plaza del Cristo** or **Parque Gonfaus**, is not as interesting as some of the older squares in town as it has no buildings of architectural interest and even the benches are broken.

North of the centre

Museo Provincial Ignacio Agramonte① *Av de los Mártires 2 esq Ignacio Sánchez, T32-282425, Tue, Wed, Thu and Sat 1000-1730, Fri 1200-2000, Sun 1000-1200, US$2,* first built as a cavalry barracks in 1848, was converted into the **Hotel Camagüey**

from 1905-43, but there are still cannon, water troughs and *tinajones* in the garden.
After considerable restoration the museum was inaugurated on 23 December 1955 (the anniversary of Agramonte's birth). There are exhibitions of archaeology, with copies of drawings and artifacts found in the caves of the Sierra de Cubitas (see below), natural history (lots of dusty stuffed animals and birds), paintings and furniture of the 19th and 20th centuries, but nothing special.

Southeast of the centre

The **Parque Casino Campestre**, on the eastern side of the Río Hatibonico, was the first place in Cuba to hold cattle shows. In the 19th century it was used for fairs, dances and other social activities but in the 20th century its purpose and structure was changed. Trees have been planted and there are monuments to independence fighter Salvador Cisneros Betancourt, to the Unknown Soldier, and to teachers. Next to the park there is a monument erected in 1941 to Barberán and Collar, the first pilots to cross the Atlantic at its widest point, in a flight from Seville. It took them 39 hours and 55 minutes.

Around Camagüey

Without your own transport, it may be easier to take an excursion, for further details see Activities and tours. There is a **Crocodile farm** ① *9 km from Senado, just north west of Minas, 0900-1700, US$1*, where endangered species are preserved. There are walking tours of the **Sierra de Cubitas**, a protected area 35 km north of Camagüey, where you can visit caves with Amerindian drawings and see much endemic wildlife and lots of birds. The tour lasts all day and is hot and tiring, minimum eight people, two expert guides, take a hat, good walking boots and lots of water. **King Ranch**, 80 km from Camagüey on the way to Santa Lucía, offers rodeo, horse riding and cheap accommodation.

Playa Santa Lucía → *Colour map 3, grid B3*

Santa Lucía is a beach resort 112 km northeast, or two hours by road, from Camagüey, where the sand stretches some 20 km along the northern coast near the **Bahía de Nuevitas**. This is a beautiful beach, protected by an offshore reef which contains over 50 species of coral and is much sought after by divers (see Diving and marine life, page 62). The water is clear and warm, with an average temperature of 24°C. You can sometimes see dolphins near the shore and there are flamingoes in the salt flats (*saliñas*) inshore. The province is the second largest salt producer in the country (after Guantánamo) and the area is principally scrub, swamp and salt flats. It is a lovely place to come and relax but be aware that it is remote, there is no real town as such, although plenty of people live here, and excursions inland can therefore be time-consuming and expensive. Most people who stay here are on all-inclusive package tours for a week or so and see little of Cuba. However, hotel tour desks can offer you day trips or longer excursions by land, sea or air to anywhere in Cuba.

Eight kilometres from Santa Lucía there is **Playa Los Cocos**, which is even better than Santa Lucía. There is a broad sweep of beach with a fishing village, La Boca, at one end and beach bars at the other end by the channel which leads to Nuevitas. There are lots of coconut palms after which the beach gets its name. The sand here is very white and the water crystal clear. There are a few rocky bits at the edge of the water but it is mostly sandy, gently sloping and safe for children. The bars and seafood restaurants (fresh lobster for less than US$11) will rent you sunbeds, US$1. Use insect repellent against the small, black, biting insect known as a *jején*; the bites hurt at the time you are bitten but they only start to itch like mad the next day.

Across the channel, west of Playa Los Cocos, is **Cayo Sabinal**, reached by road from Nuevitas. Boat trips will be organized by hotel tour desks in Santa Lucía. Hemingway was inspired to write that it was a marvellous place where the wind from the east blows night and day, and the territory as virgin as when Columbus arrived on these shores. Things haven't changed much since then. There are beautiful beaches of white sand which are practically deserted and the cay is a wildlife reserve housing the largest colony of pink flamingoes in the Caribbean, plus many other birds that are rare or endangered elsewhere. There is pleasant accommodation available in cabins, but lots of mosquitoes. There are seafood restaurants along the beaches of Playa Brava (the better beach) and Playa Los Pinos. **Rumbos** do a day trip from Camagüey for US$45, T32-294807/297229, or you can take a bus to Nuevitas and arrange a private car to the cay for about US$10.

Florida → *Colour map 3, grid B1.*

Some 46 km northwest of Camagüey on the road and railway to Ciego de Avila, is Florida, a town of some 40,000 inhabitants, with hospitals and clinics, a museum, art gallery, *Casa de Cultura*, cinema, hotel and restaurants. There are a couple of sugar mills, some factories making construction materials and textiles and a brewery. Tour buses pass through here, but few foreigners stop long. However, there are a number of lagoons in the area and Florida is used as a base for shooting and fishing expeditions. The **reservoirs Porvenir** and **Muñoz** nearby and **Mañana de Santa Ana**, southeast of Camagüey, are used for organized six-hour trout fishing sessions. The area is also popular for shooting duck, quail, doves and guinea fowl, among other game birds, so if you stay at the local hotel, **Horizontes La Casona de Florida**, you may find your fellow guests are hunters. The other hotel, **Islazul Hotel Florida**, is used by **Víazul** as a pit stop for lunch on the way from Trinidad to Santiago, but the guests are all Cubans on a family holiday.

Nuevitas & Playa Santa Lucía

Sleeping	Club Caracol **5**	Club Santa Lucía **3**
Brisas Santa Lucía **1**	Club Sabinal los Pinos **6**	Escuela Santa Lucía **4**

Guáimaro → *Colour map 3, grid B3.*

Heading southeast by road towards Las Tunas, you can stop in Guáimaro, just before the provincial border. It is a small town about 80 km from Camagüey, with a population of about 20,000 and a lively agricultural fair, *Feria Agropecuaria*, every early October, when stalls are set up in the park and rows of people sell roast pork at the side of the street. However, it is notable for its historical connections: Carlos Manuel de Céspedes was elected first president of the Republic here by the constituent assembly of 1869. The assembly's other task was to draw up the first Cuban constitution. Seventy years later the town got round to commemorating the event with a monument in Parque Constitución dedicated to the men who fought for Cuban independence including Céspedes and José Martí.

● Sleeping

Camagüey centre *p279, map p282*
Hotels
C-D Gran Hotel (Islazul), Maceo 67, entre Ignacio Agramonte y General Gómez, T32-292093-4, comazul@teleda.get.cma.net Colonial style, built 1939, renovated 1997, very smart now, central, breakfast included, a/c, fan, cable TV, fridge, good bathroom, best rooms with balcony overlooking Maceo, security box rental, car hire, small swimming pool with children's area, restaurant on top floor, good view, also piano bar, 24-hr café with entrance from street (see Entertainment).
D Colón (Accor/Islazul), República 472 entre San José y San Martín, T32-283346/283368. Old style built in 1920s, beautifully painted in blue and white, marble staircase, long thin hotel on 2 floors round central well, rocking chairs overlook patio bar and restaurant, rooms with 1 or 2 beds, a/c, TV, phone, good bathroom, lobby bar, friendly staff.
D-E Plaza (Islazul), Van Horne 1, entre República y Avellaneda, T32-282413/282457. 67 rooms with TV, fridge, colonial building right by railway station, grim exterior, brown and cream, not all rooms have a/c, more expensive rooms face the front, with balcony, but rooms at the back are away from traffic noise, mediocre restaurant, bar, **Altamira** travel agency on the ground floor next to the shop, see Acitivities and tours, below.
E Puerto Príncipe (Islazul), Av de los Mártires 60 (República) y Andrés Sánchez (Francisco Aguero), La Vigía, T32-282490/282403, near museum and railway station. Modern block, functional, no charm, 77 rooms, a/c, bar, very slow restaurant, choose a room away from the nightclub on roof open until 0130 every night.

E-F América, Avellaneda esq San Martín, T32-282135. Small, cosy hotel with a/c, nice variety of dishes in the restaurant, bar.
E-F Isla de Cuba (Islazul), O Primelles 453 esq San Estéban, T32-292248/291515. In the heart of the city, 43 rooms, 2 grades.

Casas particulares
Rooms cost US$15-20, depending on commission, breakfast usually US$2-3, dinner US$5-7 if available.
E Hospedaje Colonial Los Vitrales, Avellaneda 3 entre Gral Gómez y Martí, T32-295866. Run by Rafael Requejo, an architect, and his family. Rafael speaks English and is full of stories about the architectural history of the house, which has a courtyard and colonial kitchen off it. Despite the lack of modern conveniences, good traditional meals are served, with beans and rice cooked the way they have been for centuries. 2 rooms with very high ceilings, a/c, fan, fridge, big bathroom, hanging space for laundry, own water tank giving good pressure, garage. In case of overspill, Rafael's sister has a legal room for rent upstairs through the garage.
F Caridad García Valua, Oscar Primelles 310 A entre Bartolomé Masó y Padre Olallo (Pobres), T32-291554. 2 rooms with private bathrooms, a/c or fan, fridge, garden, clean and nice.
F Casa Blanca, San Ramón 201 altos, entre Heredia y Santa Rita, T32-293542. Run by Blanca Navarro Castro and very welcoming, chatty family. 1 large room with double and single bed covered with bright pink shiny bedspread, private bathroom, a/c, fan, no

view, dark but comfortable, with tiled floors and high ceilings, laundry service. English spoken plus a little of other languages. Breakfast and dinner about US$10. Also in the same building, Casa Amelia, interconnecting apartments which makes them feel like 1 house, 5 mins' walk to railway station.

F **Casa Manolo**, Santa Rita 18 (El Solitario) entre República y Santa Rosa, T32-294403. Run by Migdalia Carmenates y Manolo Rodríguez, 2 rooms, a/c, fan, ensuite bathrooms, hot shower, patio, laundry US$2, garage US$2, nice house, newly painted, positive atmosphere, used by travel agency **Aventura del Mondo**.

F **Casa Rosello**, Carlos M de Céspedes 260 (Hospital) entre Hnos Agüeros y San Ramón, T32-292143/296879, ask for Pedro. 2 beautiful rooms, bathroom, owner practices *Santería* and will show you some interesting things, garage opposite, US$1 per night.

F **Deysi Leyva**, Santa Rita 16A, 1st floor, entre República y Santa Rosa, T32-293348. Extremely nice. On this street there are several *casas particulares* all together, note that those with the best decoration (not listed) are not necessarily the nicest places.

F **Jorge Rovirosa**, Cristo 2C entre Cisneros y Lugareño, T32-298305. Right by the cathedral and very central. Fabulous 1910 house, cavernous entrance hall with wrought iron gates inside the front door, marble staircase, very grand but dark and dilapidated. Apartment upstairs, 1 room, light and bright, lots of air, open windows, tiled floors, high ceilings, view over city. Jorge and/or his wife speak English, German and French, but his mother does not. Breakfast US$3, dinner US$6-7.

F **Jorge Saez Solano**, San Ramón 239 entre San Martín y Heredia, T32-286456. 2 rooms each with double and single bed, shared good bathroom between them, communicating doors, noisy a/c, fan, bedside light but poor light in rooms, nylon sheets rather small, 'sexy' posters on the walls, hot water if turned on in advance, laundry on request, friendly family, no *chicas* allowed, don't touch the Dobermann! Good food, not greasy, no beans.

F **Tania Rent-a-Room**, San Ramón 285 entre San José y San Martín. A/c, very nice family, can arrange trips to Santa Lucía.

Around Camagüey *p285*

D **Hotel Camagüey** (Horizontes), Carretera Central Este Km 4.5, T32-287267, roberto @hcamaguey.cmg.tur.cu Good condition, modern, Soviet-influenced architecture, pool, disco show, bar in the lobby and on 2nd floor, cafeteria, buffet restaurant US$10, car hire.

Playa Santa Lucía *p285, map p286*

The Santa Lucía resort is part of the Cubanacán group (www.cubanacan.cu), including joint venture hotels, restaurants, shopping centre, watersports, discos and other amenities. All the hotels are all-inclusive and prices are per person sharing a double room. Standards vary, but they all offer a/c, TV, entertainment, sports and tours. It is possible to stay in *casas particulares* at Playa Santa Lucía and Playa Los Cocos, but they are illegal.

AL **Brisas Santa Lucía**, T32-365120, aloja@cvientos.stl.cyt.cu 400 rooms of which 4 are wheelchair accessible, 8 suites. All the usual facilities you'd expect of a 4-star hotel.

B-C **Club Caracol**, T32-365158, secre@vita club.stl.cyt.cu 3 star, on the sea front in large gardens, 150 2-storey *cabañas* with sea view.

B **Club Santa Lucía**, T32-365145, aloja@coral .stl.cyt.cu Newish, low buildings and cabins, 3 star, considered one of the best with 108 rooms and suites on the beach, 144 garden rooms and suites, buffet and à la carte restaurant, snack bar, disco, pool with children's area and swim-up bar, games room, bicycle and scooter hire, lots of activities and trying to cater for all ages.

D-E **Escuela Santa Lucía**, T32-365184, aloja@tararaco.stl.cyt.cu The furthest hotel north and also a staff training centre. 2 star, one of the cheapest (US$25-35 per room without breakfast), very basic, 30 rooms, rather tatty but redeemed by personal touches, TV, restaurant, bar. Helpful staff, but services rather erratic. Decent budget option.

E **Club Sabinal Los Pinos** (Rumbos), Playa Los Pinos, Cayo Sabinal, T32-287047, T32-44754. Price (per person) includes 2 meals, 5 2-star cabins, bathroom, radio, bar, restaurant, horse rental, taxis, credit cards accepted.

Florida *p286*

E **Islazul Hotel Florida**, Carretera Central Km 536, on main road from Ciego de Avila to Camagüey, outskirts of town, T32-53011.

Popular with Cuban families on holiday. Large pool, bar, restaurant, snack bar, nightclub, music day and night around the pool, used by **Víazul** as a lunch stop.

Guáimaro *p287*
F **Guáimaro**, on the east side of town on the Carretera Central, T32-82102. Tired and crumbling, 40 rooms.

Camping
The Reservations office for **Campismo Popular** is at Av de la Libertad 208 entre Pancha Agramonte y Domingo Puentes, La Caridad, Camagüey, T32-296855. All the sites in the province of Camagüey are technically reserved for national tourism. Those inland have river bathing, but there is one on the north coast at Punta Ganado, east of Playa Santa Lucía, T32-336289.

⊘ Eating

Camagüey centre *p279, map p282*
Restaurants have a reputation for reheating leftovers, *paladares* can be expensive, *casas particulares* are best for fresh, wholesome cooking. In the city centre renovation of colonial buildings has led to a proliferation of smart, state-run restaurants with fairly mediocre food but in very attractive locations. There are several shops where you can buy food, but to find out how the locals cope, go to the *Agromercado* near the river. As well as fruit and vegetables there is a small place where you can order cooked food and lots of people will try to sell you snacks.
$$ **Don Ronquillo**, in covered area at the back of **Cubanacán Galería Colonial**, Ignacio Agramonte esq República, daily 1100-1500 and 1800-2200. Used by tour parties with set lunch and live music for US$10, reasonably priced, most dishes US$5-10, beer US$1, *mojito* US$1, menu lists *pollo gorden blue* (sic) for US$9.85.
$ **Parador de los Tres Reyes**, T32-295888, and **Campana de Toledo**, T32-295888. 2 small colonial-style **Rumbos** restaurants on Plaza San Juan de Dios serving Spanish food, pleasant, live music. The latter has tables overlooking the square or in the courtyard, chicken/fish US$5-6, *moros y cristianos* US$1.50. Open for lunch and dinner, but tour parties mean they are busy at lunchtime.

Cafés and snack bars
$ **Cafetería Ditú**, on República by Parque Aróstegui overlooking the railway line. Loud music but convenient if waiting for a train. Alternatively you can sit on one of the shady benches in the Parque and train spot.
$ **Doñaneli**, Maceo entre Ignacio Agramonte y E Gómez, opposite Gran Hotel, T32-296394, daily 0700-2200. Snacks, bakery and sweets.
$ **El Paradero**, near the railway station, cafeteria, bar and bakery open 24 hrs.
$ **Las Arecas**, *Gran Hotel*, Maceo. A good 24-hr snack bar on the ground floor, entrance on Maceo.
$ **La Volanta**, on Parque Agramonte, daily 1200-2300. Basic Cuban food, no frills, and you will be asked to pay in dollars.
$ **Pizzería La Piazza**, Agramonte on the corner with Maceo. You can pay in pesos but there may be a queue at lunchtime.
$ **Rancho Luna**, on the east side of Plaza Maceo, daily 1200-1400 and 1800-2200. Serves basic Cuban food.

West of the centre *p284*
$$$ **El Ovejito**, at the entrance to Plaza del Carmen, T32-292524. Quite elegant and lovely situation, US$10-30, *moros y cristianos* US$4, *mojito* an extortionate US$5.50.

Playa Santa Lucía *p285, map p286*
There are good café grills at Playa los Cocos, serving good fish and seafood at reasonable prices. As well as the state-run restaurants and cafés, there are also *paladares*, ask *coche* drivers for recommendations, which are better value, although beware that not all of them legal.
$$ **Las Brisas**, near the junction in the residential area, T32-36349. Creole.
$$ **Luna Mar** at the Centro Comercial, T32-36284. Passable pizzas, but avoid the fish.
$$ **Vía Appia**, Residencial Santa Lucía, T32-36101. Italian, open lunch and dinner.
$ **Alondra**, T32-36146. Ice cream on the beach.

⊘ Bars

Camagüey centre *p279, map p282*
Bar El Cambio, on the northeast corner of Parque Ignacio Agramonte. This one-time gambling den now has lottery artwork on the walls, *mojito* US$2, you can expect to be approached here with offers of 'private' restaurants. A good view of the cathedral.

Bar Las Ruinas, on west side of Plaza Maceo. Set in ruins and shady trees.

Gran Hotel (see above) has several bars with entertainment: **Piano Bar Marquesina**, US$5 for 2 people Mon-Fri, US$10 per couple on Sat and Sun, includes 2 meals and beer or rum; **Bar Piscina 1920**, US$3 per person (US$1 entrance, US$2 drinks), or US$10 Sat and Sun per couple including meal, beer/rum, with ballet acuático at 2130; **Bar El Mirador**, US$1 per person.

🕐 Entertainment

Camagüey centre *p279, map p282*
Cabaret
Galería Colonial, Ignacio Agramonte y República. Cabaret 3 times a week. Can be rented for private functions.

Cinema
Three cinemas: **Casablanca**, T32-292244 and **Encanto**, T32-295511, next door on Ignacio Agramonte, and **Guerrero**, T32-292874.

Live music and disco
Every Sat night a *Noche Camagüeya* is held along República, when the street is closed to traffic and there is music everywhere and traditional food. On Sun morning there are activities in Parque Casino Campestre, including live music.
Casa de la Trova, on the west side of Parque Agramonte between Martí and Cristo. Folk and traditional music, closed Mon. Courtyard and bar, while at the entrance is a souvenir shop where you can buy music.
Disco Café, Independencia entre Martí y Plaza Maceo. Good late-night place.
Disco Labarra, República entre O Primelles (San Estéban) y Santa Rita, opposite the *Cadeca*. Popular with a younger crowd.

Theatre
Teatro Principal, on Padre Valencia 64, T32-293048. The Ballet de Camagüey, ranked 2nd in the country after Havana's ballet company, often performs here.

Playa Santa Lucía *p285, map p286*
Live music and disco
Disco La Jungla, Centro Comercial, by Hotel Club Santa Lucía, T32-365145. Hotels lay on lots of daytime and evening entertainment and organized activities.

🛍 Shopping

Camagüey centre *p279, map p282*
Art
El Cartel, Cisneros entre Hermanos Agüero y Martí. Marvellous collection of original screen prints from the 1960s and 1970s, many featuring Che and Fidel, as well as countless movie posters in the distinctive Cuban style. Some of the original prints are for sale, kept in a dusty cupboard. They are in poor condition but well worth US$2 each. The owner will show you around the workshop if you ask.

Dollar shops
Artex and other dollar shops on Maceo, Agramonte, República and on Cisneros, just north of Parque Agramonte. Maceo is a particularly busy street, with **Centro Comercial Alemán** on Plaza Maceo, selling clothes, furniture and electro-domestic goods and other stores, **Coppelia** ice cream, fast food outlets and the **Gran Hotel** running up to Plaza de la Solidaridad.
Galería Colonial (Cubanacán), Ignacio Agramonte esq República. Located in a restored colonial mansion. Shops and services include **Casa del Tabaco**, restaurant **Don Ronquillo**, café **Mamá Inés**, snack bar **Las Arcadas**, nightclub **Patio Colonial**, tourist bureau, toilets. Used by tour parties but pleasant place to pause around town.

Handicrafts
Gallery Expo-sale on the side of the Plaza de los Trabajadores.

Photography
Fotovideo Camagüey, Maceo 76, T32-287261, daily 0900-1700.
Photo service is on Agramonte esq López Recio, T32-296468, daily 0900-1700. There is also a branch on Gen Gómez entre Independencia y Maceo.

West of the centre *p284*
Caracol La Casa del Artesano, on Plaza del Carmen, Mon-Sat 0930-1720. Handicrafts.

Playa Santa Lucía *p285, map p286*
Centro Comercial, T32-365291. The usual tourist shops selling clothes, rum, cigars, souvenirs etc, with ice cream, bar and snack bar to help pass the time.

⤳ Activities and tours

Diving

At Playa Santa Lucía there are 37 dive sites at depths of 5-40 m in the area including a daily shark feeding site in the channel between Playa Los Cocos and Cayo Sabinal about 20 m offshore. There is a concrete area by the *guardia* station and steps down into the water. Up to 20 sharks congregate at a depth of some 26 m by the wreck of a Spanish galleon at 35 m; some of them swim in between the divers. No one wears any protection. However, you have to wait for the current, when the tide is on the turn and there is only a 45-min window of opportunity. **Shark's Friends** (Cubanacán Náutica), Playa Santa Lucía, T32-365182. Dive centre charging US$70 for shark feeding, or it can be arranged 'privately' for US$25. US$162 for a 5-dive package, US$290 for 10, US$60 for a resort course, US$365 for open water certification and US$250 for advanced certification. **DadoSub** (Ecotur), is at Club Santa Lucía, T32-336109, dieppasub@cmg.colombus.cu

Snorkelling

Catamarans leave twice daily at 1000 and 1400, from the pier just north of Escuela Santa Lucía, for the reef. US$20 including all gear and soft drinks on board. Recommended for a great snorkelling trip.

Watersports

Most watersports are available at the hotels but **Cubanacán Náutico** has boat rental and other watersports, T32-36404.

Tour operators

Altamira, on ground floor of Hotel Plaza, Camagüey, T32-283551, imagencu @ip.etecsa.cu Mon-Fri 0900-1200 and 1400-1600. For Víazul reservations, hotels, special offers for beach breaks, air tickets with **Cubana, Iberia, Air Europa**. **Cubatur**, 5ta Paralela 417, Florat, Camagüey, T32-261668. There is also an office on Ignacio Agramonte, opposite Cine Casablanca, T32-254785, daily 0900-1200 and 1300-1700. Tours for individuals start from Playa Santa Lucía, nothing available from Camagüey except for groups. 3 terminals for internet access with US$5 prepaid card for 3 hrs. Many tours, including to Cayo Sabinal and Santa Lucía.

Havanatur, Monteagudo entre Carretera Central y Cuba, Alt Casino, Camagüey, T32-281564/283606. Also a desk in the **Gran Hotel**, contact Jorge Omar Miranda Sánchez, T32-283664, sergio.alvarez@cimex .com.cu He is very knowledgeable but out on tours most of the time. He should be at the desk, daily 0730-0930 and 1630-2000. **Rumbos**, López Recio 108, Camagüey, T32-294807, 32-297229, Mon-Fri 0800-1800. **Cubatur**, Playa Santa Lucía T32-336291. **Fantástico**, Playa Santa Lucía, T32-336412. **Havanatur**, Playa Santa Lucía, T32-365332. **Rumbos**, Playa Santa Lucía, T32-336106.

⊝ Transport

Air

Any bus/truck going to Nuevitas, Minas or Playa Santa Lucía from Parque Finlay by the railway station will pass the Ignacio Agramonte International Airport (CMW). The airport is 9 km from the centre on the road to Nuevitas, T32-261000. **Cubana** flies daily from Havana, connecting with flights from **Mexico**, and once a week from **Montréal**. There are also charter flights from **Toronto** and **Europe** depending on the season. There is a small airstrip at Playa Santa Lucía, Joaquín de Agüero, for **Aerotaxi** services.

Airlines Cubana, República 400 esq Correa, T32-292156/291338, Mon-Fri 0815-1600, . Also at Playa Santa Lucía, in Club Mayanabo, T32-365352. **Aerotaxi**, at Santa Lucía airport, T32-61573.

Bus

The Interprovincial bus station is southwest of the centre along the Carretera Central Oeste, esq Perú. **Víazul**, T32-272346/271646, stops here on its **Havana-Santiago** and **Trinidad-Santiago** routes. Other cheaper buses also along this route, but they may be full when they arrive. A truck to **Las Tunas** is 5 pesos. **Astro**, T32-271668.

Car hire

Havanautos is at Hotel Camagüey, T32-272239, and at the airport T32-261010/287068. At Playa Santa Lucía, there are rental desks at the hotels or just outside them. **Cubacar**, T32-36464. **Havanautos**, T32-26188.

Petrol stations There are **Servi Cupet** gas stations by the river on Carretera Central with Av de la Libertad, and a couple of blocks further south on the other side of the Carretera Central; at the junction as you arrive at Playa Santa Lucía; Carretera Central y Francisco V Aguilera, Florida; Carretera Central y Martí, Guáimaro; Agramonte entre Albisa y Medrano, Nuevitas; Carretera de Santa Cruz del Sur 304; Carretera Central y Vía Blanca, Camagüey. Also an **Oro Negro** gas station at Carretera de Nuevitas Km 6.5.

Taxi

Cubataxi, T32-281247/298721 in Camagüey. Av Principal La Concha, T32-336196 in Playa Santa Lucía. **Taxi OK**, at Playa Santa Lucía, T32-36464. An official taxi will cost US$45 from **Camagüey-Playa Santa Lucía**, but you can arrange a private car for US$30 for a day trip. Ask at your *casa particular*. From **Playa Santa Lucía** to **Playa los Cocos**, expect to pay US$5-6.

Bicitaxis in the city charge about US$1 per person, fix price in advance. **Horse-drawn carriages** are used at Playa Santa Lucía for local taxi journeys; **Playa Santa Lucía** to **Playa los Cocos**, US$20 return.

Train

Schedules and fares must be confirmed, trains cannot be relied on. Railway station, T32-292633/281525. Train ticket agency, T32-283214. Foreigners pay in dollars at **Ladis** office upstairs above the main ticket office opposite Hotel Plaza. The station is divided into long distance, south of the railway by Hotel Plaza, and short distances within the province, north of the railway between Joaquín de Agüero and Manuel Benavides. The *especial* from **Havana** gets in to **Camagüey** at 0048 on its way to **Santiago**, 6 hrs, US$12.50. Trains to **Havana** daily at 2219 and Mon, Wed and Fri at 1933, 10 hrs, US$21, stopping at **Guayos** (for **Sancti Spíritus**) at 2230, US$6.50. Daily to **Bayamo** and **Manzanillo** at 0527, to **Holguín** at 2322, to **Morón** at 1208.

⊕ Directory

Camagüey centre *p279, map p282*

Banks

Banco Financiero Internacional is on Plaza Maceo, T32-294846. For all financial and exchange services including cash advances on credit cards. Efficient, cool, Mon-Fri 0800-1500 except last working day of the month 0800-1200. There is a **Cadeca** for currency exchange and TCs on República 353 entre Primelles y Santa Rita, T32-295220. The **Banco de la República** is on República opposite Iglesia La Soledad. **Bandec** is on Plaza de los Trabajadores, Mon-Fri 0800-1400, Sat 0800-1200, Visa accepted. Also in the residential area of Playa Santa Lucía where the workers live; hotels will change money if you need it. Only US dollars accepted at the beach.

Hospitals and clinics

The **Policlínico Finlay** is on Av Carlos J Finlay heading towards the airport. **Policlínica Pirra** is squeezed between the railway station and the Agramonte museum. The **Provincial Hospital** is west of the centre, T32-291902 /282012. **Amalia Simoni Clinic** is out on the road to Nuevitas, just past the junction with Circunvalación, T32-261011/261941.

At Playa Santa Lucía there is an **International Clinic**, Residencia 4, T32-366203, F32-365300.

Internet

Cubatur, see tour operators above, has 3 terminals using prepaid cards, US$5 for 3 hrs, slow and inefficient service. The hotels have internet service for guests.

Pharmacy

24-hr pharmacy on the corner of Avellaneda y Primelles, Camagüey.

Post office

The central Post Office is just on the corner of the Plaza de los Trabajadores on Cisneros, next to Casa Natal Ignacio Agramonte. At Playa Santa Lucía there is a post office by Servi Cupet at the main junction.

Telephone

Etecsa is on Avellaneda 271 and 308, T32-281709. The **Centro de Llamadas de Larga Distancia** has phones and fax. At Playa Santa Lucía **Etecsa** is by Servi Cupet at the main junction. Email is available.

Useful addresses and numbers

Immigration, T32-336225.

Las Tunas → *Colour map 3, grid B4. Population: 120,000.*

Victoria de las Tunas, also known as Las Tunas, or even just Tuna, was founded in the 1750s, but was never more than a market town until Las Tunas became a province in its own right in 1975 and needed a provincial capital. Travellers could be forgiven for not noticing this small, agricultural province on their way from Camagüey to Holguín or Bayamo, as only about 65 km of the road actually passes through it. On the other hand, the provincial capital would make a convenient break in the journey, or you could get well off the beaten track by visiting the beaches of the irregular northern coast, indented by three large bays. Las Tunas boasts 35 virgin beaches, of which the main one, Playa Covarrubias, has fine, white sand and is protected by a 3-km coral reef. Hotel construction is making it easier to stay in this area, which so far does not have the enclave atmosphere of many of Cuba's beach resorts. ▸▸ *For Sleeping, Eating and other listings, see pages 295-296.*

Ins and outs

Getting there There is a domestic airport outside **Las Tunas**, but no international flights land here. Las Tunas is on the long-distance **bus** and **train** routes from Havana to Santiago de Cuba. It is easy enough to get there but more difficult to get out, as most of the buses are full when they pass through. The long-distance bus terminal is 1 km from the town centre and closer than the railway station, 2.5 km away, but both are within walking distance if you haven't got much luggage. **Bicitaxis** and **coches** are available. ▸▸ *For further details, see also Transport, page 296.*

Getting around The town of Las Tunas is small and you can **walk** around it in a day at a leisurely pace. Motorized or horse-drawn **taxis** are available if you are based further out at *Hotel Las Tunas*, where there is also **car hire**. The provincial bus station for bus services to local towns and villages is beside the railway station. Taxis will take you on excursions.

Tourist information The large hotels have information bureaux but there is not much on offer here.

Sights

City centre

The town centre is effectively the junction of three roads, the tree-lined Vicente García (the Carretera Central), Angel Guardia and Francisco Varona, at the Parque Vicente García, where there is a small church. There is a memorial to General Vicente García just off the Parque and his name crops up frequently in the town, because he led the struggle for independence in the area in 1868 and captured the town in 1876. The old centre of Las Tunas, the *casco histórico*, is being renovated.

The Carretera Central linking Havana with the east of the country runs through the middle of town, although there is now a Circunvalación running round the south so that you can avoid the centre all together if you want to.

West of the centre

In 1976 a **Cubana** plane en route from Caracas to Havana was blown up just after take-off from a stop in Barbados by a bomber who left a device under his seat when he disembarked in Barbados. Seventy-three people, including the Cuban fencing team, were killed. To this day no one has been charged in connection with the incident. The **Memorial a los Mártires de Barbados**ⓘ *Calle Lucas Ortiz 344 entre Teniente Peiso y Mártires de Barbados, T31-47213. US$1,* located in a museum in the park along Vicente García by the river, contains photos of all the victims around the walls. Three members of the fencing team came from Las Tunas and the museum is in the house of one of them. The 25th anniversary of the bombing, in 2001, coincided with the terrorist attack on the World Trade Center in New York, providing Cuba with extra publicity in its campaign for justice.

Opposite the Parque, the **Museo Provincial General Vicente García**ⓘ *Calle Francisco Varona entre Angel Guerra y Lucas Ortiz, T31-48201,* displays local history. The **Memorial Mayor General Vicente García González**ⓘ *Calle Vicente García 5 entre Francisco Vega y Julián Santana, T31-45164,* is the birthplace of the general.

The birthplace of a local 19th-century poet has been made into a museum, the **Casa Natal Juan Cristóbal Nápoles y Fajardo,** on Lucas Ortíz. He was one of the greatest creators of the Cuban *cucalambé* style which started in the 19th century but continues today as a niche cultural genre based on improvization. Every year a music festival is held in Las Tunas, *La Jornada Cucalambeana,* with singers of country music, improvization and other artists honouring this and other writers of *cucalambé* (see Festivals and events, below). There is also plenty of salsa and dancing, local food stalls and lots of beer and rum.

Around Las Tunas

The province is only 6,589 sq km of mostly low lying farming land, although the central part of the province around the city is part of the Holguín ridge and more hilly. There are three large bays on the northern coast: **Bahía de Manatí**, **Bahía de Malagueta** and **Bahía de Puerto Padre de Chapata**, which offer safe harbour and fishing ports. You can see flamingoes and other water birds in the Bahía de Malagueta. To get there, drive yourself, hire a driver for the day or see if there is an organized tour from one of the hotels.

The southern coast opens onto the **Golfo de Guacanayabo** and is marshy with mangroves. Beef cattle and sugar cane are among the main agricultural activities, while the UN Development Programme (UNDP) is helping to develop milk production. Close to Las Tunas you can get out to the **Motel El Cornito**, see Sleeping, where you can relax, walk or fish in the river and reservoir.

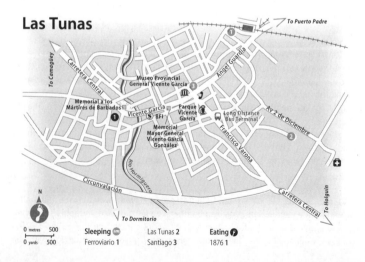

Las Tunas

To Puerto Padre

To Camagüey
Carretera Central

Museo Provincial
General Vicente García

Angel Guardia

Memorial a los
Mártires de Barbados
Vicente García
BFI
Parque
Vicente
García
Long Distance
Bus Terminal
Av 2 de Diciembre

Memorial
Mayor General
Vicente García
González

Francisco Varona

Río Hormiguero

Circunvalación

Carretera Central

To Holguín

N

To Dormitorio

0 metres 500
0 yards 500

Sleeping 😊
Ferroviario **1**

Las Tunas **2**
Santiago **3**

Eating 🍴
1876 **1**

The main town on the north coast is **Puerto Padre**, tucked in at the end of the bay of the same name. Unusually there are fresh water springs here, right next to the sea shore. Overlooking the water is the **Fuerte de la Loma**, a stone fortress built in 1869 with four circular towers, a moat and a drawbridge. It saw active service during the Wars of Independence and during the Revolution, when it was used by Batista's troops until it was taken on 25 December 1958. Some colonial buildings dating from the 1860s remain in the town, which has a wide boulevard leading down to the Malecón where there is a restaurant. If you ask around there will no doubt be a *casa particular* where you can stay if you have to. There are two daily buses from Las Tunas from the provincial bus station next to the railway station, but it is easier to hire a driver for a day trip and take in a beach as well.

Further afield, you can drive to the north coast to the beaches on **Punta Covarrubias**, **Playa Las Bocas** or **Playa La Herradura**. There are no buses and little tourist development along this stretch of coast and you are likely to have the place to yourself. On **Playa Covarrubias**, west of Puerto Padre, there is a new four-star all-inclusive hotel, **Villa Covarrubias** (Gran Caribe). So far this is the only hotel but more hotel construction is planned. The beach is white sand and protected by a reef which has created sand banks and shallow water, beautifully clear and safe. **Playa Las Bocas** is at the eastern bank of the mouth of the Bahía de Puerto Padre on a small bay with golden sand and a few palm trees. Crowds are almost non-existent although at weekends you will find Cubans who have their own transport enjoying themselves here. A basic beach bar sells pizza and soft drinks for pesos, but don't rely on it, take some supplies of your own. **Playa La Herradura** is east of here and is another unspoilt sandy beach with few facilities. There is no public transport to any of these beaches and it is best to hire a car or taxi.

● Sleeping

City centre *p293, map p294*
Hotels
F **Ferroviario**, opposite the railway station, T31-42601. 20 rooms in old hotel.
F **Santiago**, Angel Guardia 112, T31-43396. 32 rooms, just off Parque Vicente García.

Casas particulares
F **Alejandro Cordero Pupo**, Calle 50 entre Francisco Varona y Francisco Vega, La Loma, T31-48198. Alejandro is a civil engineer and his wife Maylyn is an architect and they live in a house which they designed and built a few years ago. 2 rooms to rent with ensuite bathrooms, a/c, 2 mins' walk from bus station, only Spanish spoken, helpful, kind.

Around Las Tunas *p294*
Hotels
AL **Villa Covarrubias** (Gran Caribe), Playa Covarrubias, west of Puerto Padre, T31-55530, jose@vcova.esilt.colombus.cu 4-star all-inclusive hotel, 122 rooms in *cabañas* on the beach with lots of sporting facilities available on land and in the water and a nightclub.

E **Las Tunas**, Av 2 de Diciembre y Carlos J Finlay, T31-45014, F31-45169, on a hill on the road out to the hospital, southeast of the town. 142 rooms in modern 4-storey block, restaurant, cafeteria, pool (not always filled), car rental.
F **Motel El Cornito**, 7 km west of town, off Carretera Central, T31-45015. 129 rooms in blocks or bungalows, basic and uncomfortable but attractive setting in park with bamboo groves and reservoir, fishing in the Río Hormiguero, restaurant, evening entertainment, amusement park next door.

Camping
The reservations office for **Campismo Popular** is on Adolfo Villamar esq Angel Guardia, Playa Covarrubias, T43-47001. Technically reserved for national tourism, it is still worth a try to get in to one of the beach sites, although the cabins are very basic. On the south coast, at Guayabal, Carretera a Playa Guayabal, Amancio Rodríguez, T31-96101, next to a little river and close to a sugar export terminal. On the north coast, at Los Pinos, Carretera Manatí a Playa La Boca,

Manatí, T31-21923. Just west of here is the bay of Nuevas Grandes, where manatee live. Playa Corella, Carretera a Playa La Llanita, Jesús Menéndez, T31-55447. A large site with 116 cabins on one of the best beaches in the province. Inland, Aguada de Vázquez, Carretera a Puerto Padre, Las Delicias, Poblado de Vázquez, Puerto Padre, T31-59106. Shady trees and river bathing.

🍴 Eating

City centre p293, map p294
Paladares are a better bet than the state restaurants, but these change frequently.
$ **1876**, Vicente García, near the park by the river, daily 1200-2300. Specializes in pork.
$ **Doña Neli**, on Francisco Varona entre Flora y Menocal, T31-46527, daily 0700-2200. Bakery, snacks, pastries and sweet things,
$ **Majibacoa**, in the Hotel Las Tunas, T31-45014. The food is not bad for a hotel.
$ **Rey Mar**, Francisco Varona entre Colón y Carretera Central, T31-44923. Fish and seafood, open for lunch and dinner.
$ **Rumbos**, on the main road in the old part of town, open 24 hrs. **Rumbos** restaurant, good for snacks and light meals.

Around Las Tunas p294
$ **Sierra Cristal**, on the Malecón, Puerto Padre, T31-52583, daily 1130-0100. Seafood restaurant.

🎭 Entertainment

City centre p293, map p294
Casa de la Cultura, Vicente García 8 entre Francisco Vega y Francisco Varona.

Around Las Tunas p294
Anacaona, Puerto Padre. A nightclub on the Malecón esq Paco Cabrera, which accepts credit cards.

🎉 Festivals and events

Jun or **Jul** There is a **Fiesta Cucalambé** at the Motel El Cornito for folk music, see p294.
Dec Agricultural fair in La Tunas.

☎ Transport

Local
Most local transport is by **horse and cart** or other non-motorized transport such as *bicitaxis*.

Air
There is an airport, Aeropuerto Hermanos Ameijeiras (VTU), T31-42484, 11 km from Las Tunas, which receives **Cubana** flights twice a week from **Havana**.
Airlines Cubana, Lucas Ortiz esq 24 de Febrero, T31-42702, or at the airport, T31-43266.

Bus
The bus station is just south of the main Parque on Francisco Varona, T31-43801. Long-distance buses are already full when they pass through Las Tunas and you just have to hope that someone is getting off here. Local buses use the terminal near the railway station. A truck to **Camagüey** costs 5 pesos.

Car hire
There is a **Havanautos** desk in the Hotel Las Tunas, T31-45014.
Petrol stations Cupet-Cimex fuel stations at Carretera Central Oeste Km 2, Las Tunas, and at Av Libertad 156, Puerto Padre. Oro Negro service station at Francisco Varona entre Lora y Menocal, Las Tunas.

Train
The railway station is northeast of the centre, with daily trains to **Holguín, Santiago, Matanzas** and **Havana**.

ℹ Directory

Banks Banco Financiero Internacional on Vicente Guardia on your left as you head out towards Camagüey in a modern concrete and dark glass building, Mon-Fri 0800-1500.
Telephone Telephone office on Angel Guardia, just east of the Parque.

For an explanation of the sleeping and eating price codes used in this guide, see inside the front cover. Other relevant information is provided in Essentials, pages 48-53.

Holguín and Granma

Footprint features

Introduction

The countryside of Holguín is attractive, hilly and covered with luxuriant vegetation. There are picture book views of hillsides dotted with Royal palms, towering over thatched cottages, called bohíos, while the flatter land is green with swathes of sugar cane. The city of Holguín is unassuming and pleasant, with a huge central square. The local people take pride in the tourist developments of Guardalavaca; which now include the largest hotel in Cuba. But unlike Varadero there is no wall-to-wall hotel strip. The north coast is indented with pretty horseshoe-shaped bays and sandy beaches, protected by a coral reef.

Columbus is believed to have landed at the Bahía de Bariay on 28 October 1492, which he claimed was the most beautiful country he had ever seen. The indigenous people probably thought so too, since archaeological explorations have shown that there were primitive cultures here some 6,000 years ago. Seboruco man is thought to have been the first inhabitant of what is now the province of Holguín.

The province of Granma occupies the western end of the Sierra Maestra and the flatlands and swamps to the north of the mountains. It was named after the boat that brought Castro and his comrades to Cuba to launch the Revolution. The area is studded with memories of the guerrilla struggle and the hills are full of evocative plaques commemorating the events immediately after their landing in 1953, but it has been largely neglected as far as tourism is concerned. This is one province where you will need to change a few dollars into pesos and where hassling of tourists is rare. The capital of the province is Bayamo, which has good transport links and from where hiking into the mountains is organized, while Manzanillo is its main port.

★ Don't miss...

1 Gibara Climb the Silla de Gibara for a glorious view of the bay where Columbus landed in 1492, page 304.

2 La Loma de La Cruz Puff your way up the 458 steps to the cross and admire the spectacular view over Holguín and beyond, page 303.

3 Plaza Central Sit on one of the many benches in the evening and watch the citizens of Holguín enjoy the cool air to the strains of music from the Casa de la Trova, page 301.

4 Alto de Naranjo Hike from here up into the Sierra Maestra to visit Castro's mountain base during the Revolution, page 315.

5 Playa Las Coloradas The site where the revolutionaries landed in the yacht, *Granma*, is an essential destination, page 320.

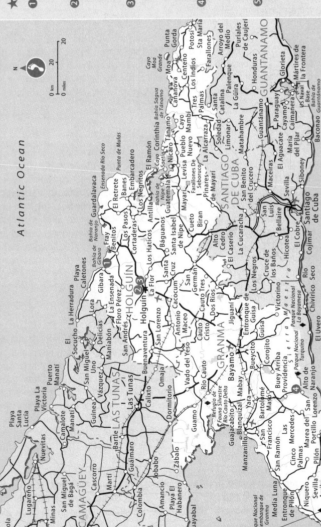

Holguín and Granma

Ins and outs

Getting there

Air Holguín has an international airport accessible for either the north-coast hotels or Bayamo. Manzanillo has an airport but it receives scheduled flights only once a week from Havana. **Rail and road** Both cities are on the main rail and bus routes from Havana to Santiago de Cuba and transport links are good. Manzanillo is less accessible, as you have to change bus or train in Bayamo.▶▶ *For further details, see page 300, page 314 and page 319.*

Tourist information

All the hotels around Guardalavaca have tourist desks which can provide information as well as tours. There are tour operators in Holguín and Bayamo (see Activities and tours, page 312), but you will get better advice from your *casa particular* if that is where you are staying.

Best time to visit

The driest season is from December to April. Hurricane season technically starts in June, but most storms arrive between September and November. Rain can fall at any time of year, usually in the afternoons. Holguín is developing a reputation as a good venue for festivals, with a local cultural event in January and an Ibero-American festival in October.

Holguín → *Colour map 3, grid B5. Population: 250,000.*

Holguín was founded in 1545, but most of the architecture in the centre dates from the 19th and 20th centuries. There are many statues and monuments to national heroes, several of which are around Plaza de la Revolución, on the edge of the city, the location of the modern City Hall and the Provincial Communist Party building. The town was named after García Holguín, a captain in the Spanish colonization force. It officially received the title of Ciudad de San Isidro de Holguín on 18 January 1752, when the population numbered 1,426. The city has a university, a paediatric hospital, coffee roasting plant, brewery and baseball stadium and is busy, although all traffic moves at the pace of the thousands of bicycles that throng the streets. There are several attractive excursions to be made from the city, with easy access to some of the best beaches in the country.▶▶ For Sleeping, Eating and other listings, see pages 308-313.

Ins and outs

Getting there Holguín has an international airport 8 km from town, a taxi ride into the centre. Most foreigners are on their way to the Guardalavaca beach resort and are transported by tour bus to their hotels. There are scheduled **flights** from Amsterdam, Dusseldorf, Frankfurt, London, Paris, Havana (US$82), with connections from many Mexican cities, and Santiago, which can be useful if you plan to do a two-centre holiday and use Holguín as a base for exploring the east of the island. The city is on the main Havana to Santiago **railway** line with daily **train** services in each direction. It is better served by long-distance buses. **Víazul** stops here on its Havana to Santiago and Trinidad to Santiago routes and runs **buses** to Guardalavaca for a day on the beach.▶▶ *For further details, see Transport, page 313.*

Getting around It is easiest to **walk** around the centre as traffic is very slow, but for going further afield you can hop on a horse-drawn **coche**, or hire a **bicitaxi**. Tour agencies, such as **Rumbos** offer organized excursions but if you want to go on your own, **car hire** is available.

Sights

City centre

Holguín is known as the 'city of the parks', five of which, **Parque Infantil, Parque Carlos Manuel de Céspedes** (also known as Parque San José), the **Plaza Central** (Plaza Gen Calixto García), **Parque Peralta** and **Parque José Martí**, lie between the two main streets: Antonio Maceo and Libertad (Manduley). There is a statue of **Carlos Manuel de Céspedes** in the park named after him: he is remembered for having freed his slaves on 10 October 1868 and starting the war of independence. The 1820 church, **Iglesia de San José**, is in **Parque Carlos Manuel de Céspedes** .

The Plaza Central is named after **General Calixto García Iñiguez** (statue in the centre), who was born in Holguín in 1839 and took part in both wars of independence. He captured the town from the Spanish in 1872 and again occupied it in 1898 after helping the US forces defeat the colonial power in Santiago de Cuba. His statue is in the centre and his birthplace, one block from the plaza, is now a museum, **Casa Natal de Calixto García** ① *Calle Miró 147, Mon-Fri 0800-1700, Sat 0800-1300, US$1*. The building is a *monumento nacional* but the museum has a collection of dusty, faded exhibits and newer models of battles for lovers of army games.

> *There are about 100 guaraperas in Holguín, selling guarapo (sugar cane juice) for 1 peso. You'll find them in doorways or at windows.*

Around the plaza are the **Commander Eddy Suñol Theatre** (he fought against Batista) and the **library** ① *Mon-Fri 0800-2100, Sat 0800-1800, Sun 0800-1300*, a modern building with a spiral staircase, which hosts special events on Sundays. Also on the plaza is **Galería Bayado** where you can buy ceramics, carvings and furniture. To the rear of the *Galería*, there is a courtyard where you can enjoy music and singing in the evening. At the **Casa de Cultura** there are handicrafts for sale, and dancing. On the north side of the square is the **Museo Provincial** ① *Mon-Fri 0900-1700, Sat 0900-1300, US$1, US$3 with camera*, known as *La Periquera* (parrot cage) because of the brightly coloured soldiers known as *periquitos* (parakeets) who used to stand guard outside when the building was used as an army barracks in the 19th century. It was built between 1860 and 1868 and is now a National Monument. On 30 October 1868, 500 armed *independistas* attacked the building shouting ¡Viva Cuba! but failed to take it because of its strategic defences. The most important item on display here is the Hacha de Holguín, a pre-Columbian axe head carved with the head of a man, measuring 350 mm in length and 76 mm at its widest point. It was found in 1860 on a hill around the city and is believed to be about 500 years old. It has become the symbol of Holguín.

The plaza is most active at night when families, friends and lovers enjoy the cooler air, sitting on the hundreds of benches or strolling around. Children leap all over the place and it is great for rollerskates, while music from the *Casa de la Trova* competes with a heavy-duty sound system on another corner.

Off the square, the **Museo de Ciencias Naturales** ① *Maceo 129, Sun-Thu 0900-1700, Sat 1300-1700, US$1*, is full of stuffed animals, including a manatee, snakes, giant turtle, nearly all the indigenous birds of Cuba and a huge shell collection. Rather macabre, with human and horse foetuses in jars, but popular. The building is almost more interesting than the exhibits, with neoclassical pillars, pretty turquoise tiles on the outside, sitting lions and two 'moorish' turrets, all newly painted greeny turquoise and white.

Parque Peralta is another square between Maceo and Manduley, named after Julio Grave de Peralta, who led the Holguín independence struggle against Spain in 1868, although it is usually called the Parque de las Flores. The **Cathedral** is on this

● *One of the foremost artists in Cuba, Cosme Proenza Almaguer, lives in Holguín, T24-423934.*
● *He is a post-modernist painter, taking his inspiration from legends and fantasies and depicting phantasmagorical creatures, gnomes, medieval lakes and caravels.*

square, built in 1720 but frequently altered or improved. It has recently been renovated. On 8 September there is a procession celebrating the day the Virgen de la Caridad appeared in the Bahía de Nipe, before she was taken to Santiago. The oldest

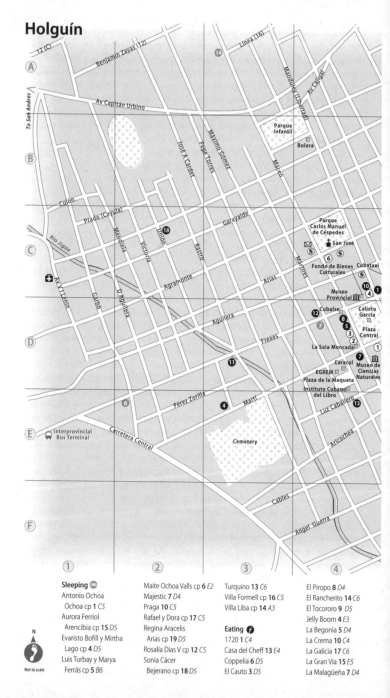

Holguín

N
Not to scale

① *Morales Lemus entre Arecochea y Cables.* Major renovation work is taking place to restore the **Plaza de la Maqueta** southwest of Plaza Central between Mártires and Máximo Gómez and make it into a major tourist attraction. The old market is being reconstructed in the centre to become a theatre, and shops, art galleries and a hotel are in progress around the outside. It has been designed with artists in mind and round the square are humorous touches: telegraph poles are carved like totem poles, against one of which is a statue of a dog peeing; another statue depicts a woman with a shopping basket and on a balcony is a man looking over the railing. On the south side is the **Instituto Cubano del Libro** ① *Mon-Sat 0800-2000, Sun 0900-1200*, a printing house and an art shop stocking oils, acrylics and other art materials, as well as the Tienda Mona Lisa (Artex) for music, books and souvenirs. On the east side work is in progress on a new hotel, **Don José**, with an *artesanía* downstairs. On the north side, **EGREM** has a music shop, **La Flor de Holguín**, selling CDs and musical instruments, while next door is Caracol's **La Cohoba**, for cigars, rum and coffee, very smart, credit cards accepted.

North of the centre

Above the city is **La Loma de la Cruz**, a strategic hill which used to have a cross on top until Hurricane Georges blew it down in 1998. On 3 May 1790, a Franciscan priest, Antonio de Alegría, came with a group of religious people and put up the cross, 275 m above sea level, 127 m above the town. All the streets of the town were laid out from that strategic point, which has a lookout tower, built by the Spanish during the 10 Years' War. In 1929, stone steps were begun up the hill, not finished until 3 May 1950. Every 3 May locals celebrate the *Romerías de la Cruz de Mayo*. There is a road round the side of the hill, but if you wish to walk up straight up the 458 steps, there are lots of benches for resting on. The way is lit up at night with street lights. Candles are lit and offerings of coins are made, but you are more likely to meet gangs of boys waiting for tourists than religious devotees. A policeman is usually on patrol in the morning.

La Pampa **18** *C2*
Pico Cristal **2** *D5*
Ramón **11** *D3*
Rombo **12** *D4*

Entertainment ♪
Café Cantante **4** *C4*
Casa de la Cultura **2** *D4*

Casa de la Trova **3** *D4*
Casa del Tango **6** *C4*
Teatro Comandante Eddy Suñol **1** *D4*
UNEAC **5** *D5*

An interesting local industry you can visit is the doll factory, **Fábrica de Muñecas Cubanas** ① *Av Cajigal entre Narciso López y Cervantes, Mon-Fri 0900-1600*. Further along the same road, Av Cajigal, about 1km from the Parque Infantil on the road to Gibara, is an organ factory, **Fábrica de Organos**, which you can also visit during working hours to see how they make the instruments.

Around Holguín

Holguín lies in the east of the country, stretching along the north coast and indented by many bays. The capital, Holguín, lies in a range of hills that stretch from Las Tunas to the coast at Punta de Mulas, while the eastern part of the province takes in the foothills of the Sierra del Cristal and the Montañas de Nipe-Sagua-Baracoa. Further to the east of the province is the hugely important nickel and cobalt plant with shipping facilities at Moa, which is receiving large amounts of foreign investment, particularly from Canada.

Mirador de Mayabe

The Mirador de Mayabe is a popular excursion. A restaurant and hotel have been built on a hillside a few kilometres out of town with a splendid view over the valley and the whole city. Water towers stand out like mushrooms in the distance. The restaurant has good Cuban food, open air but under cover and the usual strolling musicians. There is a swimming pool perched on the edge of the hill and beside it a bar, where Pancho, the beer-drinking donkey entertains guests. He is confined in a very small pen beside the bar and it is unlikely that the quantity of beer does him any good, but apart from an air of boredom he seems quite healthy and happy. This is actually Pancho II, as the first Pancho was killed in a car accident and a younger model had to be found and trained to drink beer. **La Finca Mayabe** has a second restaurant, normally open only for tour parties, with a *bohío*, and a collection of chickens, turkeys, ducks etc, which you might find around a typical farmer's house.

Gibara → *Population: 16,000.*

About 32 km north of Holguín on the coast is the pretty little town of Gibara. It is believed that Columbus first landed near here at Cayo Bariay on 28 October 1492, where a monument was erected to mark the 500th anniversary (see below). The hill nearby, the Silla de Gibara, he referred to as shaped like a saddle and it became a landmark and navigation reference point. Hike up to **El Cuartelón** (*El Mirador*) from where you get an excellent view of the Bahía de Gibara, the town with its higgledy piggledy deep red-tiled roofs punctuated by palm trees and the beach to one side. The town was not founded until 1817, but it became an important port for the area and there is still a thriving fishing industry, specializing in lobsters. The main square has a fine row of big African oak trees around it and in front of the pretty yellow church with two red domes there is a Carrara marble replica of the Statue of Liberty. In the town there are many large and pleasant old houses with open porches and stained-glass windows dating from the 19th century and there is a sweeping Malecón. On Independencia there are two museums, the **Museo Municipal** and the **Museo de Historia Natural**, which have exhibitions about the area. There are a number of *casas particulares* and a *paladar*, **Casa Colonial**, Independencia 20, in front of the Museo Municipal. Ramón Acosta Ricardo speaks (teaches) English and German and can be contacted here for information about the area. Ask around in town for boat trips so you can get a good view of the bay and the Silla from the sea. About 18 km northwest of Gibara along the coast, you come to **Playa Caletones**, a reasonable beach where natural rock pools have formed to make swimming pools.

Cayo Bariay

Cayo Bariay is not an island, but a round peninsula hanging onto the main island by a spit of land. At the tip is the **Monumento Encuentro Dos Culturas**, a monument erected in 1992 to Columbus' landing and the meeting of two cultures in 1492. There is a beach, Playa Cayo Bariay, and a restaurant, **El Mirador**. The area is popular with Cubans on holiday. Across the water is Playa Blanca and the **Hotel Don Lino** on Playa Don Lino.

Guardalavaca and around → Colour map 3, grid B6.

Guardalavaca has been developed as a tourist resort along a beautiful stretch of coastline, indented with horseshoe bays and sandy beaches. Numbers of visitors are rising fast as new hotels are built. In the winter season 2003-04, some 10,000 tourists a day were expected, arriving on 48-50 flights a week. The resort is in several parts. The older part is rather like a village with apartments for workers. There are a few shops, small craft market, discos (**Ecos Nocturno, La Roca**), bank (**BFI**), telephones, **Photo Service**, restaurant, pizza place (**Pizza Nova**) and bus stop. On the beach you can hire surfboards and windsurfers and there are beach bars and public toilets. This is where you come for a day trip from Holguín. The newer **Sol Meliá** hotels are further west on the beach **Estero Ciego** (also referred to as Playa Esmeralda). They are very isolated and there is nothing to do outside the hotels. Nevertheless, Estero Ciego beach is idyllic, a very pretty horseshoe shape with a river coming down to the sea in the middle and rocks at either end providing good snorkelling opportunities. There is a reef offshore for diving, which is very unspoilt and has a lot to offer. The hills surrounding the beach are green and wooded, helping to make the **Sol** hotels here unobtrusive.

> *The area is developing fast with many new hotels being built, but you will need your own car, bike or taxi to explore.*

West of the **Sol Río de Mares** there is a nature trail, **Sendero Ecológico Las Guanas**, which has a cave and a mirador, with lots of information in English and Spanish on the vegetation, fauna and Amerindians. Although interesting, there have been many complaints about the US$10 fee charged to walk along the trail. Just before the entrance there is a path down to your left, about 10 m to **Playa El Tiburonario**, a nice beach and despite its name there are no sharks.

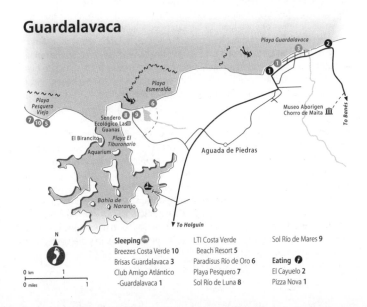

Guardalavaca

Sleeping		
Breezes Costa Verde **10**	LTI Costa Verde Beach Resort **5**	Sol Río de Mares **9**
Brisas Guardalavaca **3**	Paradisus Río de Oro **6**	**Eating**
Club Amigo Atlántico -Guardalavaca **1**	Playa Pesquero **7**	El Cayuelo **2**
	Sol Río de Luna **8**	Pizza Nova **1**

Holguín and Granma Guardalavaca and around

Bahía de Naranjo

The lagoon in the Bahía de Naranjo has been developed as a small marina. Near the mouth of the lagoon is an aquarium, 10 minutes by boat from the dock, with dolphins and a sea lion, and a restaurant. A visit here is often included in tours of the area with a show. An evening excursion costs US$45, including dolphin show, extra US$20 to swim with the dolphins, lobster supper and an Afro-Cuban show (see also page 68). At the mouth of the bay on the west side, is **El Birancito**, a replica *finca* of where Fidel Castro was born.

Playa Pesquero

West along the coast, Playa Pesquero Viejo used to be a lovely beach, but this is the area of greatest recent development with massive hotels being built. The east end of the sandy beach is better for children as there are strong currents and deceptive sand bars to the west. There is a lifeguard on duty even out of season. The hotels have completely changed the character of the beach. More are still being built, both here and on Playa Pesquero Nuevo.

Chorro de Maita

A few kilometres from Guardalavaca on a hill with a wonderful view, is the **Museo Aborigen Chorro de Maita** ① *Mon-Fri 0900-1700, Sun 0900-1300, US$2 entrance, US$1 per photo, plus US$5 per film, US$5 video, small* Artex *shop with souvenirs, a* small but well-presented museum displaying a collection of 56 skeletons dating from 1490-1540, exactly as they were found. One is of a young Spaniard of about 22 years of age with his arms crossed for a Christian burial, but the rest are Amerindians, buried in the Central American style, lying flat with their arms folded across their stomachs. Excavations took place in 1986 and a total of 108 skeletons were found (including the Spaniard), but they are not all displayed here. The aborigines had malformed skulls from birth, which can be seen clearly. The tallest was 1 m 75 cm, although the average was 1 m 56 cm.

Almost opposite the museum is a replica of a **Taíno village** (*US$5*) with statues of Amerindians going about their daily activities. If you are on an organized tour you may be taken to see the little village primary school just down the hill and you will pass the rural clinic where the doctor lives and works, looking after his allotted 120 families. A farmer at the bottom of the hill is pleased to see visitors and show them around his land, where he grows enough food for his extended family. According to Cuban rules he is allowed to keep everything he grows on his 7 ha, but if he wants more land he has to give a proportion to the state. It is interesting to see how he grows his fruit and vegetables, with herbs dotted around, and he is likely to take his machete to bits of his produce for you to taste. The livestock are kept close to the house and fed coconuts. Ask to see his 1948 Plymouth car, which is a treasure.

Banes

It is a pleasant drive about 30 km from Guardalavaca to Banes over the hills through rolling fields of sugar interspersed with Royal palms. This town is not usually on the itineraries of tour parties even though its church, **Iglesia de Nuestra Señora de la Caridad** was the site of the marriage of Fidel Castro to Birta Díaz Balart on 12 October 1948. Having visited the Museo Aborigen Chorro de Maita, however, you may be interested to see the **Museo Indocubano Bani** ① *Gen Marrero 305 y Av José Martí, Tue-Sat 0900-1700, Sun 0800-1200, US$1*, which has a good collection of pre-Columbian artifacts, probably the best in Cuba. The town of Banes was originally the site of the Bani chieftancy and the museum contains treasures discovered by the many archaeological digs in the area.

Mayarí and around → *Colour map 3, grid B5/6. Population: 23,000.*

On the road from Holguín to Baracoa is the small town of Mayarí founded in 1814 on the river of the same name. It is the sort of place people pass through on their way round the coast to Moa or inland and up into the mountains to Santiago de Cuba, but hardly anyone bothers to stop. The setting is very pretty, with the Sierra del Cristal as a backdrop. Six kilometres from Mayarí is a large cave, **Farallones de Seboruco**, where, in 1945, an archaeological exploration revealed evidence that it had been used by people living there 5,000 years ago. Inland and up in the hills the soil turns to a deep red; known as *mocarrero*, it is 85% iron. Visit the scientific station at the **Jardín de Pinare National Park**. There are trails in the park through 12 different ecosystems. The **Salto de Guayabo** is 85 m high, one of the highest waterfalls in Cuba, and there is a tremendous view across the fall, down the valley to the Bahía de Nipe. Seek local information on where to walk.

Finca Birán

ⓘ *T24-286116/286114, to speak to Alcides Leyva, the director. You need your own car to get here as it is well off the beaten track.*

In the foothills of the Sierra del Nipe, southwest of Mayarí, is the birthplace of Fidel Castro: Finca Birán, which, it is estimated, some 20,000 people visited in the 12 months to mid-2003. If coming from Holguín or Santiago de Cuba, take the turning east to Birán at Marcané Uno (just south of Loyaz Hechevarría) along a road with pot holes like caverns. If you can take your eyes off the road, the sierra provides a fantastic backdrop. On arrival in the village take the first left and drive for 1.5 km until on your left on the corner you come to a little white house with brown shutters and cactus in the fence. Turn left and drive to the end, where you arrive at the gateway of the Finca Birán (formerly Las Manacas) where Fidel grew up. Although he has written of happy childhood memories, Castro has shown little attachment to the place. It was the first farm to be expropriated after the Revolution, Castro had signed plans to flood the buildings under a reservoir in the 1960s before Celia Sánchez intervened to save it, and it was only in November 2002 that it was quietly opened to the public officially, in recognition of demand. In deference to his distaste for the cult of personality, it is called the **Birán Historic Site**, with no mention of his name in the title. The houses are mustard yellow and on stilts. The house where he was born and lived until he was 14 is straight ahead. It is a reconstruction as the original was destroyed by fire, but the walls are lined with family photos of Fidel as a boy. In the grounds are the former little school house, the teacher's house, bakery, cinema, and huts for the Haitian cane cutters. The tombs of Castro's parents are adorned by marble angels and can be clearly seen at the entrance to the buildings. The centenary of the birth of Castro's mother, Lina, was marked in 2003 by the presentation to the President at Finca Birán, of a book about the birth of the estate and its development by his father, Angel Castro: *Todo el Tiempo de los Cedros*, by journalist Katiuska Blanco. The presentation was attended by Fidel, his elder brother Ramón, and his sisters Angela and Agustina Castro Ruz.

Moa → *Colour map xx. Population: 30,000.*

The coastal road continues east to Moa, where there is a huge nickel plant and it is very industrialized. Cuba is currently the sixth largest producer of refined nickel in the world, but it has more than a third of the world's known reserves. The Moa Bay plant is jointly owned by **Sherritt International** and the Cuban government and operated by **Cubaniquel**. The Pedro Alba mine was built in 1944 by the Americans and the Moa Bay nickel plant was opened in 1959, but after the Revolution it was nationalized in 1960. **Sherritt** now produces an intermediate product in Cuba: nickel and cobalt contained in sulphide, which is then shipped to Canada and ends up as part of its Canadian refined output.

The journey from Moa to Baracoa is 74 km and takes about two hours, depending on whether you are in a truck or car. **Víazul** is considering starting a bus service from Holguín to Baracoa via Moa now that a collapsed bridge has been repaired, but the road is still not in good order. It is a spectacular ride along the coast with the mountains of the **Cuchillas de Moa** and the **Cuchillas de Toa** coming down to the sea, indented by many rivers and bays. The highest peak is the **Pico del Toldo**, at 1,175 m. From the Bahía de Taco to Baracoa the drive is beautiful, with luscious coconut palms, mountains, thatched houses and little coves with thin patches of white sand lapped by the aquamarine sea. It takes about 1 hour 25 minutes from Moa to Maguana, see page 361 for Playa Maguana.

● Sleeping

Holguín centre *p301, map p302*
Hotels
Praga and **Majestic** only occasionally take foreigners and have little to recommend them. Famous guests at the Majestic in the 1950s included Fidel Castro in room 13 and the Mexican singer Jorge Negrete, but now it is more of a short-stay hotel, painted red.
D-E **Pernik** (Islazul), Jorge Dimitrov y Plaza de la Revolución, T24-481011, F24-468141. 202 rooms, mostly overnighters passing through, shops, bar, restaurant (food not recommended), empty swimming pool, TV, a/c, nice view from top-floor rooms, small bathrooms, adequate.
D-E **Villa El Bosque** (Islazul), just off Av Jorge Dimitrov, Plaza de la Revolución, T24-481012, comazul@teleda.get.cma.net 69 rooms in spread out villas, patio garden, fridge, basic shower room, TV, a/c, also 2 suites C, good security, car rental, large pool, El Pétalo disco.
F **Turquino**, on Martí, T24-462124. 40 rooms with bath, TV, basic.

Casas particulares
E **Villa Liba**, Maceo 46 esq 18, T24-423823, villaliba@yahoo.es A very special place run by Jorge Mezerene and his wife Liba, who between them speak some English, Italian and a little French. Liba is super-efficient and can sort out any difficulty for you. She is also a walking information bureau and knows what is going on and where. Modern house in quiet residential area within walking distance of the centre. 2 rooms with double and single bed, a/c, fan, bedside lights, good wardrobe, phone interconnects with kitchen for room service, TV and video if you want it, patio with tables and rocking chairs under mariposa flowers and grapevines. Huge tank for constant water. Excellent food, good for vegetarians.

F **Antonio Ochoa Ochoa**, Morales Lemus 199 entre Martí y Frexes, T24-423659. Spanish-style house with courtyard, light and airy, 2 big rooms with high ceilings, old but good bathrooms, 3 generations live here, with the sons and their families upstairs on the roof, English spoken by Antonio's sons, welcoming family, discounts for long stays, a/c, fan, hot water, large towels, laundry.
F **Aurora Ferriol Arencibia**, Martí 102 entre Morales Lemus y Narciso López, T24-461191. 1 private room with double bed, a/c, fan, bathroom with new tiles, breakfast US$2, dinner from US$4.
F **Evaristo Bofill and Mirtha Lago**, Luz Caballero 78 Altos entre Miró y Morales Lemus. 2 large rooms, very clean, private bathroom, a/c, terrace, friendly and helpful family who make you feel at home and enjoy a good laugh.
F **Luis Turbay y Marya Ferrás**, Agramonte 68 entre Progreso y Río Marañón, T24-461000. The whole of the 1st floor is for guests, 2 bedrooms with double bed in each, huge kitchen, 2 bathrooms, a/c, TV, VCR, very good but often occupied by long-stay visitors. Friendly owners, very welcoming, good breakfast, laundry service.
F **Maite Ochoa Valls**, Frexes 332 Altos esq Carbó, T24-423694. 1 room, a/c, kitchen, can close it off from the rest of the house, popular with long-term stays, very private.
F **Rafael y Dora**, Miró 125A entre Frexes y Aguilera, T24-422090, www.cuba-individual.com 2 rooms, the smaller blue room is pleasant, the second room is dark with no window, bathroom alongside screened by a curtain for privacy to make an ensuite, new tiles. Good mattress, table and chairs, bathroom with hot water, a/c, fan.

F Regina Aracelis Arias, Morales Lemus 140 entre Martí y Frexes, T24-423204. 1 room with own sitting room, fridge, fan, bathroom, area for drying clothes, very private and huge.

F Rosalía Días V, Frexes 176 entre Miró y Morales Lemus, T24-423395. Excellent location, big room with bathroom, a/c, run by charming elderly lady.

F Sonia Cácer Bejerano, Miró 181 entre Martí y Luz Caballero, T24-423296. The house doesn't look much from the outside but inside it is huge, with an internal patio covered with creeper and a garden at the rear where there are roses and cacti. Sonia has 2 rooms to let on the ground floor and her son 2 more upstairs in a separate apartment. TV and fridge in 1 room opening onto garden, both rooms have double and single bed, a/c, fan. Juice and coffee free, meals available.

F Villa Formell, Morales Lemus 189 entre Martí y Frexes, T24-422218. Run by Deisy Formell Berrillo, who has 1 room to let with double bed, large bathroom, hot water, a/c, fan, fridge, clothes drying area and chickens out the back. Meals available.

Around Holguín p304
Hotels
D Villa Don Lino (Cubanacán), Playa Blanca, T24-30259, F24-30427. Recently renovated. Good for the price, quite clean, good beach, reasonable food, price includes breakfast. Cubans come here on holiday and there are *cabañas* for rent.

D-E El Mirador de Mayabe (Islazul), T24-422160, T/F24-425347, several kilometres outside the town. Has 24 rooms in cabins under the trees, tiled floors, a/c, TV, wooden furniture, fridge, hot water, adequate bathroom, quiet, also a suite**C** and 4 rooms in a house at the top of the hill with a fantastic view.

Casas particulares
F Angelina Avial Rodríguez, Villa Miguel, J Peralta 61 entre J Mora y Mariana Grajales, Gibara, T24-34211. 2 different rooms on the Malecón, terrace, parking, friendly.

Guardalavaca p305, map p305
Hotels
LL Paradisus Río de Oro, T24-30090-4 and **L-AL Sol Río de Luna y Mares**, T24-30060, are 3 all-inclusive hotels in the Sol Meliá group, www.solmeliacuba.com, on Playa Esmeralda.

The 5-star **Río de Oro** has 292 junior suites and 2 luxury, private houses at US$600 a night. The former **Sol Río de Luna** and **Sol Río de Mares** are now run as one 4-star resort. Guests at the **Río de Oro** can use the facilities at the other 2 hotels, but those at the 4-star hotels may only use each other's. All offer a/c, TV, restaurants, snack bars and bars, pools, tennis, football (grass pitch), beach volley ball, bicycles, scooters and cars for rent, windsurfing, catamarans, sailing school, snorkelling, dive centre, gym, sauna, massage, organized entertainment, some of it excruciating. There is also a *Campo de Golf* and mini zoo.

LL-AL Brisas Guardalavaca (Cubanacán), T24-30218, reserva@brisas.gvc.cyt.cu All-inclusive, 437 good-sized sea view or inland rooms, doubles, triples, villas and mini-suites, a/c, satellite TV, phone, balcony, 3 restaurants, 3 bars, non-motorized watersports, small man-made beach, nice pool, organized entertainment, gym, tennis, bicycles, kids' camp, tour desk, car rental, internet access.

L-B Club Amigo Atlántico-Guardalavaca (Cubanacán), T24-30180, ventas@club amigo.gvc.cyt.cu Amalgamation of 2 hotels, 747 rooms, villas, bungalows, renovated but still only 3 star. Shop around for good deals, not all agencies offer the same prices. Best position right on beach, OK for vegetarians, bicycles, windsurfing, pedalos, sailing, diving, snorkelling, gym, entertainment, shops, pool, tennis, internet access.

Playa Pesquero p306
Hotels
There are several all-inclusive hotels; **Breezes Costa Verde** (SuperClubs-Gaviota), T24-30520, **LTI Costa Verde Beach Resort** (LTI-Gaviota), T24-30510. A **Club Med** is being built and the 944-room, 5-star **Playa Pesquero** (Gaviota), T24-30530, opened in 2003.

Banes p306
Hotels
F Motel Oasis, just west of the town, T24-3447. 28 rooms, restaurant and bar, used mostly by Cubans.

Mayarí p307
Hotels
There is a peso hotel in town, but if you need a stop in the area you would do better to drive another 30 km south and up into the

hills. Alternatively, if you prefer the beach, go northeast to Cayo Saetía, where there is a small resort hotel.

C Pinares de Mayarí (Gaviota), T24-53305, F24-30126. Mountain lodge style, rustic timber and stone, isolated, pool, tennis, volleyball, gym, massage, bike rental, nature trails, pine trees, lake, restaurant, bar, billiards, horseriding, mostly used by eco-tour groups, check before arriving that they are open as they sometimes close if no party is expected.

B Villa Cayo Saetía (Gaviota), T24-42350, F24-30126. On the island in the Bahía de Nipe. There are some lovely beaches here and it is popular with day-trippers from Guardalavaca hotels who come by noisy Russian helicopter. There are facilities for visiting yachts at the Base Náutica, VHF 16, and boat rental. It is also promoted as a place to shoot wild fowl and hunt introduced animals such as zebra and antelope. The restaurant specializes in exotic meat as well as creole food.

Moa p307
Hotels
E Miraflores (Islazul), west of the town on a hill, T24-66125, F24-66332. Comfortable hotel, a modern block close to the smelter workers' apartment buildings, pool, freezing a/c in restaurant, US$1 for secure car parking.

Casas particulares
There are no legal *casas particulares* and if you arrive in a rental car you won't be able to stay in an illegal one either as the car will be a dead giveaway.

Camping
The Reservations office for **Campismo Popular** is at Mártires 85 entre Frexes y Martí, Holguín, T24-422881, and at Leyte Vidal, Mayarí, T24-52186. There is 1 site that accepts foreigners:
F Silla de Gibara, La Caridad, Rafael Freyre, T24-421586. Up in the hills with a large swimming pool, 42 cabins, hiking, cycling and horseriding, not far from the beach at Cayo Bariay.

2 other sites are technically reserved for Cubans: **F Puerto Rico Libre**, Playa Puerto Rico Libre, Banes, T24-96918, and **F Río Cabonico**, Carretera a Mayarí, Vía de Sagua de Tánamo, Cabonico, Mayarí, T24-594118.

⊙ Eating

Holguín centre *p301, map p302*
Restaurants
$$$-$$ 1720, Frexes esq Miró. Rumbos restaurant, bar, shows, information, souvenirs, in nicely restored blue and white building. The restaurant, on the right as you go in, is called **Les Parques** and is gloriously elegant with tablecloths, white china and roses on the table, but you don't need to dress up. The food is average but the service OK. The menu ranges from chicken, pork and lamb at US$5-6 to beef at US$8 and lobster at US$22. Plenty of wine on display. The bar is on the other side of the courtyard.

$$ El Rancherito, Frexes y Fomento, daily 1200-1500 and 1800-2200. Cuban cuisine, good but nothing startling.

$ Casa del Cheff, Luz Caballero entre Máximo Gómez y Mártires, close to Plaza de la Maqueta, daily 1230 until everyone stops eating. Good, simple seafood restaurant with a good reputation.

$ Coppelia, on Parque Peralta. Very popular, open 1000-2200, closes 1700 Thu.

$ El Cauto, Martí esq Morales Lemus, daily 1200-2400. On the corner, pleasant, reasonable *criollo* food, beer, rum, pizza, accepts pesos and dollars.

$ El Piropo, Maceo, on the park beside Luz de Yara dollar store. Good ice cream, well regarded.

$ El Tocororo, on Parque Central, T24-468588, open 24 hrs. Rumbos-run, cheap toasted sandwiches, wooden sculpture above door.

$ La Begonia, on Plaza Centralis, a Rumbos cafeteria. Outdoors under a flowering creeper, very pretty, good for a Mayabe beer, meeting place for *jineteras*.

$ La Crema, on Libertad just north of Plaza Central. A bakery and sweet shop.

$ Pico Cristal, corner of plaza with Libertad, T24-425855, daily 1200-1500 and 1830-2245. On 3 floors, cafetería on ground floor, open 24 hrs, usual range of fastish food, disco *Diskaraoke* on 1st floor 2100-0100, restaurant **Pico Cristal** on top floor, international and Cuban food, lots of chicken, some fish.

$ Rombo, Frexes 226 entre Máximo Gómez y Mártires, T24-468056. Cafeteria serving soggy pizza and pasta, fills a hole, dollars only.

Paladares

$ Jelly Boom, Martí 180, near the cemetery, T24-424096, daily 1200-2300, lunch only on request so phone in advance. Supposed to be one of the best in town, the usual *criollo* food, ask around for others.

$ La Galicia, Martí entre Fomento y Cervantes, in front of Turquino, no phone. 4 tables, small, *criollo* food.

$ La Gran Vía, Cables y Morales Lemus. Reasonable food, open for lunch and dinner until the last customer goes.

$ La Malagüeña, Martí entre Maceo y Mártires. 4 tables, can get very busy at night at weekends, long queue, pesos or dollars.

$ La Pampa, Unión entre Cuba y Garayalde, T24-422938, daily 1200-2100. Run by Paco, good *criollo* food.

$ Ramón, Rastro 57 entre Frexes y Pérez Zorilla, next to the telephone *cabina*. Ramón is the owner, good food, specializes in seafood.

$ Taberna Pancho, close to Plaza de la Revolución on Av Jorge Dimitrov, round the corner from the Hotel Pernik, T24-481868, see Sleeping above, daily 1215-1600 and 1815-2200. Serves beer and a reasonable burger, rustic style, heavy wooden furniture and lots of barrels, traditional music.

Around Holguín *p304*
Restaurants

$$ Compay Gallo, 3 km out of Holguín on the way to Guardalavaca, on the right, T24-30132. Spanish *quinta* style, *típico*, in the countryside, pleasant surroundings, traditional music. Good for a lunch stop, but also open for dinner.

$$ Mirador de Mayabe, Villa Mirador de Mayabe, T24-422160, open for lunch and dinner. Popular with tour parties for lunch, see above.

Paladares

$ Casa Colonial, Independencia 20 in front of the Museo Municipal, Gibara. Run by Rolando Cajigal, popular, seafood dishes and 2 rooms to rent.

Guardalavaca *p305, map p305*

There are restaurants in the *Centro Comercial* but no *paladares* in the area. Alternatively there are lots of beach bars between the *Atlántico* and *Scuba Cuba*. Most restaurants

in the hotels offer buffet meals which get very dull after a few days.

$$$-$$ El Cayuelo, short walk along coast from Las Brisas, T24-30422, daily 0900-2300. Good for lobster.

$$$-$$ Pizza Nova, Centro Comercial, in garden looking down to sea, T24-30137 (delivery), daily 1100-2300. Nice location, dining outside on circular terrace under a roof or small indoor seating if a/c preferred. Good pizza, nothing like you'll find on the street. Prices range from US$4.85-19.60, for basic, small cheese and tomato to large lobster pizzas. There is also chicken, meat, fish, lobster tail (US$25), pastas (with lobster) in a similar range of prices.

$$ Mongo Villa, Playa Esmeralda, beyond the mini zoo on the same road. Makes a change from the hotels.

◉ Entertainment

Holguín centre *p301, map p302*
Music

Cabaret El Bariay, at the end of Frexes beyond the river. Show with live performers and taped music, dancing.

Cabaret Nocturno, on road to Las Tunas, Km 2.5, T24-425185, Wed-Mon 2100-0200. Show with different Latin American music followed by salsa and dance music disco.

Café Cantante, Frexes esq Libertad. Live traditional music, *trova*, beer.

Casa de la Trova, on Plaza Calixto García between Casa de la Cultura and La Begonia, Tue-Sun. Good music and dance, notice board outside announcing what's on that night, small stage, bar, *salón*, you can hear it all from the plaza outside.

Casa del Tango, Maceo esq Arias on Parque Céspedes. Operates like a Casa de la Trova but there is only tango.

UNEAC, Libertad entre Martí y Luz Caballero, open until late, depending on the event. A magnificent restored colonial building with tables and chairs in central courtyard and now the major cultural venue in town. Art exhibitions, video shows daily except Mon, cultural and artistic events.

Theatre

Teatro Comandante Eddy Suñol on Parque Calixto García. Closed for renovation. A new theatre is being built in Plaza La Maqueta.

☸ Festivals and events

Jan Semana de la Cultura Holguinera is a week of cultural activities with artists invited from other provinces. Prizes are given in poetry, art, video, theatre etc.
3 May Romerías de la Cruz de Mayo, see Sights, North of the centre, p303 above. Also in May is the **Festival de Cine Pobre de Gibara**, a cinema festival.
Oct In the last week of Oct the **Fiesta de la Cultura Iberoamericana** is held, which each year is dedicated to one Latin American country and one province in Spain. There is a parade through the city and cultural events, organised by the *Casa Iberoamericana*, Arias entre Libertad y Maceo, Parque Céspedes.

○ Shopping

Holguín centre *p301, map p302*
Fondo de Bienes Culturales, Frexes, on Parque Central next to museum. Arts and crafts, prints and original art work, high quality. In renovated mansion with patio at rear where there is a café.

La Sala Moncada art gallery, on Parque Central and **Galería Holguín**, on Parque Céspedes, under the chess academy, host art exhibitions and sales. **Dollar shops** selling food and household goods on Plaza Central and Parque Céspedes, Mon-Sat 0830-1800, Sun 0830-1230.

Guardalavaca *p305, map p305*
Handicraft stalls are set up daily outside the shops in the Centro Comercial. Lots of wooden carvings and crochet work.

▲ Activities and tours

Caving and climbing

At *paladar* **El Colonial**, see above, Ramón Acosta can be contacted. He speaks (teaches) English and German and is very informative about the area. He can put cavers in touch with a local group of espeleologists to explore the underwater rivers and pools found in caves about 10 and 18 km from Gibara. An adventure park covering 36 sq km has been built by **Gaviota**, which includes a *rocódromo*, for vertical climbs, cave exploration, potholing and cave diving although there are other activities for the less able too. A network of cable cars will allow those who prefer not to climb to get up the Silla de Gibara for a good view.

Diving

There are dive shops on the beaches, offering courses and fun dives. On the beach at Playa Guardalavaca is **Scuba Cuba**, which charges US$35 for 1 dive, less for more, ie US$69 for 2 dives. An ICUC Open Water certification course costs US$350. Most of the big resort hotels offer diving as a package or on an individual basis. **Eagle Ray**, is the dive centre at the **Club Amigo Atlántico-Guardalavaca**, see p309, with a capacity for 11 divers and visiting 32 named sites between 5 and 40 m deep. The **Sea Lovers Diving Centre** at Playa Esmeralda has dives at 0900 and 1400 (US$30, US$140 per 5 dives, equipment US$10 or US$35 per 5 dives), and snorkelling trips at 1100 (US$8, plus US$5 for equipment), several good dive sites on the reef offshore, can be rough at times, no jetty so you have to swim and carry tank and gear out to boat. Good, well-maintained equipment and safety record.

Indoor games

Bolera, Parque Infantil, Holguín. Bowling, and other indoor games, US$0.50 entrance.

Marina

The lagoon in the Bahía de Naranjo has been developed as a small marina with 9 moorings, fuel, water, electricity (VHF16), where sailing trips and fishing expeditions can be arranged. You can stay here, there are 2 rooms on Cayo Naranjo (Gaviota), T24-30132, F24-30433.

Watersports

Watersports are offered at Guardalavaca but safety is not good with life-jackets not always offered or worn. The lifeguard on duty is not always in his chair. Hobie cats US$10 per hr, windsurfers and kayaks US$5 per hr, pedalo bikes US$2 per hr. Catamaran trips from Playa Guardalavaca US$69 with lobster lunch. For details of diving, fishing and boat excursions, contact **Cubanacán Náutica**, Playa Guardalavaca, T24-30185, cubanacan.nautica@cnautic.gvc.cyt.cu

Tour operators

The tour desks in the hotels have lots of excursions on offer along the coast or inland, even to Santiago de Cuba. Alternatively you can hire a car, scooter or bike, or contract a local private driver to take you wherever you want, for example, to Gibara for US$25 return with the option of having a meal with a Cuban family. Private operators cannot pick you up from a hotel in Guardalavaca, so meet in the Centro Comercial or on the main road. **Cubatur**, Hotel Guardalavaca, Room 626, T24-30171, holguin@cubatur.cu Tours and excursions for hotel guests and other tourists. **Havanatur**, Frexes 172 entre Morales Lemus y Narciso López, T24-468438, Mon-Fri 0830-1630. Excursions, minibus rental, transfers, guides, hotels and flights to Miami (salida definitiva). **Rumbos**, in the 1720 building on Frexes on the Parque Central.

⊖ Transport

Local
The family vehicle is a bicycle with side car – dad does all the work, mum sits alongside with the baby while seats on the cross bar and behind are for older children. There is very little motorized public transport. The city is choked with **bicitaxis**, **horse-drawn buses** and **taxis**, charging 50-80 centavos.

Long distance
Air The Frank País International Airport (HOG) is 8 km from Holguín, T24-425271. It receives scheduled and chartered flights from abroad and from **Havana** to take visitors out to the beach at **Guardalavaca**. There is also the Orestes Acosta Airport (MOA), 3 km from Moa, T24-67678, which has 1 scheduled Cubana service a week from Havana.
Airlines Aerotaxi, at the airport, T24-462512. **Cubana** is in Edif Pico de Cristal, Libertad esq Martí, Policentro, T24-461610, F24-468111. In Moa, the **Cubana** office is at Av del Puerto, Rpto Rolo Monterrey, T24-67916.
Bus The interurban bus terminal, notable for the number of horses, rather than vehicles, is on Av de los Libertadores opposite the turning to Estadio Calixto García. Buses or shared taxis to **Gibara** leave from here at 0650 and 1750. The interprovincial bus terminal is west of the centre on the Carretera Central. You can walk along Frexes from the centre, but it is a hot walk with luggage. A *bicitaxi* costs US$2. **Víazul** and **Astro** buses stop here. **Víazul**, T24-422994, runs buses to **Guardalavaca** beach from this

terminal daily at 0830, 1 hr, US$6, returns 1900, be there 30 mins before departure and check in advance that it is running.
Car hire Available at the large hotels; **Cubacar**, at Guardalavaca, T24-30389. **Havanautos**, at the airport, T24-43934. **Micar**, is in the Cristal building and at Guardalavaca, T24-421652. **Rex** is at the airport, T24-464644. **Transtur**, at La Begonia on the Parque Central, T24-468559, rents scooters and bikes (Rentamoto). **Vía Rentacar**, at the Sol hotels, T24-30060.

The road from Holguín past Rafael Freyre to Guardalavaca is broad with a good surface, lined with trees and empty of traffic. There is a cart track on either side for oxen and horses. The *Amarillos* are at every junction, organizing lifts on trucks; other people improvize with bikes or motorbikes.
Taxi Cubataxi, Miró, entre Aguilera y Frexes, T24-423290. Good service, not expensive. Turistaxi, at the Hotel Pernik, T24-481011.

⊙ Directory

Holguín centre *p301, map p302*
Banks
Bandec, Arias 159, Mon-Fri 0800-1500. Cadeca, just south of Cristal building on Libertad, Visa, MasterCard. Banco Financiero Internacional, Libertad just north of the Plaza Central, Mon-Fri 0800-1500, last working day of the month 0800-1200, MasterCard, Visa, Tran$card. Bancrédito, Parque Céspedes, Mon-Fri 0800-1500, Visa, MasterCard.

Hospitals and clinics
The main hospital is west of the town centre on Av V I Lenin. A new hospital is being built, very slowly. East of the centre is a paediatric hospital. There are also medical services at the hotels **Pernik** and **El Bosque** and at the beach resort hotels around Guardalavaca.

Internet
Facilities are few in Holguín. **Hotel Pernik** has access at US$5 per hr, daily 1200-2400. Guardalavaca hotels have access for guests.

Post office
Maceo, opposite Parque Céspedes. There is a small Post Office with telephones and DHL on Libertad, Plaza Central, Mon-Fri 1000-1200 and 1300-1600, alternate Sat 0800-1500.

Bayamo → Colour map 3, grid C4. Population: Approximately 150,000.

Bayamo is a low-key, unexciting sort of place, where tourism is of little importance. It is the capital of the province of Granma, named after the boat that brought Castro and his comrades to Cuba to launch the Revolution. Visitors come here on their way to somewhere else, either to the Sierra Maestra for some hiking, or to the port city of Manzanillo and the Granma landing site on the coast. The history of the guerrilla struggle is palpable throughout the area with constant reminders of the landing in 1953. The province occupies the western end of the Sierra Maestra and the flatlands and swamps to the north of the mountains. Many of the country's major rivers drain into the Golfo de Guacanayabo, the longest being the Río Cauto. The southern coast has the best beaches and several resort hotels are clustered around Marea del Portillo at the foot of the mountains, where there are watersports, sailing and diving, but otherwise the area has been largely neglected as far as tourism is concerned.

Everything is sold in pesos, even in the established bars along General García. If you stop over in Bayamo, you can drink daiquirís for about 5 pesos each (US$0.25).

Bayamo was the second town founded by Diego Velázquez in November 1513 and has been declared a Ciudad Monumento Nacional. However, it was burnt to the ground by its own population in 1869 as an act of rebellion against the colonial Spanish; consequently the town has little to offer in the way of very old colonial architecture, with many uninteresting low, box-like buildings reminiscent of provincial suburbs in Spain. Nevertheless, it is a cheerful town and there is often something going on, with makeshift stages put up for concerts or other festivities. Every Saturday there is a Noche Cubana, *when the whole of General García fills with stalls, ad hoc bars, pigs on spits, and the restaurants all put tables on the road.* ▸▸ *For Sleeping, Eating and other listings, see pages 316-319.*

Ins and outs

Getting there There is a small airport, Carlos Manuel de Céspedes (BYM), 16 km from the centre, but it only receives **flights** from Havana, twice a week. International air passengers fly to Holguín and get the bus from there. Bayamo is on the main road and railway between Havana and Santiago so there are regular **buses** and **trains** from both ends of the island. Holguín is only 70 km away and there is frequent traffic between the two cities. ▸▸ *For further details, see Transport, page 319.*

Getting around Traffic is slow and moves at the speed of horses, as **coches** are a common and cheap form of transport. You will be able to **walk** around the centre, which is quite small, but a **coche** or **bicitaxi** is useful to get out to the **Carrusel Sierra Maestra**, 7 pesos, see page 317. A bicitaxi from the bus station to the centre is US$1, a taxi US$2. **Car hire** is available for excursions or there are organized tours.

Tourist information The tourist bureau at the **Carrusel Sierra Maestra**, see page 317, is very helpful with information on all tours in this area. Alternatively, if you are staying in a *casa particular*, your host family will probably know everything you want to find out.

Sights

City centre

The National Anthem of Cuba (*Himno Nacional*) was written by a poet from Bayamo and one of the city's squares is named the Plaza del Himno Nacional. On 20 October 1868, Bayamo was declared capital of the Republic in Arms and the National Anthem was sung. However, on 12 January 1869, the patriotic inhabitants set fire to the town rather than let it fall into the hands of the Spanish colonial rulers. This patriotism has led Bayamo to be called the 'birthplace of the Cuban nation' and it has been declared a National Monument. Background to this can be seen at the **Casa de la Nacionalidad Cubana**① *Plaza del Himno 36 entre Antonio Maceo y Padre Batista, T23-424833*. The **Iglesia de Santísimo Salvador** in the Plaza del Himno Nacional is a 16th-century church which was badly damaged by the 1869 fire, but is currently under restoration. Only a side chapel, the Chapel of Dolores (1740) with a giant *retablo* is open.

The local museum is the **Museo Provincial** ① *Maceo 55, T23-424125, Tue-Sat 0800-1400, Sun 0900-1300*, which has one room on natural history, an exhibition of architectural history, and a room on the war of independence. Next door is the **Casa Natal de Carlos Manuel de Céspedes**① *Maceo 57 entre Donato Mármol y José Joaquín Palma, T23-423864, Tue-Sat 0900-1700, Sun 0900-1200, US$1*, a museum dedicated to the life of the main campaigner of the 1868 independence movement. The 'Father of the Homeland' was born here on 18 April 1819. It is the only two-storey house to survive the fire of 12 January 1869. There are exhibits on the history of the founding of Bayamo up to the death of Céspedes in combat. Parque Céspedes is named in his honour.

On the corner of Amado Estévez and José Martí is the site of the first cemetery established in Cuba on 5 January 1798. Also here is the ruin of San Juan Evangelista, founded at the same time as the city, but destroyed by the 1869 fire. Only the tower survived. In the park is a monument to Francisco Vicente Aguilera, 1821-77, one of the rebels in the 1868 war, and a '*retablo*' to '*los héroes*'. The first Baptist church in Cuba, founded 17 May 1705, is on the corner of Maceo and Marmol.

Around Bayamo

Parque Nacional Sierra Maestra

From Bayamo you need to get a *guagua* (two a day) or truck (very crowded) to Bartolomé Masó and hitch a lift from there (not much traffic) 20 km up into the hills to Santo Domingo. This is time consuming and hard work. If you are cycling it is strenuous and you will need a good level of fitness and cycling experience. The road is mountainous and there are several demanding hill climbs and steep descents. Take care to control your speed. You will pass **Camping La Sierrita** on the left after 4½ km, then cross Río Providencia at 11 km. (You can stay at La Sierrita, but you will have to book at the **Campismo** office in Bayamo first, see below. It is not always open though.) In Providencia village, turn left at the T-junction and begin a steep 4½-km climb. There are excellent views at the top and time to get your breath back before the very steep descent, with a left hand bend at the bottom crossing the bridge over the Río Yara, leading to *Villa Santo Domingo*. It is easier to hire a private driver, which will cost about US$40 to and from Bayamo, but he will take you direct to the National Parks office (just uphill from *Villa Santo Domingo*), which is some way from the village, in time to get a guide for the day.

All tours start at 0900, so you need to get there before then to arrange things. To the Comandancia de la Plata costs US$11 per person, while to Pico Turquino it is US$33 for a two-day hike. If you are lucky, there will be a party staying at the hotel and you and your guide can join their truck (US$2 tip to the driver on the return) for the 5-km drive up the steepest road in Cuba to the car park at **Alto de Naranjo**, at 950m. Alternatively you can walk it. If you are all fit and fast walkers going by truck you can be back at the Parks office by 1400, but more likely it will take longer than that. From Alto de Naranjo, there is a path to the left to Pico Turquino and a path to the right for the 3-km walk to the **Comandancia de la Plata**, Castro's mountain base during the Revolution. 3 km does not sound like a lot, but this hike is not for the unfit. Parts are steep and very muddy. You need to be prepared to wash everything you stand up in afterwards, including your shoes. Take lots of water and snacks, there is no lunch.

Halfway along the path you come to the **Casa Medina**, where you rest for a bit in the shed where they dry coffee beans. You have to leave your camera here. Photography is not allowed at the camp, ostensibly because Castro wants people to come and see for themselves what it was like to hide out in the mountains during the Revolution. The Medina family was the first to help the guerrillas during the Revolution and the Osvaldo Medina Quintet, which entertained the troops, still continues to perform. It is alleged that even now, Castro drinks coffee from this region to the exclusion of all others. Once you get to the command station you are shown a small museum and other wooden buildings in the camp. Castro's bedroom, campbed and kitchen are here. It is all very evocative and atmospheric, helped by beautiful surroundings up in the mountains, where you can see the Cuban trogon and other birds in the forest. This trip is a highlight of any tour of Cuba and not to be missed.

Pico Turquino (see page 339) can also be visited from Alto de Naranjo. This is a two-day hike, with one day to get up to the peak and the second day to come back the same way or carry on over the mountains to the coast west of Santiago. Camping Joaquín is the overnight stop. All trips have to be fully guided in the National Park, so if you want to do a two-day hike it is best to arrange it in advance. There are other walks available on demand, depending on your abilities and what you are interested in. The guides are all knowledgeable but don't expect them to speak any languages other than Spanish.

Dos Ríos

ⓘ *Carretera Jiguaní-San Germán Km 21, to the northeast of Bayamo, reached by bus to Jiguaní at 0710, 80 centavos, 50 minutes, then bus from Jiguaní to Dos Ríos at 0900, 1 peso. It arrives at 0950 and returns at 1015, but this gives you enough time to see the memorial.*

Other excursions in the area include a morning's visit to the national monument where José Martí was killed on 19 May 1895 at **Dos Ríos** . The memorial path is lined with *lluvia de fuego* flowers and lots of yellow *mariposas*, the national flower. Note that the bus does not depart from where you got off, but from further up the road. You will probably see people waiting at the departure point along the former runway, now the road, created for Fidel's centenary memorial visit in 1995. The **Jardín Botánico de Cupaynicú** is on the outskirts of the town of Guisa. It is in a very mountainous region and difficult to get to but worth the effort for the beautiful setting. The garden has a lot of ornamental plants but also a collection of edible and medicinal plants and palms of all shapes and sizes. There is a large area of native forest and scientists are studying the flora to see what benefit they can be to man. Car hire or private driver required to get here.

● Sleeping

Bayamo *p314, map p318*

Hotels

E **Royalton** (Islazul), on Maceo 53 y Joaquín Palma, very central location, T23-422290, F23-424792. The building dates from the 1940s and has been elegantly renovated as a 3-star hotel. 33 rooms, a/c, private bathrooms, phones, restaurant, lobby bar and terrace bar open each night, toilets beyond reception.

Casas particulares

F **Ana Martí**, Céspedes 4 entre Maceo y Canducha Figueredo, T23-425323. 2 rooms, although one is a bit difficult to get up to, clean and good.

F **Olga Celeiro Rizo**, Parada 16 (altos) entre Martí y Mármol, above Cubana office, T23-423859. Olga and her husband José Alberto are most hospitable and helpful in arranging excursions. 2 bedrooms share bathroom, extra bed on request, comfortable, balcony off sitting room for watching the world go by in the plaza below. Good food, excellent sweet potato chips, substantial breakfast.

F **Ramón Enrique Alvarez Sánchez**, Pío Rosado 22 entre Ramírez y Av Fco Vte Aguilera, T23-423984. Enormous rooms, a/c, private bathroom, wife Carolina is a good cook.

Around Bayamo *p315*
C-D **Carrusel Sierra Maestra** (Cubanacán), Carretera Central Km 1.5 via Santiago de Cuba, 2 km from city centre, T23-482230, sierra@bayamo.cyt.cu 204 rooms, delightful post-Revolution 1960s building, kitsch interior, avoid rooms overlooking noisy pool, plenty of nightlife, 3 bars, disco, mostly Cubans, helpful staff, car hire, credit cards accepted.
E **Villa Bayamo** (Islazul), Carretera Manzanillo Km 5.5, T23-423102/423124. 34 rooms and 10 cabins, 2 star.
E **Villa Santo Domingo** (Islazul), Santo Domingo, Bartolomé Masó, T LD-375. 20 rooms in cabins, some of which are damp, 1 star, a/c, TV, bar, restaurant, barbecue, games room, parking, credit cards accepted. There is good walking in the area along paths and trails and it is a great place to get close to nature with lovely views up in the mountains.

Camping
The Reservations office for **Campismo Popular** is at Gen García 215, T23-4242000.
F **La Sierrita**, Carretera Santo Domingo Km 8, Bartolomé Masó, LD-326. Technically for Cubans only, but foreigners are usually allowed if there is room. You get a basic cabin with bathroom. Rural, beside the river, but Cubans on holiday can be noisy. This river is prone to flash flooding during rainstorms.
F **Los Cantiles**, Minas de Harlem, Jiguaní, T23-424862. Cabins by the Río Cautillo which cuts through limestone hills making natural pools for river bathing.

🍴 Eating

Bayamo *p314, map p318*
Restaurants
1513, Gen García esquina General Lora, T23-425921, daily 1200-2200. Small but recommended by Bayameses. Cuban cuisine.
Bayamo, in Villa Bayamo (see above), T23-423102, daily 1900-2215. International and *criollo* food. Also **Bar Terraza**.
La Casona, Plaza del Himno Nacional, behind the church in a corner, daily 1300-2200. Nice wooden bar, pizzas or spaghetti for 5 pesos,

courtyard at the back covered with flowering vine, lots of green lizards, delightful.
Tropicrema, Parque Céspedes, daily 0900-2200. Cake and 2 scoops of ice cream, 1.80 pesos, very good and popular.

Paladares
There are *paladares* and bars along Gen García, all charge in pesos, although increasingly foreigners are being asked for dollars, best every Sat night during *Noche Cubana*, some only open on Sat.

🎭 Entertainment

Bayamo *p314, map p318*
Live music and dancing
Sat nights all year round are given over to the *Noche Cubana*, when Gen García becomes an open air bar and eating place with dozens of stalls setting out tables in the street and selling food and drinks in pesos, accompanied by traditional and modern music.
Amor Bayamés, Hotel Royalton, T23-422290. Night club, 2100-0100.
Cabaret Bayamo opposite Hotel Sierra Maestra, on Carretera Central, T23-421698, daily 2100-0200.
Casa de la Trova, on the corner of Maspote and José Martí. Shows during the afternoon and every night, quite touristy in high season.
La Bayamesa, Hotel Sierra Maestra, T23-482230. Disco, daily 2100-0200.

🛍 Shopping

Bayamo *p314, map p318*
There are cheap peso nicknacks in a few shops along Gen García.

Bookshop
Librería Cuba Nueva, Gen García 56, Mon-Sat 0800-1200 and 1300-1700. Dollar bookshop, postcards, dictionaries.

Dollar shops
Cubalse, just south of bus station. Food.
El Arte, Gen García 63, Mon-Sat 0830-1800, Sun 0830-1300.
La Creación, Parque Céspedes, Mon-Sat 0900-1800, Sun 0900-1230.
La Marquesita, opposite the bus station.
Las Modas, Gen García 111, Mon-Sat 0900-1200, 1330-1730. Shoes, shampoo, food.

La Violeta, Gen García 151 esq Figueredo, Mon-Sat 0900-1740, Sun 0900-1200. Largest dollar store with clothes and food,

Photography
Photo Service, Gen García 223, Mon-Sat 0800-2200. Also Av Frank País, entre Figueroa y 2, T23-427332.

▲ Activities and tours

Tour operators
Islazul has an office on Gen García 207, daily 0830-1700. You can also get tourist information in **Hotel Sierra Maestra** and occasionally maps, but it is difficult to get information about day trips.

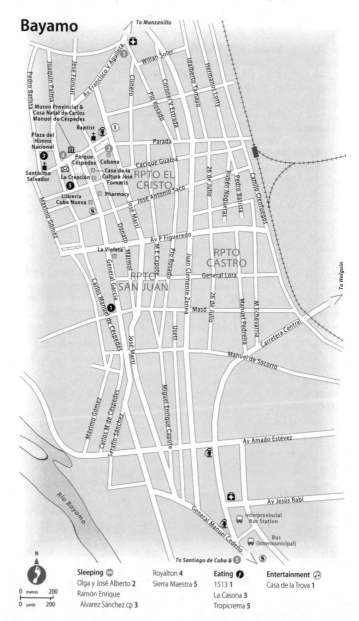

Bayamo

Sleeping
Olga y José Alberto **2**
Ramón Enrique
 Alvarez Sánchez cp **3**

Royalton **4**
Sierra Maestra **5**

Eating
1513 **1**
La Casona **3**
Tropicrema **5**

Entertainment
Casa de la Trova **1**

⊙ Transport

Air

Carlos Manuel de Céspedes airport is 4 km out of town, T23-423695; flights to **Havana** twice a week. **Airlines** Cubana at José Martí 58 entre Parada y Rojas, T23-423916.

Bus

The terminal is on the corner of Carretera Central and Jesús Rabí, T23-424036. **Víazul** passes through Bayamo on its **Havana** to **Santiago** route at 0925 and 0445, returning west at 1725 and 2210. From **Trinidad** to **Santiago** it comes through at 1825, returning 2140.

Astro services direct from **Bayamo** to **Havana** at 2000, US$36; from **Santiago** to **Matanzas** via **Bayamo** at 1845, US$31, to **Cienfuegos** at 1920, US$25, to **Santa Clara** at 1915, US$22, to **Ciego de Avila** at 1955, US$14, to **Las Tunas** at 1400, US$5. Buses from **Bayamo** to **Santiago** at 0600, 0720 and 1410. If you miss a bus or it is full, another one may turn up unannounced, or ask around the terminal for a shared truck or car to **Santiago**. Bus to **Jiguaní**, 4 daily, 80 centavos, 50 mins, or get a truck.

Car hire

Havanautos offices in Cupet Cimex. **Petrol stations** El Especial, T23-427375 and La Bujía, T23-52089.

Horse and cart

7 pesos to Carrusel Sierra Maestra.

Train

Station is at Saco y Línea. Daily trains to **Santiago**, **Havana** and **Manzanillo**.

❶ Directory

Banks Banco Nacional de Cuba, Saco y Gen García. **Bandec**, Gen García 101. Visa and MasterCard, Mon-Fri 0800-1500. **Cultural centres** Casa de la Cultura José Fornaris, Gen García 15, T23-422209. Casa de la Cultura Josué País, Heredia 204 entre San Félix y San Pedro. Casa de la Cultura Miguel Matamoros, Lacret 653. Galería de Arte, José Martí 224. Galería Provincial, Gen García 174 esq Luz Vázquez, T23-423109. **Pharmacy** Farmacia Principal Municipal, 24-hr pharmacy at Gen García 53. **Post office** Parque Céspedes, as is the telephone office, on the side opposite the church.

Manzanillo → *Colour map 3, grid C3. Population: 100,000.*

Manzanillo is a small seaside town and principal port of Granma province with not much to offer to the foreign tourist. It is rather lacking in character and atmosphere, but its one advantage is that due to lack of tourism, visitors will not be subject to the constant attention and hassle common in tourist destinations; the people of Manzanillo seem completely uninterested in the activities of foreigners in their midst and you can stroll about the town at your leisure virtually ignored. Another advantage of the absence of tourism is that you can pay for nearly everything in pesos, so for the budget traveller who wants to hang onto dollars for later, Manzanillo is a good stop-off point. ▸▸ *For Sleeping, Eating and other listings, see pages 321-322.*

Ins and outs

Getting there All long-distance transport is via Bayamo, unless you want to try for the once a week **flight** to and from Havana. At Bayamo you connect with **buses** and **trains** running from east to west along the island.

Getting around The town is not very big so you can walk around it or take a **bicitaxi** or **coche** for longer distances. **Car hire** is available for excursions to the Granma landing site and other local attractions if you don't want to go on a tour.

Tourist information The hotel is your best bet for information, or talk to local people. Tourism is not promoted in Manzanillo.

The **Malecón** is disappointing, being a grey stretch of stony beach lined with the odd concrete shell housing a cheap peso restaurant where you may be the only customers for lunch. The Malecón leads to the centre of the village, around the **Parque Céspedes**. Here is the **glorieta** (gazebo), maintained in pristine condition and considered a symbol of the city. The square is surrounded by restaurants and snack bars, all of which charge in pesos. On José Martí there are cheap stalls selling essential commodities for Cubans, also the usual mini-*paladares*. The **Casa de la Trova** is the centre of nightlife on Saturdays, and you can mingle with Cubans in a natural environment, without feeling segregated in a tourist-only exclusion zone, as in the big cities. A small, colonial church, the **Iglesia de la Purísima Concepción**, is on Maceo, overlooking Parque Céspedes. The **Museo Histórico Municipal** is on José Martí 226, with artefacts of the *conquistadores* in one section and relics of the clandestine struggle in the other.

Parque Nacional de Demajagua

The ruins of the **Demajagua sugar mill** are in the hills about 10 km south of Manzanillo. This is the place where, in 1868, Carlos Manuel de Céspedes cast the first stone in the First War of Independence by liberating his slaves and shouting "¡Viva Cuba Libre!". The mill was named after the bell used to call the slaves to work, which then became the symbol of the Revolution when Céspedes set off to rebel against Spanish rule.

Southwest Granma to Cabo Cruz → *Colour map 3, grid C3.*

From Manzanillo a road follows the coast along the Golfo de Guacanayabo to the tip of the peninsula at Cabo Cruz and the Parque Nacional Desembarco del Granma. After 50 km you come to the small town of **Media Luna**, home to the **Museo Celia Sánchez**, a small but worthy testament to this influential player in the Revolution. Celia Sánchez was a key figure at the beginning of the Revolution and it was partly because of her support that the *Granma* landing was not a complete disaster. Contrary to expectations, Batista's troops were waiting for the yacht and the revolutionaries had to scatter into the hills. Despite being in great danger, Sánchez, who lived locally, managed to get messages to the different groups and they were able to reunite.

Another 23 km brings you to to **Niquero** where there is accommodation in a nice hotel with great views of the sea in one direction and a sugar mill in the other from its rooftop bar. From Niquero a dirt road leads to the spot where Castro's 82 revolutionaries disembarked from the yacht, *Granma*, on 2 December 1956 in a mangrove swamp just southwest of **Playa Las Coloradas**, see The Beaches below. By the dirt road is a small park where a replica of *Granma* can be seen and a 2-km concrete path through the swamp takes you to a rather ugly concrete jetty and a plaque marking the occasion. (The real Granma is in Havana). Every year on 2 December, hundreds of youths re-enact the whole journey from Mexico, disembarking here and heading off into the Sierra Maestra, worth visiting at that time. The dirt road ends at **Cabo Cruz** at the tip of the peninsula. The **Parque Nacional Desembarco de Granma**, which extends from the southwestern coast of the eastern region to the Sierra Maestra has been declared a UNESCO world nature site, largely because of the Cabo Cruz marine terraces (see Geology and landscape).

Between Niquero and Media Luna there is a turning southeast across the peninsula, following the Río Sevilla for much of the way, to **Pilón** (population 12,000), a small town with a harbour on the south coast. Just before **Ojo de Agua**, there are three separate signs and plaques marking the spots where three groups of men who disembarked from *Granma* crossed the road in underground water conduits, before heading into the Sierra Maestra. The signs have the emblems of five palms in a heart, because the men arranged to reassemble at a place called **Cinco Palmas**. The spot near Ojo de Agua has the actual conduit through which Fidel and his group went, sitting at the side of the road. At Pilón the road joins up with the coast road from Santiago de Cuba.

Only 90 km from Manzanillo, **Playa Las Coloradas** is a reasonable excursion. The **Hotel Guacanayabo** will organize a bus trip there in high season, but only with a minimum of 30 people. They also run day trips to **Cayo Perla** for US$15 per person, or less for a large group, including food. There is a nice beach, but nothing else. The best beaches in this area are on the south coast around **Marea del Portillo** where there are a few hotels offering diving and other watersports. The sand is grey because of its volcanic origins and gets hot at midday, but the scenery is spectacular with palm-fringed bays at the foot of the mountains of the Sierra Maestra and the deep blue of the Caribbean Sea.

● Sleeping

Manzanillo *p319, map p321*
Hotels
E Guacanayabo (Islazul), Av Camilo Cienfuegos, T23-54012. 112 basic a/c rooms with private bathroom, Visa/MasterCard, car hire, post office, 24-hr doctor, very helpful, change TCs, views of pool from most rooms, full of noisy children during holidays, very loud disco music all day and evening, staff not used to foreign tourists. To get to town centre, walk down steps to the right of the entrance, down the street to seafront and catch a horse and cart. The tourist bureau in the hotel has some day trips but out of Cuban holiday season they probably won't be running.

Casas particulares
Casas particulares can easily be arranged in the town centre, just hang around Parque Céspedes until you are approached.

Southwest Granma *p320*
D Villa Punta Piedra, (Cubanacán), Carretera Pilón, T23-597009. 2 star, 8 km east of Pilón.

E Niquero (Islazul), Martí esq Céspedes, Niquero, T23-592498. 2 star, 26 rooms, a/c, restaurant, bar, parking.

The beaches *p321*
At Marea del Portillo 15 km east of Pilón, popular with Canadian package tours:
A-B Farallón del Caribe, (Cubanacán), Km 14, T23-597081, dsk@hfarcar.cyt.cu All-inclusive, 4 star, 140 rooms, a/c, TV, hot water, phone for international calls, diving, watersports, tennis, car and bicycle rental, nice position. Prices per person.
C-D Club Amigo Marea del Portillo, (Cubanacán), Carretera Granma Km 12.5, T23-597103, dsk@hfarcar.cyt.cu All-inclusive, 3 star, 130 rooms, hot water, phone, tennis, beach volleyball, watersports, car rental, shop. Prices per person.

Camping
F Las Coloradas (Cubamar), Playa Las Coloradas, Carretera de Niquero Km 17, T LD-0004. Reservations at **Campismo Popular** in

Manzanillo centre

Golfo de Guacanayabo

Parque Masó

Av 1 de Mayo

Sariol

Villuendas

la Purísima Concepción

Parque Carlos Manuel de Céspedes

Museo Histórico Municipal

Mártires de Viet-Nam

Luz Caballero

Plácido

Estadio Wilfredo Pagés

Marti

J M Gómez

Merchan

To Train Station

Not to scale

Entertainment ☺
Casa de la Trova **1**   Costa Azul **2**

Holguín and Granma Manzanillo: listings

Bayamo or through **Cubamar** in Havana. International tourism is welcome here in the 28 1-star cabins that sleep 4-6. On the beach, very convenient for all the sights, with music, entertainment, bikes and horseriding. Spaces for camper vans.

🍴 Eating

Manzanillo *p319, map p321*

All the restaurants charge in pesos; most of them are in and around Parque Céspedes, but avoid the cheaper establishments with just a concrete bar and plastic plates as you run the risk of a stomach infection. Other restaurants have very basic menus of 2 or 3 dishes. There is a nice coffee bar on the corner of Maceo and Merchan and a snack bar with large terrace opposite. There are mini-*paladares* all along José Martí, selection not good, but ice creams (1 peso) are nice.

$ **El Golfo**, Av 1 de Mayo, T23-53158, open for lunch and dinner. Seafood a speciality.
$ **Las Américas**, Maceo 83, T23-530443, daily 1200-1500 and 1800-2100. *Criollo* menu.

🎭 Entertainment

Manzanillo *p319, map p321*

The **Casa de la Trova** is on the corner of Masó y Merchan. **Costa Azul** on Av 1 de Mayo y Narciso López, T23-53158, has a cabaret show 2100-0100. There is also a folklore music show at the art gallery building on the south corner of Parque Céspedes on Thu at 2030.

🛍 Shopping

Manzanillo *p319, map p321*

Two **souvenir shops** on Parque Céspedes, 1 of them has Che Guevara T-shirts for US$4, compared with US$15 in the hotel, also a small but interesting selection of **books**, mostly on revolutionary history.

🏔 Activities and tours

Watersports
Watersports, scuba diving, snorkelling and sailing can be arranged at the **Marea del Portillo resorts**. Scuba diving is with **Centro de Buceo Albacora** who take up to 8 divers to 17 sites at depths of 5-40 m.

🚍 Transport

Local
Plenty of 1950s **American cars** at the bus station, 10 pesos to the hotel. **Horses and carts** from the hotel to the centre, 1 peso.

Long distance
Air The Sierra Maestra (MZO) airport is 12 km from the city, T23-54984. It has international status but only receives scheduled **Cubana** flights once a week from **Havana**. **Airlines** Cubana is on Maceo 70 entre Merchan y Villuendas, T23-2800.

Bus The bus station is at Km 2 on the Bayamo road. To **Bayamo** at 0600, 1500, US$2.50; also daily buses to Havana and **Santiago de Cuba**.

Car hire Cubacar, Carretera de Pilón, Km 14.5, T23-594085. **Havanautos**, at the Cupet-Cimex. **Petrol stations**: La Bujía fuel station, Carretera Central y Circunvalación, Manzanillo, T23-52089.

Taxi Taxi OK, Carretera de Pilón, Km 14.5, T23-594085.

Train Station is 10 blocks east of Parque Céspedes on José Martí. It is at least 2 hrs to **Bayamo** where the train links up with the **Havana-Santiago** line and all stations in between. The train to **Santiago** is second class, so services limited, no snacks available, take everything you need for a long journey. Departs 0625, should be daily but technical problems mean it is usually every other day, 8 hrs, US$5.75 (sometimes you can pay in pesos). If you have a bicycle go the day before to buy ticket, US$7.95, at the **Comercial de UB Expreso** office next to the train station, Mon-Fri 0800-1130, 1330-1700, Sat 0800-1130.

☎ Directory

Manzanillo *p319, map p321*
Hospitals and clinics Hospital Celia Sánchez Manduley, Av Camilo Cienfuegos, 10 mins' walk from Hotel Guacanayabo. Medical services for foreigners are free but take an interpreter if you don't have good Spanish. Doctor on call 24 hrs at **Hotel Guacanayabo**, can treat minor ailments. **Pharmacy** Prescriptions can be taken to the pharmacy in the hospital, where you pay in pesos (antibiotics and drops for an ear infection only cost 5 pesos).

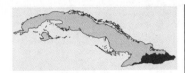

⁑ Footprint features

Santiago and Guantánamo

Introduction

This is the most mountainous part of the country, dominated by the Sierra Maestra, which runs along the foot of the island with several protected areas and National Parks, providing a habitat for many rare creatures. The highest point is Pico Turquino, 1,974 m. The Sierra Maestra also provided shelter for Castro and his band of guerrillas during the Revolution and his command post can still be visited if you have enough puff and strength of leg. This part of the island is hot – in more ways than one – there is no shortage of steamy nightlife. There is a very Caribbean feel to life here, partly because of the influx of migrants from other islands over the centuries, who brought their music and other cultural influences.

Santiago de Cuba, the second most important city in the country, is one of the oldest towns on the island, nestling in an attractive bay surrounded by mountains. It is a vibrant, cultured city with plenty of music. It is the place to come for carnival in July, a raw, ebullient celebration. Sleepy Guantánamo came to the world's attention in 2002 when the US naval base on the coast nearby was chosen to incarcerate prisoners from the conflict in Afghanistan. The crowd-puller in this most easterly province, however, is Baracoa, a laid-back, friendly place, hemmed in by pine-clad mountains. It's one of the best places to come for beaches, rivers, hiking, coconuts, chocolate and seafood, topped off by an active nightlife scene with lots of traditional and contemporary music.

★ Don't miss...

1 Carnival Visit Santiago in July when the city throbs with the beat and the heat of carnival, page 349.

2 El Cobre The shrine of Cuba's patron saint, the Virgen de la Caridad, is built over a working copper mine, page 338.

3 La Tumba Francesa Experience Guantánamo's traditional folk dancing and music originating in Haiti, pages 356 and 358.

4 Mirador de Malones See the US naval base and prison at Guantánamo through binoculars, page 355.

5 La Farola Drive to Baracoa along the spectacular 48-km viaduct, built out from the mountainside amid lush tropical scenery, pages 359 and 360.

6 Río Yumurí Take a boat trip up the river, which flows through deep canyons, page 362.

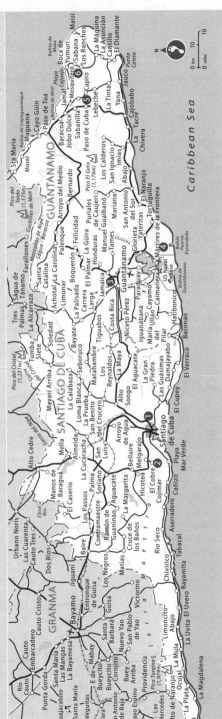

Caribbean Sea

0 km 10
0 miles 10

Ins and outs

Getting there

Santiago is the end of the line for the main road and rail links from Havana and has domestic and international air services. There are several daily buses, trains and flights from the west end of the island and good connections if you want to fan out to Guantánamo, Baracoa and other towns in the region. ▸▸ *See also Getting there, Santiago page 326, Guantánamo page 355 and Baracoa page 359.*

Tourist information

Tour agencies such as **Cubatur** can give information on how to get to where you want to go and offer organized tours as well as make reservations for transport and lodging. *Casas particulares* are a good source of information on cultural and entertainment matters and often offer unofficial transport and recommend places to stay in other towns.

Best time to visit

Without doubt, July is the most exciting time of year to visit Santiago, for its carnival and anniversary celebrations for the attack on the Moncada Garrison in 1956. However, this is also the hottest time of year in an already hot city. The foundation of Baracoa is celebrated in mid-August and there is plenty going on. Although hurricane season officially starts in June, you are most likely to get storms from September to November, when you should be prepared for all your travel plans to be disrupted. The coolest time is from December to February, although if a cold front comes down from the eastern seaboard of the USA, anywhere on Cuba's north coast, such as Baracoa, can expect high seas and some rain.

Santiago de Cuba → *Colour map 3, grid C6.*

Santiago de Cuba, near the east end of the island, 970 km from Havana, is Cuba's second city, with its own identity and charm. Its culture is different from Havana's, with more emphasis on its Afro-Caribbean roots and Santería plays a large part in people's lives. There are regional differences in the music, partly because of past immigrants from the former French colony of Saint-Domingue, now Haiti. Carnival is an experience worth going out of your way for, with energetic dancing, parades, music and increasingly sophisticated costumes as the economy improves.

The city centre is cluttered, with the feel of an overgrown country village, featuring many beautiful pastel-coloured buildings in much better condition than many of those in the capital. It is not a colonial gem along the lines of Havana or Trinidad and there is heavy industry around its edge but it does have an eclectic range of architectural styles from colonial to art deco. The Vista Alegre barrio is an outstanding example of a leafy Cuban suburb, with grand art nouveau buildings, an early 20th-century contrast to the Mudejar style of the city centre. Visit the Maqueta de la Ciudad, a scale model of the city by the Casa de Velázquez, for an overview of the city's development. ▸▸ *For Sleeping, Eating and other listings, see pages 342-353.*

Ins and outs

Getting there International and domestic **Cubana flights** arrive at the Antonio Maceo airport, 8 km south of the city on the coast. On arrival you are greeted by several taxi drivers, some of whom even manage to get right into the arrivals building; these are unofficial taxis but reasonably priced and safe. Official and unofficial taxis shuttle passengers into town for around US$5-8, depending on the company and the distance. Daily **rail** services to and from Havana link Santiago with all the major towns lying along the main rail route through the country. The new railway station is central, opposite the rum factory on Avenida Jesús Menéndez, and within walking distance of many *casas particulares* and some hotels in the centre. There are several daily **Víazul buses** from Havana, with morning and afternoon departures, and one from Trinidad, via many places of interest worth stopping off along the way. The long-distance bus terminal is to the north of the city, by the Plaza de la Revolución, some 30 minutes' walk to Parque Céspedes. Outside you will find **taxis**, **colectivos**, **trucks**, **buses** and horse-drawn **coches** to take you to your destination. Arriving at night is not a problem as there are always taxis waiting for business.➔ *For further details, see Transport, page 351.*

Getting around   Urban **buses** cost 20 centavos. There are also horse-drawn **coches**, 1 peso, **motorbikes**, US$1, and **bicitaxis**, US$1, for short journeys around town. Plaza Marte is a central hub for lots of local transport. For excursions there are buses and/or **trucks** on some routes out of town but it is easier to negotiate a day trip with a driver who can take you to your destination. Make sure everything is agreed and clear before you set off, as drivers have a reputation for moving the goalposts when you're a long way from base. **Car hire** is available if you want to drive yourself. The city is easy to **walk** around with many of the sights congregated around the centre. It takes about 20-30 minutes to walk from Parque Céspedes to the Hotel Santiago and 30 minutes from the parque to the bus station.

Best time to visit   Santiago's position at the foot of the mountains means that it is more protected from breezes than places along the north coast and is consequently several degrees hotter than Havana. This is not a problem in winter, but in the summer months of July and August it can be stifling. The song *Calor in Santiago* by Conjunto Rumba Habana sums it up perfectly: *"¡Candela, fuego, me quemo, el calor me está derritiendo!"* – "Candle, fire, I'm burning, the heat is melting me!" Unfortunately, this coincides with carnival in July, which just has to be the best time to visit Santiago. Nearly the whole month is taken up with festivities, starting with the Festival del Caribe, which runs into carnival in the third week with Santiago's patron saint's day on 25 July. Everything stops on 26 July, National Rebel Day and the anniversary of the attack on the Moncada barracks, then continues the next day.

History

Santiago de Cuba was one of the seven towns (*villas*) founded by Diego Velázquez. It was first built in 1515 on the mouth of the Río Paradas but moved in 1516 to its present location in a horseshoe valley surrounded by mountains. It was Cuba's capital city until replaced by Havana in 1553 and capital of Oriente province until 1976. During the 17th-century Santiago was besieged by pirates from France and England, leading to the construction of the Castillo del Morro, still intact and now housing the piracy museum, just south of the city. Because of its location, Santiago has been the scene of many migratory exchanges with other countries; it was the first city in Cuba to receive African slaves, many French fled here from the slaves' insurrection in Haiti in the 18th century and Jamaicans have also migrated here from the neighbouring island. Santiago is more of a truly ethnic blend than many other towns in Cuba.

It is known as the 'heroic city' (*Ciudad Héroe*), the cradle of the Cuban Revolution, the Rebel City, or '*capital moral de la Revolución Cubana*'. Many of Cuba's heroes in both the 19th and 20th centuries were born here and started insurrections in the city and the surrounding mountains. The national hero, José Martí, is buried in Santa Ifigenia cemetery, just west of the city. The city played a major role in the early days of the Revolution in the 1950s and boasts two major landmarks of the clandestine

⁞ The Padre Pico steps in Santiago

The revolution in Haiti at the end of the 18th century brought a large influx of French immigrants to Cuba, many of whom settled in the south west of Santiago de Cuba in an area known as Loma Hueca. They built a theatre there called El Tivoli, the name by which the neighbourhood came to be identified. The hill leading up to the Tivoli area was so steep that it had to be paved in staggered form, and these steps were named Loma de Corbacho, after the grocery store on one of the corners.

Decades later, in the Republic's first year, Emilio Bacardí, in his function as mayor, had the steps renovated. Locals wanted them to be named in his honour, but he proposed the name 'Padre Pico', in memory of Bernardo del Pico, a priest who had helped the poor in Santiago.

The Padre Pico steps gained further historical status when Castro chose their strategic location to fire the opening shots in his first offensive against Batista in 1956. As well as all that history, the steps give commanding views of the bay and the mountains around Santiago, and now form an essential part of any walking tour of the city.

struggle: the Moncada Garrison, now a school and museum, scene of Fidel Castro's first attack on the Batista regime in 1953, and **La Granjita Siboney**, the farmhouse where 129 revolutionaries gathered the night before the attack on the Garrison, which is also now a museum.

Sights

City centre

The small **Parque Céspedes** is at the centre of the town and everything revolves around it. Most of the main museums are within easy walking distance. The **Hotel Casa Granda** flanks the east side and the Cathedral, the white **Santa Iglesia Basílica Metropolitana** ① *Heredia entre Félix Pena y Gen Lacret (entrance on Félix Pena), daily 0800-1200, services: Mon, Wed 1830, Sat 1700, Sun 0900, 1830,* is on the south side. The first building on the site was completed in 1524 but four subsequent disasters, including earthquakes and pirate attacks, meant that the cathedral was rebuilt four times. The building now standing was restored in 1818, with more new decoration added in the early 20th century.

The west side of the park is occupied by a rather ugly bank, next to the beautiful 16th-century **Casa de Diego Velázquez**. The house where Diego Velázquez lived is now one of the best museums in Santiago, the **Museo de Ambiente Histórico Cubano** ① *Félix Pena 612, at the northwest corner of Parque Céspedes, T22-652652, Sat-Thu 0900-1700, Fri 1400-1700, US$2, with guided tour in English, French or German, camera fee US$1 per photo.* It is the oldest house in Cuba, started in 1516, completed 1530. Velázquez, Cuba's conqueror, lived on the top floor, while the ground floor was used as a contracting house and a smelter for gold. It has been restored after its use as offices following the 1959 Revolution and is in two parts, one from the 16th century, and one from the 18th century. Each room shows a particular period, demonstrating the development of Cuban material culture, featuring furniture, china, porcelain, crystal; there is also a 19th-century extension.

On the north side the **Casa del Gobierno** features a strong Moorish influence, particularly in the patio. This building is not open to the public, but is used for government functions.

The **Museo Provincial Emilio Bacardí** ① *Entrance on Pío Rosado esq Aguilera, two blocks east of the Parque, opposite the Palacio Provincial, T22-628402, Tue-Sat 1000-2000, Sun 1000-1800, Mon 1200-2000, guided tour in English, US$2,* was named after industrialist Emilio Bacardí Moreau, its main benefactor and collector of much of the museum's contents. This was the second museum founded in Cuba and has exhibits from prehistory to the Revolution downstairs, one of the most important collections of Cuban colonial paintings upstairs, while outside on one side there is a reconstruction of a typical colonial street front and a nice courtyard. The archaeology hall has mummies from Egypt and South America, including a Peruvian specimen over 1,000 years old. The Egyptian mummy dates back to the 18th dynasty, 2,000 years ago, and was personally acquired by Emilio Bacardí and brought back to Cuba. There are also exhibits of ancient art, ethnology, documents of the history of Santiago and a hand-made torpedo used by the rebels during the first war of independence in the 19th century.

On Heredia near the Casa de la Trova is the **Casa Natal de José María Heredia,** the birthplace of Santiago's most famous poet (see box, page 408). It is now a cultural centre and there is a poetry workshop here on Fridays from 1700. The **Museo de Música** is above the Casa de la Trova (see Entertainment).

If you are not going to be in town in July, you can get a flavour of the carnival by visiting the **Museo del Carnaval** ① *Calle Heredia esq a Carnicería, T22-626955, Tue-Sat 0900-1800, Sun 0900-1200, US$2.* The museum exhibits a dusty collection of instruments, drums and costumes from Santiago's famous July carnival. There are also lots of photos and newspaper cuttings but with no explanation of their significance. Every afternoon except Saturday you can feel the beat of the *bata* drums when the folklore group, *19 de Diciembre,* perform in the courtyard, US$1.

Plaza Dolores is worth noting as a point of reference if walking east from Parque Céspedes. It is known as 'Bulevar', although it is really just a widening of Aguilera. It has a coffee house, **La Isabelica,** on the corner and an ice cream stall, **Kikiriki,** open daily 1100-2300. It's the most popular of the plazas for an evening's gossip and where you're most likely to be approached by Cubans. It's also popular with musicians.

The **Museo de la Lucha Clandestina** ① *at the top of Padre Pico steps, Calle Gen Rabí 1 entre Santa Rita y San Carlos, T22-624689, Tue-Sun 0900-1700, US$2,* was founded to mark the 20th anniversary of the armed uprising in Santiago, Central Ermita and other parts of Oriente on 30 November 1956. The museum highlights the support given by the local urban population during the battle in the Sierra Maestra and has an exhibition of the citizens' underground struggle against the dictatorship. Housed on two floors, exhibits revolve around Frank País, from his early moves to foment a revolutionary consciousness to his integration into the Movimiento 26 de Julio under Fidel Castro. A guide speaking 'Spanglish' will take you round if you can't read Spanish. The building was originally the residence of the Intendente, then was a police HQ, a key target of the 26 July revolutionary movement. It is now completely restored after having been stormed and gutted during the Revolution. It is a beautiful yellow building with a marvellous courtyard and affords good views of the city. On Saturday afternoon the courtyard is the venue for conferences, performances and other cultural activities relating to the city's French roots. Many of the French staff of the Alliance Française attend.

To get a good idea of the layout of the city, visit the **Maqueta de la Ciudad** ① *Corona entre San Basilio y Santa Lucía, Tue-Sun 0900-2100, US$1, small dollar bar.* This is a scale model similar to the one in Havana. Nearby is the **Centro Cultural Francisco Prats** ① *Corona entre Heredia y San Basilio, guided tour.* This is a newly remodelled colonial house exhibiting personal belongings of the brilliant investigator.

There are several interesting churches in the centre: **Iglesia de la Santísima Trinidad (Carmen),** on Félix Pena y San Jerónimo, built in the late 18th century with some neoclassical features; two blocks west is **Iglesia San Francisco,** on Calle San Francisco, also 18th century; **Iglesia de Santa Lucía,** Santa Lucía esquina Pío Rosado,

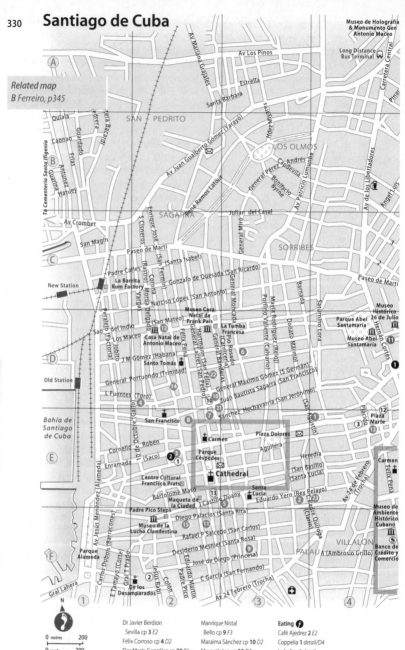

a small church worth visiting in order to see the architecture in the surrounding streets; three blocks south of the Museo de la Lucha Clandestina is **Iglesia de los Desamparados**, on General T Prado; **Iglesia Santo Tomás** is an 18th-century church on Habana y Félix Pena.

North of the city centre

Ten minutes' walk north from the centre of Santiago is the **Bacardí rum factory**, or La Barrita, but you can only go in the shop and bar, the factory is closed to visitors since tourists 'stole' the technology by taking too many photos. Ron Caney is made here. There is also a small **Museo del Ron** ① *San Basilio 358 esq Carnicería, near Parque Céspedes, T22-623737, Mon-Fri 0900-1700, US$2 including 2 cl of rum.*

Also near the factory is the **Museo Casa Natal de Frank País** ① *General Banderas 226 y Los Maceos, T22-652710.* This museum is in the birthplace of the leader of the 26 July movement and of the armed uprising in Santiago on 30 November 1956, who was shot on 30 July 1957. He is considered a great hero of the Revolution and his face is often seen on posters and hoardings alongside that of Che, Fidel and other leaders. His tomb is in Santa Ifigenia cemetery.

Another revolutionary hero, but this time from the 19th century, is celebrated at the **Casa Natal de Antonio Maceo** ① *Los Maceo 207 entre Corona y Rastro, T22-623750, Mon-Sat 0900-1700, US$1.* The house was built between 1800 and 1830, and was the birthplace, on 14 June 1845, of Antonio Maceo y Grajales, one of the greatest military commanders of the 1868 and 1895 wars of independence. The museum houses his biography and details his 32 years' devotion to the struggle for independence.

Plaza Marte

Plaza Marte, a short walk up Aguilera from Parque Céspedes, is a pick-up and drop-off point for most urban transport. Go there if you want to get a taxi/moped late at night. The bus stop for other *repartos*, including Vista Alegre, is on the

Santiago de Cuba centre

La Casa Natal de José María Heredia

José Martí said of Heredia: "The first poet in America is Heredia. Only he has captured in his poetry the sublimity, fire and ostentation of its nature. He is as volcanic as its entrails and as calm as its mountain peaks." In his short but eventful life Heredia created a poetic canon that transformed the form and content of Latin American poetry.

Jose María de Heredia y Campuzano was born on 31 December 1803 in Santiago de Cuba, the city his parents had fled to from Santo Domingo in 1801 from the invading Haitian troops. He had an itinerant childhood, the family being constantly uprooted by his father's work; they left their first house in Santiago de Cuba when Heredia was only three years old. He then spent time in the USA and Santo Domingo, as well as Havana and Matanzas. At the age of 20 he was exiled to the USA for his involvement in an independence conspiracy. There he wrote his ode 'Niagara', establishing him as a world-class poet. His death in Mexico aged 36 cut short a tragic life in exile for a man devoted to his country.

The house where Heredia was born still stands, at Heredia y San Félix, in spite of efforts by the colonial rulers of the 19th century to have it demolished. An association made up of influential people like Emilio Bacardí succeeded in buying the house, agreeing to hand over its restoration to the municipal government in 1902. Today, it has regained its original prestige as a national monument and is the most important of the numerous other cultural sites on Calle Heredia, the street formerly called Calle Catedral. The house is a now museum dedicated to the poet's life, as well as a cultural centre and meeting point for contemporary local poets.

corner of Aguilera and Plaza Marte. Plaza Marte is a quieter spot to sit than Parque Céspedes; sometimes musicians play and there's an ice cream stand. Baseball fans come here to dissect the latest matches and loudly proclaim their points of view. Children under 10 will enjoy the plaza at weekends in the late afternoon when there are rides around the square on kids' bikes or in little goat carts, as well as other entertainment paid for in pesos.

North of Plaza Marte, **Parque Abel Santamaría** is a small square commemorating one of Fidel's comrades who was captured by Batista's troops and had his eyes gouged out. The park is on the site of the hospital he was occupying at the time of his capture. The remains of the hospital have been made into the **Museo Abel Santamaría** ① *Gen Portuondo (Trinidad) esq Av de los Libertadores, T22-624119, Mon-Sat 0900-1700*. It was inaugurated on the symbolic date of 26 July 1973 on the 20th anniversary of the attempted overthrow of the Batista regime and has seven rooms exhibiting furniture from the old hospital, clothing and personal possessions of the revolutionaries and other things linked with the history of the place. Two blocks east, the former Moncada Garrison is now the **Museo Histórico 26 de Julio** ① *Av Moncada esq Gen Portuondo, T22-620157, Tue-Sat 0900-2000, Sun 0900-1300, US$2, guided tour in English, French, Italian, camera fee US$1, video camera US$5*. The Garrison was attacked (unsuccessfully) by Castro and his revolutionaries on 26 July 1953. Most of the men were captured, tortured and murdered. Fidel was caught later and imprisoned before being exiled. When the Revolution triumphed in 1959,

● *Compay Segundo's trademark Panama hat was auctioned for more than US$17,000 to*
● *cigar aficionados. The money was allocated to the island's healthcare system.*

the building was turned into a school. To mark the 14th anniversary of the attack, in 1967 one of the buildings was converted to a museum, featuring photos, plans and drawings of the battle. Exhibits include personal items of the Revolutionaries, weapons used in the attack on the Moncada Garrison and during the battles in the Sierra Maestra. There is a homemade gun built by Che Guevara and a waistcoat that belonged to José Martí, an earlier hero. Bullet holes, filled in by Batista, have been reconstructed on the outer walls. A guided visit is highly recommended to help you understand the brutality and carnage of the Batista regime.

Plaza de la Revolución

One of Cuba's foremost revolutionaries of the 19th century, General Antonio Maceo, is honoured in the **Plaza de la Revolución Mayor General Antonio Maceo**. The plaza to the northeast of the centre, has a dramatic monument to the Revolution made of galvanized steel in searing, solid Soviet style, and a gargantuan bronze statue of the general on horseback surrounded by huge iron machetes rising from the ground at different angles. Fidel has made many stirring speeches from the platform and you can picture the plaza filled to capacity to hear him. It was also where the Pope said Mass in his 1998 visit, where rallies were held demanding the repatriation of the Cuban boat boy Elián González in 2000, and the five Cuban heroes imprisoned in the USA in 2002-03, and where parades are held every 1 May on international Labour Day. The long-distance bus terminal is opposite the plaza and you can't miss the monument when departing by bus.

The **Museo de Holografía** ① *T22-643768, Mon-Sat, 0900-1700, Sun 0900-1300, US$1,* is housed below the monument in the Plaza de la Revolución. It features holograms, mostly of things associated with the Revolution and with General Maceo. A guided tour (in Spanish) shows you where the Pope rested after his speech in the plaza.

Ferreiro

The junction of Victoriano Garzón and Avenida Las Américas, where the hotels **Santiago** and **Las Américas** are situated, is known locally as Ferreiro, after the family that owned a large part of the surrounding area and emigrated to the USA after the Revolution. From here, you can catch a bus to any part of town and get a taxi, official or otherwise. Take care at night, as the three small squares at this junction are not lit. North of here along Avenida de las Américas is the **Bosque de los Héroes** ① *Av de las Américas entre M y L, Ampliación de Terrazas, Mon-Sat 0900-1700.* In this park, a block from **Hotel Las Américas**, is the first monument in Latin America devoted to the memory of Che Guevara and his Cuban comrades who died in Bolivia. The architectural sculpture leaves shadows as the sun's rays change during the day, giving different images of the heroes. At night it is strikingly illuminated.

To the east of Ferreiro off Avenida Manduley, in Reparto Vista Alegre, are several interesting museums. The **Centro Cultural Africano Fernando Ortíz** ① *Av Manduley 106, 0900-1700,* displays items of African culture. The **Casa del Caribe** ① *Calle 13 esq Calle 8, T22-642285,* is a world-renowned cultural centre. If you are interested in *Santería*, there is a musical and religious ceremony at 0930 on Wednesdays.

The **Museo de la Religión** ① *Calle 13 206, esq Calle 10, 1 block from Casa del Caribe, Mon-Sat 0830-1700, free, knowledgeable English-speaking guide, Mateo, US$2,* displays religious items particularly concerning *Santería*. There are no written explanations of the exhibits, not even in Spanish, so it is best to ask for a guide. The **Museo de la Imagen** ① *Calle 8 106, esq 5, T22-642234, Mon-Sat 0900-1700, US$1,* displays cameras, photographs, cine (film) and television.

Cementerio Santa Ifigenia

① *Av Crombet, Reparto Juan G Gómez, T22-632723, daily 0800-1730, US$1, US$1 for cameras, price includes guided tour in Spanish and English.*

This grand and well-kept cemetery northwest of the city features José Martí's mausoleum, a huge structure with a statue of Martí inside, designed to receive a shaft of sunlight all morning. Martí is surrounded by six statues of women, representing the six Cuban provinces of the 19th century. In 2003, the mausoleum was awarded the national prize for monumental restoration. Along the path leading up to the mausoleum are signposts commemorating successful independence battles, each decorated with a quote by Martí. There is an elegant changing of the guard ceremony every 30 minutes, free. Also in the cemetery is the grave of Frank País, a prime mover in the revolutionary struggle, and other notable figures, such as Céspedes, the Bacardí family and the mother and widow of Maceo. There is a monument to the Moncada fallen and the tomb of Cuba's first president, Tomás Estrada Palma. More recently, it is the burial place of the famous musician, Compay Segundo, one of the stars of the *Buena Vista Social Club*, who was born in Santiago and died in Havana in 2003. It is said by some that Castro could be laid to rest here. Well worth a visit.

South of Santiago

The Ruta Turística runs along the shore of the Bahía de Santiago to the **Castillo del Morro**, a clifftop fort and World Heritage Site since 1997 with the **Museo de la Piratería** ① *T22-691569, US$4, US$1 for cameras, taxi to El Morro, US$10 round trip with wait, bus 212 from Plaza Marte or opposite the cinema Rialto, Parque Céspedes, stops in front of embarkation point for Cayo Granma,* a museum of the sea, piracy and local history, charting the pirate attacks made on Santiago during the 16th century. Pirates included the Frenchman Jacques de Sores and the Welshman Sir Henry Morgan and you can see many of the weapons used in both attack and defence of the city. The fort

Around Santiago de Cuba

has many levels and fascinating rooms whose purpose can be guessed easily, such as the prison cells, the chapel and the cannon-loading bay. From the roof you can admire the thrilling views over the Bay of Santiago and Cayo Granma and you can follow some 16th-century steps almost down to the waterline. There is a narrow, grass-covered passage that eventually leads down to a small beach, which you can also get to by road. There is a good restaurant on a terrace with a great view, main dish US$6, and a cannon fire at sunset every evening.

Transport along the road passes the ferry at Ciudadmar to the resorts of **Cayo Granma** and **La Socapa** in the estuary (hourly, 10 centavos each way, 10 mins). Cayo Granma was originally Cayo Smith, named after its wealthy owner; it became a resort for the rich. Now most of its 600 inhabitants travel to Santiago to work. There are no vehicles; there are a couple of *paladares* serving seafood in an idyllic setting looking across the bay towards Santiago, ask around, US$6 for a fish meal and a beer.

Along the road to Gran Piedra look out for small monuments to fallen heroes of the Revolution. They are in groups of three and their names and occupations are carved on boulders or sculptures.

East of Santiago

La Gran Piedra and around

Excellent excursions can be made to **La Gran Piedra** (26 km east)
ⓘ *US$1 to climb.* From this viewpoint it is said you can see Haiti and Jamaica on a clear day, more likely their lights on a clear night. It is a giant rock weighing 75,000 tonnes, the third largest solid rock in the world (according to the Guinness Book of Records), 1,234 m high, and reached by climbing 454 steps from the road (only for the fit). The view is tremendous and buzzards circle around you. Hand-carved wooden curios are sold by artisans on the steps. There are no buses but a private car will charge you about

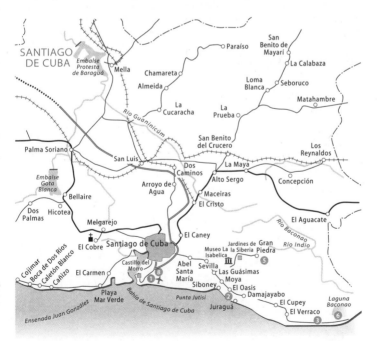

US$15 there and back (the tour desk in any hotel will arrange a tour, good value). Two kilometres before La Gran Piedra are the **Jardines de la Siberia**, on the site of a former coffee plantation, an extensive botanical garden; turn right and follow the track for about 1 km to reach the gardens.

The **Museo La Isabelica** ① *Carretera de la Gran Piedra Km 14, Tue-Sat 0900-1700, Sun 0900-1300, US$2,* is a ruined coffee plantation once owned by French emigrés from Haiti, the buildings of which are now turned into a museum. It was named a World Heritage Site in 2000. It houses the former kitchen and other facilities on the ground floor with farming tools and archaeological finds. Upstairs is the owners' house in authentic 19th-century style. On view on the ground floor are instruments of slave torture. After the slave revolt in Haiti, large numbers of former slave owners were encouraged to settle in the Sierra de la Gran Piedra. This influx led to the impact of Haitian/French culture on Santiago, especially in music. Here they built 51 *cafetales*, using slave labour. During the Ten Years' War (1868-78) the revolutionaries called for the destruction of all the *cafetales*. The owner, Victor Constantin Cuzeau, named the plantation after his lover and house slave, but when Céspedes freed the slaves he fled and Isabelica was thrown by the former slaves into a burning oven.

Siboney to Juraguá

On the Carretera Siboney at Km 13½ is **La Granjita Siboney** ① *T22-639168, Tue-Sun 0900-1700, US$2,* the farmhouse used as the headquarters for the revolutionaries' attack on the Moncada barracks on 26 July 1953. It now has a museum of uniforms, weapons and artefacts used by the 129 men who gathered here the night before, as well as extensive newspaper accounts of the attack. The road is lined with stone tributes commemorating the spots where revolutionaries were killed.

Siboney ① *take bus 214 from near bus terminal, trucks depart from Av de los Libertadores outside the maternity hospital 1 peso,* 16 km east of Santiago, is the nearest beach to the city with a reef just offshore which is great for snorkelling. It gets very crowded at weekends when trucks disgorge passengers every 45 minutes. There

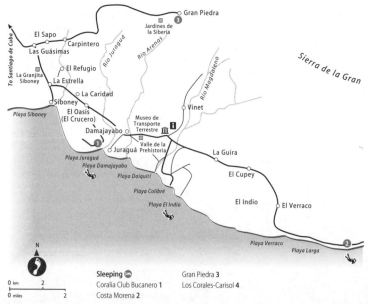

Siboney - Baconao

Sleeping 🛏
Coralia Club Bucanero **1**
Costa Morena **2**

Gran Piedra **3**
Los Corales-Carisol **4**

is a certain amount of hassling on the beach. The accommodation office is at the entrance to the village. You will be approached with offers of private rooms to rent and there are numerous street food stalls and *paladares*, mostly frequented by Cubans, although you will be charged in dollars.

About 20 km from Santiago, or half way between Siboney and Juraguá, look for a sign on the left to **Finca El Porvenir** ① *Carretera de Baconao Km 18, US$1*, a nice freshwater swimming pool with a bar and restaurant serving *comida criolla* from 1000-1800. The pool looks a bit green at first, but is actually clean and a wonderful place to stop off and cool down after sweating along the dusty highway.

Juraguá is an even nicer beach than Siboney; it is a bit rundown and not really geared towards tourism but further development is projected in this area. There is a bar if you are desperately thirsty. You can also scuba dive here and there are two dive shops offering dive packages and certification.

Valle de la Prehistoria and around

At Km 6½ on the Carretera Baconao is the **Valle de la Prehistoria** ① *T22-639239, US$2, extra US$1 to take photos*, a huge park filled with life-size carved stone dinosaurs and stone age men. Great for the kids but due to the total absence of shade it is like walking around a desert. Take huge supplies of water and try to go early or late. You can get quite a good view of the monsters from the main road as you pass by. Nearby is **Mundo de Fantasía**, a small amusement park also good for kids. Admission appears to be free, ask the stone clown at the entrance! Also in the area is the recommended old car and trailer museum, **Museo de Transporte Terrestre** ① *Carretera Baconao Km 8½, Daiquirí, turn left at the junction for Playa Daiquirí, T22-639197, US$1 entrance plus US$1 for a camera*. The old classic American cars are not particularly well kept, although some of the best of them are now being brought out to be used as taxis in Santiago to entertain the tourists. Others, however, are in serious need of proper restoration. **Daiquirí** beach (turn right at Km 25) is beautiful and quiet but the resort there is now reserved for the military. The next beach, 1 km after Daiquirí, is **Colibrí**, featuring a seawater swimming pool and a pebble beach. However, this has now been developed as a health spa and retreat and foreign tourists are no longer allowed entry. Continuing east at Km 35 is **Comunidad Artística Verraco**, a small artists' community, where you can buy original pieces of artwork.

Baconao

On this stretch of the coast, there is the **Acuario de Baconao**, an Aquarium and Dolphinarium ① *US$5, three sea-lion and dolphin shows daily, at 1000, 1130 and 1445, however small the audience*. The show is of a high standard, although controversial, and visitors are invited to dive in and play with the dolphins for an extra US$20, for about 10 minutes. The aquarium has many species of fish as well as turtle and sharks (feeding time is spectacular). There is a basic refreshment bar where you can get a sandwich for US$1 and a beach, with trees for shade but no facilities, if you want a quick dip while waiting for the next dolphin show. See also page 68 in Essentials for further information about dolphinariums in Cuba. **Playa Cazonal** is a very high quality beach for this area. Wear something on your feet when swimming and avoid standing on the coral reef. **Laguna Baconao** ① *US$1 to enter the Laguna Baconao area,* is a large murky lake in a beautiful setting. Flanking the lake is a crocodile sanctuary, but they are kept in small enclosures with barely enough water to drink. Admission includes a boat ride to a floating bar in the middle of the lake. There are no buses to **Parque Baconao,** a private car can be hired for a whole day. There is a military checkpoint at Baconao and sometimes the road is closed, making it impossible to get through to Guantánamo by this route.

West of Santiago

El Sanctuario de Nuestra Señora de la Caridad del Cobre
Ten kilometres west of Santiago is El Sanctuario de Nuestra Señora de la Caridad del Cobre ('El Cobre')① *there is no bus, so either hire a car and driver, about US$8, or get on a truck at the bus station for a few pesos*, where the shrine of Cuba's patron saint, the Virgen de la Caridad del Cobre, is built over a working copper mine. The story goes that in the 17th century, three fishermen were about to capsize in Nipe Bay, when they found a wooden statue of the Virgin Mary floating in the sea. Their lives were saved and they brought the statue to its current resting place above the altar. Downstairs there are many tokens of gratitude left by Cubans who have been helped by the Virgin in some way, for example, for their son to escape to Miami on a raft, in some medical problem or in some sporting event. It is quite common to see nuns dragging the infirm from a minivan into the church. There is a pilgrimage here on 7 September, the eve of the patron saint's day. Women with exposed shoulders are not admitted, so don't wear skimpy tops here, although they do hire rather attractive coveralls if you forget. Watch out for the touts swarming around you when you get out of the car; they will try to sell you souvenirs and pieces of copper. It is probably best to take a bit of copper and offer 50 cents or some pesos, otherwise they will be waiting for you when you leave the church. Fortunately they are not allowed inside.

Mar Verde to El Francés
There is a small, busy beach about 10 km west of Santiago called **Mar Verde**; then **Bueycabón**, which is nothing special, and then **Caletón Blanco**, (30 km west of Santiago), which is a nice beach, mostly frequented by Cubans. Like all the beaches in this area, it is quite narrow, with white sand, but no facilities. A seawater swimming pool next to the sea has the remains of a diving board. Hold your breath as youths throw themselves 2 m or so into the air above the pool, getting the distance they need over the water to avoid being smashed on the pool's edge. When they are not doing that, the pool is a pleasant place to take a dip if you want the Caribbean without the waves. Further along is **El Francés**, said to be the best beach in the west.

El Saltón
About 35 km inland from El Francés, near **Cruce de los Baños**, you will find El Saltón (see Sleeping, below), a mini-resort advertised as 'stress relief', where there is a waterfall and several natural pools to bathe in. Originally designed as a health spa, you don't have to be ill to stay there now. It is in a fantastic location in the Sierra Maestra and set into the side of a mountain some way down a track with a picturesque waterfall and nothing else around it. A great place for a massage in a very relaxing environment.

El Uvero and around

Further west from Santiago the wonderful coastal road runs along the base of the Sierra Maestra with beautiful bays and completely deserted beaches, some with black sand. It is only possible to visit by car and a sturdy one is recommended as parts of the road are gravel and unsealed. Many of the villages have connections with historical revolutionary events. **El Uvero**, about 60 km from Santiago, Carretera Granma, has a monument marking the attack by Castro and his men on the Batista troop HQ on 28 May 1957. The building that was attacked is now a small museum ① *s/n entre Escuela Simbólica y Campo Deportivo*.

It is 20 km from El Uvero to Ocujal and about 7 km from there to Las Cuevas (before La Plata), from where you can climb up to **Pico Turquino** (1,974 m). This is the highest peak in the Sierra Maestra. There are only two legally established and maintained accesses to the mountain, from Las Cuevas and from Alto de Naranjo. A guide is mandatory and costs US$15. You set out at 0630 and, depending on your level of fitness and speed, come down at 1730, just before dusk. If you need accommodation in the area, you can ask around in Ocujal and Las Cuevas, or there is a campsite at La Mula, east of Ocujal.

Cycling from Santiago de Cuba to Manzanillo

→ *3 days, 247 km, this route is a moderate to challenging graded cycle ride with some steep hills.*

Cycle through the lush, heavily forested hills of the Sierra Maestra and cross the Río Yara lowlands, characterized by rice fields and Royal palms, to Manzanillo. Cycle back along the same route or return by train from Manzanillo to Santiago. You will have to change trains in Bayamo (see page 319). Mountain bikes are strongly recommended for this route, since there are sections of badly broken road surfaces with numerous potholes. Each day ends at a designated hotel, although in Bayamo and Manzanillo there is ample opportunity to stay at a *casa particular*. The ride starts from the **Hotel Las Américas**. You should arrange to carry a packed lunch with you each day, since food stops are thin on the ground, and ensure that you pack some additional bottled water.

‼ *For further information on cycling in Cuba, see Essentials page 58.*

Day 1 Santiago de Cuba to El Saltón

→ *A demanding 87 km ride on hilly terrain.*

Plan to start the ride at 0745 after a filling early breakfast. The route detours to visit the El Cobre church. The day's ride ends at **Hotel El Saltón**, set in a beautiful valley surrounded by lush forests. There is a waterfall and a natural pool in the hotel grounds. Sit and relax under the waterfall for an invigorating revival.

0 km Leave **Hotel Las Américas**. Turn right onto the dual carriageway. Keep straight on. Pass the baseball stadium Guillermón Moncada on the right. At 1½ km go straight across at the crossroads and pass the dominating bronze monument of Antonio Maceo in the Plaza de la Revolución on the left. At 3 km pass Sala Polivalente Alejandro Urgellés on the right.

5½ km Pass under a bridge and soon after keep to the right. Pass under the fading sign 'Bayamo 110 km'. Stay on this road. The road starts to climb. Pass Josué País García military school on the right.

13 km Turn left at the T-junction. Pass through the small village **El Pajuil**. At 16 km cross a bridge and enter **Melgarejo**. There is a petrol station on your left. Immediately after turn left, signed **El Cobre**. You can see the church (see page 338) in the distance. Enter the village and turn right at the crossroads at 18 km. Follow this road round to the right at the fork, leading to the church. Return through the village and retrace your steps to the main road. The petrol station is now on the right. Turn left onto the main road.

23 km Pass through **Puerta de Moya**. The road starts to climb steeply. There are good views of El Cobre to the left. At the summit pass an armoured tank monument on the left. Stay on this road and go down the hill. Cross **Río Frío**. At 34 km pass through **La Clarita** village.

36 km Turn left at the junction. There is no signpost. It is marked by a small kiosk under a tree and a bus shelter just past the junction on the right. (If you miss the turning you will continue to Bellaire village.) Cross the bridge. Take care, the road surface is broken. Stay on this road passing through the small villages of **Hicotea** and **La Unión**. At 40½ km pass Escuela Carlos Pillot Quiroga on the left.

43 km Enter **Dos Palmas**. Pass **Escuela Rubén Díaz Martínez** on the right. Keep straight on up the hill. The suggested lunch stop is at the small park with shady trees and benches on the right. There is an ice cream stall opposite. Continue straight through Dos Palmas. Pass a cemetery on your left. From here the road surface has badly deteriorated, there are large potholes and erosion. There are several steep climbs and descents in this mountainous section.

53 km Pass through **Guadalupe**. Stay on this road. At 57 km climb a short hill and enter **El Pilón**. There is a *panadería* (bakery) on the left. After Pilón there is a steep downhill followed by a short steep climb and a second, more serious 3-km climb. There are coffee plantations and guava trees on either side of the road.

68 km Enter **Las Minas** a small mining village. After 4 km pass through **Arroyo Rico**. Pass Argenis Burgos school on the right. Cross the bridge and keep straight on.

75½ km Pass Guillermo Domínguez school on the right. Pass a coffee drying plant, Planta de Beneficio, on the right and cross a bridge. Immediately after, turn left towards **Cruce de los Baños**. Follow the road down to the town. At about 79 km pass the sign 'Tercer Frente' municipality.

80 km Enter **Cruce de los Baños**. At the main junction turn right signed 'El Saltón and Filé'. Pass petrol station El Mambí on the right and bear left. Pass a school on your left with pink and white walls.

83 km Enter **Filé**. Pass a rural doctor's surgery (*Médico de la Familia*) on your left. Cross the bridge. Pass the children's playground on the right. At the crossroads turn left at 83.5 km. A cafeteria is on the left-hand corner. Stay on this road for about 3 km to **Hotel El Saltón**.

Day 2 El Saltón to Bayamo → *67 km*

Hilly to undulating and flat terrain. The route continues through the Sierra Maestra. As you progress northwards the terrain becomes undulating. There are numerous potholes and road surfaces are poor. The road flattens out as you follow the main road west to Bayamo. The day's ride ends at the **Hotel Sierra Maestra** (see page 317).

0 km Leave the hotel and retrace your steps to **Filé**. At the crossroads at 3 km, with the cafeteria on your right, turn left to **Matías**. Pass the *farmacía* and entrance to the baseball pitch on the left. The road climbs steeply upwards, followed by a steep downhill. Cross an open bridge, pass through a small village and enter Matías at 8.5 km. Pass José Martí Pérez school on the left. Bear right at the junction. Pass hospital Esteban Caballero on the right. Leave town.

15 km Pass Rosa P Eclere school on the right. After a 2-km climb you reach the top of the hill. There are dramatic views of the plains with Royal palms. Go downhill and cross a bridge. Pass banana plantations and small *bohíos*.

18½ km Enter **Los Negros**. At the junction turn left to Baire. Pass *Combinado de Servicios* (Laundromat) on the left and continue straight across at the offset crossroads. Pass a park and water tower, both on the right. Continue straight at the junction and pass a *Video Salón* on the right. Leave town and stay on this road. Enter **La Candelaria** village at 27 km.

29 km Cross a bridge and enter **Baire**. Stay on this street, turn right at the junction with an arrow indicating a right turn. There is a single-storey building with three windows and shutters on the opposite corner. (If you miss the turning the road surface soon deteriorates.) Keep straight on. At the main crossroads turn left onto the Carretera Central signed Jiguaní. (Contramaestre is to the right.) Pass a *policlínico* and a park on the right. Leave Baire and stay on this road. This is a main road and carries heavy traffic. Pass under a railway bridge.

35 km Enter **Granma Province**. (Soon afterwards pass a turning for **Hotel El Yarey** to the right.) At 41.5 km bear left at the fork and follow the main road. This bypasses Jiguaní. Cross a bridge with white-washed walls. At 49 km enter **Santa Rita**. There is a tree-lined avenue through the town and a park on the left. Continue on the main road. Pass a petrol station and several *guarapo* (sugar cane juice) stalls on the left. Pass restaurant **La Caridad** on the right. Leave town and stay on this road.

55 km Cross **Río Cautillo**. **Restaurante Cautillo** is on the right. Continue on the main road to Bayamo. Pass through **Entronque de Guisa** and an industrialized zone on the outskirts of Bayamo. At 63½ km pass an electricity generating plant on the left. Enter **Bayamo** at 65 km. **Hotel Sierra Maestra**, with tall Royal palms in the grounds, is on the left at 67 km.

Day 3   Bayamo to Manzanillo → *96 km*

You should plan to start the ride at 0745 after a filling early breakfast. Today's route is flat, following quiet country roads to Bartolomé Masó with the Sierra Maestra mountains to the left, then heading northwest to Manzanillo. The day's ride ends at the **Hotel Guacanayabo**.

0 km Leave the hotel and turn left onto the main road. Go straight across at the traffic lights. Pass the **Servi Cupet** petrol station (green logo) and shortly afterwards El Rápido (red logo) on the right. Follow the road round to the right. At 1.2 km turn left at the crossroads, signed 'Manzanillo and Las Tunas'. Go straight across at the traffic lights and continue straight on this road. Leave town and pass through open parkland.

3 km At the crossroads, turn left signed 'Yara, Manzanillo and Niquero'. Pass an artificial insemination cattle station at 6.2 km.

8 km Bear right at the fork. Cross **Río Mabay** at 10 km. At 16 km bear left at the fork. There is a small store selling refreshments in US$. Stay on this road.

20 km Cross two bridges in quick succession. After the second there is a sign for Buey Arriba. At the T-junction turn left. Pass José Martí Pérez school on the right. Enter **Sanicu** at 22½ km. There are banana plantations to the left and the Sierra Maestra looms in the distance. At 24 km pass a cemetery on the left and at the fork with the poster of Che bear right to Bartolomé Masó. (Buey Arriba is to the left here.) There are usually roadside stalls here selling food for Cuban pesos.

24½ km Cross a bridge and stay on the road. Tall Royal palms dot the open landscape. At 27½ km enter **Bartolomé Masó** municipality. Pass through sugar cane fields. Cross two bridges at about 40½ km and 42½ km. Take care, as the road starts to deteriorate rapidly here with numerous potholes and broken surfaces. At 43 km pass through **San Juan Uno** and about 1½ km later go through **Sabana Larga**. At 45 km bear left at the fork signed Santo Domingo, cross a bridge and enter **Valle Verde** village.

48½ km At the crossroads go straight on towards **Las Mercedes** (Bartolomé Masó is to the right). Stay on this road. Continue straight on at the fork towards Las Mercedes. Pass Combate del Cerro. At 50½ km cross **Río Yara**. Soon after, pass **Planta Cuba Café** on the right, a coffee drying farm. Go straight across the crossroads. Pass rice fields and at 54 km pass Abel Santamaría school on the right. Lake Paso Malo is on the left.

54½ km Enter a small village. There is a roadside stall selling *guarapo frío* on the right in pesos. This is the recommended lunch stop. There are places to sit nearby, next to the bust of José Martí. At 54 km cross **Río Arroyón** and enter **Caney de las Mercedes**. Pass El Caney Ciudad school and a playground on the right. Stay on this road. Pass hospital Mariano López on the left.

58 km Fork right at the junction to Cayo Espino. (Las Mercedes is to the left here.) Go down the hill. The surface begins to deteriorate here. Pass through **La Biajaca** village. Pass 7 de Diciembre school on the right. At 63 km cross **Río Jibacoa** and pass a sign for **Campismo El Saltón** on the left.

64 km Go up the small hill and turn right. There are potholes and no signpost. Immediately after the turning there are some small *bohíos* on the right. The road surface starts to deteriorate and in places has completely eroded.

66 km Enter **Cayo Espino**. Pass a school on the right and a small church on the left. There is a playground on the right with some shade. **Restaurant La Familia** is on the left. Continue straight on. Pass through a changing landscape of sugar cane fields, banana plantations, rice fields and orange groves. This is a rich agricultural area and there are many tractors on the road.

75½ km Pass through **Palmarito** village. The route is now straight and flat to Manzanillo. At 83½ km enter **El Pozón**. Stay on this road. Pass a turning on the right, signed Sierra Maestra Airport, and continue. At 92½ km pass through La Gota. Pass **Empresa de Conservas** (on right). Enter **Manzanillo**.

94½ km At the crossroads (there is a cemetery entrance opposite), turn left on to the *Circunvalación* (ring road) *Camilo Cienfuegos*. Pass the *Politécnico* on the left. At the next crossroads, immediately after the **Servi-Cupet** petrol station on the right, continue straight across. Continue down the hill to **Hotel Guacanayabo** on the right.

⬤ Sleeping

Santiago de Cuba centre *p328, map p330*
Hotels
L-A Casa Granda, (Gran Caribe/Accor, managed by Sofitel), Heredia 201 entre San Pedro y San Félix, on Parque Céspedes, T22-686600, F22-686035. Elegant building opened in 1914 and patronized by many famous movie stars and singers, as well as sports champions Joe Louis the boxer and Babe Ruth the baseball player. 4 star, renovated and expanded in 2000. A/c, fax service, laundry, car hire, satellite TV, pool, post office, 1 room for handicapped people, **Havanatur** and **Asistur** offices. Excellent central location with terrace bar and café, overlooking park, 5th-floor bar with even better views over city (US$2 to go up 2000-0100 if you are not staying at the hotel, but that buys your first cocktail), restaurant and café, open 0800-2400, good. Disco (karaoke) at the side of the hotel, US$1.
D Gran Hotel, Enramada 312 entre San Félix y San Pedro, T22-653020, www.granhotel stgo.cu Training school for tourism workers (Formatur), 2 star, very central and newly rebuilt on a shopping street. 27 rooms, a/c, TV, hot water, mini bar, restaurant and cafeteria.
D-E Hostal Islazul, San Basilio 403 entre Calvario y Carnicería, T22-651502. A new hotel in baby blue, close to the historical centre, nice decor with lots of plants and

stylish pieces of furniture. 8 large and very comfortable rooms, a/c, fridge, private bathroom, hot water, satellite TV, security box, minibar, 24-hr restaurant serving *criollo* and international food.
D-E Libertad, Aguilera 658 entre Pizarro y Plácido, Plaza de Marte, T22-627710. Unprepossessing hotel on busy street, 17 rooms, CP, a/c, 1 suite, TV, lobby bar and restaurant serving *criollo* and international food, nothing to write home about, terrace and bar 1600-0400. Internet access.

Casas particulares
Touts around Parque Céspedes, also near all hotels and at the railway terminal exit. Note that it is increasingly common to offer a good-value package of dinner, bed and breakfast for around US$30-40 for 2 people.
D Orestes González Campos, Gral Portuondo (Callejón de Trinidad) 651 ¼ esq Moncada, T22-626305, norka@ncm. uo.edu.cu Price is for dinner, bed and breakfast for two people, excellent value. Pink colonial house with white columns, high ceilings. 2 bedrooms have no proper windows but effective a/c and fan, good beds, private bathroom, good food and plenty of it. Within walking distance of Parque Céspedes or Museo 26 de Julio, but quiet with no traffic noise.

E-F **Félix Corroso**, San Germán 165 entre Rastro y Gallo, T22-653720. Known as Garden House, 2 rooms, a/c, fan, nice garden, breakfast US$3, dinner US$6-8.

E-F **Irma y Umberto**, Santa Lucía 303 entre San Pedro y San Félix, T22-622391, close to Parque Céspedes. Brother and sister live in huge house with their respective families, large room sleeps 3, private bathroom, patio.

E-F **Manrique Nistal Bello**, Princesa 565 entre Carnicería y Calvario, T22-651909, abarreda@abt.uo.edu.cu 1 room with 1 bed, another with 2 beds, bathroom, fridge, good food in large portions, some English spoken.

E-F **Marta Franco**, Corona 802 bajos entre San Carlos y Santa Rita, T22-651882. Very central, about 100 m west of Cathedral, apartment on ground floor of fairly modern block. 2 rooms, 1 with a/c, bathroom between them, hot shower, breakfast US$3, dinner US$6, meals taken in family room, very good food, helpful and friendly family.

F **Aída Morales Valdés**, Enramada 565 entre San Agustín y Barnada, T22-628612. Room with private bathroom, a/c, very good food, friendly family, central, only 1 block from Plaza Marte.

F **Amparo Hernández**, Santa Rita 161 entre Corona y Padre Pico, T22-623208. Extremely pleasant place and nice woman who also cooks really well. Well known and always full.

F **Dinorah Rodríguez Bueno and William Pérez**, Diego Palacios (Santa Rita) 504 entre Reloj y Clarín, T22-625834. Dinorah speaks a little English, independent room with ensuite bathroom, a/c, good food, patio, William is a historian and full of knowledge on cultural matters, both of them are excellent sources of information and very helpful, 10-min walk from Parque Céspedes.

F **Dr Javier Berdion Sevilla**, Corona 564 Apto B entre Enramadas y Aguilera, T22-622955. 2 rooms, double bed, a/c, hot water, shared bathroom, fridge, balcony, terrace, great view of the bay.

F **La Casona Colonial**, San Francisco 303 (Sagarra) entre San Bartolomé y San Félix, T22-622517, arlexjorge@yahoo.com Run by Arlex Rojas Cruz and Jorge and their gorgeous sausage dog, Bebe. 2 rooms with shared bathroom in a lovely colonial house with an internal patio. Little natural light but rooms are large and comfortable. Breakfasts are good.

F **Liliam**, Hechavarría (San Jerónimo) 308 entre Hartmann (San Félix) y Lacret (San Pedro), T22-627236. Small, independent apartment, 2 bedrooms with twin beds, kitchen and bathroom, owner lives downstairs.

F **Lourdes de la Gómez Beaton**, Félix Pena 454 entre San Jerónimo y San Francisco, T22-654468. Large old house with patio, excellent accommodation in 2 rooms, bathroom, hospitable hostess.

F **Maraima Sánchez**, Hartmann entre Sagarra y Máximo Gómez, T22-652728. 2 double rooms, shared bathroom, use of kitchen, family atmosphere, very clean.

F **Margot's Inn**, San Fermín 207 entre Maceo y San Mateo. On the way from the railway station to the town centre very near the Casa Natal de Antonio Maceo, quiet neighbourhood. Margot is in her 70s and lives with her son, Tony, an English teacher, nice people, 1 room sleeps 3 if you have a child, shower, hot water, a/c, fridge.

F **Maruchi**, San Félix 337 entre San Germán y Trinidad. Good location close to the centre, colonial house with large courtyard and beautiful vegetation. 2 large, quiet rooms, 1 with fridge, private bathrooms, a/c. Maruchi is a researcher at Casa del Caribe with a wide knowledge of Afrocuban religions and Cuban culture. Speaks fluent English and French.

F **Migdalia Gámez Rodríguez**, Corona 371 entre San Germán y Trinidad, T22-624569. Large, private room with shower, fan, quiet, friendly, great food.

F **Reynaldo Gascon Mirabent**, Clarin 157 A (Padre Quiroga) entre Rey Pelayo y Sta Lucía, T22-624859. Only Spanish spoken. Cold and warm water. 1 room, double bed. Very friendly and helpful. Dinner, breakfast and beer available.

Ferreiro *p333, map p345*

Hotels

AL Meliá Santiago de Cuba (Cubanacán), Av Las Américas entre 4 y M, Reparto Sueño, T22-687070, www.meliasantiago decuba.solmelia.com Built in 1991, the 15-floor hotel's modern design stands out like a beacon and is quite a landmark with its red, white and blue colour scheme. 5 star, 302 rooms and suites, some for non-smokers and the physically handicapped, 24-hr room service, excellent breakfast buffet US$9, lots of bars and restaurants, good view of city from roof top bar, swimming pools open to day visitors for US$10, tennis, sauna, car hire, has business centre with internet access, post office and will change almost any currency into dollars, staff exceptionally helpful and friendly.

B-C Las Américas (Horizontes), T22-642011, F22-687075, Av de las Américas esq Gen Cebreco, easy bus/truck access to centre, taxis around bus stop opposite hotel. Rebuilt, 68 rooms, 2 mini-suites, lively, high-quality restaurant, variety of dishes, non-residents may use pool where they have cultural shows every night, helpful Rumbos agent, nice reception staff, safety deposit, **Havanautos** and **Transtur**, **Cadeca**, shop, bicycle hire.

D Villa Santiago de Cuba (Gaviota), Av Manduley 502, entre 19 y 21, Reparto Vista Alegre, T22-641368/641346, F22-687166. 3 star, car hire, tourist office, nearby pool for guests, quiet, no credit cards.

Casas particulares

D Flor María González, J 314 entre Av Las Américas y 6, Reparto Sueño, upper floor, T22-645568, fmgc@cnt.uo.edu.cu Price for dinner, bed and breakfast, 1 large room with ensuite bathroom, hot water, a/c, fan, TV, desk. Flor María is a very knowledgeable professor at the Oriente University and her husband speaks English and Russian.

E-F Rubén Rodes Estrada, 10 410 entre 15 y 17, Reparto Vista Alegre, T22-642611. Run by great (gay) couple, house painted red and yellow, giant cactus outside and inside, hot water, good food, US$5 huge breakfast and US$10 evening meal even bigger. They also have a good self-contained flat for the same price.

F Emilia Brooks, 6 110 entre 3 y 5, Reparto Vista Alegre, upper floor, T22-643195. Good location close to **Las Américas** hotel. 1 room with ensuite bathroom, hot water, a/c, fridge, terrace, quiet, pleasant host.

F Odalys Turro Tejeda, 6 401 entre 15 y 17, Reparto Vista Alegre, upper floor, T22-642911. Independent large room with en suite bathroom, a/c, hot water, fan, TV, garage, use of kitchen, close to **Doña Nelly** and Cubalse supermarket.

F Omar Frómeta, Anacaona 194 entre Alfredo Zayas y Bravo Correoso, Santa Bárbara. Nice apartment, very clean and quiet, a/c, hot water, terrace, balcony, private bathroom, fridge, use of kitchen. Santa Bárbara is a peaceful neighbourhood, a leafy green suburb. It is not difficult to get into town and it is close to all sights around Ferreiro. Not all the houses have a phone and often there is only 1 in the block.

F Rita María, 3 102 entre Av Manduley y Carretera del Caney, Vista Alegre, T22-614263. Colonial house (Villa Victoria), good location near **Las Américas** hotel, 2 large bedrooms, a/c, private bathrooms, hot water. Beautiful courtyard where very tasty food is served.

South of Santiago *p334, map p334*
Hotels

B-C Carrusel Versalles (Cubanacán), Carretera del Morro Km 1, near airport, US$2 taxi from centre, T22-691016, F22-686245. 3-star, in residential area with views to mountains in the distance, but not particularly attractive and rather dated, 72 rooms, singles, doubles, triples and suites, faded glory, staff can be unhelpful, US$1 for visitors to use pool, but expensive pool-side snack bar.

D Balcón del Caribe (Islazul), Carretera del Morro Km 7 ½, next to Castillo del Morro, T22-691011, F22-692398. Three-star, 72 rooms and 20 bungalows on a cliff overlooking the sea, quiet, pool, tourist office, simple Cuban food, cold water in bungalows, pleasant but inconvenient for the town.

East of Santiago *p335, maps p334 and p336*
Hotels

AL LTI Los Corales – Carisol (Cubanacán), T22-356113-5, reserva@carisol.scu.cyt .cu 3 star, 120 rooms and 46 junior suites, a/c, minibar, TV, all-inclusive, buffet and à la carte restaurant and cafeteria, pool, diving, beach volleyball, tennis, car and bicycle hire, childcare, near Playa Cazonal.

B-C Hotel San Juan (Horizontes), Km 4½ Carretera a Siboney, T22-687156, hotel@sanjuan.scu.cyt.cu Out of town (taxi to the centre US$3-4, private car US$2-3) but nice location, the former *Leningrado* is right beside the site of one of the last battles of the 1898 War of Independence, now the Parque Histórico Militar La Loma. The remains of a huge ceiba tree (it fell down in a storm in 2000) are in the grounds, beneath which Spain and the USA signed the surrender of Santiago on 16 July 1898. A complex with cabins, 107 nice rooms, some triples, large, clean, intermittent hot water, large pool, bar, restaurants, good breakfast, high quality by Cuban standards, queues at weekends and during festivals, car hire.

C Coralia Club Bucanero, (Gran Caribe), Carretera Baconao Km 4, Arroyo La Costa, 15 miles from the airport, T22-686363-4, F22-686070. 3-star, 200 all-inclusive rooms (price code per person) with some triples set in pleasant gardens with pool over looking the sea. Food is reasonable. Good dive centre here with dynamic instructors, beautiful dive sites and good visibility, also great snorkelling. US$5 for non-guests to enter the hotel incl 2 drinks, US$25 each dive or less for more dives, nice little beach with canyon behind.

C Costa Morena (Islazul), Carretera Baconao, km 38½, Sigua, T22-686126, F22-686155. 3

star resort with 115 simple, functional rooms **345** on both sides of the road (used to be two hotels), car hire, Visa accepted, scuba diving.

C-D Gran Piedra (Horizontes), Carretera de la Gran Piedra Km 14, T22-686147, near the Gran Piedra. Up in the hills, lovely setting, great views. 2 star, 22 simple rooms in stone bungalows with a bedroom, kitchen, sitting room, bathroom and balcony. You don't have to cook for yourself, though, as the restaurant and bar serve the usual Cuban fare.

West of Santiago *p338, map p334*
Hotels
AL-A Brisas Sierra Mar-Los Galeones (Cubanacán), on Playa Sevilla, Carretera de Chivirico Km 60, T22-29110, reservat@smar.scu.cyt.cu 234 all-inclusive rooms in two locations: **Sierra Mar** is on the beach, while **Los Galeones** is up on the hillside. **Sierra Mar** is a modern 200-room resort in terraced style, a/c, satellite TV, small beach, watersports, freeform pool on terrace

Ferreiro

0 metres 100
0 yards 100

with bar and good sea view, 2 restaurants, 3 bars, shop, rental bikes, many activities such as horse rental, helicopter ride into the mountains, sports, gymnasium, kids' club, children are welcome, tours and car hire, weddings arranged free of charge including cake, champagne, marriage certificate and public notary. **Los Galeones** is for singles and couples over 16 only, marketed to honeymooners, weddings arranged free of charge, and considered by some to be the best of the coastal resorts in this area. 34 rooms including 1 suite on a cliff overlooking the Caribbean, lovely location, a/c and fan, satellite TV, 300 winding steps lead down to the sea, restaurant serves good food, bar, sauna, massage, gym, special scuba training pool, bowling, volleyball, car and bike rental, courtesy bus to **Sierra Mar**, a taxi from the airport costs about US$50. Snorkelling is good in this area.

C-D Carrusel El Saltón, Carretera a Filé, Puerto Rico, Tercer Frente, near Cruce de los Baños, about 35 km inland, T22-56495, comercial@hsierra.grm.cyt.cu Very relaxing, there is a waterfall and several natural pools to bathe in. Originally designed as a health spa, and still great for a massage, in a fantastic location in the Sierra Maestra and set into the side of a mountain some way down a track with nothing else around it. The 22-room hotel is clean and nice with good service and an open air rustic restaurant, but the highlight is its picturesque waterfall, beside which you can have barbecues.

🍴 Eating

Santiago de Cuba centre *p328, map p330*
Restaurants

All the hotels have restaurants, some of which are very good, such as in the **Meliá Santiago de Cuba**. In local restaurants the main dish is chicken, usually fried but sometimes with a garlic and onion sauce. A half chicken with fried green plantain (*tostones*), sweet potatoes (*boniato*) or chips costs 25 pesos, rice and beans (*congri*) 2 pesos, salad 3 pesos, beer 10 pesos. You can find this sort of meal at the **Doña Yuya** chain, where they also serve things like smoked pork chops (*chuletas de cerdo ahumado*), veal (*ternera*) or thin steak (*bistec de palomilla*), costing around 25 pesos.

$$$-$$ La Casa de Don Antonio, Aguilera entre Calvario y Reloj, Plaza Dolores, T22-652205, daily 1200-2400. Nice decor, bar inside serving all kinds of Cuban cocktails, complimentary welcome cocktail, tasty *criollo* food, reasonable prices with dishes from US$2.10 for starters to US$28.

$ Las Enramadas, Búlevar (Plaza Dolores), T22-652205. Good atmosphere, cheap, basic food, nice setting, open 24 hrs.

$ La Taberna de Dolores, Aguilera esq Reloj, T22-623913. Spanish food, 1900-2400, reasonable at around US$5 for main course.

$ Santiago 1900, San Basilio entre San Félix y Carnicería. Basic but excellent meals at bargain price of around US$4 including drinks, pesos and dollar equivalent acceptable.

Paladares

Most of the official *paladares* have closed because of taxes and regulations and there are now only 2 left. However you may get approached in the street by touts offering unofficial/illegal places to eat.

$$ Tropical, Fernández Marcane entre 10 y 9, upper floor, Tue-Sun 1800-2400. Open air, well decorated, excellent food, international style.

$ Las Gallegas, San Basilio entre San Pedro y San Félix, upper floor. Unexciting food, uncomfortable, negligent service.

Street stalls

Street stalls sell snacks in pesos, usually only open until early evening, some only at lunchtime. Most things cost 1 peso. Avoid *fritos*, they are just fried lumps of dough; most reliable thing is cheese, pork or egg sandwich; pizza is usually a dry bit of dough with a few gratings of cheese. Lots of stalls along 'Ferreiro' or Av Victoriano Garzón, these are open later than others, especially up near **Hotel Las Américas**. Also lots around bus station on Libertadores and a few along the bottom part of Aguilera, between Parque Céspedes and Plaza Dolores.

Cafés and ice cream parlours

Café Ajedrez, Enramada y Santo Tomás. Open-air café in cool architectural structure designed by Cuban architect, Walter A Betancourt Fernández. Coffee served only.

Coppelia, Félix Pena under the cathedral, Mon-Fri 1000-2100, Sat and Sun 1100-2200.

No queuing if you have dollars, also at Av de los Libertadores y Victoriano Garzón.

Helado Alondra, Garzón y 6, T22-687078, near junction with Hotel Santiago. Great ice creams and milk shakes, 0900-2200.

Isabelica, Aguilera esq Plaza Dolores, open 24 hrs. Serves only coffee, US$0.85, cigars rolled, bohemian hangout, watch out for hustlers, serious hassling by *jineteros/as*. The local speciality *Rocío del Gallo* is coffee and rum – ask for it at **Café Isabelica**.

Kíkiriki, Plaza Dolores, daily 1100-2300. Good ice cream.

Terrace Coffee Bar, Hotel Casa Granda, open 24 hrs. A pleasant place for a drink. The **Roof Garden**, at the top of the same hotel, open 2000-0300, has *mojitos* US$1.65.

Ferreiro p333, map p345
Restaurants
$$ **Pizza Nova**, Hotel Meliá Santiago, T22-687070, outside by the shops, open 1100-2400. Open air but under cover, serving surprisingly good pizzas and nothing like you get on the streets. Prices range from US$4.85 for a small cheese and tomato pizza to US$19.60 for a large one with lobster, while pastas cost from US$5.75 to US$11.95 with lobster. You can also have chicken, meat or fish dishes if you are not seeking a pizza fix.

East of Santiago p335, maps p334 and p336
Restaurants
$$ **Sito de Compay Segundo**, Calle Montenegro s/n, Siboney, T22-39325, daily 1200-2100. The house where the musician, Compay Segundo, was born is now a restaurant serving international and *criollo* food, with dishes from US$1.50 to US$28.

♥ Bars

Santiago de Cuba centre p328, map p330
Baturro, Aguilera esq San Félix. Snacks, bar, nice atmosphere and reliable prices.
El Farito, Av de los Libertadores y Trinidad. 24-hr bar and cafetería.
Kontiki, Enramada esq San Pedro. A dark bar popular with Cubans and visitors,
Las Columnitas, 1 block from Enramada, San Félix y Callejón del Carmen. Outdoor dollar bar and café. Beware of double measures here, guaranteed to get you salsa-ing before the end of the evening.

☻ Entertainment

Santiago de Cuba centre p328, map p330
Cabaret
Cabaret San Pedro del Mar, Carretera del Morro Km 7 ½, T22-691287, Islazul-run, US$5 taxi. US$5 entrance, reasonable food.
Club Tropicana Santiago, Autopista Nacional Km 1½ , T22-687020, (restaurant 1200-2200), taxi, US$8-10. Local show with emphasis on the Caribbean and Santiaguerans, different from Havana's version and considered one of the best shows in Cuba, disco after the show, open 2000-0300, closed Mon, US$50. There is a restaurant with a limited menu and drinks aren't cheap.

Cinema and theatre
Check locally for cinema programmes and theatre performances.
Cine Cuba, Gral Lacret entre Aguilera y Enramada.
Cine Rialto, Santo Tomás entre San Basilio y Heredia.
Teatro Heredia, Av de los Desfiles on the other side of Av de las Américas from the Plaza de la Revolución. You can hear live boleros and other traditional music in Café Cantante, in the theatre, 2100 Fri-Sun, US$5.

Clubs and music venues
See also Cultural centres, p354.
Buró de Información Cultural, Plaza Marte. Poetry, dance, live music in its patio bar.
Casa de la Música, Corona 564 entre Aguilera y Enramada, T22-652227. Taped music during the day 1000-1900. Live Cuban music every night 2200-0230 and Sat-Sun 1500-1900, US$5 entrance, sale of CDs and tapes, worth trying.
Casa de las Tradiciones, Rabí entre José de Diego (Princesa) y García (San Fernando), open 2030-0100, closed Tue, US$1. Also known as **La Casona**. Large colonial house with central patio, live music for listening and dancing to, *son, trova, boleros*, 1500-2300, small bar.
Casa de la Trova, Heredia 208, around the corner from Casa Granda, T22-623943. Traditional Santiagueran *trova, son* and *boleros*, all live, 1930-2130, US$3. Great upstairs dance floor and seating area with tables and chairs on the balcony. Downstairs is also used.

Daiquirí

The recipe for the Daiquirí cocktail was first created by an engineer in the Daiquirí mines near Santiago de Cuba. Known as a Daiquirí Natural (1898), it includes the juice of half a lime, half a tablespoon of sugar, 1½ oz light dry rum and some pieces of ice, which you put in a shaker, shake and serve strained in a cocktail glass, with more ice if you want.

The idea of using shaved ice came later, added by Constante, the bartender at El Floridito in the 1920s. It was a favourite of Ernest Hemingway; he described it in his book, Islands in the Stream, and drank it in the company of Jean-Paul Sartre, Gary Cooper, Ava Gardner, Marlene Dietrich, and Tennessee Williams among others.

The recipe for this Daiquirí includes 1½ tablespoons of sugar, the juice of half a lime, some drops of maraschino liqueur, 1½ oz light dry rum and a lot of shaved ice. Put it all in a blender and serve in a champagne glass.

Other refinements are the strawberry Daiquirí, the banana, peach or pineapple Daiquirí or even the orange Daiquirí, made with the addition of fruit or fruit liqueur. The resulting mound of flavoured, alcoholic, crushed ice should be piled high in a wide, chilled champagne glass and served with a straw – aaah!

Casa del Caribe (see Cultural centres, below) on 13 154 esq 8, T22-642285. Live Afro-Cuban music and dance at weekends.
Casa de los Estudiantes, Heredia, near Casa Granda. Live music Sun 1330, always popular, US$1. Two daily shows of music, morning and evening, traditional, acoustic son music, open until 2400, US$1 and worth it, nice venue in beautiful building with patio where the bands play at night, also bar. Very friendly and welcoming, the bands are excellent and dancing is encouraged, particularly at night when you can expect hassle from locals wanting to dance with you.
Club La Iris, Aguilera 617 entre Paraíso y Barnarda, T22-654910. Disco and karaoke daily 1000-1600, 2200-0300, US$2, snack bar, 24 hrs, great for that *bocadito* at 0400 when everything else is shut.
Disco Bar/Club 300, Aguilera entre San Félix y San Pedro, T22-653532, daily 1900-0300. Live and recorded music, snack bar.
Rincón de Santiago and **Café Cantante** in the Hotel Santiago, daily 2000-0200, US$6. Every drink including bottled water costs US$6.
El Patio de Artex, Heredia 304 entre Carnicería y Calvario, T22-654814. Home of painters, Félix and José Joaquín Tejada Revilla, often live music with fantastic local bands, lots of dancing, friendly, 2200-0200.

Los Dos Abuelos, Pérez Carbo 5 frente a Plaza de Marte, T22-623302. EGREM agency, rocks with live traditional son and boleros from 2130 until dawn and encourages visitors to join in, US$2. Also snack bar with tasty small meals, the *daiquirís* are a winner.
Sala de Conciertos Dolores, Plaza Dolores. Classical and choral concerts.

Dance performances
Ballet Folklórico Cutatumba, Enramada, at Museo del Carnaval, 2 blocks west of Parque Céspedes. There is a superb show Sun 1030, US$3 – unmissable.
Cabildo Teatral, Enramadas y Calvario, upstairs. Information bureau Mon-Sat 0900-1700. Tickets on sale 1 hr beforehand, small bar in patio. Folklore and theatre combined in an extraordinary performance of bands (hip hop, pop) and groups from Santiago. Don't miss the performance of Fátima Paterson and her theatre company. Very popular among youngsters.
Grupo Folklórico del Oriente, San Francisco y San Félix, folk groups play daytime till lunchtime, then again in the evening.

If you want to learn to play the drums, a recommended conga/bongo teacher is **Manuel Semanat Bell** (El Rápido), Habana 819 entre Barnada y San Agustín. He started a

• Music in Santiago de Cuba

Santiago is overflowing with musical talent. Even the cockerels crow in time to the *son*. Santiago is *son*'s spiritual home. At the **Casa de la Trova** on Calle Heredia images of old *soneros* look down on the musicians, as elegant Santiaguerans lose themselves in the dance and the rum flows freely. Although Cuba's most famous groups rarely venture out to Santiago (the impressive Heredia theatre has a reputation for turning on the sound halfway through the night), the city has enough supreme musicians of its own. The ancient and ironically named *Estudiantina Invasora*, the young *Grupo Turquino* and the multi-talented *Sonora La Calle* are all worth catching.

Rumba in Santiago has its place in the carnival parade. While the band takes a rest, the *Columbia Santiaguera* strikes up for the dancers. There is also a regular *rumba* on Sunday mornings at the **Museo del Carnaval** on Heredia (almost opposite the *Trova*).

For a calmer session you can enjoy choral, orchestral and chamber music at the **Sala Dolores** (on Plaza Dolores). There is an annual *Festival Internacional del Coro* in December.

You can experience Santiago's African roots at the occasionally wonderful *peñas* at the **Casa del Caribe** on Calle B or the **Casa de Africa** on the evocatively named Avenida Manduley, both in Vista Alegre. Stunning shows by Cutumba, Cocoyé and Guillermón Moncada celebrate all of Oriente's music and dance traditions. Other groups, such as the Cabildo Isuama and the Tumba Francesa, keep alive the memories of Africa.

July in Santiago is super hot, and so is the music. In early July, the Festival del Caribe brings groups from all over the Caribbean for street shows, theatre events and a big parade. Carnival follows almost immediately, when the *comparsas* and *paseos* parade their congas around the streets in spectacular style, past stages set up for live bands and kiosks selling beer and *frituras*. See Festivals, page 349, for details.

To conga properly you'll need your wooden sandals (*chancletas*), curlers, shorts and a boob tube (*bajo y chupa*, literally 'down and suck'). To join the musicians you need the brake drum off a 1953 Chevy. Maybe it's better simply to *arrollar y gozar*.

drumming school in London and has played in Europe on several occasions. He is very enthusiastic and even complete beginners can have a wonderful time.

⊛ Festivals and events

15-19 May Festival de Baile is a vibrant street festival.

Mid-May Festival de la Canción Francesa is a contest in which students of the Alliance Française sing in French. The first three places go to the national contest in Havana and the prize is a month's trip to France, all expenses paid.

1st week in Jul Festival del Caribe begins with theatre, dancing and conferences and continues later in Jul to coincide with the Moncada celebrations on 26 Jul.

18-27 of Jul Carnival is already in full swing by the Moncada celebrations on 26 Jul (as it was in 1953, the date carefully chosen to catch Batista's militia drunk and off-guard and use the noise of the carnival to drown the sound of gunfire). Carnival always lasts 1 week between the 18 and 27 July, taking in Santiago's patron saint's day, 25 Jul and stopping traditionally for the rather more serious Moncada celebrations on 26 Jul, continuing on 27 Jul. This carnival is regaining its former glory and is well worth seeing. Wear no jewellery, leave all valuables behind. The other provinces are represented, installing an area in Reparto

Sueño where they sell food and drink typical of each province. Each *municipio* organizes different activities, music, dancing, cabaret etc in different parts of the city, even in the sea, with beer, food and kiosks. There are competitions and parades, with rivalry between the *comparsas* (congas) and *paseos* (*grupos de baile*). The whole city is covered in lights and all the doors are decorated. The parades and floats are judged from 2100 and pass down Garzón where there are seats for viewing. To get a seat go to the temporary Izlazul office behind the seating area on the south side of the road between 1800 and 2000. It starts at 2100, US$2 for a tourist seat. Good views possible if you queue early. Visit the Museo del Carnaval, see pxxx, to get the feel of it. Photos, costumes and musical instruments depict the history of the carnival and the cultures that influenced it.

Sep Festival del Pregón is also known as *Frutas del Caney*, a festival of song when people dress up in traditional costumes and sell fruit in the street while singing.

Sep/Oct Festival de la Trova is a festival of folk music, the exact date each year depends on funding.

Dec Festival Internacional del Coro is a festival held every 5 years.

New Year's Eve You will find *son* bands playing in Plaza Marte and surrounding streets. Just before midnight everyone moves toward Parque Céspedes and sings the National Anthem. On the stroke of midnight the Cuban flag is raised on the Casa de Gobierno, commemorating the anniversary of the first time it was flown in 1902 when the Republic of Cuba was proclaimed. Afterwards, there's all-night drinking and dancing on the streets and in local bars.

O Shopping

Santiago de Cuba centre *p328, map p330*
Art galleries and artesanía
Handicrafts and books are sold on the street on Heredia entre Hartmann y Pío Rosado.
Casa de la Artesanía, under cathedral in Parque Céspedes, T22-623924, daily 0800-1730, also on Lacret 724 entre San Basilio y Heredia.
Cubartesana, Félix Pena esq Masó under the cathedral.

Salón Artexanda, Heredia 304 entre Pío Rosado y Calvario.
Fondo Cubano de Bienes Culturales, Lacret 704 esq Heredia, T22-652358, fbcstgo@cult.stgo.cu Paintings, antiques and art works.
Galería 1927, Ateneo Cultural, Santo Tomás 755 entre Santa Rita y Santa Lucía, T22-651969, daily 0900-2000.
Galería de Arte Universal, C entre M y Terrazas, Vista Alegre, open Tue-Sun 0900-1700. Exhibition and sale of art work.
Galería El Zaguán, Heredia, opposite Casa Granda hotel and next to Rumbos, open daily 0900-2000.
Galería la Confronta, Heredia entre Carnicería y San Félix. Contemporary art.
Galería Oriente, San Pedro (Lacret) 653 entre Heredia y Aguilera, underneath the Hotel Casa Granda on Parque Céspedes, contemporary art, open Tue-Sun 0900-1700. Exhibition and sale of contemporary art.
Galería Santiago, San Pedro esq Heredia.

Bookshops
Ho Chi Minh at the top of Enramada. Peso bookshop.
Librería Amado Ramos Sánchez, Enramadas y San Félix, Mon-Sat 0900-1800. Contemporary Cuban literature of all types, pay in pesos.
Librería Internacional, on Heredia under the cathedral, open 0800-2000. A selection of paperbacks in English and postcards.

Clothes
La Maison, Av Manduley. Expensive European clothes for dollars.

Food
Several dollar stores can be found in the Parque Céspedes area, ask for 'shopping', especially on Saco. There are dollar shops on Plaza del Marte and on Garzón near **Helado Alondra**. There is a food market on Ferreiro opposite **Hotel Las Américas**. Herbs, spices and *Santería* items can be bought on Mon and Thu at Gen Lacret y Gómez.
Casa de Miel, Gen Lacret. Sells honey.
Doña Neli, Aguilera at Plaza Marte, just down from **Hotel Libertad**. Good bread shop (dollars).

Panadería El Sol, Plaza Marte entre Saco y Aguilera.

La Bombonera, near Parque Céspedes on Aguilera entre Gen Lacret y Hartmann, open Mon-Sat 0900-1800, Sun 0900-1200. Dollar store selling food.

Photography

Photoclub, Enramada y San Félix, T22-65355. **Photoservice** has several shops: on Gen Lacret (San Pedro) entre San Basilio y Heredia, under the Cathedral, T22-622226; on Félix Pena entre Aguilera y Enramada; on Victoriano Garzón esq 5, Reparto Santa Bárbara, across from **Hotel Las Américas**, T22-686344. Expensive, US$1 per film and US$0.45 per photo, washed-out colours.

Music

Artex, Heredia 304. Music and videos as well as postcards and cultural items for dollars.

Casa de la Música, Corona entre Enramada y Aguilera.

Casa de la Trova, see above, Heredia y San Félix.

Enramadas and **Siglo XX**, Enramada. Records, books, clothes, jewellery, ornaments etc in pesos.

▲ Activities and tours

Baseball

Played Nov-Apr at the Estadio Guillermo Moncada on Av Las Américas, T22-641090/641078.

Diving, fishing and waterports

Bucanero Scuba Diving Center, at the Bucanero Hotel, Juraguá, 5-dive package, US$139; resort course, US$60; CMAS Open Water certification US$365; Advanced certification, US$250.

Marina Punta Gorda, Calle 1 A 4, Punta Gorda, T22-691446, F22-686108, VHF 16 and 72. 30 moorings, boat repairs, commissary, fuel, water, showers, restaurant, boat rental, fishing, dive centre, windsurfing, catamarans, banana boat, waterbicycles.

Sigua Scuba Diving Center, at Playa Sigua. The same prices as *Bucanero* above.

Hunting

Can be done (birds) around Parque Baconao, contact **Coto El Indio**, T22-643445.

Tour operators

Cubanacán, offices in the hotels **Meliá Santiago de Cuba, Versalles, Los Corales, Sierra Mar-Los Galeones** and at the airport. Head office T22-643445, F22-687209.

Cubatur, Victoriano Garzón entre 3 y 4, T22-652560, santiago@cubatur.cu daily 0800-1200, 1300-2000, is helpful with knowledgeable guides and excellent value. Also offices in **Hotel Meliá Santiago de Cuba** and at the airport. Easy to book Víazul tickets, air tickets as well as tours, car hire, tourist cards and hotel reservations.

Havanatur main office is on Av Raúl Pujol, T22-643603, with other offices at the airport, in the hotels **Meliá Santiago de Cuba, Casa Granda, Bucanero**. Offering the same as **Rumbos** but slightly more expensive. They have very good guides who are fluent in most European languages.

Rumbos Cuba, Heredia opposite Casa *Granda*, T22-624823, open 0800-1700 for tours and later for car hire. Organized city tours with guide, also day trips to destinations around Santiago. Prices vary according to season and number of people, tour to La Gran Piedra US$35 for 1 person, US$25 per person for 2 people, US$20 per person for 3, then progressively lower to 10 people when it stays the same however many there are. Cheaper to take a taxi. Also flights and trips to Jamaica and Santo Domingo.

⊖ Transport

Air

Airport Antonio Maceo (SCU), is 8 km from town, T22-691014/691830, F22-86184. Daily flights to/from **Havana** with **Cubana**, US$108 and **Aerocaribbean**, US$105, also **Baracoa** (Sun), **Holguín** (Sat, Sun), **Trinidad** (Tue) and **Varadero** (Mon). **Cubana** also has international flights to **Santiago** from **Madrid** and **Paris**, and Aerocaribbean has flights from **Montego Bay, Jamaica, Port-au-Prince, Haiti,** and **Santo Domingo, Dominican Republic**. There are connecting flights from **Mexico** via **Havana**.

Airlines Aerocaribbean next to Rumbos on San Pedro entre San Basilio y Heredia. **Aerotaxi** at the airport, T22-6422186/6426343. **Cubana**, Félix Pena 673 entre Heredia y San Basilio, near the cathedral, Mon-Fri 0900-1700, Sat

0900-1400, T22-624156/651579/622290.
Local and inter-Caribbean flights (some
destinations) can also be booked at tour
operators while **Cubanacán Express**, Calle 6
entre L y M, Reparto Sueño, T/F22-687221,
express@stgocub.scu.cyt.cu sells tickets for
**Aerocaribbean, Air France, Air Jamaica
Express, Air Europa, Cayman Airways,
Cubana,** and **Iberia**.

Bus
Local There is a regular bus service
between Plaza Ferreiro (top of Av Victoriano
Garzón) and Plaza Marte/Parque Céspedes.
Buses, 20 centavos. If there is no sign of a
bus, catch a truck, ask driver the destination,
pay flat rate of 1 peso. Horse-drawn *coches*
are also 1 peso. Bus number 214 goes to
Playa Siboney; 207 to Juraguá; no bus at
present to Parque Baconao; no bus to El
Cobre, but many trucks go there from the
main bus terminal.

Long distance Terminal near Plaza de
la Revolución at the top of Av de los
Libertadores/Carretera Central. **Víazul**,
T22-628484, is in an office to the left of the
bus departure area, with a blue door, open
0700-2100, closed Sun afternoon, but if you
turn up 30 mins before departure you can
buy your ticket. Note that for buses to
Baracoa demand can be great in high
season. Get your ticket the day before (or Sat
for a Mon journey). Once a busload of tickets
has been sold no more will be sold that day
but if you turn up at 0500 the next morning
they usually put on more buses depending
on demand. On your return you can only buy
tickets on the day of travel because the
number of seats depends on how many
buses have come from Santiago, but queue
early. See p 44 for timetable. For an
overnight journey wear trousers and a fleece
if you have one, as the a/c is very cold and
even **Víazul** is not comfortable at night. If
you want to travel with **Astro** on more local
services, you can queue jump by paying in
dollars, but if the **Astrobus** is full you will not
get a seat with any currency, so it is best to
get there either the day before or at least a
couple of hours in advance. Buy ticket in
Astro office on Yarayo (the 1st street on the
left going north from the terminal) before
boarding, open daily 0600-1400. **Astro** to
Bayamo 0940, 1040, 1730 daily, US$5, 3 hrs,

20 mins; to **Niquero** 0700 daily; to **Holguín**
1100 alternate days; to **Moa** 0720 alternate
days; to **Pilón** 0720 alternate days.

If you go by *camión*/truck and pay in
pesos it is 5 pesos to Guantánamo, 10 pesos
to Bayamo and 15 pesos in a *colectivo* to
Guantánamo. Trucks are available outside
the terminal to most destinations, drivers
shout destination prior to departure, pay in
pesos. For a long journey avoid trucks
without any kind of cover, or you will burn.

Car hire
At the airport: **Havanautos**, T22-651056,
airport T22-686161; **Transautos**, T22-692245;
Vía Rent-a-Car T22-687278. These and other
agencies in Hotel Casa Granda, Hotel
Santiago, Villa Santiago de Cuba, Hotel San
Juan, Hotel Las Américas. **Vía Rent a Car** in
Rumbos office opposite Casa Granda,
T22-624646, also at Carretera del Caney y
Calle 15, Reparto Vista Alegre, T22-641465.
US$192 for 4 days plus US$40 for insurance.
On return beware of US$10 charge for dirty
exterior, US$20 for dirty interior and US$16
for scratches on the paint work caused by
flying stones. **Havanautos**, agency at La
Punta service station, T22-639328.

Taxi
Local There are 3 types: **Turistaxi** are the
most expensive, eg US$8 from airport to
town centre; **Taxis OK** owned by Cubanacán
are also expensive; **Cubataxi**, T22-651038/9,
are the cheapest (name on windscreen), eg
airport to town US$5. The taxi fare from the
bus station to Plaza Marte is US$1, to Parque
Céspedes US$2, from the centre out to Santa
Bárbara US$3. The bus company, **Víazul**, has
a minibus which often meets long-distance
services at the bus station and runs as a taxi
to hotels and *casas particulares* in the centre,
US$2 per person. You can also get a private
taxi, lots hang around Parque Céspedes and
Plaza Marte, but they will charge about the
same as a **Cubataxi**. For a longer journey,
you can negotiate a price, eg Castillo del
Morro, US$10. However, get a written quote
if possible as even **Cubataxis** have been
known to renege on their agreements and
demand more and/or return to Santiago.
You will be continually offered private taxis
every time you go out, particularly near any
of the hotels or plazas.

Bicitaxi Transport can be arranged at Plaza Marte for about US$1. *Bicitaxis* cost US$0.50.

Train
The station is opposite the rum factory on Av Jesús Menéndez. Book tickets in advance from basement office in new terminal. Relatively easy and quick, unlike the journey itself when delays of 16 hrs or more are frequent. Do not enter the waiting room area but walk in from the left and there is a guard on the door. If there is a queue for tickets he will make you wait outside. Train travel is not as reliable or comfortable as bus travel. Take sweater for Havana journey, freezing a/c. Daily to **Havana**, see also under Train, Havana, for fares and services.

⊙ Directory

Santiago de Cuba *p328, map p330*
Banks
It is possible to get US dollar cash advance on credit cards (non-US) at **Banco Financiero Internacional**, Av Las Américas entre I y J, Reparto Sueño, T22-686252, Mon-Fri 0800-1600, they also change foreign currency and TCs. **Banco de Crédito y Comercio**, Parque Céspedes, Santo Tomás entre Aguilera y Heredia and Lacret esq Aguilera, efficient service for credit card advances and changing TCs in European currencies into dollars, 2.5% commission. **BICSA**, Enramada opposite Plaza Dolores, for changing foreign currency and TCs. **Banco Popular de Ahorro**, Plaza Dolores, 0800-1500, Visa and MasterCard, ATM, prompt service, also a newly built branch on Victoriano Garzón esq 3. TCs can be changed in any hotel except those in the Islazul chain; commission is usually 2-3%. **Meliá Santiago de Cuba** has a *Cadeca* in its shopping precinct (also Post Office, pharmacy, tour operators, gift shops) daily 0900-2000, will change virtually any cash currency into dollars. TCs can be changed in the **Havanatur** office in Casa Granda. **Hotel Las Américas** has a *Cadeca* in the lobby open daily 0800-1800 (although there is often no one there at lunchtime), for currency exchange, TCs, Visa, Mastercard advances. In the **Asistur** office under Casa Granda you can get cash advance on all major credit cards including American Express and Diners Club; they will also change American Express TCs, the only place that will

do so in all Cuba. Do not change dollars on the street. There is a *Cadeca* on Aguilera close to Plaza Dolores. If you want to buy *pesos Cubanos,* change no more than US$5-10 for a 2- 3-week stay.

Hospitals and clinics
Clínica Internacional, Av Raúl Pujol esq 10, T22-642589. Outpatient appointments, laboratory, dentist, 24-hr emergencies, international pharmacy, especially for tourists, everything payable in dollars, US$25 per consultation, the best clinic to visit to be sure of immediate treatment.

Internet
Etecsa has an office under the cathedral on the corner of Parque Céspedes, Félix Pena y Heredia, open 0700-2300 daily. Only 3 terminals, converted to the prepaid card system in 2003, some have better connection than others so if you can't get through on one machine, ask to try another. Also 2 international phone booths and 2 domestic. **Hotel Las Américas**, 2 terminals in the hotel lobby, US$2 per 30 mins. Bar alongside if you have to wait your turn. **Meliá Santiago de Cuba**, business centre off the entrance. The best place in terms of quality and quantity of machines where there are 6 computers, US$5 per hr, and connection is usually good.

Language schools
The Universidad de Oriente, on the outskirts of town (see Essentials, page 25).

Laundry
Abatur, Av de Céspedes, near Hotel Santiago. Most *casas particulares* will also offer laundry on request, prices vary.

Pharmacies
There is a pharmacy next door to the **Casa de la Trova** on Heredia. The **Hotel Meliá Santiago de Cuba** has a well-stocked pharmacy but it is expensive.

Post office
The main post office is on Aguilera y Clarín, daily 0700-2000, where you can make phone calls within Cuba and buy international phone cards. There is email service but no internet access. The **Casa Granda** has its own post office, as does **Hotel Sol Meliá Santiago**. For a

courier service, **Cubanacán Express**, Calle 6 entre L y M, Reparto Sueño, T22-687221, express@stgocub.scu.cyt.cu offers good service at reasonable prices. There is also **DHL**, opposite the bar, *El Baturro*, near Plaza Céspedes, which has email facilities.

Telephone

You cannot make collect calls from hotels, only from private houses. **Etecsa** is on . Aguilera, just before Plaza Dolores, open 24 hrs. For calls outside Santiago, **Centro de Comunicaciones Nacional e Internacional**, Heredia y Félix Pena, by the cathedral.

Useful addresses

Cultural centres Casa de Africa, Av Manduley. Includes craftwork shop and has Afro-Cuban music in the evenings. **Casa del Caribe**, 13 154 esq 8, Vista Alegre, T22-642285. Extensive library of Caribbean subjects, publishes magazine called *Caribe*, Afro-Cuban music and dance Sat nights, great authentic *folkórico*. **Centro de Estudios Africanos Fernando Ortiz**, Av Manduley y 5, Vista Alegre. US$1 entrance, artefacts and research centre. **Hermanos Saiz**, Heredia, cultural centre that promotes poetry. **El Tívoli**, Santa Rosa y Jesús Rabí. Promotes influence of French culture, named after

neighbourhood where French settled in 18th century, fleeing from slave uprising in Haiti. **La Conga de los Hoyos**, Moncada y Av José Martí. Specializes in conga music, promotes the festival of 24 Jun with conga drummers in the streets. **La Tumba Francesa**, Los Maceo 501 esq Gen Banderas, Mon-Sat 0800-1600, with dance displays Tue, and Thu 2030, US$2. Like its counterpart in Guantánamo, celebrates Haitian influence on Cuban culture, with traditional costumes, music, dancing and handicrafts. **UNEAC**, Bartolomé Masó y Pío Rosado. National art and literature centre. **Fire** Martí 517, T22-623242. **Immigration** Asistur, Hotel Casa Granda, Heredia esq San Pedro, T22-686600. For all health, financial, legal and insurance problems for foreign tourists. **Inmigración y Extranjería**, Av Raúl Pujol y 1, Reparto Santa Bárbara, Mon and Fri 0900-1200, 1330-1630, Tue, Wed and Thu 0900-1200, in summer holiday mornings only. Go to **Bandec** on Parque Céspedes y Aguilera and buy special stamp (*sello*) for US$25, then return to Immigration for paper work (15 mins). **Police** T116. Central police station is Unidad 2, Corona y San Gerónimo. Near to the hotels Santiago and Las Américas is **Unidad 4**, on Aguilera near the hospital and the market.

Guantánamo

Guantánamo → *Colour map 4, grid C1.*

Guantánamo, the capital of the most easterly and most mountainous province of the same name, has one major difference from other Cuban colonial towns. The large influx of Haitian, French and Jamaican immigrants in the 19th century means that the architecture has much less of a Spanish colonial feel; the narrow, brightly coloured buildings with thin wooden balconies and wrought ironwork are more reminiscent of New Orleans than Madrid. This is also reflected in the local musical rhythms, notably the Tumba Francesa, a colourful folk dance tradition originating in Haiti, based in the centre of the town. The city is close to the US naval base of Guantánamo (which cannot be easily visited from Cuba). It is so little a part of the town that you will not, except in conversation, come across it unless you make a specific trip to Mirador de Malones to view it through binoculars. The range of the Montañas de Nipe-Sagua-Baracoa runs through the province, ending at the Atlantic Ocean on the northern coast and the Caribbean Sea to the south. The area is notable for its many endemic species of fauna and flora and it is one of the most beautiful parts of the island. ▶▶ *For Sleeping, Eating and other listings, see pages 357-356.*

Ins and outs

Getting there There are **flights** from Havana at the crack of dawn five days a week, which then turn around and head straight back again. Guantánamo is some 80 km from Santiago on the Baracoa road. **Víazul** and **Astro** have **buses** from Santiago to Baracoa via Guantánamo and to other destinations. The **Víazul** bus is usually full at weekends and it can be difficult to get on another bus if you want to break your journey in Guantánamo, so seat reservation in advance is essential. **Train** services are better, with daily trains to and from Santiago, Havana and Holguín, but you can't rely on their punctuality.▶▶ *For further details, see Transport, page 357.*

Getting around The town is small enough to walk around but there are horse-drawn *coches* for longer distances. A taxi or organized excursion is required if you want to go to one of the look outs to see the American base. A number of streets have had their names changed, but locals often do not even know the official title. Avenida de los Estudiantes is known as Paseo, while Bartolomé Masó is known as Carretera.

Best time to visit It is hot any time of the year, but humidity increases in the summer months and the risk of storms is higher from September to November.

History

The town of Guantánamo was founded in 1819 and was called Santa Catalina del Saltadero del Guaso until 1843. It lies north of the Bahía de Guantánamo, between the Jaibo, Bano and Guaso rivers which flow into the bay. Guantánamo is a pleasant, fairly well-restored colonial town.

The US naval base was established at the beginning of the 20th century, when Cuba was a protectorate of the USA following independence from Spain, in the area known as Caimanera at the mouth of the bay. Although the USA relinquished its right to intervene in Cuban affairs in 1934, it retained its naval base on a lease which expires in 2033. Cuba considers the occupation illegal but has taken no action to

● *The annual rent for the US Naval Base at Guantánamo Bay is 2000 gold coins, equivalent*
● *to US$4,085, or US$0.01 per square metre. Since March 1959 Cuba has never cashed a rent cheque, demanding instead the return of the land.*

eject the American forces. In early 2002, the US base came to the world's attention when al-Qaida and Taliban prisoners were transferred there from Afghanistan under heavy guard to await military trial following the war against the Taliban. Huge metal cages were built to incarcerate the prisoners and security at the base was tighter than ever. International condemnation of the treatment of the prisoners (who were not awarded the status of prisoners of war and while being held outside US territory were therefore outside the rule of law) gathered pace during 2003. Although 20 prisoners were repatriated in November 2003, they were replaced by 20 more. None of the prisoners had faced trial at that time.

Sights

The central square is the **Plaza Martí**, shaded by laburnum trees, with a church, the Iglesia Parroquial Santa Catalina, in the centre. The two roads running north–south either side of the plaza, General Pérez and Calixto García, contain some of the most attractive colonial houses. The Post Office and the **Casa de la Cultura** are on the west side and the **Tumba Francesa** on the east (see page 356). Two kilometres north, the **Plaza de la Revolución** has a modernist carved stone monument to the heroes of all the wars of independence. The **Museo Municipal** ① *José Martí 802 entre Francisco Aguilera y Prudencio del Prado, Tue-Sat 0800-1800, Sun 0800-1200,* housing artefacts from the history of Guantánamo, is in a former colonial prison built in 1861-62. There is also a small museum near the Plaza de la Revolución which contains the space capsule in which the first Cuban went into space. South of the centre is the **Casa Natal Regino Boti** ① *Bernabé Varona 405, entre José Martí y Pedro Agustín Pérez.* Boti was a notable poet, essayist, historian and artist. He was born here on 18 February 1878 and lived and worked all his life in the same house.

Around Guantánamo

There is a day tour taking in Guantánamo city, **La Tumba Francesa**, Zoológico de Piedra and Changüí (a traditional form of music played on a farm a short distance from the city while visitors have a good lunch, join in the dance and meet the musicians). The **Zoológico de Piedra** ① *Carretera a Yateras Km 18,* is an outdoor museum of carved stone animals, set in a beautiful hillside location with tropical vegetation. Many are bizarre, from tiny stone lizards to huge bison. All are carved directly from the rocks in their natural setting and you can buy miniature replicas from the sculptor on the way out. The tour is organized by **Havanatur,** with an excellent guide in an air-conditioned minibus, daily during high season, Tuesday and Saturday in low season, 0900 outside **Hotel Guantánamo,** approximately US$30. There is also a trip, with the same sights, going on to Baracoa on the same day.

◉ Sleeping

Guantánamo *p355, map p354*

E **Casa de Los Ensueños**, Ahogados esq 15 Norte, Reparto Caribe, T21-326304. 3 rooms, a/c, TV, bar, 24-hr room service.

E **Guantánamo** (Islazul), Av Ahogados, esq 13 Norte, Plaza Mariana Grajales, Reparto Caribe, T21-381015, F21-382406, 15 mins' walk from the centre. Plaza Mariana Grajales, created in 1985, is an important post-Revolutionary square, a complex of artistic and architectural monuments. 3-star, 142 rooms, Soviet-style architecture, pool, clean, a/c, 2 bars and busy restaurant, food average, nightclub, disco,

mostly Cuban clientele, staff pleasant and helpful, tours arranged to see the naval base.

F **Elsye Castillo Osoria**, Calixto García 766 entre Prado y Jesús del Sol. Rooms with a/c, TV, fridge, sitting room, private and secure in central location.

F **Lisette Foster Lara**, Gen Pedro A Pérez 661 entre Jesús del Sol y Prado. Central, close to plaza, a/c, hot water, secure.

F **Osmaida Blanco Castillo**, Gen Pedro A Perez 664 entre Paseo y Narciso Lopez, T21-325193. If you get the nasty room without windows, ask for another. Outside seating, dinner US$5.

Around Guantánamo *p356*

D **Caimanera** (Islazul), Loma Norte, Caimanera, T21-91414, F21-99520. On a slight rise overlooking the bay and the sea, 3-star, 17 basic rooms and cabins but pleasant location, a/c, TV, bar, restaurant, pool. The closest you'll get to the US base.
E **Villa La Lupe** (Islazul), Carretera El Salvador Km 3 ½, T21-382612. 2-star, just outside Guantánamo on the Río Bano in a pleasant countryside location with lots of trees, 50 functional rooms in reasonably attractive modern blocks called cabins, reached by concrete staircases, a/c, TV, few luxuries but there is a decent pool and a squash court, peaceful atmosphere, bar, restaurant.

Camping

Empresa Campismo Popular, Bartolomé Masó 809 entre 4 y San Gregorio, T21-326552. Oficina de Reservaciones, Crombet entre Martí y Gen Pedro A Pérez. There is a campground at Yacabo Abajo, Carretera Baracoa Km 45, before you get to Imías, T21-80289, on the coast where it is very dry and rocky with a backdrop of barren hills, 18 cabins sleeping 4-6, but unless you are very persuasive you will probably be told it is for Cubans only.

❼ Eating

Guantánamo *p355, map p354*
Plenty of *paladares*, most of whom charge in pesos although they will, of course, accept dollars. Price should be about 45 pesos per person, but some raise it for tourists. Two *paladares* on Av de los Estudiantes (Paseo) and a number of street stalls selling pork sandwiches for 5 pesos, some are there every day, all of them at weekends. Other *paladares* off Plaza Martí in the centre.

Around Guantánamo *p356*
$ **Mirador de Malones**, Carretera de Boquerón, T21-41386, daily 1200-2200. If you are visiting the Mirador, you can get something to eat here. Cuban food.

❻ Entertainment

Guantánamo *p355, map p354*
The is a **cinema** on Av de los Estudiantes, on the corner of the road to *Hotel*

Guantánamo. Live **music** can be heard at the **Casa de la Cultura**, Gen Pérez, southwest corner of Plaza Martí, and the **Tumba Francesa**.
The **Casa de la Cultura** also holds exhibitions of photography and painting, usually run by **UNEAC**, José Martí near Plaza Martí.

❺ Shopping

Guantánamo *p355, map p354*
A couple of good peso **bookshops**, one just off Plaza Martí on Calixto García, much better stocked than those in Havana or Santiago. The demand is not so high here for literature, so several classics have been sitting on the shelves for years. **Tumba Francesa** (see above) sells good-quality Haitian-style **handicrafts** and souvenirs; the shop is right on Plaza Martí, opposite the church. There are dollar shops in the Guantánamo and Caimanera hotels. Also *Zun-Zun* on Maceo y Aguilera.

▲▲ Activities and tours

Cycling

Contact **Josué Gaínza Matos**, Calle B 233 entre 7 y 8, Imías, Guantánamo, president of the local club, **Grupo de Ciclo Turismos La Farola**.

Tour operators

There are *burós de turismo* in the hotels in Guantánamo that can arrange tours to Mt Malones, where you can view the US base through Soviet binoculars. **Islazul** office is on Los Maceo entre Narciso López y Paseo.

❺ Transport

Air

Aeropuerto Mariana Grajales (GAO) is 16 km from Guantánamo, off the Baracoa road. Scheduled flight Mon, Wed, Fri, Sat at 0530 from **Havana**, returning 0845, plus Sun 0840 (1155). **Cubana** is at Calixto García 817 entre Prado y Aguilera, T21-34533.

Bus

The bus terminal, T21-326016, is 5 km southwest of the centre. Private cars and taxis run from the train and bus station to Hotel Guantánamo/town centre, US$1. Daily bus to **Havana**, 4 buses to **Santiago**, 1 bus to **Baracoa**. Víazul stops here on its

Music in Guantánamo

The name of Guantánamo is known the world over, thanks to the song *'Guajira Guantanamera'* which is the climax of the show for all but the most principled groups. (The way to look cool and Cuban is to cry "AE SALA", after the first 'Guantanamera' and "SONGOLOQUESONGO" after the second). The words to the verses are noble and mournful, based as they are on the poetry of José Martí. *'Guajira'* is a rural style of *son* and is similar to the simple, improvizing *'Nengón'*, which developed in the mountains surrounding Guantánamo. The Valera Miranda family, still living in the hills, have kept this style alive. In Guantánamo itself, *Nengón* became the *'Son Changüí'* which, with its African thumb bass (*Marimbula*) and old style bongos, has stayed true to the roots of the original son. *Changüí* is tremendously complex, with backbeats, cross rhythms and constant bongo improvization but for many it is the most beautiful form of *son*. Catch it at the *Casa de la Trova*. Local grandad made good Elio Revé Matos (1930-97), created a new *changüí* which brought him national fame (and a contract with Peter Gabriel) during the 1970s and 1980s. His background, like many Guantanamerans, is in the coffee plantations established in the sierra by French landowners following the Haitian Revolution in 1791. The *Tumba Francesa de Santa Catalina* was created during the 1890s by newly freed blacks in order to preserve the rich cultural heritage that had been developed on the plantations. One of only three such organizations still surviving (the other two being in Santiago and Sagua de Tánamo), the Tumba Francesa in Guantánamo still fulfils its original purpose. To the urgent rhythms of the Premier drums and the wooden percussion instrument the *Catá* (both of which originated in the Dahomeyan region of Africa), the elderly patrons recreate the dances of their great-great-grandparents. The singer (*Composé*) organizes the dance, calling the musicians to order and setting in train the ancient movements of the *Mason*, *Yuba* or *Frente*. Queen of *Composé* was Tecla Benet Danger, the only woman *Catá* player in Cuba, who died recently, having sung and played until the age of 91.

Santiago-Baracoa route, depart Santiago 0730, 3 hrs 15 mins, US$6, depart Baracoa 1415, 6 hrs, US$10.
 Camiones to **Santiago** leave from the bus station. Bargain hard. *Camiones* to **Baracoa** leave from La Punta, 7 km from bus station (take a taxi), 4-5 hrs, 5 pesos, extremely uncomfortable, but cheap.

Car hire
Havanautos office is at Cupet Cimex gas station at Prado esq 6 Este, the beginning of the Baracoa road.

Train
The station is in the centre on Calixto García. Daily trains to **Santiago**, **Havana** and **Holguín**. About 5 daily trains to **Caimanera**.

❶ Directory

Guantánamo *p355, map p354*
Banks Banco de Crédito at Calixto García esq Carretera, Mon-Fri 0800-1500. *Cadeca*, Calixto García esq Prado, Mon-Sat 0830-1800, Sun 0800-1300. **Post office** On the west side of Plaza Martí. DHL is in the post office.

● *For an explanation of the sleeping and eating price codes used in this guide, see inside the*
● *front cover. Other relevant information is provided in Essentials, pages 48-53.*

Baracoa → *Colour map 4, grid B2.*

Baracoa is the tourist hot spot of the east – small, low-key and attractive, surrounded by rich, tropical forests. It is the perfect place to come and spend a few relaxing days on the beach. Alternatively you can be more energetic and go hiking in the mountains or explore the many rivers that wind their way through canyons to the sea. It is well worth the trip from Santiago (five hours' drive) for the scenery of the 48-km section of road known as 'La Farola', a viaduct that winds through lush, bright green pine forests in the mountains and then descends steeply to the coast. If you are in an open truck it feels like a roller coaster as it bends and swoops at speed down the mountains. Look out for people selling cucurucho, *a delicious mixture of coconut, fruit and sugar served in a cone of palm leaves.*▶ *For Sleeping, Eating and other listings, see pages 363-366.*

Ins and outs

Getting there There is an airport but **flights** are notoriously difficult to book, even in Havana, as times change frequently and **Cubana** often doesn't know when the planes are going. It is usually easier to book a tour with an agency as they have greater access to seats. There is no **railway**. It is best to travel by **road** from Santiago, with buses and trucks from there via Guantánamo. **Víazul** runs a daily bus service from Santiago. The bus station is within walking distance of the town centre. There is a road from Holguín round the coast through Moa, which is interesting if you are driving yourself and you can do a circular route via Guantánamo and Santiago back to Holguín, or vice versa. As we went to press there were only trucks between Baracoa and Moa (buses Moa–Holguín), however now a damaged bridge has been repaired, **Víazul** is considering a service Holguín–Baracoa.▶ *For further details, see also Transport, page 366.*

Getting around The best way to get around Baracoa is on foot or by *bicitaxi*. Most of them wait on Maceo outside the **Fondo de Bienes Culturales**; they charge US$1 to go almost anywhere. Getting from Porto Santo into town is difficult as there are no *bicitaxis* or taxis outside the hotel. Unless you get reception to call you a cab, walk down to the *barrio* at the bottom of the hill and wait around on the bridge for a *bicitaxi*.

History

Christopher Columbus arrived in Baracoa on 27 November 1492. He planted a cross, now housed in the church, and described a mountain in the shape of an anvil (*yunque*), which was thereafter used as a point of reference for sailors. The first maps of Cuba drawn by an Englishman showed the **Yunque de Baracoa** mountain, copies of which can be seen in the museum. Baracoa was the first town founded by Diego Velázquez. On 15 August 1511, he bestowed the settlement with the name Nuestra Señora de la Asunción de Baracoa and, for four years, it was the capital of Cuba. Between 1739 and 1742, Baracoa's three forts were built. The oldest, **El Castillo**, also known as Seboruco, or Sanguily, is now the *Hotel Castillo*. The others were **Fuerte de la Punta**, now restaurant *La Punta*, and **Fuerte Matachín**, now the municipal museum. Baracoa became a refuge for French exiles after the revolution in Haiti and they brought with them coffee and cacao farming techniques, as well as their own style of architecture, which contributed greatly to the buildings we can see now; as in Guantánamo, they have much less of a Spanish colonial style than in other towns in Cuba. The French also created the first drinking water plant. In 1856, Carlos Manuel de Céspedes spent five months in isolation in Baracoa as a punishment. The war of independence of 1895 saw many revolutionaries disembarking at Baracoa. Up until

Myths and legends of Baracoa

Economic growth picked up in Baracoa at the beginning of the 20th century with bananas. A railway was built to transport them and trade in bananas was established with the USA. However, two diseases endemic to bananas wiped out the industry in 1945. Superstitious blame was placed on a mysterious man called 'El Pelú', who had arrived in Baracoa in 1897. Children had laughed at his strange appearance and people threw stones and, offended, he had placed a curse on the village. No one took any notice of it until the banana crisis of 1945. Even today, people still refer to the 'curse of El Pelú' and in Baracoa El Pelú is generally held to bring bad luck.

In the 1930s, 'La Rusa' arrived in Baracoa. Magdalena Rovieskuya was the daughter of a general in the Russian aristocracy, who had left Russia in 1917 to travel the world. She came to Baracoa, built a hotel (still called *La Rusa*) on the Malecón and became very popular with the local people, who affectionately called her 'Mimá'. In the 1950s she was on the point of leaving but decided to stay and give her full support to the Revolution. She helped the Red Cross and supplied funds for the rebels to buy arms. Fidel and Che stayed in her hotel during the clandestine struggle. She died in 1978, on her deathbed donating a diamond bracelet to the *Festival Mundial de Los Estudiantes*.

There are many species of flora and fauna endemic to the Baracoa area and it is famous for its multicoloured snails, called *polimitas*. Legend has it that they came to Baracoa to find peace and took their bright colours from the sun, earth, sea and sky. They are sometimes sold around Boca de Yumurí, but they are now rather rare.

A local story explains the origin and size of the Río Toa, the widest river in Cuba. It is believed there was an Indian tradition to banish naughty children to the mountains to learn good behaviour. Once there, the grief-stricken children cried so much that their torrent of tears formed a river.

the 1960s, it was really only accessible by sea until the viaduct, **La Farola**, was built. This is one of the most spectacular roads in Cuba, 30 km long, joined to the mountain on one side and supported by columns on the other.

Land and environment

The name Baracoa is an Amerindian word meaning 'existence of the sea', also known as 'land of water' – it is the wettest region in Cuba with annual rainfall of 2 m in the coastal zone to 3.6 m in the middle and upper Toa Valley. The area is a UNESCO biosphere reserve, with more than 10 rivers, including the **Río Toa**, 120 km long and the widest river in Cuba, see Around Baracoa page 363. Another river, the **Río de Miel**, carries the legend that if you swim in it you will come back to Baracoa one day. There are many beautiful waterfalls, 120 different types of tree and lots of coconuts. Some 80% of Cuba's coconut production comes from here. Whitewater rafting is possible down the Río Toa, with different levels of difficulty. Baracoa has 56 archaeological sites, with traces of the three Amerindian groups who lived there: the Siboney, the Taíno and the Guanturabey (See page 382). There is one surviving community of 300 Amerindians, called the **Yateras**, dating back to the Spaniards' arrival. They are integrated with the rest of society but only marry among themselves and maintain their traditions. They live in an isolated region along the shores of the Río Toa, but a visit can be organized through Alejandro Hartmann in the Museo Municipal, minimum six people.

The **Parque Central**, or **Parque Independencia**, is halfway down Antonio Maceo, one of the main streets in town. It has many peso stalls selling good snacks and sandwiches at lunchtime and evening; there is also a **Rumbos** bar. All the young people hang out here every night. It is great for people-watching but you will get pestered a lot by harmless hustlers with rooms to rent, pesos to exchange, etc, unless you are with Cubans, in which case you'll be left alone. It is the hub of activity every Saturday, when Antonio Maceo fills up with stalls selling food and drink and the whole town comes out to dance to street musicians and have a party, or *noche Cubana*. The **Iglesia de la Asunción** on the Parque was built in 1512, burned down by the French in 1652, and rebuilt in 1805. The church contains the cross, known as the **Cruz de la Parra**, said to have been planted there by Columbus. Catholics and restorers have carved off slices over the years, with the result that the cross has diminished to almost half its former size. Belgian historians confirmed in 1989 that the cross did indeed date from Columbus' time. The best time to be sure of finding the church open is during Mass on Sunday.

The **Museo Municipal** ① *Fuerte Matachín, daily 0800-1800, US$2*, is in the Matachín fort at the end of the Malecón to the east of the town (turn right as you come in from La Farola). It is a small museum with interesting but rather antiquated displays on the history of the town from prehistoric times to memorabilia of La Rusa (see box, page 360) who died in 1978. There is a large cauldron for making sugar and the only armaments magazine of its type in Cuba dating from 1739. In 1838, the Queen of Spain presented Baracoa with its own coat of arms, now on display in the museum. The English-speaking conservation officer, Daniel Salomón Paján, is happy to give further information on local history and legends.

Around Baracoa

Boca de Miel and around

The delightful tropical village of Boca de Miel is within walking distance of Baracoa. Head east past the stadium, along the beach, and then turn north and cross a large bridge. You can buy fruit and watch the men fish. Around the bay is Playa Blanca, which is a bit rocky and you can find coloured shells. Boys in the area and vendors on La Farola sell *polimitas*, see box, page 360.

Playa Duaba

Playa Duaba is a point 6 km from Baracoa where the river meets the sea; you can swim in both and eat at **Finca Duaba**, where the food is good but the service not fantastic. You can hire horses here. Historically, Duaba is notable for being the place where General Antonio Maceo landed on 1 April 1895 to start the second War of Independence. There are waterfalls on the Río Duaba, reached by driving along a rocky road from Baracoa to the entrance by a campsite (**El Yunque**, Santa Rosa de Duaba 456), where you will be met by people wanting to guide you. A guide is needed for the 45-minute walk (take water) as you need to cross the river at a certain point and scramble up rocks. Depending on your haggling skills you will have to pay US$5-8. Excellent excursion, unspoilt and no other tourists.

Playa Maguana

Playa Maguana, is a beautiful white-sand curving beach 22 km northwest from Baracoa. The trees come right down to the sand, so there is shade under them or among the sea grapes growing further along the beach. The sand shelves quite steeply into the sea, which can be rough at certain times of the year, particularly if there is a storm or a cold front coming down from the USA. This is the Atlantic, not the

Caribbean, but the water is warm and inviting and, once you're in there, is a tremendous view looking inland to the mountains. Be very careful never to leave your things unattended and do not take valuables such as passports and tickets to the beach. They will be stolen. On the other hand, there is a security patrol and if you notice the theft in time, you may get your stuff back. It happens. There are many families living near the beach who will cook lunch for you and a beach *paladar* serving seafood, **Set del Mar**. Hygiene is not a top priority. You can hire beach chairs, US$0.50 per hour or US$2 for the day.

Río Yumurí

The Río Yumurí is 30 km east of Baracoa. This is the most spectacular of Baracoa's rivers, running through two deep canyons. There is an organized trip which includes a visit to a farm where they cultivate cacao, but even private drivers will do these sort of things too. Fishing trips can also be arranged in the village of Yumurí. If you don't want to take a tour, rent a private car (US$10) or take a *colectivo* taxi or truck to the Río Yumurí where the road ends. A canoe will ferry you across or you can hire one to take you upriver for US$2 per person. There are always guides on hand. You can continue walking upriver and swim, very quiet and peaceful.

El Yunque

You can hire a guide to take you to the top of El Yunque, 575 m above sea level, to view the breathtaking scenery and panorama of banana and coconut palms. Do not

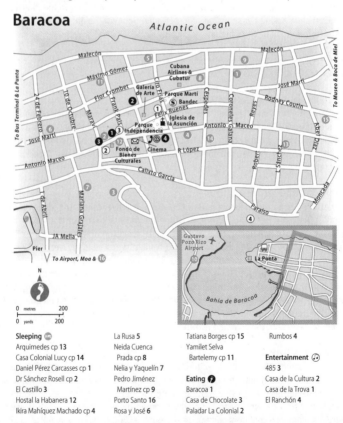

Baracoa

Sleeping 🛏
Arquimedes cp **13**
Casa Colonial Lucy cp **14**
Daniel Pérez Carcasses cp **1**
Dr Sánchez Rosell cp **2**
El Castillo **3**
Hostal la Habanera **12**
Ikira Mahíquez Machado cp **4**

La Rusa **5**
Neida Cuenca
  Prada cp **8**
Nelia y Yaquelín **7**
Pedro Jiménez
  Martínez cp **9**
Porto Santo **16**
Rosa y José **6**

Tatiana Borges cp **15**
Yamilet Selva
  Bartelemy cp **11**

Eating 🍴
Baracoa **1**
Casa de Chocolate **3**
Paladar La Colonial **2**

Rumbos **4**

Entertainment 🎵
485 **3**
Casa de la Cultura **2**
Casa de la Trova **1**
El Ranchón **4**

attempt it if you are not fit, it is a long, hard slog in tremendous heat and you will need plenty of water and good boots. Easier is the long walk up the **Río Toa** through the UNESCO biosphere forest, followed by a 45-minute return boat journey along Cuba's widest river. **Terrazas de Yara** are caves featuring ancient cave drawings, which you can visit only on an organized tour.

Punta de Maisí

The most eastern point of Cuba, Punta de Maisí, is only 80 km from Haiti across the Windward Passage, and on a clear night you can see the lights of the neighbouring island from the lighthouse here. There are caves on the point: La Patana, Los Bichos and Jaguey, which the Taínos used for ceremonial purposes and have left drawings on the walls. They were first explored in 1945 by Dr Antonio Nuñez Jiménez, who discovered that the temperature inside is very high. Hire a car, taxi or private driver to get there.

◉ Sleeping

Baracoa *p359, map p362*
Hotels
A-D Porto Santo (Gaviota), T21-45105, F21-45135. 57 rooms, 3 suites, a/c, bath, TV, restaurant, bar, shop, beautiful swimming pool, car hire, next to airport, beach, peaceful atmosphere, friendly but service weak.
C-D El Castillo (Gaviota), Calixto García, Loma del Paraíso, T21-45165, F21-45223. 34 a/c rooms with bath, phone, TV in lobby lounge, pool (US$3 for use by non-residents) with great views, parking, friendly staff, food OK, excellent views, feeling of grandeur, very good breakfast included.
C-D Hostal La Habanera, Maceo esq Frank País, T21-45273, F21-45226, rumbcoa @enet.cu Glorious pink colonial building converted to a hotel in 2003. If you want a central hotel with style this is the place. Friendly staff, excellent service. 10 rooms, a/c, cable TV, hot water, room service, internet access, massage room, snack bar, nightclub El Café1511, **Rumbos** information and tours.
E-F La Rusa (Islazul), a bright yellow building on the Malecón, Máximo Gómez 13, T21-43011, islazul@gtmo.cu Named after the Russian lady, Magdalena Menasse (see box, page 360), who used to run the hotel and whose photos adorn the walls; famous guests have included Fidel Castro, basic rooms, average food, nice location.

Casas particulares
There are alleged to be 200 casas particulares in Baracoa now.
F Arquimedes, Rubert López 87 entre Limbano Sánchez y Ramón López, T21-43291. Run by Arquimedes and Bárbara,

a/c, hot and cold water, great food with lots of fish in coconut and other local dishes, room has own entrance off the street or you can come in through the house.
F Casa Colonial Lucy, Céspedes 29 entre Rubert López y Maceo, T21-43548. One of the nicest places to stay, Lucy has a delightful colonial house with lovely views over the town and the sea from the roof terrace. 2 rooms with high ceilings, private bathroom, fridge, a/c, hot water, great food, organizes trips.
F Casa Ernesto, Libertad 13 entre 1 Abril y M Grajales, 5 mins' walk from Plaza Independencia towards Hotel Porto Santo. Room with a/c, big breakfast included, dinner of traditional food from the region (fish in coconut milk), bike rental US$2 per day.
F César Labori Balga, Martí 81 entre 24 de Febrero y Coliseo, T21-433227. A very welcoming and delightful family with a separate apartment with its own off-street entrance. 2 double bedrooms, bathroom, hot water, a/c, small porch overlooking lush courtyard garden with chatty parrot. Eldest son, César, runs this *casa* and mother Concepción cooks lovely local dishes; fresh fish in coconut milk, lamb and excellent coffee from her father's farm.
F Daniel Pérez Carcasses, Coroneles Galana 6 entre Flor Crombet y Martí, T21-43274. Near the sea, private roof and room with new shower and a/c, nice family, good cooking.
F Dr Sánchez Rosell, Maceo 123 entre Frank País y Maravi, T21-43161. Friendly couple, private bathroom, fan, extremely clean, breakfast and dinner.

F **Ikira Mahíquez Machado**, Maceo 168-A entre Céspedes y Ciro Frías, T21-42466. 2 rooms, also separate part of the house with kitchen and garage, friendly family.

F **Inés Morgado Terán**, Maceo 51 entre Peralejo y Coliseo, T21-43292. Room with private bathroom, a/c, no English spoken but Inés and her husband are warm and helpful.

F **Miriam Zolla Montoya**, Martí 301, T21-43529. Extremely hospitable, comfortable, a/c, good food offered.

F **Neida Cuenca Prada**, Flor Crombet 194 esq Céspedes, T21-43178. Upstairs rooms better than the one downstairs, kind and generous family, wonderful food and reasonably priced.

F **Nelia y Yaquelín**, Mariana Grajales 11 entre Julio A Mella y Calixto García, T21-42652. Three generations of a delightful family offer a simple but comfortable place to stay, sea views, new, private bathroom, small room, breakfast US$2, dinner US$5, both delicious and more than you can eat.

F **Pedro Jiménez Martínez**, Flor Crombet 213 entre Coroneles y Reyes. Extremely nice family, great food, will cook anything you want, huge portions.

F **Rosa Quintero y José Alvarado**, Martí 87 entre 10 de Octubre y 24 de Febrero, T21-42205. Colonial single-storey house with high ceilings, although the guest suite is at the back in a newer extension with low ceilings, fan and a/c essential. 2 beds in bedroom, bathroom has new tiles and good fittings but poor water pressure in the hot shower. Own dining room with fridge opens on to garden and clothes washing and drying area. Friendly, helpful family who can offer transport and excursions, good food.

F **Sol E Gamboa Muguercia**, Emiliano Corrales 39 entre Libertad y Mariana Grajales. 1 room, a/c, double bed, good food, in quiet area away from centre, family atmosphere.

F **Tatiana Borges**, Rodney Coutin 46 entre Abel Diaz y Moncada, T21-43674. Pleasant room with balcony and your own entrance. Very nice people, dinner possible.

F **Williams Montoya Sánchez**, Martí 287, T21-42798. Very hospitable, a/c, car parking, US$1, car cleaning US$2, also for non-guests.

F **Yamilet Selva Bartelemy**, Frank País 6 entre Máximo Gómez y Flor Crombet, T21-42724, yamito2002@yahoo.es Despite being a seaside town, this is one of the few houses to have a sea view from 2 light and bright rooms. 1 room has 2 beds, the other is smaller with 1 bed and bigger bathroom, hot shower, sea breezes, a/c, fan, in hospitable household with charming couple, secure, comfortable, dinner US$5-7, breakfast US$2-3, excellent.

Around Baracoa *p359*

C **Villa Maguana** (Gaviota), Carretera a Moa Km 22½. There is no phone, only a radio connection from **Hotel El Castillo** in Baracoa, so you need to book from there. The only place to stay on the beach, Playa Maguana. 2-star bungalow accommodation, with only 4 double rooms and a restaurant in 2003, although more are being built which will be of a higher specification, breakfast included.

❷ Eating

Baracoa *p359, map p362*

The isolation of Baracoa has led to an individual local cuisine, mostly featuring coconut milk and fish. Don't miss the *cucurucho*, also known as *pastel de coco* or *coco con chocolate*. These are wrapped in dried palm leaves in a clever cone shape with a carrying handle and are sold at the roadside up in the hills on La Farola. You can get 2 for US$1. They also sell cocoa balls the size of a tennis ball, 3 for US$1, which are delicious for making hot chocolate or using in cakes. Lots of *paladares*, many of which are well established, most offer pork, chicken, fish, turtle, some offer lobster, all of a high standard.

$ **Baracoa**, Maceo 129. Old colonial house with large dining room serving basic *criollo* food in pesos with chicken and pork costing less than US$1. Side dishes like *congrí* or *plátano* cost only 3 pesos, cucumber 1 peso.

$ **Casa de Chocolate**, Maceo esq Maraví. Serves a local version of hot chocolate with water, sugar and salt. Not to everyone's taste but worth trying just in case. Only 30 centavos a cup. Cuban pesos essential, no US dollars accepted. Snacks available. You can buy chocolate in town made by the Baracoa chocolate factory – a bit dry and gritty but with good flavour. The factory was opened by Che in 1963 on the Moa road out of town.

$ **Fuerte La Punta**. The fort at La Punta, which juts out into the bay west of the town, has been converted to a pleasant, breezy, open-air restaurant, with rustic tables and chairs inside the fort looking out through the cannon holes to the sea. Nice setting, reasonably priced food, fish in coconut milk US$6, *pollo frito* US$1.20, sandwiches US$2, spaghetti US$1.20, ice cream US$0.70.

$ La Colonial, José Martí 123, T21-45391. Excellent candlelit subdued atmosphere, extensive menu.

$ Rumbos, Parque Independencia. 24-hr bar with outside seating under a flowering vine for shade. Fast food with terminally slow service, spaghetti, pizza, sandwiches, chicken. Also scooters for rent.

🎭 Entertainment

Baracoa *p359, map p362*
Live music and dancing
Artex El Patio, in the Fondo de Bienes Culturales (see Cultural centres). Bar with live music, outdoor seating. Snack bar run by Rumbos open all day until 2300, also beer. Rumbos also has a 24-hr bar in the Parque Independencia with live or taped music, dance floor, snacks and drinks, seating in the shade of a trailing begonia.
Casa de la Cultura, Maceo 124, T21-42364. Live music on its patio. Programme varies from day to day, with young local talent given the chance to shine. Nightly show of Afro-Cuban music by Bararrumba, which is highly recommended, US$1, very interesting to see all the costumes and instruments.
Casa de la Trova, Felix Ruenes esq Ciro Frías. Traditional music, Tue-Sun from 2100, US$1 entry, US$2 for a *mojito* or *Cuba libre*, good *son* and friendly atmosphere. Seats around the edge but many people stand on the street and look through the windows (until it rains). Dancing in the centre. The local girls won't dance, so foreign women are approached to partner the men. Dancers always in demand.
Cuatro ochenta cinco (485), Félix Ruenes, bar with live band every night, US$1, great fun, everyone gets up to dance. Disco playing western music next door.
Dancing Light, Maceo just before Parque Central. Disco for young Cubans although tourists will not feel out of place, drinks in dollars for tourists, quite a small place but lively, check out breakdancing show nightly by local youths.
El Ranchón, up the hill above Calixto García. All the young people move up here after the

Casa de la Trova and other places close. Open-air disco with live and taped music, 2100-0300, although it doesn't really get going until after 2400. Great view over Baracoa and out to sea. Watch out for all the steps if you've been hitting the rum.
La Punta, in the fortress, see Eating above. 24-hr bar.
La Terraza Cabaret, at Casa de la Cultura, Martí opposite Casa del Chocolate. Show starts at 2330, disco afterwards, US$1.
Porto Santo and **El Castillo**. Nightly dancing and live music at these 2 hotels, the former is livelier, see Sleeping above.

Cinema and events
Cineteatro El Encanto, Maceo, next to Parque Central. Shows movies and hosts cultural events.

🎪 Festivals and events

Baracoa *p359, map p362*
Last week in Mar Semana de la Cultura promotes the cultural traditions of the area with lots of music and dancing going back to the roots of Cuban *son*. **Fiesta del Kiribá** is a farmers' fiesta, particularly coffee farmers. **Carnival** follows the next week.
12-15 Aug **Fiesta de las Aguas** celebrates the foundation of Baracoa on 15 Aug 1511. There are conferences and courses about history and tradition, architecture, archaeology, traditional dancing, environmental events related to the Humboldt National Park, *Cayambeda* (legend of the Rio de Miel), demonstrations by *Treseros* (guitarists) and the **Feria de Arte Popular**.

🛍 Shopping

Baracoa *p359, map p362*
There is a **bookshop** on José Martí 195.
Fondo de Bienes Culturales (see Cultural centres in Directory, below). Handicrafts.
Galería de Arte Eliseo Osorio, Felix Ruenes. Art for sale, art exhibitions and special events, such as the **Concurso Guayacán**, wood carving demonstrations and exhibitions 6-8 Nov.

🥾 Activities and tours

Baracoa city tour US$4, Saltadero (35 m waterfall) US$8, El Yunque US$18, Playa Maguana US$7, Toa US$8, Duaba US$8

(Toa and Duaba, peasant farms and boat trips), Yumurí US$12 (fishing village, cocoa plantation and boat trip).

Cubatur, in the office of Cubana, José Martí 181, T21-42171. Tickets and reservations, transfers and tours.

Gaviota, at the Hotel Castillo, T21-43665, and Hotel Porto Santo, T21-45106. Usual tours.

Havanatur, at the Fondo de Bienes Culturales, Maceo 120, T21-43627. The usual range of services, tickets and tours.

Rumbos Cuba, Hostal La Habanera, T21-45155, rcubar@enet.cu Tickets for **Víazul**, **Cubana**, **Aerocaribbean**, transfers, phone cards, hotel and restaurant reservations. The only agency to offer multilingual guides (English, French, Italian, German, Tony Mas, representative and guide), trips to El Yunque, waterfall, Boca de Yumuri, Playa Maguana. New adventure tourism with rafting on the Toa (2½ hrs) and Challenge Toa/Duaba, a combination of hiking, *cayucas*, kayaks, bikes.

⊖ Transport

Air

Airport 100 m from **Hotel Porto Santo**. There are 2 scheduled **Cubana**, José Martí 181, T21-45374, flights a week from **Havana**, US$120, on Thu (0840, returning 1200) and Sun (0410, returning 0900), and an **Aerocaribbean** flight on Thu (1030 returning 1405). **Aerocaribbean** also flies from **Santiago** on Thu (1030, 1305). All times subject to frequent change.

Bus

Main bus terminal at the end of Martí near Av de los Mártires, T21-43889, for buses to **Havana, Santiago, Camagüey, Guantánamo**. Make sure you reserve in advance at busy times and that your name is down on the list, *plano*, otherwise your reservation will not be valid. **Víazul** has a service to **Santiago** at 1415, arriving 1900, US$15, departing Santiago 0730, arriving Baracoa 1215, via Guantánamo, see p352 for details of tickets and queues. Trucks to **Guantánamo**, **Moa** and other destinations from 2nd bus terminal on Coroneles Galan, a couple of blocks inland from the Parque.

Car hire

There is a **Servi Cupet** station near the museum on Martí, closed Sun.

Playa Maguana *p361*

A battered **Víazul minibus** leaves Parque Independencia daily at 1000, returning 1700, US$2 one way. **Cocotaxi** charges US$14 return or US$15 if they wait for you. A normal taxi charges US$17-20. Alternatively, hire a private car for about US$12-13, 1 hr on an unpaved road.

① Directory

Baracoa *p359, map p362*

Banks Banco Nacional de Cuba is on Maceo but will change only TCs, you cannot get cash advance on credit cards. **Porto Santo** and **El Castillo** hotels both change TCs. **Cultural centres** Fondo de Bienes Culturales, Maceo 120, T21-43627. As well as a tasteful souvenir shop full of local artists' work, wooden carvings, paintings etc, information about local artists; Baracoa has its own school of *artesanía*, where artists train in traditional methods using wood and coconut shell, producing the work on sale in the shop. The very friendly and helpful English-speaking Alberto Matos Llime is worth talking to if you have any questions about local history and culture. **Hospitals and clinics** Hospital Octavio de la Concepción y de la Pedraja, on Carretera Guantánamo. Policlínica, in the small *barrio* next to Hotel Porto Santo, where you pay in pesos, there is also a dentist here. Clínica Dental, in Barrio de la Punta, near the port. **Internet** Etecsa, Maceo, opposite Parque Independencia. Internet service with 4 terminals using prepaid cards, US$6 per hour, valid only in Baracoa. **Pharmacies** There is a 24-hr pharmacy on Maceo 132. **Post office** Maceo 136, open 0800-2000. **Telephone** Etecsa Centro de Llamadas, Maceo, opposite Parque Independencia. Phone boxes for domestic and international calls using prepaid phone cards.

💡 Footprint features

Introduction

The Isla de la Juventud, or Isla – as it is known – looks as though it belongs on a scorched-edged pirates' map of old, the parchment bearing a single cross indicating buried gold. Apparently such tales of treasures still abound as it was once a lair for British and French corsarios. Its history as a temporary home for Castro (in prison), for Martí (in exile), for the US Navy (another naval base) and for residents from other communist countries (as students) makes the island a curious destination for the traveller keen to get off the beaten track. Its modern-day appeal lies in the exceptional diving off the west coast, the ancient caves and its natural setting.

As a one-time prison island, there has been very little development, and what there is has been concentrated around Nueva Gerona, its main town, and the port area. There are few reasons to stay here if you are not interested in diving, as the swimming is poor compared with other Cuban beaches. The island is a good place to go for a weekend out of Havana, although if you plan to see the whole island you will need more than one weekend.

Cayo Largo, on the other hand, is a sun, sea and sand destination, where all-inclusive is the order of the day and you are totally isolated from the rest of Cuba. It is so little a part of Cuba that both euros and US dollars are the accepted currencies and Cuban pesos are invisible. Everyone comes here on a package deal, for one day, two days or a week, for no other reason than to enjoy the idyllic beaches with pale golden sand and perfect conditions for swimming, sailing and other watersports.

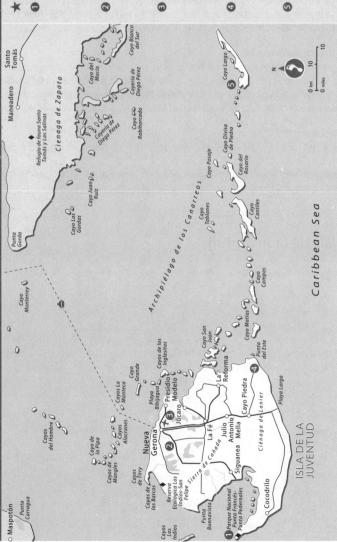

ISLA DE LA
JUVENTUD

Maspotón

Punta
Carragua

Cayos de
los Barcos

Cayos
Los
Indios

Cayos
del Hambre

Cayo de
la Pipa

Cayos
de Tirry

Cayos
de Manglés

Cayo
Monterrey

Cayos
Alacranes

Cayos La
Manteca

Cayo
Grande

Cayos de los
Inglesitos

Playa
Bibijagua

Nueva
Gerona

Presidio
Modelo

Júcaro

Reserva
Ecológica Los
Indios-San
Felipe

Sierra de Canada

La Fé

Julio
Antonio
Mella

Siguanea

Parque Nacional
Punta Francés-
Punta Pedernales

Punta
Buenavista

Cocodrilo

Ciénaga de Lanier

Cayo de Piedra

La
Reforma

Punta
del Este

Playa Largo

Cayo San
Juan

Cayo Matías

Cayo
Campos

Cayo
Cantiles

Archipiélago de los Canarreos

Cayo
Tablones

Cayo Pasaje

Cayo Divisa
de Piedra

Cayo del
Rosario

Cayo Largo

Caribbean Sea

Punta
Gorda

Cayo Las
Gordas

Cayo Juan
Ruiz

Refugio de fauna Santo
Tomás y Las Salinas

Ciénaga de Zapata

Maneadero

Santo
Tomás

Cayo del
Macio

Cayo Blanco
del Sur

Cayería de
Diego Pérez

Cayo de
Rabihorcado

Cayería de
Diego Pérez

N

0 km   10
0 miles 10

The Islands Introduction

★ Don't miss...

1 Punta Francés The underwater scenery in the marine reserve is marvellous and some of the best dive sites in the Caribbean are here, page 376.

2 Finca El Abra The national hero, José Martí, spent his exile at this farm where there is now a museum, page 373.

3 Presidio Modelo Political opponents to the dictatorship, including Fidel Castro and the Moncada rebels, were incarcerated in this 'model prison', page 373.

4 Cueva del Punta del Este The most important Amerindian drawings in the Caribbean can be found here, page 374.

5 Cayo Largo Charter a yacht and sail around the cays or make the most of the beach life and watersports, page 378.

Ins and outs

Getting there

Air There are daily flights from Havana which connect with international flights, notably from 15 Mexican cities. Cayo Largo del Sur can be reached by air from other resort areas such as Varadero. **Sea** You can also get to Isla de la Juventud by sea, via the ferry or catamaran, but Cayo Largo del Sur can only be reached by sea if you have your own boat. ▸▸ *For further details, see Isla de la Juventud below and Cayo Largo page 378.*

Getting around

Road Hired car or taxi is the usual method of transport, unless you book a tour through an agency. There are several public buses on Isla de la Juventud. If you are not in a hurry you can pick up a horse-drawn *coche*, or go by bicycle. The south of Isla de la Juventud is an exclusion zone and you need a permit to enter. **Sea** There is no inter-island transport and to get from the Isla to Cayo Largo you need a private yacht.

Tourist information

Rumbos and **Ecotur** agencies on Isla de la Juventud are good for information and tours. The hotels on Cayo Largo have *burós de turismo* and **Cubanacán, Cubatur, Havanatur** and **Rumbos** are all represented. The website www.cayolargodelsur.cu has a section on the Isla, although most of it is on Cayo Largo, worth investigating.

Best time to visit

The driest time of year is between December and April. From June you can expect increased humidity and rain, with the risk of tropical storms or hurricanes from September until November. There is usually a sea breeze at any time of year to cool things down and the islands are not as hot as the mother island of Cuba.

Isla de la Juventud

Sleeping
El Colony 1

Isla de la Juventud

The Isla de la Juventud (Isle of Youth) is in the Gulf of Batabanó, 97 km from the main island. Much of the island is flat, with a large area taken up with swamp in the Ciénaga de Lanier in the southern half of the island. The northern half is more hospitable and here there are marble hills near the capital, Nueva Gerona, and the slate hills of Sierra del Cañada in the west. The area around the Presidio is particularly beautiful, with its low green hills and citrus plantations. Mangroves line much of the coast, a haven for wildlife and migrating birds. The south coast's white-sand beaches are currently inaccessible but are zoned for tourism development, though not in the short term. There is, so far, no infrastructure and the area can be visited only with official permission, but roads are virtually non-existent. The beaches on the west coast have black sand. ▶▶ For Sleeping, Eating and other listings, see pages 375-377.

Ins and outs

Getting there The Rafael Cabrera airport (GER) is nearly 5 km from town and there are daily scheduled 40-minute **flights** from Havana in **Cubana Antonov AN-24** (or AN-26 turbo prop) aircraft. An interesting way of getting to the island is by the passenger **ferry** or **catamaran** from Surgidero de Batabanó on the mainland south coast. There is a morning crossing and a midday crossing. The early morning ferry takes three hours, and the catamaran one hour, US$11. Do not even think about visiting the Isla, as it is known, without booking your transport off the island again. The plane and ferry are totally oversubscribed and security has been quadrupled since two attempted hijacks in March 2003. ▶▶ See also Transport, page 377.

Getting around Travel to anywhere on the island can be difficult although nearly every car will turn into a **taxi** on request. Fares within Nueva Gerona and to main hotels are about US$2. The best way to see the island is to hire a **private car** with a driver/guide, which costs about US$60-90 a day depending on the season. It is worthwhile renting a car and driver/guide simply for the drive as there are some particularly beautiful areas with green rolling hills and citrus plantations. A good day's sightseeing will take in the Model Prison, the crocodile farm and the **Hotel El Colony**, where you can hire a kayak for an hour. If you hope to see the whole island, plan to spend more than a weekend, particularly if you want to see all the caves. Roads are generally in good condition. **Motorbike hire** from the hotels is US$7 per hour. Local transport is often by **horse and cart** (recommended for short distances), the drivers are willing to show you the sights and give you an impromptu history lesson. You cannot drive south of Cayo Piedra into the military exclusion zone without a permit, which can be obtained from **Ecotur** and **Rumbos**, see below. **Ecotur**, is recommended as a means of getting around the island, with trips to the south and chances of spotting a wild orchid that smells like chocolate.

History

The Isla was always an enclave, whether populated by pirates post-Columbus, or by US businessmen and communities of Japanese farmers in the first quarter of the 20th century. In recent decades, its population has been swelled by tens of thousands of Cuban and Third World students, giving rise to the modern name of **Isle of Youth**. Early aboriginal inhabitants called it Camaraco, Ahao or Siguanea. The abundant pine and later casuarina (Australian pine) trees gave rise it the name Isla de Pinos (Isle of Pines), by which it was known officially before the revolutionary authorities renamed it, and local inhabitants (and their baseball team) are still called *pineros* by other Cubans. It earned its place in world literature as the supposed model for Robert Louis Stevenson's *Treasure Island*. Yet another, unofficial, name, La Isla de las Cotorras (Island of the Parrots) is a reminder of just one of the feathered species that inhabit the island's pinewoods, though the Ciénaga de Lanier marshland extending east–west across the island is the chief magnet for ornithologists. Columbus named the island San Juan Evangelista (St John the Evangelist) when he arrived in June 1494. In the 16th and 17th centuries its use as a base by French and British pirates (including Welshman Henry Morgan who later gained respectability as governor of Jamaica) earned it another name, the Isla de Piratas (Isle of Pirates).

Place names like Estero de los Corsarios date from that era, as does Punta Francés, the lair of the French pirate Leclerc. Francis Drake also fought the Spaniards in the surrounding seas, and wrecked galleons from this era add interest to modern-day diving. The biggest draw, however, is the superb coral reef, acclaimed by Jacques Cousteau and others. Spain colonized the island in the 19th century, naming it Colonia Reina Amalia, but from the 19th century until the Revolution its main function was as a prison and both José Martí and Fidel Castro served time there.

After the Revolution, youth brigades were mobilized to plant citrus. Schools for international students, mostly from Africa (Mozambique, Angola, South Africa, Ethiopia) and Vietnam were built along the highway. Students started their studies at secondary level and returned to their countries at technical or postgraduate level. Their education was free. Students were taught on the basis of work and study and contributed to citrus cultivation. All the schools are now closed. Now the major economic activities are citrus cultivation and processing (in conjunction with Chilean capital), marble quarrying (mainly for tourism and export), fishing and tourism. The Delita mine has estimated deposits of 1,750,000 oz of gold and close to 14,000,000 oz of silver. The Isla is the centre of administration for the 2,398-sq-km 'Special Municipality', which includes Cayo Largo and the Archipiélago de los Canarreos.

Nueva Gerona → *Colour map 1, grid C5.*

The capital, Nueva Gerona, dates from the 19th century and remains the only substantial settlement. Surrounded by small rounded hills, it is a pleasant, laid-back country town with a slow pace. The recent proliferation of private tourist-related businesses means that it is not as isolated as it used to be. Most development has taken place post-1959 (the island's entire population was just 10,000 in 1959), so there are few historically interesting buildings. The town centre is set out on the grid system where each block is about 100 m, with even-numbered streets running east–west and odd numbered ones north–south. The **Río Las Casas** runs through the town heading northwards out to sea; this has traditionally been the main route to the Cuban mainland. The boat that served as a ferry from the 1920s until 1974, *El Pinero*, has been preserved by the river at the end of Calle 28. It ferried Castro off the island when Batista's amnesty secured his release.

Sights

The **Parque Central** is two blocks west of the river, between Calles 28 and 30, and 37 and 39. The Parque attracts 'retired' men during the day and comes alive at night; it is also a good place to enquire about cars and guides. Ask anyone, as everyone has a contact. The church of **Nuestra Señora de los Dolores** is on the north side of the square. A church was first built on this site in 1853 but was blown away by a hurricane in 1926. The present one, in colonial style, was built in 1929. Padre Guillermo Sardiñas, parish priest here in the 1950s, was the only priest to join Fidel Castro on his revolutionary campaign in the Sierra Maestra, leaving the Isla in 1957 to take up arms. The **Museo Municipal** ① *Calle 30 entre 37 y Martí (39), on the south side of the Parque Central,*

T46-323791, Mon-Fri 0900-2200, Sun 0900-1300, US$1, is housed in the former Casa de Gobierno, built in 1853, one of the oldest buildings on the island. It has a small historical collection of items of local interest.

To make the most of a day in town, you could ask the local ICAP (Cuban Institute for Friendship with the Peoples) office to arrange visits to places of social interest, where the rarity of visitors ensures a genuine welcome. A visit to the pottery, **Fábrica de Cerámica**, on Calles 37 y 30, near *Coppelia*, whose design department seems to be stuck in a time-warp, should be considered a last resort.

The **Museo de la Lucha Clandestina** ① *Calle 24 entre 43 y 45, Tue-Sat 0900-1700, Sun 0800-1200*, has a collection of photos and other material relating to the Revolution and the uprising against the dictator, Batista. The **Planetario y Museo de Ciencias Naturales** ① *Calle 41 4625 y 54, T46-323143, Tue-Thu 0800-1900, Fri 1400-2200, Sat 1300-1700, Sun 0900-1300, US$2*, has exhibits relating to the natural history, geology and archaeology of the island, with a replica of the cave painting.

Around Nueva Gerona

Outside the town, 3 km west just off the road to La Demajagua, is **Casa Museo Finca El Abra** ① *Tue-Sat 0900-1630, Sun 0900-1300, US$2, US$1 camera*. The excellent guide is Rolando Fonseca. Spanish only spoken. There are two white posts at the entrance otherwise it is not signed. It is a pleasant walk from town or take a horse-drawn *coche*. This is where José Martí came on 13 October 1870, after serving one year of a six-year sentence in prison in Havana. His father knew the finca owner, José María Sardá and his wife Trinidad Valdés Amador de Sardá and Sardá knew people in government. Martí's transfer to the finca was arranged on condition he did not leave it. He returned to Havana on 18 December 1870. In 1926 a hurricane destroyed the finca, which is in a lovely setting with a backdrop of hills, approached along an avenue of oak trees, and so most of it is not original. However, the floor of Martí's bedroom is original. You can see the contents of the house and kitchen and some of Martí's belongings. The 96 descendants of the Catalan military man-turned-finca owner still live in the area, some of them actually living at the finca. There are plenty of exhibits relating to the finca and the life of Martí but it's much more interesting if you speak Spanish as the guide can bring the exhibits to life, especially the stories about the love triangle that Martí found himself in between his wife-to-be and a Guatemalan lady.

About 4 km east of Nueva Gerona is the **Presidio Modelo** (the Model Prison) ① *Reparto Chacón, T46-325112, Tue-Sat 0900-1630, Sun 0900-1300, US$2, US$1 camera*, built 1925-32 by the dictator Gerardo Machado to a high-security 'panopticon' design first developed by Jeremy Bentham in 1791 to give total surveillance and control of the inmates. It is a sinister and impressive sight of huge circular buildings, very atmospheric, especially towards dusk and, although the building is now decaying, you can still imagine the horrors of incarceration here. You can wander around the guard towers and circular cell blocks and see the numbered, tiered cells. The four circulars had 465 cells with two men to a cell. On the sixth floor of each circular were 15 punishment cells. Men would be placed naked in the cell for nine days without bread or water and then sent to work outside. The circular in the centre was the dining room. All the wooden tables have been removed, but the metal supports remain. They randomly creak and moan which is horribly eerie.

Pictures, beds and belongings have been carefully preserved. Inmates have included many fighters in the independence struggle, 350 Japanese Cuban internees in the Second World War, and Fidel Castro and fellow Moncada rebels imprisoned 1953-55. Fidel and the other Moncada prisoners were held for 19 months in the medical wing, which is now the museum. Replacement beds have been installed and each bed is accompanied by a photograph and a potted history of all the Moncadistas including details of whether they are still alive. Fidel was removed from this wing to a separate room after singing to Batista through a window on one of his visits. Fidel's bed is not the original but the bathroom with the chink of light with which Fidel read and wrote are authentic. Castro returned in 1959 to propose the development projects which were to transform it into the Isle of Youth. He closed the prison in 1967 and it became a school for a while before being turned into a museum.

The **Balneario Santa Rita** at Santa Fé, T46-397961, is scheduled to open in April 2004 with full services for tourists including two thermal pools. Also in April an **Aldea Aboriginal** is going to be built nearby as well as a **Jardín de Cactus**. Close to Santa Fé is **La Jungla de Jones** ① *Tue-Sun 0900-1700, US$2.* North Americans Harry Jones and Helen Rodwan came to the island in 1902 to set up a botanical garden with a wide range of trees from around the world. One of the most beautiful areas is a natural, bamboo cathedral. Mr Jones died in 1938 in an accident and Mrs Jones was murdered in 1960 by escapees from the Presidio Modelo.

Playa Paraíso is a white-sand beach in the north of the island with a restaurant, which is a little nicer, but not much, than **Playa Bibijagua**, which has black sand. You will be hassled on the beach here. The only hotel there is now a shell but there is a small café in the grounds, otherwise there are no facilities.

The **Cueva del Punta del Este** ① *59 km southeast of Nueva Gerona, transport by rental car or by an organized excursion,* contains paintings attributed to the original Siboney inhabitants. They were discovered in 1910 by a shipwrecked French sailor and contain 235 pictures on the walls and ceilings, painted long before the arrival of the Spanish. They are considered the most important pictographs in the Caribbean

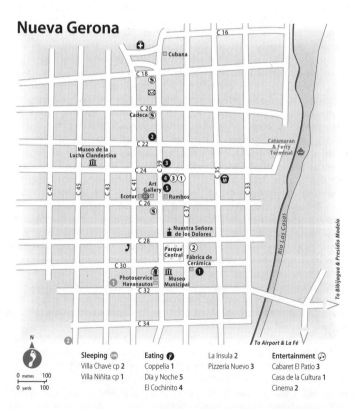

Nueva Gerona

The Islands Isla de la Juventud

N

0 metres 100
0 yards 100

To Bibijagua & Presidio Modelo

To Airport & La Fé

Río Las Casas

Cubana

C 16
C 18
C 20
Cadeca
C 22
Museo de la Lucha Clandestina
C 24
C 39
Art Gallery
Ecotur
Rumbos
C 26
C 37
Nuestra Señora de los Dolores
C 28
Parque Central
Fábrica de Cerámica
C 30
Photoservice Havanautos
Museo Municipal
C 32
C 34
Catamaran & Ferry Terminal
C 35
C 33
C 47
C 45
C 43
C 41

Sleeping
Villa Chave cp **2**
Villa Niñita cp **1**

Eating
Coppelia **1**
Día y Noche **5**
El Cochinito **4**

La Insula **2**
Pizzería Nuevo **3**

Entertainment
Cabaret El Patio **3**
Casa de la Cultura **1**
Cinema **2**

and have been declared a national monument. It is believed that they might represent a solar calendar. There are seven caves in total.

Well worth a visit is the **Cocodrilo** crocodile farm ① *US$3*, a one-hour drive (any car) south and west from Nueva Gerona, including several kilometres of dirt road. You have a guided tour by the knowledgeable caretakers (in Spanish) of the hatchery and the breeding pens where the crocodiles stay for 4-5 years until they are released.

🛏 Sleeping

Nuevo Gerona *p372, map p374*
The best option price-wise is to stay in *casas particulares*. People will approach you at the ferry dock, or at the bus terminal in Havana (they will get a commission), so don't fret if you haven't reserved.

Hotels
C-D **Rancho el Tesoro**,1 km south of Nueva Gerona, in woods close to the Río Las Casas, T46-323035. 60 rooms in blocks. Unappealing no pool but you can use the one at Villa Isla.
D **Villa Isla** (Gaviota), on the outskirts of Nueva Gerona on the road to La Fé beside the river, T46-323290. The foyer wins the ugliest and strangest foyer in Cuba award but the pool is great. 20 rooms, single and triple available, extra cots for children, a/c, fridge, TV, phone, pool where national swimming team trains, poolside bar, restaurants, squash court and gymnasium, disco Thu-Sun 2130-0400, techno music, young crowd, dance and aerobics classes advertized, the nicest dollar place to stay if you are not diving or on a package, Havanautos for car and motorcycle rental.

Casas particulares
F **Villa Chave**, Calle 45 3406 entre 34 y 36, T46-324292. Run by the kind family of Isabel y Onil. Good breakfasts and enormous suppers. Bathroom is shared between the 2 rented rooms.
F **Villa Niñita**, Calle 32 4110 entre 41 y 43, T46-321255, zerep@web.correosdecuba.cu Run by the friendly Viviana y Alina Pérez Castanedo. Occasionally their father Gilberto, a charming and interesting man, is there. Excellent self-contained apartment above family home with separate entrance and kitchen and terrace with great views.

Around Nueva Gerona *p373, map p370*
C-E **El Colony** (Marinas Puertosol), T46-398282/398181, www.cuba.tc/Cuba Scuba_PuertoSol_Colony.html 40 mins by road from Nueva Gerona's small airport, very isolated, once part of the Hilton chain, established as a diving hotel before Cuba reappeared on the world tourist map, diving centre with access to 56 buoyed diving locations. Swimming and snorkelling not great because of shallow water and sea urchins, you have to wade a long way before it is deep enough to swim, but beach is white sand. 77 a/c rooms in main block and *cabañas*, in need of renovation, single and triple available, discounts for stays of over a week, TV. Lovely setting, pool, 3 restaurants, snack bar, store, basket ball, volleyball, tennis and squash courts, horseriding, disco Saturdays 2100-0600, car rental, excursions, busy with package tourists, so accommodation could be hard to find. It has its own bus service, US$3.

🍴 Eating

Nuevo Gerona *p372, map p374*
Restaurants
There are very few *paladares*. The best bet is to eat in your *casa particular*, where you can get an excellent meal for US$5-6. At the **Mercado Agropecuario** at Calles 24 y 35, you can get fresh fruit and vegetables and there are a few basic places to eat in this area where you can pay in pesos.
$$-$ **Cabaret El Dragón**, Calles 39 y 26, Mon-Thu 1600-2200, Fri-Sun 1600-0030. Chinese and Cuban food, bar, cabaret at weekends, deluxe atmosphere, upscale crowd.
$$-$ **El Cochinito**, Calles 39 y 24. State run, daily 1400-2200, specializes in pork with dishes ranging from US$1-9. There's an airy

📌 *While in prison, Fidel wrote* La Historia Me Absolverá *on cards that he had been sent by his family. He wrote in between the lines with lemon juice and sent them back to his family who would iron them to make the writing appear.*

dining room but food displayed in a cabinet at the entrance looks really unappetizing. You can sit on real cowskin chairs though.
$$-$ La Insula, Calles 22 y 39, Sun-Fri 1530-2230, Sat 1530-2100, café open Sun-Fri 1200-0130, Sat 1200-2100. Probably the most upmarket place in town and popular with travellers. The food is of a high standard and the staff are friendly. You might want to avoid the karaoke nights as the staff will try and get you to join in!
$$-$ Pizzeria Nuevo Virgínia, Calles 24 y 39. Pizzas, hot dogs, friendly.
$ Coppelia, Calles 37 y 32. Ice cream.
$ Día y Noche, Calle 39 entre 24 y 26, open 24 hours. *Bocaditos* for a dollar and fried chicken for US$1.10.

◑ Bars

Nuevo Gerona *p372, map p374*
Casa de los Vinos, Calles 20 y 41, Mon-Wed 1400-2200, Fri-Sun 1400-2400. Popular peso drinking spot with grapefruit, melon, tomato and grape wines, last orders 2300, so order early, wine served in earthenware jugs, advisable to take glasses, avoid the snacks.
Taberna Gerona, Calles 39 y 22, daily 1100-2100. Cuban food and pub atmosphere, very friendly, strictly pesos.

◉ Entertainment

Nuevo Gerona *p372, map p374*
Cabaret El Patio, Calle 24 entre 37 y 39, daily 2100-0200, cabaret, 2 shows nightly at weekends, at 2200 and 0100, entry US$3, US$10, Fri, Sat, Sun, lots of Cubans.
Casa de la Cultura, Calles 37 y 24. Check the schedule posted outside for dance events.
La Movida, Calle 34 entre 18 y 20. Outdoor disco, US$3, Cubans pay in pesos, young student crowd, starts at 2200.
Villa Gaviota, Thu-Sun, 2130-0400, entry US$1. Disco, cave-like atmosphere, picks up after midnight, young crowd, techno music.

◉ Festivals

Mar Nueva Gerona has a grapefruit festival and week-long fiesta around 13 Mar which marks the end of the US hold on the island (13 Mar 1926).

◓ Shopping

Nuevo Gerona *p372, map p374*
Art For local artwork there is the **Centro de Desarrollo de las Artes Visuales**, Calles 39 y 26. **Bookshops Librería Frank País**, Calles 22 y 39. Mostly Spanish books.
Handicrafts Mercado Artesanal at Calles 24 y 35. **Photography Photoservice** Calle 39 entre 30 y 32, T46-324640.

▲ Activities and tours

Diving
For diving information contact the **Hotel Colony**, see above. The **Centro Internacional de Buceo El Colony** has excellent facilities including underwater photography, and there is a recompression chamber. All dives are boat dives and, as most of the sites are quite a long way from the marina, lunch is usually on board before your second dive. The area around **Punta Francés** in the west is probably the best, with caves, tunnels and all manner of sea creatures including turtles, which are protected. There are over 40 different corals and innumerable fish. The area is a marine reserve; you may only dive with an official operator. **Ecotur**, see tour operators below, offers cheap accommodation and diving deals.

Fishing
Fishing is not allowed in the marine reserve, but the **Marina El Colony**, below, can arrange for a fishing trip to the south of the island.

Marina
Marina El Colony has mooring for 15 boats, maximum draft 2.5m, VHF channels 16, 19, 68 and 72, a liveaboard, *Spondylus*, with a capacity for 10 divers and other facilities. Watersports are available, such as catamarans, US$10 per hr, a 2-person kayak, US$6 per hr and a single kayak, US$4 per hr.

Tour operators
Ecotur, Calle 26 entre 39 y 41, T46-327101, ecoturisla@hotmail.com www.cayolargodelsur.cu/ecotur/home.htm daily 0800-1700. Trips to the south of the island include La Cañada, Los Indios, El Cocodrilo, Punta del Este, Rincón del Guanal, Jacksonville, with chances to see chocolate scented wild orchids and the tocororo bird plus deer. Prices are US$12.50-15

per person if you have a car or they can hire you a car for US$65-67.50 per day. If more than 4 people a minibus needs to be hired. All trips must be booked at least 1 day in advance because permits must be secured for visits to the southern part of the island. Also sells tours for **Hotel Colony** at cheaper prices: seafari, snorkelling, diving and you can take advantage of the hotel's transport service, US$3. Internet US$5 per hr, flights arranged. Guides speak English, Italian, French and German and are all naturalists. Run by the helpful Neray Pavel.

Rumbos, Calles 39 y 26, T46-323947. Sells permits to visit the southern part of the island as well as standard tour agency services.

⊖ Transport

Air

Rafael Cabrera airport (GER), T46-322690. There are 2 or 3 scheduled 40-min flights a day from **Havana**. Daily at 0600 and 1750 (the latter connecting with flights from 15 **Mexican cities**, Mon, Wed, Fri Sun also at 1415. They return at 1210, 1900 and 1525 respectively, so you could do a day trip if you wanted. Fare US$32 1 way, book in advance. **Aerotaxi** to **Pinar del Río** like a flying bus, but suspended in 2003 because of hijacking. **Airlines** Cubana at Calle 39 1415 entre 16 y 18, Nueva Gerona, T46-324259, Mon-Fri 0800-1600, closed 1300-1400. Aerotaxi at airport, T46-322300.

Bus

Buses run to **La Fé**, the **Hotel Colony**, **Playa Bibijagua**, and there is a bus marked 'Servicio Aereo', which runs between the **airport** and the cinema in Nueva Gerona, but don't rely on any of these to run on a regular basis.

Car hire

Havanautos has an office in Nueva Gerona at Calles 32 y 39, T46-324432, but the dollar hotels also have car hire desks, daily 0700-1900. Between US$70-87 a day with insurance. **Petrol stations** Cupet-Cimex fuel station is at Calles 39 y 30.

Ferry/catamaran

From the side entrance of the main bus station in Vedado, Havana, there is a little booth for the company **Viajero**. Either ring for instructions, T7-8781841, which is advisable to

check times and to find out whether you need to go the day or several days beforehand because of availability problems (In Batabanó, T62-83845). If you turn up on the departure day you will need to be there at 0900 to collect a valueless ticket for which you must have your passport. Then you need to return to the office window for a bus pass at 1140. The bus leaves at 1230 and arrives at 1330. The scheduled ferry/ catamaran departure is at 1400. You may or may not need to pay the 2 peso bus fare there and back depending on the *chofer*. At the port, there are some small buildings to the right of the waiting room area where you need to go to buy your passage in dollars, US$11, 1 way. From there you and everyone else will be checked, rechecked, checked and checked again. There is a 20-kg weight limit and they are fairly strict about it. You will also have to pass your stuff through an X-ray machine. Bring all food and drink as the Cuban cafeteria will not sustain you (unless you imagine cigarettes will) should you suffer delays because of the boats which is common. If you have not organized your return trip, which is highly inadvisable, you need to go to **Agencia Sta María**, Oficina de Correo, Calle 53 entre 39 a y 8, Mercado de Abel, in Nueva Gerona, T46-322270. This is where boat tickets are sold in dollars but only from 1400. You cannot obtain dollar tickets at the port unless in an extreme emergency. There is a return ferry (with cold a/c but a film showing to pacify you) or catamaran at 0700 and 1200. Because of 2 hijackings of planes in March 2003 security is tight with the counter-revolutionary police (Brigada Especial) on all transport. This contributes to delays.

Taxi

Turistaxi, at Hotel El Colony, T46-398282.

⊕ Directory

Nuevo Gerona *p372, map p374*

Banks Banco de Crédito and Comercio, Calles 39 y 18, Mon-Fri 0800-1500. **Caja Popular de Ahorro**, Calles 39 y 26, Mon-Fri 0800-1700. **Cadeca**, Calles 20 y 39, Mon-Sat 0830-1800, Sun 0830-1200. **Pharmacy** Calles 39 y 24, Mon-Fri 0800-2200, Sat 0800-1600. Take plenty of insect repellent, particularly if you are heading for the Ciénaga or out to the Hotel Colony.

Cayo Largo → *Colour map 2, grid.*

Cayo Largo is at the eastern end of the Archipiélago de los Canarreos, 114 km east of Isla de la Juventud and 80 km south of the Península de Zapata. It is a long, thin, coral island, 26 km long and no more than 2 km wide. There are beautiful white sandy beaches protected by a reef, all along the southern coast which, together with the crystal clear, warm waters of the Caribbean, make it ideal for tourism. A string of hotels lines the southern tip of the island and these are practically the only employers on the island so that its economy depends entirely on tourism. The northern coast is mostly mangrove and swamp, housing hungry mosquitoes as well as numerous birds (pelicans being the most visible) and iguanas. There are few Cubans on the island and the westernized, "all-inclusive" nature of the place doesn't really recommend it to anyone wanting to see Cuba. On the other hand, if you want a few days on the beach with nothing but watersports to entertain you, then you should enjoy the resort.▸▸ For Sleeping, Eating and other listings, see pages 379-380.

Ins and outs

Getting there and around **Flights** come in from Milan, Frankfurt, Toronto and Montréal and there are daily flights to and from Havana with weekly **excursions** from other tourist centres, such as Varadero, Cienfuegos, Pinar del Río, Trinidad and Santiago de Cuba. A day trip from Havana is US$109 including transfers and lunch but you have to pay extra for watersports and boat trips; a two-day, one-night package with meals, drinks, transfers and a half-day snorkelling excursion costs US$185. You can hire a **car** or **bicycle** from your hotel to explore Cayo Largo, or book a place on an organized **tour** to see the island and some of the smaller cays.▸▸ *For further details, see Transport page 380.*

Tourist information There are tourist information bureaux in the hotels which will sell you excursions and tell you whatever you need to know. For online information, www.cayolargodelsur.cu

Around the island

The best beach on the island is **Playa Sirena**, which faces west and is spared any wind or currents, which sometimes affect the southern beaches. It is also spared any hotels along its 2 km of white sand and so everyone comes on a day trip. Snorkelling and scuba diving can be done at Playa Sirena, 10 minutes' boat ride from the hotels, and there is a

Cayo Largo

Sleeping	Sol Club Cayo Largo 5	Villa Coral 4	Villa Marinera 3
Isla del Sur 1	Sol Pelícano 2	Villa Lindamar 6	Villa Soledad 7

restaurant for lunch. Snorkelling is also good further east at **Playa Los Cocos,** which you can reach by bicycle. If there is a problem with the weather and the currents become dangerous, red flags will be flown to forbid swimming. Turtles lay their eggs at **Playa Tortuga** in the northeast, and there is a turtle farm at Combinado northwest of the airstrip. Tame iguanas can be spotted at another nearby cay, **Cayo Rico** (day trips available from Cayo Largo) and also on the appropriately named **Cayo Iguana**. Hotel expansion is planned to cater for watersport tourism. **Cayos Rosario** and **Avalos,** between Juventud and Largo, have not yet been developed.

◉ Sleeping

All the hotels are all-inclusive and good-value package deals can be arranged from abroad as well as from Havana. Prices are only a guide. Packages can be as low as US$400 per person for 4 nights, including air and ground transport from Havana. You may have to wear a coloured plastic bracelet to indicate which package you are on. Prices include 3 meals and free use of all water sports and other activities such as tennis, horseriding and volleyball. Always check what is included in your package. Medical facilities, laundry, Post Office and fax services are all available. For more information, www.barcelo.com www.grancaribe.cu www.solmeliacuba.com There is no private accommodation on the island and you will not need any pesos.

LL Barceló Cayo Largo del Sur Resort, comercial.cl@solymar.gca.tur.cu Opened December 2003. 4 star, 306 luxury rooms with every comfort and amenity.

L Sol Club Cayo Largo, T45-48260, director.comercial.sol@solmeliacuba.com 296 cool blue, huge rooms with balconies and all the facilities for an active beach holiday you could imagine: diving, snorkelling, swimming pools for adults or children, tennis, volleyball, football, archery, bowls, boules, indoor games, gymnasium; and things to pamper yourself: Jacuzzi, turkish bath, massage, beauty parlour. Also several restaurants and bars, currency exchange, tour desk, car rental and taxis.

L Sol Pelícano, T45-48333, jefe.reservas.spl@solmeliacuba.com 307 rooms colourfully renovated by Sol Hotels, bright and cheerful with a huge pool and all the same facilities as the sister hotel. Good for families and scuba divers.

L Villa Lindamar, T45-48111, reserva@isla.cls.tur.cu One of the older developments, 4 star, A-frame thatched rooms.

L-AL Isla del Sur/Eden Village, T45-48111, www.edenviaggi.it A smaller 3-star hotel with only 57 rooms, 1 of the first to be built but recently updated and repainted. Large rooms with balconies and 2 double beds. Lots of sports and entertainment and the usual facilities. Run in conjunction with **Villa Coral,** see below.

L-AL Villa Coral/Eden Village, T45-48111, reserva@isla.cls.tur.cu 3 star, 55 rooms, à la carte restaurant.

L-AL Villa Soledad, T45-48111, reserva@isla.cls.tur.cu 24 rooms, 3 star, only a buffet restaurant here and limited facilities on site.

AL Villa Marinera, T45-48213, gcom@puertosol.cls.tur.cu 10 rooms in log cabins with veranda, 3-star, good sunset watching with view over sea.

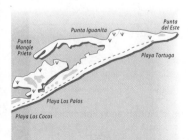

◐ Eating

There are several buffet restaurants and thatched snack bars (*ranchones*) attached to the hotels. The food is quite good and plentiful. À la carte restaurants have to be booked. You will not find any *paladares* here but there is lots of lobster. Alcoholic drinks are included in the all-inclusive package. Most of the cocktails are rum-based and sweet. Frequently essential ingredients are not available. Beer is often the best bet.

⊕ Entertainment

There is usually evening entertainment in the hotels.
D'prisa 'Diego Grillo', T45-48305, open 2000-0200, taped and traditional music.
Taberna El Pirata, T45-48213, Bar open 24 hrs, taped and traditional music.

▲ Activities and tours

Diving
Good but perhaps not as spectacular as in some other areas of Cuba (see Diving and marine life, page 63). There is an extensive reef with gorgonians, sponges and lots of fish, while north of the island you will find large pelagics. Diving, snorkelling and glass bottom boats are all available. Hotels will arrange diving through **Marina Puertosol**, see below.

Fishing
There is deep sea fishing for marlin and other big fish, with international fishing tournaments held here. Contact the marina, see below.

Marina
The **Marina Puertosol Cayo Largo del Sur** at Combinado has 50 moorings for visiting yachts, who don't have to buy a tourist card to come here if they are not going on to anywhere else in Cuba, because the island is a free port. To clear customs, call the marina on VHF 6, or maritime security (*seguridad marítima*) on VHF 16. T45-48213, gcom@puertosol.cls.tur.cu There are showers, laundry service, restaurant and bar for yachties.

Sailing
Sailing is popular and there is a bareboat yacht charter fleet, available by the day for longer rental. Other watersports include windsurfing, kayaking, jet skis, catamarans, and banana rides.

Tour operators
Cubanacán, Villa Coral, T45-48280, cbcanviajes@cayolargo.cls.tur.cu
Cubatur, Isla del Sur, T45-48126, amael@cubatur.cls.tur.cu
Havanatur, Villa Soledad, T45-48215, olgapu@cimex.com.cu
Rumbos, Villa Soledad, T45-48327, rumbos@isla.cls.tur.cu

⊖ Transport

Air
There are several charters and scheduled international flights to Vilo Acuña International airport (CYO). A highlight for some people is the journey there on a 60 year-old Antonov AN-2 bi-plane with a cruising altitude of 1,200 m, very scenic and a wonderful experience, though perhaps not for nervous fliers. **Aerogaviota**, T45-48364, flies from Aeropuerto Playa Baracoa, **Havana**, a former military air base.There are also charter flights from Varadero, or by light plane or boat from **Isla de la Juventud**. **Aerotaxi** at the airport, T45-48364/48100. **Cubana**, T45-48141.

Car hire
Havanautos and **Transautos** at the Hotel Pelícano. Motorcycles, bicycles, and jeeps are also available. **Transtur**, T45-48245, direccion@transtur.cls.tur.cu Scooters for hire at US$7 for 1 hr or US$3 per hr if hiring for more than 3 hrs. Daily rates available. Jeeps for US$22 for 1 hr or US$59 for 12-24 hrs. Daily and weekly rates available, including fuel and insurance. Taxi service at US$0.75 per km.

① Directory

Banks There are no banks but the hotels have currency exchange desks if you need them. Euros and US dollars are accepted everywhere. You will not need Cuban pesos. **Hospitals and clinics** Clínica Internacional, Pueblo Turístico, T45-48238, clinica@cayolargo.cls,tur.cu 24-hr emergency service, X-rays, pharmacy, home visits, massages. Also medical stations at Hotels Pelícano, Sol Club Cayo Largo and Villa Iguana.

Background

⁛ Footprint features

History

Precolumbian society in Cuba

The recorded history of the Caribbean islands begins with the arrival of Christopher Columbus' fleet in 1492. Knowledge of the native peoples who inhabited Cuba before and at the time of his arrival is largely derived from the accounts of contemporary Spanish writers and from archaeological examinations as there is no evidence of indigenous written records.

The Amerindians encountered by Columbus in Cuba and the other Greater Antilles had no overall tribal name but organized themselves in a series of villages or local chiefdoms, each of which had its own tribal name. The name now used, 'Arawak', was not in use then. The term was used by the Amerindians of the Guianas, a group who had spread into Trinidad, but their territory was not explored until nearly another century later. The use of the generic term 'Arawak' to describe the Amerindians Columbus encountered arose because of linguistic similarities with the Arawaks of the mainland. It is therefore surmised that migration took place many centuries before Columbus' arrival, but that the two groups were not in contact at that time. The time of the latest migration from the mainland, and consequently, the existence of the island Arawaks, is in dispute, with some academics tracing it to about the time of Christ (the arrival of the Saladoids) and others to AD 1000 (the Ostionoids).

The inhabitants of Cuba and the other Greater Antilles were generally referred to as Taínos, but there were many sub-groupings. The earliest known inhabitants of the region, the Siboneys, migrated from Florida (some say Mexico) and spread throughout the Bahamas and the major islands. Most archaeological evidence of their settlements has been found near the shore, along bays or streams, where they lived in small groups. The largest discovered settlement has been one of 100 inhabitants in Cuba. They were hunters and gatherers, living on fish and other seafood, small rodents, iguanas, snakes and birds. They gathered roots and wild fruits, such as guava, guanabana and mamey, but did not cultivate plants. They worked with primitive tools made out of stone, shell, bone or wood, for hammering, chipping or scraping, but had no knowledge of pottery. The Siboneys were eventually absorbed by the advance of the Arawaks migrating from the south, who had made more technological advances in agriculture, arts and crafts.

The people now known as Arawaks migrated from the Guianas to Trinidad and on through the island arc to Cuba. Their population expanded because of the natural fertility of the islands and the abundance of fruit and seafood, helped by their agricultural skills in cultivating and improving wild plants and their excellent boat-building and fishing techniques. They were healthy, tall, good looking and lived to a ripe old age. It is estimated that up to 8 million may have lived on the island of Hispaniola alone, but there was always plenty of food for all.

Their society was essentially communal and organized around families. The smaller islands were particularly egalitarian, but in the larger ones, where village communities of extended families numbered up to 500 people, there was an incipient class structure. Typically, each village had a headman, called a *cacique*, whose duty it was to represent the village when dealing with other tribes, to settle family disputes and organize defence. However, he had no powers of coercion and was often little more than a nominal head. The position was largely hereditary, with the eldest son of the eldest sister having rights of succession, but women could and did become *caciques*. In the larger communities, there was some delegation of responsibility to the senior men, but economic activities were usually organized along family lines, and their power was limited.

: Cuba fact file

Population 11,224,321 (2002).

Density 100.9 per sq km.

Birth rate Per 1,000 population 12.08, (2002). Urban 75% (2001). Male 50.1% (2000). Ethnic composition: mixed 51%, white 37%, black 11%, other 1% (1994).

Health Infant mortality 6.2 per 1,000 live births (2001), the lowest in Latin America. 63,642 doctors, one per 176 inhabitants. 7.4 hospital beds per 1,000 inhabitants (1997). Life expectancy (2002), male 74.2 years, female 79.15 years. Caloric intake as % of FAO requirement, 99%.

Language Spanish.

National flower *Mariposa*, butterfly flower, a jasmine, symbol of purity and rebellion in the Wars of Independence.

National bird Tocororo, Cuban trogon, with the red, white and blue colours of the Cuban flag.

National tree Palma real, Royal palm, typical of the Cuban landscape.

Economy Gross national product (market prices) US$25.9 bn (2002), per capita US$2,307 (estimated).

Tourism 1,686,716 visitors (2002).

The division of labour was usually based on age and sex. The men would clear and prepare the land for agriculture and be responsible for defence of the village, while women cultivated the crops and were the major food producers, also making items such as mats, baskets, bowls and fishing nets. Women were in charge of raising the children, especially the girls, while the men taught the boys traditional customs, skills and rites.

The Taínos hunted for some of their food, but fishing was more important and most of their settlements were close to the sea. Fish and shellfish were their main sources of protein and they had many different ways of catching them – from hands, baskets or nets to poisoning, shooting or line fishing. Cassava was a staple food, which they had successfully learned to leach of its poisonous juice. They also grew yams, maize, cotton, arrowroot, peanuts, beans, cacao and spices, rotating their crops to prevent soil erosion.

Cotton was used to make clothing and hammocks (never before seen by Europeans), while the calabash tree was used to make ropes and cords, baskets and roofing. Plants were used for medicinal and spiritual purposes, and cosmetics such as face and body paint. Also important, both to the Arawaks and later to the Europeans, was the cultivation of tobacco, as a drug and as a means of exchange. It is still of major economic importance in Cuba today.

They had no writing, no beasts of burden, no wheeled vehicles and no hard metals, although they did have some alluvial gold for personal ornament. The abundance of food allowed them time to develop their arts and crafts and they were skilled in woodwork and pottery. They had polished stone tools, but also carved shell implements for manioc preparation or as fish hooks. Coral manioc graters have also been found. Their boatbuilding techniques were noted by Columbus, who marvelled at their canoes of up to 75 ft in length, carrying up to 50 people, made of a single tree trunk in one piece. It took two months to fell a tree by gradually burning and chipping it down, and many more to make the canoe.

The Arawaks had three main deities, evidence of which have been found in stone and conch carvings in many of the Lesser Antilles as well as the well-populated Greater Antilles, although their relative importance varied according to the island. The principal male god was Yocahú, yoca being the word for cassava and hú meaning 'giver of'. It is believed that the Amerindians associated this deity's power to provide cassava with the mystery of the volcanoes, for all the carvings – the earliest out of shells and the later ones of stone are conical. The Yocahú cult was wiped out by the Spaniards, but it is thought to have existed from about AD 200.

The main female deity was a fertility goddess, often referred to as Atabeyra, but she is thought to have had several names relating to her other roles as goddess of the moon, mother of the sea, the tides and the springs, and the goddess of childbirth. In carvings she is usually depicted as a squatting figure with her hands up to her chin, sometimes in the act of giving birth.

A third deity is a dog god, named Opiyel-Guaobiran, meaning 'the dog deity who takes care of the souls of the immediately deceased and is the son of the spirit of darkness'. Again, carvings of a dog's head or whole body have been found of shell or stone, which were often used to induce narcotic trances. Many of the carvings have holes and Y-shaped passages which would have been put to the nose to snuff narcotics and induce a religious trance in the shaman or priest, who could then ascertain the status of a departed soul for a recently bereaved relative.

One custom which aroused interest in the Spaniards was the ball game, not only for the sport and its ceremonial features, but because the ball was made of rubber and bounced, a phenomenon that had not previously been seen in Europe. Roman Catholicism soon eradicated the game, but archaeological remains have been found in several islands, notably in Puerto Rico, but also in Hispaniola. Excavations in the Greater Antilles have revealed earth embankments and rows of elongated upright stones surrounding plazas or courts, pavements and stone balls. These are called *bateyes*, *juegos de indios*, *juegos de bola*, *cercados* or *corrales de indios*. Batey was the aboriginal name for the ball game, the rubber ball itself and also the court where it was played. The word is still used to designate the cleared area in front of houses in the country.

The ball game had religious and ceremonial significance but it was a sport and bets and wagers were important. It was played by two teams of up to 20 or 30 players, who had to keep the ball in the air by means of their hips, shoulders, heads, elbows and other parts of their body, but never with their hands. The aim was to bounce the ball in this manner to the opposing team until it hit the ground. Men and women played, but not usually in mixed sex games. Great athleticism was required and it is clear that the players practised hard to perfect their skill, several, smaller practice courts having been built in larger settlements. The game was sometimes played before the village made an important decision, and the prize could be a sacrificial victim, usually a prisoner, granted to the victor.

The Amerindians in Cuba were unable to resist the Spanish invasion and were soon wiped out by disease, cruelty and murder. The Spanish exacted tribute and forced labour while allowing their herds of cattle and pigs to destroy the Amerindians' unfenced fields and clearings. Transportation to the mines resulted in shifts in the native population which could not be fed from the surrounding areas and starvation became common. The 500 years since Columbus' arrival have served to obliterate practically all the evidence of the indigenous civilization in Cuba.

Spanish conquest

Cuba was visited by Cristóbal Colón (Christopher Columbus) during his first voyage to find a westerly route to the Orient on 27 October 1492, and he made another brief stop two years later on his way from Hispaniola to Jamaica. Columbus did not realize it was an island when he landed; he had heard from the inhabitants of the Bahamas, where he first made landfall, that there were larger islands to the south where there was gold, which he hoped was Japan. He arrived on the north coast of 'Colba', but found little gold. He did, however, note the Amerindians' practice of puffing at a large, burning roll of leaves, which they called *tobacos* or *cohiba*.

The Arawaks told Columbus of the more aggressive Carib tribe and he headed off towards the eastern islands to find them, discovering *La Isla Española*, or Hispaniola, which occupied the Spanish for the next few years with attempted settlements, feuds, rebellions and other troubles. On future expeditions, more settlers were brought from Spain to Hispaniola; adventurers who wanted to get rich quick and return to Spain. Although most died of tropical diseases, enough survived to impart their own European viruses on the Amerindians, decimating the local population. The Spaniards also demanded a constant supply of Amerindian labour which they were ill equipped to provide, having previously lived in a subsistence barter economy with no experience of regular work. The Spaniards' cruel treatment of the native inhabitants led to many of them losing the will to live. On the other hand, the need for a steady supply of labour pushed the Spanish into further exploration of the Indies. Slavers went from one island to another in search of manpower. Puerto Rico was conquered in 1508, Jamaica in 1509 and Cuba in 1511. From there they moved on to the mainland to trade in slaves, gold and other commodities.

Cuba was first circumnavigated by Sebastián de Ocampo in 1508, but it was **Diego Velázquez** who conquered it in 1511 and founded several towns, called *villas*, including Havana. From Cuba, Velázquez sent out two expeditions in 1517-18 to investigate the Yucatán and the Gulf of Mexico. On the basis of their information he petitioned the Spanish Crown for permission to set up a base there prior to conquest and settlement. However, before the authorization came through from Spain, his commander, Hernán Cortés, set off without permission with 600 men, 16 horses, 14 cannon and 13 muskets to conquer Mexico, leaving Velázquez in the lurch.

The first African slaves were imported to Cuba in 1526. Sugar was introduced soon after but was not important until the last decade of the 16th century. When the British took Jamaica in 1655 a number of Spanish settlers fled to Cuba, already famous for its cigars. Tobacco was then made a strict monopoly of Spain in 1717 and a coffee plant was introduced in 1748. The British, under Lord Albemarle and Admiral Pocock, captured Havana and held the island from 1762-63, but it was returned to Spain in exchange for Florida. Up until this point, the colony had been important largely as a refuelling depot for Spanish ships crossing the Atlantic, but the British occupation and the temporary lifting of Spanish restrictions showed the local landowning class the economic potential of trading their commodities with England and North America.

Independence movement

Towards the end of the 18th century, Cuba began its transformation into a slave plantation society. After the French Revolution, there were slave revolts in the French colony of Haiti, which became the first independent black republic. French sugar planters fled what had been the most profitable colony in the Caribbean and settled across the water in Cuba, bringing their expertise with them. Cuba soon became a major sugar exporter and, after 1793, slaves were imported in huge numbers to work the plantations. The island was under absolute military control with a colonial elite that made its money principally from sugar. The tobacco monopoly was abolished in 1816 and Cuba was given the right to trade with the world in 1818. Independence elsewhere in the Spanish Empire bred ambitions, however, and a strong movement for independence was quelled by Spain in 1823. By this time the blacks outnumbered the whites in the island; there were several slave rebellions and little by little the

Creoles (or Spaniards born in Cuba) made common cause with them. On the other hand, there was also a movement for annexation by the USA, Cuba's major trading partner, supported by many slave owners who had a common interest with the southern states in the American Civil War. The defeat of the South and the abolition of slavery in the USA ended support for annexation.

By the 1860s Cuba was producing about a third of the world's sugar and was heavily dependent on African slaves to do so, supplemented by indentured Chinese labourers in the 1850s and 1860s. Although Spain signed treaties under British pressure to outlaw the Atlantic slave trade in 1817 and 1835, they were completely ignored by the colony and an estimated 600,000 African slaves were imported by 1867. Independence from Spain became a burning issue in Cuba as Spain remained intransigent and refused to consider political reforms which would give the colony more autonomy within the empire.

On 10 October 1868, a Creole landowner, **Carlos Manuel de Céspedes**, issued the *Grito de Yara*, a proclamation of independence and a call to arms, while simultaneously freeing his slaves. The first war of independence was a 10-year rebellion against Spain in the eastern part of the island between 1868 and 1878, but it gained little save a modest move towards the abolition of slavery. In 1870, the **Moret Law** freed all children of slaves born after 1868 and any slave over 60, but complete abolition was not achieved until 1886. In 1878, the **Convention of Zanjón** brought the civil war to an end. This enabled Cubans to elect representatives to the Spanish *cortes* (parliament) in 1879, but did not suppress the desire for independence. Many national heroes were created during this period who have become revolutionary icons in the struggle against domination by a foreign power. Men such as de Céspedes, Máximo Gómez and the mulatto General Antonio Maceo have inspired generations of Cuban patriots and are still revered with statues and street names in nearly every town and city on the island. One consequence of the war was the destruction of much agricultural land and the ruin of many sugar planters. US interests began to take over the sugar plantations and the sugar mills and, as sugar beet became more important in Europe, so Cuba became more dependent on the market for its main crop in the USA.

From 1895 to 1898, rebellion flared up again in the second war of independence under the young poet and revolutionary, **José Martí**, who had organized the movement from exile in the USA, together with the old guard of Antonio Maceo and Máximo Gómez. José Martí led the invasion but was killed in an ambush in May 1895 when the war had barely begun, and Maceo was killed in 1896. Despite fierce fighting throughout the island, neither the Nationalists nor the Spanish could gain the upper hand. However, the USA was now concerned for its investments in Cuba and was considering its strategic interests within the region. When the US battleship *Maine* exploded in Havana harbour on 15 February 1898, killing 260 crew, this was made a pretext for declaring war on Spain. Spain offered the independence fighters a truce but they chose instead to help the USA to defeat the colonial power. American forces (which included Colonel Theodore Roosevelt) were landed, a squadron blockaded Havana and defeated the Spanish fleet at Santiago de Cuba. In December 1898 peace was signed and US forces occupied the island. The Nationalists had gained independence from Spain but found themselves under **US military occupation** for four years and then with only limited independence granted to them by the USA.

During the occupation, the USA put the Cuban administration and economy back to rights. It eliminated a famine, introduced improved sanitation and helped to eradicate yellow fever with the scientific discoveries of a Cuban doctor, Carlos J Finlay. State education was introduced, the judiciary was reformed and an electoral system for local and national government was introduced. In 1901, an elected assembly approved a liberal constitution which separated Church and state and guaranteed universal adult male suffrage.

: Our Man in Havana

Graham Greene's first visit to Cuba was in 1957 to research his book *Our Man in Havana*. He was originally going to set it in Lisbon, but decided on a more exotic location; he planned to sell the film rights to the novel before it was even written. He immediately took a liking to the unlimited decadence Havana had to offer, and spent much of his time at the Shanghai Theatre, a club which featured live sex shows. Greene's former connections with the British SIS (Secret Intelligence Service) gave him access to political society. He based some of the characters in 'Our Man' on Batista's soldiers: Captain Segura, with his cigarette case made of human skin, was based on the real-life Capitán Ventura. The plot of the novel involves a vacuum cleaner salesman being mistaken for a secret agent, who for fear of being discovered as a fraud, tries to carry out the orders given to him by providing diagrams of vacuum cleaner parts, pretending they are in fact the plans for an arsenal of nuclear weapons.

Greene's training as a secret agent allowed him to infiltrate all levels of political life: he made contact with Castro's rebel forces in the Sierra, offering them any help they needed. He was asked to smuggle a suitcase of warm clothes, to help them survive the freezing night-time temperatures of the Sierra Maestra, through customs on a Havana-Santiago flight.

In 1959, when Greene arrived for the second time in Havana to assist director Carol Reed in the filming of his novel, the Revolution had already triumphed. Greene's small act of support in 1957 had not been forgotten, and Castro gave his personal seal of approval to the film, although he felt it didn't capture the full extent of Batista's evil.

The **Republic of Cuba** was proclaimed in 1902 and the Government was handed over to its first president, **Tomás Estrada Palma,** the elected candidate of José Martí's Cuban Revolutionary Party, on 20 May. However, the new Republic was constrained by the **Platt Amendment** to the constitution, passed by the US Congress, which clearly made it a protectorate of the USA. The USA retained naval bases at Río Hondo and Guantánamo Bay and reserved the right of intervention in Cuban domestic affairs, but granted the island a handsome import preference for its sugar. The USA intervened several times to settle quarrels by rival political factions but, to quell growing unrest and a reassertion of pro-independence and revolutionary forces, repealed the Platt Amendment in 1934. The USA formally relinquished the right to intervene but retained its naval base at Guantánamo. (The lease on Guantánamo Bay expires in 2033.) Resentment against the USA for its political and economic dominance of the island lingered and was a powerful stimulus for the Nationalist Revolution of the 1950s.

Dictatorship

Even after the repeal of the Platt Amendment, the USA dominated the Cuban economy. Around two thirds of sugar exports went to the USA under a quota system at prices set by Washington; two thirds of Cuba's imports came from the USA; foreign capital investment was largely from the USA and Cuba was effectively a client state. Yet, despite the money being made out of Cuba, its people suffered from grinding rural poverty, high unemployment, illiteracy and inadequate healthcare. The good life, as enjoyed by the socialites in the casinos and bars of

Havana, highlighted the social inequalities in the country and politics was a mixture of authoritarian rule and corrupt democracy.

From 1924 to 1933 the 'strong man' **Gerardo Machado** ruled Cuba. He was elected in 1924 on a wave of popularity and set about diversifying the economy and investing in public works projects. However, a drastic fall in sugar prices in the late 1920s led to strikes and protests which he forcefully repressed. In 1928 he 'persuaded' Congress to grant him a second term of office, which was greeted with protests and violence from students, the middle classes and labour unions. Widespread Nationalist popular rebellion throughout Machado's dictatorship was harshly repressed by the police force. The USA was reluctant to intervene again, but tried to negotiate a deal with its ambassador. The Nationalists called a general strike in protest at US interference and Machado finally went into exile. The violence did not abate, however, and there were more strikes, mob attacks and occupations of factories, which the new government was unable to quell. In September 1933, a revolt of non-commissioned officers including **Fulgencio Batista**, then a sergeant, deposed the government and installed a five-member committee chosen by the student movement, the *Directorio Estudiantil*. They chose as president a professor, **Dr Ramón Grau San Martín**, but he only lasted four months before Batista staged a coup. Batista then held power through presidential puppets until he was elected president himself in 1940.

Batista's first period in power, 1933-44, was characterized by Nationalist and populist policies, set against corruption and political violence. Batista himself was a mulatto from a poor background who had pulled himself up through the ranks of the military and retained the support of the armed forces. He was also supported by US and Cuban business interests while gaining control of the trade unions by passing social welfare legislation, building low cost housing and creating jobs with public works projects. The students and radical Nationalists remained opposed to him, however, and terrorism continued. In 1940, a new Constitution was passed by a constituent assembly dominated by Batista, which included universal suffrage and benefits for workers such as a minimum wage, pensions, social insurance and an eight-hour day.

In 1944, Batista lost the elections to the candidate of the radical Nationalists: Dr Ramón Grau San Martín, of the Partido Revolucionario Cubana-Auténtico, who held office from 1944-48. His presidential term benefited from high sugar prices following the Second World War, which allowed corruption and political violence to continue unabated. Grau was followed into the presidency by his protégé, **Carlos Prío Socarrás**, 1948-52, a term which was even more corrupt and depraved, until Batista, by then a self-promoted general, staged a military coup in 1952. Constitutional and democratic government was at an end. His harshly repressive dictatorship was brought to a close by **Fidel Castro** in January 1959, after an extraordinary and heroic three-year campaign, mostly in the Sierra Maestra, with a guerrilla force reduced at one point to 12 men.

Revolution

The dictator, Batista, was opposed by many, but none more effective than the young lawyer, Fidel Castro, the son of immigrants from Galicia and born in Cuba in 1926. He saw José Martí as his role model and aimed to continue the Revolution Martí had started in 1895, following his ideals. In 1953, the 100th anniversary of José Martí's birth, Castro and a committed band of about 160 revolutionaries attacked the Moncada barracks in Santiago de Cuba on 26 July. The attack failed and although Castro and his brother Raúl escaped, they were later captured and put on trial. Fidel used the occasion to make an impassioned speech, denouncing corruption in the ruling class and the need for political freedom and economic independence. The

⁞ Fidel Castro Ruz

Now in his 70s, Fidel Castro has spent more than half his life as president, *jefe* (chief) and supreme *comandante* of Cuba. He has passed from being the world's youngest ruler in 1959 to the longest serving head of state. He has outstayed eight US presidents and survived hundreds of assassination attempts, and is still non-committal about his future, saying he will stay in office as long as his country needs him. It is reported that he still exercises regularly, swims, scuba dives, plays ball games and works long hours, but his speeches are now shorter, quieter and less passionate. His longest speech went on for seven hours, but Cubans were regularly called upon to listen to his rhetoric for four or five hours. Dramatic pauses have replaced the fire and arm waving of his youth, he moves more slowly and on medical advice has given up his trademark cigar. Rumours circulate of heart troubles and arthritis. Nevertheless, he still travels to international summit meetings and conventions and, in 1996, was received by the Pope in an historic photo opportunity which made him look almost sprightly in comparison with his host. He has always been instantly recognizable for his beard, now thinning and grey, and his military fatigues, although these are now occasionally replaced when abroad by a sober suit.

Castro's father came from Galicia in Spain. Fidel was born in Cuba in 1926 and became a lawyer, running his own practice until he took up the revolutionary cause. His first armed uprising with 150 insurgents was launched on the Moncada barracks in Santiago de Cuba on 26 July 1953.

The attack was repelled, many rebels were killed and the others including Castro faced 15 years' imprisonment on the Isla de Pinos, now the Isla de la Juventud. However, in 1955 the dictator Batista granted an amnesty to political prisoners and Castro chose exile in the USA and later in Mexico, where he met the Argentinian, Che Guevara, one of the most influential members of the rebel group. From there he launched his second incursion, sailing from exile on the cabin cruiser, *Granma*, and landing in Cuba on 2 December, 1956, with over 80 revolutionaries, including his younger brother, Raúl, and Che, who fought alongside him. The uprising was crushed by the military but 12 men, including Castro, escaped into the mountains. There they organized the 26 July Movement, named after the 1953 uprising, and began guerrilla warfare while gradually building up popular support. Although Raúl was a Marxist-Leninist, Fidel campaigned on a Nationalist platform and only later turned to Communism. The campaign slogan was *libertad o muerte* (freedom or death), rather than the subsequently adapted version, *patria o muerte* (the homeland or death) in 1960 and then *socialismo o muerte* (socialism or death). On 17 March 1958 he called for a general revolt. His popularity and forces had grown steadily and they pushed on towards Havana. On 1 January 1959 Batista fled the country and a provisional government was established. Castro initially renounced office, but was prevailed upon to become prime minister and later president.

Background History

speech has gone down in history for its final phrase, "History will absolve me", and a revised version, smuggled out of prison on the Isle of Pines, became the basis of a reform programme. In 1955, the Castros were given an amnesty and went to Mexico. There Fidel continued to work on his essentially Nationalist revolutionary programme, called the **26 July** Movement, which called for radical social and economic reforms and a return to the democracy of Cuba's 1940 constitution. He met another man of ideas, an Argentine doctor called Ernesto Guevara (see box, page 231), who sailed with him and his brother Raúl and a band of 82 like-minded revolutionaries, back to Cuba on 2 December 1956. Their campaign began in the Sierra Maestra in the east of Cuba and after years of fierce fighting Batista fled to the Dominican Republic on 1 January 1959. Fidel Castro, to universal popular acclaim, entered Havana and assumed control of the island.

Communism and the 1960s

From 1960 onwards, in the face of increasing hostility from the USA, Castro led Cuba into socialism and then Communism. Officials of the Batista regime were put on trial in 'people's courts' and executed. The promised new elections were not held. The judiciary lost its independence when Castro assumed the right to appoint judges. The free press was closed or taken over. Trade unions lost their independence and became part of government. The University of Havana, a former focus of dissent, and professional associations all lost their autonomy. The democratic constitution of 1940 was never reinstated. In 1960, the sugar centrales, the oil refineries and the foreign banks were nationalized, all US property was expropriated and the Central Planning Board (*Juceplan*) was established. The professional and property-owning middle classes began a steady exodus which drained the country of much of its skilled workers.

CIA-backed mercenaries and Cuban emigrés kept up a relentless barrage of attacks, but failed to achieve their objective. In March a French ship carrying arms to Cuba was sabotaged. At the burial of the victims, Castro first used the slogan, 'Patria o Muerte'. Diplomatic relations were re-established with the USSR, North Korea and Vietnam, while China and Cuba signed mutual benefit treaties. Meanwhile, the USA cancelled Cuba's sugar quota and put an embargo on all imports to Cuba.

At the beginning of 1961, the USA severed diplomatic relations with Cuba and encouraged Latin American countries to do likewise. This was the year of the **Bay of Pigs** invasion, a fiasco which was to harden Castro's political persuasion. On 14 April 1961, some 1,400 Cuban emigrés, trained by the CIA in Miami and Guatemala, set off from Nicaragua to invade Cuba with the US Navy as escort. On 15 April, planes from Nicaragua bombed several Cuban airfields in an attempt to wipe out the air force. Seven Cuban airmen were killed in the raid, and at their funeral the next day, Fidel Castro addressed a mass rally in Havana and declared Cuba to be socialist. On 17 April the invasion flotilla landed at Playa Girón and Playa Larga in the Bahía de Cochinos (Bay of Pigs), but the men were stranded on the beaches when the Cuban air force attacked their supply ships. Two hundred were killed and the rest surrendered within three days. The invaders' aircraft also took a beating when 11 were shot down, including all the B-26 bombers flown from Nicaragua. A total of 1,197 men were captured and eventually returned to the USA in exchange for US$53 million in food and medicine. In his May Day speech, Fidel Castro, who had personally taken control of the defence of Cuba, confirmed that the Cuban Revolution was socialist.

The US reaction was to isolate Cuba, with a full trade embargo and heavy pressure on other American countries to sever diplomatic relations. Cuba was expelled from the Organization of American States (OAS) and the OAS imposed economic sanctions. Crucially, however, across the border in both Canada and Mexico, governments refused to toe the line and maintained relations (a policy which has now borne fruit for many Canadian and Mexican companies at the expense of US businesses). Nevertheless, in 1961-62, the trade embargo hit hard, shortages soon appeared and by March 1962 rationing had to be imposed.

⁑ An exploding cigar and other 1960s plots

The number of CIA-backed attempts on Castro's life is legendary, the most extraordinary stories so far published being about trying to kill him with an exploding cigar, or putting a special powder in his shoes to make his beard fall out. But, failing to assassinate or maim him, the US administration in the 1960s put an extraordinary amount of effort into trying to discredit him. Many covert plans were put forward to Operation Mongoose, an anti-Castro destabilization project at the Pentagon. One plan, codenamed Operation Dirty Trick, was to blame Castro if anything went wrong with US space flights, specifically John Glenn's flight into orbit in 1962. The Pentagon was to provide 'irrevocable proof' that if anything happened it was the fault of Cuban Communists and their electronic interference. Another idea was to sabotage a US plane and claim that a Cuban aircraft had shot down a civilian airliner. Yet another was to sink a US warship and blame that on Castro.

None of these came to anything, but sabotage did take place. Cuban emigré groups received help from a special CIA budget to destroy Castro's Cuba. In 1960, a French ship carrying a cargo of armaments from Belgium was blown up in Havana harbour, killing 81 people and wounding hundreds of others. Pressure was put on British companies by the USA to stop them trading with Cuba. Having 'discouraged' British ships from transporting a cargo of British Leyland buses and spare parts, but having failed to get the deal cancelled, it was therefore more than coincidental that an East German ship carrying the equipment was rammed in the Thames. Cuba has claimed other sabotage, such as supplying asymmetrical ball bearings to damage machinery, and chemical additives in lubricants for engines to make them wear out quickly. As classified documents of the Kennedy administration are released, more and more bugs keep crawling out of the woodwork.

At this stage, Cuba became entangled in the rivalry between the two superpowers: the USA and the USSR. In April 1962, Russian President **Kruschev** decided to send medium-range missiles to Cuba, which would be capable of striking anywhere in the USA, even though all Castro wanted were short-range missiles he could point at Miami to deter invasion. In October, President JF Kennedy ordered Soviet ships heading for Cuba to be stopped and searched for missiles in international waters. This episode, which became known as the **Cuban Missile Crisis**, brought the world to the brink of nuclear war, defused only by secret negotiations between JFK and Kruschev. Kennedy demanded the withdrawal of Soviet troops and arms from Cuba and imposed a naval blockade. Without consulting Castro and without his knowledge, Kruschev eventually agreed to have the missiles dismantled and withdrawn on condition that the West would guarantee a policy of non-aggression towards Cuba. In November, Kennedy suspended the naval blockade but reiterated US support for political and economic aggression towards Cuba. In the following year he made a speech in Costa Rica, in which he stated, "We will build a wall around Cuba", and Central American countries agreed to isolate the island.

Castro's decision to adopt Marxism-Leninism as the official ideology of the Revolution was followed by the fusion of the 26 July Movement with the Communist Party, at that time known as the Popular Socialist Party (PSP). The PSP had opposed the Revolution until the final stages of the overthrow of the Batista dictatorship and it took several years and two purges before the 'old' Communists were expunged and the new Communist Party was united behind the new official ideology. In October 1965, a restructured **Cuban Communist Party** (PCC) was founded and Cuba has been Communist ever since.

Economic policy during the 1960s was largely unsuccessful in achieving its aims. After a spell as head of the Central Bank, Che Guevara was appointed Minister of Industry, a key position given that the government wanted to industrialize rapidly to reduce dependence on sugar. However, the crash programme, with help from the USSR, was a failure and had to be abandoned. Sugar was king again but productivity plummeted and there were poor harvests in 1963-64. The whole nation was called upon to achieve a target of 10 million tonnes of sugar by 1970 and everyone spent time in the fields helping towards this goal. It was never reached and never has been, but the effort revealed distortions in the Cuban economy which in effect increased the island's dependence on the Soviet Union. Castro jumped out of the frying pan into the fire: he escaped domination by the USA only to replace it with another superpower.

Social policy

Rationing is still in place and there are still shortages of consumer goods. However, the Revolution's social policies have largely been successful and it is principally these achievements that have ensured the people's support of Castro and kept him in power. Education, housing and health services have been greatly improved and the social inequalities of the 1940s and 1950s have been wiped out. Equality of the sexes and races has also been promoted, a major change in what was a *machista*, racially prejudiced society. Infant mortality fell to 7.3 per 1,000 live births in 1997, on a par with many industrialized countries. In 1961 300,000 Cubans volunteered to go out into the countryside, as part of a literacy campaign, to teach their comrades how to read and write. On 22 December of the same year, Cuba was declared free of illiteracy. Considerable emphasis is now placed on combining productive agricultural work with study: there are over 400 schools and colleges in rural areas where the students divide their time between the fields and the classroom. Education is compulsory up to the age of 17, and free, while access to higher education has been granted to all.

1970s Soviet domination

During the second decade of the Revolution, Cuba became firmly entrenched as a member of the Soviet bloc, joining COMECON in 1972. Technicians came from Eastern Europe and Cubans were trained in the USSR. The Communist Party grew in strength and size and permeated all walks of life, influencing every aspect of Cubans' day to day living, while putting more central controls on education and culture. The Revolution was institutionalized along Soviet lines and the Party gained control of the bureaucracy, the judiciary and the local and national assemblies. Communist planners controlled the economy and workers were organized into government-controlled trade unions. A new socialist constitution was adopted in 1976. In 1971-75 the economy grew by about 16% a year, but fell back after then and never recovered such spectacular growth rates again.

Cuba's foreign policy during this period changed from actively fomenting socialist revolutions abroad (such as Guevara's forays into the Congo and Bolivia in the 1960s) to supporting other left wing or third world countries with combat troops and technical advisers. Some 20,000 Cubans helped the Angolan Marxist government to defeat a South African backed guerrilla insurgency and 15,000 went to Ethiopia in the war against Somalia and then the separatist rebellion in Eritrea. Cuban advisers and medical workers went to Nicaragua after the Sandinista overthrow of the Somoza dictatorship in 1979; advisers and workers went to help the left wing Manley government in Jamaica and to the Marxist government in

Grenada (until expelled by the US Marines in 1983). In September 1979, Castro hosted a summit conference of the non-aligned nations in Havana, a high point in his foreign policy initiatives.

The decade also marked a period of intellectual debate at home and abroad about the path the Revolution was taking. In 1971, the poet **Herberto Padilla** was arrested for cultural deviation and forced to confess his crimes against the Revolution. His treatment and cultural censorship brought accusations of Stalinization of cultural life. The Padilla affair split the Hispanic intellectual world, with writers such as Octavio Paz and Carlos Fuentes of Mexico, Mario Vargas Llosa of Peru and Juan Goytisolo of Spain renouncing their support for the Revolution, while Gabriel García Márquez of Colombia and Julio Cortázar of Argentina reaffirmed their support. Free expression was stifled and during this time the best Cuban art and literature was produced by emigrés. The debate widened to include civil liberties and political rights, and official secrecy made it difficult to gauge accurately the persecution of political prisoners, religious believers, intellectual opponents and homosexuals.

Constitution and government

In 1976 a new constitution was approved by 97.7% of the voters, setting up municipal and provincial assemblies and a National Assembly of People's Power. The membership of the Assembly was increased to 589 in 1993, candidates being nominated by the 169 municipal councils, and elected by direct secret ballot. Similarly elected are members of the 14 provincial assemblies, all for five-year terms. The number of Cuba's provinces was increased from six to 14 as a result of the decisions of the First Congress of the Communist Party of Cuba in December 1975. Dr Fidel Castro was elected President of the Council of State by the National Assembly and his brother, Major Raúl Castro, was elected First Vice-President.

1980s dissatisfaction and flight

By the 1980s, the heavy dependence on sugar and the USSR, coupled with the trade embargo, meant that the expected improvements in living standards, 20 years after the Revolution, were not being delivered as fast as hoped and the people were tiring of being asked for ever more sacrifices for the good of the nation. In 1980, the compound of the Peruvian embassy was overrun by 11,000 people seeking political asylum. Castro's answer to the dissidents was to let them go and he opened the port of **Mariel** for a mass departure by sea. He also opened the prisons to allow prisoners, both political and criminal, to head for the USA in anything they could find which would float. It was estimated that some 125,000 embarked for Miami, amid publicity that it was the criminals, delinquents, homosexuals and mental patients who were fleeing Cuba. At the same time huge demonstrations were organized in Havana in support of the Revolution. Some relaxation in controls was allowed, however, with 'free markets' opening alongside the official ration system.

This was the decade of the Latin American debt crisis and Cuba was unable to escape the pressures brought to bear on its neighbours. Development projects in the 1970s had been financed with loans from western banks, in addition to the aid it was already receiving from the USSR. When interest rates went up in 1982, Cuba was forced to renegotiate its US$3.5 billion debt to commercial banks and, in 1986, its debt to the USSR. The need to restrain budget spending and keep a tight control over public finances brought more austerity. The private markets were stopped in 1986 and the people were once more asked for voluntary labour to raise productivity and achieve economic growth. Excess manpower, or unemployment, was eased by sending thousands of Cubans abroad as internationalists to help other developing countries, whether as combat troops or technicians.

Castro and the UN

In 1960, Fidel Castro visited the UN for the first time since becoming leader of Cuba. Relations with the USA were becoming sour and the hotels in New York were wary of giving lodging to the new government in case of reprisals from Cuban exiles and other potential violence. Hotels refused to accept his booking without a large deposit, which he refused to pay. Undeterred, Castro led his party to buy tents and headed for Central Park, where he intended to pitch camp, declaring he was still a *guerrilla comandante*. They never got there, however, for a young black leader called Malcolm X persuaded them to come with him to Harlem, where he found them rooms in the rundown Hotel Theresa in the heart of the black district. In addition he promised them security and protection from the emigrés provided by his black Muslims. It was a great occasion and Castro held court at the hotel, receiving eminent visitors such as Nehru and his daughter Indira Gandhi, Nasser, Kruschev and others, while also mingling with the public. His performance at the General Assembly was memorable: the audience was forced to listen to a speech lasting 4½ hours.

Thirty five years later, he made another visit to the UN and went back to Harlem, although he lodged at the Cuban UN mission. Discarding the sober suit he wore to the UN General Assembly (where this time he was limited to a five-minute address but received a longer ovation than President Clinton for a speech which expressed the broad resentments of the Third World), he donned his military fatigues and cap and went to talk to an all-ticket audience at the Abyssinian Baptist Church about Cuba's educational and health achievements. Although he was again excluded by polite society (he was not invited to President Clinton's reception for 149 heads of state and left off the guest list for Mayor Giuliani's dinner party) he was courted by no less than 230 US business people and invited to lunch by the Rockefeller family.

The **collapse of the Communist system** in the Eastern European countries in the late 1980s, followed by the demise of the USSR, very nearly brought the end of Castro's Cuba as well. Emigrés in Miami started counting the days until they would re-enter the homeland and Castro's position looked extremely precarious. There were signs that a power struggle was taking place at the top of the Communist Party. In 1989, General Arnaldo Ochoa, a hero of the Angolan campaign, was charged with drug trafficking and corruption. He was publicly tried and executed along with several other military officers allegedly involved. Castro took the opportunity to pledge to fight against corruption and privilege and deepen the process of rectification begun in 1986.

The Soviet connection

Before the collapse of the Soviet system, aid to Cuba from the USSR was traditionally estimated at about 25% of GNP. Cuba's debt with the USSR was a secret: estimates ranged from US$8.5 billion to US$34 billion. Apart from military aid, economic assistance took two forms: balance of payments support (about 85%), under which sugar and nickel exports were priced in excess of world levels and oil imports were indexed against world prices for the previous five years, and assistance for development projects. About 13 million tonnes of oil were supplied a year by the USSR, allowing 3 million to be re-exported, providing a valuable source of foreign earnings. By the late 1980s up to 90% of Cuba's foreign trade was with centrally planned economies.

US relations

Before the Revolution of 1959, the USA had investments in Cuba worth about US$1,000 million, covering nearly every activity from agriculture and mining to oil installations. Today all American businesses in Cuba, including banks, have been nationalized; the USA has cut off all imports from Cuba, placed an embargo on exports to Cuba, and broken off diplomatic relations. Promising moves to improve relations with the USA were given impetus in 1988 by the termination of Cuban military activities in Angola under agreement with the USA and South Africa. However, developments in Eastern Europe and the former USSR in 1989-90 revealed the vulnerability of the economy (see Economy, page 398) and provoked Castro to defend the Cuban system of government; the lack of political change delayed any further rapprochement with the USA. Prior to the 1992 US presidential elections, President Bush approved the Cuban Democracy Act (Torricelli Bill), which strengthened the trade embargo by forbidding US subsidiaries from trading with Cuba. Many countries, including EC members and Canada, said they would not allow the US bill to affect their trade with Cuba and the UN General Assembly voted in November in favour of a resolution calling for an end to the embargo. The defeat of George Bush by Bill Clinton did not, however, signal a change in US attitudes, in large part because of the support given to the Democrat's campaign by Cuban emigrés in Miami.

1990s crisis and change

In an effort to broaden the people's power system of government introduced in 1976, the central committee of the Cuban Communist Party adopted resolutions in 1990 designed to strengthen the municipal and provincial assemblies and transform the National Assembly into a genuine parliament. In February 1993, the first direct, secret elections for the National Assembly and for provincial assemblies were held. Despite calls from opponents abroad for voters to register a protest by spoiling their ballot or not voting, the official results showed that 99.6% of the electorate voted, with 92.6% of votes cast valid. All 589 official candidates were elected. Delegates to the municipal assemblies of people's power serve a two-year term. Delegates are directly nominated in neighbourhood meetings (the PCC does not put forward candidates), and ballot boxes are guarded by primary school children. Provincial delegates and national deputies are elected for a five-year term. The slate consists of up to 50% of the municipal delegates and the remainder selected by a national commission on the basis of proposals from the mass organizations. In the October 1997 elections, 97.6% of the electorate voted and 92.8% of the votes were valid (7.2% blank or spoiled).

Economic difficulties in the 1990s brought on by the loss of markets in the former USSR and Eastern Europe, together with higher oil prices because of the Gulf crisis, forced the government to impose emergency measures and declare a special period in peace time (1990-94). Rationing was increased, petrol became scarce, the bureaucracy was slashed and several hundred arrests were made in a drive against corruption. In 1993, Cuba was hit on 13 March by a winter storm which caused an estimated US$1 bn in damage. Agricultural production, for both export and domestic consumption, was severely affected. In mid-1994, economic frustration and discontent boiled up and Cubans began to flee their country. Thousands left for Florida in a mass exodus similar to that of Mariel in 1980 on any craft they could invent. It was estimated that between mid-August and mid-September 30,000 Cubans had left the country, compared with 3,656 in the whole of 1993. In contrast, the number of US visas issued from January-August was 2,059 out of an agreed maximum annual quota of 20,000. Eventually the crisis forced President Clinton into an agreement whereby the USA was committed to accepting at least 20,000 Cubans a year, plus the next of kin of US citizens, while Cuba agreed to prevent further departures.

As the economic crisis persisted, the government adopted measures (some of which are outlined below) which opened up many sectors to private enterprise and recognized the dependence of much of the economy on dollars. The partial reforms did not eradicate the imbalances between the peso and the dollar economies, and shortages remained for those without access to hard currency.

Cuba then intensified its economic liberalization programme, speeding up the opening of farmers' markets throughout the country and allowing farmers to sell at uncontrolled prices once their commitments to the state procurement system were fulfilled. Importantly, the reforms also allowed middlemen to operate. It had been the emergence of this profitable occupation which had provoked the government to close down the previous farmers' market system in 1986. Markets in manufactured goods and handicrafts also opened and efforts were made to increase the number of self-employed.

US pressure in the 1990s

In 1996, a US election year, Cuba faced another crackdown by the US administration. In February, Cuba shot down two light aircraft piloted by Miami emigrés, allegedly over Cuban air space and implicitly confirmed by the findings of the International Civil Aviation Organization (ICAO) report in June. The attack provoked President Clinton into reversing his previous opposition to key elements of the Helms-Burton bill to tighten and internationalize the US embargo on Cuba and on 12 March he signed into law the Cuban Freedom and Democratic Solidarity Act. The new legislation allows legal action against any company or individual benefiting from properties expropriated by the Cuban government after the Revolution. Claims on property nationalized by the Cuban state extended to persons who did not hold US citizenship at the time of the expropriation, thus including Batista supporters who fled at the start of the Revolution. It brought universal condemnation: Canada and Mexico (NAFTA partners), the EU, Russia, China, the Caribbean community and the Río Group of Latin American countries all protested that it was unacceptable to extend sanctions outside the USA to foreign companies and their employees who do business with Cuba. In 1997, the EU brought a formal complaint against the USA at the World Trade Organization (WTO), but suspended it when an EU/US agreement was reached under which Clinton was to ask the US Congress to amend Title IV of the law (concerning the denial of US entry visas to employees and shareholders of 'trafficking companies'). Clinton was also to carry on waiving Title III (authorizing court cases against 'trafficking' of expropriated assets).

In 1999, Human Rights Watch (hrwdc@hrw.org) produced a report that strongly criticized the US embargo, arguing that it had helped Castro to develop and maintain his repressive regime, restricting freedom of speech, movement and association. It had also divided the international community, alienating Washington's potential allies who, it argued, should be working together to push for change in Cuba. The same year, the UN Human Rights Commission expressed concern about 'continued repression' in Cuba, following the trial and conviction of four Cubans for sedition. They were jailed for receiving funds and instructions from the USA aimed at obstructing foreign investment. A civil suit brought in Cuba claimed US$181 bn in damages from the US government for its aggressive policing over the previous 40 years, causing the deaths of 3,478 Cubans. The case was seen partially as a retaliation for the Helms-Burton Law.

Recent events

A spate of bombings targeted at the tourist industry caused alarm in 1997. The first was in April at the hotels **Meliá Cohiba** in Havana, followed by one in July at the **Capri** and another at the **Nacional**. The **Meliá Cohiba** was hit again in August, while in September three hotels on the seafront were bombed and an Italian was killed by flying glass. In an extraordinarily successful piece of detective work, it only took about a week for the Interior Ministry to announce it was holding a former paratrooper from El Salvador, Raúl Ernesto Cruz León, who confessed publicly on TV to working as a mercenary and planting six bombs. He did not say who he was working for, but it was assumed in Cuba that the Miami-based Cuban American National Foundation (CANF) was behind the bombings. Two Salvadorians were sentenced to death in 1999 for their part in the 1997 bombing campaign.

1997 was the 30th anniversary of the death of Che Guevara in Bolivia, whose remains were returned to Cuba in July. The country held a week of official mourning for Che and his comrades in arms. Vast numbers filed past their remains in Havana and Santa Clara, where they were laid to rest on 17 October. In December 1998 the remains of the 10 more guerrillas killed in Bolivia in 1967 were also interred in the Che Guevara memorial in Santa Clara (see page 227). They included Haydée Tamara Bunke, known as Tania, who was believed to be Che's lover.

In January 1998, the Pope visited Cuba for the first time. During his four-day visit he held open-air masses around the country, attended by thousands of fascinated Cubans encouraged to attend by Castro. The world's press was represented in large numbers to record the Pope's preaching against Cuba's record on human rights and abortion while also condemning the US trade embargo preventing food and medicines reaching the needy. The visit was a public relations success for both Castro and the Pope. Shortly afterwards, 200 prisoners were pardoned and released.

In November 1999 a six-year-old boy, Elián González, was rescued from the sea off Florida, the only survivor from a boatload of illegal migrants which included his mother and her boyfriend. He was looked after by distant relatives in Miami and quickly became the centrepiece of a new row between Cuban emigrés, supported by right wing Republicans, and Cuba. The US Attorney General, Janet Reno, supported the decision, by the US Immigration and and Naturalization Service (INS) on 5 January 2000, that the boy should be repatriated and reunited with his father in Cuba by 14 January, but she postponed the deadline indefinitely to allow for legal challenges. Mass demonstrations were held in Havana in support of Elián's return but legal manoeuvres by US politicians stalled any progress and caused further disputes. Amid enormous controversy, the US authorities seized Elián on 22 April and reunited him with his father, who had travelled to the USA earlier in the month with his second wife and baby. The family finally took him home, amid celebrations in Cuba, where the boy had become a symbol of resistance to the USA.

The election of George W Bush to the US presidency was bad news for any prospects of a thaw in relations with the USA. A crackdown on spies was ordered and in June 2001, five Cubans (arrested in 1998) were convicted of conspiracy to commit espionage and murder in a US Federal Court in Miami. Castro referred to them as 'heroes', who he said had not been putting the USA in danger but had been infiltrating Cuban-American anti-Castro groups and defending Cuba. Their faces are on billboards across Cuba and their case is still part of the propaganda war between Cuba and the USA. The prisoners known as the 'Miami Five' are being held in separate prisons across the USA and are being denied access to their families because their wives have been denied US visas. A motion for a retrial was filed in 2003.

However, 2001 saw the first commercial export of food from the USA to Cuba, with a shipment of corn from Louisiana. In two years a total of US$328 million in beans, rice, chicken and other goods have been sold by US farmers to Alimport, Cuba's food-buying agency. Even the state of Texas joined in, with the Texas Cuba Trade Alliance forecasting sales of US$30 million from that state alone in 2004. The debate on the lifting of sanctions was fuelled by the visit of former US President Jimmy Carter in 2002 and an ever-increasing number of Americans travelled to the island, legally or illegally. However, the thaw came to a grinding halt in 2003 when Castro had three ferry hijackers executed and imprisoned 75 journalists, rights activists and dissidents, many of whom had allegedly been encouraged by the head of the US Interests Section in Havana. Amid universal condemnation, the EU announced a review of its relations with Cuba and curtailed high-level governmental visits. The hard line stance is intensifying in the run-up to the next US presidential elections. In 2002, Osvaldo Paya, leader of the dissident Varela project (Felix Varela was an independence hero), delivered a petition with 11,020 signatures to the National Assembly demanding sweeping political reforms, but it was dismissed. Undeterred, Paya submitted a second petition in October 2003 with 14,384 signatures, calling for a referendum on freedom of speech and assembly and amnesty for political prisoners. At the same time, the US administration announced a clampdown on its citizens travelling to the island. Immigration and Customs officers were ordered to carry out the letter of the law, with thousands of baggage searches and the first prosecutions were announced. In January 2004, the USA cancelled semi-annual migration talks as relations deteriorated.

Economy

Following the 1959 Revolution, Cuba adopted a Marxist-Leninist system. Almost all sectors of the economy were state controlled and centrally planned, the only significant exception being agriculture, where some 12% of arable land was still privately owned. The country became heavily dependent on trade and aid from other Communist countries, principally the USSR (through its participation in the Council of Mutual Economic Aid), encouraged by the US trade embargo. It relied on sugar and, to a lesser extent, nickel for nearly all its exports. While times were good, Cuba used the Soviet protection to build up an impressive, but costly, social welfare system, with better housing, education and healthcare than anywhere else in Latin America and the Caribbean. The collapse of the Eastern European bloc, however, revealed the vulnerability of the island's economy and the desperate need for reform. A sharp fall in GDP of 35% in 1990-93, accompanied by a decline in exports from US$8.1 billion (1989) to US$1.7 billion (1993), forced the government to take remedial action and the decision was made to start the complex process of transition to a mixed economy.

Transformation of the unwieldy and heavily centralized state apparatus has progressed in fits and starts. The government initially encouraged self-employment to enable it to reduce the public sector workforce, but Cuban workers are cautious about relinquishing their job security. Some small businesses have sprung up, particularly in the tourism sector, but numbers of registered tax payers have fallen. Free farm produce markets were permitted in 1994 and these were followed by similar markets at deregulated prices for manufacturers, including goods produced by state enterprises and handicrafts. Cubans are now allowed to hold US dollars and in 1995 a convertible peso at par with the US dollar was introduced, which is fully exchangeable for hard currencies. There has been considerable success in reducing the fiscal deficit, which was bloated by subsidies and inefficiencies. Financial services are being overhauled to cater for the accumulation of capital by owners of small businesses, who currently operate in cash. Less than half of all Cubans have a bank account and dollar savings accounts have not yet proved popular, partly, it is believed, because they do not want the Government to trace the source of their income. In 1997 legislation was approved to transform the **Banco Nacional de Cuba**; the **Banco Central de Cuba** was established on 28 May 1997 to assume the central banking functions of the **Banco Nacional**, which continues as a commercial bank.

Although commercial relations with market economies were poor in the late 1980s, because of lack of progress in debt rescheduling negotiations, Cuba made great efforts in the 1990s to improve its foreign relations. The US trade embargo and the

Health

Free healthcare is provided to all Cubans by the state as their right. In the 1960s the state took on the task of curing the population of many infectious diseases, despite having lost half of its 6,000 doctors, who left the country after the Revolution. Mortality rates were high and attention was focused on eradicating specific diseases, improving ante-natal and post-natal care and training large numbers of doctors and other health care workers. Health facilities in operation before the Revolution were consolidated into a single state health system. In the 1970s, there was more emphasis on community healthcare, and polyclinics were set up with specialist services around the country. Positive results were soon evident as mortality rates fell and life expectancy rose. By the 1980s, policy had shifted again, this time towards preventive medicine rather than curative care. Mass immunization programmes were carried out and screening became regular practice. In 1985 the Family Doctor programme was started to take pressure off the hospitals and clinics and provide continuity of care. Each doctor cares for 120 families as well as collecting health and social information on all patients, providing the state with a database on the health of the nation.

The results of this attention to health care are staggering. Cubans may be poor and live in inadequate housing but their health is equal to that of industrialized countries. 95% of the population has been vaccinated against 12 diseases and several (such as polio, diphtheria, measles and mumps) have been eliminated from the island completely. Between 1986 and 1993, the entire population was tested for HIV and the 'sexually active' population is still tested annually. No cases of HIV positive new-born babies have been recorded since 1998 as a result of ante-natal screening. At the end of 2001 the infant mortality rate was reduced to a record low of 6.2 per 1,000 live births, a rate as good as that of Canada. As a result of the intensive training of doctors, there is now a better doctor/patient ratio than anywhere in the world except Israel.

Healthcare is now also an export item. Cuba's expertise is sought by developing countries worldwide. Cuban doctors work abroad in teams to provide specific services and foreign medical students come to Cuba to receive training. The Carlos J Finlay Medical Detachment was set up in the 1980s to prepare community doctors and in the first graduation year it included 147 graduates (out of a total of 3,440 that year) from 45 different countries. The Detachment was named after the 19th century Cuban physician who discovered the mosquito as vector of yellow fever. In 1996, South Africa requested the services of 600 English-speaking Cuban doctors under a three-year contract to make up a shortfall caused by the emigration of South African doctors. Cuban emergency medical teams have helped overseas with hurricane relief and other natural disasters. Some 16,000 victims of the Chernobyl nuclear disaster, mostly children, have been treated by Cuban medical institutions. (Cuba has done more for the Chernobyl victims than all the rest of the world put together.)

Exports of medicines and vaccines are also substantial: Brazil has bought the meningitis vaccine from Cuba; in 1996 it was proposed Cuba's debt to Venezuela, of around US$46 million, should be amortized with revenue earned from medicines exported to that country; and an agreement with Vietnam involves the Cuban import of rice in exchange for sales of medical and pharmaceutical products. Exports of pharmaceuticals are now around US$100 million a year and rising.

associated inability to secure finance from multilateral sources led the government to encourage foreign investment, principally in joint ventures. All sectors of the economy, including sugar and real estate, are now open to foreign investment and in some areas majority foreign shareholdings are allowed. Some 400 foreign companies are now established in Cuba, with capital from 38 countries in 26 economic sectors, mostly in tourism, oil, mining and telecommunications. The leading investors are from Spain, Canada, France, Italy and Mexico. Bilateral investment promotion and protection agreements have been signed with 12 nations including Italy, Spain, Germany and the UK. Under new legislation passed in 1996, free-trade zones are being established, the first one at Havana with others at Cienfuegos, Mariel and Wajay, outside Havana. Some 75% of production must be exported but the rest can be sold in Cuba on the dollar market. Employees are paid in pesos. The external accounts remain weak. Foreign debt is around US$11 billion (excluding debt to former members of COMECON – Russia claims Cuba owes it US$20 billion), and Cuba's dependence on high-interest, short-term trade finance is a burden. Cuba is ineligible for long-term development finance from multilateral lending agencies because of the US veto. Low sugar and nickel prices, relatively high oil prices, a decline in tourism after the 11 September 2001 terrorist attack and massive hurricane damage in 2002 all hindered recovery from the economic crisis of the 1990s.

There is a huge gap between those who have access to dollars and those who live in the peso economy, which has encouraged highly skilled professionals, such as doctors, to give up their training and become waiters or tourist guides. At the same time there is resentment at being physically excluded from tourist enclaves and beaches such as Varadero; Cubans who do not work there are stopped at check points and turned away if they do not have the right papers. Tourists also find the situation confusing; package holiday visitors spend only dollars while independent travellers cope with pesos.

Sugar is the major crop and earns around US$430 million in foreign exchange. However, the industry has consistently failed to reach the targets set with output falling from 8 million tonnes in 1990 to 3.2 million tonnes in 1998, the lowest for 50 years. World prices then fell to a 12-year low, while poor weather and shortages of fertilizers, oil and spare parts limited any great improvement in income. In 2003, 71 of the country's 156 sugar mills were closed and the land under production cut by 60%, with consequent severe job losses.

Citrus is now an important agricultural export with production of around 1,850,000 tonnes a year. Production is mostly in the centre and west of the island and in the Isla de la Juventud. Cuba became a member of the International Coffee Agreement in 1985 and produces about 22,000 tonnes of coffee a year but exports are minimal. Drought and disease have limited expansion. Tobacco is a traditional crop and Cuban cigars are world famous, but this too has suffered from lack of fuel, fertilizers and other inputs. Production is recovering with the help of Spanish credits and importers from France and Britain. A Spanish company has taken a shareholding in the cigar exporting company, Habanos SA, to boost sales abroad.

Diversification away from sugar is a major goal, with the emphasis on production of **food** for domestic use because of the shortage of foreign exchange for imports. The supply of food for the capital has greatly improved, partly with the introduction of city vegetable gardens, *agropónicos*, but the main staple, rice, is still imported to make up a shortfall in domestic production caused by inefficiencies. The beef herd declined in the first half of the 1990s because of the inability to pay for imports of grains, fertilizers and chemicals. Production is now less intensive, with smaller herds on pastures, and numbers are beginning to rise again. Similarly, milk production is also increasing. The opening of farmers' markets in 1994 has helped to stimulate diversification of crops and greater availability of foodstuffs, although shortages still remain. Drought in the east, hurricanes and flooding have all in recent years affected crops of beans, grains, vegetables and fruit.

The sudden withdrawal of oil supplies, when trade agreements with Russia had to be renegotiated and denominated in convertible currencies, was a crucial factor in the collapse of the Cuban economy. Although trade agreements involving oil and sugar remain, Cuba had to purchase oil from other suppliers with extremely limited foreign exchange. As a result, Cuba stepped up its own production: foreign companies explore for oil on and off-shore and investment has borne fruit, with over 92% of electricity generated by domestic oil and gas and half of all consumption met by domestic production, but shortages of fuel remain.

Mining is attracting foreign interest and in 1994 a new mining law was passed. Major foreign investors include Australian (nickel), Canadian (gold, silver and base metals) and South African (gold, copper and nickel) companies. About half of nickel and cobalt production comes from the Moa Bay plant, a Canadian-Cuban joint venture.

Tourism is now a major foreign exchange earner and has received massive investment from abroad. New hotel projects are coming on stream and many more are planned. Most of the development has been along the Varadero coast, where large resort hotels attract package tourism, but Cayo Coco and Cayo Guillermo are undergoing major construction. Despite political crises, numbers of visitors have risen steadily from 546,000 in 1993 to 1.7 million in 2002, generating revenues of US$1.85 billion. The target is for 7 mn tourists a year by 2010, bringing earnings of about US$11.8 billion. It is estimated that if the travel ban were lifted in the USA, some one million American tourists would immediately book holidays in Cuba.

Culture

Art

Until the 19th century Cuban artists were mainly concerned with emulating the styles fashionable in Spain at the time, to gain favour with their colonial rulers. But then painters began to develop styles that were endemic to the island. Even at the end of the 19th century, when Impressionism was revolutionizing painting in France, the Cuban style still retained its roots in the academic tradition of landscape and portrait painting. One of the artists known for his major contribution to the emerging Cuban style of painting was **Leopoldo Romañach**, born near Coralillo in Villa Clara in 1862, although he spent most of his life abroad.

It was the 1920s that saw Cuban artists finally developing their own avant-garde movement and the art magazine *Avance* made its appearance in 1927. **Víctor Manuel**'s (1897-1969) 1924 painting *Gitana Tropical*, with its echoes of Cézanne and Gaugin, caused a sensation when the public first saw it. Now it has become the painting that symbolizes the beginning of modernism in Cuban art. US encroachment on the failing Cuban sugar industry in the 1920s led to a new nationalism among artists and intellectuals, with painters looking to Afro-Cuban images for inspiration. The generation of painters of 1927-1950 are known as La Vanguardia. They combined the modernism of post-Impressionist European artists with the vibrant landscapes and people found in Cuba. Today, their paintings are worth a small fortune and there is a ready market in forgeries.

Wifredo Lam (1902-82) is still Cuba's most famous painter. He spent many years in France and Spain, becoming friends with Picasso and André Bréton, who introduced him to primitive art. Lam blended synthetic cubism, African masks and surrealism to create an essentially Cuban vision. Although he did most of his major work in Cuba, he always intended to show those outside Latin America the reality there.

⁙ The Cuban Revolution and culture

The Cuban Revolution has had a profound effect on culture, both on the island itself and in a wider context. Domestically, its chief achievement has been to integrate popular expression into daily life, compared with the pre-revolutionary climate in which art was either the preserve of an elite or, in its popular forms, had to fight for acceptance.

The encouragement of painting in people's studios and through a national art school, and the support given by the state to musicians and film-makers, has done much to foster a national cultural identity. This is not to say that the system has neither refrained from controlling what the people should be exposed to (eg much Western pop music was banned in the 1960s), nor that it has been without its domestic critics (either those who lived through the Revolution and took issue with it, or younger artists who now feel stifled by a cultural bureaucracy).

Furthermore, while great steps have been made towards the goal of a fully integrated society, there remain areas in which the unrestricted participation of blacks, women and homosexuals has yet to be achieved. Blacks predominate in sport and music (as in Brazil), but find it harder to gain recognition in the public media; women artists, novelists and composers have had to struggle for acceptance; homosexuals have suffered persecution, particularly in the 1970s, and many gay intellectuals have fled the country. Nevertheless, measures are being taken in the cultural, social and political spheres to rectify this situation and the last decade of the 20th century saw a considerable relaxation in prejudices.

Amelia Peláez (1896-1968) looked west for her inspiration, to the mural painting of Mexico, although her early work was influenced by Matisse, Braque and Picasso. Her brightly coloured murals can be seen in the Tribunal de Cuentas building and the Office of the Comptroller in Havana. It was this divergence of influences that characterized Cuban art during the 1940s.

Carlos Enríquez (1900-57) lived in Cuba, New York, Paris and Madrid, while his style evolved through surrealism to expressionism.

René Portocarrero (1912-85) was one of the few painters not to be influenced by the movements in Europe. His big colourful paintings incorporate Afro-Cuban imagery. He travelled to Haiti, Europe and the USA and worked with ceramics and murals.

Mariano Rodríguez (1912-90) studied under Mexican muralists. His most popular work is his series 'Gallos' (roosters) produced in the 1940s and he exhibited widely in the USA.

Mario Carreño (1913-99) was a nomad for the first half of his life, working as a graphic artist in Spain, a muralist in Mexico, a painter in Paris before the war and an abstract painter in New York after the war, with only visits to his homeland. In 1957, he took up permanent residence in Chile and lived there until his death.

The 1950s and 1960s saw a big influence on painting of imagery from the cinema; a major group of artists around this time were known as the *Grupo de los Once*, and included **Luis Martínez Pedro** (1910-90), originally an architect who exhibited his paintings worldwide and designed theatre sets and costumes for contemporary dance, and **Raúl Milián** (1914-86), who didn't start painting until 1952 and never worked in oils, preferring water-based inks.

The Revolution had a strong influence on developments in the art world: the first national art school was founded in the early 1960s; and in 1976 the Escuela Superior de Arte was founded. These institutions gave more people access to the serious study of applied art. **Raúl Martínez** (1927-95) was the most well known of the Cuban Pop Artists. Unlike their North American contemporaries, the imagery of Cuban Pop Art came from the ubiquitous faces of revolutionaries, seen on murals all over Cuba.

The 1970s was the most difficult era for artists in Cuba, with many political restrictions on their work; of the few that made it past the censors, **Flavio Garciandia** (1954-) was the most notable, producing paintings which mixed abstract and figurative styles together.

The 1980s saw the emergence of conceptual art in Cuba, as elsewhere, and many alternative groups were formed, such as *Artecalle* – street art. There was also the *Puré* group, the most important member being **José Angel Toirac**, (1966-) who famously put Castro's image on Marlboro cigarette advertisements and Calvin Klein's Eternity. Though most of the better-known artists were now abroad, the art scene still flourished. Some, like the sculptor **Alejandro Aguilera** (1964-), distorted patriotic symbols in a confrontational way. In Cuba, as in other parts of the world, the 1980s was a decade in which everything was questioned and deconstructed. The 1990s saw the rise of performance art as a means of expression. **Carlos Garaicoa** is one of the bigger names in this field, already having taken part in the *1997 Havana Biennal* along with **Tania Bruguera**, who had also exhibited in the *1996 Sao Paulo Biennal*. Many alternative galleries have sprung up recently, the best being 'Aglutinador', run by two well-known artists from the 1980s, **Sandra Ceballos** and **Esequiel Suárez**. The gallery is in their house in the Vedado area of Havana. The 1990s also saw a return to painting, after the vogue for installation of the 1980s. This reflects the economic need, during the special period (see History, page 395), for artists to make saleable objects again, although it also has its conceptual roots in post-modernism.

The **Museo Nacional Palacio de Bellas Artes** reopened in 2001 and is essential viewing for anyone interested in colonial and modern Cuban art (see page 92). The national collection is divided between two buildings in Old Havana, one for Cuban art and the other for world art, with many pieces having been in private collections before the Revolution. Other state-run galleries in Havana are the **Centro de Desarrollo de las Artes Visuales** and the **Wifredo Lam Centre**, which has shows by contemporary artists. You can also see some small exhibitions of avant-garde work at the **Casa de Las Américas**. Look out for the many small private galleries around Old Havana and Central Havana as well. In the provinces there are several places where you can see local artists exhibit their work, either in galleries or in provincial museums.

Architecture

The oldest house in Cuba still standing today is Diego Velázquez's residence in Santiago, built in 1522. However, the most important architectural works of the 16th century were the forts of Havana and Santiago, built in response to the many pirate attacks Cuba suffered. The original fort on the site of the **Castillo de la Real Fuerza** in Havana was burnt to the ground in 1555 by the French pirate Jacques de Sores. Felipe II commissioned a new fortress but the work was delayed when the architect was replaced in 1562 by Francisco de Calona, who completed the reconstruction in 1582. The building is a technological marvel, considering the primitive resources available when it was built: the walls are 6 m thick and 10 m high, with huge triangular bulwarks at each corner; a drawbridge leads over the wide moat to the vaulted interior. The early 17th century saw the construction of two castles in Havana and Santiago, by the Italian architect Juan Bautista Antonelli. They are both known as **Castillo del Morro**, and both still stand. Also built in the 17th century were the Havana city walls. One and a half metres thick and 10 m high, they ran for nearly 5,000 m around the edge of the bay. A few fragments remain at Calle Egido y Avenida del Puerto.

Korda and the making of an icon

Alberto Díaz Gutiérrez (1928-2001) was the son of a railway worker and tried a variety of jobs before turning to photography as a way of meeting beautiful women. The scheme worked; he established himself as a fashion photographer and married one of Cuba's most beautiful models. He took the name 'Korda' because he thought it sounded like Kodak and set up a studio in Havana where he lived the lifestyle of the successful and famous.

The 1959 Revolution changed his world completely and he became converted to the cause after a photographic expedition into the countryside that year. He saw at first hand the grinding poverty of the peasants and the inequality caused by the dictatorship. Instead of fashion pictures for *Vogue*, he took photos of the new leadership, which he sold to the newspaper, *Revolución*. He followed Castro, Che and their entourage around the country giving speeches and holding rallies or joining workers in the sugar harvest. On one of these occasions he took the photo of Che which was to make him world famous and convert the Argentine into an icon to inspire student revolutionaries for a generation. The occasion was the funeral in 1960 of 100 dock workers who were killed when a French freighter loaded with arms exploded in Havana harbour. Interpreted as a CIA-backed terrorist attack, the Cubans were furious and grief stricken at the funeral and Che's expression reflects the mix of emotions he felt as he surveyed the crowd before taking his leave. Korda's photo was rejected by *Revolución*, but it was precious enough to him to hang it on the wall of his studio for years.

In 1967, Korda received a visit from the Italian publisher, Giangiacomo Feltrinelli, to whom he gave a print of the photo as a present. The matter might have rested there if Che had not been killed in Bolivia a few weeks later. A Ministry of the Interior official discovered the photo and hung a huge version of it on the building overlooking the Plaza de la Revolución where it served as a backdrop for Castro when he paid homage to his friend and colleague. Images of the event were screened on televisions all round the world and Feltrinelli realised what could be done with such a powerful picture. Without permission and without paying Korda a cent, Feltrinelli printed millions of posters of the photo which later adorned student rooms and were carried in demonstrations in Europe and Mexico in the late 1960s. This single image of Che has been used on posters, T-shirts, hats, books, cards and any number of other items to reinforce revolutionary thought or just to sell goods with the aid of a beautiful young man with a stern but wistful gaze. In December 1999 an exhibition in Paris called '*100 Photographs of the Century*' had Korda's photo of Che on the cover of the catalogue, in recognition of its impact.

For 20 years Korda did nothing about his copyright and received no royalties. It was only in 1998 when Smirnoff advertised a vodka with the picture of Che and the slogan 'Hot and Fiery' that he decided to take action. Incensed that Che should be used to advertise alcohol when he didn't even drink, Korda took the advertising and picture agencies to court and won. When damages were paid in 2000 he donated them to the Cuban health service to buy medicines for Cuban children, as he believed Che would have done. He died of a heart attack in Paris while attending an exhibition of his work and was buried in Havana. Despite a huge photographic legacy including an underwater record of Cuba as well as fashion and news photos, it is for the single photo of Che Guevara that he will always be known.

Baroque

The most notable Baroque building in Havana is the **cathedral**; completed in 1777, it features an eccentric, undulating façade, asymmetrical towers, and wooden-ribbed vaulting over its three naves. The increased power enjoyed by the church in the 17th and 18th centuries led to bishops such as Diego Evelino de Compostela having a big say in city planning, with the result that many churches were built during this period. The gardens of Evelino's house in Calle Compostela, Havana, were the site of the first baroque church in Havana, **Iglesia de Nuestra Señora de Belén**, completed in 1718 and currently under restoration. The classic baroque façade features a nativity scene framed within a shell. Diego de Compostela also built the **Colegio de San Francisco de Sales** in Havana. A typical central patio, surrounded by thick columns and slatted doors, receives rainbows of light from the *mediopuntos* – semicircular windows with fan-shaped stained glass.

The **San Francisco de Asís** church in Old Havana was rebuilt in the baroque style in 1730. When a 40-m tower was added it became one of the highest religious buildings in Latin America. It is no longer a church and only the exterior, in particular the Escorial style of the façade, retains the baroque splendour of its day.

Colonial mansions

In a typical Spanish colonial house of some wealth, there was a series of large, airy rooms on the first floor surrounded the central patio, based on the Sevillian style; the ground floor was reserved for warehouses and shops, and the *entresol*, between the ground and first floors, was where the slaves lived. Ornate carved *rejas* adorned the windows, and half-doors set with coloured glass divided the rooms. A good example in Havana is **Casa de La Obra Pía**, on Obrapía and Mercaderes.

Neoclassical

The first neoclassical building in Havana was the **Templete**, a small doric temple on the Plaza de Armas. In the early 19th century, the cathedral in Havana had its baroque altars removed and replaced with neoclassical ones by Bishop Juan José de Espada. There are three fine neoclassical buildings in Matanzas: the cathedral, the **Iglesia de San Pedro Apóstol**, and the theatre. Many elaborate country houses were built around this time, for example **Quinta de Santovenia** near Havana, now an old people's home. Its inlaid marble floor, fountains and wrought-iron *rejas* are typical of the neoclassical period. The **Palacio de Aldama** (Amistad y Reina in Central Havana) has a stunning neoclassical interior with fine decorated ceilings. It is now the *Instituto de Historia de Cuba*.

20th century

One of the most notable art nouveau buildings is the **Palacio Velasco**, on Capdevila esquina Agramonte in Central Havana. Built in 1912, it is now the Spanish Embassy. There are also many good examples of art deco in Havana; the best is the **Edificio Bacardí** on Avenida de las Misiones, Old Havana (now renovated and looking fabulous), built in 1929 by the founder of Bacardi rum, and the neo-Renaissance **Casino Español**, now the Palacio de Los Matrimonios, on Paseo de Martí (Prado). The **Capitolio** was the brainwave of former dictator Machado, who sought to demonstrate his allegiance to the USA by erecting a copy of the Capitol building in Washington DC. Built in 1932, it has a 62-m dome and a 120-m very ornate entrance hall.

More examples of 1930s architecture can be seen in Santiago, where there are some attractive art deco buildings on the Malecón, as well as the **Palacio Nacionalista**. The **Vista Alegre** neighbourhood, begun in 1906, contains some outstanding examples of art nouveau, notably the Palacio de Pioneros. This pink building on Manduley entre 9 y 11 was one of the Bacardí family residences.

Aquiles Capablanca was the most popular architect of the 1950s. His **Tribunal de Cuentas** in Havana is one of the most admired 20th-century buildings in Latin

America. He also built the **Office of the Comptroller**, in Plaza de la República. Both buildings feature murals by well-known artist Amelia Peláez. Capablanca employed many elements inspired by Le Corbusier, whose influence can also be seen in residential work of the 1950s; conical designs called paraboloids were incorporated in the roof, whose purpose was to allow fresh air to circulate in the building. These avant-garde designs were combined with a revival of the colonial construction around a central patio, which hadn't been used for 70 years. The **Tropicana** nightclub, built by Max Borges Jr in 1952, was another work of stunning originality: exotic, sinuous curves on the shell-like structure are combined with tropical vegetation and the architect's own sculptures.

Post-Revolution

The Revolution saw less construction of new buildings than the conversion of former emblems of the Batista dictatorship into more functional buildings for public benefit. This happened with the **Moncada Garrison** in Santiago, now a school and museum, and the **Capitolio** in Havana, now a library and museum. Some new structures did appear, such as the **School of Plastic Arts**: started in 1961 by Ricardo Porro, and completed after his defection by Vittorio Garatti in 1965, it has been described as resembling a stretched-out woman's body, with breast-like domes and curved walkways. Another good example of post-Revolution creativity is the **Coppelia** ice cream parlour, by Mario Girona, completed in 1966.

Soviet influence and materials after the Revolution saw the appearance of the grey monolithic buildings associated with the former USSR. However, the negative aura of such buildings in Eastern Europe has often much to do with the climate. Many similar buildings in Cuba, for example state-run hotels built during the 1960s and 1970s, have such wide, open-plan interiors and vast windows, often coloured with modernist stained glass, that the effect is entirely positive, allowing light and air to move freely through the building. The **Hotel Sierra Maestra** in Bayamo and the **Hotel Guacanayabo** in Manzanillo are good examples of this.

An excellent way to get an overall picture of the architecture of Havana is to visit the Maqueta de La Habana, on Calle 28 113 entre 1 y 3, Miramar. This is a detailed model of the city with a scale of 1 m = 1 km, covering all its buildings dated by colour from the colonial period to the present.

Literature

The earliest known work of Cuban literature was a poem called *Espejos de paciencia*, published in 1605 by **Silvestre de Balboa**. An epic *canto* about the struggles between a Spanish bishop and a French pirate, it is an esteemed work for its time, though it now retains only historical value. Early schools of writers in Cuba were too influenced by Spanish literature to produce anything essentially Cuban and it was not until the first half of the 19th century that poets begin to formulate a voice of their own: the first collection of verse by a native Cuban was **Ignacio Valdés Machuca's** (1792-1851) *Ocios poéticos*, published in 1819.

José María Heredia y Heredia (1803-39) is considered the turning point for Cuban letters. His *Meditación en el teocalli de Chobula* (1820) marked the beginning of Romanticism, not only in Cuba, but in the Spanish language. He was also the first of many Cuban writers to be involved in the struggle for independence. He was expelled from the country for his part in anti-colonial conspiracies, and wrote most of his work while in exile in Mexico and the USA.

Cuba's most prolific woman writer was **Gertrudis Gómez de Avellaneda** (1814-73). Her anti-slavery novel *Sab* (1841) was the first of its kind to be published anywhere in Latin America, its theme predating *Uncle Tom's Cabin* by a decade. A glut

of abolitionist novels followed, the most notable being *Cecilia Valdés* (1882) by **Cirilio**
Villaverde (1812-94). The poet **Domingo Delmonte** (1804-53) led a protest against Cuba's continued acceptance of slavery after its official abolition in 1815, and many writers had to publish their anti-slavery novels in New York.

The most influential figure in Cuba's struggle for independence was **José Martí** (1853-95). He was deported to Spain in 1880 for his part in the independence movement. He later died in battle during the second War of Independence in 1895. He wrote *Versos Sencillos* (1891), based on the drama of his own life, while in exile in the USA. Martí also wrote highly acclaimed prose, which appeared in political journals published in Argentina and Venezuela. Many of his prophesies about Cuba's political future have been fulfilled.

Two poets associated with the transition from romanticism to modernism are **Enrique Hernández Miyarés** (1859-1914) and **Julián del Casal** (1863-93). The latter, influenced by Baudelaire, praised the value of art over nature in *Hojas al Viento* (Leaves in the Wind, 1890). His posthumous *Bustos y Rimas* (Busts and Rhymes, 1893) has been compared with the great Nicaraguan poet Rubén Darío. Another important modernist poet was **Regina Eladio Boti y Barreiro**. Although she only published three collections of verse, she was responsible for taking Cuban poetry from modernism to post-modernism.

In the 1920s, the *negrismo* movement began, which created non-intellectual poetry based on African dance rhythms. The poet **Lydia Cabrera** (1899-1999) dedicated her life to research of Afro-Cuban culture. As well as numerous stories, in which she created a prose based on the magical-mythical beliefs passed orally through black folklore, she published many books on the ethnography and linguistics of Afro-Cubans. The *negrismo* group consisted of poets both black and white, although its most famous member, **Nicolás Guillén Batista** (1902-89), was mulatto. *Motivos de son* (1930), in which he incorporated African rhythms in his *son* poetry, is considered his best work. He joined the Communist party and after the Revolution, was made president of the Union of Cuban Writers, and declared the National Poet by Castro.

Two of Guillén's former colleagues on the Communist newspaper *Hoy* were the writers **Lino Novás Calvo** (1905-83) and **Carlos Montenegro** (1900-81). Novas Calvo is recognized as one of the finest short story writers in Latin America. He used the narrative techniques of Hemingway and Faulkner to capture the feel of Havana slang. He was the first of many writers to go into voluntary exile with the instalment of Castro's régime. *La Luna Nona y Otros Cuentos* (The Ninth Moon, 1942) is his best collection. Carlos Montenegro's *Hombres Sin Mujer* (Life Without Women) has been compared to Céline and Genet. He was jailed for life aged 18 for killing a sailor who sexually assaulted him. The novel is based on the sexual exploits of his 15 years in prison.

The major writers at the time of the 1959 Revolution were the novelists **Virgilio Piñera** (1914-79) and **Alejo Carpentier** (1904-80) and the poet **José Lezama Lima**. All publishers were merged into the National Printing Press, with Alejo Carpentier as manager. The founder of magical realism, Carpentier's early novels are among the most highly rated in Latin American literature. Many are available in English, including *Los Pasos Perdidos* (The Lost Steps), the most accessible of his richly baroque tales.

José Lezama Lima (1910-76) scandalized post-Revolution Cuba with his novel *Paradiso* (Paradise, 1966), a thinly disguised account of his homosexual experiences. Primarily a poet, Lezama was one of the driving forces behind the *criollismo* movement of the 1940s and 1950s. His rebellious, apolitical stance is an inspiration to the young Cuban poets of today, who seek to create a non-politicized poetry with a more spiritual dimension.

One of the most famous dissident novelists was **Reinaldo Arenas** (1943-90). Dogged by state security for most of his youth, he was imprisoned several times as a dissident and a homosexual, and only managed to publish his novel *El Mundo Alucinado* (Hallucinations, 1971) by smuggling the manuscript out of the country

José Martí (1853-95)

Born into a poor family in Havana, José Martí dedicated his life from a young age to rebellion against the colonial Spanish rule. The head of his school, the poet and freedom fighter Rafael Mendive, was a strong influence on him, and it was his connection with Mendive that was used as evidence for Martí's sentence of forced labour for his part in the 1868 Independence Conspiracy while he was still a boy. The experience of gross injustice, slaving in the sun with old men and young boys chained at the ankles, implanted in the young Martí a lifelong commitment to the struggle for independence from Spanish rule.

Martí's sentence was commuted to exile. He was sent to Spain in 1871-74, where aged 18 he wrote the first of many political essays, *El presidio político de Cuba*, in which he denounced the sufferings of his fellow Cubans at the hands of an authoritarian colonial rule. He completed his studies in Spain, and then went to Mexico to become editor of *Revista Universal*. From there, his continued period of exile found him teaching at the University of Guatemala in 1877. He then lived in Venezuela until 1881 and the last years of his exile were spent in the USA. He left in 1895 to join the liberation movement in Cuba, where he was welcomed as a political leader. Tragically, he was killed on 19 May that year while fighting in the War of Independence at Boca de Dos Ríos near Santiago, see also page 316.

José Martí's work was primarily concerned with the liberation of Cuba, but many of his poems focused on nature, with Man at the centre engaged in a continual process of betterment. He combined a love of poetry with a desire for his prose work to have some effect on the world; all his energies were directed towards securing a future in which justice and happiness could flourish. Although one of the greatest modernist poets, he did not share other modernists' views that the role of poetry was outside conventional society.

Martí also differed from his contemporaries in his rejection of contemporary European literature. He saw precolumbian culture as having far more importance to a Latin American poet. His views were expanded upon in his essay *Nuestra América*, in which he welcomed the contributing force of Amerindians and blacks in contemporary culture.

Martí set the tone for all his poetry with *Ismaelillo* (1882), demonstrating the simplicity and sincerity he felt was lacking in current Spanish poetry. He developed this style in 1878, with *Versos libres*, and later in his most admired collection *Versos sencillos* (1891), in which the upheavals of his own life were his biggest inspiration. Martí is perhaps best known in Europe by the song *Guantanamera* – an adaptation by Pete Seeger of Martí's verse, put to the melody of Joseíto Fernández. In Cuba, however, he is the figure head of Cuban liberation and has become an icon, deliberately exploited by Castro, of anti-colonialism,

through foreign friends. He finally escaped to Miami in the Mariel exodus, but, suffering from AIDS, he committed suicide in New York. His memoirs, *Antes Que Anochezca* (Before Night Falls) were published posthumously and have since been made into a film, see Cinema, page 418. This and his other works are available in translation. Also available in English are the works of **Guillermo Cabrera Infante**

(1929-). In 1959 he became editor of the literary weekly, *Lunes de la Revolución*, but it was closed after two years when he got into trouble with the government. In 1962, he went to Brussels as cultural attaché, but resigned in 1965 and began exile in London in 1966. His witty novel about Havana nightlife during Batista's dictatorship, *Tres Tristes Tigres*, first version 1964, second version 1967 (Three Trapped Tigers, 1971), brought him literary fame. The book won him the Premio Biblioteca Breve in Barcelona in 1964, but led to him being expelled from the Cuban Union of Writers in 1968. Conflict between artistic creativity and the Revolution exploded in the 1970s with the Padilla affair. Herberto Padilla, a poet, won a literary prize in 1971, but instead of guaranteed publication, his book of satirical and questioning poems was blocked. He was imprisoned as a counter-revolutionary and forced to make a public confession of crimes he had not committed, a humiliating act which caused an outcry among the intellectuals of Europe.

As a reaction to the political restrictions placed on writers after the Revolution, a movement of experimental literature sprang up in the 1960s, influenced by the French avant-garde and North American pop culture. **Severo Sarduy** (1937-93), who left Cuba for Paris immediately after the Revolution, was the leading member; his *De dónde son los cantantes?* (From Cuba with a Song, 1967), with its complex layering of cultural history and linguistic puzzles, is still regarded as a classic by Cuban intellectuals. Sarduy became a citizen of France in 1967 and lived there until his death.

Nowadays Cuban writers find it easier to express their ideas in public. Havana has its first legally-recognized literary group. At the centre of the group is **Reina María Rodríguez**, a poet who is already gaining admiration outside Cuba. Some of these young poets and writers see themselves as carrying on where literature left off after the 1960s, when the repressive measures of the Revolution induced a state of creative inertia and self-censorship. There is also a new generation of Cuban American writers, whose parents fled in the 1960s, who are now discovering their roots.

Music and dance

There are few countries in the world with so rich a musical heritage as Cuba. No visitor can fail to be moved by the variety of sounds that surround them, whether it be a street corner rumba or a *septeto* in the *Casa de la Trova*. Music is everywhere – it seems that nothing can happen without it.

The origins of Cuban music lie in the movement of numerous, primarily European, and African cultures. Through the inauspicious conditions of migration, enslavement, war and colonization, elements of these disparate identities have fused into a Cuban identity, forged in the villages and on plantations, in tenements and dockyards. African music and dance forms whose paths might never have crossed on their own vast continent did so in Cuba, enriching each other, and drawing also upon European forms. The mirror image is equally true with European dances finding new, African interpretations, while musicians have absorbed African harmony and chorus styles as well as rhythm. Most of today's popular genres are neither Yoruba nor French, Ekiti, Ashanti, nor Spanish, but fusions from this vast cultural gene pool.

The Cuban music most universally accepted on the island is surely the **son**, which, in spite of its more urban variations and offspring, remains essentially rural. Played by Cuba's oldest and youngest musicians, it is a principal root of salsa, and, however unlikely it might at times seem, also *timba*. In its various forms *son* still thrives both in the countryside and cities throughout the island, pointing to the nascent character of urban culture. *Son* began its life in Oriente where old songs from Spain combined with African call-and-response choruses. The syncopated notes of the guitar and *tres* (a small guitar-like instrument) contributed to other genres such as *guaracha*, full of satire and humour, and soon evolved new ones such as the *guajira*, resulting in the famous '*guajira*

Alicia Alonso and the Ballet Nacional de Cuba

Although there was dancing in Cuba during the Spanish colonial period, with occasional visiting companies from Spain, ballet was not seen until 1842, when the great Romantic ballerina Fanny Elssler appeared at the Teatro Tacón. Performances by touring companies followed, including a visit by Anna Pavlova in 1917. Home-bred ballet started with the ballet evenings of the Sociedad Pro-Arte Música in 1931, whose conservatory produced Alicia Alonso and the two Alonso brothers, Alberto and Fernando, among other outstanding dancers and choreographers of their generation.

Alicia Alonso has been the most influential Cuban dancer and ballet director ever, having made her name on the world stage before returning to Cuba to direct the development of ballet. Born Alicia Ernestina de la Caridad del Cobre Martínez Hoyo in Havana on 21 December 1921, she studied in Havana and at the School of American Ballet in New York. After working on Broadway, in 1940 she became a member of the Ballet Theatre and temporarily joined the Sociedad Pro-Arte Música in Havana. She suffered periods off work because of a detached retina but returned to the Ballet Theatre in 1943 as ballerina. In 1948, she set up her own company in Havana, the Ballet Alicia Alonso, followed by a school in 1950, but continued to dance abroad, both with the American Ballet Theatre and as a guest of many other companies.

Alonso is known for her classical style and flawless technique, but she has also successfully interpreted modern roles. In New York she worked a lot with the choreographer Anthony Tudor, who once said of her during a rehearsal, "Oh, this excitable, temperamental Cuban, very savage, very primitive, you should try to be more educated!" Knowing that his remarks were hurtful, he asked when

she would start crying. "Never!" came the reply, and she kept her promise. In fact, Tudor loved her superb technique, her spirit and her combination of vulnerability and defiance, but believed that her natural expressiveness and her tendency to show all her emotion in her face was vulgar and needed to be restrained. He held that the movement itself should show the expression. A compromise was reached. One of Alonso's most famous roles was, like Fanny Elssler, that of Giselle, but she has created roles in Tudor's Undertow (1945), Alberto Alonso's Romeo and Juliet (1946), Balanchine's Theme and Variations (1947), de Mille's Fall River Legend (1948), and the title role in Alberto Alonso's Carmen (1967).

Alicia married Fernando Alonso, a dancer and ballet director, and brother of dancer and choreographer, Alberto Alonso. The three of them worked to establish the company, Ballet Alicia Alonso, which in 1961 became the Ballet Nacional de Cuba. The company became a showpiece for the Revolutionary government, even touring to the USA in 1978. The school's young dancers have a reputation for technique and artistic interpretation, winning many medals at international competitions. In Havana they perform a repertory of classical ballets, folklore-based works and modern dance at the Teatro García Lorca. Several important ballets have been especially created for the company, including Alberto Alonso's El Güije and Un retablo para Romeo y Julieta. Alonso's Carmen was originally created for the Bolshoi Ballet, but has become part of the repertory of the Ballet Nacional de Cuba.

The Festival Internacional de Ballet is usually held in October in Havana and other Cuban cities. For details, paradis@turcult.get.cma.net and bnc@cubarte.cult.cu

Guantanamera', and *nengón*. With the addition of bongo, maracas and marimbula, *nengón* developed into the style known as **son changüí**. From Guantánamo (where *changüí* is still strong), the *son* reached Havana around 1909, along with elements of the new Permanent Army, and gained there the disdain of society, which disregarded and feared it as the music of the lower, particularly black, class. Persecuted by the authorities, *son* simmered in a few black neighbourhoods, existing there through illegal parties for some ten years. However, given Society's taste for expropriating the surplus value of the lower orders' uncouth labour, it was perhaps inevitable that they would eventually appropriate also their dynamic culture. By the early 1920s, and with tasteful modifications, small *son* combos were beginning to displace the cumbersome and expensive *danzón* orchestras from La Habana's exclusive dance salons. Capturing the most gifted writers and band leaders of the time this gentrification of *son* was not entirely without benefit to its continued evolution and precipitated its spread not just across social but also national boundaries. Although few if any recordings were made of *son* prior to this, a multitude followed, and whatever criticisms one might make, they remain a rich source of material for inspiration and re-interpretation.

As the 1930s approached, **Ignacio Piñero** formed his **Septeto Nacional**. (A *septeto* is a seven-piece band, including guitars, percussion, brass, vocals, playing traditional Cuban music.) Their *sones* not only featured his exceptional vocal improvisations (honed in the large choral societies called *Coros de Clave*), but added a hot trumpet to the central rhythm of the *clave*. **Nicolás Guillén** busied himself composing *sones* and *son* was now recognized as the sound of Cuba (to stand alonside such 'exotic' names as samba, conga and tango, in Europe and the USA it was marketed as the '*rhumba*'). The *septeto* style is still heard today in the popular music bars and *Casas de la Trova*. Piñero continued to innovate by mixing styles, creating *guajira son*, *bolero son* (also popularized by Santiago's *Miguel Matamoros*) and even *son pregón son* which used Havana street cries, including the famous *echalé salsita*.

A new development in the 1930s was Arsenio Rodriguez' *conjunto* style, which marked the beginning of modern **salsa**. To the traditional *septeto* came conga drums, *timbales* (or '*paila*' – optional), piano and more trumpets. This 'big band' *son* made much of the final, wild call-and-response or *montuno* section of the song. The later *Descargas* were improvised jam sessions over strong *paila*, conga and bongo rhythms, which had major influences on US jazz. The *tumbao* played by the *tumbadoras* is derived from rumba, so salsa combines elements of the three most prominent musical traditions: *son*, *danzón* and rumba.

During the 1950s, Beny Moré emerged as *Sonero Mayor* (meaning greatest singer and lyric improviser more than interpreter of *son*) and he remains one of the most revered figures in Cuban music history. Beny and his *Banda Gigante* were as adept with the newer styles, mambo and cha cha cha, as with *son* and its variations. Of equal importance, the size of his orchestra allowed the introduction of American Big Band Jazz to the Cuban melting pot. The era also saw the arrival of such artists as **La Sonora Matancera** and **Celia Cruz**, both of whom found fame in exile. There, in the USA, Celia (died 2003) won world wide acclaim as the Queen of Salsa. Back in Cuba, **Miguel Cuní**, **Félix Chapottín** and **Lilí** forged a somewhat harder edged urban Son to serenade the arrival of Castro's nationalist Revolution.

If Cuba of the sixties is remembered more in connection with Russian nuclear missiles than for earth shattering music, the foundations were being laid for future musical revolutions. It's hard to find any virtue in the frankly awful experiments with pop music by Elio Revé and **Juan Formell**, but both talents went on to lead bands of enormous importance and popularity through the 1970s and 1980s. Formell's band, **Los Van Van**, have undergone a number of reinventions and remain very much at the cutting edge of today's music.

No less than the development of a popular education system on the island following the Revolution, US policy towards Cuba has had a powerful effect on the subsequent unfolding of popular Latin music in both countries, actually creating something of a schism. Cut off from its source, the music of Cuban exile and Portarrican communities has tended to become bogged in old musical language in the way of ex-pats, at the same time absorbing the economic ethos of the host nation. Polished and manicured and formularised, salsa has become a multi-million dollar industry in the USA and its southern sphere of influence, its product as personal as any other factory produced commodity. Cubans on the other hand have never ceased to import, fuse and re-fuse ideas from their rich musical larder and from elsewhere and, less driven by market trends, their bands tend to develop distinctive sounds. Through the 1970s and 1980s the distinctions between genres such as *son* and charanga blurred somewhat, however, while economic pressure forced the replacement of acoustic with electric bass guitar. The Baby Bass (a substitute electric upright electric bass) which is de rigueur in salsa bands was almost unheard of in Cuba. This reality alone sent Cuban music off on its own path. Some bands began to borrow heavily from funk and other urban black American styles, but overall the feel of music from this era is quite rustic. As well as the bands mentioned above, **Orquesta 440** (not to be confused with Juan Luis Guerra) stands out, as do **Son 14**, and **Adalberto Alvarez y su Son**, both the latter two being led by the same Adalberto.

Not for the first time, the new generation has continued the tradition of innovation to the point of creating a new music, **timba**. That a prominent pioneer such as Giraldo Piloto should protest his music to be merely *progressive son* alludes to the power of this revered tradition, the strength in Cuban culture of lineage principles as against individuation and, within this, the dependence of urban culture on its rural roots. Timba and Cuban rap were born not in the hills, but in the cities. They incorporate musical ideas from the outside urban world that resonate with city dwellers and certainly *timba* is the product of musicians who have enjoyed a technical training their predecessors could not have imagined. This is fundamentally urban music which perhaps has yet to become fully self aware, and you will hear little of it outside La Habana.

While *son* was appearing in Cuba's countryside, an African rhythm known as the **yuka**, which had survived on the sugar plantations, was joining forces with the Spanish *décima* and livening up the ports of Havana and Matanzas. This style soon came to be known as **rumba**. African rhythms were played on whatever came to hand: boxes used to pack fish or candles gave a good tone. Characters such as *Mama'buela* were created in mime and singers commented on current events or battled with each other for honours. This *rumba de cajón* also involved the stately *yambú* dance, where following the vocal section, a couple would mime courtship. Soon the rhythms passed onto drums, the large *tumba* providing a solid bass, the conga a repeated cross rhythm which was accompanied by brilliant improvisations on the small *quinto*. There are other terms like *llamador, trabajador, tres dos*, and *tres golpes* to describe the deeper sounding drums, which seem to be named after their role in the rumba. To this was added a pair of *claves* and a struck length of bamboo known as the *guagua* or *cata*. The more sexual dance form known as *guaguancó* (still the main rumba style) demanded more rapid playing. Great rumberos emerged, such as **Florencio Calle**, **Chano Pozo**, **Estéban Latrí** and **Celeste Mendoza**, as well as groups who specialized in rumba, such as **Los Papines**, **Conjunto de Clave y Guaguancó** and the well-travelled **Muñequitos de Matanzas**, who used the rhythms of the Abakuá religion in their rumbas. The *Muñequitos* also play the Matanzas style known as *Columbia*. This rumba echoes African solo dancing, involving an element of danger such as the use of knives. Even faster playing underpins a singing style which makes use of Bantu phrases and ends in a call-and-response.

Music on TV

A most encouraging aspect of Cuban culture is that live music is paramount. Rather than tinny speakers placed high up on walls, most cafés, hotels, bars and even airports will have a live band serenading the punters. However, those who find themselves in front of a (working) television will not be disappointed.

Music is everywhere in Cuba and there are a host of specials on Cubavision to look out for. A 'must see' for salsa fans is *Mi Salsa* on Sunday nights, which regularly showcases a top Cuban band as well as showing the latest salsa artists on video. This follows on from *Palmas y Cañas*, the *campesino* programme which features rural son and the *controversio* style of musical debate, as well as advice on herbal teas... Tuesday night has both *Encuentro*, a collection of music from across Latin America, and *A Capella*, which shows old film of Cuban greats such as Matamoros or Tata Güinés. On Wednesday you can hear Cuban stars talk about their influences in '*Tiempos*', while *En FM* on Friday nights is the *Top of the Pops* of Cuban music – the chart is compiled by phone-in requests. Anyone who has struggled with a Cuban phone will realize what a triumph of patience this is. Saturday night kicks off with the excellent *Contacto*, a two-hour arts magazine which has a regular live band and discussion with top musicians. A wonderful *Contacto* moment occurred when Ken Loach (in Havana for the film festival) enjoyed the music and then proceeded to struggle with inane 'are you liking Cuba' questions, having previously sat in silence during an in-depth discussion (in Spanish) with Gutiérrez Alea on the influence of Italian New Realism on revolutionary Cuban Cinema! *Contacto* is followed by the hugely popular comedy show *Sabadazo*; *Los Van Van*, *La Charanga* or other star bands finish off the show with a blast of brilliant son. Along with whole nights dedicated to musical rallies, Christmas specials and New Year concerts, TV is a great chance to see the bands you might have missed live. If you can't get near a TV, Saturday radio (*Rebelde*) rocks to some great salsa.

Go on, have a night in.

Rumba is a playfully competitive art form, although sometimes the competitiveness is not always so playful. The men, particularly the '*guapos*', or 'hard guys', take it very seriously and people do get hurt, sometimes even killed. The rhythms have got faster, break dancing and karate moves have been incorporated into the dance, *rumberos* sing about the special period; in this way, rumba survives as a true reflection of Cuban street life.

Matanzas is also the birthplace of the **danzón**. The popular *Típica* orchestras, influenced by the great cornettist **Miguel Faílde**, added subtle African rhythms to the European Contradanza, along with a call-and-response *montuno* section, creating a balance between formal dance and syncopated rhythm, almost a Cuban ragtime. The **Orquesta Típica** slowly changed, adding piano and further percussion, while the 1920s saw a new arrival, the *Charanga Francesa*. Of French Haitian descent, this was another development of the *típica*, featuring wooden flute and strings as well as *pailas*. It is in this format, so different from its origins, that *danzón* is generally remembered and occasionally interpreted. It was the beginning of the **Charanga** style developed by contemporary Cuban groups such as **Orquesta Aragón** and **Los Van Van**.

During the 1940s and 1950s, **Orestes López** (*Cachao*) and the violinist **Enrique Jorrín** created the new mambo and **cha cha cha** styles directly from *danzón*. These

Background Music & dance

☷ Ten classic timba/salsa nueva CDs

1 **Azúcar Negra**, Andar Andando (Bis Music, 2000). After this first recording lead singer Haila from Bamboleo went her own way. Here you will find the most eloquent expression of *timba* at high tide.

2 **Bamboleo**, *Yo No Me Parezco a Nadie* (Ahí Na'Ma', 1998). Imagine two loud young women busting into a cabaret where a highly accomplished band is earning its daily bread. The girls bustle their way on stage, where, disarmed by decorum, nobody can prevent them from taking over the show. Undeniably lowering the tone, it nevertheless works out for the better as inspired by this raw energy, the band now realize their potential. Rough and smooth in perfect harmony, that was Bamboleo at their best.

3 **Conexión Salsera**, *Muy Caliente Para Tí* (EGREM, 1997). Featuring Danny Lozada en route for La Charanga Habanera, this is subtle in its use of contrasting chorus and lead vocal styles, beautifully focused percussion, and some of the greatest Cuban piano work on record. All quite understated, great for dancing Casino.

4 **Giraldo Piloto y Klimax**, *Oye Como Va* (Eurotropical, 2000). Piloto pilots his band through seamless changes of genre and style, a kind of aural painting. More a musician's than a popular band, the trajectory is towards jazz-rock-funk-*timba* fusion and in this field Piloto has no company let alone equals. Probably one of the greatest CDs released ever.

5 **Isaac Delgado**, *El Malecón (La Formula)* (Bis Music/Ahí Na'Ma', 2000). The king of salsa nueva when he pulls his finger out, you will find here a fistful of cracking dances, and a lot more besides. Songs tend to have long gentle intros, then the bass lets rip under a steaming rhythm section.

driving rhythms are still popular all over Cuba, and were fundamental to the explosion of Latin music and dance worldwide.

The **canción habanera** is regarded as the first truly Cuban vocal style. Emerging in the 1830s as a mixture of the so-called *tongo congo* rhythm and Spanish melodies, it had its greatest exponent in **Eduardo Sánchez**. *Habaneras* were also composed by **Eduardo Lecuona**, a pianist who was internationally feted during the 1930s and 1940s.

Another *canción* style, involving simply a singer and a guitar, was developed during the 19th century in Oriente by **Pepe Sánchez**. His simple, beautiful songs, such as *Rosa No 1* and *Rosa No 2*, inspired others such as María Teresa Vera and the remarkable **Sindo Garay**, who claimed to be the only man who had shaken the hand of both Jose Martí and Fidel Castro! The romantic style known as bolero soon developed from *canción*.

Realizing the potential for expression offered by *canción*, young musicians like **Silvio Rodríguez**, **Sara González** and **Pablo Milanés** created the **nueva trova**. Their songs reflect the path of the Revolution, **Silvio**'s '*Playa Girón*' telling its own story. '*Pablito*' is an exceptional composer and interpreter, especially of Guillén's poetry.

Cuban **jazz** is exceptionally healthy. **Orquesta Irakere** continue to renew themselves, inspired by the pianistic genius of Jesús 'Chucho' Valdéz, while **Grupo Afro-Cuba** fuse jazz with traditional Cuban rhythms, including the *bata* drums of *Santería*. Among the generation of the 1980s and 1990s the incredible pianist **Gonzalo Rubalcaba** is supreme, composing pieces using *danzón* rhythms amongst others. The annual Jazz Festival in Havana was for years attended by **Dizzy Gillespie**,

6 **David Calzado y La Charanga Habanera**, *Tremendo Delirio* (Universal 1997). For many, the definitive *timba* CD, certainly none of the bands that formed from the CH's subsequent split have produced anything comparable. With the addition of Danny Calzado, it is phenomenal.

7 **Los Van Van**, *Te Pone La Cabeza Mala* (Caribe, 1997). Van Van's finest moment. Juan Formell and band had developed and ran parallel along with *timba*. They offer here the most complex crowd-pleasing music you could hope to find, music that seeks the highest common denominator while remaining truly popular. Singer Mayito shines through the frontline.

8 **Manolín** (El Médico de la Salsa), *De Buena Fé* (Caribe, 1997). Opportunist El Médico is a psychiatrist without a very good voice who turned to singing. Having attempted to straddle the Cuba/Miami divide, Manolín settled in the States after suffering power cuts during his gigs and other such 'accidents' on the island. Musically, this CD has enormous depth in its arrangements, a master class in *timba* percussion, keyboard, chorus and bass, so who cares if he can't sing?

9 **NG La Banda**, *En La Calle* (Qbadisc, 1989). The one that started it all. Here you will find the young Issac Delgado, Giraldo Piloto, El Tosco, and the 'terror brass'. Such explosions are rare and this one hasn't dated a second. A million miles both from what preceded and what succeeded it.

10 **Paulo FG**, *Una Vez Más….Por Amor* (2000). Paulito runs the gamut between sublimely complex sophisticated *timba*, and slushy *salsa romántica* and ballads. This penultimate CD contains a good handful of ultra smooth *timba* tracks that almost slide in one ear and out the other.

whose influence is evident in the playing of Cubans such as **Arturo Sandóval** and has recently heard British jazzers giving their all. Less well known but of no less virtue as the above are **Los Terry**, a family-based band which plays an unusually rural form of Latin jazz. Lacking the polish of its New York equivalent that tends to struggle self-consciously to integrate Afro-Cuban elements, **Los Terry** have nothing to prove. If their jazz is elementally powerful, it is also totally absorbing in its complexity, dipping into Afro-Cuban folklore intuitively and naturally, rather than to make a point.

The rhythms and songs of **Santería** remain strong across the island. The three African *bata* drums are regarded as the most complex of all to master and the rhythms, each assigned to a particular deity, accompany the singing in old Yoruba. **Merceditas Valdés** is loved throughout Cuba for her interpretation of these songs. Meanwhile, '*bembe*' parties on Saints' days are accompanied by singing and drumming. The singer **Lázaro Ros** has developed a band, **Síntesis**, who combine traditional *Santería* music effectively with jazz rock.

The music of the Cuban **carnival**, recently revived following the debilitating effects of the special period, is truly exhilarating. Both Havana and Santiago have their own styles of **conga**, the thunderous music which drives on the parade. During August in Havana, the conga drums, bells and bass drums of groups such as **Los Dandy La Jardinera**, support brass players as they belt out popular melodies, the lanterns spinning in the dancers' hands. In Santiago, each *barrio* is represented by massed ranks of *bocué* drums, bass drums and brake drums. The cloaked and masked revellers of Los Hoyos and San Agustín sing in response to the wailing *corneta china*, a remnant of Cuba's

Chinese communities. Other bands' *paseos* combine brass players with the usual barrage of percussion during the late July festivities.The carnival procession usually features the old *Cabildos*, whose drums keep alive the rhythms of Africa. In Oriente, the *Tumbas Francesas* parade the rhythms and dances developed by Africans in Haiti, before the 18th-century Revolution forced yet another move across the ocean.

All of this music can be heard in Cuba now: at the *Casas de La Trova*, at the *Focos Culturales*, in the theatres and the cafés, in the parks, the backyards and on the streets. From *changüí* to cha cha cha, from rumba to bolero, from *son* to *Santería*, the music of Cuba is gloriously, vibrantly alive.

The rise and decline of timba and salsa nueva

"*Que sabrosura viva, tremenda expresividad,*" echoes the chorus, following an opening riff from '*los metales del terror,*' surely the scariest horn section ever. La Habana circa 1989 and like never before, a new band is rocking the city with a tribute to the neighbourhoods. This is not salsa as we've known or might expect it. The structure and feel are fresh and innovative, actually disconcerting. Isn't it jazz or some weird form of rock? You have to pay attention though because this band overflows with virtuosity, breaking tradition consciously, rather than from incompetence. Not a slow number but it feels laid back, grounding you with heavy *tumbadoras*, driving kit drums and bass, lifting you with blinding horn riffs, and there's a vocalist whose ease of delivery sends your head swimming. "*¿Quién se come el calamar? La gente de Miramar*" asks and answers the chorus. Then half the band cuts out leaving the bass booming and growling under syncopated thumps, to a rhythm section which has taken almost as much from jazz-rock and funk as its Afro-Cuban roots. Almost as much. The percussion breakdown or '*bomba*' in salsa makes its debut.

This was **NG La Banda**, as they said with characteristic modesty, '*la que manda,*' a talent concentrate from which some of Cuba's current leading artists emerged to form bands in their own right. The working title of '*bomba-son*' evolved through the 1990s and onwards with new bands and ideas taking shape from an unprecedented pool of talent. Each has added new ingredients to this urban fusion, lending diversity that defies homogenisation. Today the music has become known loosely as *timba*.

Not by chance, the pioneers of **NG** (new generation) **La Banda** were drawn largely from two other bands with histories in pushing forward the frontiers of traditional Cuban music. Though not necessarily for dance music, **Irakere** has been acclaimed internationally for its fusions of jazz with funk, disco, rock and Afro-Cuban rhythm. On the other hand **Los Van Van** had enjoyed 20 years or so as Cuba's number one dance band, combining elements of pop and pan-Caribbean rhythm within a modernized Charanga band. When some of these two bands' strongest elements got together, then the result was bound to be explosive. Principal among the founders was the multi-talented director **José Luís Cortés** (El Tosco) who lays claim with equally gifted **Giraldo Piloto** (now with his own band, *Klimax*) to be the inventor of this new music.

The emergence of *timba* rested upon the state education system and changing conditions of life no less than upon Cuba's traditions and gifted musicians. These days a musician or arranger's innate talent is complemented with the discipline of a comprehensive academy training. Not that they're stuffed shirts or anything. Through the early and mid 1990s the dissemination and development of technique and style among musicians continued, each innovation tested in the street practices and rehearsals that maintain contact between the public and even the most prestigious bands. A shouted joke or taunt from the crowd is transformed in a moment to a chorus line and improvised around. It becomes the line that hooks you when you hear the record; the symbiotic relationship between the bands and their audience gives inspiration to musicians while elevating to the stage the lives, dreams and preoccupations of Havana's youth. As such, and along with more familiar subjects, songs abounded about prostitution, the virtues of soya mince, girlfriends disappearing with rich foreign men and just the struggle to

⁞ Buying music

Obviously on your return from Cuba you will want to transform your little room into the local *Casa de la Trova* and invite all the neighbours round for a *traguito* of Havana Club rum. Luckily there is a large choice of music available, on video, cassette and CD. The state record company EGREM has shops alongside recording studios in the main towns. Every hotel should stock tapes at least of the major artists. Thanks to a distribution deal with a French company, much of the EGREM back catalogue is seeing the light of day again under the name of ARTEX, in a series of well-balanced compilations and major reissues. ARTEX is involved in all cultural marketing so they too have shops in every town centre, which stock posters, crafts and books alongside the sound and vision. The dollar shops such as Cubalse will also have a good range. The series *El Son Es Lo Más Sublime* features an extensive history of the genre and there are excellent series on rumba, *danzón*, *bolero*, Cuban jazz, conga and folkloric styles, as well as the latest by **Van Van**, **El Médico** and the others. These should also be for sale, along with recordings by house bands, in the *Casas de la Trova*. Occasionally the booksellers on street corners and in the plaza will have old vinyl discs (probably unplayable) and you might even chance upon one of the newly emerging second-hand record stores for those rare '*descarga*' sessions. These are sometimes worth it for the sleeves alone. You'll need to know the dollar/peso exchange rate to buy, though. If you fancy a go yourself, EGREM shops stock a range of mass produced Afro-Cuban instruments: conga drums, bongos, claves and suchlike, which are reasonably priced, especially compared with prices in Europe. You'll need to watch your baggage allowance though (and your back muscles as you stagger home). If you don't have time for record shopping, or you want to brush up on your *son* before you go, the Latin American craft shop Tumi (Tumi Music Ltd, 8/9 New Bond Street Place, Bath, BA1 1BH, T01225-462367, F01225-444870) are now distributing the best of EGREM's compilations in Britain. For people with a taste for the new generation of music from La Habana, Timba Merchant is your best bet in the UK. Call or email for a catalogue of contemporary CDs (T020-7790 4693, timbamerchant@hotmail.com).

There are also three wonderful and all-embracing compilations: *Cuban Counterpoint – A History of Son Montuno, A Carnival of Cuban Music* and *Afro-Cuba, An Anthology*; all out on the Rounder label. It's difficult to find a book purely about Cuban music in English. The best at the moment is the study of salsa *Havana Heat, Bronx Beat*, by Hernando Calvo Ospina. If your Spanish is up to it, you could try the short essays (and lovely pen sketches) *Música por El Caribe*, by Helio Orovio. María Teresa Linares' *La Música y El Pueblo* is a classic and the African roots are brilliantly explored in *Los Cabildos y la Fiesta Afrocubanos del Día de Reyes*, by Cuba's pioneering ethnologist Fernando Ortíz. All these should be adequate for the new lending library attached to your recently opened '*Casa de la Trova experience*'. The neighbours will be ecstatic.

survive. Presented with irony, and the facility of street wit, *timba* constituted an antidote to the escapism of ubiquitous *tele-novelas* (soap operas). It is pop music in the truest sense of the word and it has shaken salsa to its foundations.

Lagging a little behind *timba*, **salsa nueva** emerged as a music to bridge the gap between old and new. Integrating with salsa elements of *timba* such as syncopated bass lines and sparing use of a shouted chorus, it is more restrained and comprehensible to a traditional salsa ear. Eschewing the more nihilistic trends of incessant *bloques* (percussion breaks), structural shifts and breakdowns, it is also easier to dance to for anyone who needs something solid to hang on to. What culminated in a wave of inspired, original, infectious music around 1997, three years later had reached maturity, and was promising to extinguish in a final blast. Everything subsequently has been little more of an afterglow, although if you prefer sophistication and balance to youthful exuberance it is in this later period that you'll find a spattering of truly timeless gems. While bands of lesser originality begin to repeat themselves or go all out for the Latin pop market, some of the greatest band leaders are restrained by the confines of dance music, even for a musically sophisticated people like the Cubans. Each exploration by the likes of **Giraldo Piloto** might continue breaking musical boundaries, but ultimately estranges them from the mass audience upon which they once depended. Their music is just too complex and never settles into comforting recognizable formulas. In this context **Cuban rap** makes its appearance. First to make waves were **Orishas**. In spite of a hip hop parody stage act, their first CD fused rap to powerful effect with the morose nostalgia of the *guajira*. Another notable is **Clan 537** whose more recent hit '*Quien Tiró La Tisa?*' is stunning more in its social than musical content. Officially, racism and class prejudices do not exist in Cuba, although they are deeply ingrained in Cuba's people and culture. However restrained by American standards, **Clan 537** show their resentment of this reality as frankly as *timba* artists in their day dealt with the problems they could.

Timba will never disappear though. Many bands whose reputations are built on other genres have nodded *timba*'s way and, in doing so, have incorporated its innovations into the mainstream. This is where *timba* now lies, so don't be surprised to hear syncopated electric bass lines and percussion breakdowns from the younger generation of *son* bands. Neither has the standard of musicianship upon which *timba* depended disappeared. It has merely lost focus for its employment. Many now wait in anticipation of the next wave.

Cinema

One of the great success stories of the Cuban Revolution is the Cuban film industry. The Film Institute, known familiarly as **ICAIC** (Cuban Institute of Cinematographic Art and Industry), was set up by the new government in March 1959, only three months after the victory of the Revolution. Headed by **Alfredo Guevara**, it aimed to produce, distribute and show Cuban films to as wide a domestic audience as possible, to train film-makers and technicians, and to promote film culture generally. Open to anyone with an interest in film, excepting pro-Batista collaborationists, the institute built up an industry with an international reputation within 10 years, virtually from scratch.

Before the Revolution, films had been made in Cuba by foreign companies or amateurs. The staple diet of the Cuban filmgoer, even in 1959, was Hollywood movies. In the early 1960s, after the Bay of Pigs episode (1961) and the missile crisis (1962), several film directors (including **Néstor Almendros**), cinematographers and technicians, left the island, taking their precious equipment with them. Adequate government funding, which depended on the fluctuating Cuban economy, and state-of-the-art training and technology, became critical problems following the US trade embargo. The majority of the crew working on **Tomás Gutiérrez Alea**'s comedy *The Twelve Chairs*, for example (the assistant director, director of cinematography, camera operator, focus puller, camera assistant and continuity girls), were first-timers. Yet in learning to make the most of their scant resources, the Cuban film-makers introduced striking new techniques which, in addition to their youthful enthusiasm, improvisation and revolutionary focus, created a forceful impact on the world of film. Five Cuban films won international awards in 1960 alone. As Francis Ford Coppola remarked, "We don't have the advantage of their inconveniences". Measures such as the launch of the film journal *Cine cubano*, the inauguration of the **Havana Cinemateca** (1960), a national network of film clubs, and a travelling cinema (*cinemóvil*) showing films to peasants in remote rural districts, the nationalization of the film distribution companies, and the 1961 literacy campaign enabling 700,000 viewers to read the subtitles of undubbed foreign films for the first time, placed cinema at the forefront of revolutionary cultural innovation. Even the posters, designed under the auspices of ICAIC by individual artists, became world famous.

The types of films made during the 1960s were national, nonconformist and cheap. **ICAIC** aimed to keep as independent a criteria as possible over what constituted art, and encouraged imaginative, popular films, directly relevant to the Revolutionary process and challenging the mass culture of acquiescent consumption. The preferred format was the documentary shot on 8-mm or 16-mm film (40 were made in 1965), honed to perfection by **Santiago Alvarez**, but there were a good number of excellent features too: *Cuba Baila* (Cuba Dances), *Historias de la Revolución* (Stories of the Revolution), *El Joven Rebelde* (The Young Rebel, based on a script by Zavattini), *La Muerte de un Burócrata* (Death of a Bureaucrat) and *Aventuras de Juan Quinquin* (The Adventures of Juan Quinquin), the most popular feature in Cuba of all time, until the release of *Fresa y Chocolate* (Strawberry and Chocolate).

In 1967, the film director **Julio García Espinosa** published his seminal essay *For an Imperfect Cinema* which, with the work of **Octavio Getino** and **Fernando Solanas** in Argentina and **Glauber Rocha** in Brazil, laid the basis of the New Latin American cinema movement, also known as **Third Cinema**, a key concept in film culture today. Cuban cinema reached its high point in 1968, with groundbreaking films such as *Lucía* (Lucia) and *Memorias del Subdesarrollo* (Memories of Underdevelopment) and, in 1969, *La Primera Carga al Machete* (The First Charge of the Machete). Cuban film-makers, a number of whom had been trained in the **Centro Sperimentale** in Rome in the 1950s, were influenced predominantly by Italian Neorealism, French New Wave Cinema and *cinéma verité* – British Free Cinema (Tony Richardson and Lindsay Anderson), and the Soviet classics. Films shot on location, with hand-held cameras featuring ordinary people engaged in a revolutionary process, have remained the trademarks of classic Cuban cinema ever since.

By the 1970s, however, uncomfortable questions were being asked about the appropriateness of avant-garde art for the needs of the Cuban mass public. Tensions between creative artists and government bureaucrats exploded in the **Padilla affair** (1970), resulting in a five-year government clampdown. **ICAIC's** production programme was reduced to three features a year, while young, often amateur film-makers (average age 36), were favoured over the more experienced. Nevertheless, important films were produced, tending to focus on women's issues, historical and/or multiracial themes (particularly slavery and African-Cuban culture), with a view to consolidating a strong, cohesive sense of national identity. The black film director **Sergio Giral's** *El Otro Francisco* (The Other Francisco) and Gutierrez Alea's *La Ultima Cena* (The Last Supper), both depicting the courage and resistance of Cuban slaves, black director Sara Gómez's *De Cierta Manera* (One Way or Another), highlighting the problem of *machismo* among black men, and Pastor Vegas' *Retrato de Teresa* (Portrait of Teresa), denouncing sexist attitudes in post-revolutionary society, all date from this period.

In 1976, the **Ministry of Culture** was set up, ushering in yet another episode in Cuban film history. In 1982, **Julio García Espinosa** took over from Alfredo Guevara as the Head of **ICAIC**, and the organisation was incorporated into the ministry. Until 1980 it had been self-financing. Nevertheless, despite the increasing influence of the Hollywood format (favouring sentimental melodrama and romance), perhaps indicative of a deeper crisis of belief, films still tended to be critical of Cuban social

❖ Films

If you know Spanish (and even if you don't) the following comedies are a must: *La Muerte de un Burócrata* (Death of a Bureaucrat, Gutiérrez Alea, 1966), in which a worker is mistakenly buried with his identity card. His widow needs it to claim her pension but when the family try to exhume the body officially they are caught up in a Kafkian tangle of bureaucracy forcing them to dig up the body themselves. When the body starts to smell, they try to bury it again, with hilarious results. This is a side-splitting, but no less serious, criticism of state officialism.

The social satire *¡Plaff!* (Splat!, Juan Carlos Tabío, 1988) picks up on the same theme. A woman dies of a heart attack when an egg is thrown at her. Who threw the egg and why? This parody of a detective film delves deep into social issues, such as the Cuban housing crisis and the scarcity of resources, while lampooning "imperfect cinema". The preference for foreign imports is ridiculed when a home-made polymer made from pig shit at the Institute of Excrement is proved to be far superior to a Canadian brand. The highlight of the film, however, is when the director of the Institute asks for a new filing cabinet, to store the letters he has written asking for a new filing cabinet.

Adorables Mentiras (Adorable Lies, Gerardo Chijona, 1991) is a much more poignant comedy. An unsuccessful scriptwriter tries to impress a young streetwalker by pretending to be a film director, while she in turn deceives him by pretending to be a professional actress. The complex web of sex, lies and audiotape unravels when the writer's wife, who thinks he's gay, is delighted to find out he is having an affair with a woman. But the objective of this apparently farcical charade is deadly serious. Cuban society of the 1980s is shown to be rife with petty corruption, resulting from self-delusion and material constraints. Young people are urged to face reality and get on with their lives, even if it means painful compromise.

reality. Production figures increased to some six features a year during the 1980s, many of these co-productions with countries such as Mexico and Spain. By the end of the 1980s there were 60 million film goers, each Cuban visiting a cinema on average six times a year. The Cuban audiences, mostly young white-collar workers, technicians and specialists, tend to be educated and demanding. A network of video clubs and libraries were set up in the 1980s to meet their needs.

In the late 1980s, **ICAIC** recovered its independence and was restructured on the basis of three 'creation groups' each under an experienced film director in charge of encouraging and training young film makers. But, as Cuba moved into the **'Special Period'** (1990-94) in response to the fall of the Eastern block and the intensified US trade embargo, **ICAIC** faced another crisis. After the release of a controversially critical film, *Alicia en el Pueblo de Maravillas* (Alice in Wonderworld), in a climate of political tension, moves were made to incorporate the Institute into Radio and Television, directly controlled by the **Central Committee of the Communist Party**. This strategy was actively resisted by leading filmmakers, such as Gutiérrez Alea, the plans were scrapped, and Alfredo Guevara was appointed director once more. Paradoxically, at a time when resources were scarcer than ever before, **ICAIC** produced its most successful film ever, *Fresa y Chocolate* (Strawberry and Chocolate, 1993), suggesting, perhaps, that the best Cuban films are made when circumstances are at their worst.

Daniel Díaz Torres followed his *Alicia* hit with *Kleines Tropikana* (Little Tropicana, Cuba/Germany/Spain, 1997), a hilarious pastiche of Gutiérrez Alea films and a fitting homage to the master. This satirical snapshot of Cuban xenophobia, played by the actors starring in *Alicia* and Vladimir Cruz *(Fresa y Chocolate)*, features a detective fiction writer, a dead German tourist and a British hippy girl, cleverly targetting European audiences. In fact, Cuban cinema maintains an exceptionally high international profile, as demonstrated in the 1999 London Latin American Film Festival where a dozen Cuban films and documentaries were screened (including several classics mentioned here). Music, laughter and social critique dominate the scene. Films of the late 1990s to watch out for are **Fernando Pérez**'s award-winning *La vida es silbar* (Life is to whistle, Cuba/Spain, 1998), **Manuel Herrera**'s *Zafiros locura azul* (Zafiros [Sapphires], Blue Madness, 1998) and **Juan Carlos Tabío**'s *El elefante y la bicicleta* (The Elephant and the Bicycle, 1998), all of which starred **Luís Alberto García** ('*Plaff*!' and '*Adorables mentiras*'). He is only in his thirties, but he has already acted in some 35 films. The first film is yet another sharp-edged comedy about life's illusions and disappointments, a bitter-sweet genre that the Cubans have made their own. As might be expected, the three protagonists (a dropout, a nurse and a ballet dancer) all have sexual hang-ups and are seen attempting to make sense of their chaotic lives in today's Havana. The second film is a musical biopic partly produced in the USA, again starring García. It tells the story of Miguel Cancio (the producer's father), founder of the 1960s quartet **Los Zafiros** who developed a unique blend of up-beat r&b and bolero music.

The international explosion of Cuban music, old and new, has led to a trend in Cuban musical documentaries. The film that has made the greatest impact in recent years is without doubt **Wim Wender**'s documentary *Buena Vista Social Club* (Cuba/Germany, 1998), a nostalgic reconstruction of the lives and times of the band of the same name, whose original members are now in their 80s and 90s. The late **Rubén González**'s piano playing, **Ibrahim Ferrer**'s crooning, accompanied by **Ry Cooder** on guitar (with his son, **Joaquín Cooder**, on drums) practising for two gigs in Amsterdam (April 1998) and New York (July 1998) and – above all – the stunning colour photography are quite unforgettable. Two Grammy Award winning CDs are available: *Buena Vista Social Club* (WCD050) and *Buena Vista Social Club Presents Ibrahim Ferrer* (WCD055). The rhythmic soundtrack of *Tropicola* (Cuba 1998), directed by **Steve Fagin**, is exciting too, although this film is more concerned with today's problems in Cuba: the harmful effects of tourism and the dollar economy. Entirely different, but just as Cuban, is the wonderfully evocative short *Misa cubana* (Cuban Mass, Cuba, 1998), a collage of 16th- and 17th-century sacred music with a score written by maestro **José María Vitier**.

Cuba has once again hit the headlines in several films made about the island in the USA and elsewhere. First there was *Cosas que dejé en la Habana* (Things I left in Havana, 1998) by Spanish film director **Manuel Gutiérrez Aragón** starring Jorge Perugorría (of *Fresa y Chocolate* fame). The film, funny yet critical, tells the story of three Cuban sisters who come to Madrid in search of a better world but are exploited by their aunt who, among other things, tries to marry the youngest girl to her gay son. Then **Roger Donaldson**'s political thriller *Thirteen Days* starring Kevin Costner, released in 2000, presented yet another version of the 1962 Cuban Missile Crisis, when the world was pushed to the brink of nuclear war. Despite its length (over two hours), the film received favourable reviews and was screened in Cuba. Costner and the producers were invited to dinner with Fidel and then collaborated with **ICAIC** to get the film put on in the island.

The most controversial film about Cuba in recent years (when aren't films about Cuba controversial?) is **Julian Schabel**'s *Before Night Falls* (2001) which is loosely based on the autobiography of gay Cuban writer **Reinaldo Arenas**' *Antes que anochezca* (Barcelona, 1992) (Before Night Falls, London, 1993). Arenas was born near Holguín in 1943 and was self taught. After the Revolution he was given posts in the National Library and as editor of the famous *Gaceta de Cuba* (1968-74). His first novel was published in Cuba in 1967, but

Background Cinema

Tomás Gutiérrez Alea (1928-96)

The two most famous Cuban films, *Memorias del Subdesarrollo* (Memories of Underdevelopment, 1968), on the role of the intellectual in society, and *Fresa y Chocolate* (Strawberry and Chocolate, 1993), about gay issues in Cuba, were made by the director who has contributed more than any other to Cuban cinema.

Tomás Gutiérrez Alea made over 12 features and 13 documentaries/shorts. His films vary from the hilarious *La Muerte de un Burócrata* (Death of a Bureaucrat, 1966) to the sentimental romance *Hasta Cierto Punto* (Up to a Point, 1984). Except for *Cartas del Parque* (Letters from the Park, 1988), based on a screenplay by Gabriel García Márquez, they all have a sharp critical edge.

Gutiérrez Alea started filming in 1947, then studied at the *Centro Sperimentale* in Rome in 1953. His first serious work was a 1955 documentary on the charcoal workers, confiscated by the Batista police. During the Revolution he played a leading part organizing the cinema section of the Revolutionary army and made (with García Espinosa) the first post-victory documentary, *Esta Tierra Nuestra* (This Our Land). His first feature film,

Historias de la Revolución (Stories of the Revolution) dates from 1960.

Since then, Gutiérrez Alea has won many international awards and retrospectives of his work have been shown across the world (including San Francisco, New York, Toronto and New Delhi).

Repeatedly, particularly in the late 1980s, he was refused entry into the USA. Yet in 1994, *Fresa y Chocolate* was nominated for an Oscar in the best foreign film category. Made primarily for a domestic market, it stages the dramatic encounter between a young Communist student and a gay intellectual. Both are patriotic Cubans but, while the student embraces the culture of Che and Fidel, the intellectual identifies with the refined artistic world of pre-Revolutionary Cuba. Each learns from the other, but the intellectual, hounded by the authorities, finally seeks political asylum in Europe. Gutiérrez Alea's last film, the road movie *Guantanamera* (1995), which returns to the macabre comedy format of *La Muerte de un Burócrata*, was completed shortly before his death. The leading actress in both films was his wife, Mirta Ibarra.

in the early 1970s he ran into trouble with the authorities and was imprisoned for two years (1974-76). He left Cuba in the Mariel exodus of 1980 and was employed in the USA as a literature professor. He contracted HIV and committed suicide in New York in 1990. His autobiography, although beautifully written, is hyperbolical (he boasts of having had 5,000 gay sexual encounters before the age of 25) and especially hostile to Castro. It should not be read as documentary fact, as several of Arenas' Cuban friends and colleagues have since pointed out. The film represents events at an even further remove from historical reality, yet has been widely reviewed as the most recent indictment of Castro's apparently brutal government. In other words, the film is deliberately politically biased. This is not to say it is not a good film; it is, but it is fiction and should be viewed as such. The Spanish actor Javier Bardem, playing Arenas, is powerful and convincing. He won several awards for his role, including the Best Actor at the Venice International Film Festival (2000) and the National Society of Film Critics (2001); the film also features famous Hollywood actors (Sean Penn, Johnny Depp) in cameo roles. Although the camera work is excellent, if you don't know Arenas's story you may be confused by the complex plot.

In Cuba, meanwhile, veteran film-maker **Humberto Solás** (*Lucía*, 1968; *Cecilia*, 1981 and many other films) brought out *Miel para Oshún* (Honey for the Goddess Oshun, 2001), the story of a Cuban, Roberto (played by Jorge Perugorría, yet again), who was taken to the USA as a child after the Revolution and returns 30 years later to find his mother. Like Alea's *Guantanamera*, this is a road movie, more notable for its outstanding photography of the Cuban landscape than for its penetrating character analyses. Another award-winning film released in 2001 is **Juan Carlos Tabío**'s comedy, *Lista de Espera* (Waiting List), scripted by Senel Paz and Arturo Arango and starring Vladimir Cruz (of *Fresa y Chocolate* fame) and Jorge Perugorría (now playing a blind man). The action takes place in a remote, dilapidated bus station. The passengers wait and wait for a bus but they are all full so they try and repair an old Soviet wreck in a collective effort to repair the broken dream. The bus is a metaphor for the better times that never materialize and the passengers' solidarity a comment on the resilience and blind optimism of those that try to make things work despite all odds.

At the 2002 International Film Festival, the largest crowds queued to see *Balseros* (Rafters), a film documentary about seven Cubans who set sail for Miami in 1994, a time of economic crisis when Castro allowed thousands to flee on any home- made craft for Florida. Their stories show the pain of leaving families behind and the culture shock of living and working long hours in the USA. Directors **Carles Bosch** and **Josep Domenech** presented a frank account of the poverty driving Cubans to leave, but also the harsh reality of life elsewhere. In 2003, one of the most talked about films was a silent movie directed by **Fernando Pérez**, *Suite Habana*, a documentary of a day in the life of the city and its inhabitants, with a sound track limited to music and city noises. It can be interpreted as either a subversive criticism of Castro's system, or as a tribute to the courage and resilience of Habaneros, struggling against all odds to survive without losing their revolutionary dreams.

Four new films are in the works, in co-production with Spain: *Perfecto Amor Equivocado, Bailando Cha Cha Cha, Ellos Son,* and *El Bárbaro del Ritmo*, the last one about Beny Moré with sound track by Chucho Valdés and Juan Manuel Ceruto. In short, the Cuban film industry is progressing well in the 21st century and the International Film Festival (Festival Internacional del Nuevo Cine Latinoamericano, festival@icaic.inf.cu) is still a major event that should not be missed.

Religion

The major characteristic of Cuban culture is its combination of the African and European. Because slavery was not abolished until 1886 in Cuba, black African traditions were kept intact much later than elsewhere in the Caribbean. They persist now, inevitably mingled with Hispanic influence, in religion: in *Santería*, for instance, a cult which blends popular Catholicism with the Yoruba belief in the spirits that inhabit all plant life. This now has a greater hold in Cuba than orthodox Catholicism, which has traditionally been seen as the religion of the white, upper class: opposing independence from Spain in the 19th century and the Revolution in the 1950s.

The Roman Catholic Church

Church and State were separated at the beginning of the 20th century when Spain was defeated by the USA and a constituent assembly approved a new constitution. The domination of the USA after that time encouraged the spread of Protestantism, although Catholicism remained the religion of the majority. Nevertheless, Catholicism was not as well supported as in some other Latin American countries.

⁞ The Orishas

Every *toque de santo* begins and ends with the evocation of **Elegguá**, lord of the roads and crossroads and guardian of our destiny, dressed always in red and black. In the calendar of Christian saints he is equated with the Child of Prague. Most powerful *orisha* of all is red-clad **Changó**, lord of fire, thunder, war, drums and virility, who is syncretized with St Barbara. *Santeros* believe he was born of **Yemayá**, alter ego of the Virgin of Regla, Havana Bay's patron saint. Dressed in blue and white, she is mistress of the seas and goddess of motherhood.

Oggún (St Peter) is another war god and patron of blacksmiths. Brother to **Changó**, he is also his rival for the affection of **Yemayá**'s sensual dancing sister **Ochún**, the yellow-clad goddess of rivers and springs, beauty and sexual love. Christianized as the Virgin of Charity of El Cobre, she is Cuba's patron saint. Her shrine at the Basilica of El Cobre, outside Santiago de Cuba, is always filled with fragrant *mariposas*, the national flower, and the walls are hung with countless offerings from those whose prayers have been answered, including crutches, sachets of Angolan earth brought by returning veterans, a medallion left by Fidel Castro's mother after his safe return from the guerrilla struggle, and Hemingway's Nobel Prize.

Olofi or **Olorun**, syncretized as both the Eternal Father and the Holy Spirit, is the supreme creator of all things, but, say *santeros*, takes little interest in our world, and long ago handed over the care of it to **Obatalá** who, dressed all in white like his devotees or *hijos* (children), is god of peace, truth, wisdom and justice. In Christian guise he is Our Lady of Mercy. His son is **Orula** (colours: yellow and green), syncretized as St Francis of Assisi and others. Known also as **Ifá**, he is the ancient, implacable lord of divination. Unlike other **orishas**, who 'descend on' and possess their *hijos*, he communicates only with the *babalawo* or priest who interprets his predictions. Divination of what the future holds is a central feature of Regla de Ocha, and may be achieved through casting the *ékuele*, a set of eight pieces of turtle or coconut shell.

Other popular *orishas* include **Oyá** (St Teresa of Ávila), mistress of the winds and lightning, queen of the cemetery; and **Babalú Ayé**. Dressed in bishop's purple, covered in sores, limping along on crutches and followed by stray dogs, he is the deity of leprosy and venereal and skin diseases. Every 17 December thousands of his followers, including the halt and lame and those fulfilling a promise in thanks for a favour received, make the pilgrimage to the chapel of St Lazarus, his Christian manifestation, at El Rincón on the southern outskirts of Havana.

Few villages had churches and most Cubans rarely went to mass. Even before the Revolution, the Church was seen as right wing, as most of the priests were Spanish and many of them were supporters of General Franco and his fascist regime in Spain.

After the Revolution, relations between the Catholic Church and Castro were frosty. Most priests left the country and some joined the emigrés in Miami, where connections are still strong. By the late 1970s, the Vatican's condemnation of the US embargo helped towards a gradual reconciliation. In 1979, the Pope was invited to visit Cuba on his way back from a trip to Mexico, but he also received an invitation from the Cuban emigrés in Miami. Caught between a rock and a hard place, the Pope opted to go to the Bahamas instead. In the 1980s, Castro issued visas to foreign priests and missionaries and allowed the import of bibles, as well as giving permission for new churches to be built.

In 1994, Cardinal Jaime Ortega was appointed by the Vatican to fill the position left vacant in Cuba since the last cardinal died in 1963. A ban on religious believers joining the Communist Party has been lifted and Protestant, Catholic and other church leaders have reported rising congregations. In the archdiocese of Havana, there were 7,500 baptisms in 1979 but this figure shot up to 34,800 in 1994.

In 1996, Fidel visited Pope John Paul II at the Vatican and the Pope visited Cuba in January 1998. Castro has stated in the past that there is no conflict between Marxism and Christianity and has been sympathetic towards supporters of liberation theology in their quest for equality and a just distribution of social wealth. During the Pope's visit to Brazil in October 1997, he criticized free market ideology which promotes excessive individualism and undermines the role of society, which he further emphasized in his visit to Cuba. The two septuagenarians clearly share common ground on the need for social justice, although they are poles apart on the family, marriage, abortion and contraception, let alone totalitarianism and violent Revolution. At the Pope's request, Castro decreed 25 December 1997 a public holiday, initially for one year only, but it is now a regular event. Christmas Day was abolished in the 1960s because it interfered with the sugar harvest; a whole generation has grown up without it and many people were unsure of its religious significance when it was reinstated. Nevertheless, artificial Christmas trees sold out and tinsel and religious imagery were to be found in many homes.

Afro-Cuban religion

From the mid-16th century to the late 19th century, countless hundreds of thousands of African slaves were brought to Cuba. Torn from dozens of peoples between the Gulf of Guinea and southern Angola, speaking hundreds of languages and dialects, they brought from home only a memory of their customs and beliefs as a shred of comfort in their traumatic new existence on the sugar plantations. The most numerous and culturally most influential group were the Yoruba-speaking agriculturalists from the forests of southeast Nigeria, Dahomey and Togo, who became known collectively in Cuba as *lucumí*. It is their pantheon of deities or *orishas*, and the legends (*pwatakis*) and customs surrounding these, which form the basis of the syncretic Regla de Ocha cult, better known as **Santería.**

Although slaves were ostensibly obliged to become Christians, their owners, anxious to prevent different ethnic groups from uniting, turned a blind eye to their traditional rituals. The Catholic saints thus spontaneously merged or syncretized in the *lucumí* mind with the *orishas*, whose imagined attributes they shared.

While the Yoruba recognize 400 or more regional or tribal *orishas*, their Cuban descendants have forgotten, discarded or fused together most of these, so that today barely two dozen regularly receive tribute at the rites known as *toques de santo* (see box, page 424).

Santería, which claims to have at least as many believers as the Roman Catholic Church in Cuba, in all walks of life including Communist Party members, enshrines a rich cultural heritage. For every *orisha* there is a complex code of conduct, dress (including colour-coded necklaces) and diet to which his or her *hijos* must conform, and a series of chants and rhythms played on the sacred *batá* drums.

Santería is non-sectarian and non-proselytizing, co-existing peacefully with both Christianity and the **Regla Conga** or **Palo Monte** cult brought to Cuba by *congos*, slaves from various Bantu-speaking regions of the Congo basin. Indeed many people are practising believers in both or all three. Found mainly in Havana and Matanzas provinces, **Palo Monte** is a much more fragmented and impoverished belief system than **Regla de Ocha**, and has borrowed aspects from it and other sources. Divided into several sects, the most important being the *mayomberos*, *kisimberos* and *briyumberos*, it is basically animist, using the forces of nature to perform good or evil magic and predict the future in

The Afro Trail

It is not so long since traditionalist believers were scandalized when the renowned jazz and salsa band **Irakere** started to use the sacred *cueros batá* (the three drums used in *Santería* rites) on stage. In these times, when all's fair in the scramble for tourist dollars, you may well find a more-or-less Disneyfied all-singing, all-dancing version of *lucumí* or congo ceremonies on offer as part of your hotel's entertainment. Enjoy the spectacle but season liberally with salt.

Alternatively you can witness expertly choreographed and largely genuine performances of Yoruba and Congo devotional and profane song and dance, as well as the intricacies of the *real rumba* in all its variants, at the Sábado de la Rumba sessions put on by the **Conjunto Folklórico Nacional** on Saturday afternoons at their Calle 4 headquarters in Vedado (see box, Music in Havana, page 129). Despite the colourful trappings, this is only incidentally a spectacle for tourists, who are regularly outnumbered by the Cubans fervidly chorusing the *santero* chants in Yoruba and swaying to the infectious *guaguancó*. The **Casa de África** (Obrapía 157, entre San Ignacio y Mercaderes, Old Havana, Tue-Sun 1300-2000) is an untaxing and pleasant way to get a glimpse of the wealth of African cultures, in Cuba and in Africa itself. As well as small collections from various African countries, it houses the Afro-Cuban devotional artifacts collected by the late Don Fernando Ortiz, the founding father of Afro-Cuban ethnographic studies.

Also worth a visit is the **Museo Municipal de Regla** (Martí 158, entre Facciolo y Piedra, Regla, Mon-Sat 0930-1830, Sun 0900-1300). The most atmospheric way to reach Regla is by *lanchita* (ferry) across the bay from the terminal near the Plaza de Armas. The collection of history of African religions in Cuba, formerly in the **Museo Histórico de Guanabacoa** (Martí 108, entre Versalles y San Antonio) in the district popularly regarded as the Mecca of Afro-Cuban cults, is now in the Casa de Africa. Any *habanero* afflicted by aches and pains or generally down in the mouth will sooner or later be advised, "What you need is a trip to Guanabacoa."

ceremonies involving rum, tobacco and at times gunpowder. The focus of its liturgy is the *nganga*, both a supernatural spirit and the earthenware or iron container in which it dwells along with the *mpungus* or saints. **Regla Conga** boasts a wealth of complex magic symbols or *firmas*, and has retained some exciting drum rhythms.

The **Abakuá Secret Society** is, as its name suggests, not a religion but a closed sect. Open to men only, and upholding traditional *macho* virtues, it has been described as an Afro-Cuban freemasonry, although it claims many non-black devotees. Found almost exclusively in Havana (particularly in the Guanabacoa, Regla and Marianao districts), and in the cities of Matanzas, Cárdenas and Cienfuegos, it has a strong following among dock-workers; indeed, outsiders often claim its members have *de facto* control over those ports. Also known as **ñañiguismo**, the sect originated among slaves brought from the Calabar region of southern Nigeria and Cameroon, whose Cuban descendants are called *carabalí*. Some **ñáñigos** claim the society was formally founded in 1836 in Regla, across the bay from Havana, but there is evidence that it already existed at the time of the 1812 anti-slavery conspiracy. **Abakuá** shares with freemasonry the fraternal aims of mutual assistance, as well as a series of seven secret commandments, secret signs and arcane ceremonies involving special vestments.

Land and environment

Geology and landscape

Geologically at least, Cuba is part of North America; the boundary between the North American and Caribbean plates runs east–west under the Caribbean Sea to the south of the island. Along the plate margin is a deep underwater rift valley, which runs between Cuba and Jamaica. This feature is quite close to the Cuban coast to the south of the Sierra Maestra, with water plunging to 6,000 m only a few miles offshore. Earth movements along the plate boundary make the eastern region of Cuba the most earthquake-prone part of the country, with earthquakes in Bayamo in 1551 and Santiago de Cuba in 1932.

Current plate movements are pushing Cuba to the west and the Caribbean plate to the east. What is now the Sierra Maestra in southern Cuba was probably joined 40 million years ago to geologically similar areas on the north coast of Haiti and the Dominican Republic. Plate movements since then have caused a displacement of around 400 km. Cuba is also being tilted gradually to the north. The northern coastline is gradually emerging from the sea. Old coral reefs have been brought to the surface, and now form much of the coastline, so that much of the northern coast consists of coral limestone cliffs and sandy beaches. A short way inland, old cliff lines marking stages of coastal emergence form a series of coral terraces, one of which runs just northeast of the **Hotel Nacional** in Havana. There are well-developed series of old cliff lines and coral terraces on the southeast tip of the island near Baracoa and to the west of Santiago near Cabo Cruz. By contrast the southern coastline is being gradually submerged, producing a series of wetlands and mangroves running from the Ensenada de Cortés in the west to the Gulf of Guacanayabo in the east, with fewer sandy beaches than the north of the island.

During the glacial periods of the last million years, sea levels worldwide fell by about 120 m; as much of the world's water was locked up in the northern ice sheets. The shallow seas which now form Cuba's continental shelf were dry land, and the coastline generally followed the line of Cuba's 4,000-plus offshore islands: the Sabana island chain to the north and the Canarreos and Jardines de la Reina to the south. At this time, central Cuba was separated from the Bahamas by a narrow channel, about 32 km wide.

Cave systems which formed during glacial periods in what were then coastal limestone plains have since been flooded by the sea. In coastal areas such as the western Guanahacabibes peninsula and Playa Girón, there are small, deep lakes known to English-speaking geologists as Blue Holes where these submerged cave systems meet the surface.

There is no clear agreement about Cuba's more distant geological origins. The curve of the island follows the line of a collision in the Cretaceous period around 100 million years ago between an arc of volcanic islands and the stable Bahamas platform which then formed the southern edge of the North American plate. There is disagreement about whether this arc faced north or south, and about how the collision took place. But the powerful forces associated with the process produced a complex pattern of folding and faulting, while many rocks were greatly altered by heat and pressure. Many of Cuba's rocks predate this collision. These include the Caribbean's only pre-Cambrian rocks, metamorphics more than 900 million years old in the province of Santa Clara; and the Jurassic limestones, around 160 million years old, which form the Sierra de los Organos.

After the collision, what is now Cuba was submerged for long periods, and there were new deposits of limestone and other rocks. For most of the tertiary period, from 35 million years ago, Cuba was a series of large islands and shallow seas, emerging as a single land mass by the start of the Pliocene period five million years ago. Limestones of various types cover about two-thirds of the island. In most areas, there is a flat or gently rolling landscape. The most common soils, both formed on limestone, are terra rossa, stained bright red by iron oxides, and vertisols, black, fertile, and developing deep cracks during the dry season.

There are three main mountain areas in the island. In the west, the Cordillera de Guaniguanico is divided into the Sierra del los Organos in the west, with thick deposits of limestone which have developed a distinctive landscape of steep-sided flat-topped mountains; and the Sierra del Rosario in the east, made up partly of limestones and partly of lavas and other igneous rocks. Another mountainous area in central Cuba includes the Escambray mountains north of Trinidad, a double dome structure made up of igneous and metamorphic rocks, including marble.

The Sierra Maestra in the east has Cuba's highest mountains, rising to Pico Turquino (1,974 m) and a different geological history, with some rocks formed in an arc of volcanic activity around 50 million years ago. Older rocks include marble, and other metamorphics. The country's most important mineral deposits are in this area; nickel mined near Moa is the third largest foreign currency earner, after tourism and sugar.

For those interested in further information on the physical and human geography of Cuba, the *Nuevo Atlas Nacional de Cuba* (Geocuba, Calle F y 13, Havana, T7-323494) provides a beautifully produced series of detailed thematic maps on every possible topic down to the distribution of ants and spiders, with informative commentaries.

Climate

Like most Caribbean islands, Cuba has a tropical marine climate, with temperatures averaging 22-26°C over most of the country, and rainfall generally around 1,000-1,400 mm. The rainfall total sounds high by European standards but is achieved by high intensity showers, not a slow steady drip. Havana and most coastal areas have rain on fewer than 80 days a year. Rainfall is more than 2,000 mm in the three mountainous areas of western, central and eastern Cuba; the highest total of 3,400 mm is recorded in the highest parts of the Sierra Maestra, where the mountain climate also produces lower temperatures of around 16°C. By contrast, the coastline south of the Sierra Maestra, around Guantánamo Bay, is a rain shadow area with rainfall around 600 mm and the highest average temperatures in the country.

Completely cloudless days are most common in the dry season, which runs from December to April. As Cuba is relatively close to the North American continent, cold fronts in winter can also produce heavy rain, strong winds, rough seas and quite low temperatures on the north coast. Lows of 6-12°C are reached in an average year; 2°C has been recorded in exceptional conditions. For most of the year, the northeast trades keep temperatures comfortable, but daytime highs of up to 36°C are sometimes recorded in summer. Very hot conditions are most frequent in the eastern interior of the island.

The rainy season runs from May to October, with rainfall slightly lower in the middle of this period (July and August) than in May and June or September and October. Even in the wettest months, most days have dry, relatively clear weather.

Cuba is in the hurricane belt, although the chances of any part of the island being hit in a particular year are quite low, and satellite weather systems give several days' warning of an approaching storm. Hurricane risk is greatest from June to November.

Flora and fauna

When the Spanish arrived at the end of the 15th century, more than 90% of Cuba was covered with forest. When Fray Bartolomé de las Casas visited the island, he said "*La isla tiene de luengo cerca de 300 leguas y se puede andar toda por debajo de los árboles*" (the island is 300 leagues long and you can walk the length of it beneath the trees). However, clearance for cattle raising and sugar cane reduced this proportion to 54% by this figure. Some 75% of the land is now savannah or plains, 18% mountains and 4% swamps. The mesophytic semi-deciduous tropical woodland which covered most low-lying areas was hardest hit by forest clearance. Besides semi-deciduous woodland, vegetation types include rainforest, coastal and upland scrub, distinctive limestone vegetation found in the Sierra de los Organos and similar areas, savannah vegetation found on nutrient-deficient white silica sands, pine forests, xerophytic coastal limestone woodland, mangroves and other bird-rich coastal wetlands.

Cuba is characterized by extraordinarily high rates of biodiversity and endemism, particularly concentrated in four regions: the **Montañas de Moa-Nipe-Sagua-Baracoa**, which have the greatest diversity in all the Caribbean and are among the highest in the world, and 30% of the endemic species on the island; **Parque Nacional Sierra de los Organos** and the **Reserva de la Biósfera Sierra del Rosario** come a close second, with high rates of endemism, followed closely by the **Reserva Ecológica del Macizo de Guamuhaya**. There is a high proportion of endemic species, found only in Cuba, one region of Cuba, or in the extreme case of some snail species, only on one small mountain in the Sierra de los Organos. Around half the plant species, 90% of the insects and molluscs, 82% of the reptiles and 74 bird species are endemic.

Why the high proportion of endemics? Cuba has a five million-year history as an isolated land mass, with species following their own evolutionary path. There are also a number of specialized environments with geological or soil constraints such as chemical toxicity, poor water retention, low nutrient retention, on ultrabasic igneous rocks, silica sands and limestones. A catalogue is in preparation of all the flora and fauna found in Cuba's protected areas as well as a large percentage of those outside the reserves.

Flora

There are over 7,000 plant species in Cuba, of which around 3,000 are endemic, and 950 plant species that are endangered, rare, or have become extinct in the last 350 years. Oddities in the plant world include the **Pinguicola lignicola**, the world's only carniverous epiphytic plant; the **cork palm** (*Microcycas colocoma*), an endemic living fossil which is a threatened species; and the **Solandra grandiflora**, one of the world's largest flowers, 10 cm across at the calyx and 30 cm at the corolla.

There are around 100 different palm trees in Cuba, of which 90 are endemic. The Royal palm (*Roystonea regia*) is one of four species of *Roystonia*; it is the national tree and can be seen in the countryside throughout the island. Cubans use the small, purple fruits to feed pigs, as they are oily and nutritious. They develop in bunches below the crown shaft, which can weigh 20-25 kg. They would naturally drop one by one when ripe, but they are usually harvested before then by *trepadores*, men who skilfully climb the trunk of the palm by means of two slings, one supporting the thigh and another supporting a foot. You can also see many flowering trees: pines, oaks, cedars etc, although original forest is confined to some of the highest points in the southeast mountains and the mangroves of the Zapata Peninsula.

There are a multitude of flowers and in the country even the smallest of houses has a flower garden at the front. The **orchid** family includes some 300 endemic species, but more are constantly being discovered. You can find orchids all over the island, especially in the mountainous regions, some of which live above 700 m. There is one tiny orchid, *Pleurothallis shaferi*, which is only 1 cm, with leaves measuring 5 mm and flowers of only 2 mm. The orchidarium at Soroa has over 700 examples of orchids and other flowers. To complement the wide variety of butterflies that can be found here, the butterfly flower, **mariposa**, a type of jasmine, has been named the national flower.

Fauna

Animal life is also varied, with nearly 14,000 species of fauna, of which 10% could be on the verge of extinction: 250 vertebrate species are endangered, rare or have become extinct in the last 350 years. The total number includes 54 mammals (40% endemic), 330 species of birds (8 genus, 22 species, 32 endemic sub-species), 106 reptiles (81% endemic), 42 amphibians (93% endemic), over 1,700 molluscs (87% endemic), 7,000 insects and 1,200 arachnids, as well as a variety of marine species.

There are no native large mammals but some genera and families have diversified into a large number of distinct island species. These include mammals such as the **hutia** (*Capromys*: 10 species, *jutía* in Spanish), a rodent, **bats** (26 species, Cuba has more species of bat per sq km than all North America) and the protected **manatee** with more than 20 breeding groups, mostly in the Ciénaga de Zapata and north of Villa Clara. Reptiles range from three types of crocodiles including the **Cuban crocodile** (*Crocodylus rhombifer*) now found only in the Ciénaga de Zapata (there is a farm on the Zapata Peninsula) to iguanas to tiny salamanders. An **iguana**, *Cyclura nubila*, found only in Cuba and the Cayman Islands, is in danger of extinction. Cuba claims the smallest of a number of animals, for instance the **Cuban pygmy frog** (*Eleutherodactylus limbatus*, 12 mm long, one of some 30 small frogs), the **almiquí** (*Selenodon cubanus*, a shrew-like insectivore, the world's smallest mammal, found only in the Sierra de Nipe-Sagua-Baracoa), the **butterfly** or **moth bat** (*Natalus lepidus*, 186 mm, 2 gm, often confused with moths at night, it eats mosquitoes) and the **bee hummingbird** (*mellisuga helenae*, 63 mm long, called locally the *zunzuncito*). The latter is an endangered species, like the **carpintero real woodpecker** (*Campephilus principalis*), the **cariara** or **caracara** (*Caracara plancus*, a hawk-like bird of the savannah), the **pygmy owl** (*Glaucidium siju*), the **Cuban green parrot** (*Amazona leucocephala*) and the **fermina**, or **Zapata wren** (*Ferminia cerverai*). Less attractively, there is also a **dwarf scorpion** (*Microtytus fundorai*, *alacrán* in Spanish, 10 mm long).

The best place for **birdwatching** on the island is the Zapata Peninsula, where 170 species of Cuban birds have been recorded, including the majority of endemic species. In winter the number increases as migratory waterbirds, swallows and others visit the marshes. The area around Santo Tomás contains rare birds such as the **Zapata rail**, the **Zapata wren** and the **Zapata sparrow** (*Torreornis inexpectata*, or *cabrerito de la Ciénaga*). The national bird is the forest-dwelling **Cuban trogon** (*Priotelus temnurus*, the *tocororo*), partly because of its blue head, white chest and red underbelly, the colours of the Cuban flag. Other good birdwatching places include La Güira and Soroa, west of Havana, Cayo Coco on the north coast and Najasa, southeast of Camagüey (contact local biologist Pedro Regalado), but there is no shortage of opportunities for spotting endemics anywhere on the island.

Protected areas

The first national park, the **Parque Nacional Pico Cristal**, was established in 1930, but with little regulation and less financing. Conservation only really got started in Cuba with the passing of Law 27 in 1980, which provided funds and legislation to set up more parks. They started in the **Sierra Maestra**, where there are now 13 parks, reserves and refuges. In 1985, UNESCO started working with Cuba in selecting first class sites, collecting data on biodiversity and endemic species, highlighting the need to give priority to conservation and give total protection in some areas. Within a year a co-ordinating committee had set out financing needs and donations began to come in to develop the first international reserves in Cuba. Four biosphere reserves were established as pilot programmes and education programmes were offered to neighbouring communities on conservation and sustainable development. In 1991, a consultative group was formed which set up a new **Sistema Nacional de Areas Protegidas** (national system of protected areas) and proposed 73 reserves. Overnight, 12% of Cuba's territory was protected, taking in 96% of vegetation and 321 species of vertebrates. Cuba also ratified the Cartagena Agreement for the protection of the marine environment and certain UNESCO conventions on World Heritage sites and Biosphere Reserves. In 1995, a new strategy was adopted, reorganizing the

! Crocodiles

The endemic crocodile in Cuba, the *Rhombifer*, was facing extinction under the Batista dictatorship and it was only in 1959 after the Revolution that it gained a reprieve. A serious effort was made to set up farms and breed the species, with a programme to release some of the offspring into the wild.

There are now several crocodile farms around the island, but one of the most visited by tourists is at Guamá in the Zapata peninsula (see page 209). Here the animals are graded according to size and age and there are 25 sections containing a total of some 2,000 crocodiles. A visitor will see only a small part of the farm, with a selection of crocs on display, from a group of 5-10 months old measuring less than a metre, to one of four years old with his mouth tied up so that he can be made to pose to be touched and photographed. The path circles some ponds in which you can see fully grown

monsters which can live up to 100 years. They often lounge on the banks with their mouths open to regulate their temperature, giving you a good view of their teeth.

A crocodile reaches maturity at six years, laying eggs in the spring. It eats only once a week and its diet in Cuba is enlivened by dead or sick and dying domestic animals brought by their owners for disposal. As farmed creatures, the crocodiles' skin, meat and teeth are used and exported.

According to CITES they are endangered in the wild, but by farming them Cuba now has thousands of crocodiles in captivity. These farmed animals are used for meat and their skins are used in leather goods, but there is a CITES ban on the export of crocodile products. You will find farmed crocodile on menus in a few places in Cuba, which you can try if you wish. Wild crocodile is not permitted.

national environmental plan with the formation of 12 institutions. The key agency is the Centro Nacional para las Areas Protegidas (CNAP), which, together with the Centro Nacional para la Administración Ambiental and the Centro Nacional para la Información, now has responsibility for the protection of the natural environment.

A new environmental law passed in 1997 strengthened the legal framework for wildlife conservation. There is now a comprehensive system of protected areas covering 30% of Cuba, including its marine platform, and incorporating examples of more than 96% of Cuba's vegetation types, 95% of plant species and almost all terrestrial vertebrates. There are 11 categories of protection: *reserva natural, parque nacional, reserva ecológica, elemento natural destacado, reserva florística manejada, refugio de fauna, parque natural, área natural turística, área protegida recursos manejados, área protegida de uso múltiple* and *área protegida sin categoría*. These areas include 14 national parks and four UNESCO biosphere reserves: **Guanahacabibes** in the extreme western tip of the island; the **Sierra del Rosario**, 60 km west of Havana; **Baconao** in the east and **Cuchillas del Toa**. However, not all legally established conservation areas have any infrastructure, personnel or administration in place.

In practice, Cuba's record on preservation of species is not perfect. Crocodiles, highly endangered at the time of the Revolution were subsequently protected and breeding programmes were set up. Now that numbers have been brought to a healthy level in captivity, crocodiles are farmed, killed for their meat, skin and teeth, which are exported. Black coral, protected by CITES, is openly sold as jewellery. Despite the SPAW agreement, to which Cuba is a signatory, dolphins are caught in the wild and kept in dolphinariums for tourists' amusement or allegedly exported to other Caribbean islands for the same purpose.

Isla de la Juventud's land and marine wildlife

Fauna and flora
There are many endemic birds on the Isla de la Juventud and also many migrating water fowl, particularly in the Ciénaga de Lanier, the second largest swamp in the Cuban archipelago, where you can also find crocodiles. There are few facilities for birdwatchers and roads are very poor in the south, but on the other hand keen twitchers and birds alike find it remarkably unspoilt.

Diving and marine life
Underwater there are even more attractions, with some of the best scuba diving in the whole country (see Diving and marine life, page 63). The Centro Internacional de Buceo (International Scuba Diving Centre) El Colony has excellent facilities including underwater photography, and there is a recompression chamber. All dives are boat dives and, as most of the sites are quite a long way from the marina, lunch is usually on board before your second dive.

The area around Punta Francés in the west is probably the best, with caves, tunnels and all manner of sea creatures including turtles, which are protected. There are over 40 different corals and innumerable fish. The area is a marine reserve and you may only dive with an official operator, not on your own. You may not fish around here, but the marina can arrange for a fishing trip round to the south of the island if you wish.

The Marina El Colony has mooring for 15 boats, maximum draft 2.5m, VHF channels 16, 19, 68 and 72, a liveaboard, Spondylus, with a capacity for 10 divers and other facilities. Accommodation on land is at the Hotel El Colony. Other watersports are also available at the El Colony, such as catamarans, US$10 per hour, a two-person kayak, US$6 per hour and a single kayak, US$4 per hour.

National parks

Parque Nacional Alejandro de Humboldt 59,771 ha in the Montañas de Toa, near Moa, ranging in altitude from 20 m to 1,168 m, and now being established with assistance from the German NGO, Green Gold. It is the nucleus of the **Cuchillas del Toa UNESCO Biosphere Reserve**, and basically the union of a group of reserves: Cupeyal del Norte, Ojito de Agua, Jaguaní, Alto de Iberia, Taco and Yamaniguey. This tropical woodland has examples of 16 of Cuba's 28 vegetation types and has the highest rate of endemism, with 150 species found only in this area. Of the 64 species of birds that have been recorded, 12 are endemic. Endangered species include the *carpintero real*, the *almiquí*, the Cuban kite (*Chondrohierax wilsonii*, known in Spanish as the *gavilán caguarero*), the Cuban parakeet (*Aratinga euops*, or *catey* in Spanish), the Cuban parrot (*Amazona leucocephala*, or *cotorra* in Spanish) and the manatee.

To locate the national parks, see the colour maps at the back of this guide. For more information, see: www.dtcuba.com/esp/naturaleza_parques.asp

Parque Nacional Turquino 17,450 ha national park in the Sierra Maestra, including Cuba's highest mountains: the Pico Turquino (1,974 m), the Pico Suecia (1,934 m) and the Pico Cuba (1,872 m), it is managed in collaboration with WWF Canada. This park contains humid montane forest and has a high percentage of endemics, *Juniperus saxicola* trees, fruit-bearing *Rubus turquinensis*, and small frogs, *Eleutherodactylus albipes* and *Eleutherodactylus turquinensis*.

Parque Nacional Desembarco de Granma Includes the marine terraces of Cabo Cruz, 25,764 ha, which is managed in collaboration with WWF Canada. This is the world's second biggest series of marine coral terraces, a staircase-like formation of 22 old shorelines and sea cliffs formed on emerging coral coast, with dry tropical forest and mangrove. There have been 58 endemic plant species recorded here and the fauna includes species like the primitive lizard (*Cricosaura typica*) and a brightly coloured snail (*Ligus vittatus*), which only lives in a small area of the park. There is a network of interpretative paths, archaeological sites with petroglyghs and pictographs, manatees, and diving on the offshore reef.

Parque Nacional La Bayamesa   21,100 ha in the Sierra Maestra around Pico Bayamesa (1,730 m), north of Uvero, but there is no administration in place yet.

Parque Nacional La Mensura Pilotos (Pinares de Mayarí) 5,340 ha in the Altiplanicie de Nipe of pine forests with traditional coffee and livestock farming, while also home to 460 endemic species. There are interpretative paths, some ecotourism and you can see parrots.

Parque Nacional Pico Cristal   16,010 ha in the Sierra de Cristal of pine forest and broadleaved humid tropical forest, where you can find parrots and nightingales (*Myadestes elizebeth*) and possibly the *almiquí*. There is no administration yet in place. This was the first protected area in Cuba, dating from 1930, although it was never managed as such until recently.

Parque Nacional Caguanes   22,690 ha (5,387 on land and 17,303 under water) in the Cayería Caibarién Caguanes, a group of small islands just offshore. Cayo Caguanes, which gives its name to the park, has 25 caves on only 1.1 sq km and is joined to the mainland by mangroves. Some caves have endemic invertebrates and a rare fresh water sponge has been found in flooded caves. They are also sites of prehistoric interest, with cave drawings and dozens of archaeological sites. The park is also home to one of the 10 colonies in Cuba of sandhill cranes, known locally as *grulla* (*Grus canadensis nesiotes*), a tall, long-legged bird with a long neck which it stretches out in front of it when flying.

Parque Nacional Viñales   21,600 ha in the Sierra de los Organos, with the distinctive *mogotes*. There is no administration in place for these limestone uplands with extensive cave systems (Santo Tomás and Palmarito are thought to be the largest in the Caribbean) and distinctive xerophytic vegetation, where you can find sierra palm (*Gausio princeps*), ceibón (*Bombracopsis cubensis*) and cork palm (*Mycrocicas calocoma*). Several types of snails have become so isolated that they live only on one part of a *mogote*.

Parque Nacional Marino Punta Francés, **Punta Pedernales**   17,924 ha of marine platform going down to 200 m, with untouched coral formations and abundant flora and fauna. There is no park management as such, but it is looked after by the International Diving Centre at **Hotel Colony**, Isla de la Juventud.

Reserva Ecológica Los Indios-San Felipe   A 3,050-ha reserve on the white-sand plains of Isla de la Juventud, administered in collaboration with WWF Canada. As well as exceptional bird life, there is pine-covered savannah with 24 endemics and the carniverous plants of the genera *drosera*, *pinguicola* and *utricularia*. Many plants and trees have adapted to become resistant to fire. As a result of management and protection of the area, it is now the site of one of the largest nesting groups of Cuban parrot, and is another of the sites for the sandhill crane.

Reserva Ecológica El Naranjal   3,068-ha reserve in the Guamuhaya mountains at an altitude of 70-870 m, where you can find the Cuban parrot, the Cuban parakeet and the *jutía conga* (*Capromys pilorides)*. Over 600 plant species have been recorded here, of which 22% are endemic and 12 are found nowhere else. An area of 12,494 ha in the Guamuhaya mountains (or Sierra del Escambray) is classified as **Paisaje Natural Protegido Topes de Collantes**, or protected natural landscape. Topes de Collantes is a popular hiking excursion from Trinidad. Abundant rainfall encourages mosses, lichens, ferns, orchids and other vegetation, home to many birds and invertebrates.

Reserva Ecológica Punta Negra-Punta de Quemados   On the Maisí marine terraces are 3,972 ha of the world's largest and best developed system of marine coral terraces, with 27 levels and the driest natural environment in Cuba, many endemic, and some unique plants. A substantial part of the first three levels is included in the reserve. There is no administration yet in place.

Refugio de Fauna Santo Tomás y Las Salinas These are two reserves which form the basis of the 70,277-ha **Parque Nacional Ciénaga de Zapata**. They are still being defined and established but there is rich bird life here, in what is the largest wetland in the Caribbean. More than 170 species of birds have been recorded. At Las Salinas there are huge populations of waterbirds and at Santo Tomás there are two species found nowhere else in the world, the Zapata rail, known as the *gallinuela de Santo Tomás* (*Cyanolimnas cerverai*), and the Zapata wren, known as ferminia (*Ferminia cerverai*). The Zapata rail is dark, with a mixture of olive brown on top, slate grey underneath and on its forehead and cheeks, without any spots or streaks, except for white tips to its flank feathers and conspicuously white under its tail. Its bill is green, with red at its base, it has red feet and very short wings, so it does not fly very well. The Zapata wren measures 16 cm, it has short wings and a long tail, has a spotted head, greyish brown back with black bars and whitish underparts. It lives in the dense bushes and hardly ever flies but it has a loud voice, with a varied, musical warbling. There are also crocodiles (*Crocodylus rhombifer*), which are endemic, and the manatee, or sea cow.

Refugio de Fauna Silvestre Río Máximo 12,500 ha of mangroves on the north Camagüey coast, with saline and freshwater lakes and semi-deciduous coastal woodlands. It is a major site for flamingoes with two colonies of some 4,000 birds and the world's largest nesting population. There is also a large population of the American crocodile (*Crocodylus acutus*). Largest of all, however, is the number of water fowl which migrate here in season, when tens of thousands of duck (*Anas*, 11 species), glossy ibis (*Plegadis falcinellus*), white ibis (*Eudocimus albus*) (both known locally as *cocos*), roseate spoonbill (*Ajaia ajaia*) and other birds can be seen.

Refugio de Fauna Silvestre Río Cauto Delta Just north of Manzanillo, 60,000 ha of mangroves, hypersaline and freshwater lakes and wetlands, which are rich in bird life as well as home to flamingoes and the American crocodile.

Refugio de Fauna Silvestre Hatibonica 5,220 ha refuge overlooking the US naval base at Guantánamo Bay, with sparsely vegetated hill country and varied fauna including iguanas (*Cyclura nubila nubila*) and endemic cacti. Strange wind-blown, variegated rock formations, called *Monitongos*, characterize this arid landscape. There is an interpretative path: Los Monitongos.

Area Protegida de Recursos Manejados Cayos del Norte de Villa Clara 17,500-ha protected area above and below water down to 20 m in the Sabana de Camagüey archipelago, part of **Parque Nacional Cayo Guillermo Santa María**. Wildlife includes the second largest colony of manatees in the country around the Cayos del Pajonal, hutia or *jutía rata* (*Capromys auritus*) on Cayo Fragoso, flamingoes on Las Picuas, iguanas on Cayo Cobo and endemic birds and reptiles on Cayo Francés and Cayo Santa María.

Reserva de la Biósfera Guanahacabibes On the extreme western tip of the island, covering 101,500 ha of 'dogstooth' landscape of bare limestone, with scattered pockets of soil and dry coastal evergreen and semi-deciduous woodland. Terraces and beaches are interspersed along the coast. There are two well-established nuclei of the biosphere reserve, **Reserva Natural El Veral** and **Reserva Natural Cabo Corrientes**, where an ecological station carries out research.

Reserva de la Biósfera Sierra del Rosario 25,000 ha of the Sierra del Rosario mountain range, with the best example of evergreen forest in western Cuba. There are three nuclei in the reserve, El Salón, Las Peladas and Las Terrazas, where there is an ecological station and the local community is directly involved with protecting the environment. Bird watching is rewarding and you may see the bee hummingbird. There are nearly 800 plant species, of which 34% are endemic.

Reserva de la Biósfera Baconao 80,000 ha along the foothills of the Sierra Maestra, stretching east from Santiago de Cuba to Laguna Baconao. The reserve includes many tourist facilities such as hotels, a dolphinarium, the Valle de la Prehistoria and others, but the fauna and flora in the park are varied, with many endemic species.

Further reading

Culture

Calder, Simon and **Hatchwell, Emily**, *In Focus: Cuba, A Guide to the People, Politics and Culture*, Latin America Bureau (ISBN 0-906156 -95 -5). One of an excellent series of books on Latin America and the Caribbean, covering history, economics, politics and culture.

Daniel, Yvonne, *Rumba, Dance and Social Change in Contemporary Cuba* (1995), Indiana University Press. Also in the series: *Blacks in the Diaspora* (ISBN 0-253-31605-7, paperback ISBN 0-253-20948-X). A good general book on Cuba as well as on music, portrait of life on the streets, the author is a professional dancer who completed her research in 1991.

Lumsden, Ian, *Machos, Maricones and Gays, Cuba and Homosexuality* (1996), Temple University Press, Philadelphia, also published in the UK by Latin American Bureau (ISBN 1-56639-371-X). Very readable account of the attitudes of Cubans towards gays since the days of slavery, with related treatment of blacks and women.

Pérez Sarduy, Pedro and **Stubbs, Jean** (Editors), *AfroCuba, an Anthology of Cuban Writing on Race, Politics and Culture* (1993), Ocean Press, Melbourne, Australia, also by the Latin American Bureau (ISBN 0-906156-75-0). Collection of fiction, theatre, poetry, history and political commentary, dealing with the relationship between Africa and Cuba.

Guía de Arquitectura La Habana Colonial, La Habana (1995), Sevilla. Useful guide to Old Havana, with maps, ground plans and photos.

Fiction

See Literature (p406) for further information on noteworthy Cuban novelists and poets.

Arenas, Reinaldo, *Antes que Anochezca* (Before Night Falls, 1994, Viking). Autobiography of a homosexual growing up in Cuba after the Revolution, facing persecution, censorship and imprisonment. Arenas left Cuba in the Mariel boat lift but never settled in the USA, finally committing suicide in 1990 aged 47, when dying of AIDS.

Cabrera Infante, Guillermo, *Tres Tristes Tigres* (1967), (Three Trapped Tigers, 1989, Faber & Faber). One of the funniest novels in Spanish, a tableau of Havana's nightlife in the time of Batista, written after the author emigrated.

Calvo Ospina, Hernando, *Salsa! Havana Heat, Bronx Beat* (1995), Latin American Bureau. An avid salsa dancer traces the development of modern salsa from the slave ships to New York commercial cut-throat business, via *son*, jazz and cha cha cha. Other Latin styles are covered, including Colombian *cumbia* and Dominican Republic *merengue*.

Ferguson, James, *A Traveller's History of the Caribbean* (1998), Windrush Press. Concise and easy to dip into, from Columbus to Castro, with interesting asides on recent issues such as drugs trafficking, characters such as Fidel and the US influence and intervention throughout the Caribbean.

García, Cristina, *Dreaming in Cuban*, (1992) Flamingo, London, (1982) Knopf, New York. Cuba as seen by three generations of women, the grandmother who stayed behind, the daughter who emigrated to the USA and the granddaughter, who returns to visit.

Greene, Graham, *Our Man in Havana: An Entertainment* (1958), William Heinemann. Spy thriller set in Havana at the end of the Batista regime as the Revolutionaries close in.

Gutiérrez, Pedro Juan, *Dirty Havana Trilogy*, translated by Natasha Wimmer (2001), Faber and Faber. Pedro Juan gives up his job as a reporter to re-educate himself in his attitude to life and what makes him happy. This involves lots of sex, drugs, rum, music and other good things in life, highly explicit and with insights into what makes Havana tick.

Miller, T, *Trading with the Enemy: a Yankee travels through Castro's Cuba* (1996). Set in the early 1990s this is a sharply observed travelogue. Detailing Miller's encounters with colourful Cubans from bartenders to baseball players, it steers away from political issues.

Roy, Maya, *Cuban Music* (2002), Latin American Bureau. Comprehensive and accessible, all you wanted to know about the historical and ethnic roots of Cuban music, the political dimension and the artists involved. Rumba, *danzón, son, guaracha*, are all explained. It includes the Buena Vista Social Club phenomenon.

Background Further reading

Smith, Stephen, *Land of Miracles* (1998), Abacus. A quirky travelogue set in the Special Period when times were hard and the Cubans had to be inventive to survive. Written by a British TV Channel 4 reporter, whose search for the real Cuba turns into a search for Castro.

History and society

Collier, Simon, Skidmore, Thomas E and Blakemore, Harold (Editors), *The Encyclopaedia of Latin America and the Caribbean* (1992), Cambridge University Press, 2nd edition. Useful reference book which includes cultural, geographical and economic information on Cuba in the Latin American context.

Ferguson, James, *The Traveller's Literary Companion, The Caribbean* (1997), Windrush Press. A good introduction to Cuban literature and writings on Cuba, with chapters by Jason Wilson. Includes a good reading list.

Parry, JH, Sherlock, PM and Maingot, Anthony, *A Short History of the West Indies* (1987), Macmillan. Academic but very readable.

Stubbs, Jean, *Cuba, the Test of Time* (1989) Latin American Bureau, London (ISBN 0-906156-42-4). Short historical and economic analysis of the first 30 years of the Revolution, still useful even without the upheaval of the 1990s.

Thomas, Hugh, *Cuba, or the Pursuit of Freedom* (2002), Eyre and Spottiswoode, London. First published in 1971, this is the best history book specifically on Cuba.

Williamson, Edwin, *The History of Latin America* (1992), Penguin, London. Excellent general history of Cuba's colonial past and independence and revolutionary struggles, set in the context of the Spanish Empire and independent Latin American republics.

Religion

There is a vast array of reading matter on Afro-Cuban religions, most of which is in Spanish. Those titles published in Cuba are available in dollars at large hotel bookstores (eg the Habana Libre), or at Librería Fernando Ortiz (opposite the Habana Libre, esq 23 y L), or possibly at La Moderna Poesía in Old Havana, esq Obispo y Bernaza. Ediciones Unión has its own bookshop at the UNEAC (Unión de Escritores y Artistas de Cuba)

headquarters Calle 17 351, esq H, Vedado. Casa de las Américas is on Av 3 y G, Vedado. Letras Cubanas has its own bookshop in the Palacio del Segundo Cabo, O'Reilly 4 (Plaza de Armas, Old Havana).

Barnet, Miguel, *Cultos afrocubanos: la regla de Ocha, la regla de Palo Monte* (1995), Ediciones Unión, Havana.

Bolívar, Natalia, *Los orishas en Cuba*, Editorial Unión, Havana.

Bolívar, Natalia and González Díaz de Villegas, Aróstegui & Carmen, *Mitos y leyendas de la comida afrocubana* (1993), Colección Echú Bi, Editorial de Ciencias Sociales, Havana.

Cabrera, Lydia, *El Monte: Igbo, Finda, Ewe Orisha, Vititi Nfinda* (Colección del Chicherekú, Ediciones Universal, 3090 SW 8th Street, Miami, Florida, ediciones@kampung.net, 1992, first published in Havana 1954); *Reglas de Congo: Palo monte mayombe* (Ediciones CR, Miami, Florida, 1979).

Feijóo, Samuel, *Mitología cubana* (1985), Editorial Letras Cubanas, Havana.

González-Wippler, Migene, *Santería – the religion: a legacy of faith, rites and magic* (1994), Llewelyn Publications, St Paul, Minnesota, *Legends of Santería* (1994), Llewelyn Publications, St Paul, Minnesota.

Martí, Agenor, *Mis porfiados oráculos* (1992), Fuentetaja Ediciones, Madrid.

Núñez Cedeño, Rafael A, *The Abakuá secret society in Cuba: language and culture* (1988), Hispania, vol 71, no 1.

Ortiz, Fernando, *Los negros esclavos* (1987), Editorial de Ciencias Sociales, Havana. *Los bailes y el teatro de los negros en el folklore de Cuba* (1985), Letras Cubanas, Havana.

Rodríguez, Enrique Sosa, *Los ñáñigos* (1982), Casa de las Américas, Havana.

Wildlife

Flieg and Sander, *A Photo Guide to the Birds of the West Indies*, http://johnbirding.wolweb.nl A report on a private birding trip to Cuba in 2001 with maps and photos of sites, GPS locations and species list.

Garrido and Kirkconnel, *Birds of Cuba* (2000) Helm/Black, London, or Cornell University Press. Essential if you are visiting only Cuba.

Raffaele et al, *A Guide to the Birds of the West Indies* (1998), Princeton University Press. Birdwatching in the wider Caribbean, thorough and heavy.

Footnotes

Basic Spanish for travellers

Learning Spanish is a useful part of the preparation for a trip to Latin America and no volumes of dictionaries, phrase books or word lists will provide the same enjoyment as being able to communicate directly with the people of the country you are visiting. It is a good idea to make an effort to grasp the basics before you go. As you travel you will pick up more of the language and the more you know, the more you will benefit from your stay.

General pronunciation

Whether you have been taught the 'Castilian' pronunciation (*z* and *c* followed by *i* or *e* are pronounced as the *th* in *think*) or the 'American' pronunciation (they are pronounced as *s*) you will encounter little difficulty in understanding either. Regional accents and usages vary, but the basic language is essentially the same everywhere.

Vowels

a	as in English *cat*
e	as in English *best*
i	as the *ee* in English *feet*
o	as in English *shop*
u	as the *oo* in English *food*
ai	as the *i* in English *ride*
ei	as *ey* in English *they*
oi	as *oy* in English *toy*

Consonants

Most consonants can be pronounced more or less as they are in English. The exceptions are:

g	before *e* or *i* is the same as *j*
h	is always silent (except in *ch* as in *chair*)
j	as the *ch* in Scottish *loch*
ll	as the *y* in *yellow*
ñ	as the *ni* in English *onion*
rr	trilled much more than in English
x	depending on its location, pronounced *x, s, sh* or *j*

Spanish words and phrases

Greetings, courtesies

hello	*hola*
good morning	*buenos días*
good afternoon/evening/night	*buenas tardes/noches*
goodbye	*adiós/chao*
pleased to meet you	*mucho gusto*
see you later	*hasta luego*
how are you?	*¿cómo está?¿cómo estás?*
I'm fine, thanks	*estoy muy bien, gracias*
I'm called...	*me llamo...*
what is your name?	*¿cómo se llama? ¿cómo te llamas?*
yes/no	*sí/no*
please	*por favor*
thank you (very much)	*(muchas) gracias*
I speak Spanish	*hablo español*
I don't speak Spanish	*no hablo español*
do you speak English?	*¿habla inglés?*
I don't understand	*no entiendo/no comprendo*
please speak slowly	*hable despacio por favor*
I am very sorry	*lo siento mucho/disculpe*
what do you want?	*¿qué quiere? ¿qué quieres?*
I want	*quiero*
I don't want it	*no lo quiero*
leave me alone	*déjeme en paz/no me moleste*
good/bad	*bueno/malo*

Basic questions and requests

have you got a room for two people?	*¿tiene una habitación para dos personas?*
how do I get to_?	*¿cómo llego a_?*
how much does it cost?	*¿cuánto cuesta? ¿cuánto es?*
I'd like to make a long-distance phone call	*quisiera hacer una llamada de larga distancia*
is service included?	*¿está incluido el servicio?*
is tax included?	*¿están incluidos los impuestos?*
when does the bus leave (arrive)?	*¿a qué hora sale (llega) el autobús?*
when?	*¿cuándo?*
where is_?	*¿dónde está_?*
where can I buy tickets?	*¿dónde puedo comprar boletos?*
where is the nearest petrol station?	*¿dónde está la gasolinera más cercana?*
why?	*¿por qué?*

Basic words and phrases

bank	*el banco*
bathroom/toilet	*el baño*
to be	*ser, estar*
bill	*la factura/la cuenta*
cash	*el efectivo*
cheap	*barato/a*
credit card	*la tarjeta de crédito*
exchange house	*la casa de cambio*
exchange rate	*el tipo de cambio*
expensive	*caro/a*
to go	*ir*
to have	*tener, haber*
market	*el mercado*
note/coin	*el billete/la moneda*
police (policeman)	*la policía (el policía)*
post office	*el correo*
public telephone	*el teléfono público*
shop	*la tienda*
supermarket	*el supermercado*
there is/are	*hay*
there isn't/aren't	*no hay*
ticket office	*la taquilla*
travellers' cheques	*los cheques de viajero/los travelers*

Getting around

aeroplane	*el avión*
airport	*el aeropuerto*
arrival/departure	*la llegada/salida*
avenue	*la avenida*
block	*la cuadra*
border	*la frontera*
bus station	*la terminal de autobuses/camiones*
bus	*el bus/el autobús/el camión*
collective/fixed-route taxi	*el colectivo*
corner	*la esquina*
customs	*la aduana*
first/second class	*la primera/segunda clase*
left/right	*izquierda/derecha*
ticket	*el boleto*
empty/full	*vacío/lleno*
highway, main road	*la carretera*
immigration	*la inmigración*
insurance	*el seguro*
insured person	*el asegurado/la asegurada*

to insure yourself against	asegurarse contra
luggage	el equipaje
motorway, freeway	el autopista/la carretera
north, south, west, east	el norte, el sur, el oeste (occidente), el este (oriente)
oil	el aceite
to park	estacionarse
passport	el pasaporte
petrol/gasoline	la gasolina
puncture	el pinchazo/la ponchadura
street	la calle
that way	por allí/por allá
this way	por aquí/por acá
tourist card/visa	la tarjeta de turista/visa
tyre	la llanta
unleaded	sin plomo
waiting room	la sala de espera
to walk	caminar/andar

Accommodation

air conditioning	el aire acondicionado
all-inclusive	todo incluido
bathroom, private	el baño privado
bed, double/single	la cama matrimonial/sencilla
blankets	las cobijas/mantas
to clean	limpiar
dining room	el comedor
guesthouse	la casa de huéspedes
hotel	el hotel
noisy	ruidoso
pillows	las almohadas
power cut	el apagón/corte
restaurant	el restaurante
room/bedroom	el cuarto/la habitación
sheets	las sábanas
shower	la ducha/regadera
soap	el jabón
toilet	el sanitario/excusado
toilet paper	el papel higiénico
towels, clean/dirty	las toallas limpias/sucias
water, hot/cold	el agua caliente/fría

Health

aspirin	la aspirina
blood	la sangre
chemist	la farmacia
condoms	los preservativos, los condones
contact lenses	los lentes de contacto
contraceptives	los anticonceptivos
contraceptive pill	la píldora anticonceptiva
diarrhoea	la diarrea
doctor	el médico
fever/sweat	la fiebre/el sudor
pain	el dolor
head	la cabeza
period/sanitary towels	la regla/las toallas femininas
stomach	el estómago
altitude sickness	el soroche

Family

family	*la familia*
brother/sister	*el hermano/la hermana*
daughter/son	*la hija/el hijo*
father/mother	*el padre/la madre*
husband/wife	*el esposo (marido)/la esposa*
boyfriend/girlfriend	*el novio/la novia*
friend	*el amigo/la amiga*
married	*casado/a*
single/unmarried	*soltero/a*

Months, days and time

January	*enero*
February	*febrero*
March	*marzo*
April	*abril*
May	*mayo*
June	*junio*
July	*julio*
August	*agosto*
September	*septiembre*
October	*octubre*
November	*noviembre*
December	*diciembre*
Monday	*lunes*
Tuesday	*martes*
Wednesday	*miércoles*
Thursday	*jueves*
Friday	*viernes*
Saturday	*sábado*
Sunday	*domingo*
at one o'clock	*a la una*
at half past two	*a las dos y media*
at a quarter to three	*a cuarto para las tres/a las tres menos quince*
it's one o'clock	*es la una*
it's seven o'clock	*son las siete*
it's six twenty	*son las seis y veinte*
it's five to nine	*son cinco para las nueve/las nueve menos cinco*
in ten minutes	*en diez minutos*
five hours	*cinco horas*
does it take long?	*¿tarda mucho?*

Numbers

one	*uno/una*
two	*dos*
three	*tres*
four	*cuatro*
five	*cinco*
six	*seis*
seven	*siete*
eight	*ocho*
nine	*nueve*
ten	*diez*
eleven	*once*
twelve	*doce*
thirteen	*trece*
fourteen	*catorce*

fifteen	*quince*
sixteen	*dieciséis*
seventeen	*diecisiete*
eighteen	*dieciocho*
nineteen	*diecinueve*
twenty	*veinte*
twenty-one	*veintiuno*
thirty	*treinta*
forty	*cuarenta*
fifty	*cincuenta*
sixty	*sesenta*
seventy	*setenta*
eighty	*ochenta*
ninety	*noventa*
hundred	*cien/ciento*
thousand	*mil*

Food

avocado	*el aguacate*
baked	*al horno*
bakery	*la panadería*
banana	*el plátano*
beans	*los frijoles/las habichuelas*
beef	*la carne de res*
beef steak or pork fillet	*el bistec*
boiled rice	*el arroz blanco*
bread	*el pan*
breakfast	*el desayuno*
butter	*la mantequilla*
cake	*el pastel*
chewing gum	*el chicle*
chicken	*el pollo*
chilli pepper or green pepper	*el ají/el chile/el pimiento*
clear soup, stock	*el caldo*
cooked	*cocido*
dining room	*el comedor*
egg	*el huevo*
fish	*el pescado*
fork	*el tenedor*
fried	*frito*
garlic	*el ajo*
goat	*el chivo*
grapefruit	*la toronja/el pomelo*
grill	*la parrilla*
guava	*la guayaba*
ham	*el jamón*
hamburger	*la hamburguesa*
hot, spicy	*picante*
ice cream	*el helado*
jam	*la mermelada*
knife	*el cuchillo*
lime	*el limón*
lobster	*la langosta*
lunch	*el almuerzo/la comida*
meal	*la comida*
meat	*la carne*
minced meat	*el picadillo*
onion	*la cebolla*
orange	*la naranja*

pepper	*el pimiento*
pasty, turnover	*la empanada/el pastelito*
pork	*el cerdo*
potato	*la papa*
prawns	*los camarones*
raw	*crudo*
restaurant	*el restaurante*
salad	*la ensalada*
salt	*la sal*
sandwich	*el bocadillo*
sauce	*la salsa*
sausage	*la longaniza/el chorizo*
scrambled eggs	*los huevos revueltos*
seafood	*los mariscos*
soup	*la sopa*
spoon	*la cuchara*
squash	*la calabaza*
squid	*los calamares*
supper	*la cena*
sweet	*dulce*
to eat	*comer*
toasted	*tostado*
turkey	*el pavo*
vegetables	*los legumbres/vegetales*
without meat	*sin carne*
yam	*el camote*

Drink

beer	*la cerveza*
boiled	*hervido/a*
bottled	*en botella*
camomile tea	*té de manzanilla*
canned	*en lata*
coffee	*el café*
coffee, white	*el café con leche*
cold	*frío*
cup	*la taza*
drink	*la bebida*
drunk	*borracho/a*
firewater	*el aguardiente*
fruit milkshake	*el batido/licuado*
glass	*el vaso*
hot	*caliente*
ice/without ice	*el hielo/sin hielo*
juice	*el jugo*
lemonade	*la limonada*
milk	*la leche*
mint	*la menta/la hierbabuena*
rum	*el ron*
soft drink	*el refresco*
sugar	*el azúcar*
tea	*el té*
to drink	*beber/tomar*
water	*el agua*
water, carbonated	*el agua mineral con gas*
water, still mineral	*el agua mineral sin gas*
wine, red	*el vino tinto*
wine, white	*el vino blanco*

Index

Map index

Credits

Footprint credits

Editor: Caroline Lascom
Map editor: Sarah Sorensen
Picture editor: Robert Lunn

Publisher: Patrick Dawson
Editorial: Alan Murphy, Sophie Blacksell, Sarah Thorowgood, Claire Boobbyer, Felicity Laughton, Davina Rungasamy, Laura Dixon
Proofreading: Sarah Chatwin
Cartography: Robert Lunn, Claire Benison, Kevin Feeney
Series development: Rachel Fielding
Design: Mytton Williams and Rosemary Dawson (brand)
Advertising: Debbie Wylde
Finance and administration: Sharon Hughes, Elizabeth Taylor

Photography credits

Front cover: Alamy (Tuk tuk in front of sign)
Back cover: Powerstock (La Habana cigars)
Inside colour section: Claire Boobbyer, Julio César Muñoz, Robert Harding, Powerstock, R Williams.

Print

Manufactured in Italy by LegoPrint
Pulp from sustainable forests

Footprint feedback

We try as hard as we can to make each Footprint guide as up to date as possible but, of course, things always change. If you want to let us know about your experiences – good, bad or ugly – then don't delay, go to www.footprintbooks.com and send in your comments.

Publishing information

Footprint Cuba
4th edition
© Footprint Handbooks Ltd
March 2004

ISBN 1 903471 90 7
CIP DATA: A catalogue record for this book is available from the British Library

® Footprint Handbooks and the Footprint mark are a registered trademark of Footprint Handbooks Ltd

Published by Footprint
6 Riverside Court
Lower Bristol Road
Bath BA2 3DZ, UK
T +44 (0)1225 469141
F +44 (0)1225 469461
discover@footprintbooks.com
www.footprintbooks.com

Distributed in the USA by
Publishers Group West

Acknowledgements

This fourth edition was revised and updated with the welcome help of a team of researchers. Sarah Cameron and Claire Boobbyer of Footprint travelled the length and breadth of the island between them but the real hard labour was carried out by our friends in Cuba: Federico and Yamelis Llanes were of invaluable help in Havana, battling against constantly changing phone numbers in their quest for accuracy; Omelio Moreno in Santa Clara, with additional input from Yuri Montano, gave us the benefit of his experienced eye and thorough updating of the text; Julio Muñoz in Trinidad checked, revised and checked again; Juan Carlos Otaño in Pinar del Río kept his ear to the ground with frequent bulletins on what was going on; Grethel Suárez Sánchez in Santiago again provided us with the benefit of her wide knowledge of that area; Iliannis Vera Londres was of tremendous help in Baracoa; Carlos and Guillermo Ochoa opened many doors in Holguín. We are also grateful to the many casa particular owners who helped provide information and insight into the current state of affairs in Cuba and developments in tourism there.

Claire Boobbyer would like to thank the following for their advice: Hostal Alma and Casa Manolo in Matanzas, Pedro Rodríguez Carmenate in Varadero, Armando and Leonor Martínez in Cienfuegos and Fran and Vilma in Santiago.

Specialist contributors
Art, architecture and literature by **Gavin Clark**.
Music by **Dave Willetts**, with additional material by **Rufus Boulting-Vaughan**.
Cinema by **Catherine Davies**, with assistance from **Steve Wilkinson**.
Diving by **Martha Watkins Gilkes** and **Eleonora de Sabata**.
Che Guevara by **Patrick Symmes**.
Cycling by **Simon Bull**.
Health by **Dr Charlie Easmon** and **Dr David Snashall**.
Afro-Cuban religion by **Meic Haines**.
Geology and climate by **Mark Wilson**.
Responsible travel by **Mark Eckstein**.

Thanks are also due to the following readers who have kindly sent us up to date information: Laure Ayosso (UK); Christopher P Baker (email); Sebastian Beaume (USA); Smeyers Bram (Belgium); Carla Burshtein (Canada); Sarah Crawford (UK); Mike Curtis (UK); Frank DeLia (Germany); Aldo Diethelm (Switzerland); Benoit Fontaine (Canada); Catherine Fouquet & Michael Hall (UK); Nicole Fraefel & Peter Spreiter (Switzerland); Lee Haas (Canada); Andrea Haker (Holland); Francis Stephen Hayde (UK); Alex Henney (UK); Lewis Herbert (email); Alexei Kirk (UK); Stefan Kleineisen (Austria); Dirk Lübbert (Germany); Anders Lundgren (Sweden); Caro Matla (Holland); Benjamin Moser (Netherlands); Nicole Motzer (Switzerland); Christine & Frank Mueller (Germany); Ronan O'Connor (Eire); Isobel & Robin Patchett (Canada); David Pickles (UK); Cari Platis (email); Alexander Prager & Stefania Lanfranchini (Germany); Ute Schmidt (Germany); Fiona Seath (UK); Jeff & Sheelagh Smith (UK); Matthew Smith (UK); Ernst Soldan (Germany); Lucy Tilney (UK); Peter Walsh (email); Barbara Ward (UK); Louisa Williams UK); Beate Weber (Germany); Lucy Williams & Mark Woodward (UK); E C Wilson (UK); Fabrizio Valenzano (UK).

Complete title listing

Footprint publishes travel guides to over 150 destinations worldwide. Each guide is packed with practical, concise and colourful information for everybody from first-time travellers to travel aficionados. The list is growing fast and current titles are noted below.

Available from all good bookshops and online

www.footprintbooks.com

(P) denotes pocket guide

Latin America and Caribbean
Argentina
Barbados (P)
Bolivia
Brazil
Caribbean Islands
Central America & Mexico
Chile
Colombia
Costa Rica
Cuba
Cusco & the Inca Trail
Dominican Republic
Ecuador & Galápagos
Guatemala
Havana (P)
Mexico
Nicaragua
Peru
Rio de Janeiro
South American Handbook
Venezuela

North America
Vancouver (P)
New York (P)
Western Canada

Africa
Cape Town (P)
East Africa
Libya
Marrakech & the High Atlas
Marrakech (P)
Morocco
Namibia
South Africa
Tunisia
Uganda

Middle East
Egypt
Israel
Jordan
Syria & Lebanon

Australasia
Australia
East Coast Australia
New Zealand
Sydney (P)
West Coast Australia

Asia
Bali
Bangkok & the Beaches
Cambodia
Goa
Hong Kong (P)
India
Indian Himalaya
Indonesia
Laos
Malaysia
Nepal
Pakistan
Rajasthan & Gujarat
Singapore
South India
Sri Lanka
Sumatra
Thailand
Tibet
Vietnam

Europe
Andalucía
Barcelona
Barcelona (P)
Berlin (P)
Bilbao (P)
Bologna (P)

Britain
Cardiff (P)
Copenhagen (P)
Croatia
Dublin
Dublin (P)
Edinburgh
Edinburgh (P)
England
Glasgow
Glasgow (P)
Ireland
Lisbon (P)
London
London (P)
Madrid (P)
Naples (P)
Northern Spain
Paris (P)
Reykjavík (P)
Scotland
Scotland Highlands & Islands
Seville (P)
Spain
Tallinn (P)
Turin (P)
Turkey
Valencia (P)
Verona (P)

Also available
Traveller's Handbook (WEXAS)
Traveller's Healthbook (WEXAS)
Traveller's Internet Guide (WEXAS)

Footnotes Complete title listing

Advertisers' index

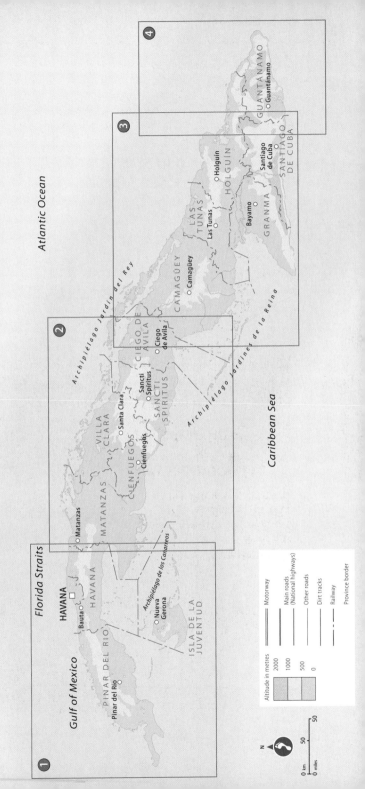

Cuba

Atlantic Ocean

Florida Straits

Gulf of Mexico

Caribbean Sea

PINAR DEL RIO
○ Pinar del Río

HAVANA
□ HAVANA
○ Bauta

MATANZAS
○ Matanzas

VILLA CLARA
○ Santa Clara

CIENFUEGOS
○ Cienfuegos

SANCTI SPIRITUS
○ Sancti Spíritus

CIEGO DE ÁVILA
○ Ciego de Ávila

CAMAGÜEY
○ Camagüey

LAS TUNAS
○ Las Tunas

HOLGUÍN
○ Holguín

GRANMA
○ Bayamo

SANTIAGO DE CUBA
○ Santiago de Cuba

GUANTÁNAMO
○ Guantánamo

Archipiélago Jardín del Rey

Archipiélago Jardines de la Reina

Archipiélago de los Canarreos

ISLA DE LA JUVENTUD
○ Nueva Gerona

① ② ③ ④

N

0 km 50
0 miles 50

Altitude in metres	
2000	
1000	
500	
0	

Motorway
Main roads (National highways)
Other roads
Dirt tracks
Railway
Province border

Map 1

Gulf of Mexico

Archipiélago de los Colorados y de Santa Isabel

Cayo Levisa
Palma Rubia
Cayo Arenas
Manuel Sanguily
Cayo Inés de Soto
Puerto Esperanza
El Rosario
Parque Nacional La Güira
Cayo Jutías
La Palma
Pico Grande (521m)
San Cayetano
San Andrés
Santa Lucía
Parque Nacional Viñales
Antón
Pan de Azúcar (616m)
Viñales
Punta Tabaco
Minas de Matahambre
El Moncada
Pilotos
Consolación del Sur
Dimas
Pons
Herradura
Cayo Rapado Grande
Llanura del Norte
Santa Rita
Sumidero
Cabeza
Aguas Claras
Cayo de Buenavista
Sierra de los Órganos
Arroyos de Mantua
Pinar del Río
Mazón
Las Ovas
Puerta de Golpe
PINAR DEL RÍO
Mantua
Alonso de Rojas
San Juan y Martínez
Llanura del Sur
La Coloma
Playa el Guanal
Las Clavelinas
Guane
El Corojo
Las Canas
Golfo de Guanahacabibes
Isabel Rubio
Boca de Galafre
Punta de Cartas
Playa La Salina
Las Canas
Bolívar
Las Colorados
Sandino
Bailén
La Fé
Punta El Cajón
Cayos de la Leña
Reserva de la Biósfera Guanahacabibes
Manuel Lazo
Cayos de San Felipe
Cabo de San Antonio
Las Tumbas
La Bajada
Vallecito
Las Martinas
Cayo Real
Cayo El Coco
Caleta Larga
Bahía de Corrientes
María La Gorda
Caba Corrientes

N

0 km   20
0 miles   20

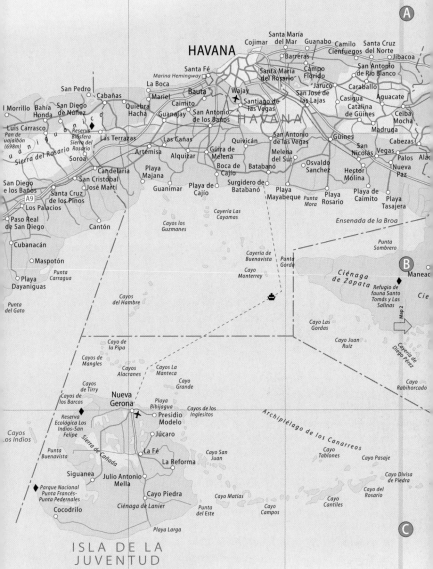

Florida Straits

A

Santa María
del Mar
Cojimar   Guanabo Camilo   Santa Cruz
HAVANA   Cienfuegos del Norte
Barreras   Jibacoa
Santa Fé   Campo   San Antonio
Marina Hemingway   Santa María Florido Jaruco de Río Blanco
La Boca   Bauta   del Rosario   Caraballo
San Pedro Cabañas Mariel   San José de Casigua Aguacate
Quiebra Caimito   Wajay Santiago de las Lajas Catalina Ceiba
San Diego Hacha   las Vegas   de Güines Mocha
de Núñez   Guanajay San Antonio   HAVANA   Madruga
Luis Carrasco   de los Baños   Güines
Pan de   San Antonio
uajaibón Reserva   Las Cañas   Güira de de las Vegas   San Cabezas
(698m) Biosfera Las Terrazas   Quivicán Melena Nicolás Vegas Palos Ala
Sierra del Artemisa Alquízar   Melena   Nueva
Soroa Rosario   Boca de del Sur Osvaldo Héctor Paz
Candelaria   Playa   Cajío Batabanó Sánchez Molina
San Diego San Cristóbal Majana   Surgidero de Playa   Playa de Playa
e los Baños José Martí Guanimar Playa de Batabanó Mayabeque Playa Caimito Tasajera
A9   Cajío   Punta Rosario
Santa Cruz   Mora
Paso Real de los Pinos Cantón   Ensenada de la Broa
de San Diego
Cayería Las
Cubanacán   Cayería Cayamas   Punta
Sombrero
Maspotón   Punta Cayos los   Ciénaga
Carragua Guzmanes   Cayería de   de Zapata   Maneac
Playa   Buenavista Punta   Refugio de Cie
Dayaniguas Punta   Cayo   Gorda   fauna Santo
del Gato   Monterrey   Tomás y Las
Salinas
Cayos   Cayo Las
del Hambre   Gordas
Cayo de   Cayo Juan
la Pipa   Ruiz
Cayos de   Cayos Cayos La
Mangles Alacranes Manteca
Cayo
Cayos Nueva Grande   Cayo
de Tirry Gerona Playa   Rabihorcado
Cayos Bibijagua Cayos de los
de los Barcos Presidio Inglesitos
Reserva Modelo   Archipiélago de los Canarreos
Ecológica Los Júcaro
Indios-San
Felipe La Fé   Cayo San Cayo
Punta Sierra de La Reforma Juan Tablones Cayo Pasaje
Buenavista Cañada
Siguanea Julio Antonio   Cayo Divisa
Mella   Cayo Matías   de Piedra
Parque Nacional Cayo Piedra   Cayo del
Punta Francés- Ciénaga de Lanier Punta Cayo Rosario
Punta Pedernales Cocodrilo del Este Campos Cayo
Cantiles
Playa Larga

ISLA DE LA
JUVENTUD

Caribbean Sea

4   5   6

B

C

Map 2

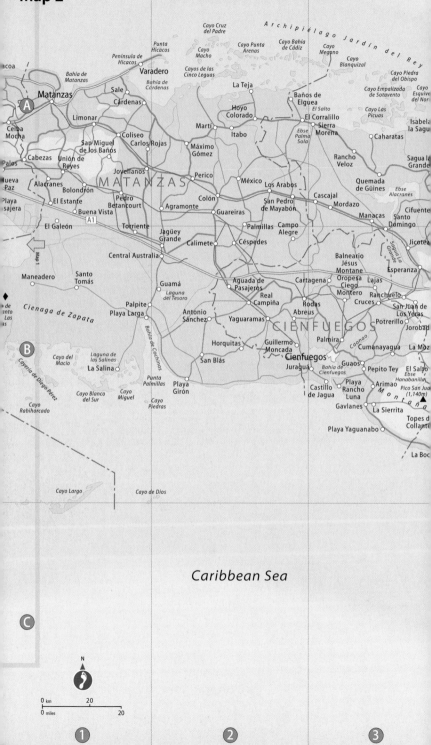

Caribbean Sea

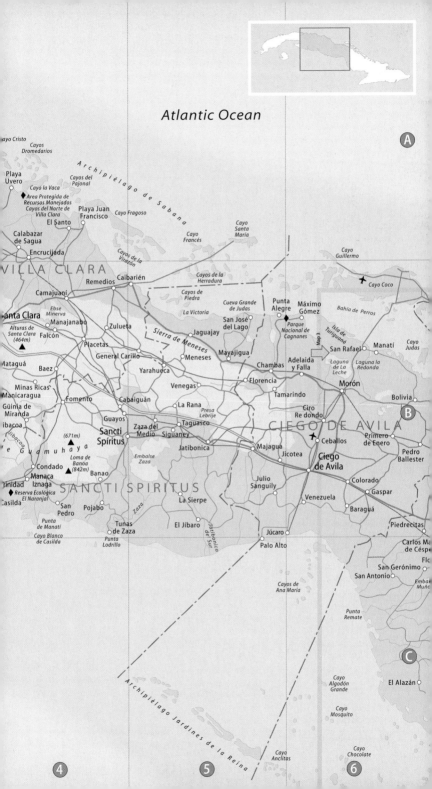

Map 3

Cayo Coco

Bahía de Perros

Isla de Turiguanó

Cayo Paredón Grande

Archipiélago de Camagüey

Cayo Mégano Grande

Cayo Romano

Cayo Cruz

San Rafael

Manatí

Cayo Judas

Bahía de Jigüey

Laguna de La Leche

Laguna la Redonda

Morón

A

CIEGO DE AVILA

Bolivia

Ciro Redondo

Ceballos

Primero de Enero

Pedro Ballester

Playa Jiguey

Llanura del Norte de Camagüey

Cayo Guajaba

Ciego de Avila

Colorado

Brasil

Esmeralda

Punta Cruz

Punta Piedra

nezuela

Gaspar

Mamentuabo

Embalse Porvenir

Playa Piloto

Refugio de Fauna Silvestre Río Máximo

Punta Central

Punta Maternillos

Baraguá

Sierra de Cubitas

Cubitas

Sola

CAMAGÜEY

Cayo Sabinal

Punta de Prácticas

Piedrecitas

Senado

Playa Santa Lucía

Carlos Manuel de Céspedes

Florida

(330m) ▲

Noel Fernández

Lugareño

Nuevitas

San Gerónimo

Caonao

Minas

San Antonio

Embalse Muñoz

Altagracia

San Miguel de Bagá

Camalote

Camagüey

Presa Amistad Cubano-Búlgaro

Punta Remate

Vertientes

Jimaguayú

Ignacio

Embalse Mañana de Santa Ana

Sibanicú

Cascorro

B

Cayo Algodón Grande

Presa Jimaguayú

Hatuey

Najasa

Martí

Guáimaro

Bartle

Cayo Mosquito

Llanura del Sur de Camagüey

Colombia

Jobabo

Cayo Chocolate

LAS TUNAS

Iagua Tres

Amancio

Dormitorio

Laberinto de las Doce Leguas

Cándido González

Haiti

Guayabal

Playa El Habanero

Zábalo

Cayo Las Caguamas

Cayo Cabeza del Este

Santa Cruz del Sur

Cayo Granada

Cayo Media Luna

Cayo Mosquito Grande

Blanquizal

Manzanillo

Las Novillas

C

Caribbean Sea

Troya

Campechuela

San Francisco

San Ramón

Israel Licea

N

Media Luna

Cienaguilla

Entronque de Pilón

Bahía de Niquero

Niquero

Sevilla

Vicana Arriba

La Habanita

| 0 km | 20 |
| 0 miles | 20 |

La Marea de Limones

Sevilla Arriba

Cinco Palmas

Marea del Portillo

Portillito

Las Coloradas

Parque Nacional Desembarque de Granma

Pilón

Punta Farallones

Mota Uno

1

2

Cabo Cruz

Punta del Inglés

Alegría de Pío

Ensenada El Real

Ensenada Ojo del Toro

Punta Hicacos

3

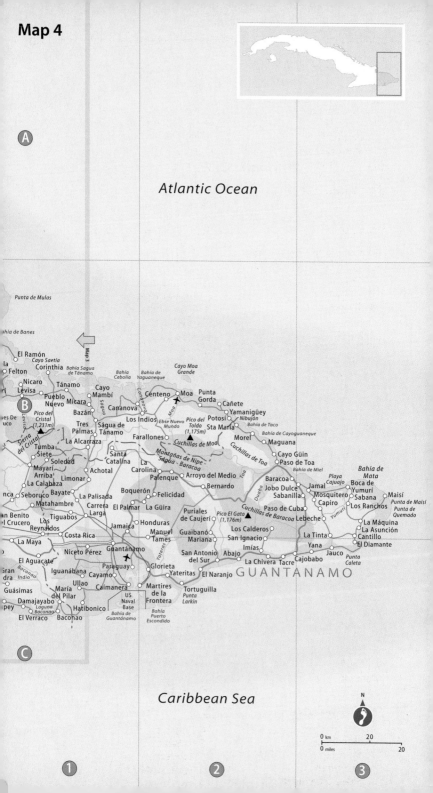

Map symbols

Administration

- ☐ Capital city
- ○ Other city/town
- International border
- Regional border
- Disputed border

Roads and travel

- ── Main road (National highway)
- ── Unpaved or *ripio* (gravel) road
- ---- 4WD track
- ······ Footpath
- Railway with station
- ✈ Airport
- 🚌 Bus station
- Ⓜ Metro station
- - - - Cable car
- ╫╫╫╫ Funicular
- ⛴ Ferry

Water features

- River, canal
- Lake, ocean
- Seasonal marshland
- Beach, sand bank
- Waterfall

Topographical features

- Contours (approx)
- Mountain
- Volcano
- Mountain pass
- Escarpment
- Gorge
- Glacier
- Salt flat
- Rocks

Cities and towns

- Main through route
- Main street
- Minor street
- Pedestrianized street

Tunnel and street symbols

- ⅀ ⊐ Tunnel
- → One way street
- ⅏⅏⅏⅏ Steps
- ⅀ Bridge
- Fortified wall
- Park, garden, stadium
- 💤 Sleeping
- 🍴 Eating
- 🍸 Bars & clubs
- 🎭 Entertainment
- cp Casa particular
- ▇ Building
- ▫ Sight
- ⛪ Cathedral, church
- Chinese temple
- Hindu temple
- Meru
- Mosque
- Stupa
- ✡ Synagogue
- ℹ Tourist office
- 🏛 Museum
- ✉ Post office
- Police
- Ⓢ Bank
- @ Internet
- ♪ Telephone
- Ⓜ Market
- Hospital
- P Parking
- Petrol
- Golf
- [A] Detail map
- ◁A Related map

Other symbols

- ⸪ Archaeological site
- ◆ National park, wildlife reserve
- Viewing point
- Ⓐ Campsite
- Refuge, lodge
- 🏰 Castle
- Diving
- Deciduous/coniferous/palm trees
- Hide
- Vineyard
- Distillery
- Shipwreck
- ⚔ Historic battlefield

For a different view of Europe, take a Footprint

❝❞ Superstylish travel guides – perfect for short break addicts.
Harvey Nichols magazine

Discover so much more...
Listings driven, forward looking and up to date. Focuses on what's going on right now. Contemporary, stylish, and innovative approach, providing quality travel information.